The
COMPLETE
COOK

The
COMPLETE
COOK

EDITED BY SOPHIE HALE
& JOSEPHINE BACON

NEW
BURLINGTON
BOOKS

A QUINTET BOOK

This edition published in 1990
by New Burlington Books
6 Blundell Street
LONDON N7 9BH

ISBN 1 85348 227 7

This book was designed and produced by
Quintet Publishing Limited
6 Blundell Street
LONDON N7 9BH

Designer: Phil Mitton
Editors: Susie Ward, Fanny Campbell, Shaun Barrington

Typeset in Great Britain by
Lynne Shippam, QV Typesetters

Printed in Italy by Fratelli Spada SpA

Contents

Introduction   6

Hors d'Oeuvres and Snacks   8

Soups   30

Eggs, Milk and Cheese   52

Fish and Seafood   70

Poultry and Game   96

Mutton and Lamb   122

Beef and Veal   138

Pork and Ham   156

Pasta, Rice and Dumplings   170

Vegetable Dishes   192

Salads   214

Cold Desserts and Sweets   234

Hot Desserts   274

Cakes, Biscuits, Pastries and Breads   292

Drinks   346

Confectionery   356

Sauces, Dressings and Marinades   366

Pickles and Preserves   382

Appendix   390

Index of Recipes   393

Introduction

HOW TO USE THIS BOOK

THE COMPLETE COOK is a practical guide to success in the kitchen and at the table — whether you are preparing a simple meal for two or a grand feast for ten. Over a thousand recipes — from scrumptious soups to mouth-watering desserts, from summer salads to winter casseroles, and from Austrian Bagels to Yorkshire Curd Tart — offer a wide variety of culinary choices, both to the traditional and to the more adventurous home cook.

The book is divided into 18 sections that cover appetizers or starters, such as Soups and Hors d'Oeuvres and Snacks; main dishes, including Fish and Seafood, Mutton and Lamb, and Pork and Ham; accompaniments like Salads, Pickles and Preserves, and Drinks; and sweets, among them Hot Desserts, Confectionery, and Cakes, Biscuits, Pastries and Breads. The section on Eggs, Milk and Cheese presents a selection of recipes concentrating on these staple foods, using them as starters, main dishes or puddings. The section is a good starting point for one way of using this book: working from the refrigerator or freezer towards the recipe. For the last-minute cook, a quick inventory of the fridge contents and a check on the relevant contents page may produce a Savoury Cheese Strudel or a Welsh Rarebit, according to the time and ingredients available.

The colour photographs spread throughout THE COMPLETE COOK — over half of the recipes are illustrated — are useful both as guides toward achieving the desired result and suggestions as to how to garnish and serve dishes. Step-by-step instructions following the sections are also helpful, not only for their concisely worded advice on how to tackle such tasks as making a soufflé, jointing a chicken, preparing julienne vegetables or beating strudel paste, but also for their telling series of colour photographs. Many basic cookbooks give such hints to their readers in words, but viewing each stage of the real process is the next best thing to an actual cooking lesson.

THE COMPLETE COOK will guide you when it comes to basic preparation: if a recipe calls for, say, shortcrust pastry, then a full explanation of how to make it is given. Where basic recipes form a part of a dish, they are capitalized in the ingredients list to indicate their inclusion in the book as recipes in their own right. A quick glance at the index at the back of the book, or the table of contents at the start of each section, will tell you, for instance, how to go about making Vinaigrette for your Summer Avocado Salad, or Tomato Sauce for your Red Mullet Provençal, or Thick Chocolate Icing for your Habsburger Torte.

The popularity of ethnic restaurants and travel abroad have introduced Western palates to many foreign dishes in recent years, and THE COMPLETE COOK provides recipes for many of the more familiar dishes, from starters such as Hummus and Samosas, to more exotic entrées that include Lamb Dhansak, Malaysian Chicken and Thai Beef with Spinach. THE COMPLETE COOK has a truly international flavour, travelling from Western and Eastern Europe, through North and South America, to the Orient and the Middle East; and you can bring the tastes of all these nations into your own kitchen — at a much cheaper price than going out to eat.

THE COMPLETE COOK also caters for the vegetarian, starting with just simple vegetable side dishes or soups, and leading to imaginative and filling meals that appeal to vegetarians and non-vegetarians alike. Just a few such dishes are Stuffed Aubergines, Cheesy Onion Quiche, Curry Noodles and Vegetable Lasagne.

Those with a discerning sweet tooth are well provided for in THE COMPLETE COOK, with myriad delicious recipes, ranging from the quick and easy to the sophisticated — although the latter are not in the least

For the preparation of vegetables for crudités see page 29.

daunting to create, whatever you may have assumed from sampling the fare at a fancy patisserie. Whether you want to make the likes of Sailor's Delight or Nun's Pretzels, or Queen of Puddings and Gâteau des Rois — and whether you are celebrating a child's birthday or entertaining your friends — you can do it with THE COMPLETE COOK as your guide.

Where appropriate, interesting general information accompanies some of the recipes. These titbits include historical background on dishes that have been adapted from centuries-old recipes, as well as simple suggestions on what kinds of vegetables to serve with main dishes.

So, indulge yourself — and your family and guests — with the culinary treats you will find on the following pages. You won't believe how easy it is to make so many delicious dishes — and to earn so many glowing compliments!

Hors d'oeuvres and Snacks

Artichokes with Tomato Sauce 9
Stuffed Aubergines 9
Avocado with Blue Cheese 10
Summer Avocado Salad 10
Avocado Dip 10
Avocado with Honey Sauce 11
Avocado Fish 11
Chopped Calf's Liver 11
Quick Blue Cheese Pâté 11
Broad Bean Pâté 12
Stuffed Date Patties 12
Sautéed Chicken Livers 12
Chicken Livers with Avocado 12
Chopped Chicken Livers 12
Ceviche 13
Corn on the Cob with Olive Butter 13
Crudités with Hot Anchovy Dip 13
Stuffed Vine Leaves 14
Egg Salad 14
Garlic Mushrooms 14
Herring and Apple Salad 15
Chopped Herring Marseilles 15
Finnish Herring 15
German Herring Salad 15
Herring and Beetroot Salad 15
Mushroom and Herring Salad 16
Special Pickled Herring 16
Kipper Pâté 16
Lesco 16
Stuffed Melon 17
Mixed Herb Platter 17
Hummus 17
Mozzarella and Avocado Bees 17
New Potatoes with Caviar 18
Pâté Rothschild 18
Stuffed Peppers 18
Pilchard Pâté 18

Smoked Mackerel Pâté 18
Smoked Mackerel Cream 19
Shrimp-Stuffed Vine leaves 19
Prawn Bush 19
Smoked Salmon Pâté 19
Spinach and Carrot Terrine 20
Summer Lunch Bowl 20
Sweet and Sour Salmon 20
Stuffed Tomatoes I 21
Stuffed tomatoes II 21
Tuna Pâté 21
Tarama Salad 22
Vegetable Caviar 22
Vegetarian "Chopped Liver" 22
Vegetable Cream Cheese 22
Bean Pancake 23
Pork Spring Roll 23
Cheese and Garlic Straws 23
Cheese Cutlets 24
Chop 24
Devilled Eggs 24
Devils on Horseback 25
Deep Fried Pastries 25
Falafel 25
Garlic Buttered Nuts 26
Curried Vegetable Fritters 26
Savoury pasties 26
Fish Savouries with Spicy Tomato Sauce 26
Hi-Speed Pizzas 27
Green Banana Balls 27
Galloping Horses 27
Tapenade 27
Samosas 28
Wholewheat Samosas 28

Preparing Julienne Vegetables 29

Artichokes with Tomato Sauce
Serves 4

Ingredients

4 large artichokes
15-30ml/1-2 tbsp oil
1 large onion, chopped
2 cloves garlic, chopped
400-g/15-oz can tomatoes, mashed
15ml/1tbsp tomato purée
15g/2tsp fresh oregano, chopped
lemon juice
salt and freshly ground black pepper

Preparation Rinse the artichokes thoroughly under the cold tap and leave them upside down to drain. Bring a very large pan of salted water to the boil, put the artichokes in and boil fast for 30-50 minutes, depending on the size. When an outer leaf comes away at a gentle tug, the artichokes are ready.

Meanwhile, make the sauce. Heat the oil in a pan and fry the onion and garlic until transparent. Add the tomatoes, tomato purée and oregano and reduce until the sauce is of pouring consistency but not sloppy. Season with salt and pepper and a dash of lemon juice to taste.

Drain the artichokes. When cool, pull out the tiny inner leaves together with the hairy inedible "choke". Spoon in some tomato sauce.

Stand each artichoke in a pool of sauce on an individual dish and serve.

Stuffed Aubergines
Serves 4 or 8

Ingredients

4 aubergines
olive oil
1 large onion, chopped
2-3 cloves garlic, crushed
4 large tomatoes, skinned and chopped
15g/2tbsp fresh herbs, chopped
salt and freshly ground black pepper
100g/4oz Mozzarella cheese
40g/4tbsp brown breadcrumbs
a little butter

Preparation Preheat the oven to 200°C/400°F/Gas 6.
Wash the aubergines. Cut in half lengthwise and score the cut surface deeply with a knife. Sprinkle with salt and leave, cut surface down, for 30 minutes.

Meanwhile, heat 1-2tbsp oil in a pan and fry the onion and garlic until translucent. Transfer to a bowl and mix in the tomatoes and chopped herbs.

Add more oil to the pan. Rinse the aubergines and pat dry. Put them, cut surface down, in the pan and cook gently for about 15 minutes. They absorb a lot of oil, so you will need to keep adding more.

Scoop some of the flesh out of the aubergines, mash and mix it with the rest of the filling. Season well.

Pile the filling onto the aubergines and top with thinly sliced Mozzarella. Sprinkle with breadcrumbs and dot with butter. Arrange aubergines in a greased ovenproof dish and bake for 20 minutes until the cheese has melted and the breadcrumbs are crispy.

Avocado with Blue Cheese
Serves 4

This makes a delicious start to a summer meal, but can also be served as a light lunch for two. Stilton can be substituted with another mild blue cheese.

Ingredients

75g/3oz Stilton or blue cheese, crumbled	lemon juice to taste
60ml/4tbsp Mayonnaise	freshly ground black pepper
60ml/4tbsp plain yoghurt	3 ripe avocado pears, peeled
15g/2tbsp parsley sprigs	20g/2tbsp walnut pieces
	4 lettuce leaves

Preparation Mash together the cheese, mayonnaise, yoghurt and parsley. Season to taste with lemon juice and black pepper.

Halve the avocados. Remove the stones, scoop out the flesh and retain the skins. Dice flesh and put into a mixing bowl with the walnut pieces. Add the cheese dressing and mix well.

Arrange each lettuce leaf on a small plate, and spoon the avocado mixture back into four of the skins.

Summer Avocado Salad
Serves 4

Ingredients

2 ripe avocados	100g/4oz cooked prawns
15ml/1tbsp lemon juice	50g/2oz cooked long-grain rice
2 grapefruit	
1 small lettuce	1 sweet yellow pepper, seeded
1/4 cucumber	
150ml/1/4pt Vinaigrette	salt and freshly ground pepper

Preparation Peel the avocados. Cut them in half and remove the stones. Cut the flesh in slices and sprinkle with the lemon juice to prevent discoloration.

Using a small sharp knife, cut a slice from the grapefruit exposing the flesh. Cut round in strips, removing all the white pith. Cut into each section between the membranes of each slice. At the end you will have segments of grapefruit without skin. Squeeze the juice of the membranes by hand over the fruit.

Line the serving dish or dishes with washed, drained lettuce leaves and cucumber slices.

Pour some of the Vinaigrette over the grapefruit.

Mix the cooked prawns with the rice and remaining dressing.

Cut the yellow pepper in thin strips. Retaining some for the garnish, chop the remainder and mix with the rice and prawns. Season well.

Arrange the prawn and rice mixture in the dishes on the cucumber and lettuce.

Top with sliced avocado and grapefruit and serve garnished with reserved pepper rings.

Avocado Dip
Serves 3-4

Ingredients

1 large avocado	dash Tabasco
75g/3oz cream cheese	30ml/2tbsp lemon juice
1/2 small onion, finely chopped	salt and pepper

Preparation Mash the flesh of the avocado. Add the remaining ingredients, mixing them in very well. Spoon the mixture into a serving dish and cover it well. Refrigerate until required.

Serve with raw vegetables or crackers as a dip or spread.

Note Do not make this too long before you intend to serve it as avocado discolours easily.

Avocado with Honey Sauce
Serves 6-8

The sweetness of the honey, the naturally nutty flavour of the avocado and the citrus tang of the grapefruit make this an interesting combination.

Ingredients

1 onion, finely chopped	*100ml/4fl oz olive oil*
5g/1tsp dry mustard	*4 large avocados*
175ml/6fl oz honey	*1 large grapefruit, peeled,*
100ml/4fl oz lemon juice	*seeded and sectioned*

Preparation First make the honey sauce. In a large mixing bowl, combine the onion, mustard, honey, lemon juice and olive oil. Mix thoroughly. Chill for 30 minutes.

Halve the avocados and remove the stones. Cut each avocado half into wedges approximately the same size as the grapefruit sections. Remove the outer skin.

Arrange the avocado wedges alternately with grapefruit sections in small dishes. Spoon some of the honey sauce over each portion and serve.

Avocado Fish
Serves 4

Ingredients

2 avocados	*1 clove garlic, crushed*
juice of 1 lemon	*50g/2oz cooked long-grain*
100g/4oz canned tuna	*rice*
fish, drained	*rind of lemon*
150ml/¼pt natural yoghurt	*good pinch paprika*
5g/1tsp cumin powder	

Preparation Slice the avocados lengthwise. Remove the stones. Remove some of the flesh and sprinkle lemon juice into the shells and on to the flesh.

Mix the tuna with the diced avocado flesh.

In a small bowl mix the yoghurt, cumin and crushed garlic. Stir well. Add the cooked rice and the avocado and tuna mixture.

Pile the filling into the avocado shells and serve garnished with lemon rind and paprika.

Variation Substitute 100g/4oz cooked prawns for the tuna.

Chopped Calf's Liver
Serves 8

A variation of the more familiar chopped chicken liver, this recipe is a speciality of Eastern Europe.

Ingredients

125ml/4fl oz beef stock	*1 large stalk celery, finely*
450g/1lb fresh calf's liver,	*chopped*
cubed	*50g/2oz diced onions*
1 clove garlic, finely	*30ml/2tbsp sherry*
chopped	*5ml/1tsp brandy*
450g/1lb fresh chicken	*20g/2tbsp unflavoured dry*
livers, halved	*breadcrumbs*
2 hard-boiled eggs, finely	*2.5g/½tsp salt*
chopped	*5g/1tsp white pepper*
125ml/4fl oz Mayonnaise	
50g/2oz diced green	
pepper	

Preparation Heat the beef stock in a medium-sized saucepan. Add the calf's liver cubes and garlic and cook, stirring frequently, for 10 to 12 minutes, or until the liver is thoroughly cooked. Remove the liver cubes and set them aside. Discard the cooking liquid.

Put the chicken livers in a saucepan and add enough cold water to cover. Bring the liquid to boil and simmer for 15 minutes, or until the livers are thoroughly cooked. Drain well.

Put the calf's liver, chicken livers, eggs, mayonnaise, green pepper, celery, onions, sherry, brandy, breadcrumbs, salt and white pepper into a large mixing bowl. Mash the ingredients together with a fork until the mixture has a fine and even consistency. Cover the bowl and refrigerate for at least 2 hours before serving.

Quick Blue Cheese Pâté
Serves 4

If Stilton is not available use any other mild blue cheese such as Roquefort or Danish Blue.

Ingredients

225g/8oz Stilton or blue	*45ml/3tbsp Mayonnaise*
cheese, crumbled	*freshly ground black*
50g/2oz unsalted butter,	*pepper*
softened	*4 pecan halves*
30ml/2tbsp port	

Preparation Mash together or process the cheese, butter and port until smooth. Quickly mix in the mayonnaise and a little pepper.

Taste for seasoning, then spoon into four small individual dishes. Press a pecan half on top of each, then cover and chill.

Serve with hot toast and a watercress salad.

Broad Bean Pâté
Serves 4

Ingredients

350g/12oz shelled broad beans
approx. 175g/6oz cream cheese

salt and freshly ground black pepper
sprigs of mint

Preparation If the beans are old, remove the skins either before or after cooking. Boil lightly in salted water until tender.

Mash or put through a vegetable mill with enough cream cheese to make a thick paste. Season with salt and pepper. Press into individual dishes and garnish each with a sprig of mint.

Serve with triangles of wholewheat toast.

Stuffed Date Patties
Serves 6-8

This dish of stuffed dates on veal patties is traditionally served with Pickled Lemons.

Ingredients

65g/2½oz butter or margarine
450g/1lb minced veal
good pinch thyme

32 unsalted roasted almonds
32 dried dates, stoned

Preparation Melt 25g/1oz of the butter or margarine in a small pan. Add the veal and thyme and cook over a low heat for 15 minutes, or until the veal is thoroughly browned. Drain off any fat that has accumulated in the pan. Set the veal aside.

Preheat the oven to 190°C/375°F/Gas 5. When the veal is cool enough to handle, form it into 32 small patties each with a diameter of about 2.5cm (1in).

Arrange the patties on a greased baking sheet.

Insert an almond into each date. Top each veal patty with a stuffed date.

Melt the remaining butter or margarine, pour over the patties and bake in the preheated oven for 10 minutes. Serve hot.

Sautéed Chicken Livers
Serves 8

Featuring two different kinds of wine, this recipe has a decidedly Continental flavour.

Ingredients

50g/2oz chicken fat
675g/1½lb fresh chicken livers
225ml/8fl oz white wine
50ml/2fl oz dry sherry
7g/1tbsp chopped parsley
10g/1tbsp finely chopped onion

1 clove garlic, finely chopped
1 small shallot, finely chopped
good pinch salt
good pinch ground white pepper

Preparation Melt the chicken fat in a large skillet over a low heat. Add the chicken livers and sauté until browned, about 5 minutes. Add the remaining ingredients, raise the heat to medium, cover and cook for 5 minutes.

Remove the cover and cook until the liquid is almost gone, stirring occasionally.

Serve with crackers or crusty bread.

Chicken Livers with Avocado
Serves 6

Ingredients

25g/1oz butter
1 medium onion, sliced
675g/1½lb chicken livers
juice of half a lemon
50ml/2fl oz dry vermouth

150ml/¼pt yoghurt
salt and pepper
1 avocado, sliced
chopped parsley

Preparation Heat the oil, add the onion and cook until it has softened but not browned. Add the chicken livers and cook them, stirring from time to time, for about 5 minutes. Add the lemon juice and vermouth. Cover and cook for a further 8 minutes.

Stir in the yoghurt, season to taste, and cook just long enough to warm the yoghurt through. Spoon onto a shallow serving dish, lay the avocado slices along the livers and scatter with parsley.

Variation For a richer dish use sour cream instead of the yoghurt.

Chopped Chicken Livers
Serves 6-10

Ingredients

450g/1lb fresh chicken livers
50g/2oz Mayonnaise
2 hard-boiled eggs
50g/2oz chopped celery

50g/2oz chopped onion
2.5g/½tsp salt
2.5g/½tsp freshly ground black pepper

Preparation Put the chicken livers into a saucepan and cover completely with cold water. Bring to the boil and cook for 10 to 12 minutes. Drain the livers well.

In a large mixing bowl, combine the livers with the mayonnaise and eggs. Mash the mixture with a fork. Add the celery, onion, salt and pepper. Mash until the mixture has as even, fine consistency.

Put the mixture into a serving bowl, cover, and chill for at least 1 hour before serving. Serve with crusty bread, melba toast or crackers.

Ceviche
Serves 6

This dish can be traced back to the Peruvian Incas. The fish "cooks" in the lime juice.

Ingredients
225ml/8fl oz fresh lime juice
225ml/8fl oz fresh lemon juice
4 dried red chilli peppers, finely ground
2 large Spanish or red onions, thinly sliced
2 cloves garlic, finely chopped

5g/1tsp salt
good pinch black pepper
1.25kg/2½lb sole or flounder fillets, cut into 2.5-cm/1-in square pieces
1 large head lettuce

Preparation In a large glass or ceramic dish, combine the lime juice, lemon juice, ground chilli peppers, onions, garlic, salt and pepper. Stir well. Add the fish pieces and submerge them in the marinade.

Cover and chill for 4 hours. Serve cold on a bed of lettuce.

Corn on the Cob with Olive Butter
Serves 4

Ingredients
4 corn on the cob
1.25g/¼tsp sugar
50g/2oz butter
1 spring onion, washed and sliced
12 green or stuffed olives
7g/1tbsp parsley, chopped

10g/2tsp capers
salt and freshly ground pepper
15ml/1tbsp lemon juice
2.5g/½tsp grated lemon rind

Preparation Remove the hairy husk and trim the stalk end of the corn. Cook in unsalted water with the sugar for 15 minutes. The cooking time will depend on the freshness of the corn — corn freshly picked and cooked immediately may need only 5 minutes cooking time.

Melt the butter on a very low heat, add the sliced spring onion and olives, allow to cook for 1 minute. Add the parsley, capers, seasoning, lemon juice and rind.

Drain the corn and serve hot with the olive butter spooned on each.

Note If using frozen corn, follow cooking instructions on the packet.

Crudités with Hot Anchovy Dip
Serves 6-8

Ingredients
675-900g/1½-2lb crisp mixed raw vegetables, cut into manageable pieces, such as:
carrots
celery
green, red and yellow peppers
cucumber

cauliflower florets
radishes
mushrooms
Dip
100g/4oz butter
2 cloves garlic, crushed
8 anchovy fillets
300ml/½pt double cream

Preparation Prepare the vegetables and arrange them on a serving platter. Keep cold.

Prepare the dip. Heat the butter in a pan and add the garlic. Drain the anchovy fillets and pat dry with kitchen paper. When the garlic has softened, pound the anchovies into the pan until you have a smooth paste.

Beat in the cream and bring back to the boil. Cook, stirring until the dip has thickened slightly. Serve hot. If you use a small copper pan or a fondue pan, you can serve the dip in the pan you cooked it in.

Stuffed Vine Leaves
Makes approx. 60

These are usually served with a bowl of chilled yoghurt.

Ingredients

1 packet preserved vine leaves (vacuum packed)
30ml/2tbsp vegetable oil
2 large onions, finely chopped
100g/4oz brown rice, cooked
25g/1oz pine nuts, chopped
25g/4tbsp parsley, freshly chopped
1tsp mint
30g/2tbsp currants
salt and freshly ground pepper
300ml/¹/₂pt boiling water
125ml/¹/₄pt olive oil
juice of 2 lemons

Preparation Preheat the oven to 170°C/325°F/Gas 3.

Rinse the vine leaves and blanch in boiling water for 2 minutes or use according to the instructions on the packet.

Heat the vegetable oil on a low heat and cook the chopped onions for about 3 minutes, until they are translucent.

Add the cooked rice and stir gently. Add the chopped pine nuts, parsley, chopped mint, currants and seasoning.

Gradually stir in the boiling water, cover and cook for about 10 minutes, until the water is absorbed but the rice still has a bite.

Smooth the leaves on a board and arrange 1tsp stuffing on each. Fold the stem end and the sides in and roll firmly.

Line an ovenproof dish with any leaves which are left over. Put a layer of stuffed leaves in the dish, ensuring the seam side is downwards. When one layer is complete, sprinkle with oil and lemon juice.

Continue packing layers until finished, sprinkling each with oil and lemon juice. Depending on the size of dish, you may need more oil and lemon juice. Cover with foil and weight with empty baking tins to keep rolls in shape.

Cook in the preheated oven for 1 hour and remove from the heat. Allow to cool; excess liquid will be absorbed. Chill before serving.

Transfer to a serving dish and garnish with lemon wedges.

Extra rolls may be kept in the freezer for future use.

Egg Salad
Serves 6

Ingredients

6 hard-boiled eggs
60ml/4tbsp Mayonnaise
1 carrot, diced
1 large stalk celery, diced
1 small onion, finely chopped
20g/2tbsp chopped green pepper
1 large pimiento, chopped
30ml/2tbsp sweet pickle relish
15ml/1tbsp Dijon-style mustard
2.5g/¹/₂tsp celery salt
5ml/1tsp Worcestershire sauce
5g/1tsp cayenne pepper
5g/1tsp paprika
lettuce

Preparation In a large mixing bowl, combine all the ingredients except the paprika. Mix roughly with fork until the consistency, texture and colour of the mixture is even throughout.

Arrange the egg salad on a bed of lettuce. Sprinkle with paprika. Chill for 10 minutes before serving.

Garlic Mushrooms
Serves 4

Ingredients

16 open mushrooms, about 3cm/1¹/₂in across
2 slices wholewheat bread, crumbled
125ml/¹/₄pt warm milk
4 cloves garlic
75g/3oz fresh mixed herbs, chopped
a little oil
salt and freshly ground black pepper
few sprigs of watercress

Preparation Preheat the oven to 180°C/350°F/Gas 4.

Wipe the mushroom caps clean. Remove, chop and reserve the stalks.

Soak the breadcrumbs in milk until soft, then squeeze out excess milk.

In a mortar, pound the garlic with herbs and enough oil to make a paste. Pound in the stalks. Mix together with the breadcrumbs and season well with salt and pepper.

Spoon the filling into the mushroom caps and arrange them in a lightly oiled ovenproof dish. Bake for about 15 minutes in the preheated oven until mushrooms are soft and juicy and filling has crisped a little on the top.

Serve hot, garnished with sprigs of watercress.

Herring and Apple Salad
Serves 4

Ingredients
1 jar (approx. 350g/12oz)
 pickled herring
150ml/¼pt sour cream
1 large crisp apple, sliced

Preparation Drain the liquid from the jar of herrings and cut them into slices. Add the onions from the jar together with the apple and sour cream. Mix all together well.

Refrigerate until required and serve with black bread if possible.

Chopped Herring Marseilles
Serves 6-8

Ingredients
8 large salt herring fillets
75g/3oz finely chopped
 onion
2 apples, peeled, cored and
 finely chopped
3 hard-boiled eggs, finely
 chopped
60ml/4tbsp vinegar
3 slices white bread,
 trimmed and shredded
10g/2tbsp sugar
40ml/2½tbsp olive oil

Preparation Soak the herring overnight in cold water in a large mixing bowl. Drain well and chop finely.

In a mixing bowl combine the herring with the remaining ingredients. Mix thoroughly until the consistency is even throughout. Cover and chill for at least 4 hours before serving.

Finnish Herring
Serves 4

Ingredients
140g/5oz curd cheese,
 preferably home-made
60ml/4tbsp cream
15ml/1tbsp French
 mustard
15g/1tbsp sugar
fresh dill to taste
1 hard-boiled egg, chopped
1 jar (approx. 350g/12oz)
 pickled herring

Preparation Mix everything except the herrings together very well. Add a little of the liquid from the herrings if the mixture is very stiff.

Drain the rest of the liquid from the herrings and cut the herrings into slices, together with their onions. Add the herrings and onions to the mixture and stir to coat the herring well. Refrigerate until required.

German Herring Salad
Serves 4

You can use a jar of pickled herring or any other herring you can obtain at a delicatessen. Use more herring if you like and add some small pieces of cold meat, such as roast beef. This sounds an odd combination but is surprisingly good.

Ingredients
3 salt herrings, filleted and
 very finely chopped
2 large cooked potatoes,
 very finely chopped
1 large cooked beetroot,
 very finely chopped
1 large cooking apple,
 peeled and very finely
 chopped
1 large pickled cucumber,
 very finely chopped
150ml/¼pt sour cream
watercress to garnish

Preparation Combine all the ingredients and mix well. Pack the mixture into a small ring mould if you like and refrigerate it until required. Unmould it and put some watercress in the centre of the ring.

Herring and Beetroot Salad
Serves 6

This piquant herring salad is a delicious way to start a meal. Serve it on a bed of lettuce with thin rounds of crusty bread.

Ingredients
400-450g/14-16oz herring
 fillets
75g/3oz cooked beetroot,
 diced
3 spring onions (including
 tops), diced
30ml/2 tbsp white wine
 vinegar
2.5g/½tsp dried tarragon
2.5g/½tsp dried dill
30ml/2tbsp olive oil
50ml/2fl oz lemon juice
2.5g/½tsp black pepper
50ml/2fl oz orange juice
15ml/1tbsp Dijon-style
 mustard

Preparation Combine all the ingredients in a blender or food processor and chop finely.

Spoon the salad into a serving bowl, cover tightly and refrigerate for at least 1 hour before serving.

Mushroom and Herring Salad
Serves 6-8

Ingredients

575g/1¼lb beetroot,
  cooked and diced
450g/1lb new potatoes,
  cooked and diced
450g/1lb canned pear
  sections, drained and
  cut into small pieces
1kg/2lb bottled herring
  pieces, drained
2 medium onions, finely
  sliced

250ml/8fl oz red wine
  vinegar
2.5g/½tsp black pepper
good pinch salt
75g/3oz mushrooms,
  quartered
450ml/16fl oz sour cream
125ml/4fl oz white wine

Preparation Toss all the ingredients together in a large mixing bowl. Cover and chill for at least 3 hours before serving.

Special Pickled Herring
Serves 6

Ingredients

675g/1½lb pickled herring
  (rollmops)
100ml/4fl oz raspberry
  vinegar
100g/4oz small onions,
  diced

5g/1tsp freshly ground
  black pepper
2.5g/½tsp tarragon
100ml/4fl oz white wine
100g/4oz cooked peas

Preparation Drain the herring well and set aside. Discard any onions or other ingredients packed with the herring.

Put the raspberry vinegar, onions, pepper, tarragon and white wine in a large glass or ceramic, but not metal, bowl.

Add the herring, which should be completely covered by the liquid; if not, add equal amounts of white wine and vinegar until the herring is covered. Cover the bowl and chill for at least 12 hours.

Just before serving, add the peas to the herring and marinade and mix gently.

Kipper Pâté
Serves 6-8

Ingredients

450g/1lb kipper fillets
225g/8oz curd cheese
5g/1tsp paprika

juice of 1 lemon
pepper

Preparation Poach the kipper fillets, drain them and remove the skin.

Liquidize them with the curd cheese, paprika and lemon juice until smooth and season to taste. Spoon into individual pots or one serving dish.

Refrigerate until required, and serve with toast and lemon wedges.

Variation To make a softer mixture, add a little cream.

Lesco
Serves 6-8

Ingredients

75ml/5tbsp chicken fat
1 medium onion, finely
  chopped
2 cloves garlic, chopped
1kg/2lb tomatoes, skinned,
  seeded and coarsely
  chopped
675g/1½lb green peppers,
  seeded and cut into
  strips

2.5g/½tsp salt
5g/1tsp black pepper
30g/3tbsp paprika
50g/2oz black olives,
  stoned and diced
225g/8oz tomato purée
675g/1½lb beef sausage,
  thinly sliced
6-8 eggs

Preparation Melt the chicken fat in a large saucepan. Add the onion and garlic and cook for 10-12 minutes over a low heat.

Add the tomatoes, green peppers, salt, pepper, paprika and olives. Turn the heat up to medium, cover and cook for 15 minutes.

Add the tomato purée and sausage. Reduce the heat to low and simmer, covered, for 30 minutes.

After the Lesco has cooked for 25 minutes, fry the eggs on both sides until the whites are firm.

Serve the Lesco in soup bowls, topping each portion with a fried egg.

Stuffed Melon
Serves 6

This delicious first course takes an ordinary melon and turns it into something special.

Ingredients
3 oranges, peeled, seeded and sectioned
1 large pink grapefruit, peeled, seeded and sectioned
90ml/6tbsp Triple Sec or other orange-flavoured liqueur
45ml/3tbsp grenadine syrup
100g/4oz fresh pomegranate seeds
7g/1tbsp finely chopped fresh mint
3 small cantaloupe melons, halved and seeded

Preparation In a small mixing bowl, combine the orange and grapefruit sections, Triple Sec, grenadine syrup, pomegranate seeds and mint. Refrigerate for 1 hour.

Spoon the fruit mixture evenly into the cantaloupe halves.

Mixed Herb Platter
Serves 6

This delightful dish of fresh herbs and feta cheese is the traditional Iranian way to begin a meal. Serve with pitta bread.

Ingredients
medium-sized bunch flat-leaved parsley
small bunch mint sprigs
small bunch spring onions
75g/3oz fresh chives
small bunch fresh tarragon
small bunch coriander leaves
small bunch watercress
2 small heads chicory
225g/8oz feta cheese, broken into small pieces

Preparation Arrange the ingredients in piles on a large platter, preferably silver or pewter.

Hummus
Serves 6-8

This garlicky chick-pea dip is a favourite appetizer in the Middle East. Serve it with warmed pitta bread or crudités.

Ingredients
450g/1lb cooked chick-peas, drained
125g/4oz tahini (sesame seed paste)
1 medium-sized onion, quartered
100ml/4fl oz fresh lemon juice
2 cloves garlic, chopped
2.5g/½tsp dried coriander
2.5g/½tsp ground cumin
2.5g/½tsp salt
2.5g/½tsp freshly ground black pepper
22.5ml/1½tbsp water
20g/3tbsp fresh parsley, coarsely chopped

Preparation Put the chick-peas, tahini, onion, lemon juice, garlic, paprika, coriander, cumin, salt, pepper and water into a food processor or electric blender. Blend until smooth and creamy.

Pile the hummus into a serving dish and garnish with the parsley.

Mozzarella and Avocado Bees
Serves 2

Ingredients
1 ripe avocado
100g/4oz Mozzarella cheese
15ml/1tbsp olive oil
15ml/1tbsp tarragon vinegar
salt and freshly ground black pepper

Preparation Cut the avocado in half and remove the stone. With a spatula carefully remove the flesh from each half of the avocado in one piece.

Lay the avocado halves flat-side downwards and cut horizontally into 1-cm/½-in slices.

Cut semi-circular slices of the same width from the Mozzarella, with 4 extra semi-circles for wings.

Arrange the cheese slices between the avocado slices to form the striped body of the bee, and arrange the wings at the sides.

Mix the oil and vinegar together and season well. Pour over the bees and serve.

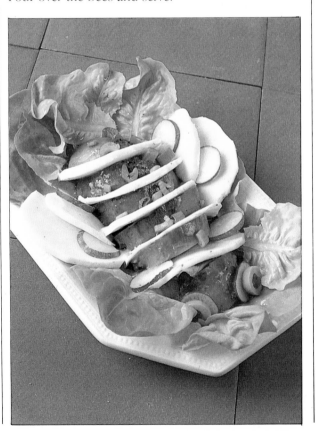

New Potatoes with Caviar
Serves 6

Ingredients

6 medium-sized new
 potatoes
25g/1oz black caviar or
 lumpfish roe
25g/1oz red caviar or
 lumpfish roe

8 hard-boiled egg yolks,
 crumbled
3 lemons, quartered

Preparation Cook the potatoes in a large pot of boiling water until they are tender, about 20 to 30 minutes. Drain well.

When the potatoes are cool enough to handle, cut them in half lengthwise. Scoop a small pocket out of each half with a teaspoon.

Fill six of the potato halves with the black caviar; fill the remaining halves with the red caviar. Sprinkle the crumbled egg yolks over each potato.

Put both a red and black potato half on each plate and garnish with lemon wedges.

Pâté Rothschild
Serves 6-8

Ingredients

450g/1lb fresh chicken
 livers, finely chopped
450g/1lb fresh calf's liver,
 finely chopped
2 eggs, beaten
75g/3oz cooked haricot
 beans, mashed
30ml/2tbsp lemon juice
60ml/4tbsp cream

1 clove garlic, finely
 chopped
bay leaf, crumbled
good pinch salt
good pinch black pepper
50ml/2fl oz chicken fat
50ml/2fl oz brandy
50ml/2fl oz dark sherry

Preparation Preheat the oven to 190°C/375°F/Gas 5. Put all the ingredients in a large wooden mixing bowl and combine thoroughly.

Pack the pâté mixture into a small loaf pan. Smooth the top. Bake for 1½ hours.

Remove the pâté from the oven and leave it to cool. Invert the loaf pan and turn out the pâté.

Cover and chill for at least 3 hours before serving.

Stuffed Peppers
Serves 4

Ingredients

2 large green peppers (or 1
 red and 1 green)
225g/8oz ricotta cheese
1 small pickled cucumber,
 finely chopped

7g/1tbsp chopped parsley
7g/1tbsp chopped dill
salt and pepper
crisp lettuce to serve

Preparation Remove the stalk end of the peppers and discard the cores and seeds. Mix the ricotta with the pickled cucumber, parsley, dill and salt and pepper.

Stuff the mixture into the peppers and refrigerate for several hours. With a very sharp knife, cut the peppers into slices about 1cm/½in thick.

Serve the pepper slices on a bed of crisp lettuce.

Variation Use curd or cottage cheese instead of ricotta, or a mixture of low-fat soft cheeses.

Pilchard Pâté
Serves 4-6

This pâté can also be used as a dip or as a stuffing for tomatoes or celery.

Ingredients

350g/12oz canned
 pilchards in tomato
 sauce
175g/6oz cottage cheese

30ml/2tbsp lemon juice
1 clove garlic, crushed
salt and pepper

Preparation Blend everything together well until smooth. Chill.

Either serve in individual pots, garnished with a slice of tomato or some parsley, or turn the mixture into a serving dish.

Smoked Mackerel Pâté
Serves 3-4

This makes a very firm pâté — you can make a softer mixture by adding more yoghurt. It would then make a dip, for carrot sticks etc. This freezes very well.

Ingredients

approx. 225g/8oz smoked
 mackerel fillets
125ml/¼pt yoghurt
10g/2tsp grated
 horseradish

15ml/1tbsp lemon juice
salt and pepper

Preparation Skin the fish and remove any bones. Liquidize all the ingredients together. Spoon into individual dishes or one serving dish. Refrigerate until required.

Serve with toast and lemon wedges.

Smoked Mackerel Cream
Serves 4

Ingredients
large 300g/10oz smoked
  mackerel fillet
juice of 1 lemon
1 clove garlic, crushed
30ml/2tbsp vegetable or
  olive oil

25g/1oz cream cheese
15g/2tbsp parsley, finely
  chopped
salt and freshly ground
  pepper

Preparation Remove the skin from the mackerel and check for any bones which may be left. Mash in a bowl with a fork. Sprinkle with the lemon juice.

Mix the crushed garlic, oil and cream cheese in a bowl. Gradually add the fish and the parsley. (Alternatively feed the ingredients into a food processor and mix for a few seconds.) Season well.

Serve in small ramekins with triangles of brown toast and lemon wedges.

Shrimp-Stuffed Vine Leaves
Serves 8

Ingredients
olive oil
1 large onion, chopped
1 clove garlic, chopped
50g/2oz green pepper,
  chopped
50g/2oz carrot, chopped
150g/6oz brown rice

600ml/1pt water or stock
salt and freshly ground
  black pepper
225g/8oz peeled shrimps
15g/2tbsp parsley, chopped
soy sauce to taste
1 packet vine leaves

Preparation Preheat the oven to 180°C/350°C/Gas 4.

Heat a little oil in a pan and fry the onion and garlic until soft. Stir in the green pepper, carrot and rice. Pour on the water or stock. Bring to the boil and season with salt and pepper. Cover and turn the heat down low. Simmer without stirring for about 40 minutes.

Stir in the shrimps and cook for a further 10 minutes until liquid has been absorbed and rice is tender. Stir in the parsley and season with soy sauce to taste.

Divide the mixture between the vine leaves and roll into tight parcels.

Pack the vine leaves in an ovenproof dish. Pour enough olive oil over to coat, cover the dish and bake for 30 minutes until heated through.

Prawn Bush
Serves 4

Ingredients
24 large prawns, cooked,
  in shells

bunch of parsley or
  watercress

Preparation Arrange the prawns or shrimps with the tails over the rim of a large glass goblet.

Stand on a glass plate and make a garland with the remaining prawns or shrimps and parsley or watercress round the plate.

Serve with Mayonnaise or Aïoli.

Smoked Salmon Pâté
Serves 3-4

Ingredients
100g/4oz smoked salmon
  pieces
15g/2tbsp fresh parsley,
  chopped
freshly ground black
  pepper

juice of 2 lemons
25g/1oz cream cheese
30ml/2tbsp double or
  whipping cream

Preparation Select a few small pieces of smoked salmon and retain for garnish. Pound, sieve or blend the remainder, then add a good shake of black pepper and lemon juice and mix well.

Add the smoked salmon and chopped parsley to the cream cheese and double or whipping cream. Mix well.

Serve in small ramekins with triangles of toast.

This mixture can also be piped on crackers or toast to serve as canapés decorated with small curls of smoked salmon.

Spinach and Carrot Terrine
Serves 4-6

Ingredients

1kg/2lb spinach, washed,
*   stalks removed*
2 egg whites
5g/1tsp salt
freshly ground white
*   pepper*
nutmeg
ground ginger
125ml/4fl oz double cream

Filling

400g/14oz carrots, peeled
*   and trimmed*

2 egg whites
5g/1tsp salt
freshly ground white
*   pepper*
125ml/4fl oz double cream
butter to grease the terrine
*   dish*
250ml/8fl oz Chaudfroid
*   Sauce*
carrot cutouts to decorate
aspic to finish

Preparation Squeeze the spinach into a heavy-bottomed pan, cover and cook with only the water adhering to the leaves over a low heat for 5-8 minutes, stirring occasionally. When soft, allow to cool. Squeeze out the excess liquid and then purée in a blender.

Gradually beat the egg whites into the spinach. Add the salt, pepper, nutmeg and ginger to taste. Stand the bowl over ice and beat in the cream a little at a time.

Cut up the carrots and cook in salted water until tender. Make up the carrot filling just as you made up the spinach mixture.

Grease the terrine dish and carefully fill it with alternate layers of spinach and carrot mixture. Cover the dish with foil and stand it in a roasting tray of simmering water in the oven. Cook for 45 minutes. Allow to cool.

When the terrine is cool, cover the top of it with a layer of chaudfroid sauce. When this has set, decorate with carrot cutouts and glaze with aspic.

Summer Lunch Bowl
Serves 1

This is lovely and refreshing for a warm summer's day — add an ice cube if necessary to cool it down.

Ingredients

225g/8fl oz yoghurt or
*   smetana or a mixture of*
*   yoghurt and sour cream*
slices of cucumber
chopped green (spring)
*   onion*

chopped chives
15g/1tbsp cream cheese
1 radish
salt and pepper

Preparation Add the vegetables and chives to the yoghurt in a pretty bowl. Crumble in the cream cheese. Season to taste. Serve well chilled.

Variation Add the raw vegetables of your choice to the yoghurt.

Sweet and Sour Salmon
Serves 8

Ingredients

3 medium onions, sliced
3 lemons, sliced
175ml/6fl oz honey
50g/2oz seedless raisins
bay leaf
8 thin salmon steaks
5g/1tsp salt

700ml/1¼pt water
8 crushed ginger snaps
*   (brandy snap biscuits)*
100ml/4fl oz cider vinegar
70g/2½oz sliced blanched
*   almonds*

Preparation Combine the onions, lemon slices, honey, raisins, bay leaf, salmon steaks, salt and water in a large saucepan. Cover and cook over a low heat for 30 minutes. Remove the fish.

Add the ginger snaps, vinegar and almonds to the fish stock. Cook over a low heat. Stir until smooth. Pour over the fish, and serve either warm or cold.

Stuffed Tomatoes I
Serves 4

Ingredients

4 large tomatoes, peeled   lemon juice
100g/4oz cream cheese   10g/1tbsp grated onion
milk   pepper
30g/2tbsp lumpfish roe

Preparation Cut the tops off the tomatoes, scoop out the seeds (reserve the tops and seeds for use in a soup).

Mix the cream cheese with a little milk, just to soften it. Add the lumpfish roe and lemon juice to taste. Stir in the grated onion. Season with pepper (you shouldn't need salt as the roe will be fairly salty).

Mix everything together well and stuff the tomatoes with the mixture. Refrigerate until required.

Serve on crispy lettuce with some hot French bread.

Stuffed Tomatoes II
Serves 4

Ingredients

4 large tomatoes   1 fresh green chilli, seeded
50g/2oz long-grain rice,   and sliced
  cooked   2.5g/½tsp curry powder
salt and freshly ground   (optional)
  pepper   25g/1oz almonds, chopped
30ml/2tbsp oil   2.5g/1tsp chopped fresh
1 large onion, sliced   coriander or parsley
1 green pepper, seeded and   50g/2oz cooked minced
  sliced   beef, lamb or chicken

Preparation Remove the top of the tomatoes. Scoop out the centres into a bowl.

Add the cooked long-grain rice. Season well.

Heat the oil and fry the onion over a low heat for 3 minutes. Add the sliced pepper and chilli. Sprinkle with the curry powder and continue cooking for 2 minutes. Add the chopped almonds.

Finally sprinkle in the chopped coriander or parsley. Add the meat and mix well.

Fill each tomato with the rice mixture. Brush the tomatoes with oil. Then cook in the oven for about 15 minutes at 180°C/350°F/Gas 4.

Tuna Pâté
Serves 2-3

Ingredients

175-g/6-oz tin tuna fish   50ml/2fl oz double cream
1 clove garlic, crushed   1 drop Tabasco sauce
2.5g/½tsp cayenne   freshly chopped parsley to
30ml/2tbsp fresh lemon   taste
  juice   salt and pepper to taste

Preparation Drain the tuna fish.

Mash with all the other ingredients and season to taste.

Turn into a dish and refrigerate for 3 hours.

Tarama Salad
Serves 6-8

Ingredients

3 large potatoes
45ml/3tbsp milk
100g/4oz red caviar or
 smoked cod's roe
90ml/6tbsp water

50ml/2fl oz lemon juice
1 small onion, finely
 chopped
150ml/6fl oz olive oil

Preparation Peel and dice the potatoes. Cook them in boiling water until very soft, about 20 minutes.

Drain the potatoes and put them into a mixing bowl. By hand or with an electric beater, mash the potatoes, slowly adding the milk, until smooth.

Add the caviar or cod's roe and water to the potatoes. Mix well.

Add the lemon juice and onion to the mixture and mix briefly. Slowly beat in the olive oil.

Continue to beat until a smooth paste is formed.

Serve with cucumber and tomato slices and warmed pitta bread.

Vegetable Caviar
Serves 6-8

Serve this delectable vegetarian dish in exactly the same way as real caviar — by itself, accompanied by thin slices of dark bread and perhaps a squeeze of lemon.

Ingredients

1 small aubergine, peeled
1 small marrow, halved
 and seeded
3 large green peppers,
 seeded
2.5g/½tsp salt
2.5g/½tsp black pepper

2.5g/½tsp finely chopped
 garlic
45ml/3tbsp lemon juice
90ml/6tbsp vegetable oil
90ml/6tbsp vegetable oil
20g/3tbsp fresh parsley,
 finely chopped

Preparation Preheat the oven to 245°C/475°F/Gas 9. Put the aubergine, marrow and green peppers in a baking dish. Bake for 30 minutes and remove the peppers. Bake the marrow and aubergine for 15 minutes longer.

Cut the peppers into strips. Cut the aubergine into cubes. Scoop the pulp from the marrow and discard the skin.

Combine the aubergines, peppers and marrow in a medium-sized mixing bowl. Chop and mix thoroughly until the mixture is well combined. Add the salt, black pepper, garlic, lemon juice, vegetable oil and parsley. Blend thoroughly.

Chill for at least 2 hours before serving.

Vegetarian "Chopped Liver"
Serves 6

Ingredients

200g/8oz chick peas,
 cooked and drained
200g/8oz red kidney
 beans, cooked and
 drained
1 hard-boiled egg, finely
 chopped
100g/4oz canned mackerel
 fillets in tomato sauce

100g/4oz finely chopped
 onion
40g/1½oz finely chopped
 onion
25g/1oz slivered carrot
30ml/2tbsp lemon juice
15ml/1tbsp red wine

Preparation Combine all the ingredients in a large wooden chopping bowl. Mash them into a paste with a fine and even consistency.

Spoon the mixture into a serving bowl. Cover and chill for at least 2 hours. Serve with crackers, dark bread or on a bed of lettuce.

Vegetable Cream Cheese
Makes approx. 350g/¾lb

Ingredients

225g/8oz cream cheese
2 green (spring) onions,
 chopped
2 carrots, grated
2 radishes, chopped
2 sticks celery, chopped

small piece fennel, chopped
½ green pepper, chopped
7g/1tbsp chives, chopped
2.5g/½tsp paprika
salt and pepper

Preparation Combine all the ingredients and mix well.

Use the mixture as an hors d'oeuvre, served in small bowls, or as a spread for open sandwiches (try pumpernickel or rye bread or raisin malt loaf).

Bean Pancake
Makes 16

Ingredients
225g/8oz split or whole
  beans, washed
50g/2oz glutinous rice
30ml/2tbsp soy sauce
10g/1tbsp roasted sesame
  seeds, crushed
2.5g/½tsp bicarbonate of
  soda
100g/4oz bean sprouts,
  blanched and dried
1 clove garlic, peeled and
  crushed
4 spring onions, trimmed
  and chopped

100g/4oz cooked lean
  pork, shredded
salt and pepper to taste
sesame oil for frying
Sauce
50ml/2fl oz soy sauce
1 clove garlic, peeled and
  crushed
30ml/2tbsp rice vinegar
2 spring onions, finely
  sliced lengthwise
pinch of sugar

Preparation Pick over then soak the mung beans and glutinous rice in water for at least 8 hours.

Rinse well, removing as many green skins as possible, drain, then put into a food processor and grind to a batter the consistency of double cream. Add soy sauce, sesame seeds and bicarbonate of soda.

When ready to cook, add the bean sprouts, garlic, spring onion and pork. Season to taste. Heat the sesame oil in a pan. Spoon or ladle in just over 150ml/¼pt of the mixture and, using the back of a spoon, spread it into a thick pancake. Drizzle a little of the sesame oil over the surface, cover and cook over a medium heat until the underside is cooked.

Now invert a lightly oiled plate over the pancake. Remove from the heat and turn the frying pan over so that the pancake is on the plate. Slip the pancake, uncooked-side down, back into the pan, and continue cooking for a further 3-4 minutes.

Keep warm while cooking the remaining batter and serve in quarters with the dipping sauce, made by blending together its ingredients.

Pork Spring Roll
Makes 20

Ingredients
25g/1oz onions, chopped
  finely
3 cloves garlic, crushed
1cm/½in ginger, scraped
  and shredded
2 red chillies, shredded
oil for frying
225g/8oz pork, finely
  minced
5g/1tsp turmeric

10 spring roll wrappers, cut
  in half
flour and water paste to
  seal
Sauce
100ml/3½fl oz vinegar
1½ cloves garlic
salt and black pepper
6 pieces chilli, sliced

Preparation Fry the onions, garlic and ginger with the chillies and oil. Add the pork, cook for 5 minutes, stirring until the meat changes colour. Add seasoning and turmeric. Cook for 2 minutes, and cool.

Fill rolls, sealing with flour and water paste. Then deep fry in hot oil until they turn crispy and brown.

Mix together all the sauce ingredients and serve in a small bowl as a dip for the rolls.

Cheese and Garlic Straws
Makes 20

Ingredients
225g/8oz Puff Pastry
juice of 2-3 garlic cloves
50ml/2fl oz milk
5g/1tsp paprika

15g/1tbsp Parmesan
  cheese, grated
salt and cayenne pepper

Preparation Roll out the puff pastry on a floured board into a rectangle, as thinly as possible.

Stir the garlic juice into most of the milk and brush the pastry with half of it.

Mix the paprika and Parmesan, and season with a little salt and cayenne. Sprinkle half of it over one half of the pastry.

Fold the pastry and roll out as thinly as possible.

Repeat with the remaining garlic milk and Parmesan mixture and roll out to a rectangle not more than 6mm/¼in thick. Brush with milk and cut into strips about 1cm/½in wide and 15cm/6in long.

Arrange the straws, at least 2.5cm/1in apart, on greased baking sheets and bake for 7 to 10 minutes in a preheated 220°C/425°F/Gas 7 oven until well-risen and golden brown.

Serve warm, piled onto each other, log cabin style.

Cheese Cutlets
Makes 6

Ingredients

15ml/1tbsp Ghee or butter
250ml/8fl oz milk
175g/6oz cottage cheese
100g/4oz semolina
1 medium onion, finely
  chopped
2 green chillies, seeded and
  finely chopped

7g/1tbsp chopped
  coriander leaves
2.5g/¹/₂tsp salt
30g/2tbsp flour
125ml/4fl oz milk
breadcrumbs
oil for deep frying

Preparation Melt the ghee or butter over medium heat, add the milk, cottage cheese, semolina, onions, chillies, coriander leaves and salt and mix thoroughly. Stirring constantly, cook until the mixture leaves the sides and a ball forms, about 3-4 minutes.

Spread the mixture 1.5 cm/³/₄ in thick on a greased baking tin. Cut into 2.5-cm/1-in squares and chill for about 2 hours.

Make a smooth batter with the flour and milk. Dip each square in the batter and then roll it in breadcrumbs.

Heat the oil and deep fry the cutlets for 2-3 minutes over a high heat till crisp and golden. Serve with chutney.

Chop
Spicy minced lamb wrapped in potato
Makes approx. 20

Ingredients

30ml/2tbsp oil
1 large onion, finely sliced
2 cloves garlic, crushed
1.25cm/¹/₂in ginger, grated
4g/³/₄tsp ground turmeric
2.5g/¹/₂tsp chilli powder
5g/1tsp salt
good pinch of salt
10g/1tbsp raisins
  (optional)
10ml/2tsp vinegar
450g/1lb minced lamb

5g/1tsp Garam Masala
1 egg (lightly beaten)
breadcrumbs
oil for shallow frying
900g/1¹/₄lb potatoes, peeled
  and boiled
5g/1tsp ground, roasted
  cumin
2.5g/¹/₂tsp ground, roasted,
  dried red chillies
  (optional)

Preparation Heat the oil in a large frying pan over a medium high heat. Add the onion, garlic and ginger and fry for 4-5 minutes, stirring constantly, until the onion becomes pale gold.

Add the turmeric, chilli powder, salt, sugar, raisins (if used) and vinegar, mix thoroughly with the onion and fry for 1 minute. Add the lamb and mix with the spices.

Cover, lower heat, and, stirring occasionally, cook for about 20 minutes. Remove the cover, turn the heat up and, stirring constantly, cook until all the liquid has evaporated and the lamb is dry.

Mix in the garam masala, remove from the heat, and set aside to cool.

Mash the potatoes with the cumin, ground chilli (if used) and salt. Divide into about 20 balls.

Take a ball and make a depression in the middle with your thumb, to form a cup shape. Fill the centre with the meat mixture and re-form the potato ball, making sure no cracks appear. Make all the Chop in this manner.

Dip in the egg, one at a time, and roll in the breadcrumbs.

Heat the oil over a very high heat in a large frying pan and fry until golden brown, turning once after about a minute.

Devilled Eggs
Makes 8

Ingredients

4 hard-boiled eggs, halved
  lengthwise
15g/1¹/₂tbsp onions, finely
  chopped
2 green chillies, seeded and
  finely chopped
7g/1tbsp coriander leaves,
  chopped

2.5g/¹/₂tsp salt
30g/2tbsp mashed potato
oil for deep frying
15g/1tbsp plain flour
50ml/2fl oz water

Preparation Remove the yolks and mix with the onions, chillies, coriander leaves, salt and mashed potatoes. Put the mixture back into the egg whites. Chill for 30 minutes.

Heat the oil in a pan over high heat. While the oil is heating up make a batter with the flour and water. Be careful not to allow the oil to catch fire.

Dip eggs into the batter and gently put into the hot oil. Fry until golden, turning once. Drain and serve warm.

Falafel
Chick-Pea Balls
Serves 4

Ingredients
225g/8oz chick-peas
3 cloves garlic, finely chopped
1 onion, finely chopped
5g/1tsp ground cumin
5g/1tsp ground coriander
15g/2tbsp fresh parsley, finely chopped
15ml/1tbsp tahini paste
2 eggs, beaten
lemon juice
wholewheat flour mixed with wheatgerm for coating
oil
cayenne pepper
olives, gherkins, pickled peppers (optional)

Preparation Soak the chick-peas overnight, then cook in boiling water until they can be mashed with a fork.

In a large bowl, mash the chick-peas with the garlic, onion, cumin, coriander, parsley and tahini. Add enough egg and lemon juice to make a dough.

Form the dough into 3-cm/1½-in balls, roll in flour and wheatgerm to coat and fry in hot oil until crispy. Drain on kitchen paper.

Serve hot or cold with a dip of tahini paste mixed with olive oil and lemon juice, and sprinkled with cayenne pepper. Serve with olives, gherkins and pickled peppers if you like. Alternatively, stuff the falafel into envelopes of pitta bread with a salad of shredded leaves, peppers and a few chopped chilli peppers.

Devils on Horseback
Makes 12

Ingredients
12 prunes, soaked
6 slices streaky bacon
12 cocktail sticks

Preparation Put the soaked prunes in a small saucepan, cover with water, bring to the boil and simmer for 5 minutes. Drain and allow to cool slightly.

Remove the stones from the prunes and reshape.

Cut the rind from the bacon, cut each slice in half and smooth out with a spatula. Put a piece of foil on the grill pan and arrange the slices of bacon on the foil. Cook for 2 minutes under a hot grill. Do not allow to crisp.

When slightly cooled, wrap the bacon pieces around the prunes and finish cooking under the grill or in the oven if more convenient.

Secure with cocktail sticks, and serve hot with pre-dinner drinks.

Deep Fried Pastries
Makes 12

Kalonji is also known as nigella. It is a small black seed and can be purchased at Indian grocers.

Ingredients
100g/4oz flour
2.5g/½tsp salt
pinch kalonji
pinch ground roasted cumin
20ml/1½tbsp oil
50ml/2fl oz hot water
oil for deep frying

Preparation Sieve the flour and salt together. Mix in the cumin. Rub in the oil.

Add enough water to make a stiff dough. Knead for 10 minutes until soft and smooth.

Divided the dough into 12 balls. Roll each ball into thin rounds 10cm/4in across. Make 5 or 6 small cuts in the rounds.

Heat oil in a frying pan over medium heat. Add a pastry round and fry until crisp and golden. Drain on paper towels. Serve warm with chutney.

HORS D'OEUVRES AND SNACKS

Garlic Buttered Nuts
Makes 225g/8oz

Ingredients
225g/8oz shelled almonds, cashews or peanuts, or a mixture
25g/1oz butter
15ml/1tbsp oil
2-3 cloves of garlic, finely crushed
rock salt

Preparation Loosen and remove the almond skins by pouring boiling water over them and refreshing in cold water. Toast the peanuts briefly and rub off the brown skins.

Melt the butter and oil with the garlic in a heavy frying pan and toss the nuts in it over a moderate heat for 3 to 5 minutes or until they are crisp and golden.

Drain on kitchen paper towels and sprinkle with rock salt. Serve warm.

Variation For Devilled Garlic Nuts, add a little cayenne to the rock salt.

Curried Vegetable Fritters
Makes 20

Ingredients
60g/4tbsp chick-pea (gram) flour
10ml/2tsp oil
5g/1tsp baking powder
2.5g/½tsp salt
75ml/3fl oz water
Any of the following vegetables can be used:
aubergines, cut into very thin rounds
onions, cut into 3mm/⅛-in rings
potatoes, cut into very thin rounds
cauliflower, cut into 1.5-cm/¼-in florets
fresh chilli, left whole
pumpkin, cut into thin slices
green pepper, cut into thin strips
oil for deep frying

Preparation Mix all the batter ingredients together and beat until smooth.

Wash the slices of vegetables and pat dry.

Heat the oil in a wide frying pan till very hot.

Dip each vegetable slice into the batter and lower into the hot oil. Put as many slices as you can in the oil. Fry till crisp and golden.

Drain and serve with Coriander Chutney.

Savoury Pasties
Makes 20

Ingredients
350g/12oz Puff or Shortcrust Pastry
milk or beaten egg to seal
deep fat for frying
15ml/1tbsp oil
½ small onion, peeled and chopped
1 clove garlic
100g/4oz minced pork
½ spicy sausage, finely chopped
7.5ml/½tbsp tomato purée
1 hard-boiled egg, chopped
15-25g/½-1oz raisins
4 stuffed olives, cut into rings
1 small gherkin, chopped
seasoning

Preparation Make the pastry or thaw if you are using frozen. Cover and leave to rest in the refrigerator while preparing the filling.

Heat the oil and fry the onion and garlic without browning. Add the minced pork and stir until the meat browns. Add the sausage and tomato purée. Cover and cook very gently for 10-15 minutes. Draw from the heat and leave to cool, then stir in the hard-boiled eggs, raisins, olives, gherkin and seasoning to taste. Leave to cool completely.

Roll out the pastry on a floured board and cut into 10-cm/4-in rounds. Divide the filling between them. Damp the edges half-way round, then fold into a half circle. Seal the edges by knocking up with the back of a knife, then flute them or mark with the prongs of a fork, to seal.

When all the pasties are made, fry in hot oil for 10 minutes until golden and cooked through. Drain thoroughly on absorbent kitchen paper and serve hot or warm.

Variation Instead of deep frying the pasties, you can bake them at 220°C/425°F/Gas 7 in a preheated oven for 12 minutes.

Fish Savouries with Spicy Tomato Sauce
Serves 4

Leftover poached salmon, trout or canned fish such as tuna or salmon can be used.

Ingredients
225g/8oz fish, cooked
25g/1oz butter
1 small onion, peeled and sliced
225g/8oz potatoes, cooked and sieved
2 drops Tabasco sauce
5ml/1tsp tomato ketchup
salt and freshly ground pepper
7g/1tbsp chopped parsley
1 egg, beaten
dried breadcrumbs
oil for frying
150ml/¼pt Spicy Tomato Sauce

Preparation Make sure that all the bones are removed from the cooked fish.

Melt the butter and sweat the onion until tender. Add the potatoes, seasoning and parsley to the onion in a bowl, and finally add the fish and mix well.

Mix with a little of the beaten egg. Add a few drops of water to the remaining egg. Flour the hands and form the mixture into small balls and chill in the refrigerator.

Roll the fish balls in the egg and water mixture, and then in the dried crumbs. Fry the balls in deep fat or in a frying pan one-third filled with oil which has been heated.

Arrange on a plate. Spear the balls with cocktail sticks and serve around a dish of hot Spicy Tomato Sauce.

Hi-Speed Pizzas
Makes 4 small pizzas

Ingredients
225g/8oz flour
2.5g/¹⁄₂tsp salt
5g/1tsp baking powder
60ml/4tbsp olive oil
water to mix
250ml/8fl.oz Concentrated
 Tomato Sauce
good pinch fresh marjoram
 or 2.5g/¹⁄₂tsp dried
 oregano

50g/2oz stoned black
 olives
175g/6oz Cheddar cheese,
 thinly sliced
1 clove garlic, finely
 chopped

Preparation Sift together the flour, salt and baking powder, and add the oil and enough water to make a very sticky dough.

Divide into 4 and press each piece into a well-oiled 15-cm/6-in round pizza or pie pan.

Top each with the tomato sauce, marjoram or oregano, olives and cheese, and sprinkle with the garlic.

Bake for 15 to 20 minutes in a preheated 230°C/450°F/Gas 8 oven until the dough is cooked and the cheese is browned and bubbling.

Variation You can add chopped ham, crisp bacon, strips of salami, sliced button mushrooms or sliced red pepper.

Green Banana Balls
Makes 8

Ingredients
1 green banana, halved
1 fresh green chilli, seeded
 and chopped
3g/¹⁄₂tbsp chopped
 coriander leaves

2.5g/¹⁄₂tsp salt
10g/1tbsp chopped onion
5g/1tsp plain flour
oil for deep frying

Preparation Boil the banana till soft. Peel and cool.

Mash the banana with the chilli, coriander leaves, salt, onion and flour. Divide the mixture into 8 small balls and flatten.

Heat the oil and fry the balls, turning once, till crisp and golden.

Galloping Horses
Fried Pork and Fruit Snacks
Makes 16

Make up the filling just before using — it binds together better when still warm.

Ingredients
20ml/1¹⁄₂tbsp peanut or
 vegetable oil
1 clove garlic, peeled and
 crushed
1 red chilli, seeded and
 chopped
few stems fresh coriander,
 stems chopped and
 leaves reserved
175g/6oz pork with a
 reasonable proportion of
 fat to lean, finely minced
25g/1oz salted peanuts,
 crushed coarsely with
 pestle and mortar

15ml/1tbsp Worcestershire
 sauce
15g/1tbsp brown sugar or
 to taste
freshly ground black
 pepper
pieces of fresh pineapple
mandarin segments, cut
 almost through vertically
 and opened out like a
 book, skin-side down.
canned lychees, well
 drained

Preparation Heat the oil in a wok, fry the garlic and chillies without browning, then add the coriander stems. Now add the meat and cook until the colour changes. Add the peanuts, fish sauce if used, sugar and pepper. Continue cooking, stirring occasionally, for 10 minutes or until the mixture is cooked but not too dry.

Arrange the pieces of prepared fruit on a serving dish and top each with a spoonful of the pork mixture. Lightly press with fingers to stick.

Garnish with the reserved coriander leaves. Serve.

Tapenade
Serves 6

Ingredients
100g/4oz black olives
2-3 cloves of garlic,
 coarsely chopped
75g/3oz canned anchovies

10g/1tbsp capers
100ml/4fl oz olive oil
medium French loaf, thinly
 sliced.

Preparation Stone and coarsely chop the olives and blend them with the garlic, anchovies and capers, adding the oil gradually.

Toast the bread on one side. Spread the untoasted side thickly with the mixture and cook under a hot grill until the edges are well browned. Serve warm.

This can also be served on fingers of crisp, buttered toast.

Samosas
Makes 20

Ingredients

45ml/3tbsp oil
pinch whole cumin seeds
450g/1lb potatoes, diced
   into 1-cm/½-in cubes
1 fresh green chilli, seeded
   and finely chopped
pinch turmeric
2.5g/½tsp salt
75g/3oz peas

5g/1tsp ground roasted
   cumin

Dough
225g/8oz plain flour
5g/1tsp salt
45ml/3tbsp oil
approx. 100ml/3½fl. oz hot
   water
oil for deep frying

Preparation To make the filling, heat the oil in a heavy frying pan over medium high heat and add the cumin seeds. Let them sizzle for a few seconds.

Add the potatoes and green chilli and fry for 2-3 minutes. Add the turmeric and salt and, stirring occasionally, cook for 5 minutes.

Add the peas and the ground roasted cumin. Stir to mix. Cover, lower heat and cook a further 10 minutes until the potatoes are tender. Cool.

For the dough, sieve together the flour and salt. Rub in the oil. Add enough water to form a stiff dough. Knead for 10 minutes until smooth.

Divide into 12 balls. Roll each ball into a round of about 15cm/6in across. Cut in half.

Pick up one half, flatten it slightly and form a cone, sealing the overlapping edge with a little water. Fill the cone with 1½tsp of the filling and seal the top with a little water.

Continue making the samosas until all the ingredients are used up.

Heat oil in a frying pan over medium heat. Put in as many samosas as you can into the hot oil and fry until crisp and golden.

Drain and serve with a chutney.

Wholewheat Samosas
Makes 16

Ingredients

225g/8oz wholewheat
   flour
2.5g/½tsp salt
60ml/4tbsp oil
60ml/4tbsp water

Filling
15ml/1tbsp oil
100g/4oz minced lamb
1 potato, peeled, cooked
   and diced

2g/1tsp fresh mint,
   chopped
pinch coriander
pinch curry powder
salt and freshly ground
   pepper
45ml/3tbsp water
20g/2tbsp cooked peas
15ml/1tbsp yoghurt
oil for deep frying

Preparation Sprinkle the flour and salt into a bowl and pour the oil over the flour. Rub in with finger tips, as if making Shortcrust Pastry, until the mixture is in fine crumbs. Gradually add the water and mix to a stiff dough.

Turn on to a floured work surface and knead for a few minutes, until smooth. Put the dough in an oiled polythene bag and allow to stand for at least 30 minutes.

To make the filling, heat the oil in a frying pan and brown the lamb, separating the minced meat with a spoon or fork.

Add the diced potato, mix with meat, sprinkle with mint, coriander, curry powder and season well. Fry for 2 minutes. Add the water and cook for 5 minutes on a low heat.

Add peas and yoghurt. Allow to cool. Taste for seasoning.

Knead the dough on a floured surface for 2 minutes. Roll into a sausage shape and divide into 8. Put the other pieces of pastry back into the oiled bag while making the samosas.

Flatten into an 18-cm/7-in square, using a rolling pin. Cut into two triangles. Wet the open ends with cold water and seal one side.

Fill the open end with the mixture, seal the edge well. Flute the wide edge with the finger tips and press the other two edges with floured fingers to form an even strip. Shape and fill remaining dough as described.

Heat the oil to 190°C/360°F in a deep pan. Fry two or three at a time, turning from time to time. Drain on kitchen paper.

Serve hot as an appetizer or as a light meal with salad.

These can be made even smaller and used as cocktail snacks.

Julienne Vegetables

1 Slicing vegetables such as carrots and celery for crudités like this makes the hors d'oeuvres more attractive. (Steamed Julienne vegetables look highly professional as part of the main dish). Square off the sides of root vegetables so that they are block-shaped.

2 Slice finely, using a good, sharp knife.

3 Stack the slices and slice again into 'matchsticks'. Soaking Julienne vegetables in iced water makes them curly.

Soups and Stocks

Avocado Soup 31
Aubergine Soup 31
Cold Apple Soup 31
Bean Soup 31
Beetroot and Cabbage Borscht 32
Hearty Beef Soup 32
Chilled Borscht 32
Broccoli and Orange Soup 32
Carrot and Coriander Soup 33
Chard Soup with Lentils 33
Celeriac Soup 33
German Carrot Soup 33
Oriental Chicken Soup 34
Cheese and Onion Soup 34
Cold Cherry Soup 34
Jellied Lemon Chicken Soup 34
Chicken in the Pot with Soup 35
Clam Chowder 35
Corn Chowder 35
Midwest Corn Chowder 36
Fish Chowder 36
Courgette and Fennel Soup 36
Cock-A-Leekie Soup 37
Cream of Corn Soup 37
Cucumber Soup 37
Persian Cucumber Soup 37
Garlic Chicken Soup 38
Garlic Soup 38
Fruit Soup 38
Fish Soup 38
Gazpacho 38/39
Green Soup 39
Harvest Soup 39
Kohlrabi and Chicken Soup 40
Curried Lentil Soup 40

Family Lentil Soup 40
Lentil and Tomato Soup 41
Curried Marrow Soup 41
Cream of Mushroom Soup 41
Mushroom Soup 42
Pork Soup with Ginger 42
Green Pea Soup 42
Green Pea and Lettuce Soup 43
French Onion Soup 43
Potato Soup 43
Cheesey Potato Soup 44
Russian Egg Drop Soup 44
Scotch Broth 44
Scotch Barley Soup 44
Shellfish Bisque 45
Sour Soup 45
Spinach Soup 45
Cold Tomato Soup 46
Fresh Tomato and Vodka Soup 46
Vegetable Cream Soup 47
Quick Chilled Summer Soup 47
Vegetable Garlic Basil Soup 47
Consommé 47
Watercress Soup 48
Country Vegetable Soup 48
Scholar's Vegetable Soup 48
Chicken.Broth 49
Watercress and Potato Soup 49
Chicken Stock 50
Brown Stock 50
Waste-Nothing Vegetable Stock 50
Court-Bouillon 50
Fish Stock 50

Making a stock 51

Avocado Soup
Serves 4

Ingredients
2 large ripe avocados
600ml/1pt yoghurt
1 clove garlic, crushed

juice of 1 lemon
salt and pepper

Preparation Halve the avocados, remove the stones and peel them. Blend all the ingredients together. Serve very well chilled, garnished with chives if desired.

The thickness of the soup will depend as much on the size of the avocados as the thickness of the yoghurt used. You can thin it down with a little milk or cream if you need to.

Aubergine Soup
Serves 6-8

This unusual soup shows a touch of Turkish influence.

Ingredients
100ml/4fl oz olive oil
75g/3oz mushrooms, quartered
1 large onion, coarsely chopped
1 large tomato, cut into eighths
1 large aubergine, peeled and diced

700ml/1¼pt beef stock
2.5g/½tsp dried parsley
pinch salt
pinch white pepper
pinch dried thyme
pinch dried marjoram
pinch grated nutmeg

Preparation Heat the olive oil in a large pot over a low heat. Add the mushrooms, onion and tomato and sauté for 10 minutes.

Add the remaining ingredients to the pot. Cover and simmer for 35 to 40 minutes. Serve hot.

Cold Apple Soup
Serves 4-6

Fruit soup is popular throughout Central Europe. This version could be also made with plums, pears, peaches or cherries.

Ingredients
3 medium/450g/1lb cooking apples, peeled and cored
150ml/¼pt water
75g/3oz sugar
juice of ½ lemon
15g/1tbsp cinnamon

2 whole cloves
pinch salt
15ml/1tbsp white wine
450ml/¾pt yoghurt
150ml/¼pt sour cream (optional)

Preparation Cube the apples and cook them with the water, sugar, lemon juice, cinnamon, cloves and salt until they are soft. Remove the cloves.

Mash the apples and leave them to cool. Add the wine and yoghurt to the apples and mix together well.

Serve well chilled, with the sour cream if desired.

A thinly sliced red-skinned apple can be used as a garnish.

Bean Soup
Serves 4-6

Ingredients
225g/8oz haricot beans
15-30ml/1-2tbsp oil
1 onion, chopped
1 clove garlic, chopped
2 carrots, chopped
2 stalks celery, sliced
200g/7oz tomatoes, peeled (or a small can)

1 slice lemon
soy sauce
salt and freshly ground black pepper
parsley

Preparation Soak the beans overnight. Bring to the boil in a large pan of water (about 1l/1¾pts) and simmer until tender.

Meanwhile, heat oil in a frying pan and cook onion and garlic until soft. Add carrots, celery and tomatoes, in that order, stirring all the while.

Tip vegetables into the pan with the cooked beans. Add the slice of lemon and soy sauce. Taste and adjust seasoning.

Heat through and serve sprinkled with chopped parsley. The soup may be partly puréed if you like.

Beetroot and Cabbage Borscht
Serves 6-8

The perhaps unlikely combination of beetroot and red cabbage makes a deliciously rich and hearty soup. The addition of the sausages makes it into more of a meal. Although the sour cream is not cooked with the soup, it is an essential part of it.

Ingredients
butter or margarine
2 rashers bacon, chopped
450g/1lb cooked beetroot, peeled and diced
30g/2tbsp flour
30ml/2tbsp vinegar
675g/1½lb red cabbage, finely shredded
bay leaf
1 clove garlic, crushed
1 tbsp sugar
2l/3½pt beef stock
salt and pepper
450g/1lb spicy sausages, chopped (optional)
150ml/¼pt sour cream

Preparation Heat the butter and fry the bacon. Add the beetroot and toss it for 1 minute. Add the flour and stir well off the heat. Return to the heat and add the vinegar, mixing it in well.

Add the cabbage, bay leaf, garlic, sugar, stock, salt and pepper. Bring to the boil and then simmer, covered, for 1 hour, adding a little more stock if necessary. If you are using the sausages, add them 5 minutes before serving.

Serve hot with a generous spoonful of sour cream in each bowl.

Hearty Beef Soup
Serves 8

Ingredients
450g/1lb beef brisket or chuck, thinly sliced
450g/1lb beef bones, split into pieces
1 large turnip, diced
1 onion, quartered
2 stalks celery, finely chopped
1 carrot, halved
30g/1oz chopped green pepper
pinch salt
pinch black pepper
30g/4tbsp chopped chives
50ml/2fl oz wine
1.9l/3¼pt water
225g/8oz egg noodles

Preparation Put all the ingredients except the noodles into a large soup pot. Bring to a boil, reduce the heat and simmer, tightly covered, for 5-6 hours. Add the noodles.

Raise the heat to medium and cook for a further 12-15 minutes. Serve hot.

Chilled Borscht
Serves 6

Ingredients
450g/1lb cooked beetroot, peeled
900ml/1½pt chicken with the stock
juice of 1 lemon
300ml/½pt sour cream
dill
salt and pepper

Preparation Liquidize the beetroot, with the stock, lemon juice, half of the sour cream, dill, salt and pepper. You can make the mixture as smooth as you like, but you may prefer to leave it a little chunky with small pieces of beetroot floating in it.

Refrigerate as long as possible (overnight is best) and serve well chilled with the remaining sour cream and perhaps a couple of ice cubes in each bowl.

Broccoli and Orange Soup
Serves 6

Ingredients
450g/1lb broccoli, chopped
1 medium onion, chopped
15ml/1tbsp oil
juice of 2 oranges
900ml/1½pt chicken stock
15g/1tbsp cornflour
30ml/2tbsp water
150ml/¼pt single cream
salt and pepper
grated orange rind

Preparation Reserve some small pieces of broccoli for garnish.

Heat the oil and cook the onion until it has just softened but not browned. Add the broccoli and stir. Cook, covered, for a few minutes and then add the orange juice and stock. Bring to the boil, cover and simmer for about 20 minutes, until the broccoli is soft. Purée the soup in a blender.

Mix the cornflour and water to a smooth paste and stir into the soup, adding the cream, with salt and pepper to taste. Return the soup to the heat and cook for a further 5 minutes.

Serve, garnished with the reserved broccoli and orange rind.

Use frozen broccoli if fresh is not available. If you prefer, this soup can be served cold.

Carrot and Coriander Soup
Serves 6

Ingredients

25g/1oz butter
1 medium onion, sliced
675g/1½lb carrots, sliced
5g/1tsp ground coriander
900ml/1½pt vegetable
stock

150ml/¼pt sour cream
salt and pepper
fresh coriander or parsley

Preparation Heat the butter, add the onion and cook until it has just softened but not browned. Add the carrots and ground coriander and stir well. Leave the carrots to cook gently for 3 minutes. Add the stock and bring the mixture to the boil, then simmer, covered, for 25 minutes.

Liquidize the soup, adding the sour cream. Adjust the seasoning. Serve very cold, garnished with fresh coriander or parsley

Use a chicken stock if preferred. Herb bouillon cubes are very good for this soup.

Chard Soup with Lentils
Serves 6-8

Kale or fresh spinach may be substituted for the chard.

Ingredients

400g/14oz brown lentils
1.9l/3¼pt water
50ml/2fl oz olive oil
2 large onions, finely
chopped
6 cloves garlic, coarsely
chopped
130g/4½oz Swiss chard
leaves, torn, tough stems
removed

25g/1oz chopped fresh
coriander
2.5g/½tsp salt
pinch black pepper
50ml/2fl oz lemon juice

Preparation Pick over the lentils and wash them. Put the lentils into a large saucepan and add the water. Cover and cook over a medium heat for 1 hour.

When the lentils have cooked for 50 minutes, heat the olive oil in a frying pan over a low heat. Add the onions, garlic and chard and sauté for 8 minutes, stirring constantly.

Add the chard mixture to the lentils. Add the coriander, salt, pepper and lemon juice and stir well. Cover the saucepan and simmer over a low heat for 20 minutes. Serve hot.

Celeriac Soup
Serves 6-8

Ingredients

1.5l/2½pt chicken stock
2 large celeriac, peeled
and sliced
65g/2½oz coarsely
chopped celery

50g/2oz chopped leeks
1 small endive, chopped
2 large carrots, diced
2.5g/½tsp salt
2.5g/½tsp white pepper

Preparation In a large soup pot, bring the chicken stock to a boil. Add the remaining ingredients, reduce the heat to low and simmer for 40 minutes. Serve hot.

German Carrot Soup
Serves 4-6

Carrots, apples and onions may seem an odd combination, but this delicious soup is a traditional dish along the Rhine.

Ingredients

450g/1lb carrots, peeled
and sliced
bay leaf
1l/1¾pt chicken stock
5g/1tsp brown sugar
75g/3oz butter
3 medium onions, peeled
and halved

1 large cooking apple,
peeled, cored and sliced
salt and freshly ground
pepper
a little lemon juice
a little chopped chervil

Preparation Put the carrots into a large pan with the bay leaf, chicken stock, and brown sugar. Bring to a boil, then simmer until nearly tender.

Meanwhile, heat the butter in a frying pan, add the sliced onions and apples with a little salt and pepper. Fry until soft and golden brown. Add the contents of the frying pan to the carrots, and continue cooking until all the vegetables are very soft. Strain and reserve the liquid. Remove the bay leaf.

Sieve or liquidize the vegetable mixture until very smooth. Return to the liquid. Reheat and adjust the seasoning, adding a little lemon juice if necessary.

Serve sprinkled with chopped chervil.

German Carrot Soup

Oriental Chicken Soup
Serves 6

Serve prawn or shrimp crackers with this slightly spicy, unusual soup.

Ingredients

2 chicken joints, skinned	1 large green pepper,
1 medium onion, peeled	seeded and coarsely
and quartered	chopped
2.5cm/1in root ginger,	25g/1oz Chinese egg
peeled and sliced	noodles
1l/1¾pt good chicken or	soy sauce
vegetable stock	freshly ground pepper
	2 spring onions, sliced, to
	garnish

Preparation Wipe the chicken joints and place in a large pan. Add the onion and ginger to the pan with the stock. Bring to the boil, then cover and simmer gently for 20 minutes, or until the chicken is very tender. Remove from the heat and allow to cool slightly.

Remove the onion from the pan, then lift out and bone the chicken joints. Reserve the meat. Skim any fat from the liquid left in the pan.

Add the pepper to the liquid in the pan. Finely chop the reserved chicken, and add to the pan with the noodles and a little soy sauce and ground pepper. Bring back to the boil, then simmer gently for 5 minutes. Taste for seasoning, and add a little more soy sauce if necessary.

Spoon into individual bowls and garnish with the sliced spring onions.

Cheese and Onion Soup
Serves 4-6

Ingredients

15-30ml/1-2 tbsp oil	175g/6oz Cheddar cheese,
2 medium onions, sliced	grated
1.2l/2pt stock	salt
225g/8oz potatoes	soy sauce

Preparation Heat the oil in a large saucepan and stir-fry onions until lightly browned. Add stock and bring to the boil

Meanwhile, peel the potatoes and grate them into the saucepan. Turn down the heat and simmer until potatoes have cooked and soup has thickened.

Add the grated cheese, stirring to melt. Season to taste with salt and soy sauce.

Serve with wholewheat bread and a crisp green salad.

Cold Cherry Soup
Serves 8

This unusual soup is made using both red and black cherries and is served cold.

Ingredients

900ml/1½pt cold water	30ml/2tbsp lemon juice
350g/12oz sugar	250ml/8fl oz red wine
pinch cinnamon	pinch dried dill
500g/18oz fresh or canned	2.5g/½tsp ground white
red cherries, stoned	pepper
500g/18oz fresh or canned	30ml/2tbsp tepid water
black cherries, stoned	15g/1tbsp arrowroot

Preparation In a medium-sized saucepan, combine all the ingredients except the tepid water and arrowroot. Bring to a boil over a medium heat. Partially cover the saucepan and reduce the heat to low. Simmer for 1 hour.

In a small bowl, combine the arrowroot and tepid water. Stir well. Stir the mixture into the soup and turn the heat up to medium. Continue stirring until the soup begins to bubble. Reduce the heat to low. Simmer the soup, uncovered, for 2 minutes.

Pour the soup into a glass bowl and chill for 1 hour. Serve cold.

Jellied Lemon Chicken Soup
Serves 4

Ingredients

900ml/1½pt chicken stock	5g/1 tsp sugar
25ml/5tsp gelatine	150ml/¼pt sour cream
175ml/6fl oz lemon juice	

Preparation Bring the stock to the boil, remove from the heat, sprinkle over the gelatine and stir to dissolve. Add the lemon juice and sugar and stir well.

Leave this to cool and when it is beginning to set, whisk in the sour cream. Pour into individual dishes or glasses and leave to set firm. The mixture may separate into two layers, but this will simply add to its charm.

Chicken in the Pot with Soup
Serves 6-8

This dish, the queen of all chicken soups, is traditionally served with Kreplach and Matzo Balls.

Ingredients

2 large parsley sprigs	5 carrots, halved
1 large parsnip	1-kg/3-lb chicken, cut into
1 small leek	pieces
dill sprig	5g/1tsp salt
2.4l/4pt water	2.5g/¹⁄₂tsp black pepper
2 stalks celery, halved	pinch ground white pepper
2 large onions, halved	65g/2¹⁄₂oz fine egg
	noodles

Preparation Tie the parsley, parsnip, leek and dill together with kitchen string.

Fill a large soup pot with the water. Add the bunch of vegetables and herbs and the celery, onions, carrots and chicken pieces. Bring the liquid to the boil. Add the salt, black pepper and white pepper. Reduce the heat to low. Simmer for 1 hour 45 minutes.

Remove and discard the bunch of vegetables and herbs. Add the egg noodles to the pot. Simmer for 10 minutes, stirring occasionally.

Serve the soup with the vegetables and chicken pieces in large deep bowls.

Clam Chowder
Serves 4

Ingredients

1-2 dozen clams or 1 can	1 stalk celery, diced
clams	100g/4oz potato, diced
150ml/¹⁄₄pt white wine	salt and freshly ground
300ml/¹⁄₂pt water	pepper
bay leaf	few sprigs fresh thyme or
bouquet garni	2.5g/¹⁄₂tsp dried thyme
100g/4oz bacon	4-6 fresh tomatoes, skinned
25g/1oz butter	or 425-g/15-oz can
1 medium onion, diced	tomatoes
2 leeks, washed and	7g/1tbsp chopped parsley
chopped	8 cream crackers, crushed
1 green pepper, seeded,	
blanched and diced	

Preparation Poach fresh clams for about 10 minutes in the white wine and water with a bay leaf and bouquet garni added. If using canned, poach for 5 minutes.

Cut the streaky bacon into small pieces. Melt the butter in a saucepan and add bacon. After about 2 minutes add the onion, leeks, diced pepper, diced celery and diced potato. Sweat the vegetables for about 6 minutes then add the clam liquor with seasoning, thyme and chopped tomatoes.

Make the liquid up to approximately 900ml/1¹⁄₂pt with water. Bring the soup to the boil, reduce heat and simmer until the vegetables are tender. Add the clams a few minutes before serving.

Serve the chowder sprinkled with crushed crackers and parsley.

Corn Chowder
Serves 4

Ingredients

4 slices streaky bacon	600ml/1pt chicken stock
1 medium onion, peeled	salt and freshly ground
and diced	pepper
1 potato, peeled and cubed	300ml/¹⁄₂pt milk
350g/12oz can corn	drop Tabasco
kernels or frozen corn	7g/1tbsp chopped parsley

Preparation Remove any rind from the bacon slices and cut into small pieces.

On a low heat cook the bacon in a saucepan in its own fat. When there is a little fat in the pan, turn up the heat and allow to crisp. Add the onion and fry for 1 minute.

Add the potato cubes, stir round, then add half the corn with the chicken stock and seasoning. Bring to the boil and simmer for 30 minutes. Allow to cool slightly and liquidize the soup in a blender or food processor.

Return to the saucepan and stir in the milk and the remaining corn. Heat through over a low heat. Add Tabasco and taste for seasoning.

Serve sprinkled with chopped parsley.

Midwest Corn Chowder
Serves 4-6

Ingredients

175g/6oz finely chopped
  bacon
1 onion, chopped
50g/2oz sliced celery
225g/¹/₂lb diced potatoes
425ml/³/₄pt water
1 bay leaf

5g/1tsp salt
pinch black pepper
425ml/³/₄pt milk
150ml/¹/₄pt whipping
  cream
175g/6oz corn, cut from
  the cob

Preparation In a saucepan, sauté the bacon until well browned. Stir in the onion and cook for a further 2 minutes. Add the celery, potatoes, water, bay leaf and salt. Simmer gently until potatoes are tender, about 20-30 minutes.

In a small bowl mix the flour with 1tbsp milk. Stir until smooth and add to potato mixture. Add the remaining milk and stir. Heat the soup until it thickens.

Slowly stir in the cream and corn. Heat mixture gently but thoroughly. Add the black pepper, stir, and serve.

Fish Chowder
Serves 4

Ingredients

450g/1lb white fish, boned
25g/1oz butter
1 large onion, peeled and
  finely chopped
1-2 cloves garlic, peeled
  and crushed
4 potatoes, peeled and
  diced
400-g/14-oz can tomatoes
few sprigs of thyme
few sprigs of parsley

1-2 bay leaves or 1
  bouquet garni
salt and freshly ground
  black pepper
pinch cayenne pepper
300ml/¹/₂pt hot water
150ml/¹/₄pt milk
8 plain crackers, crushed
7g/1tbsp chopped parsley

Preparation Make sure the fish is boned as far as possible, as most people object to fish bones. Cut into even-sized pieces.

Melt the butter and sweat the onion, crushed garlic and diced potato for about 5 minutes. Add the can of tomatoes with the herbs and seasoning. Pour in the hot water.

Bring to the boil and simmer for about 20 minutes, or until potatoes are cooked. Add the fish for about the last 10 minutes of cooking. Taste for seasoning and make sure all the fish is cooked. Add the milk and stir over a low heat for a few minutes.

Put the crackers in the bottom of the soup bowls and pour over the soup. Sprinkle with chopped parsley. Serve with warm French bread or crispy rolls.

Courgette and Fennel Soup
Serves 4-6

This Italian soup is delicious served with garlic bread.

Ingredients

1 bulb fennel, approx.
  225g/¹/₂lb
5ml/1tsp lemon juice
50g/2oz butter or
  margarine
450g/1lb courgettes, sliced
1 medium onion, sliced

salt and freshly ground
  pepper
25g/1oz flour
600ml/1pt good chicken or
  vegetable stock
150ml/¹/₄pt single cream
chopped chives or parsley

Preparation Trim the fennel and quarter. Cook in boiling salted water with the lemon juice until tender — about 20 minutes. Drain thoroughly.

Heat the butter or margarine in a large pan and add the sliced vegetables with a little salt and pepper. Cover, and cook slowly for 15 minutes. Slice the drained fennel and add to courgette mixture. Raise the heat and cook, stirring constantly for 1 minute, then stir in the flour, followed by the stock. Bring to the boil, then cover and simmer for 20 minutes.

Strain the soup, reserving the liquid. Sieve or liquidize the vegetables until smooth. Return to the pan with the liquid and the cream. Reheat, adding more stock or water if the soup is too thick, and taste for seasoning.

Sprinkle with the chopped chives or parsley just before serving.

Cock-A-Leekie Soup
Serves 4

Ingredients

1 large chicken joint or 1 chicken carcass	1l/1¾pt water
1 onion, peeled	25g/1oz brown rice
bay leaf	100g/4oz prunes, soaked in water
bouquet garni	450g/1lb leeks, washed
salt and freshly ground pepper	7g/1tbsp chopped parsley

Preparation Put the chicken joint or cooked carcass with the quartered onion in a saucepan. Add the bay leaf and bouquet garni with a sprinkling of seasoning. Pour on the water and bring to the boil. Simmer for 1 hour.

Strain into a bowl, remove the chicken joint, skin it and chop the meat into small pieces. If using a carcass, remove any meat left and leave aside.

Skim any fat from the stock and return to the saucepan. Make up to 1.2l/2pt with water or more chicken stock.

Sprinkle in the brown rice, bring to the boil and simmer until the rice is almost cooked, approximately 20 minutes. Add the prunes and continue cooking for 5 minutes.

Make a cross through the centre of each leek, having first removed any discoloured outside leaves. Wash thoroughly under a running tap. Chop into slices about 5mm (¼in) thick. Add to the soup. Cook on a simmering heat for a further 10-15 minutes. Stir in the cooked chicken and heat through.

Serve hot, garnished with parsley.

With wholewheat bread, this makes an excellent snack meal.

Cream of Corn Soup
Serves 8

Ingredients

50g/2oz butter or margarine	500g/18oz canned or cooked sweetcorn
40g/1½oz onion, finely chopped	5g/1tsp salt
30g/2tbsp flour	black pepper to taste
900ml/1½pt milk	

Preparation Melt the butter or margarine in a saucepan. Add the onions and sauté for 3 minutes. Stir in the flour and milk. Slowly bring the mixture to a boil and add the corn, salt and pepper.

Cook over a low heat for 15 minutes, and serve hot.

Cucumber Soup
Serves 4

Ingredients

1 large cucumber, peeled	salt and pepper
600ml/1pt yoghurt	walnuts, chopped (optional)
dill or mint	

Preparation Remove a thumb-length piece of cucumber and reserve it. Cut the rest of the cucumber into chunks. Liquidize it with the yoghurt, herbs, salt and pepper.

Refrigerate the soup and serve very cold, with the reserved cucumber diced finely. Scatter some chopped walnuts over the soup if desired.

Variation Use half milk, half yoghurt and include a pickled cucumber, chopped, 100g/4oz diced cooked chicken, plenty of chopped fresh herbs and 2 chopped hard-boiled eggs.

Persian Cucumber Soup
Serves 4

Ingredients

1 large cucumber, finely grated	2 hard-boiled eggs, finely chopped
600ml/1pt yoghurt	1 large clove garlic, crushed
30ml/2tbsp tarragon vinegar	5g/1tsp sugar
dill	150ml/¼pt cream
30ml/2tbsp raisins soaked in 30ml/2tbsp tea for 1 hour	salt and pepper

Preparation Combine all the ingredients and stir thoroughly. Refrigerate for a minimum of 3 hours and serve very cold.

Variation You may prefer to substitute mint or tarragon for the dill, and add chopped apples, celery, fennel or radishes.

Garlic Chicken Soup
Serves 8

The simple yet pungent flavour of this traditional country soup was thought to arouse the taste buds for the courses to follow. This recipe can be traced back to the 17th century.

Ingredients

1.5l/2½pt chicken stock	100g/4oz onion, chopped
50ml/2fl oz white wine	10g/1tbsp spring onion,
450g/1lb chicken, boned,	chopped
skinned and shredded	
250g/9oz garlic cloves,	
peeled and quartered	

Preparation Combine the chicken stock, white wine and shredded chicken meat in a medium-sized saucepan. Simmer over a low heat for 15 minutes.

Add the garlic cloves, chopped onions and spring onions to the soup. Simmer for 10-12 minutes longer and serve.

This soup is especially good with chunks of crusty French bread.

Garlic Soup
Serves 6-8

Variations on this rich and tasty soup are found throughout the Spanish-speaking world.

Ingredients

100ml/4fl oz olive oil	1.75l/3pt boiling water
8 cloves garlic	10g/2tsp salt
5g/1tsp paprika	5g/1tsp fresh ground black
pinch cayenne pepper	pepper
6 slices stale white bread,	6 eggs, beaten
cubed	

Preparation Heat the olive oil in a large heavy saucepan. Add the garlic and sauté until golden brown. Stir in the paprika and cayenne pepper. Add the bread cubes and sauté until they are firm and golden. Carefully add the boiling water to the pan, making sure the fried bread cubes are not broken. Add the salt and pepper. Cover the pan and simmer for 1 hour.

Slowly pour the beaten eggs into the pan, stirring constantly. Simmer until the eggs are firm. Serve at once.

Fruit Soup
Serves 6

This fruit soup can be made with nearly any fruit in season.

Ingredients

2 ripe peaches, halved and	150g/6oz strawberries
stoned	100g/4oz ripe cherries,
4 ripe plums, halved and	stoned
stoned	50ml/2fl oz lemon juice
3 ripe apricots, halved and	900ml/1½pt water
stoned	100g/4oz sugar
2 apples, peeled, cored and	225ml/8fl oz white wine
halved	350ml/12fl oz sour cream

Preparation Put the fruit, lemon juice, water and sugar in a large pot. Simmer, covered, over a medium heat for 25 minutes.

Turn the heat off. Mash the fruit with a fork into a paste. Add the wine. Simmer over a low heat for 5 minutes.

Chill and add a dollop of sour cream to each bowl of soup just before serving.

Fish Soup
Serves 8-10

Deliciously light and savoury, this Russian fish soup is traditionally made during the summer and autumn months.

Ingredients

1.75l/3pt water	100ml/4fl oz heavy cream
250g/9oz onions, finely	200ml/8fl oz white wine
chopped	pinch white pepper
4g/2 tsp fresh parsley,	1 clove garlic, crushed
finely chopped	2 large cucumbers, peeled
pinch lemon rind, finely	and sliced
grated	400g/14oz tomatoes,
bay leaf	peeled, seeded and diced
pinch black pepper	75g/3oz black olives,
450g/1lb halibut steaks,	stoned and halved
diced	

Preparation In a very large soup pot, combine the water, onions, parsley, lemon rind, bay leaf and black pepper. Bring the liquid to a boil, reduce the heat and simmer for 2 minutes.

Add the fish to the pot and simmer for 5 minutes. Reduce the heat to low and simmer for a further 5 minutes.

Add the cream, white wine, white pepper, garlic, cucumbers and tomatoes. Simmer over a low heat for 5 minutes. Do not let the soup boil.

Remove the pot from the heat. Stir in the olives. Leave the pot to stand for 30 seconds. Stir again and serve.

Gazpacho
Serves 4-6

The basic soup is very smooth and icy, and the guests add garnishes of their choice until the soup is very thick, and full of crunchy vegetables.

Ingredients

675g/1½lb ripe tomatoes, peeled and seeded
2-3 cloves garlic, peeled
6 slices crustless wholewheat bread, diced
1 green pepper, cored, seeded and quartered
1 red pepper, cored, seeded and quartered
60ml/4tbsp good olive oil
60ml/4tbsp red wine vinegar
1 large cucumber, peeled
1 large Spanish onion, peeled and quartered
600ml/1pt tomato juice
12 ice cubes
salt and freshly ground pepper
few drops Tabasco

Garnishes
1 small cucumber, peeled and chopped
1 red pepper, cored, seeded and chopped
1 green pepper, cored, seeded and chopped
6 spring onions, trimmed and sliced
2 tomatoes, peeled and chopped
garlic flavoured croûtons (optional)

Preparation Either process or liquidize the tomatoes until smooth. With the machine still running, drop in the garlic, diced bread, peppers and gradually add the oil and vinegar. Cut the cucumber into 2.5-cm (1-in) chunks and add with the onion to the mixture. Process until the soup is very smooth.

Tip into a bowl, stir in the tomato juice and ice cubes and season to taste with salt, pepper and Tabasco. Chill until ready to serve. If the soup seems too thick, add more ice cubes.

Spoon the soup into individual bowls. Arrange bowls of vegetables and croûtons, if used, on a tray, so everyone can help themselves.

Green Soup
Serves 4-6

This is a useful way of using up odd amounts of vegetables which tend to lurk in the refrigerator. Use any green vegetables you have in whatever quantity you like — this is only a rough guide.

Ingredients

15ml/1tbsp oil
1 medium onion, sliced
2 large/225g/8oz courgettes, sliced
225g/8oz spinach, washed and picked over
handful of sorrel, washed and picked over
½ bunch watercress
900ml/1½pt chicken stock
150ml/¼pt sour cream
1 egg yolk
salt and pepper

Preparation Heat the oil, add the onion and cook until it has just softened but not browned. Add the vegetables and stock. Stir and bring to the boil and then simmer, covered, for 20 minutes.

Mix the sour cream with the egg yolk. Liquidize the soup, adding the sour cream mixture slowly. Adjust the seasoning. Serve hot or cold.

Harvest Soup
Serves 4-6

Ingredients

5-10ml/1-2tsp oil
1 onion, chopped
350g/12oz pumpkin, peeled and diced
250g/8oz carrots, sliced
2 potatoes
juice of ½ lemon
1l/2pt stock
salt and freshly ground black pepper
1 courgette, sliced (optional)
50g/2oz runner beans, sliced (optional)
basil leaves

Preparation Heat the oil in a large saucepan and fry the onion until translucent. Add pumpkins, carrots and potatoes and pour the lemon juice over. Sweat, covered, for 5 minutes.

Add stock and seasoning and simmer until potatoes are cooked. Blend or part-blend the soup. If liked, add courgettes and beans and simmer for a further 4 minutes. Check seasoning.

Serve garnished with basil leaves. This soup can also be served sprinkled with Parmesan cheese.

Harvest Soup

Kohlrabi and Chicken Soup
Serves 8

Fresh kohlrabi, a root vegetable, can be purchased at most well-stocked greengrocers.

Ingredients

*1.3 kg/3lb chicken, cut
  into pieces
3 medium onions, halved
1.9l/3¼pt chicken stock
1 leek
2.5g/½tsp salt
pinch black pepper
500g/18oz fresh kohlrabi,
  peeled and cut into
  small pieces*

*25g/1oz fresh parsley,
  coarsely chopped
40g/1½oz margarine
50ml/2fl oz white wine*

Preparation Put the chicken, onions, chicken stock, leek, salt and pepper in a large soup pot. Simmer, covered, over a medium heat for 50 minutes. Add the kohlrabi, parsley, margarine and wine. Simmer, covered, for an additional 35 minutes. Remove the chicken and use it in another dish. Serve the soup hot.

Curried Lentil Soup
Serves 4-6

Serve with wholemeal bread and cheese to make a filling, nutritious meal.

Ingredients

*175g/6oz lentils
2 medium onions, finely
  chopped
2 cloves garlic, finely
  chopped
2.5cm/1in root ginger,
  peeled and finely
  chopped
1 fresh green chilli, seeded
  and finely chopped
30ml/2tbsp oil
2.5g/½tsp ground
  coriander
2.5g/½tsp ground cumin
pinch cayenne pepper, to
  taste*

*2 stalks celery, coarsely
  chopped
1 red pepper, cored, seeded
  and coarsely chopped
4 medium tomatoes, peeled
  and coarsely chopped
100g/4oz rindless, streaky
  bacon (optional),
  coarsely chopped
1.2l/2pt chicken or
  vegetable stock
salt and freshly ground
  black pepper
fresh coriander leaves,
  chopped*

Preparation Pick over the lentils, wash thoroughly and leave to drain. Mash or blend the onions, garlic, ginger and chilli to form a thick paste.

Heat the oil in a heavy pan and quickly fry the ground coriander, cumin and cayenne pepper. After 5 seconds, add the onion paste and fry for a further 5 seconds. Add the celery, red pepper, tomatoes and bacon, if used, and stir-fry for 1 minute.

Stir in the lentils, stock and salt and pepper to taste. Bring to the boil, then cover and simmer for about 40 minutes. Taste for seasoning, then stir in the fresh, chopped coriander.

Serve very hot with warm, crusty bread and cheese.

Family Lentil Soup
Serves 4

Ingredients

*30ml/2tbsp oil
1 large onion, peeled
1 carrot, scraped
2 sticks celery, washed
250g/8oz red lentils,
  washed
1 sprig parsley*

*1 bay leaf
1 bouquet garni
salt and freshly ground
  pepper
1.2l/2pt stock
7g/1tbsp chopped parsley
wholewheat bread croûtons*

Preparation Heat the oil over a low heat in a large saucepan.

Dice the vegetables finely, add to the oil and allow to cook for 4 minutes.

Add the lentils, parsley, bay leaf, bouquet garni, seasoning and stock. Bring to the boil and simmer gently for about 35 minutes, until the lentils are cooked. If necessary, skim the surface from time to time.

Taste for seasoning and adjust. Serve with chopped parsley sprinkled on top and a dish of croûtons.

Variation Cream of Lentil Soup can be made by liquidizing the soup and reheating slowly with 60ml/4tbsp milk and 30ml/2tbsp cream.

Lentil and Tomato Soup
Serves 4

Ingredients

100g/4oz red lentils	1l/1¼pt stock or water
1 large onion, peeled	bay leaf
1 small turnip, peeled	bouquet garni
1 parsnip, peeled	salt and freshly ground
2 stalks celery, washed	pepper
450-g/15-oz can tomatoes	wholewheat croûtons
	7g/1tbsp chopped parsley

Preparation Wash and rinse the lentils, removing any discoloured or black pieces.

Chop the vegetables roughly into even-sized pieces.

Put the lentils, vegetables, tomatoes and stock or water into a large saucepan with the bay leaf and bouqet garni. Season well.

Bring the soup to the boil and remove and skim. Lower the heat to allow liquid to simmer for about 35 minutes, until vegetables and lentils are tender. Allow to cool slightly.

Liquidize the soup in a blender or food processor or rub through a mouli-legumes. If the mixture is too thick, add a little more stock, milk or water. Reheat and taste for seasoning.

Serve with wholemeal bread croûtons and a sprinkling of chopped parsley.

Curried Marrow Soup
Serves 6

Ingredients

15ml/1tbsp oil	1l/1¼pt chicken stock
1 large onion, chopped	30ml/2tbsp yoghurt
20g/2tbsp curry powder	30ml/2tbsp mango chutney
1 small marrow (about 675g/1½lb), peeled and chopped	

Preparation Heat the oil, add the onion and cook until it has just softened but not browned. Stir in the curry powder and cook it for 1 minute. Add the marrow and stir well. Add the stock.

Bring to the boil and then simmer until the marrow is soft.

Blend the soup and return it to the pan. Keep warm while you mix the yoghurt and chutney together. Stir into the soup and serve immediately.

If you prefer to make this in advance, don't add the yoghurt mixture until you reheat it. You could serve a little desiccated coconut with this and additional chutney if desired.

Cream of Mushroom Soup
Serves 4-6

Ingredients

350g/12oz mushrooms	bay leaf
50g/2oz butter	30ml/2tbsp white wine
1 small onion, peeled and finely chopped	15g/1tbsp wholemeal flour
1l/1¼pt chicken stock	salt and freshly ground pepper
bouquet garni	60ml/4tbsp whipping cream
	pinch paprika

Preparation Wash the mushrooms and retain two for garnish. Chop the remainder roughly.

Heat half the butter in a large saucepan on a low heat. Add the onion and cook for 3 minutes. Add mushrooms and stir for a further 2 minutes.

Add the stock, bouquet garni, bay leaf and white wine. Bring to the boil and simmer for 15 minutes. Allow to cool slightly.

Liquidize the soup in a blender or food processor. If this is not possible, pass through a wide-meshed sieve or mouli-legumes.

Heat the remaining butter in a cleaned saucepan, add the flour until a roux (a paste of flour and butter) is made. Cook for 1 minute, then gradually add the mushroom soup, stirring briskly. Season well. Add half the cream just before serving.

Mix the remaining cream with the paprika. Pour the soup into bowls and swirl the cream mixture on top. Decorate with the reserved mushrooms, sliced. Serve with fresh wholewheat bread.

Mushroom Soup
Serves 4

Ingredients

.25g/1oz butter
1 large onion, sliced
350g/12oz mushrooms,
  sliced
grated nutmeg

15g/1tbsp flour
450ml/¾pt chicken stock
300ml/½pt yoghurt
30ml/2tbsp sherry
  (optional)

Preparation Heat the butter and cook the onion until it has just softened but not browned. Add the mushrooms, stir and leave them to cook for 2 minutes. Add the butter if necessary.

Add nutmeg to taste and the flour and stir well. Slowly add the stock, stirring until the mixture is smooth. Bring to the boil and then simmer for 5 minutes. Stir in the yoghurt and just warm it through.

Add the sherry and serve hot.

Pork Soup with Ginger
Serves 6

The ginger greatly enhances the flavour of this soup. The fish sauce and vinegar are also evident, but do not overpower. It is quite a meal in itself, with all the meaty pieces.

Ingredients

1.5l/2½pt pork or chicken
  stock
30ml/2tbsp light soy sauce
1 clove garlic, peeled and
  crushed
2.5cm/1in ginger, scraped
  and sliced
1 medium-sized onion,
  peeled and sliced
15g/1tbsp sugar
15ml/1tbsp fish sauce
  (optional)
15ml/1tbsp lime juice or
  vinegar

100g/4oz pork fillet,
  shredded finely
100g/4oz pig's liver, cut
  into small pieces
  (optional)
15-30g/1-2tbsp seasoned
  cornflour
30-45ml/2-3tbsp oil
seasoning
spring onions or coriander
  leaves

Green Pea Soup

Preparation Simmer the stock and soy sauce together while preparing the other ingredients.

Pound the garlic, ginger and onion together in a pestle and mortar or blender and add them to the stock. Cook for 5 minutes, then add the sugar, fish sauce, if used, and lime juice or vinegar.

Dip the pork and liver pieces in seasoned cornflour. Fry in hot oil until the meats change colour, keeping the pieces of meat as separate as possible. Pour off any excess oil and add the meats to the soup. Simmer for 20-30 minutes or until the meat is tender.

Taste for seasoning and serve garnished with chopped spring onions or coriander leaves.

Green Pea Soup
Serves 4

Ingredients

225g/8oz dried green peas
25g/1oz butter
1 large onion, diced
900ml/1½pt stock or water
¼tsp sugar
salt and freshly ground
  pepper

5g/1tsp chervil
bay leaf
bouquet garni
125ml/¼pt milk
60ml/4tbsp single cream

Preparation Soak the dried peas in cold water overnight.

Melt the butter in a large saucepan. Add the onion and cook over a low heat for 4 minutes.

Add the peas with ⅔ of the stock or water, bring to the boil and simmer until cooked. (This will take about 35 minutes.) Allow to cool slightly.

Liquidize the peas in a blender or food processor or pass through a mouli-legumes. Return to the saucepan, add the sugar, seasoning and herbs.

Over a low heat, add the remaining stock or water and simmer for 10 minutes. Gradually add the milk and continue cooking on a low heat for a further 5 minutes. Remove the bouquet garni and bay leaf, taste for seasoning. Stir in the cream just before serving.

Serve with slices of wholewheat bread, brown rolls or croûtons.

Variation Use frozen peas for this recipe if preferred. Reduce initial cooking time to 15 minutes.

Green Pea and Lettuce Soup
Serves 4

Ingredients

900ml/1½pt chicken stock
  or water
1 large potato, peeled and
  sliced
225g/8oz frozen peas
2 spring onions or 1 small
  onion, peeled
1 bay leaf
1 bouquet garni

sprig parsley
salt and freshly ground
  pepper
1 lettuce, washed
30ml/2tbsp single cream
10g/1tbsp spring onion,
  chopped

Preparation Put the stock or water in a large saucepan. Add the potato, bring to the boil and simmer for 15 minutes.

Add the frozen peas and simmer for a further 5 minutes.

Chop the spring onions or finely chop the onion if spring onions are not available.

Add the onions, bay leaf and bouquet garni and sprig of parsley with some seasoning.

Gradually add the lettuce, torn into strips, and simmer for a further 10 minutes.

Allow to cool slightly and liquidize in a blender or food processor or rub through a mouli-legumes.

Taste for seasoning and reheat if serving hot. Garnish each bowl with a swirl of cream and a little chopped spring onion.

French Onion Soup
Serves 8

Served in individual bowls topped with melted cheese, this soup is a French classic.

Ingredients

30ml/2tbsp vegetable oil
50g/2oz butter
1kg/2lb onions, coarsely
  chopped
15g/2tbsp flour
1.9l/3¼pt stock or water

2.5g/½tsp salt
12 slices Swiss cheese
16 thin slices cut from a
  French loaf
10ml/2tsp olive oil
2 cloves garlic, finely
  chopped

Preparation Heat the vegetable oil and butter in a large deep saucepan. Add the onions and sauté over a medium heat for 5 minutes. Reduce the heat to low and simmer for a further 20 minutes, stirring frequently.

Sprinkle the onions with the flour and continue cooking, stirring constantly, for 3 minutes.

Add the vegetable stock and salt. Simmer, covered, for 35 minutes over a low heat. While the soup simmers, coarsely chop 4 of the cheese slices. Preheat oven to 165°C/325°F/Gas 3.

Brush the bread slices with the olive oil and arrange them in a single layer on a baking sheet. Sprinkle the bread with the garlic and the chopped cheese. Bake for 15 minutes and set aside.

When the soup is done, place 2 bread slices in each of 8 individual deep soup bowls. Fill each bowl with soup and top with a slice of cheese. Place the bowls on the centre rack of the oven and raise the heat to 175°C/350°F/Gas 4. Bake for 5 to 7 minutes or until the cheese begins to soften and turn brown.

Remove the bowls from the oven, allow to cool for 1 minute and serve.

Potato Soup
Serves 6

Ingredients

75g/3oz butter
1 onion, finely chopped
450g/1lb potatoes, cubed
1 carrot, grated
salt to taste
2.5g/½tsp white pepper

5g/1tsp caraway seeds
725ml/1¼pt water
30g/2tbsp cream of wheat
725ml/1¼pt milk
20g/3tbsp chopped parsley
100ml/4fl oz sour cream

Preparation Melt the butter in a saucepan and brown the onions.

Add the potatoes, carrot, salt, pepper and caraway seeds. Stir until all the ingredients are slightly soft. Add the water and bring to the boil. Stir in the cream of wheat and cook over a low heat for 20 minutes, stirring frequently.

Add the milk and parsley, bring to boiling point, and serve with the sour cream.

Cheesy Potato Soup
Serves 4-6

Ingredients

75g/3oz butter or
 margarine
450g/1lb potatoes, peeled
 and sliced
2 large onions, sliced
2 cloves garlic, chopped
salt and freshly ground
 pepper

1l/1¾pt beef stock
100g/4oz Cheddar cheese,
 grated
thin slices toasted French
 bread with a little extra
 grated cheese

Preparation Heat the butter or margarine in a large, heavy pan and add the sliced vegetables with a little salt and pepper. Stir well, cover and simmer for about 10 minutes, or until the vegetables are softened and slightly golden in colour. Add the stock and simmer gently for 15 to 20 minutes, or until the soup has thickened and the vegetables are very tender.

Strain the soup, reserving the liquid.

Sieve or liquidize the vegetables until smooth, then return to the liquid with the grated cheese. Reheat, stirring constantly until the soup is thick and creamy. Taste for seasoning.

To serve, toast bread and then cover with extra grated cheese, then grill until brown and bubbling. Spoon the soup into warmed bowls, and float cheese-topped toast slices on top.

Russian Egg Drop Soup
Serves 8-10

Ingredients

1.9l/3¾pt chicken stock
400g/14oz chicken, cooked
 and shredded
50ml/2fl oz white wine
300g/10oz fine egg noodles
2.5g/½tsp salt

pinch dill
65g/2½oz finely chopped
 celery
2 large carrots, quartered
sprig parsley
4 eggs, well beaten

Preparation Pour the chicken stock into a large saucepan. Add the chicken meat, wine, egg noodles, salt, dill, celery, carrots and parsley. Bring the soup to the boil. Reduce the heat and simmer for 18-20 minutes over a low heat.

Bring the soup back to a furious boil. Beat the eggs in with a fork. Remove the pan from the heat when the eggs become cloud-like, and serve immediately.

Scotch Broth
Serves 4-6

Ingredients

450g/1lb scrag end of
 lamb
1l/1¼pt water
salt and freshly ground
 pepper
bay leaf
30-45g/2-3tbsp pearl
 barley

30g/2tbsp dried peas,
 soaked
2 carrots, scraped
1 large onion
1 small turnip, peeled
3 leeks, washed
7g/1tbsp chopped parsley

Preparation Put the trimmed meat in a large saucepan with the water, 5g/1tsp salt, pepper and bay leaf. Add the pearl barley and peas. Bring to the boil and simmer for 1 hour. Remove the meat and cut into small pieces.

Cut the carrots into dice, the onions into small dice and the turnip into slices and then small dice. Cut a cross down the leeks and wash thoroughly, then slice.

Skim away any fat that has risen to the surface of the broth. Add the carrots, onions and turnips and bring back to the boil and skim. Simmer for a further 15-20 minutes. Then add the leeks and cook for a further 10 minutes with the meat.

Skim any fat from the surface with kitchen paper. Toss in the chopped parsley, and serve with slices of wholemeal bread.

Scotch Barley Soup
Serves 8

Ingredients

75g/3oz butter or
 margarine
6 carrots, grated
3 onions, coarsely chopped
2 turnips, cubed

1.9l/3¾pt water
350g/12oz pearl barley
5g/1tsp salt
black pepper to taste
chopped parsley

Preparation Melt the butter or margarine in a large saucepan. Add the carrots, onions and turnips and sauté for 5 minutes. Add the water and bring to a boil.

Add the barley, salt and pepper. Cook over a low heat for 2 hours. Stir in the parsley and serve.

Sour Soup
Serves 8

This unusual soup gets its savoury flavour from the veal.

Ingredients

15ml/1tbsp olive oil	*2 beaten eggs*
1 large carrot, finely chopped	*2 slices bread, soaked in water and squeezed out*
40g/1½oz celery, chopped	*2.5g/½tsp salt*
2 onions, diced	*pinch black pepper*
350ml/12fl oz water	*40g/1½oz cooked rice*
15g/½oz chopped parsley	*½tsp fresh dill, chopped*
900ml/1½pt sauerkraut or pickled cucumber juice	*675g/1½lb minced veal*

Preparation Heat the olive oil in a large saucepan over a medium heat. Add the carrots, celery and onions and sauté for 8 minutes, stirring frequently. Add the water and parsley to the saucepan and bring to a boil. Cook for 1 minute. Add the sauerkraut or cucumber juice and reduce the heat slightly. Cook for 15 minutes.

In a large mixing bowl, combine the eggs, bread, salt, pepper, rice, dill and veal. Mix with a fork until the consistency is even. Form the veal mixture into balls approximately 2.5cm (1in) in diameter.

Drop the meatballs into the simmering soup and reduce the heat to low. Simmer for 40 minutes and serve.

Shellfish Bisque
Serves 4

Ingredients

24 large prawns or shrimps	*3 stalks parsley*
25g/1oz butter	*30ml/2tbsp brandy*
1 medium onion, peeled and diced	*60ml/4tbsp white wine*
1 carrot, peeled and diced	*1l/1¾pt water or fish stock*
sprig of thyme or pinch dried thyme	*25g/1oz butter*
bay leaf	*25g/1oz flour*
bouquet garni	*salt and freshly ground pepper*
	60ml/4tbsp cream

Preparation Wash the prawns or shrimps thoroughly. Remove the shells and crush them in a plastic bag with a rolling pin.

Melt the butter in a saucepan and sweat the onions and carrots over a low heat for about 5 minutes, then add 8 of the prawns or shrimps.

Add thyme, bay leaf, bouquet garni and parsley at the side of the pan.

Pour the brandy into a ladle and heat, set alight and pour over the shellfish and vegetables. Add the white wine and simmer for 2 minutes.

Pour the stock into a saucepan and add the crushed prawn shells. Bring to the boil and simmer for 35 minutes.

Mix the butter and flour together with the fingertips into a paste and form into small balls.

Pass the soup through a fine sieve. Return the soup to the saucepan, and stirring over a low heat add the balls of flour and butter until the mixture has thickened. Taste for seasoning and add the rest of the prawns for the last 5 minutes cooking time.

Stir in the cream just before serving.

Variation Lobster or crayfish shells may be crushed, brought to the boil and simmered with the vegetables. Continue to make soup as in method given above. If the lobster meat has already been eaten, canned lobster may be used as a garnish or the soup may be served without the meat.

Spinach Soup
Serves 6

Ingredients

15ml/1tbsp oil	*1 clove garlic, crushed*
1 large onion, sliced	*1l/1¾pt chicken stock*
700g/1½lb spinach, washed and picked over	*300ml/½pt yoghurt*
	salt and pepper

Preparation Heat the oil, add the onion and cook until it has just softened but not browned. Add the spinach and garlic and stir. Add the stock, bring to the boil and then simmer, covered, for 15 minutes. Liquidize the soup, adding the yoghurt slowly. Adjust the seasoning. Serve hot or cold.

Use well-thawed frozen spinach if you prefer, about 450g/1lb would do.

Cold Tomato Soup
Serves 6

Ingredients
600ml/1pt tomato juice
600ml/1pt yoghurt
3 spring onions, chopped
1 green pepper, chopped

1 large tomato, skinned
    and chopped
salt and pepper

Preparation Blend the juice and yoghurt and pour the mixture into a large bowl. Add the onions, pepper and tomato and season to taste.

Serve well chilled, with some ice cubes floating in the soup.

Variations You can add or subtract ingredients to this according to what you have handy. Try sliced avocados; prawns; fresh basil; chopped olives; cucumber cut into fine dice; raw sliced mushrooms; chopped fennel; fried croûtons.

Fresh Tomato and Vodka Soup
Serves 6

An unusual start for a dinner party, this soup is equally good served hot or cold. If you don't like vodka, you can omit it, but the soup won't be quite the same.

Ingredients
75g/3oz spring onions,
    trimmed and sliced
1 medium onion, sliced
1 small fresh green chilli,
    seeded and sliced
1 clove garlic, sliced
600ml/1pt tomato juice

salt and freshly ground
    pepper
1kg/2lb ripe tomatoes,
    peeled, seeded and
    chopped
a little brown sugar
125ml/¼pt vodka
a few chopped chives to
    garnish

Preparation Put the spring onions, onion, chilli and garlic into a large pan with half the tomato juice, and a little salt and pepper. Cover and cook over low heat until the onions are very soft — about 40 minutes.

Add the tomatoes to the pan with a little brown sugar and the remaining tomato juice. Cook uncovered, over medium heat for 20 minutes. Strain the soup and reserve the liquid.

Sieve or liquidize the vegetables until very smooth. Return to the liquid, and if the soup seems too thin, reduce over high heat. Taste, and adjust the seasoning.

The soup can be served hot or chilled — either way add the vodka and chives just before serving.

Fresh Tomato and Vodka Soup

Vegetable Cream Soup
Serves 6

This delicious soup has a creamy texture yet uses no milk products.

Ingredients

50ml/2fl oz olive oil
4 cloves garlic, finely chopped
1 onion, coarsely chopped
200g/7oz green beans trimmed and quartered
125g/5oz courgettes, peeled and coarsely chopped
125g/5oz yellow squash, peeled and coarsely chopped
50g/2oz carrots, sliced
125g/5oz turnips, peeled and cubed
125g/5oz celery, coarsely chopped
350g/12oz potatoes, peeled and cubed

50g/2oz leeks, finely chopped
25g/1oz spinach, finely chopped
75g/3oz baby peas, cooked
175g/7oz butter beans, cooked
150g/6oz jellied cranberry sauce
15g/¹⁄₂oz parsley, finely chopped
15g/2tbsp fresh basil, coarsely chopped
5g/1tsp salt
pinch ground white pepper
1.5l/2¹⁄₂pt water

Preparation In a large saucepan, combine all the ingredients. Mash with a fork.

Cover and simmer for 40 minutes over a low heat. Mash again. Replace the lid and simmer for an additional 20 minutes over a low heat. Serve hot.

Quick Chilled Summer Soup
Serves 4-6

Perfect for a meal on the patio, this soup can also be taken in a thermos flask for summer picnics.

Ingredients

1 large cucumber, peeled
2 ripe avocados, peeled
juice of ¹⁄₂ lime
7g/1tbsp fresh coriander leaves, chopped
300ml/¹⁄₂pt plain yoghurt, chilled

300ml/¹⁄₂pt good chicken or vegetable stock, chilled
salt and pepper to taste
3 drops Tabasco
lime slices and a few crushed ice cubes

Preparation Cut the cucumber into 5-cm/2-in chunks, and quarter the avocados, discarding the stones. Either liquidize or process the cucumber and avocados with the lime juice, coriander and yoghurt, until very smooth. Tip into a bowl and stir in the stock.

Season to taste with salt, pepper and a little Tabasco. If necessary, add a little more lime juice, and if the soup is too thick, add a little milk, stock or water.

Chill well. Just before serving, stir in a few crushed ice cubes. Spoon into chilled bowls, and float lime slices on the top.

Vegetable Garlic Basil Soup
Serves 8

This hearty traditional French soup can be a meal in itself. Serve with crusty bread.

Ingredients

75ml/5tbsp olive oil
150g/6oz finely chopped onions
5 cloves garlic, finely chopped
2.4l/4pt water
90g/3¹⁄₂oz haricot beans, cooked
450g/1lb fresh tomatoes, peeled, seeded and coarsely chopped
150g/6oz carrots, coarsely chopped
150g/6oz new potatoes, diced

40g/1¹⁄₂oz spring onions, finely chopped
celery stalks, coarsely chopped
150g/6oz fresh green beans, trimmed and quartered
150g/6oz courgettes, thinly sliced
40g/4tbsp dried basil
30ml/2tbsp tomato purée
2.5g/¹⁄₂tsp salt
2.5g/¹⁄₂tsp black pepper

Preparation Heat 30ml/2tbsp of the oil in a large saucepan. Add the onions and garlic and sauté over a low heat for 5 minutes.

Add the remaining ingredients, including the rest of the oil, and simmer over a medium heat for 30 minutes, stirring occasionally. Serve hot.

Consommé
Serves 4

Ingredients

600ml/1pt brown stock
salt and freshly ground pepper
2 egg whites with shells
50g/2oz lean minced beef

1 small leek
15g/2tbsp parsley, chopped
30ml/2tbsp dry sherry

Preparation Make sure the brown stock is as free of fat as possible. Season well. Whisk the egg whites until slightly frothy and mix with the minced beef. Mix with 300ml/¹⁄₂pt cold stock.

Bring the remaining stock to the boil with the chopped leek and parsley. Turn the heat off. Gradually add the whisked egg and beef mixture, stirring the stock to distribute the egg mixture evenly. Add the egg shells after crushing them in a plastic bag.

Bring the mixture back to simmering point, stirring while it is heating. Stop stirring when bubbles appear on the surface and allow the egg white to come to the surface. Allow pan to simmer very slowly almost off the heat for about 10 minutes.

Arrange a sieve lined with muslin over another saucepan or bowl. Carefully pour the stock through.

Allow the consommé to stand for a few minutes, then add the sherry. Use as required.

Watercress Soup
Serves 4

Ingredients

30g/1oz butter	salt and freshly ground
1 large onion, chopped	black pepper
250g/8oz potatoes, peeled	3 bunches watercress
1.2l/2pt stock	cream

Preparation Melt the butter in a large saucepan, add the onion and cook, stirring, until transparent.

Add the potatoes, stock and seasoning. Bring to the boil, then simmer until potatoes can be mashed with a fork.

Wash watercress and discard tough stalks and yellow leaves. Reserve a few sprigs for garnish, roughly chop the rest and add to the soup. Continue cooking for 2 minutes.

Allow the soup to cool slightly, then blend in a liquidizer. Allow to cool completely. Taste and adjust seasoning.

Chill and serve with reserved sprigs of watercress and a swirl of cream.

Country Vegetable Soup
Serves 6

A hearty soup, full of natural goodness and flavour.

Ingredients

1kg/2lb mixed root vegetables — carrots, celery, Jerusalem artichokes, leeks, onions, parsnips, potatoes, swedes, turnips, etc.	2 cloves garlic, sliced
	bay leaf
	salt and pepper to taste
	300ml/½pt good chicken or vegetable stock
75g/3oz butter or margarine	a little grated cheese to garnish (optional)

Preparation Wash and prepare the vegetables, trimming and peeling where necessary, and slice them.

Heat the butter or margarine in a large pan and add the vegetables, garlic, bay leaf, and a little salt and pepper. Stir well, then cover and cook slowly for 15 minutes, stirring occasionally. Add the stock, bring to the boil, then cover and simmer gently for 30 minutes or until the vegetables are tender. Remove the bay leaf.

Strain the soup, reserving the liquid. Coarsely mash or blend half the vegetables. Add to the liquid. Sieve or liquidize the remaining vegetables until they form a thick purée. Add to the soup, reheat and taste for seasoning.

Spoon into individual bowls and serve sprinkled with grated cheese, if wished.

Scholar's Vegetable Soup
Serves 6-8

Ingredients

450g/1lb ripe tomatoes, seeded and finely chopped	5g/1tsp salt
	1 small head cauliflower, cut into florets
4 large carrots, peeled and quartered	bay leaf
300g/10oz chopped celery	2.5g/½tsp black pepper
3 leeks, cut into sections	15g/½oz diced green pepper
150g/6oz fresh green peas	4l/6½pt water
100g/4oz lentils	1 large Spanish onion, halved
	2 vegetable stock cubes

Preparation Combine all the ingredients in a large soup pot. Bring to a boil, reduce the heat to medium and simmer for 3 hours, stirring occasionally.

Serve hot in large soup bowls.

Chicken Broth
Serves 4

Ingredients

15g/½oz butter	2 stalks parsley
1 onion, peeled and diced	600ml/1pt chicken stock
3 leeks, washed	100g/4oz cooked chicken
1 bouquet garni	75g/3oz vermicelli
1 bay leaf	15g/2tbsp chopped parsley

Preparation Melt the butter in a saucepan and cook the onion over a low heat until transparent.

Prepare the leeks by removing the coarse outer leaves, trim off the coarse tops and then cut a cross down the centre of the leek, i.e., two lengthwise cuts to the white part. This enables the mud to be washed off easily under a cold running tap.

Add the leeks to the onion and stir well. Drop the bouquet garni, bay leaf and parsley stalks into the saucepan.

Pour the stock in and simmer for 10 minutes after bringing to the boil.

Taste for seasoning, add the cooked chicken and vermicelli. Simmer for a further 7 minutes then add the chopped parsley. Taste for seasoning before serving. Remove bouquet garni, bay leaf and parsley stalk.

Watercress and Potato Soup
Serves 6

Ingredients

40g/1½oz butter or margarine	2 bunches watercress
1 medium onion, chopped	600ml/1pt chicken stock
450g/1lb potatoes, peeled and sliced	425ml/¾pt yoghurt
	1 egg
	salt and pepper

Preparation Heat the butter, add the onion and cook until it has just softened but not browned. Add the potatoes and watercress. Stir and leave on a low heat for 3 minutes. Add the stock and simmer for 20 minutes. Mix the yoghurt with the egg.

When the potatoes are soft, liquidize the soup, adding the yoghurt mixture slowly. Serve hot or cold.

Chicken Stock
Makes 2l/3¼pt

Ingredients
2 onions, peeled and sliced	1 bouquet garni
2 carrots, scraped and sliced	6 peppercorns, slightly crushed
3 stalks celery	1½-kg/3-lb boiling fowl
2 bay leaves	3.5-5l/6-8pt water
2 stalks parsley	

Preparation Place all the ingredients in a large saucepan and bring to the boil. Add giblets if available, reduce heat and simmer for 1½ hours. Check that the chicken is tender, allow to cool in the stock.

Remove chicken and strain stock for use in soups and sauces.

To make chicken stock with remnants of a cooked bird use all the scraps and carcass of cooked chicken. Reduce the liquid to 2l/4pt.

Brown Stock
Makes 1.7l/3pt

Ingredients
450-g/1-lb shin of beef	1 bouquet garni
1kg/2lb beef and veal bones	1 bay leaf
2 onions, peeled and sliced	6 peppercorns, crushed
2 carrots, peeled and sliced	2.4l/4pt water

Preparation Slice the meat thinly and arrange in a roasting pan with the roughly chopped bones and vegetables. Place in a hot oven (200°C/400°F/Gas 6) to brown. After 30 minutes, when the bones and meat are brown, drain off the fat and transfer the meat and bones into a large saucepan. Add the herbs and peppercorns with the water, to the bones and vegetables.

Bring to the boil, remove any scum with a slotted spoon and allow to simmer for 1½-2 hours. Strain when cool and allow any fat to solidify on the top. Use as required — any excess can be stored in the freezer for special dishes, such as consommé.

Brown stock can also be made in smaller quantities in the oven in a casserole when it is being used for long term cooking. To make in a pressure cooker follow manufacturer's instructions.

Waste-Nothing Vegetable Stock

Ingredients
1-2tbsp oil	any vegetables past their prime, such as soft tomatoes or mushrooms
2 large onions, chopped	
1 clove garlic, chopped	
2 carrots, sliced	fresh herbs, chopped
2 sticks celery, sliced	2l/3½pts water, including any leftover from cooking vegetables, tomato juice drained from cans etc.
juice ½ lemon	
1 large potato, peeled and diced	
100g/4oz lentils, presoaked	
cabbage or cauliflower stalks	salt and freshly ground black pepper
outer leaves of cabbage, lettuce etc.	30-45ml/2-3tbsp soy sauce

Preparation Heat the oil in a large saucepan and stir-fry the onion and garlic until transparent.

Add the carrots, celery and lemon juice. Turn the heat to low, cover the pan and sweat the vegetables, stirring occasionally, for 5-10 minutes.

Add the remaining vegetables and herbs and pour over the water. Season well and simmer, covered, for about 40 minutes, until vegetables are mushy.

Blend the stock and add soy sauce to taste. Keep in the fridge to use within a couple of days or freeze in ice cube trays.

Court-Bouillon
To cook 3kg/6lb fish

Used for cooking salmon, trout, crawfish and lobster.

Ingredients
2.5l/4pt water	60ml/4tbsp white wine or white wine vinegar
10g/2tsp salt	
225g/8oz carrots, peeled and sliced	2 bouquets garnis or 2 bay leaves
225g/8oz onions, peeled and sliced	sprigs of thyme
25g/1oz parsley stalks	6 slightly crushed peppercorns

Preparation Place all the ingredients except the peppercorns in a fish kettle or large saucepan. Bring the liquid to the boil and skim.

Simmer for approximately 3-5 minutes then add the crushed peppercorns, continue simmering for a further 10-20 minutes. Allow to cool and strain through a fine sieve.

Use as required. After cooking fish in the court-bouillon the stock can be used several times if strained each time.

To store, pour into a plastic bag set in a bowl or plastic box and freeze until cooking fish again.

The bag may be taken out when frozen and sealed. This quantity is for large fish (weighing about 3kg/6lb) and may be halved for smaller quantities.

Fish Stock

To make a good fish stock, add the fish trimmings to the Court-Bouillon, leaving out the vinegar. The vegetables should not be simmered for longer than 30 minutes, or the stock will become bitter.

Note After fish has been cooked in the Court-Bouillon the liquid becomes a fish stock.

Making a Stock

The secret of stocks is slow gentle simmering. If the liquid is the slightest bit greasy, vigorous boiling will produce a murky, fatty-tasting stock. Skimming, especially for meat stocks, is vital too — as fat and scum rise to the surface they should be lifted off with a perforated spoon, perhaps every 10 or 15 minutes. Vegetables and bones should be evenly well browned — not burned — to make good brown stock.

Eggs, Milk and Cheese

Asparagus and Egg Napoleon 53
Baked Eggs with Green Peas and Cream 53
Eggs with Curly Kale 54
Bulgarian Eggs 54
Tea Eggs 54
Curried Eggs 54
Scarborough Eggs 55
Piperade 55
Lox and Onion Omelette 56
Scrambled Eggs with Smoked Salmon 56
Avocado Soufflé Omelettes 56
Omelette with Cheese and Horseradish 57
Mushroom Omelette Surprise 57
Spiced Omelette 57
Grapefruit Cheese Jelly 57
Kukuye 58
Pancakes 58
Stuffed Pancakes with Cheese and Herbs 58
Cheese and Celery Pancakes 58
Mandarin Pancakes 58
Mushroom Pancakes 59
Buttermilk Pancakes 59
Spinach Pancakes 59
Smoked Salmon Pancakes 59
Tuna Crêpes 60
Herb Roulade 60
Spinach Roulade 60

Cheese Soufflé 61
Cheese and Spinach Soufflé 61
Courgette Soufflé 61
Chicory Soufflé 61
Leek and Stilton Bake 62
Crab and Asparagus Tart 62
Summer Posy Mousse 62
Salmon and Chive Cocottes 63
Ham and Cheese Mousse 63
Crunchy Pepper and Tuna Mousse 63
Onion Tart 64
Cheesy Onion Quiche 64
Tomato and Sage Derby Quiche 64
Spinach Quiche 65
Kipper Mousse Quiche 65
Savoury Pumpkin Pie 65
Leek Quiche 66
Blue Cheese Pâté 66
Cheese and Herb Pâté 66
Date and Cream Cheese Spread 66
Welsh Rarebit 67
Vegetable Cheese Custard 67
Savoury Cheesecake 68
Broccoli and Tomato Cheesecake 68
Savoury Cheese Strudel 68

Whisking eggs and preparing a soufflé 69

Asparagus and Egg Napoleon
Serves 6

This is a kind of mille-feuilles made with a quick rough-puff pastry, and filled with asparagus and scrambled egg. The pastry can be made several days in advance and crisped up before use.

Ingredients

350g/12oz plain flour	**Filling**
good pinch salt	24 spears cooked
100g/4oz cold butter or	asparagus (fresh or
block margarine, diced	canned)
100g/4oz cold lard or	75g/3oz butter
vegetable fat, diced	9 eggs
approx. 100ml/7tbsp icy	150ml/¼pt single or
water	double cream
15ml/3tsp lemon juice	salt and freshly ground
beaten egg to glaze	pepper

Preparation First make the pastry. Lightly cut the fats into the flour and salt until the fats become thumb-nail size flakes. Stir in the water and lemon juice using a round-bladed knife, adding more water if needed. You should have a soft but not sticky, lumpy-looking dough. Wrap well and chill for about 30 minutes.

Sprinkle a work surface and rolling pin with flour, and carefully roll out the dough to a rectangle 38×13cm/15×5in. Fold the top third of the pastry down and the bottom third of the pastry up to make a three-layered square of pastry. Turn the pastry so the fold is on your left, and roll and fold the pastry as before. Wrap and chill for 15 minutes. Repeat the rolling, folding and chill procedure twice more, so the pastry has been folded a total of 6 times.

Grease 2 large baking sheets. Roll out the pastry to a rectangle 35×23cm/14×9in (or the length of your baking sheets), and 3mm/⅛in thick. Cut the rectangle in half to make 2 thin rectangles 35cm/14in long. Put on the baking sheets and prick well. Brush with beaten egg, then bake in the heated oven at 200°C/400°F/Gas 6 until golden and crispy — about 10 minutes. Cool on a wire rack, then trim off the edges, and cut each sheet into 6 strips.

When ready to eat, gently warm the pastry and asparagus tips. Melt the butter in a heavy pan. Beat the eggs till frothy with half the cream and a little salt and plenty of pepper. Tip into the pan and stir over low heat until the eggs are lightly scrambled. Remove from the heat and taste for seasoning. Stir in the rest of the cream.

Put a strip of pastry on each of 6 plates. Divide the scrambled eggs between the pastry bases, then arrange 4 spears of asparagus on top of each. Cover with the remaining pastry strips. Serve straight away.

Variation Replace the asparagus with strips of smoked salmon, cooked smoked haddock, or kipper fillets.

Baked Eggs with Green Peas and Cream
Serves 4

Ingredients

450g/1lb green peas, fresh	50g/2oz butter
(shelled weight)	salt and pepper
5g/1tsp sugar	8 eggs
springs of fresh mint	150ml/¼pt single cream

Preparation Boil the peas with the sugar and mint for 10 to 15 minutes or until just tender.

Drain, discarding the mint, and mash to a rough purée.

Stir in the butter, and season with salt and pepper to taste.

Divide the pea purée between 4 greased ramekin dishes and break 2 eggs over the top of each.

Pour the cream over the eggs and bake for 7 to 10 minutes at 200°C/400°F/Gas 6, until the eggs are just set. Serve immediately.

Variation "Mushy peas" are a woefully neglected vegetable, and this is a delicious and unusual way of serving them. Warm the contents of a 15 oz can, beat in a little butter, season with plenty of salt and pepper and proceed as for the green pea purée.

Eggs with Curly Kale
Serves 2-4

Ingredients
450g/1lb curly kale
4 eggs
25g/1oz butter
25g/1oz plain flour
300ml/½pt milk

50g/2oz Cheddar cheese, grated
salt and freshly ground black pepper

Preparation Wash the kale and discard the stalks. Pack into a saucepan with a very little water, cover and cook slowly for about 20 minutes until tender. Drain and cut up roughly with a knife and fork. Put the kale in the bottom of a heatproof serving dish and keep warm. Soft-boil the eggs.

Meanwhile, make the cheese sauce. Melt the butter in a pan and stir in the flour. Cook, stirring for a few minutes. Gradually add the milk. Continue to stir until the sauce has thickened. Add the cheese. When it melts, season.

Plunge the eggs in cold water and remove the shells. Lay them on the bed of kale and cover with the sauce. Heat the dish through in the oven or under the grill.

Bulgarian Eggs
Serves 2 or 4

Ingredients
4 eggs
300ml/½pt yoghurt
1 small clove garlic, crushed

salt and pepper
25g/1oz butter, melted
2.5g/½tsp paprika

Preparation Softly poach the eggs. Mix the yoghurt with the garlic, salt and pepper and warm it through gently but don't let it boil. Spoon it into four shallow dishes. Put one egg, well drained, into each dish.

Add the paprika to the melted butter and drizzle it onto the eggs. Serve immediately, with hot French or pitta bread.

Tea Eggs
Makes 12

Ingredients
12 eggs
10g/2tsp salt
45ml/3tbsp light soy sauce
30ml/2tbsp dark soy sauce

5g/1tsp five-spice powder
10g/1tbsp red Chinese tea leaves

Preparation Boil the eggs in water for 5-10 minutes. Remove and gently tap the shell of each egg with a spoon until it is cracked finely all over.

Put the eggs back in the pan and cover with fresh water. Add the salt, soy sauces, five-spice powder and tea leaves (the better the quality of the tea, the better the result). Bring to the boil and simmer for 30-40 minutes. Leave the eggs to cool in the liquid.

To serve, peel off the shells — the eggs will have a beautiful marbled pattern. They can be served either on their own or as part of a mixed hors d'oeuvre, whole or cut into halves or quarters.

Curried Eggs
Serves 4

Ingredients
30ml/2tbsp oil
1 large onion, finely sliced
2.5g/½tsp ground turmeric
2.5g/½tsp chilli powder

2.5g/½tsp salt
big pinch sugar
8 hard-boiled eggs
100ml/4fl oz water

Preparation Heat the oil in a frying pan over medium high heat and fry the sliced onion for 3-4 minutes until lightly browned.

Add turmeric, chilli, salt and sugar and, stirring constantly, fry for another 2-3 minutes. Add the eggs and mix until well covered with the spices.

Add the water, bring to the boil, lower heat, cover and cook for about 10 minutes until the gravy thickens.

Scarborough Eggs

Scarborough Eggs
Serves 2

This is the perfect dish for a light lunch. Accompany with plenty of crusty bread and a green salad.

Ingredients

40g/1½oz butter
1 clove garlic, crushed
5g/½tbsp parsley, chopped
½tsp fresh sage, chopped
2-3 blades fresh rosemary, bruised
½tsp fresh thyme
salt and pepper
4 fresh eggs

Preparation Melt the butter over a low heat and add the garlic, herbs and seasoning. Cook gently for about 5 minutes until the garlic is transparent.

Boil the eggs for 3½ to 4 minutes and shell them.

Add the eggs to the herb and garlic butter and turn them for a minute. Remove the rosemary blades and serve immediately.

Piperade
Serves 3-4

Ingredients

25g/1oz butter
1 medium onion, thinly sliced
1-2 cloves of garlic, crushed
1 red pepper, seeded and thinly sliced
2 large tomatoes, skinned, seeded and coarsely chopped
4 eggs
salt and pepper
a slice of hot buttered toast per person
7g/1tbsp parsley, chopped

Preparation Melt the butter in a heavy saucepan and cook the onions, garlic and pepper over a moderate heat for 15 minutes. Add the tomato and cook for a further 5 minutes.

Beat the eggs with a little salt and pepper and pour into the vegetables.

Turn down the heat and stir until the eggs are thick and creamy. Be careful not to overcook them.

Serve immediately piled on the toast and sprinkled with parsley.

Variation For a more substantial version, add 175g/6oz cubed cooked ham with the tomatoes.

Lox and Onion Omelette
Makes 4

Lox is the Yiddish name for smoked salmon, and this dish is perfect for a light lunch. It is traditionally served with toasted bagels.

Ingredients
8 eggs
225g/8oz lox (smoked salmon), cubed

1 onion, finely chopped
black pepper to taste
20g/4tsp butter

Preparation Beat the eggs in a bowl. Stir in the salmon, onion and pepper.

Melt 5g/1tsp of the butter in a small frying pan. Add a quarter of the egg mixture and cook over a low heat until the omelette has set. Keep warm while you make 3 more omelettes in the same way.

Scrambled Eggs with Smoked Salmon
Serves 2

For the most delicious breakfast there is, serve this with chilled Champagne or Buck's fizz. The secret of perfect scrambled eggs is to remove them from the heat just before they begin to set, as they will continue cooking on the plate. Have thin triangles of wholemeal toast buttered and kept hot on warmed plates so that all that remains to be done once the eggs are cooked is to pop the cork.

Ingredients
6 medium-sized eggs
  beaten with 15ml/1tbsp
  milk
freshly ground black
  pepper
25g/1oz butter

100g/4oz smoked salmon,
  cut into 1-cm/½-in
  squares
pinch cayenne
hot buttered toast

Preparation Beat the eggs with some pepper.

Melt the butter in a large heavy-bottomed frying pan over a low heat. Stir in the eggs and smoked salmon. Keep stirring, moving the spoon all over the bottom of the pan to prevent the eggs from sticking.

As soon as the eggs are thick and creamy, pile them onto the hot toast, sprinkle over a little cayenne and serve.

Avocado Soufflé Omelettes
Makes 2

Ingredients
1 green pepper
40g/1½oz butter
1 ripe avocado
few drops of lemon juice

4 eggs, separated
salt and freshly ground
  black pepper

Preparation Deseed and slice the green pepper. Heat a little of the butter in a pan and fry it until soft. Set aside.

Cut the avocado in half. Remove the stone and remove the flesh from the shell in one careful movement with a palette knife. Slice the avocado and sprinkle with lemon juice.

Beat the egg yolks and season with salt and pepper. Whisk the whites and fold the two together.

Heat half the remaining butter in a pan and pour in half the omelette mixture. Arrange half the avocado and green pepper on one side of it. When lightly set, fold the omelette in two, slide out of the pan and keep hot until you have made the second omelette in the same way. Serve immediately.

Omelette with Cheese and Horseradish
Serves 2

Ingredients
4 eggs
15ml/1tbsp water
salt and pepper to taste
a little butter
50g/2oz grated cheddar
  cheese
2.5g/1tsp fresh horseradish,
  finely chopped or grated

Preparation Mix the eggs, water, salt and pepper.
Heat the frying pan and add a touch of butter. When fairly hot pour in the eggs.
Sprinkle with the cheese and horseradish when the omelette is nearly cooked.
Serve immediately with a tomato salad.

Mushroom Omelette Surprise
Serves 2

Ingredients
100g/4oz mushrooms
approx. 150ml/¼pt milk
15g/1tbsp butter
15g/1tbsp flour
15g/1tbsp grated Parmesan
  cheese
salt and freshly ground
  black pepper
4 eggs, separated

Preparation Peel or wipe the mushrooms and slice. Put them in a small, heavy-bottomed pan with a little of the milk and poach gently until very black and juicy. Remove the mushrooms with a slotted spoon and arrange them in the bottom of a shallow greased heatproof dish about 18cm/7in in diameter.
Heat the butter in a pan and when it has melted, add the flour. Stir well and remove from the heat. Add the milk that the mushrooms have been cooked in and stir in enough extra milk to make a thick sauce. Stir in the cheese and season well.

Beat the yolks into the cheese sauce. Whisk the whites until they form soft peaks and fold into the sauce.
Pour the mixture over the mushrooms and cook under a preheated grill until the omelette is nearly set and golden on top.

Spiced Omelette
Makes 1

Ingredients
2 eggs
4 cardamoms (skinned
  and ground)
5g/1tsp coriander seed,
  finely crushed
50g/2oz chick-pea
  (gram) flour
30ml/2tbsp yoghurt
15g/1tbsp Ghee (Clarified
  Butter
parsley, chopped
  (optional)

Preparation Whisk the eggs well. Add the cardamom, coriander and flour and stir gently. Add the yoghurt and beat thoroughly. Leave to stand for 30 minutes.
Heat the ghee in a large pan and pour in the egg mixture. Tip the pan so that the egg covers the whole of the bottom of the pan. Leave for a moment or two to set the eggs.
Remove the omelette from the pan, sprinkle with chopped parsley and serve immediately.

Grapefruit Cheese Jelly
Serves 4

This can be served as an accompaniment to cold poultry or fish. It can also be served as a dessert. Use another citrus-flavoured jelly if you prefer.

Ingredients
1 large grapefruit, peeled
130g/4¼oz lime jelly
75g/3oz cream cheese

Preparation Cut the grapefruit into small chunks. Make up the jelly according to the instructions, using 50ml/2fl oz less water than the packet says. Pour half the jelly into a bowl and leave to cool before mixing with the cream cheese until smooth. Add the grapefruit. Pour the mixture into a moistened small ring mould and refrigerate until set.
Spoon on the remaining jelly (which should not set if you have left it out of the refrigerator; if it does, melt it gently and spoon over the set jelly when cooled). Refrigerate until set. Unmould before serving.

Kukuye
Serves 6

Ingredients

12 eggs	2.5g/½tsp salt
1 large onion, finely chopped	2.5g/½tsp black pepper
8 courgettes, thinly sliced	5g/1tsp sugar
7.5g/1½tsp ground turmeric	50ml/2fl oz Ghee (Clarified Butter)

Preparation Beat the eggs in a mixing bowl. Add the onion, courgettes, turmeric, salt, pepper and sugar. Mix well.

In a large frying pan, heat the clarified butter over a low heat until it is very hot. Add the egg mixture, cover, and cook for 5 to 7 minutes. If the omelette is entirely solid, remove it from the pan and serve, cut into wedges. If the omelette is still semi-solid, replace the lid and cook for a further 2 minutes.

Pancakes
Makes 8-10

Ingredients

600ml/1pt milk	2 eggs
225g/8oz flour	butter or oil for frying
pinch of salt	

Preparation Mix the milk and flour together until smooth. Add the salt and eggs and beat in well. Leave the mixture to rest for at least 15 minutes and up to 2 hours.

Heat a little butter or oil in a heavy pan (preferably one used only for pancakes). Tip out excess butter. Pour in just enough batter to coat the bottom of the pan.

Fry on one side only if the pancakes are to be filled.

Stuffed Pancakes with Cheese and Herbs
Makes 9-10

Ingredients

	Filling
40g/1½oz plain flour	450g/1lb curd cheese
40g/1½oz wholewheat flour	30ml/2tsp cream
pinch salt	1 fat clove garlic, crushed
1 egg	15g/2tbsp fresh herbs, finely chopped
125ml/4fl oz milk	10g/1tbsp spring onion, chopped
15ml/1tbsp melted butter	

Preparation To make the pancake batter, sift the flour and salt into a bowl. Make a well in the middle of it and add the egg.

Gradually beat in the milk. When half of the milk has been added, beat in the melted butter. Continue beating in the milk until you have a thin batter. Allow the batter to stand for half an hour.

Meanwhile, prepare the filling. Combine the curd cheese with the rest of the ingredients and mix well.

To fry the pancakes, oil a heavy-bottomed frying pan 18cm/7in in diameter. Put it on the heat and when it is very hot, add 30ml/2tbsp of the batter. Tilt the pan so that the batter covers the base. Cook until the pancake is beginning to brown on the underside and then turn over and cook the top. You may have to throw the first pancake away, as it will absorb the excess oil in the pan.

Continue making pancakes, keeping them warm, until all the batter is used up. Divide the filling between them, rolling the pancakes around it into a cigar shape.

Arrange the stuffed pancakes in an ovenproof dish and heat through in a moderate oven or microwave.

Cheese and Celery Pancakes
Makes 8-10

Ingredients

1 recipe Pancakes	salt and pepper
350g/12oz curd cheese	400g/14oz canned or cooked celery, drained
1 egg	
2.5g/½tsp paprika	melted butter

Preparation Make the pancakes as directed in the recipe.

Mix the curd cheese, egg, paprika, salt and pepper together well. Put a spoonful of the cheese mixture onto each pancake on the cooked side and spread it a little. Divide the celery among the pancakes. Fold each pancake into a parcel or roll it, tucking in the edges.

Put the filled pancakes in a buttered oven dish and drizzle a little melted butter over the top. Warm through in the oven at 180°C/350°F/Gas 4 for 25 minutes.

Serve with a spoonful of yoghurt or sour cream on top of each pancake if liked.

Variation Substitute cooked asparagus for the celery.

Mandarin Pancakes
Makes 10-12

Ingredients

225g/8oz strong plain flour	200ml/7fl oz boiling water
pinch of salt	45ml/3tbsp peanut or sesame oil

Preparation Sift the flour and salt into a bowl or food processor. Gradually add sufficient boiling water and a third of the oil to form a soft but not sticky dough. Knead for 2-3 minutes or 30 seconds in the food processor. Allow to rest for 30 minutes.

Divide the dough into 20-24 pieces. Roll out each evenly into 12-cm/15-in or 18-cm/7-in rounds. Brush the surface of half the rounds with oil and sandwich pairs together, matching the size as near as possible

When all the pancakes are ready, brush the surface of a heavy frying pan sparingly with oil. Even better, have two pans to speed up the process. Put the pancakes in the pan one at a time and cook over a gentle heat until the pancake is puffy but not coloured. Turn over and cook a further 2-3 minutes.

Mushroom Pancakes
Makes 8-10

Ingredients

1 recipe Pancakes	30g/2tbsp canned red
butter	pimientos, finely
1 large onion, finely	chopped
chopped	150ml/¼pt sour cream
450g/1lb mushrooms,	salt and pepper
chopped	melted butter

Preparation Make the pancakes as directed.

Melt the butter, add the onion and cook until it has softened but not browned. Add the mushrooms and cook until soft. Drain off excess liquid. Mix in the pimientos, sour cream, salt and pepper.

Put a spoonful of the mixture onto each pancake on the cooked side. Roll up the pancakes, tucking in the edges. Put the rolled pancakes in a buttered oven dish and drizzle a little melted butter over the top. Warm through in the oven at 180°C/350°F/Gas 4 for 25 minutes.

Serve with extra sour cream if desired.

Buttermilk Pancakes
Makes 8-10

These pancakes are not the paper-thin crêpe type but fairly thick and spongy. Serve them warm with extra butter and, if you like, some maple syrup.

Ingredients

225g/8oz flour	2 eggs
5g/1tsp baking powder	450ml/¾pt buttermilk
5g/1tsp bicarbonate of	60ml/4tbsp melted butter
soda	butter or oil for frying
5g/1tsp salt	

Preparation Sift the dry ingredients into a large bowl. Whisk the eggs until they are light and fluffy. Stir the buttermilk into the eggs. Fold this into the dry ingredients and mix until smooth. Add the melted butter and stir well.

Heat your pancake pan until it is very hot. Add a little fat and when it has melted, pour off any excess. Cook the pancakes (about 100ml/4fl oz mixture per pancake, depending on the size of the pan) until golden on each side. Keep pancakes warm in a low oven while you cook the rest of the mixture.

Spinach Pancakes
Makes 8-10

Ingredients

1 recipe Pancakes	1 egg
450g/1lb spinach, washed	grated nutmeg
and picked over	salt and pepper
225g/8oz cottage cheese	melted butter

Preparation Make the pancakes as directed.

Cook the spinach without any excess water. Drain it very well (between two plates is the most effective way). Mix the cooked spinach with the cottage cheese, egg, and nutmeg, salt and pepper to taste.

Spread a spoonful of the mixture on to each pancake on the cooked side. Roll or fold the pancakes, tucking in the edges well. Put the filled pancakes in a buttered oven dish and drizzle a little melted butter over the top. Warm through in the oven at 180°C/350°F/Gas 4 for 25 minutes.

Serve with a spoonful of yoghurt or sour cream on top of each pancake if you like.

Smoked Salmon Pancakes
Makes 4-6

Although this seems an extravagant recipe, the use of smoked salmon pieces instead of the more expensive whole slices should help you economize.

Ingredients

½ recipe Pancakes	1 egg
175g/6oz smoked salmon	pepper
pieces, chopped	butter
225g/8oz cream cheese	

Preparation Make the pancakes as directed.

Mix the chopped smoked salmon with the cream cheese, egg and pepper. Put a spoonful of the mixture onto each pancake on the cooked side. Roll up the pancakes, tucking in the edges. Fry the pancakes gently in butter to warm them through.

These are rather rich but would be even more delicious served with sour cream.

Tuna Crêpes
Serves 6-8

Ingredients

2×175-g/7-oz cans tuna,
  drained
50-g/2-oz can anchovies,
  drained
15g/2tbsp chopped parsley
2.5g/½tsp salt
2.5g/½tsp pepper

6 eggs, beaten
100g/4oz flour
225ml/8fl oz cold water
7g/2tsp finely chopped
  onion
30ml/2tbsp vegetable oil

Preparation In a medium-sized mixing bowl, combine the tuna, anchovies, parsley, salt and pepper. Flake with a fork and mix until evenly blended. Set the filling aside.

In another mixing bowl, combine the eggs, flour, water and onions. Mix the batter thoroughly.

Lightly grease a large heavy frying pan with the vegetable oil. Place over a medium heat. Ladle 45ml/3tbsp of the batter at a time into the pan, spreading it evenly, and cook for 3 to 5 minutes or until the crêpe is solid but still slightly moist. Place 1tbsp of the tuna filling on the crêpe and fold it over. Remove from pan and set aside on a large baking sheet. Repeat the process until all the batter and filling are used up.

Preheat the oven to 230°C/450°F/Gas 8. Put the baking sheet in the oven and bake for 8 minutes. Serve hot.

Herb Roulade
Serves 6

Ingredients

50g/2oz Cheddar cheese,
  grated
50g/2oz Parmesan cheese,
  grated
50g/2oz crustless brown
  bread, crumbled
150ml/¼pt sour cream
45ml/3tbsp full-cream milk
7g/1tbsp parsley
7g/1tbsp snipped chives
7g/1tbsp chervil
4 eggs, separated
salt and freshly ground
  pepper

Filling
45ml/3tbsp Mayonnaise
4 large lettuce leaves
30ml/2tbsp olive oil
5ml/1tsp wine vinegar
salt and freshly ground
  pepper
French mustard to taste
7g/1tbsp basil leaves,
  chopped
4 tomatoes, peeled,
  quartered and seeded

Preparation Grease a Swiss roll tin 33×23cm/13×9in and line with greaseproof or waxed paper.

Mix the Cheddar and Parmesan, bread crumbs, cream, milk, herbs and egg yolks. Whip the egg whites until stiff and mix in quickly. Add salt and pepper to taste.

Spoon into the prepared tin and bake in a preheated oven at 200°C/400°F/Gas 6 for 10 minutes, or until firm and golden. Remove from the oven and cover with a damp, clean tea-towel and leave to cool.

Turn out the roulade on to a sheet of non-stick baking paper and trim the edges. Spread the roulade with the mayonnaise and cover with lettuce leaves. In a liquidizer or food processor, quickly reduce the oil with the vinegar, salt, pepper, mustard and basil to a smooth dressing.

Arrange the tomatoes on the lettuce leaves. Spoon over the basil dressing, and roll up the roulade like a Swiss roll. Serve immediately.

Spinach Roulade
Serves 4

Ingredients

675g/1½lb fresh spinach,
  washed and picked over
15g/½oz butter
4 eggs, separated
grated nutmeg

salt and pepper
100g/4oz curd cheese
150ml/¼pt sour cream
4 spring onions, finely
  chopped

Preparation Cook the spinach without any extra water. Drain it very well (press it between two plates) and either chop the spinach very finely or blend it just enough to chop it.

Add the butter, egg yolks, grated nutmeg and salt and pepper to taste. Mix together very well. Whisk the egg whites until they are stiff. Fold a spoonful of the beaten whites into the spinach mixture to lighten it and then fold in the remaining whites. Mix through carefully. Turn the mixture into a Swiss roll tin 38×25cm/15×10in which has been lined with greased paper or foil. Bake at 200°C/400°F/Gas 6 for 10 minutes only.

While the spinach is cooking, mix the curd cheese with the sour cream and spring onions. Season to taste. Have a clean tea towel spread on a board and when the spinach mixture is cooked, turn it upside down onto the tea towel. Carefully peel off the paper or foil.

Spread the cheese and sour cream mixture over the spinach, taking care not to tear the surface. Using the tea towel to help you, roll the spinach up into a roll and onto serving plate. Serve immediately.

Although this is usually served hot, it is, in fact, very good cold.

Cheese Soufflé
Serves 4

Ingredients

50g/2oz unsalted butter
50g/2oz plain flour
225ml/8fl oz millk
5 eggs, separated
140g/5oz grated Cheddar
    cheese
salt

freshly ground white
    pepper, a generous
    amount
cayenne pepper, according
    to taste (¼tsp makes it
    quite hot)
pinch mustard powder

Preparation Melt the butter and mix in the flour. Add the milk and stir until smooth. Remove from the heat when mixture has thickened. Add the egg yolks, one at a time. Add the cheese, salt, spices, freshly ground white pepper, cayenne pepper and mustard.

Whisk the egg whites until they stand in peaks. Stir a little egg white into the cheese mixture to loosen it, then fold in the rest.

Turn the mixture into a buttered soufflé dish and bake in a preheated oven at 200°C/400°F/Gas 6 for 25 minutes, or until the soufflé is brown and risen.

Cheese and Spinach Soufflé
Serves 4

Ingredients

450g/1lb spinach, washed
    and picked over
50g/2oz butter or
    margarine
50g/2oz flour

450ml/¾pt milk
6 eggs
225g/8oz cottage cheese
grated nutmeg
salt and pepper

Preparation Cook the spinach without any extra water. Drain it very well (between two plates).

While the spinach is cooking, melt the butter and stir in the flour off the heat. Slowly add the milk and return the pan to the heat. Stir to thicken the sauce. Remove the pan from the heat. Separate the eggs and add the yolks, one at a time, mixing after each one. Add the cooked and drained spinach, cottage cheese, nutmeg, salt and pepper to taste. Mix everything together well.

Whisk the whites until they are very stiff. Take a scoop of the whites and fold it gently into the spinach mixture to lighten it a little and then incorporate the rest of the whites into it, mixing it in lightly. Turn the soufflé mixture into a greased soufflé dish measuring about 21×9cm/8¼×3½in. Bake at 190°C/375°F/Gas 5 for 30 minutes.

Test with a clean knife to see if it is ready. If the mixture is still very runny, return the dish to the oven for a further 5 minutes or so. If you like, sprinkle some grated Parmesan cheese on the top 10 minutes before the end of cooking.

Courgette Soufflé
Serves 6

French flair combines with a Middle Eastern influence to create this unusual and delicious soufflé.

Ingredients

50g/2oz butter
75g/3oz finely chopped
    onion
25g/1oz flour
225ml/8fl oz milk
15g/1tbsp grated Parmesan
    cheese
100g/4oz feta cheese,
    crumbled

450g/1lb courgettes, finely
    chopped
pinch salt
pinch black pepper
4 egg yolks
5 egg whites

Preparation Preheat the oven to 175°C/350°F/Gas 4. Melt the butter in a large saucepan over a medium heat. Add the onion and sauté for 2 minutes. Add the flour and cook for an additional 2 minutes.

Add the milk and cook, stirring constantly, until the sauce begins to bubble and thicken. Add the Parmesan and feta cheeses and stir until well mixed.

Add the courgettes, salt and pepper. Reduce the heat to low and cook for 1 minute.

Stir in the yolks one at a time. When all the egg yolks are blended, remove the saucepan from the heat.

Whisk the egg whites until they are stiff. Fold the egg whites into the courgette mixture. Pour the mixture into a buttered soufflé dish and bake for 45 minutes, or until the soufflé is puffed and browned. Serve at once.

Chicory Soufflé
Serves 4

Ingredients

3 heads of chicory
salt
15ml/1tbsp lemon juice
40g/1½oz butter
40g/1½oz flour

300ml/½pt milk
50g/2oz grated cheese
4 eggs, separated
10g/1tbsp dry brown
    breadcrumbs

Preparation Trim the chicory and cook in salted water to which you have added the lemon juice. This will stop it discolouring.

When the chicory is tender, drain and set aside. When it is cool, press the water out from between the leaves with your fingers. Chop the chicory very finely.

Meanwhile, melt the butter in a heavy-bottomed pan. Stir in the flour. Remove from the heat and stir in the milk. Return to the heat and stir until the sauce has thickened. Add the cheese and cook for a further minute. Allow to cool.

When the sauce has cooled, mix in the chicory, then the egg yolks.

Whisk the egg whites until they form soft peaks and fold into the chicory mixture. Spoon into a greased soufflé dish and sprinkle the top with breadcrumbs.

Bake in a preheated oven at 200°C/400°F/Gas 6 for 20-25 minutes until lightly set, well risen and golden on top. Serve this soufflé with a strongly flavoured salad, such as watercress garnished with slivers of orange.

Leek and Stilton Bake
Serves 4

Ingredients
450g/1lb small leeks
6 eggs
1 slice wholemeal bread, crumbled
30ml/2tbsp cider vinegar
100g/4oz Stilton cheese

Preparation Preheat the oven to 200°C/400°F/Gas 6. Trim and wash the leeks. Steam for 10-15 minutes. Lay them in a greased ovenproof dish.

Beat the eggs with the vinegar and breadcrumbs and crumble in the Stilton. Pour over the leeks and bake for 30 minutes until risen and golden.

Crab and Asparagus Tart
Serves 4

Ingredients
150g/6oz Shortcrust Pastry
2 eggs plus 1 yolk
150ml/¼pt double cream
15ml/1tbsp brandy
225g/8oz crabmeat
25g/1oz butter
25g/1oz flour
150ml/¼pt milk
30g/2tbsp grated Cheddar cheese
salt and cayenne pepper
8 asparagus spears, cooked

Preparation Roll out the pastry and line a 22-cm/8-in quiche or flan tin standing on a greased baking sheet.

Beat the eggs, cream and brandy together. Flake the crabmeat with a fork and stir into the egg mixture.

Melt the butter in a heavy-bottomed pan and add the flour. Stir and cook for a few minutes. Remove from the heat and gradually stir in the milk. Return to the heat and continue stirring until the sauce thickens. Add the cheese and seasoning.

Stir the crab mixture into the cheese sauce and pour into the flan. Decorate the top with asparagus spears, pressing them into the filling. Bake in a preheated oven at 190°C/375°F/Gas 5 for 35-40 minutes till lightly set.

Summer Posy Mousse
Serves 4

If you cannot get the herbs and edible flowers in this posy, other seasonal herbs can be substituted.

Ingredients
15g/½oz (2 envelopes) powdered gelatine
30ml/2tbsp warm water
2 eggs, separated, plus 1 egg white
150ml/¼pt double cream
100g/4oz Roquefort cheese, crumbled
45ml/3tbsp sour cream
salt and freshly ground white pepper
few drops Tabasco

The posy
nasturtium flowers and leaves
borage flowers and leaves
summer savory
springs of mint, fennel and dill

Preparation Put the gelatine and water into a small bowl and stand it in a pan of simmering water. Stir well until the gelatine has dissolved.

Beat the egg yolks with half the double cream, the sour cream and the gelatine. Mash in the cheese. Whip the remaining double cream, fold into the mixture, season and add Tabasco to taste. Chill.

Whisk the egg whites until soft peaks form. Fold them into the mixture. Oil a ring mould, pour in the mousse and chill until set.

Dip the mould into hot water, invert a plate over it and turn the mousse out. Fill the centre with a posy of edible flowers and delicate leafy herbs. Serve with brown bread.

Salmon and Chive Cocottes

Salmon and Chive Cocottes
Serves 4

Ingredients

butter
175g/6oz cooked salmon, boned
50g/2oz Cheddar cheese
3 eggs

2 egg yolks
300ml/½pt single cream
7g/1tbsp snipped chives
salt and freshly ground pepper

Preparation Butter 4 small individual dishes.

Skin and flake the salmon and divide among the dishes.

Mix together the cheese, eggs, egg yolks, cream and chives. Season, then pour over the salmon in the dishes. Place in a roasting pan half-filled with hot water. Bring to the boil on top of the stove, then bake in the heated oven at 190°C/375°F/Gas 5 for 15 minutes or until firm to the touch. Either serve at once, or leave to cool.

Ham and Cheese Mousse
Serves 4

Ingredients

1 cucumber
175g/6oz ham
175g/6oz cream cheese
10ml/2tsp mustard

2 eggs
20g/4tsp gelatine
45ml/3tbsp boiling water

Preparation Slice the cucumber and line a moistened small ring mould or dish with half the slices. Chop the ham and mix it into the cheese with the mustard and eggs.

Mix the gelatine with the water until it has dissolved. Add this to the ham mixture. Fold in the remaining cucumber slices and spoon the mixture into the prepared mould. Leave to set for a minimum of 6 hours, or overnight.

Unmould and serve with salad.

Crunchy Pepper and Tuna Mousse
Serves 6

Set in a Tupperware or plastic container instead of a glass bowl, this tangy, textured mousse makes a picnic treat.

Ingredients

225g/8oz can tuna, drained and flaked
2 hard-boiled eggs, coarsely chopped
1 red pepper, cored, seeded and coarsely chopped
1 green pepper, cored, seeded and coarsely chopped
15g/½oz butter or margarine
15g/½oz flour
150ml/¼pt milk

45ml/3tbsp water
7.5g/¼oz gelatine
150ml/¼pt Mayonnaise
150ml/¼pt double cream, whipped
30ml/2tbsp lemon juice
salt and freshly ground pepper
tomato ketchup, to taste (optional)
lemon slices or pepper rings

Preparation Mix together the tuna, eggs and peppers until well blended.

Melt the butter in a small pan, and stir in the flour followed by the milk. Bring to the boil, stirring constantly. Simmer for two minutes. Tip on to a large plate and allow the sauce to cool completely.

Meanwhile, put the water into a small pan and sprinkle in the gelatine. Leave to soak for 5 minutes, then gently melt over low heat.

Mix the cooled sauce into the tuna mixture with the melted gelatine, mayonnaise, and whipped cream. Season to taste with lemon juice, salt and pepper and tomato ketchup, if used.

Spoon into a glass bowl, cover and chill until firm. Garnish with thin lemon slices or pepper rings, and serve with a green salad and crusty bread.

Onion Tart
Serves 4

Ingredients

175g/6oz Shortcrust Pastry
15g/1tbsp butter
15ml/1tbsp oil
500g/18oz onions, finely
  chopped
2 eggs plus 1 yolk
450ml/¾pt single cream

15-30g/1-2tbsp grated
  Cheddar cheese
7-15g/1-2tbsp chopped
  parsley
salt and freshly ground
  black pepper
pinch cayenne

Preparation Heat the oven to 190°C/375°F/Gas 5.

Line a 22-cm/8-in quiche pan with the pastry.

Heat the butter and oil in a pan. Stir in the onions. Cover the pan, turn down the heat and sweat for about 5 minutes, stirring occasionally until the onions are soft and transparent.

Beat the eggs, cream and cheese togther and add the onions and parsley. Season with salt and pepper and cayenne to taste, pour into the pastry-lined pan and bake in the middle of the oven for 30-40 minutes until golden and set.

Variation For Onion and Blue Cheese Tart combine 15-30g/1-2tbsp crumbled blue cheese with the cream before beating it with the eggs. Omit the Cheddar, parsley and cayenne pepper.

Cheesy Onion Quiche
Serves 6-8

This is a favourite country recipe from Alsace.

Ingredients

100g/4oz Cheddar cheese,
  grated
140g/5oz plain flour
75g/3oz cold butter, diced
pinch each salt and
  cayenne pepper
1 egg, beaten

Filling
675g/1½lb medium sized
  onions
75g/3oz butter or
  margarine
salt and freshly ground
  pepper
bay leaf
150ml/¼pt white wine
1 egg
45ml/3tbsp milk
100g/4oz Cheddar cheese,
  sliced

Preparation First make the pastry. Mix the grated cheese with the flour, butter and seasonings, until the mixture resembles fine breadcrumbs. Pour in the beaten egg, and mix until the mixture forms a soft but not sticky dough. Turn out onto a floured surface and roll out fairly thickly, then use to line a 20-cm/8-in quiche dish. Bake blind in a preheated oven at 190°C/375°F/Gas 5 for 10 to 15 minutes or until the pastry is looking golden and crisp.

While the pastry is cooking, prepare the filling. Slice the onions. Heat the butter or margarine in a large frying pan, then add the onions, a little salt and pepper, and the bay leaf. Fry over a high heat, stirring constantly, until the onions are golden. Add the wine, and cook over medium heat, stirring frequently until all the liquid has evaporated. Remove the bay leaf. Mix the egg with the milk.

Spoon the onion mixture into the cooked pastry case, pressing the filling down well. Arrange the cheese slices on top of the onions, then carefully pour on the egg mixture. Bake in a preheated oven for 15 minutes or until the quiche is golden brown.

Serve hot or warm.

Tomato and Sage Derby Quiche
Serves 4

If Sage Derby is not available use another hard, herb-flavoured cheese. A firm goat's cheese is a very good substitute.

Ingredients

4 large tomatoes
175g/6oz Shortcrust Pastry
100g/4oz Sage Derby
  cheese

3 eggs
150ml/¼pt milk
salt and freshly ground
  black pepper

Preparation Pour boiling water over the tomatoes. After a minute the skins will begin to split. Refresh with cold water. Peel the tomatoes and slice them thickly.

Line a 22-cm/8-in quiche pan with the pastry and crumble the cheese into it. Arrange the tomato slices to cover the cheese.

Break the eggs into a bowl and lightly beat with the milk and seasoning. Pour egg mixture over the tomatoes, gently pressing them down with a fork.

Bake in the centre of a preheated oven at 200°C/400°F/Gas 6 for 15-20 minutes, until set and golden.

Spinach Quiche
Serves 4

Ingredients

175g/6oz Shortcrust Pastry
1kg/2lb spinach
25g/1oz butter
salt and freshly ground
    black pepper
nutmeg

300ml/½pt single cream
2 eggs plus 1 yolk
50g/2oz grated Parmesan
    cheese
25-50g/1-2oz mushrooms,
    sliced

Preparation Roll out the pastry and use to line a 22-cm/8-in quiche pan.

Wash the spinach and discard the tough stalks. Squeeze it into a large saucepan with the water still clinging to it and add three quarters of the butter. Cook, tightly covered, over a low heat, stirring occasionally, until soft (about 5-8 minutes).

Purée the spinach in a blender and season to taste with salt, pepper and nutmeg.

Beat the cream, eggs and cheese together and stir in the spinach. Pour spinach mixture into a prepared pie crust and arrange the mushroom slices on top. Dot with the remaining butter and bake for 30-40 minutes in a preheated oven at 190°C/375°F/Gas 5 until set and slightly browned on top.

Kipper Mousse Quiche
Serves 6-8

Ingredients

75g/3oz cornflakes,
    crushed
75g/3oz plain flour
pinch each salt and pepper
75g/3oz cold butter, diced
1 small egg, beaten

Filling
450g/1lb kipper fillets,
    cooked
225g/8oz cottage cheese
    with chives
a little lemon juice
freshly ground black
    pepper
150ml/¼pt double cream,
    whipped
lemon slices

Preparation First make the pastry. Blend together the cornflakes, flour, salt and pepper and butter, until the mixture resembles breadcrumbs. Add the beaten egg, and mix to a soft but not sticky dough.

Turn out onto a well floured board and roll out fairly thickly. Use to line a 20-cm/8-in oven-proof china quiche dish. Bake blind in a preheated oven at 190°C/375°F/Gas 5 for 10 to 15 minutes or until the pastry is crisp and golden brown. Allow to cool completely.

Meanwhile make the filling. Skin and flake the cooked, cooled kipper fillets. Liquidize or sieve the cottage cheese until smooth. Add the flaked fish with the lemon juice and black pepper. Liquidize or process until very smooth and light.

Fold this mixture into the whipped cream. Taste for seasoning, adding more lemon juice and pepper if necessary. Spoon mixture into the pastry case and chill well.

Garnish the quiche with lemon slices, and serve well chilled with lemon wedges and a cucumber salad.

Savoury Pumpkin Pie
Serves 4-6

Ingredients

175g/6oz wholewheat or
    white self-raising flour
pinch salt
30ml/2tbsp oil
water to mix

Filling
450g/1lb pumpkin flesh
4 eggs
150ml/¼pt double cream
150ml/¼pt milk
2 large tomatoes, peeled
    and chopped
7g/1tbsp chopped fresh
    basil leaves
freshly ground black
    pepper

Preparation To make the pastry sift the flour with the salt. Rub in the oil with your fingertips and add enough water to make a dough. Chill. Roll out. Line a greased 22-cm/8-in quiche pan.

Remove the rind and seeds from the pumpkin and cut into slivers. Pack into a pan with very little water and cook over a low heat, covered. Check the pan occasionally to make sure the pumpkin hasn't dried out. After about 20 minutes you should be able to mash it into a purée.

Beat the eggs with the cream and milk. Mix in the pumpkin, tomato and basil and pour into the pastry-lined pan. Bake in a preheated oven at 190°C/375°F/Gas 5 for 45 minutes until set and golden.

Leek Quiche
Serves 4

Ingredients

pie plate 20cm/8in lined with Shortcrust Pastry	*1 large onion, chopped*
25g/1oz butter	*225g/8oz cottage cheese*
450g/1lb leeks, trimmed and chopped	*3 eggs*
	salt and pepper
	pinch ground allspice

Preparation Prick the pastry case with a fork, line it with uncooked rice or beans and bake it for 10 minutes at 180°C/350°F/Gas 4. Discard the rice or beans.

Heat the butter and soften the leeks and onion in it for 5 minutes. Mix the cottage cheese with the remaining ingredients.

Cover the bottom of the lined pie plate with the cooked leeks and onions. Spoon over the cottage cheese mixture. Bake for 35 minutes.

This is equally good hot, cold, or warm.

Blue Cheese Pâté
Makes approx. 300g/10oz

This mixture is useful as a filling for fruit (especially good with pears) or choux pastry, for stuffed tomatoes or celery, or as a salad dressing, in which case add more cream or creamy milk.

Ingredients
150g/6oz curd cheese
100g/4oz blue cheese
30-60ml/2-4tbsp cream

Preparation Liquidize the cheeses with just enough cream to reach the required consistency. Refrigerate the mixture until required. It will firm up considerably.

Cheese and Herb Pâté
Makes approx. 500g/1¼lb

If you don't eat all this divine pâté, created by John Tovey of the Miller Howe Hotel in the English Lake District, just by constant "tasting", you will find it amazingly versatile — as a vegetable stuffing, a spread, slipped under the skin of a chicken before roasting, with fruit, as a dressing for hot vegetables, stuffing for veal or pork, on grilled meats. Use any available fresh herbs.

Ingredients

140g/5oz butter, melted	*7g/1tbsp finely chopped chives*
3 cloves garlic, crushed	
7g/1tbsp finely chopped parsley	*450g/1lb cream cheese*
7g/1tbsp chopped chervil	*salt and pepper*

Preparation Melt the butter slowly and leave it to cool a little. Combine all the other ingredients and gently fold in the cooled butter. Pot it and refrigerate it until needed. It keeps for several weeks if well wrapped. Use as required.

Date and Cream Cheese Spread
Makes approx. 300g/10oz

Fresh dates are so different from the more widely known semi-dried variety, familiar to us at Christmas time. They are not as sweet as the boxed ones and lend themselves to interesting combinations. This spread can be used on bread (try granary) or as a cocktail appetizer on small crackers.

Ingredients
50g/2oz cream cheese
30ml/2tbsp milk
225g/8oz fresh dates, finely chopped
15g/1tbsp finely grated lemon rind

Preparation Mix the cheese with the milk to a smooth cream. Add the dates and lemon rind and mix together well.

Welsh Rarebit
Serves 2 or 4

Ingredients

4 slices bread	50ml/2fl oz strong ale
50g/2oz butter	10ml/2tsp English mustard
225g/8oz Cheddar cheese, grated	salt and pepper to taste

Preparation Toast the bread on both sides.

Melt the butter in a heavy saucepan over a low heat. Add the cheese and ale, stirring all the time. Add the mustard, salt and pepper.

Spread on the toast and grill until browned and bubbling.

Vegetable Cheese Custard
Serves 910

Ingredients

15ml/1tbsp oil	3 eggs
1 medium onion, chopped	100g/4oz cream cheese or cottage cheese
400g/14oz canned tomatoes	100g/4oz grated Cheddar cheese
fresh basil, chopped, to taste	
salt and pepper	

Preparation Heat the oil, add the onion and cook until just softened but not browned. Drain the tomatoes (reserve the juice for use in a sauce or soup) and add them to the onion together with the basil, salt and pepper. Cook for 5 minutes, breaking the tomatoes up as they cook. Turn the contents of the pan into a lightly greased ovenproof dish.

Mix the remaining ingredients except the grated cheese together well, in a blender or food processor. Pour the mixture over the tomatoes and scatter the grated cheese on top. Bake at 180°C/350°F/Gas 4 for 30 minutes.

Variation The recipe can be adapted to use any vegetable or combination of vegetables you like: fresh tomatoes instead of canned, 450g/1lb courgettes, lightly fried with an onion and fresh marjoram and thyme added; 350g/12oz button mushrooms, lightly fried with an onion and a little grated nutmeg added; a ratatouille of onions, courgettes, aubergines and tomatoes with oregano; sautéed leeks with grated nutmeg. Try ricotta, curd cheese, or drained yoghurt instead of the cream cheese.

You may care to make a quiche with this mixture, in which case line a pie shell 23cm/9in in diameter, which has been baked for 10 minutes, with the prepared vegetables and spread the cheese mixture over the vegetables. Top with the grated cheese and bake as above.

Savoury Cheesecake
Serves 4-6

Ingredients
15g/½oz butter
1 large onion, sliced
4 eggs
225g/8oz curd cheese
225g/8oz cream cheese

15g/2tbsp chopped chives
salt and pepper
part-baked Shortcrust
Pastry case approx.
20cm/8in in diameter

Preparation Heat the butter, add the onion and cook until it has just softened but not browned. Beat the eggs until they are very light and fluffy. Mix the cheeses with the cooked onion, chives, salt and pepper. Carefully fold the cheese mixture into the beaten eggs and spoon this into the pastry case. Bake at 180°C/350°F/Gas 4 for 30 minutes, or until set.

Serve cold (preferably the next day) with a crisp salad. This freezes very well.

Broccoli and Tomato Cheesecake
Serves 4-6

Ingredients
100g/4oz wholewheat
  biscuit crumbs
50g/2oz butter, softened
Filling
225g/8oz broccoli florets
1 large tomato
350g/12oz curd cheese

salt and freshly ground
  white pepper
pinch nutmeg
2 eggs,separated
a little gelatine melted in
  warm water (optional)

Preparation Combine the crumbs and the butter and press down well into a greased 22-cm/8-in quiche pan with a loose bottom.

Steam the broccoli florets over boiling salted water until tender. Carefully slice some of the florets for decoration. Immerse the tomato in boiling water for a minute, refresh in cold water, peel and deseed.

Mash the curd cheese with most of the broccoli and the tomato and season well with salt, pepper and a good pinch of nutmeg. Beat in the egg yolks.

Whisk the whites until they form soft peaks and fold into the mixture. Pour the filling over the crumb base and bake in a preheated oven at 180°C/350°F/Gas 4 for about 20-25 minutes until slightly risen and just set.

Allow to cool. When cold, remove from the tin and decorate the top with the remaining sliced broccoli florets. Brush with the melted gelatine if you like and chill before serving.

Savoury Cheese Strudel
Serves 4

Ingredients
350g/12oz Puff Pastry
150g/6oz grated cheddar
  cheese
100g/4oz cream cheese
100g/4oz curd cheese

1 egg
chopped parsley or mint, to
  taste
salt and pepper
egg white to glaze

Preparation Roll the pastry out as thinly as possible. Mix the remaining ingredients, except the egg white, until smooth. Spread the mixture over the pastry. Fold over to make a flattish roll, sealing the edges well. Brush with the egg white. Transfer to a moistened baking sheet and bake at 200°C/400°F/Gas 6 for 20 minutes.

Serve hot, with sour cream if liked.

Whisking Eggs

Frothy Whisked, usually with a fork, just enough to mix them and prevent them pouring out of the jug or bowl separately. This makes them easier to add gradually to mixtures.

Soft Peak Whisked until the egg white will just hold its shape when the whisk is lifted, the points that are dragged up by the rising whisk flopping over softly. Used to add to fairly liquid mixtures such as cake batters or whipped cream.

Medium Peak Whisked until the egg whites will stand in peaks when the whisk is lifted, but with the tips of the peaks just flopping over like wilted leaves. For incorporating into soft mixtures such as soufflés, ice creams, sorbets and sherbets. The idea is to have the two mixtures the cook is combining as close to each other in consistency as possible. It is very difficult to add over-whisked (too stiff and too dry) egg whites to, say, a soft chocolate mousse mixture — the egg whites break up into islands and by the time you have stirred and struggled to get the mixture smooth, most of that carefully incorporated air has been knocked out.

Stiff Peak Whisked until the egg white will stand up in rigid pointed (not floppy) peaks when the whisk is lifted. Used mainly for meringue, at which point the sugar is added.

To Make a Soufflé

1 Fold not-too-stiffly whisked whites into the base. Continue until there are no large patches of egg white, then stop. Do not overmix.

2 Brush out the soufflé dish with melted butter, then — for a crusty edge — dust with breadcrumbs. Fill dish only two-thirds full.

3 A paper collar — also buttered and breadcrumbed — pinned in place will allow the soufflé to rise to the top of the dish.

4 Draw a knife through the mixture first one way then at angles to break up any air pockets.

5 Running a finger around the edge of the soufflé mixture ensures a top-hat shape when baked.

6 Carefully peel away the collar, if used, before serving.

Fish and Seafood

Fisherman's Stew 71
Fish in Bean Paste Sauce 71
Family Fish Pie 71/72
Paella Marrano 72
Gefillte Fish Patties 72
Salt-Grilled Fish 72
Stuffed Fish 73
Fish Kebabs 73
Smoked Fish Croquettes 73
Smoked Fish Salad 73
Jellied Fish 74
Spiced Fish 74
Smoked Haddock Soufflé 74
Baked Grey Mullet 74
Red Mullet Provencal 74
Devilled Herring 75
Herrings in Oatmeal with Mustard Sauce 75
Baked Salt Herring 75
"Solomon Gundy" 75
Stuffed Baked Mackerel 75
Baked Perch 76
Pike Quenelles 76
Baked Red Snapper 76
Red Snapper á la Creole 76/77
Baked Stuffed Salmon Trout 77
Poached Salmon 77
Dressed Salmon 78
Salmon en Croute 78/79
Salmon Fish Cakes 79
Rich Salmon Fish Cakes 79
Salmon with Lime and Walnut Oil 79
Salmon Cutlets with Anchovy Butter 80
Salmon Loaf 80
Salmon and Spinach Pie 80/81
Salmon Mousse 81
Coulibiac 81
Skate in Caper Sauce 82
Sardines Provencal 82
Poached Sole 82

Goujons of Sole 82
Fillets of Sole in White Wine with Mushroomss 83
Sole Dugléré 83
Sole Véronique 83
Sole Meunière 83
Grilled Squid with Lime 84
Savoury Sprats 84
Trout "Au Bleu" 84
Trout Chaudfroid 85
Trout with Almonds 85
Trout with Avocado and Ham 85
Two Trout Mousse 86
Steamed Trout with Hazelnuts and Courgettes 86
Tuna Wholewheat Rolls 87
Tuna Mousse 87
Tuna-Stuffed Potatoes 87
Whitebait 87
Whiting Bercy 87
Dressed Crab 88
Chilli Crab 88
Papaya Crab 89
Crab with Eggs 89
Baked Avocado with Crab 89
Dressed Lobster 90
Oysters à l'Americaine 90
Lobster Newburg 90
Moules Marinère 91
Oysters en brochette 91
Prawn Curry 91
Scallops au Gratin 92
Shrimp-Stuffed Courgettes 92
Scallops with Mushrooms 92/93

Selection of Fish 93
Preparation of Fish 93
To Clean and Fillet Flat Fish 93
To Clean and Bone Round Fish 94
Dressing Crab 94

Fisherman's Stew
Serves 8-10

Ingredients

1kg/2lb fresh halibut steaks	5g/1tsp grated orange peel
1kg/2lb white fish (preferably mixed), cleaned	5g/1tsp dried thyme
	7g/1tbsp parsley, coarsely chopped
1kg/2lb haddock steaks	bay leaf
1kg/2lb cod-fish steaks	pinch of saffron threads
125ml/4fl oz olive oil	2.5g/½tsp salt
2 medium onions, coarsely chopped	2.5g/½tsp black pepper
	2 green chillies, seeded and coarsely chopped
175g/6oz thinly sliced leeks	
6 cloves garlic, finely chopped	2.5ml/½tsp Tabasco
1.6l/2¾pt water	100g/4oz chopped pimiento
450ml/16fl oz white wine	30g/3tbsp unflavoured breadcrumbs
1.5kg/3lb tomatoes, peeled, seeded and coarsely chopped	350g/12oz cooked rice

Preparation Trim the skin and bones from the fish steaks. Fillet the whole fish. Cut the fish steaks and fillets into 2.5-cm (1-in) cubes. Reserve the trimmings, heads and bones.

Heat 45ml/3tbsp of the olive oil in a large saucepan. Add the onions, leeks and a third of the chopped garlic. Cook over a low heat, stirring occasionally, for 5 minutes.

Add 1.2l/2¼pt of the water, the white wine and reserved fish trimmings to the pan. Cover and simmer over a low heat for 5 minutes.

Add the tomatoes, orange peel, thyme, parsley, bay leaf, saffron, salt and pepper. Raise the heat slightly and simmer, covered, for 15 minutes. Remove the cover and simmer for a further 10 minutes.

Prepare the Rouille. Combine the remaining garlic with the green chillies, Tabasco, pimiento, remaining olive oil and breadcrumbs. Mix well.

Put the mixture into a saucepan and add the remaining water. Simmer over a moderate heat for 10 minutes. Put the sauce into a serving bowl and set aside.

When the fish broth is ready, strain it through a cheesecloth into another saucepan.

Bring the strained stock to a boil over a medium heat. Add the fish pieces and cook for 10 minutes. Reduce the heat to low and cook for a further 5 minutes.

Heat the rice through and divide it between soup bowls. Ladle the soup on top. Serve with the Rouille.

Fish in Bean Paste Sauce
Serves 2-3

Ingredients

675g/1½lb snapper or bream	5g/1tsp sugar
½ medium peeled and chopped onion	3 green chillies, seeded and roughly chopped
	300ml/½pt water
2 cloves garlic, crushed	seasoning to taste
30ml/2tbsp bean paste	spring onion or coriander leaves
15g/½oz fresh ginger	
oil for frying	

Preparation Wipe the fish, then make three slashes on each side with a sharp knife.

Pound half the onion, one garlic clove and the bean paste together until creamy. Slice and shred the ginger.

Half fry the fish in oil on both sides then lift out. Fry the reserved onion and garlic in the fat in the pan until just browning. Stir in the bean paste mixture and fry for 1-2 minutes to bring out the flavour. Add the sugar and green chillies. Cook until you can smell the aroma from the chillies.

Pour in the water. Bring to the boil then lower the fish into the sauce. Cover and cook for further 5-10 minutes or until the fish is cooked through.

Garnish with chopped spring onion or fresh coriander leaves.

Family Fish Pie
Serves 4

Ingredients

450g/1lb haddock or cod, filleted	25g/1oz flour
	salt and freshly ground pepper
approx. 300ml/½pt milk or milk and water	1kg/2lb potatoes, peeled and sliced
2 tomatoes, skinned and sliced	1 egg
	30ml/2tbsp milk
50g/2oz mushrooms, washed and sliced	parsley sprigs
50g/2oz butter	

Preparation Poach the fish in the milk or milk and water. Allow to cool in the liquid. Strain the liquid into a measuring jug and make up to 300ml/½pt if necessary for the Béchamel Sauce. Remove the skin from the fish, and flake.

Arrange the tomatoes and mushrooms on the bottom

of a pie plate. Make up the sauce using half the butter, season well, mix with the fish and pour into the pie plate.

Cook, mash or sieve the potatoes, mix with a little beaten egg and milk, season well. Pipe or pile on top of the fish mixture and dot with the remaining butter.

Bake at 180°C/350°F/Gas 4 for about 25 minutes, and serve garnished with parsley sprigs.

Paella Marrano
Serves 10

Ingredients

50ml/2fl oz olive oil	2.5g/½tsp black pepper
450g/1lb spicy beef sausage, sliced	75g/3oz finely chopped onions
350g/12oz cooked shelled shrimps or prawns	1 green pepper, seeded and finely chopped
350g/12oz cooked shelled mussels	1 large tomato, peeled, seeded and finely chopped
1kg/2lb chicken, cut into small pieces	4 cloves garlic, finely chopped
1kg/2lb white fish	600g/21oz rice
450g/1lb salmon steak, cut into small pieces	pinch of saffron threads
450g/1lb haddock fillets, cut into small pieces	1.5l/2½pt boiling water
5g/1tsp salt·	a few cooked prawns and mussels in their shells to garnish
	225g/8oz peas
	lemon wedges

Preparation In a medium-sized heavy frying pan, heat 45ml/3tbsp of the olive oil. Add the sausage slices and brown well over a low heat. Remove the sausage slices and set aside.

In the same pan, brown the chicken pieces over a moderate heat for 10 to 20 minutes, or until thoroughly cooked. Remove the pieces and set aside.

Drain the fat from the pan. Add the rest of the oil and heat over a low heat. Add the shellfish, fish pieces, salt, pepper, onions, green pepper, tomatoes and garlic. Sauté for 15 to 20 minutes or until the fish are cooked but still firm. Set aside.

Preheat the oven to 205°C/400°F/Gas 6. In a large paella pan or flameproof casserole combine the sautéed fish and vegetables with the rice, saffron and boiling water. Stir well and bring to the boil over a high heat. Remove the pan from the heat.

Arrange the pieces of sausage, prawns and mussels in their shells and the peas over the rice mixture. Bake, uncovered, for 30 minutes, or until all the liquid is absorbed.

Remove the pan from the oven and cover with a clean tea-towel. Leave it to stand for 5 minutes. Serve with lemon wedges for garnish.

Gefillte Fish Patties
Serves 8-10

Ingredients

1kg/2lb fresh white fish fillets (reserve the heads, skin and bones)	15g/1tbsp salt
	7.5g/1½tsp black pepper
	4 large onions, finely chopped
1kg/2lb fresh carp fillets (reserve the heads, skin and bones)	4 eggs, beaten
	50g/2oz matzo meal
	30g/2tbsp sugar
1kg/2lb fresh pike or trout fillets (reserve the heads, skin and bones)	2 carrots, cut into fine julienne strips
	3 carrots, peeled and cut into 2.5cm/1in rounds
1.9l/3¼pt cold water	

Preparation Put the reserved fish heads, skin and bones into a large stock pot. Add the water, 5g/1tsp of the salt, and the pepper. Bring the liquid to the boil and cook, uncovered, over a high heat for 40 minutes. Strain the fish stock into another pot and discard the heads, skin and bones.

Finely chop the fish fillets. Put the chopped fish into a large bowl and add the onions, eggs, matzo meal, sugar, remaining salt, julienne carrots and another 225ml/8fl oz cold water. Mix well until the consistency is even. Shape the fish mixture into balls about 5cm (2in) in diameter.

Bring the strained fish stock to a boil over a low heat. Add the carrot slices. Drop the fish balls into the stock and cover the pot. Simmer over a low heat for 1 hour. Remove the cover and simmer for another 45 minutes. Remove the pot from the heat and let the gefillte fish cool in the liquid to room temperature.

Remove the gefillte fish and put them into a glass or ceramic serving bowl. Strain the stock again and pour it over the fish. Add the sliced carrots from the stock. Cover the bowl and chill for 2 hours before serving. Serve with horseradish.

Salt-Grilled Fish
Serves 2

This method of cooking a whole fish is very simple and quite delicious. After marinating with salt, the fish is cooked over a high heat causing the oils and the salt to give a succulent, moist result.

Ingredients

2 small mackerel or red snapper (or any medium-sized fish), gutted, but head and tail left on	finely grated daikon (white radish or mooli) or lemon slices
	50ml/2fl oz soy sauce
salt	

Preparation Rinse and dry the fish on absorbent kitchen paper. Thread two skewers through the body of the fish as handles for grilling. Wrap the tail and fins, if liked, in small pieces of foil to prevent them burning when cooking. Sprinkle the surfaces of the fish, inside and out, with salt and leave for 30 minutes.

Grill or barbecue for at least 5-10 minutes on each side, depending on the size of the fish. The flesh should look milky and flake easily. Do not overcook.

Serve garnished with the daikon or slices of lemon and a bowl of soy sauce so that the fish can be dipped into it before eating.

Stuffed Fish
Serves 6-8

This mixture of fish stuffed with dates may seem odd, but it is very tasty.

Ingredients

75g/3oz cooked rice	black pepper to taste
65g/2½oz chopped almonds	225g/8oz dates, stoned
50g/2oz sugar	3kg/6lb firm, white-fleshed fish, cleaned
100g/4oz butter	1 onion, sliced
2.5g/½tsp ground ginger	10g/1tbsp cinnamon
salt to taste	

Preparation Preheat the oven to 175°C/350°F/Gas 4. Combine the rice, almonds, sugar, 25g/1oz of the butter, ginger, salt and pepper in a mixing bowl. Mix well. Stuff the dates with the mixture and close the openings with toothpicks. Pack the cavity of the fish with the stuffed dates.

Grease a large baking dish with the remaining butter. Put the fish in the dish and top with the onion slices. Bake until the fish flakes easily with a fork, about 25 to 30 minutes.

Remove the dates from the fish and arrange the fish on a serving platter. Arrange the dates around the fish and dust with the cinnamon.

Fish Kebabs
Serves 4

Ingredients

	Marinade
2 thick cod steaks	60ml/4tbsp oil
8 medium mushrooms	70ml/5tbsp lemon juice
8 bay leaves	salt and freshly ground pepper
8 cooked prawns or shrimps	7g/1tbsp roughly chopped parsley
1 green pepper, seeded and blanched	bay leaf
1 red or yellow pepper, seeded	1 small onion, thinly sliced in rings
2 courgettes, thickly sliced	2.5g/½tsp paprika
	225g/8oz long grain rice, uncooked
	900ml/1½pt water
	2.5g/½tsp turmeric
	a little oil
	lemon wedges
	parsley sprigs

Preparation Cut the cod steaks into 12 even-sized pieces and thread onto the skewers one piece at a time. Alternate with mushrooms, bay leaves, prawns or shrimps, squares of blanched peppers and slices of courgette.

Combine the oil, lemon juice, seasoning, parsley, bay leaf, onion and paprika and pour over the fish. Leave to marinate for at least 3 hours, turning the kebabs from time to time.

Add the water with turmeric added to the rice and cook as directed on the packet.

Paint the grill rack with oil to prevent sticking and grill the skewered food for about 4 minutes each side until the cod is cooked.

Serve on a warm bed of rice with Spicy Tomato Sauce and a crisp green salad.

Smoked Fish Croquettes
Makes 16

Ingredients

500g/1lb smoked haddock, cod or mackerel	1 hard-boiled egg
150ml/¼pt milk	few drops Worcestershire sauce
1 small onion, finely chopped, or 6 spring onions	7g/1tbsp parsley, chopped
	1 egg, beaten
725g/1½lb potatoes, peeled and cooked	100g/4oz dried breadcrumbs
	oil for frying

Preparation Poach the smoked fish in a little milk and a knob of butter. Allow the fish to cool in the liquid then remove and flake the fish into a bowl.

Chop up the spring onions and add to the fish mixture. If using an onion in place of spring onions sweat in butter until cooked but do not allow to brown.

Sieve or put the potatoes through a mouli or ricer to prevent lumps, and add 60ml/4tbsp of fish liquid. Add the chopped hard-boiled egg, Worcestershire sauce, chopped parsley, and a shake of pepper. Taste before salting as the fish may be salty. Mix the ingredients well.

With floured hands form into sausage-shape cylinders about 5cm (2in) long. Chill in the refrigerator and then coat in egg and crumbs.

Fry in hot oil and serve with crisp vegetables or a salad.

Note It is handy to make up double and store extra in the freezer until needed.

Smoked Fish Salad
Serves 6

Ingredients

125ml/4fl oz whipping cream	3 stalks celery, chopped
300g/10oz curd cheese	50g/2oz canned sweet pimientos, chopped
675g/1½lb smoked mackerel or trout, boned and skinned	15ml/1tbsp lemon juice
	salt and pepper

Preparation Whip the cream and fold it into the curd cheese. Add the fish, flaked, and the remaining ingredients, combining them all gently so as not to break the fish up too much. Refrigerate until required.

You can put the salad into a ring mould and turn it out onto a bed of shredded lettuce. Decorate it with the rest of the can of pimientos, cut into thin strips.

Jellied Fish
Serves 6

This cold fish dish is of Eastern European ancestry. Any firm white fish fillets may be used.

Ingredients

1kg/2lb fish heads and trimmings	2 onions, quartered
450ml/16fl oz water	2.5g/½tsp black pepper
225ml/8fl oz white wine	30ml/2tbsp lemon juice
1 stalk celery, diced	pinch of salt
bay leaf	30ml/2tbsp olive oil
25g/1oz coarsely chopped parsley	1kg/2lb fish fillets

Preparation Put all the ingredients except the fish fillets in a medium-sized saucepan. Bring the liquid to the boil over high heat. Reduce the heat to medium, cover, and cook for 1 hour.

Strain the fish stock through a fine sieve into another saucepan. Add the fish fillets to the fish stock, cover, and simmer over low heat for 20 minutes.

Carefully remove the fish fillets and put them in a deep dish. Pour the stock over the fish and chill until the stock jellies. Serve cold.

Spiced Fish
Serves 6

Ingredients

50ml/2fl oz lemon juice	pinch of cayenne pepper
2.5g/½tsp ground ginger	pinch of ground turmeric
2.5g/½tsp finely chopped garlic	2.5g/½tsp salt
pinch of ground cumin	225ml/8fl oz white wine
2.5g/½tsp paprika	1.5kg/3lb flounder fillets

Preparation Preheat the oven to 190°C/375°F/Gas 5. In a small mixing bowl, combine all the ingredients except the flounder fillets. Mix well.

Arrange the fillets in a large baking dish and pour the sauce over them. Bake for 15 minutes. Serve hot.

Smoked Haddock Soufflé
Serves 4

Ingredients

450g/1lb smoked haddock	pinch cayenne
300ml/½pt milk	pinch of grated nutmeg
25g/1oz butter	4 egg yolks
25g/1oz flour	30ml/2tbsp single cream
salt and freshly ground pepper	6 egg whites

Preparation Poach the smoked haddock in the milk with a quarter of the butter for about 10 minutes over a low heat until just cooked.

Drain the liquid and make up to 300ml (½pt) with a little water if necessary. Skin and flake the fish.

Melt the remaining butter in a saucepan and make a roux with the flour. Season the fish liquid and add the cayenne and nutmeg. Be careful with the salt as smoked fish can be salty. Add the fish liquor to the roux and make a thick smooth sauce. Add a little of the warm sauce to the egg yolks mixed with the cream and then return to the sauce. Add half the flaked fish.

Prepare a 17-cm/7-in soufflé dish by oiling well. Put the other half of the fish in the bottom of the dish.

Whisk the egg whites until fluffy but not too stiff and fold carefully into the mixture. Turn into the soufflé dish and cook for about 30-35 minutes at 200°C/400°F/Gas 6.

Serve immediately with a crisp salad for lunch or supper, or as the fish course or appetizer for a dinner party.

Baked Grey Mullet
Serves 4

Ingredients

1kg/2lb grey mullet, gutted and cleaned	1 small onion, peeled and quartered
50g/2oz Green Butter	fresh thyme sprigs
½ lemon, sliced	sprigs of parsley

Preparation Smear the fish inside and out with the Green Butter. Arrange the lemon slices, quartered onion, sprig of thyme and parsley in the stomach slit.

Make an S-shaped cut in the fish back and stuff the thyme sprigs into it. Bake for 25 minutes at 180°C/350°F/Gas 4.

Serve with Gribiche Sauce and extra Green Butter.

The fish may be cooked wrapped in foil, if preferred.

Red Mullet Provençal
Serves 2

Red mullet has a very delicate taste and is best prepared simply either by grilling or baking in foil. It has no gall and does not need to be gutted; indeed the liver is considered a delicacy.

Ingredients

4 red mullet	15ml/1tbsp port or sherry
25g/1oz butter	salt and freshly ground pepper
300ml/½pt Tomato Sauce	stoned black olives
1 green or red pepper, seeded and diced	lemon wedges
	4 anchovy fillets

Preparation Rub the fish with melted butter and cook under a hot grill for 2 minutes each side. Arrange in an ovenproof dish.

Mix the Tomato Sauce with the diced pepper and the port or sherry. Season the fish well and pour over it the sauce, then arrange the olives. Bake for 20 minutes at 180°C/350°F/Gas 4.

Serve either hot, garnished with lemon wedges and anchovy fillets, or chilled as an hors d'oeuvre.

Devilled Herring
Serves 4

Ingredients

4 herrings, filleted
20ml/4tsp French mustard
15g/4tsp breadcrumbs

Sauce
150ml/¼pt vegetable oil
45ml/3tbsp white wine
   vinegar
5g/1tsp capers, chopped
2.5g/½tsp tarragon, dried
1 spring onion, finely
   chopped
salt and freshly ground
   pepper

Preparation Preheat the grill. Make 3 slits in the backs of each of the boned herrings. Arrange on the grill pan.

Spread the mustard over the fish and sprinkle with breadcrumbs. Brush with a little vegetable oil and grill under a high heat for 5 minutes. Lower heat to medium and continue cooking for a further 5 minutes.

Put all the sauce ingredients in a screw-top jar and shake well. Serve separately in a sauceboat, either hot or cold.

Herrings in Oatmeal with Mustard Sauce
Serves 4

Ingredients

4 herrings, filleted
60ml/4tbsp milk
15g/1tbsp seasoned flour
1 egg, beaten

50g/2oz coarse oatmeal
oil for frying
lemon wedges
Mustard Sauce

Preparation Fillet the herrings or ask the fish shop to do this for you. Wash thoroughly under cold running water, and flatten out.

Steep the herring in the milk for about half an hour, drain and dip in seasoned flour.

Dip the fish in beaten egg and then coat generously in coarse oatmeal.

Shallow fry in hot oil, stomach side down first, until crisp and golden on either side.

Serve with wedges of lemon and Mustard Sauce. New potatoes are usually served with this dish.

Baked Salt Herring
Serves 4-6

Ingredients

4 salt herrings, cut into
   small pieces
30g/4tbsp coriander
   leaves, chopped
7g/1tbsp fresh or 5g/1tsp
   dried marjoram

pinch of salt
pinch of black pepper
1 large pimiento, finely
   chopped
7g/1tbsp parsley, chopped
175 g/6oz finely chopped
   onion

Preparation Put the herring pieces in a large glass or ceramic, not metal, baking dish. Cover the herring with the coriander, marjoram, salt, pepper, pimiento, parsley and onion. Cover the dish and marinate in the refrigerator for 6 hours.

Preheat the grill. Remove the herring pieces from the marinade and put them in an ovenproof dish. Grill them until they are lightly browned, about 15 minutes, and serve immediately.

"Solomon Gundy"
Soused Herrings
Serves 4

Ingredients

8 herrings, filleted
scant 5g/1 tsp salt
freshly ground pepper
5g/1tsp whole allspice

8 peppercorns, slightly
   crushed
bay leaf
300ml/½pt vinegar
300ml/½pt water

Preparation Fillet the herrings or ask the fish shop to do this for you. Season the inside of the washed herrings.

Roll each fish from head to tail and secure with a wooden cocktail stick or toothpick. Arrange fish in a baking dish or casserole.

Put the remaining ingredients in a saucepan, bring to the boil and simmer for 5 minutes, then allow to cool slightly.

Pour over the fish and bake in the oven at 170°C/325°F/Gas 3, covered either with foil or a lid, for about 1 hour.

Allow to cool in the liquid and serve with a green salad.

Stuffed Baked Mackerel
Serves 4

Ingredients

4 mackerel
salt and freshly ground
   pepper
30ml/2tbsp lemon juice
60ml/4tbsp oil
1 medium onion, finely
   chopped
100g/4oz gooseberries,
   fresh or canned and
   drained

30g/3tbsp breadcrumbs
7g/1tbsp chopped parsley
1tsp chopped mint
salt and freshly ground
   pepper
25g/1oz butter
lemon wedges

Preparation Clean the fish, remove head, slit down the stomach and remove backbone. Sprinkle with salt, pepper and a little of the lemon juice.

Heat half the oil and the onion, then add the gooseberries and mix well.

Mix breadcrumbs, parsley, mint, lemon juice, and seasoning together, add onion and gooseberries and mix well.

Stuff into mackerel and secure edges together with a cocktail stick or toothpick.

Put the fish in remaining oil in a casserole, dot with butter and bake at 200°C/400°F/Gas 6 for 15 minutes then reduce heat to 180°C/350°F/Gas 4 for a further 15-20 minutes until tender. Serve with lemon wedges.

Baked Perch
Serves 4-6

This recipe is traditionally made with mushat, a fish native to the Sea of Galilee. Perch is a good substitute.

Ingredients

8 large perch fillets
pinch of salt
pinch of black pepper
175g/6oz coarsely chopped
    onion
20g/3tbsp coarsely
    chopped parsley
125ml/4fl oz white wine
50ml/2fl oz lemon juice
50ml/2fl oz olive oil

Preparation Preheat the oven to 190°C/375°F/Gas 5. In a large baking tin, arrange the perch fillets skin side down. Sprinkle with the salt and pepper and top with the onion.

Combine the parsley, wine, lemon juice and olive oil in a small mixing bowl. Mix thoroughly.,

Pour half the olive oil mixture over the fish and bake for 10 minutes. Baste the fish with the remaining olive oil mixture and bake for 10 minutes longer. Serve immediately.

Pike Quenelles
Serves 4

Quenelles are traditionally made with pike but other fish can be used. It is a rather difficult dish to make by hand and is easier if a food processor is used.

Ingredients

675g/1½lb pike or grey
    mullet
4 eggs
100g/4oz flour
300ml/½pt milk
50g/2oz butter
50g/2oz suet
salt and freshly ground
    pepper
45ml/3tbsp double or
    whipping cream, lightly
    beaten
600ml/1pt Béchamel
    Sauce
15ml/1tbsp tomato purée
100g/4oz cooked, peeled
    prawns or shrimps

Preparation Remove the skin and bones from the fish, put the flesh in the food processor and pulverize.

Make a thick mixture by stirring 2 of the eggs, sieved flour and milk together. Beat briskly over a low heat, add butter and stir until a thick mixture is made, almost

like a choux pastry. Allow to cool.

Add the suet, then the flour mixture. Season, then add the yolks of the remaining 2 eggs and mix well in the processor. Add the lightly beaten cream.

Wet a board and form the mixture into small sausage-sized portions. If the mixture is not holding together add a whisked egg white.

Bring a saucepan of salted water to the boil and reduce to simmering. Drop a quenelle into the water. Cook for a few minutes (never boil) and test for flavour. Correct if necessary, then simmer the rest.

For the sauce, add the tomato purée and prawns or shrimps to the Béchamel and serve hot with the warm quenelles.

Baked Red Snapper
Serves 8

Any large white fish can be cooked in this way.

Ingredients

1 large red snapper
50ml/2fl oz red wine
    vinegar
100ml/4fl oz olive oil
225ml/8fl oz white wine
600ml/1pt water
10g/2tsp sugar
5g/1tsp salt
2 cloves garlic, finely
    chopped

Preparation Clean and fillet the fish. Reserve the head and bones. In a saucepan, combine the reserved fish trimmings with the vinegar, olive oil, wine, water, sugar, salt and garlic. Cover and simmer over a low heat for 30 minutes. Strain the fish stock mixture through a fine sieve.

Preheat the oven to 220°C/425°F/Gas 7. Put the red snapper fillets in a large baking pan. Pour the fish stock mixture over the fillets. Bake for 30 minutes. Keep warm. Pour off the cooking liquid and serve in a gravy boat on the side.

Red Snapper à la Creole
Serves 4

Ingredients

1.5kg/2-3lb red snapper or
    red mullet
salt and freshly ground
    pepper
juice of 1 lemon
few sprigs of thyme
bay leaf
sprig parsley
4 allspice berries, crushed
4 cloves

Stuffing
½ onion
25g/1oz butter
mushroom stalks from
    100g/4oz mushrooms,
    chopped
20g/2tbsp breadcrumbs
30g/4tbsp parsley, chopped
salt and freshly ground
    pepper

Sauce
150ml/¼pt white wine
25g/1oz butter
1 large onion, peeled and
    finely chopped
2 large tomatoes, peeled
100g/4oz mushrooms,
    sliced
425-g/15-oz can of
    tomatoes

Preparation Clean and wash the snapper thoroughly. Sprinkle inside and out with seasoning and lemon juice. Make an S-shaped cut in the back and stuff with thyme, bay leaf, parsley, allspice and cloves.

Make the stuffing by sweating the onion in the butter until it is translucent, about 4 minutes on a low heat. Add chopped mushroom stalks and continue cooking for a further 2 minutes. Add the breadcrumbs and 7g/1tbsp of the parsley and seasoning. Put the stuffing into the fish stomach.

Lay the fish in a flat dish and pour over the wine. Bake for about 20 minutes at 170°C/350°F/Gas 4, covered with a lid or piece of foil.

Meanwhile melt the butter in a frying pan, add the chopped onion and cook until it is transparent. Add the chopped fresh tomatoes and sliced mushrooms and cook for a few minutes on a low heat. Then add the canned tomatoes, season and simmer for about 10 minutes.

After the fish has cooked for 20 minutes pour over the sauce. Continue cooking for a further 10-15 minutes.

Serve sprinkled with extra parsley.

Variation For a truly traditional touch add oysters and shrimps with the tomatoes.

Baked Stuffed Salmon Trout
Serves 6

This recipe was originally for pike, which may be hard to obtain. It works well with any large freshwater fish.

Ingredients

1 medium onion, finely chopped	*25g/1oz grated Parmesan cheese*
75g/3oz butter	*a 2-kg/4-lb salmon trout,*
3 cloves garlic, diced	*cleaned and scaled,*
75g/3oz finely chopped mushrooms	*without backbone, but with the head and tail*
50g/2oz seasoned fresh breadcrumbs	*left intact*
50ml/2fl oz milk	*125ml/4fl oz sour cream, chilled*
6 anchovies, ground to a paste	*5g/1tsp salt*
10g/1tbsp capers	*5g/1tsp black pepper*
15g/2tbsp finely chopped parsley	*45ml/3tbsp lemon juice*

Preparation Prepare the stuffing first. In a medium-sized frying pan, brown the onions and garlic in the butter. Cook for 2 to 3 minutes. Stir in the mushrooms and cook for a further 5 minutes.

In a large mixing bowl, combine the breadcrumbs, milk, anchovies, capers, parsley and Parmesan cheese. Mix thoroughly. Set the stuffing aside.

Preheat the oven to 220°C/425°F/Gas 7. Rinse the fish inside and out, and pat completely dry. Fill the cavity of the fish with the stuffing. Pour the butter, mushrooms and onions over the fish. Bake the fish for 45 to 50 minutes, basting with the pan juices every 5 to 7 minutes.

While the fish is cooking, combine the sour cream, salt, pepper and lemon juice in a small bowl. Chill.

Remove the fish from the oven. Remove the stuffing from the cavity of the fish and put it in a large mixing bowl. Add half the fish drippings and half the onions and mushrooms from the baking pan. Mix well. Put the stuffing back into the fish. Reduce the oven temperature to 120°C/250°F/Gas ¼. Return the fish to the oven for 5 minutes.

Pour the remaining fish drippings, along with the remaining mushrooms and onions from the baking pan into a small saucepan. Add the sour cream, mix and cook over a low heat, stirring frequently until heated through. Do not allow the sauce to boil.

Arrange the fish on a serving platter. Pour some of the sauce over the fish. Serve the remainder of the fish sauce separately.

Poached Salmon
Serves 8-10

This method can also used for salmon trout and sea bass.

Ingredients

4kg/7-8lb salmon	*bay leaf*
½ lemon	*1 sprig parsley*
½ onion, halved	*cold Court-Bouillon*

Preparation Prepare the salmon by slitting the stomach and removing the insides from head to tail. Wash the cavity under cold running water. (The fish can also be gutted by removing the head and drawing the entrails out with the curved handle of a soup ladle. This means the stomach remains whole and is better to dress for a buffet table. However, many fish are bought already gutted.)

Put the lemon, onion, bay leaf and parsley sprig in the cavity.

Half fill a fish kettle with the court-bouillon and lower the fish into the liquid, bring to the boil gently and then simmer over a low heat for about 45 minutes. Remove from the heat and allow to cool for some hours in the fish liquid.

Do not cook over a high heat or the fish will split.

Remove the fish from the liquid and allow it to drain for about 1 hour if using cold, as a Dressed Salmon. Alternatively serve the salmon hot with Hollandaise or Mousseline Sauce.

Alternative Method As fish kettles are fairly large, the smallest being around 40cm (18in) long, many people do not want the expense of buying one or the storage problem for an occasional large fish. It is possible to cook a fairly large fish in a modern oven if you have a large roasting tin. Pour the court-bouillon to about a quarter of the way up the tin and place the fish diagonally across. The head may be cut off and the tail wrapped in foil to make the fish fit. Cook the head beside the fish. Pour over as much liquid as the tin will take and cover with a double sheet of foil or another large roasting tin.

Allow 10 minutes for each 450g/1lb using this method at 170°C/325°F/Gas 3. Cool as instructed above.

Dressed Salmon
Serves 8-10

The salmon will look very elegant if you use an extra cucumber, sliced wafer thin, and arrange the slices to cover all the fish flesh, overlapping like scales.

Ingredients

1 poached salmon with head and tail	12 stuffed olives
300ml/½pt aspic jelly	2 lemons
1 cucumber	watercress

Preparation Remove the top skin of the salmon and any grey bits on the pink flesh with the back of a knife. Arrange on a serving platter.

Make up the aspic jelly as directed on the packet with boiling water and allow to cool.

Paint the salmon over with the aspic and allow to set slightly. After about 30 minutes pour a little more aspic all over the fish. Allow to set.

Slice the cucumber very thinly and cut each slice in half. Cut the olives into thin slices. The lemon can be scored with a sharp knife before halving, then slicing it thinly.

Arrange the cucumber slices in a wavy pattern along one edge of the fish. Use the olives to mark the backbone. Paint each slice with aspic before arranging.

Use the halved lemon slices for the other side of the fish, then pour over another coating of almost setting aspic. Any excess aspic may be chopped and arranged round the fish when it has set.

Serve the salmon with Mayonnaise .

The fish can also be decorated with radishes, hard-boiled egg, parsley, halved lemons, etc. as you like.

Dressed Salmon

Salmon en Croûte
Serves 4

Ingredients

1.35kg/3lb tail end of salmon	25g/1oz butter
600ml/1pt Court-Bouillon	30ml/2tbsp tomato purée
1 medium onion, peeled and finely chopped	7g/1tbsp fresh parsley, chopped
6 spring onions, washed and chopped	salt and freshly ground pepper
100g/4oz mushrooms, washed and finely chopped	450g/1lb Puff Pastry, thawed if frozen
	beaten egg to glaze

Preparation Poach the salmon in the court-bouillon for about 15-20 minutes. Allow to cool in the liquid.

Remove the fish and then reduce the liquid by boiling. Skin each side and carefully remove the two top fillets of fish, then lift out the bones and two further fillets will appear underneath. The vegetables for the stuffing may be chopped in the blender or food processor.

Melt the butter in a frying pan and cook the onion and spring onions over a low heat for about 5 minutes. Add the finely chopped mushrooms and continue cooking for a further 3 minutes. Add the tomato purée and 30ml/2tbsp of the reduced fish liquid. Season well and add the parsley. Allow to cool.

Divide the pastry in two, with one piece bigger than the other, and roll out the smaller piece. Cut it into a simple fish shape with a slightly pointed nose coming out to a flat head, a rounded body and a fan tail. Make a paper pattern about 30cm (12in) long as a guideline, if necessary.

Arrange two pieces of fish on the pastry with the broad ends meeting in the middle and the narrower parts at either end. Cover with the stuffing and then

put the other two pieces of fish neatly on top.

Roll out the larger half of the pastry about 5cm (2in) bigger than the previous piece. Dampen the edges with cold water and lay over the fish, tucking the extra pastry underneath and moulding it to secure and improve the fish shape.

Cut the remaining strips of pastry into crescents for decoration and thin strips to decorate the tail with fins. Make several slits down the back to allow the steam to escape.

Arrange the decorations, paint with beaten egg and bake at 210°C/425°/Gas 7 for 20 minutes. If the pastry is browning too quickly, turn down the heat after 15 minutes.

Serve hot or warm with Hollandaise Sauce.

Salmon Fish Cakes
Makes 12

Ingredients

900g/2lb peeled and sliced potatoes	7g/1tbsp finely chopped parsley
225g/8oz cooked salmon, flaked and boned	1 egg
100g/4oz coley or haddock, cooked, flaked and boned	lemon wedges
	Coating
	1 egg
15ml/1tbsp tomato ketchup	30ml/2tbsp water
5ml/1tsp Worcestershire sauce	75g/3oz dried breadcrumbs
salt and freshly ground pepper	

Preparation Boil the potatoes until soft, drain and mash through a ricer, a large vegetable mouli or a sieve. It is important that the potato is free from lumps.

Mix the flaked fish into the potatoes, gradually add seasonings and the parsley, and bind with beaten egg.

Flour a board and, using a 5-cm (2-in) scone or cookie cutter, shape the cakes. Put them onto a tray or baking sheet and chill in the freezer or top of the fridge for at least 30 minutes.

Flour your hands and dip each cake into the beaten egg mixed with the water, and then coat with the breadcrumbs. Press the crumbs well into the cakes. Chill for a further 30 minutes.

Fry in deep fat at 190°C/375°F for about 4-5 minutes until crisp. Serve with wedges of lemon.

The fried cakes can be refrigerated or frozen.

Rich Salmon Fish Cakes
Serves 8

Ingredients

1.5kg/3lb canned salmon, drained	100g/4oz butter or margarine, softened
5g/1tsp salt	50g/2oz flour
black pepper to taste	125ml/4fl oz double cream
175g/6oz onion, chopped	175ml/6fl oz vegetable oil

Preparation Chop the salmon very finely in a mixing bowl. Add salt and pepper. Add the onions, butter, flour and cream and mix until smooth. Shape the mixture into cakes.

Heat the vegetable oil in a large heavy pan. Cook the salmon cakes in batches until golden brown on both sides.

Salmon with Lime and Walnut Oil
Serves 4

Ingredients

4 salmon steaks	100g/7tbsp chilled, unsalted butter
salt to taste	
black pepper to taste	30ml/2tbsp lime juice
rind of 1 lime	45ml/3tbsp walnut oil

Preparation Season the salmon steaks with salt and pepper. Preheat the oven to 120°C/250°F/Gas 2.

Cut the lime rind into julienne strips. Blanch strips in boiling water for 1 minute. Drain well.

Heat 2 tbsp of butter in a large frying pan. Add the salmon and sauté over a medium-high heat until lightly browned, about 4 minutes per side. Transfer the salmon to a plate, cover, and keep warm in oven.

Add the lime juice, lime rind and walnut oil to pan. Stir well and cook over a low heat until the mixture is just heated through. Whisk in the remaining butter 1 tbsp at a time. Be careful not to let the sauce get too hot. Remove the pan from the heat and let it cool slightly if necessary. The sauce should be slightly thick, the same consistency as Hollandaise sauce. Season with salt and pepper and remove from heat.

Remove the salmon from oven. Spoon sauce over steaks and serve.

Salmon Cutlets with Anchovy Butter
Serves 4

Ingredients

4 anchovy fillets	a little oil
20ml/1½tbsp milk	4 salmon cutlets
50g/2oz butter	parsley sprigs
pepper and Tabasco to taste	4 lemon wedges

Preparation First make the anchovy butter. Soak the anchovy fillets in the milk for ½ hour then mash with a wooden spoon until creamy. Cream in the butter and season. Chill until needed.

Preheat the grill to "high". Oil the grill rack.

Put a small knob of Anchovy Butter (divide a quarter of the mixture in four) on each cutlet and arrange so each gets an even heat. Grill for 4 minutes.

Turn the cutlets with a fish slice and place another quarter of the butter among the steaks. Grill on the second side for 4 minutes. Reduce the heat and allow to cook for a further 3 minutes, less if the cutlets are thin.

Serve with a quarter of the remaining anchovy butter in a neat pat on top of each cutlet. Garnish with parsley sprigs and lemon wedges.

Salmon Loaf
Serves 8-10

Ingredients

550g/1lb 4oz flour	5g/1tsp black pepper
225g/8oz unsalted butter, softened	350ml/12fl oz white wine
100g/4oz vegetable shortening	450g/1lb mushrooms, quartered
10g/2tsp salt	2 egg yolks
225ml/8fl oz iced water	225ml/8fl oz chicken broth
1kg/2lb fresh salmon, skinned and boned	60ml/4tbsp lemon juice
675g/1½lb cabbage, shredded	30g/4tbsp chopped fresh dill
225g/8oz roughly chopped onion	30g/2tbsp sugar
	4 hard-boiled eggs, chopped

Preparation In a large mixing bowl, combine the flour, a quarter of the butter, the vegetable shortening and half the salt. Mix together with a wooden spoon until the dough has a flaky texture. Add the iced water and mix until smooth. Divide the dough into 2 equal portions. Wrap each half in cling film and refrigerate for 3½ hours.

Put the salmon, remaining butter, cabbage, onion, pepper, wine, mushrooms, remaining salt, egg yolks, chicken broth, lemon juice, dill and sugar into a large saucepan. Simmer for 1 hour, or until most of the liquid has evaporated.

Flake the salmon with a fork. Stir gently and add the chopped hard-boiled eggs. Stir gently again. Set the mixture aside.

Roll out half the chilled dough on a lightly floured surface into a rectangle about 2.5cm (1in) thick. Dust with flour, and then roll the dough out into a sheet 3mm (⅛in) thick. Trim the sheet into a rectangle 20×40cm (8×16in). Repeat with the remaining dough, but trim the sheet to 25×40cm (10×16in).

Put the smaller dough rectangle on a large, greased baking sheet. Arrange the salmon filling evenly on the dough, leaving a 2.5-cm (1-in) border around the edges. Put the larger dough sheet over the filling. Press the edges of the top and bottom dough sheets together with a fork. Chill for 15 minutes.

Preheat the oven to 205°C/400°F/Gas 6. Bake the loaf for 1 hour. Serve immediately.

Salmon and Spinach Pie
Serves 4

Ingredients

450g/1lb frozen chopped spinach	5g/1tsp dill
350g/12oz salmon, poached	7g/1tbsp chopped parsley
600ml/1pt Béchamel Sauce	salt and freshly ground black pepper
2 hard-boiled eggs, chopped	225g/8oz Puff Pastry, thawed if frozen
	½ beaten egg to glaze

Preparation Cook the frozen spinach in a little salted water as directed on the packet. (If using fresh spinach you will need to cook approximately 1kg/2lb.) Drain well and line the bottom of a buttered pie plate with it.

Mix the cooked, boned and skinned salmon with the béchamel sauce (which can be made with the liquid in which the fish was poached) and hard-boiled eggs. Mix in the dill, parsley, salt and pepper and pour the mixture on top of the spinach.

Roll out the puff pastry 5cm (2in) larger than the pie plate. Cut a 2.5-cm (1-in) wide strip from the outer edge of the pastry. Brush the rim of the plate with water and fit the pastry strip round it. Lift the remaining piece of pastry over the rolling pin and transfer to the pie plate. Press the edges together and trim with a sharp knife held at an angle away from the dish. To seal the edges firmly together hold the knife horizontally towards the pie plate and make a series of shallow cuts round the edge. Flute the edges with your thumb and forefinger and pull in the flutes with the back of a knife.

To make decorative leaves cut remaining pastry into 3.5-cm (1½-in) strips using the rolling pin or ruler as a guide. Every 5cm (2½in) cut the strips at an angle to make diamond shapes. Score lines on the diamonds to make the veins of the leaves.

Make a hole in the middle of the pie by making a cross with a knife and fold back each quarter. Arrange the leaves in a decorative pattern around the middle and brush with beaten egg.

Bake in a preheated oven at 220°C/425°F/Gas 7 until pastry is well risen and golden brown — approximately 30 minutes. Cover with foil or waxed greaseproof paper if pastry shows any sign of browning too much.

Salmon Mousse
Serves 4

Ingredients

225g/8oz salmon, cooked and flaked (or use canned salmon)	lemon juice
10g/1tbsp grated Parmesan cheese	300ml/10fl oz aspic and double cream, mixed in a proportion of 3 to 1
salt and freshly ground white pepper	2 egg whites
	thin slices of unpeeled cucumber

Preparation Mix the salmon with the cheese in a blender and season with salt, pepper and lemon juice to taste.

Reserving a little of the aspic mixture to glaze the mousse, stir the rest into the fish. When the mixture is cold, beat the egg whites until they form soft peaks and fold into the fish. Turn into a greased mould or soufflé dish and chill until set.

Unmould if liked, decorate with cucumber slices and glaze with remaining aspic. Chill again before serving.

Coulibiac
Serves 4

This is an elegant Russian fish pie which has become a classic of French cuisine.

Ingredients

50g/2oz butter	2 hard-boiled eggs
450g/1lb salmon or salmon trout	grated rind and juice of ½ lemon
salt and freshly ground pepper	7g/1tbsp fresh dill or 5g/ 1tsp dried
8 spring onions, washed and chopped or 1 onion, finely chopped	7g/1tbsp parsley, chopped
	30ml/2tbsp sour cream
100g/4oz cooked rice	450g/1lb Puff Pastry, thawed if frozen
100g/4oz mushrooms, washed and sliced	1 egg, beaten

Preparation Cut half the butter into small pieces and dab over salmon, season and wrap loosely in foil. Bake in a preheated oven at 150°C/300°F/Gas 2 for 25-30 minutes. Unwrap and allow to cool.

Melt the remaining butter and add the spring onions or very finely chopped onion. Gradually stir in the cooked rice and mushrooms. Allow to cool.

Remove the skin and bones carefully from salmon and leave in large flakes. Mix with the cooked rice and mushrooms, chopped hard-boiled egg, lemon rind and juice, dill, parsley and seasoning. Lastly add the sour cream.

Roll out the pastry to 35cm×35cm (14in×14in), then divide into four 17.5-cm (7-in) squares. Put a quarter of the salmon in the middle of each square and turn dampened corners over and crimp the edges. Brush with beaten egg and bake at 220°C/450°F/Gas 8, for about 20 minutes, reducing to 200°C/400°F/Gas 6 after the first ten minutes.

Serve garnished with watercress and baked mushrooms, and accompanied by Hollandaise Sauce or a jug of sour cream mixed with fresh chives.

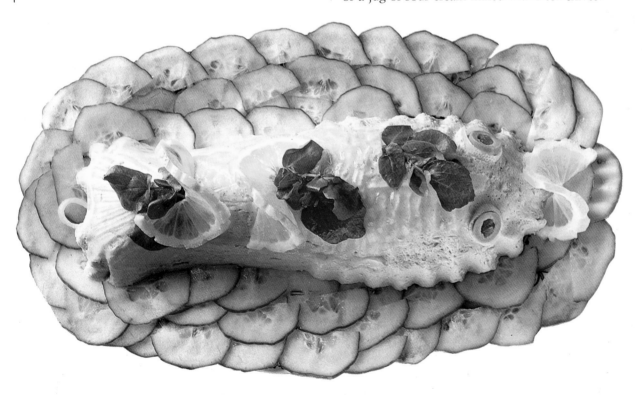

Salmon Mousse

Skate in Caper Sauce
Serves 4

Ingredients

4 wings of skate	salt and freshly ground
300ml/½pt water	pepper
15ml/1tbsp vinegar	15g/½oz butter
1 small onion, peeled and	15g/½oz flour
sliced	30g/3tbsp capers, chopped
bay leaf	15g/2tbsp fresh parsley,
	chopped

Preparation Put the skate wings in a baking dish and pour over the water, vinegar, sliced onion and bay leaf. Season with salt and pepper. Bake, covered at 180°C/350°F/Gas 4 for about 15 to 20 minutes.

In a saucepan make a roux with the butter and flour and make up to a sauce with 300ml/½pt of the fish liquor, strained from the skate. Add the chopped capers and parsley.

Pour the sauce over the fish and serve with sauté potatoes and a crisp green vegetable.

Variation If skate is unavailable use halibut or turbot.

Sardines Provençal
Serves 4

Ingredients

1kg/2lb fresh or frozen	5g/1tsp freshly chopped
sardines	parsley
salt and freshly ground	2 eggs, beaten
pepper	1kg/2lb spinach
30g/4tbsp fresh	30ml/2tbsp single cream
breadcrumbs	20g/2tbsp grated
5g/1tsp anchovy essence	Parmesan cheese
5g/1tsp mixed fresh herbs	10g/2tsp vegetable oil
or 2.5g/½tsp dried	

Preparation Allow sardines to thaw if frozen. Slit down the stomach and remove the backbone. Season each and leave open.

Mix half the breadcrumbs, seasoning, anchovy essence and herbs in a bowl and add a little of the beaten egg.

Put some of this mixture in each fish and fold over to reshape.

Blanch the spinach for 2 minutes if using fresh and for 4 if using frozen in boiling water. Drain carefully.

Season well with salt and pepper. Mix with cream and remaining egg. Arrange spinach in the bottom of an ovenproof dish with the sardines on top. Sprinkle the fish with a mixture of the remaining breadcrumbs and the Parmesan cheese. Brush with oil and bake at 180°C/350°F/Gas 4 until the fish are golden brown.

Poached Sole
Serves 6-8

Ingredients

450ml/¾pt dry vermouth	900ml/1½pt water
2 large onions, sliced	2.5g/½tsp dried thyme
4 parsley sprigs	salt
bay leaf	1.75kg/4lb sole fillets
15g/2tbsp fresh basil or 5g/	6 tomatoes
1tsp dried	4 egg yolks, beaten
10g/1tbsp black pepper	225ml/8fl oz double
140g/5oz celery, chopped	cream
	lemon slices

Preparation To make the poaching liquid, combine the vermouth, onions, parsley, bay leaf, basil, black pepper, celery, water, thyme and salt in a large pot. Simmer over a low heat for 30 minutes.

Arrange the fillets on a large square of cheesecloth. Top with the tomatoes and wrap with the cheesecloth.

Strain the stock into a fish poacher or large saucepan. Add the wrapped fish and tomatoes. Cover and simmer gently over a low heat for 10 minutes.

Remove the fish and tomatoes from the poacher. Remove the cheesecloth and arrange the fillets on a warm serving platter. Keep warm while you make the sauce.

Whisk the egg yolks and cream into the remaining stock in the poacher. Cook over a medium heat, stirring constantly, for 5 minutes or until the sauce thickens. Do not let it boil.

Pour the sauce over the fish and serve with lemon slices.

Goujons of Sole
Serves 4

Ingredients

4 sole, filleted and skinned	dry breadcrumbs
flour or matzo meal to coat	oil for frying
1 egg, beaten with 15ml/	
1tbsp water	

Preparation Cut each fish fillet into two pieces and then cut each half in strips diagonally.

Flour the strips and shake off excess. Dip in egg mixture then roll in breadcrumbs. Deep fry until golden brown.

Serve with lemon wedges or the sauce of your choice.

Fillets of Sole in White Wine with Mushrooms
Serves 4

Ingredients

4 lemon sole, filleted	sprig of parsley
150ml/¼pt white wine	4 peppercorns
150ml/¼pt water	12.5g/½oz butter
1 small onion, peeled and sliced	12.5g/½oz flour
	30ml/2tbsp single cream
6 small mushrooms	sprigs of watercress
bay leaf	

Preparation Roll the fillets of sole head to tail and arrange in an ovenproof dish.

Pour over the wine, water, onion, mushroom stalks, herbs and seasoning. Bake, covered at 170°C/350°F/Gas 4 with a buttered paper or foil or lid, for 15-20 minutes.

Strain the liquid from the fish and make up to 300ml/½pt with extra water or wine if necessary. Poach the mushroom caps in this liquid for a few minutes — remove and keep warm.

Make a roux with the butter and flour and make up a sauce with the fish liquid.

Add the cream to the sauce just before serving, pour it over the warmed fish, and serve with the mushroom caps, sprigs of watercress and, perhaps, Duchesse potatoes.

Sole Dugléré
Serves 4

Ingredients

50g/2oz butter	salt and freshly ground pepper
1 onion, peeled and chopped	150ml/¼pt white wine
3 tomatoes, peeled and chopped	12.5g/½oz flour
	1 tomato, peeled and sliced
8 sole fillets	few sprigs of parsley

Preparation Melt half the butter in a frying pan and add the chopped onions. Sweat over a low heat for a few minutes. Add the tomatoes and simmer for a further 2 minutes.

Fold each fillet in three and lay on top of the tomato and onion mixture, add seasoning and white wine and simmer for a further 12 minutes. Remove the fish to a serving dish and keep warm.

Reduce the sauce by about half over a medium heat. Make a roux with the remaining butter and flour. Add the sieved liquid to make a sauce.

Mask the fish with the sauce and serve garnished with sliced tomatoes and sprigs of parsley.

Sole Véronique
Serves 4

Ingredients

100g/4oz green grapes	6 peppercorns
50g/2oz butter	salt
½ small onion, diced	150ml/¼pt white wine or white wine and water
20g/2tbsp breadcrumbs	
salt and freshly ground pepper	25g/1oz flour
	30ml/2tbsp single cream
1kg/2lb whole sole	watercress
bay leaf	
1 small onion, peeled and sliced	

Preparation Dip the grapes in boiling water for about 5 seconds. Cut in half, remove skin and discard the seeds.

To make the stuffing, melt the butter and sweat the onion over a low heat for about 4 minutes. Mix with breadcrumbs and about half the grapes, chopped, and the seasoning.

Fillet the fish and wrap them, skinned side inwards, around stuffing. Lay in an ovenproof dish and add bay leaf, onion and seasonings; finally, pour on the wine. Add enough fish stock to come half way up the dish, and bake at 180°C/350°F/Gas 4.

When the fish is cooked, remove the fillets and keep warm. Place the liquid in a saucepan and reduce to about 150ml/¼pt. Make velouté sauce from the remaining butter, the flour, reduced fish liquor and enough milk for 300ml/½pt sauce.

Finally add the cream to the slightly cooled sauce, pour over the fish and decorate with the remaining grapes and sprigs of watercress.

Variation If sole is unavailable use plaice.

Sole Meunière
Serves 4

Ingredients

2 lemon or Dover soles, filleted	7g/1tbsp fresh parsley, chopped
50g/2oz flour	1 lemon
50g/2oz butter	

Preparation Flour the fillets of sole and shake off excess.

Melt the butter and shallow fry the fillets for about 3 minutes either side.

Arrange the fillets on a warmed serving dish and keep warm.

Add the parsley to the juices in the pan. Add a little extra butter if necessary. Pour over the fish and serve with wedges of lemon.

Savoury Sprats

Savoury Sprats
Serves 4

Ingredients

450g/1lb sprats
salt and freshly ground
  black pepper
100g/4oz cream cheese
7g/1tbsp fresh parsley,
  chopped

1 clove of garlic
1 egg, beaten with 15ml/
  1tbsp water
dried breadcrumbs
oil for frying

Preparation Remove the heads from the sprats and open down the belly slit and remove the backbone. Wash the fish under cold running water and drain on kitchen paper. Season with salt and pepper.

Mix the cream cheese with a little seasoning, chopped parsley and a crushed clove of garlic. Cream the ingredients together well.

Stuff each sprat with a little of the cream cheese mixture and shape the fish by folding over. Dip the fish in beaten egg and then in the crumbs, coating well.

Deep fry for about 3-4 minutes until golden brown. Drain on absorbent paper, and serve hot.

Grilled Squid with Lime
Serves 3-4

Ingredients

2-3 large fresh squid 750-
  900g/1½-2lb uncleaned
  weight

salt and pepper to taste
oil
6-10 wedges lime

Preparation Clean the squid (or ask the fishmonger to do it for you). Season, then brush them with oil before grilling over a barbecue for 8-12 minutes. (They can also be cooked under a grill or in a frying pan with oil.)

Slice into rings after cooking and serve hot with the lime wedges.

Trout "Au Bleu"
Serves 4

Ingredients

4 really fresh trout
1l/1¾pt well-seasoned
  Court-Bouillon, luke-
  warm
150ml/¼pt white wine
  vinegar

Preparation Gut the trout just before cooking but do not scale. Put in a wide saucepan.

Pour on the white wine vinegar and Court-Bouillon and allow to simmer for about 10 minutes. Do not allow to boil or the fish will split.

Serve with hot or warm lemon wedges and Hollandaise Sauce.

Trout "Au Bleu"

Trout Chaudfroid
Serves 4

Trout Chaudfroid

An excellent summer meal or buffet dish.

Ingredients

4 trout	canned pimiento
300ml/¹/₂pt Chaudfroid	stuff olives, sliced
Sauce	watercress
cucumber peel	

Preparation Cook the trout "au bleu" and allow to cool.

Remove the heads and top skin. Lift top fillet from fish carefully and remove the bone. Lay fillet back on the fish.

Coat with sauce. Garnish with cucumber peel cut into thin strips, diamond-shaped pieces of pimiento, and sliced stuffed olives to make flowers and leaves. Surround head end with sprigs of watercress.

Trout with Almonds
Serves 4

Ingredients

4 trout, cleaned	25-50g/1-2oz butter
125ml/4fl oz milk	100g/4oz flaked almonds
30g/2tbsp seasoned flour	4 sprigs of parsley or
	watercress

Preparation Dip the trout in the milk and then into the seasoned flour.

Melt half the butter in a frying pan and lightly fry the almonds — alternatively this can be done without butter in a non-stick frying pan. Shake and turn the almonds to brown evenly. Remove and keep warm.

Melt the remaining butter and shallow fry the trout on both sides for about 4 minutes each side. Arrange the almonds on top of the trout during the last 2 minutes of cooking.

Replace each fish eye with a sprig of parsley or watercress, and serve hot.

Variation Remove the top skin, showing the pink flesh, after cooking and arrange the almonds on top and re-heat for a few minutes under the grill.

Trout with Avocado and Ham
Serves 4

These days trout are so easily available that traditional ways of cooking them can seem a little plain. This unusual filling will transform them.

Ingredients

4×225-g/8-oz trout,	salt and freshly ground
cleaned	pepper
60ml/4tbsp lemon juice	8 thin rashers streaky
salt	bacon
1 large ripe avocado pear	30g/2tbsp flour
75g/3oz sliced lean ham	75g/3oz butter
	lemon wedges

Preparation Sprinkle the trout inside and out with half the lemon juice and a little salt.

Peel the avocado and remove the stone. Liquidize or process the flesh with the remaining lemon juice until smooth. Add the ham, and blend until the ham is finely chopped but not puréed. Season to taste. Spoon this stuffing into the fish cavities.

Stretch the bacon rashers with the back of a knife, and wrap two rashers securely round each fish. Dust the fish with the flour.

Heat the butter in a large frying pan, and fry the fish for 4 to 5 minutes on each side, till the flesh is opaque and the skin is browned.

Serve at once with lemon wedges.

Two Trout Mousse
Serves 4-6

An unusual combination of fresh and smoked trout.

Ingredients

20g/³/₄oz butter	150ml/¹/₄pt double cream
20g/³/₄oz flour	100g/4oz smoked trout
300ml/¹/₂pt milk	100g/4oz cold, poached
2 egg yolks	trout, boned
10ml/2tsp horseradish cream	2 sticks celery, finely
salt and freshly ground	chopped
pepper	lemon juice to taste
125ml/4fl oz sunflower or	¹/₂ large cucumber, peeled
safflower oil	and thinly sliced
5ml/1tsp wine vinegar	

Preparation Melt the butter in a small pan, stir in the flour, followed by the milk. Bring to the boil, stirring constantly until sauce is smooth and creamy. Simmer for 1 minute, then leave to cool completely.

In a liquidizer or food processor mix the yolks with the horseradish cream and a little salt and pepper. With the machine running, slowly pour in the oil to make a thick mayonnaise. When all the oil has been added, mix in the vinegar. Add the cooled sauce and mix well. Turn into a mixing bowl. Stiffly whisk the cream and add to the mayonnaise mixture.

Flake both types of trout, discarding the skin. Finely chop the celery. Carefully fold into the mayonnaise mixture with the fish. Add lemon juice and season to taste.

Use half the cucumber slices to line the base and sides of a 17.5-20cm (7-8in) glass soufflé dish. Spoon in half the fish mixture. Cover with a layer of cucumber slices, then the remaining fish mixture. Decorate with the remaining cucumber slices. Cover and chill for at least 2 hours.

Serve with slices of toast or buttered pumperknickel, and a green salad.

Steamed Trout with Hazelnuts and Courgettes
Serves 2

Ingredients

2×450-g/1-lb trout	bunch fresh chives
2 courgettes	100ml/4fl oz hazelnut oil
juice of ¹/₂ lemon	25g/1oz hazelnuts

Preparation Fillet the trout or ask the fishmonger to do this. Skin the fillets and put them on a plate or dish which will fit over a saucepan, for steaming, skinned side down.

Cut the courgettes into matchstick pieces and sprinkle with a little of the lemon juice. Put the courgettes on top of the fish. Steam the fish for about 8 minutes or until cooked.

Meanwhile, snip the chives into small pieces, mix with the remaining lemon juice, hazelnut oil and the hazelnuts which have been put into a blender. Alternatively, place the nuts in the blender or food processor and blend, then add the other ingredients and mix well.

Remove trout onto warmed plates and pour over them the hazelnut dressing.

Serve with boiled new potatoes and a crisp green salad.

Tuna Wholewheat Rolls
Serves 4

Ingredients

4 wholewheat rolls, crusty
25g/1oz butter or
  margarine
2 spring onions, washed
  and sliced
4 mushrooms, washed and
  sliced

1 small can tuna fish,
  drained
40g/4tbsp canned or
  cooked corn kernels
10ml/2tsp lemon juice
2.5g/½tsp paprika
salt and freshly ground
  pepper

Preparation Cut a slice from the top of each roll about 4cm (1½in) in diameter and scoop out some of the inside.

Melt the butter or margarine in a small frying pan, add the sliced spring onions and mushrooms. Allow to cook over a low heat for 2 minutes.

Remove from the heat and stir in the remaining ingredients, including the breadcrumbs from the rolls. Season to taste.

Stuff the rolls with the filling and replace the lids. Wrap each in a square of foil and bake at 200°C/400°F/Gas 6 for 10 minutes to heat through. Remove from the oven and unwrap the foil.

Serve with a crispy green salad for a light lunch.

Tuna Mousse
Serves 4

Ingredients

200g/7oz canned tuna,
  drained
15ml/1tbsp lemon juice
50ml/2fl oz Mayonnaise
50ml/2fl oz sour cream
15g/1tbsp chopped onion

7g/1tbsp parsley, chopped
10g/2tsp gelatine
100ml/4fl oz boiling water
2 egg whites
salt and pepper

Preparation Put the tuna, lemon juice, mayonnaise, sour cream, chopped onion and parsley in a food processor or blender and mix together until smooth.

Dissolve the gelatine in the boiling water. Add to the tuna mixture and mix in well. Whisk the egg whites until stiff and fold them into the mixture. Adjust the seasoning and turn the mixture into a moistened mould (a small ring mould looks nice). Refrigerate until set and then unmould.

Decorate with watercress and/or thin slices of orange.

Tuna-Stuffed Potatoes
Serves 4

Ingredients

4 large potatoes, scrubbed
4 tomatoes, skinned and
  chopped
4 spring onions, washed
  and chopped

60ml/4tbsp sour cream
salt and freshly ground
  pepper
175-g/7-oz can tuna fish,
  in oil

Preparation Make a cross on the potato skins and bake for 1 hour at 180°C/350°F/Gas 4 or until cooked.

Halve the potatoes and scoop out the cooked potato, retaining the skins.

Mix all ingredients together, season well and pile back into the potato skins.

Re-heat before serving.

Whitebait
Serves 4

Ingredients

675g/1½lb whitebait
75g/3oz seasoned flour
oil for frying

lemon wedges
parsley sprigs

Preparation Pat the whitebait dry with kitchen paper. (It is often sold frozen and when thawed needs to be dried).

Toss the fish in seasoned flour and deep fry in hot oil for a few minutes until golden brown and crisp.

Serve with lemon wedges, parsley sprigs and Tartare Sauce. Offer thinly sliced wholewheat bread and butter.

Whiting Bercy
Serves 4

Ingredients

4×300-g/10-oz whiting
50g/2oz butter
2 small onions
150m/¼pt white wine
7g/1tbsp fresh parsley,
  chopped

juice of ½ lemon
salt and freshly ground
  pepper
15g/½oz butter kneaded
  together with 15g/½oz
  flour
25g/1oz fresh breadcrumbs
lemon slices

Preparation Fillet the fish and make the fish stock with the trimmings and heads.

Fold fillets over with a small knob of butter in each and poach in the fish stock for about 8 minutes. Remove fillets and keep warm.

Melt the remaining butter and toss finely chopped onion in it for a few minutes; cook on a low heat without browning. Add the wine and allow to reduce slightly. Finally add the strained fish stock, chopped parsley, lemon juice, salt and pepper.

Bring to the boil and remove from the heat. Whisk the flour and butter mixture into the liquid.

Whisk on the heat for a few minutes until sauce thickens. Pour over fillets which have been kept warm. Sprinkle with breadcrumbs and top with little knobs of butter.

Heat through in a hot oven or brown under the grill for a few minutes.

Variation This is also a good way to cook sole or cod.

Tuna-Stuffed Potatoes

Dressed Crab
Serves 2

Ingredients

1 crab, cooked
a little olive oil
20g/2 tbsp white
  breadcrumbs
15-30ml/1-2tbsp
  Mayonnaise
2.5ml/½tsp French mustard
juice of ½ lemon

salt and freshly ground
  pepper
fresh parsley, finely
  chopped
paprika
1 egg, hard-boiled
lettuce

Preparation Put the cooked crab on a board and twist the claws until they separate from the body. Crack the claws open with a hammer. Take a skewer and remove the white meat from the claws and put in a bowl.

Take hold of the crab firmly with both hands and with the thumbs push the body section away from the shell.

Take out and discard the following: the small sac or stomach bag which is attached to the large shell, any green tinged material in the large shell and, lastly, the grey spongy parts known as "dead man's fingers".

Scrape the brownish meat from the shell into a second bowl.

Cut the body into two and scrape any white meat left into the first bowl.

Tap the shell to remove the ragged sharp edge. Wash and scrub the inside and outside of the shell thoroughly and rinse well (do not use soap). Dry off the shell and brush with some olive oil.

Mix the white breadcrumbs with the brown meat and cream well with the mayonnaise, French mustard and seasonings.

Arrange the white meat mixed with lemon juice and salt and pepper on each side of the shell and the brown meat down the middle.

Garnish with rows of chopped parsley, paprika and the separately sieved white and yolk of the hard-boiled egg.

Serve on a bed of lettuce surrounded by the small claws, with thinly sliced wholewheat bread and butter. Serve extra Mayonnaise separately, if you like.

Chilli Crab

Chilli Crab
Serves 4

Ingredients

2 cooked crabs (675g/1½lb
  each)
2.5cm/1in piece fresh
  ginger, scraped
2 fresh red chillies or 2
  teaspoons chilli sauce
2 cloves garlic, crushed
60-90ml/4-6 tbsp vegetable
  oil

225ml/8fl oz tomato
  ketchup
15g/1tbsp brown sugar
150ml/¼pt hot water
1 beaten egg (optional)
salt
fresh coriander to garnish
chunks of cucumber and
  pieces of toast to serve

Preparation Remove the large claws and turn each crab onto its back, with the head facing away from you. Use your thumbs to push the body up from the main shell. Discard the stomach sac and "dead man's fingers" (the lungs and any green matter); leave the creamy brown meat in the shell and cut in half. Cut the body section in half with a strong knife and crack the claws with a sharp tap from a hammer or cleaver. Crack, don't splinter them.

Pound the ginger, prepared chillies and garlic together. Fry in hot oil for 1-2 minutes without browning. Add tomato ketchup, chilli sauce, sugar and water, and mix well. When almost boiling add all the crab over a high heat.

Just before serving stir in the beaten egg, which will scramble in the sauce if desired; taste for seasoning and serve at once garnished with fresh coriander leaves, together with the cucumber and toast.

Crab with Eggs
Serves 4

Ingredients

100-175g/4-6oz cooked crabmeat	seasoning
5g/1tsp sugar	4 eggs, beaten
1 small piece ginger, scraped and crushed in garlic press	a little butter or oil for frying
10ml/2tsp light soy sauce	4-6 spring onions, finely chopped

Preparation Pick over the crabmeat to remove any shell or cartilage. Stir into it the sugar, ginger and soy sauce and season to taste.

Add this to the beaten eggs and scramble in fat in a pan for 1 minute.

Add spring onions and serve at once.

Baked Avocado with Crab
Serves 4

Ingredients

2 ripe avocados	10ml/2tsp tomato purée
175-g/7-oz can of crabmeat or the meat from 1 cooked crab	salt and freshly ground pepper
15ml/1tbsp lemon juice	300ml/½pt Béchamel Sauce
30ml/2tbsp white wine	7g/1tbsp parsley, finely chopped
few drops of Tabasco	

Preparation Cut the avocados in half carefully and remove the stones and some of the flesh.

Sprinkle the crab meat and chopped avocado flesh with lemon juice and white wine.

Add the rest of the ingredients to the béchamel sauce and fill the halved avocados, piling the mixture up as high as it will go without spilling.

Bake at 180°C/350°F/Gas 4 until golden brown. Serve sprinkled with chopped parsley.

Variation This dish can be made with tuna fish in place of crab.

Papaya Crab
Serves 4

Ingredients

2 ripe papayas, 275-350g/ 10-12oz each	lime or lemon juice
25ml/1fl oz whipped cream	a little white pepper
125ml/4fl oz Mayonnaise	350g/¾lb crabmeat

Preparation Split the papayas and remove the seeds and "strings".

Mix the whipped cream with the mayonnaise. As homemade mayonnaise is so much richer than a commercial brand, you may need to add a little more whipped cream to lighten it.

Flavour to taste with lime or lemon juice and a little white pepper.

Combine the dressing with the crabmeat and pile into the papaya halves.

Serve chilled.

Variation For Melon Crab use two small melons, halved and deseeded, instead of the papayas. The fragrant, orange or peach fleshed varieties of melon, such as Charentais and Canteloupe, are particularly good for this.

Baked Avocado with Crab

Dressed Lobster

Preparation Crack the pincer claws with a small hammer and take out the meat with a skewer.

Cut the lobster lengthways from head to tail using a sharp knife. Remove the stomach bag on the right side of the head and also the grey spongy parts known as "dead man's fingers".

Remove the coral, wash and retain for decoration.

Now remove all the meat from the shell. Keep the green liver meat which is edible.

Flavour the meat with lemon juice and seasoning or mayonnaise and return to the shell. Serve on a bed of lettuce.

Note Lobsters are best at about 650g-1kg/1¾-2½lbs as this will give two good servings or about 400g/¾lb meat. A well-cooked lobster will feel heavy and the tail should be curled under the body.

To prepare and cook a live lobster, first take a skewer or sharp knife and drive through the cross which is on the head. Grip the lobster firmly behind the head and plunge into a large saucepan of boiling salted water. A bay leaf, sprig of parsley or bouquet garni may be added. Cook for 15 minutes for each 450g/1lb of lobster. Allow to cool in the liquid. Leave the antennae on as they form part of the decoration if serving in the shell. When cool, twist off the claws, retaining small claws for garnish.

Oysters à l'Américaine
Serves 4

Ingredients
24 oysters
100g/4oz fresh
  breadcrumbs
50g/2oz butter

freshly ground black
  pepper
100g/4oz Gruyère cheese,
  grated

Preparation Remove the oysters from the shell and wash the deep shells throughly. Drain and wipe the oysters on kitchen paper towels.

Fry half the breadcrumbs in melted butter until golden brown. Sprinkle a few fried breadcrumbs in the bottom of the 24 deep shells. Season with pepper.

Return oysters to prepared shells, sprinkle with a mixture of breadcrumbs and Gruyère cheese and brown in the oven at 220°C/425°F/Gas 7. Serve immediately.

Lobster Newburg
Serves 4

Most hot lobster dishes are best made with freshly cooked lobster which means killing the lobster just before cooking it. For those who find this difficult the delicious Lobster Newburg is a welcome recipe as it can be made with a cooked lobster.

Ingredients
a 1-kg/2-lb lobster, cooked
25g/1oz butter
salt and freshly ground
  pepper
30ml/2tbsp brandy
3 egg yolks

125ml/4fl oz double or
  whipping cream
275g/10oz cooked rice, hot
7g/1tbsp parsley, chopped
lemon twists

Preparation Cut down the soft shell under the tail with scissors. Peel away the hard shell to leave the tail whole. Crack the claws with a small hammer and carefully remove the meat with a skewer.

Melt half the butter in a frying pan over a very low heat. Add the claw meat and the tail meat cut in sections, season well and and heat through for about 3 minutes.

Heat the brandy in a ladle and set it alight to "flambé" the lobster by pouring the lighted brandy onto the lobster meat. When the flames die down remove the pan from the heat.

In a bowl, mix egg yolks, cream and the remaining butter cut into little pieces with more seasoning.

Return the lobster meat to the lower heat and gradually pour over it the egg mixture, stirring with a wooden spoon until the sauce becomes thick and creamy.

Serve on hot boiled rice garnished with chopped parsley and lemon twists.

Lobster Newburg

Moules Marinière
Serves 4

Ingredients

approx 2kg/4lb mussels
50g/2oz butter
1 medium onion, finely
   chopped
1-2 cloves of garlic, finely
   crushed

225ml/¹/₂pt white wine
bay leaf
sprigs fresh parsley
15g/2tbsp chopped parsley
   (optional)
30ml/2tbsp cream
   (optional)

Preparation Make sure the mussels are properly prepared before cooking. They should be alive — tap with a wooden spoon and if any remain open discard at once. Wash and scrub the shells thoroughly under a cold running tap and remove the "beard". Put in a bowl of cold water and change the water several times to remove the sand.

Heat butter in a very large saucepan or frying pan. Add the chopped onion and garlic. Allow to sweat gently in the butter without browning.

Add the wine, bay leaf and sprigs of parsley. Turn up the heat and add the cleaned mussels. Shake over the heat for about 6-10 minutes until all the mussels are open.

Discard any mussels which do not open. Divide the mussels between serving bowls and, if liked, add the chopped parsley and cream to the juice. Heat for a further minute and pour over the mussels.

Serve with warm French bread and extra plates for empty shells.

Oysters en Brochette
Serves 4

Ingredients

24 oysters
300ml/¹/₂pt dry white wine
   and water
freshly ground black
   pepper
12 slices of bacon,
   de-rinded
15ml/1tbsp oil

4 slices of toast, cut in long
   strips
50g/2oz fresh white
   breadcrumbs
25g/1oz butter
3g/³/₄tsp cayenne pepper

Preparation Drain the opened oysters over a sieve lined with muslin to catch the oyster juice. Heat the wine and water and oyster liquid in a saucepan and add a shake of pepper.

Allow the oysters to remain in the liquid for a few minutes without boiling. Remove when plumped up.

Cut the bacon slices in half, stretch with a knife, and cook in a little oil over a low heat until the fat starts to run. Do not crisp.

Wrap the bacon around the oysters and thread onto skewers.

Put the skewers under a hot grill for a few minutes, turning from time to time, then put them on the strips of toast, and keep warm.

Fry the breadcrumbs in the butter until golden and mix with cayenne. Sprinkle on the brochettes and serve immediately.

Variation This recipe can also be made with mussels.

Prawn Curry
Serves 4

Ingredients

2 small potatoes, peeled
   and thinly sliced
1 onion, peeled and finely
   chopped
2 cloves garlic, crushed
15-30ml/1-2tbsp oil
20g/2tbsp curry powder
1×425-g/15-oz can
   tomatoes
15ml/1tbsp tomato purée
300ml/¹/₂pt fish stock or
   water
150g/6oz small
   mushrooms

bay leaf
bouquet garni
¹/₂ cauliflower, washed and
   broken into florets
350g/12oz prawns or
   shrimps, cooked and
   shelled
15ml/1tbsp lemon juice
salt and freshly ground
   pepper
225g/8oz long grain rice,
   cooked

Preparation Parboil potatoes for 3 minutes. Drain and set aside.

Sauté the onion and garlic in the oil for several minutes until the onion is transparent, then add the curry powder and fry, mixing with the onions for a few minutes.

Add the tomatoes, purée and fish stock or water and chopped mushroom stalks. Add herbs. Bring to the boil, then lower heat.

Add the parboiled potatoes, the cauliflower and the mushrooms to the mixture and simmer for 25 minutes.

Add the prawns or shrimps and lemon juice and simmer for a further 10 minutes on a low heat. Season to taste.

Serve on a bed of cooked rice with poppadums and chutneys.

Prawn Curry

Scallops au Gratin
Serves 4

Ingredients

8-16 scallops, depending on size	bay leaf
25-50g/1-2oz butter	bouquet garni
1 small onion, peeled and finely chopped or 6 spring onions, cleaned and chopped	salt and freshly ground pepper
	mashed potatoes
1 clove garlic, crushed (optional)	20g/³⁄₄oz butter
125ml/4fl oz white wine	20g/³⁄₄oz flour
125ml/4fl oz fish stock or water	15-30ml/1-2tbsp single cream
	20g/2tbsp fresh breadcrumbs, dried
	15g/1tbsp Parmesan cheese

Preparation Cut the scallops into slices. Melt the butter in a saucepan. Sweat the onion or spring onions and garlic over a low heat for about 3 minutes.

Add the sliced scallops, cook for a further 1 minute and then add the wine and water or fish stock with the bay leaf and bouquet garni. Season well.

Bring to the boil and turn the heat down low and simmer for about 6 minutes. Allow to cool.

Strain the liquor from the scallops, retaining the vegetables. Discard the bay leaf and bouquet garni.

Pipe a border of mashed potatoes around 8 deep, cleaned scallop shells (see Note).

Make a roux with the butter and flour, make a sauce with the fish liquor. Taste for seasoning, add cream.

Add the onion mixture, then the scallops to the sauce and divide the mixture between the shells.

Sprinkle with a mixture of breadcrumbs and Parmesan cheese. Brown in a hot oven or under the grill and serve hot.

Note If using 8 scallops, you will only need 4 shells and 15ml/1tbsp cream. One shell is sufficient for a fish course but 2 will be needed for a main course.

Shrimp-Stuffed Courgettes
Serves 2-4

Ingredients

4 courgettes	300ml/¹⁄₂pt Béchamel Sauce
100g/4oz shrimps or prawns	
1 hard-boiled egg	15g/1tbsp Parmesan cheese, grated

Preparation Cut a small slice lengthwise along the courgettes and scoop out a little of the flesh and chop it finely.

Blanch the courgettes for 2 minutes in boiling salted water.

Add the shrimps or prawns, chopped egg and chopped courgette to the Béchamel Sauce.

Fill the courgettes with the mixture and sprinkle with Parmesan cheese. Bake at 180°C/350°F/Gas 4 for 15-20 minutes.

Variation This mixture can also be used to fill 2 blanched peppers.

Shellfish Paella
Serves 4

Ingredients

450g/1lb cod or halibut	1 green pepper, seeded
600ml/1pt Court-Bouillon	150ml/¹⁄₄pt white wine and water
60ml/4tbsp oil	
2 cloves garlic, crushed	650g/1¹⁄₂pt mussels
3 medium onions, peeled	175g/6oz peeled prawns or shrimps
350g/12oz long grain rice	
pinch of saffron threads or ¹⁄₄tsp turmeric	7g/1tbsp parsley, chopped
	lemon wedges
600ml/1pt fish or chicken stock	4-8 large cooked prawns or shrimps (optional)
1 red pepper, seeded	

Preparation Poach the cod in Court-Bouillon for 5 minutes.

Put the oil in a large pan and sweat the garlic and 2 of the onions, one thinly sliced and the other finely chopped, for about 4 minutes without browning.

Add the rice to the pan and stir over the heat for a few minutes until rice just begins to colour.

Strain the cod and retain the stock. Add saffron or turmeric to the stock and pour over the rice, stirring from time to time over a low heat. Cook covered with a lid or foil for the first 10 minutes.

Blanch the peppers for 2 minutes then dice finely, add to the rice and stir well.

In another saucepan, put the other onion, finely chopped with the water and wine mixture and a good shake of pepper. Bring to the boil and add the cleaned mussels. Cook for 10 minutes until steamed open.

Add the strained mussel liquor to the rice and stir well. Cook for a further 5 minutes or until the rice is tender.

Add the chunks of white fish, prawns or shrimps and mussels.

Serve hot, sprinkled with parsley and garnished with lemon wedges. Decorate with extra prawns or shrimps if you like.

Scallops with Mushrooms
Serves 4

Ingredients

approx. 150ml/¹⁄₄pt dry white wine	2 tomatoes, skinned and chopped
150ml/¹⁄₄pt water	8 scallops, cleaned
1 small onion, peeled and sliced	20g/³⁄₄oz flour
4 peppercorns	1 egg yolk
bay leaf	15ml/1tbsp single cream
1 stalk parsley	few drops of lemon juice
100g/4oz mushrooms, washed	20g/2tbsp fresh breadcrumbs, dried
50g/2oz butter	lemon wedges
1 medium onion, peeled and finely chopped or 8 spring onions, washed and chopped	parsley

Preparation Put the first six ingredients in a saucepan, bring to the boil and simmer for about 10 minutes.

Remove the mushroom stalks and chop finely. Slice the caps, retaining 16 slices for garnish.

Melt half the butter in a frying pan and sweat the chopped onion or spring onions and chopped mushrooms stalks over a low heat for about 4 minutes. Add the tomatoes and cook for 3 minutes.

Add the sliced scallops to the strained wine mixture and poach over a low heat for about 8 minutes. Remove the scallops with a slotted spoon and then poach the mushroom slices for about 2 minutes. Strain the liquid into a measuring jug and make up to 300ml/ ½pt, if necessary, with wine or water.

Make a roux wih the remaining butter and the flour and make into a sauce with the fish liquor. Allow to cool slightly then add a little sauce to the egg yolk, mix well and return the mixture to the sauce. Stir over a low heat for about 1 minute. Allow to cool slightly, add the cream and, lastly, the sliced mushrooms.

Divide the onion, mushroom and tomato mixture between the shells or spread on the bottom of the serving dish if using one big dish.

Add the scallops to the mushroom sauce, taste for seasoning and add a few drops of lemon juice to taste. Pour into the shells or serving dish and sprinkle with crumbs and garnish with mushrooms. Heat through in the oven at 180°C/350°F/Gas 4 for 10-15 minutes.

Serve garnished with parsley and lemon wedges.

Variations Milk may be substituted for the wine.

For Curried Scallops add 5g/1tsp curry powder to the onion and tomato mixture and fry for about 1 minute over a high heat. Add the mixture to the sauce. Water or fish stock may be used in place of wine for the curry. Serve with lemon wedges.

Selection

When buying fish and shellfish absolute freshness is essential. Bright eyes and stiff flesh are the signs of fresh fish. Dull eyes and limp flesh with a slight ammonia smell indicate stale fish.

It is best to buy the fish the day it is to be cooked. Store it in the refrigerator loosely covered and try not to keep it longer than 24 hours before cooking.

Preparation of Fish

Ideally, fish should be prepared just before cooking but time does not always permit this. If it is to be cooked in a stock it is often advantageous to allow it to cool in the fish liquid.

Most people are not keen on cleaning or gutting fish and it is fortunate that fish shops are so helpful with preparation. However, for those who are prepared to do the work themselves, this is how it should be done.

To scale fish: lay fish on a piece of kitchen paper and hold by the tail. Scrape the scales away from the tail towards the head using the blunt side of a knife. Rinse under cold water.

To Clean and Fillet Flat Fish

Slit behind the head on the dark skin side, remove the entrails from the cavity and rinse in cold water. Pat dry with a clean cloth or kitchen paper. Remove the fins with a sharp knife or scissors.

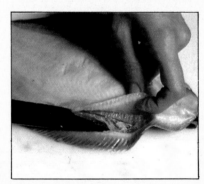

1 Begin filleting the fish by cutting into head end against the bone.

2 Cut the fillet away carefully with the skin attached to it, leaving the bone as clean as possible.

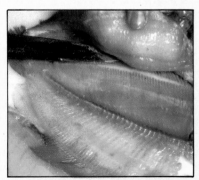

3 Turn the fish over, insert the knife at the head and carefully remove the second fillet in the same way. The flat fish is now filleted. One fillet has thick black skin, the other white skin. The bone can now be used for fish stock.

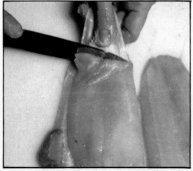

4 To skin the fish, hold the tail firmly and work fillet away from the skin from tail to head, with a sharp knife. The skin can also be used for fish stock.

To Clean and Bone Round Fish

I To clean, retaining the head, slit from under the head down to the tail.

2 Remove entrails by hooking the finger under the throat and pulling down towards the tail. Wash well. A rubber glove may be used for this step.

3 If the head is not required as with, for example, mackerel and herring, cut it off with a sharp knife before boning.

4 Slip the sharp knife under the bone on each side of the fish in turn, open and remove the bones.

5 An alternative method which may be easier for the inexperienced is to turn the fish open-side downwards. Press down on the back with the heel of the hand and loosen the bone.

6 Turn the fish over and starting at the tail end, place the blade of the knife under the bone and push along the spine to release. Feel the surface of the fish with the fingers to ensure there are no stray bones. The round fish is now ready to be cooked.

Dressing Crab

I Lay the crab on its back and twist off the claws. Then twist off the legs — do not pull them.

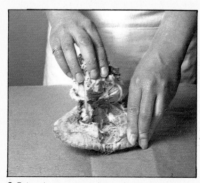

2 Prise the apron up by pulling at the pointed end near the mouth to remove the body from the shell

3 Remove the dead men's fingers. These are soft and spongy and are found at the sides of the body and stomach sac behind the head.

4 Strip out the cartilaginous membrane from the shell and discard it.

5 Remove the brown meat from the shell and put it aside. Do not mix it with the white meat from the body, legs and claws.

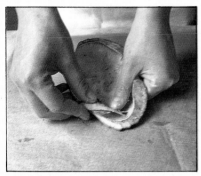  

6 With the thumbs, break the shell along the visible lines to enlarge the opening. Use a hammer if it is tough. Wash out the shell and scrub it if necessary.

7 Remove the white meat from the body, claws and legs. Crack the claws and legs with a hammer or lobster cracker. Use a lobster pick or skewer to help you extract all the flesh.

8 Mix brown meat with a little Mayonnaise (and brown breadcrumbs if you like). Spoon it down the centre of the shell. Put white meat at each end. Cover the dark meat with lines of parsley, chopped egg white and yolk.

Poultry and Game

Spanish Chicken and Rice 97
Cantonese Chicken 97
Barbecued Spiced Chicken 97
Chicken in Baked Potatoes 98
Chicken Avocado Pasta Salad 98
Chicken in Coconut Milk 98
Boned Highland Chicken 98
Chicken Curry with Noodles 99
Chicken Biryani 99
Chicken Creole 100
Chicken Casserole with Ginger 100
Chicken Casserole with Coconut Milk 101
Chicken Buried in Salt 101
Chicken Curry 101
Chicken Breasts with Sesame Seeds 101
Chicken Paprika 102
Chicken Peanut Casserole 102
Chicken with Kumquats 102
Chicken with Mushroom Lasagne 102
Chicken Satay 103
Chicken Escalopes 103
Oriental Chicken and Mushroom Stew 104
Chinese Chicken with Pineapple and Cashew Nuts 104
Cold Chicken Millefoglie 105
Chicken Stuffed with Fruit and Nuts 105
Chicken Garam Masala 105
Holiday Fried Chicken 106
Deep-fried Soy Chicken 106
Glazed Chicken Wings 106
Fried Chicken Wings 106
Double Garlic Chicken 107
Drunken Chicken 107
Jellied Chicken Salad 108

Malaysian Chicken 108
Poulet au Roquefort 108
Lemon Chicken with Wholewheat Spaghetti 108
Traditional Roast Chicken 109
Penang Chicken Curry 109
Salt-Grilled Chicken 110
Chicken with Tangerine Peel 110
Paper-Wrapped Chicken 110
Spicy Roast Chicken 111
Red-Cooked Chicken 111
Chicken in Mole Sauce 111
Tandoori Chicken 112
Sesame Chicken 112
Stuffed Poussins 112
Yakitori 112
Curry-fried Turkey 113
Devilled Turkey Legs 113
Lemon Turkey 113
Roast Turkey 113
Turkey Mole 114
Turkey Fillets in Wine Sauce 114
Peking Duck 114
Crispy Duck 115
Chinese Duck 116
Duck Breasts with Hazelnuts and Orange Potato Balls 116
Roast Duck with Spaetzle 116
Duck with Pineapple 117
Braised Coriander Duck 117
Hot Game Pie with Fried Apples and Onions 118
Pheasant Pojarski Cutlets 118

Jointing a Chicken 119
Boning a Chicken 120

Spanish Chicken and Rice
Serves 8

Rice with chicken is a classic Spanish meal, hearty and easy to prepare. Serve it with a simple salad, a glass of wine and a simple dessert.

Ingredients

25g/1oz chicken fat	4 ripe tomatoes, skinned,
2×1.5-kg/3-lb chickens, cut	seeded and finely
into serving pieces	chopped
pinch of salt	350g/12oz shelled peas
pinch of black pepper	½tsp crumbled saffron
400g/14oz finely chopped	threads
onion	20g/3tbsp finely chopped
4 cloves garlic, finely	parsley
chopped	675g/1½lb rice
15g/1½tbsp sweet paprika	1.1l/2½pt boiling water

Preparation Melt the chicken fat in a large paella pan or saucepan. Add the chicken pieces, salt and pepper and cook over a moderate heat for 40 minutes. Turn the chicken pieces frequently.

Remove the chicken pieces from the pan and set them aside.

Add the onions, garlic, paprika, tomatoes, peas, saffron and parsley to the pan. Cook over a low heat for 10 minutes, stirring frequently.

Return the chicken to the pan. Add the rice and boiling water. Stir well and bring to a boil over a high heat. Reduce the heat to low. Cover the pan and simmer for 40 minutes.

Remove the pan from the heat. Remove the lid and leave it to stand for 5 minutes before serving.

Cantonese Chicken
Serves 3

Hoisin sauce is a plum sauce widely available in supermarkets.

Ingredients

1.25-kg/2½-lb chicken	oil for deep frying
salt	spring onion curls
15g/1tbsp cornflour	cucumber slices
30ml/2tbsp sherry	hoisin sauce
30ml/2tbsp liquid honey	

Preparation Rinse the chicken inside and out thoroughly. Plunge it into a large pan of boiling water for 1 minute. Lift out carefully, drain and dry thoroughly. Tie up by the feet and dry out for 3-4 hours. Rub the skin with salt and suspend overnight in a cool, dry place.

Blend the cornflour and sherry, then stir in the honey. Rub the skin of the chicken with this mixture and leave for several hours or overnight.

Lift the chicken into a frying basket and lower into a larger pan of deep fat, lifting out several times to allow the fat to regain heat. The chicken will be cooked in 50-60 minutes and the skin will be crisp and golden.

Drain thoroughly and cut into even-sized, smallish pieces. Serve garnished with spring onions and pieces of cucumber and hoisin sauce for dipping.

Barbecued Spiced Chicken
Serves 4

Ingredients

1.5-kg/3-lb chicken, cut	5g/1tsp chilli powder
into 4 pieces	60ml/4tbsp soy sauce
8 shallots	30ml/2tbsp hoisin sauce
2 cloves garlic, peeled and	45ml/3tbsp oil
crushed	salt
1cm/½in ginger, peeled	oil for frying
and sliced	150ml/¼pt chicken stock
1 stem lemongrass	

Preparation Slash the flesh of the chicken quarters several times. Finely chop the shallots and set aside. Pound the garlic, ginger, lemongrass and chilli powder together. Mix with soy sauce, hoisin sauce and oil and pour onto the chicken pieces. Leave to marinate for 30 minutes.

Heat oil in a wok, fry the onions without browning, lift the chicken pieces out of the marinade and fry on both sides to seal. Reduce the heat, cook for 10 minutes. Transfer to the barbecue to complete cooking.

Add the marinade to the remaining ingredients in the pan. Fry, then add stock. Cook for 5 minutes and serve this sauce with the chicken.

Chicken in Baked Potatoes
Serves 4

Ingredients

4 even-sized large potatoes	60g/4tbsp sweetcorn
225g/8oz cooked chicken,	kernels, cooked
chopped	30ml/2tbsp Mayonnaise
1 green pepper, seeded and	2 tomatoes, skinned
chopped	salt and freshly ground
1 spring onion, washed	pepper
and chopped	

Preparation Wash and scrub the potato skins. Prick with a fork. Arrange on the oven shelves and bake at 200°C/400°F/Gas 6 for 45-60 minutes.

Alternatively, boil the potatoes for 15 minutes, drain and then bake in the oven for 25-35 minutes, depending on size. Potatoes can also be baked in a microwave oven – one potato will take 5 minutes but four will need 20 minutes. Crisp in the oven if liked.

Cut the potato lengthwise and scoop out some of the potato, reserve and mix with remaining ingredients. Season to taste.

Fill the potatoes and reheat for a few minutes in the oven.

Potatoes can be prepared and stuffed, then kept in the refrigerator until needed. Heat through before serving.

Chicken Avocado Pasta Salad
Serves 4

Ingredients

225g/8oz cooked pasta	salt and freshly ground
6 spring onions, washed	pepper
150ml/¼pt Mayonnaise	2 tomatoes, skinned and
2 ripe avocados	sliced
225g/8oz cooked chicken,	1 red pepper, seeded
chopped	parsley or watercress
	(optional)

Preparation Put the cooked pasta in a bowl. Chop the spring onions finely and add to the pasta with the mayonnaise.

Remove the skins from the avocados, cut them in half and remove the stones. Cut 8 thin slices for garnish and chop the remainder. Add to the pasta and mayonnaise mixture with the cooked chicken.

Season well and add a few drops of lemon juice. Place the sliced avocado in the remaining lemon juice.

Arrange the salad in a bowl which has been lined with sliced tomatoes.

Decorate with slices of blanched pepper and the sliced avocados. Arrange parsley or watercress around the dish.

Note If preparing in advance sprinkle the avocados with lemon juice.

Any wholewheat pasta shapes can be used, such as shells, spirals or short cut macaroni.

Chicken in Coconut Milk
Serves 4

Ingredients

1.4-kg/3-lb chicken, jointed	2.5-cm/1-in piece fresh
into 8 pieces	ginger
15g/1tbsp sugar	2 stems lemongrass
350g/12oz desiccated	75ml/5tbsp coconut or
coconut	vegetable oil
600ml/1pt boiling water	30g/2tbsp chilli powder or
4 small onions	to taste
2 cloves garlic	salt to taste

Preparation Rinse the pieces of chicken and dry them on kitchen paper. Put in a bowl, sprinkle with sugar and toss in the bowl to release their juices.

Dry fry 75g/3oz of coconut in a large frying pan or wok turning all the time until it becomes dry, crisp and golden. Pound with a pestle and mortar until the oil begins to show.

Turn the remaining coconut into a deep bowl and make coconut milk by pouring over it the boiling water, leaving to soak for 15 minutes, then squeezing out the liquid. Leave liquid to stand for another 15 minutes, then spoon off 60ml/4tbsp.

Peel and chop the onions and garlic and scrape and chop the ginger. Pound them with the lemongrass.

Heat the oil in the wok. Fry the pounded ingredients for several minutes to bring out the flavour. Lower the heat, add the chilli powder and cook for 3-4 minutes, stirring all the time. Add the spooned off coconut milk and salt. Stir as the mixture comes to the boil to prevent curdling. Add the chicken pieces turning frequently so that the mixture coats each piece. Reduce the heat and stir in the remaining coconut milk. Cook over a gentle heat for 45-50 minutes or until the chicken is tender.

Just before serving spoon some of the sauce into the pounded coconut. Mix well, then return this to the pan. Stir without breaking up the chicken and cook for a further 5 minutes.

Boned Highland Chicken
Serves 6-8

Ingredients

2-kg/4-lb chicken, boned	rind of 1 lemon
75g/3oz butter	juice of ½ lemon
1 large onion, peeled	60ml/4tbsp stock
2 stalks celery, washed	freshly ground pepper
100g/4oz medium oatmeal	butter or vegetable oil
15g/½oz chopped parsley	

Preparation Preheat the oven to 180°C/350°F/Gas 4.

To bone the chicken, place the chicken, breast side downwards, on the board and split the bird down the back with a very sharp knife.

Ease the skin and flesh from the carcass with the knife and fingers. Insert the knife between the ball and socket of the thigh joint and remove the sinews. Take out the thigh bones, which should come away cleanly.

Hold the joint between the finger and thumb and gradually work the meat from the drumstick. Remove the wing joint from the body and carefully work the flesh from the breastbone without cutting the skin. Remove the breastbone completely. Flatten out the bird on a board ready for stuffing.

To make the stuffing, melt the butter in a saucepan, dice the onion and cook over a low heat for 5 minutes. Remove strings from celery with a potato peeler and dice finely. Add the celery to the onion, cook for a further 3 minutes. Sprinkle in the oatmeal and stir for a few minutes with the buttery vegetables. Add parsley, lemon rind and juice. Add a little stock until the stuffing holds together.

Lay the stuffing in the cavity of the chicken, reform its shape and sew up with a trussing needle and thin string.

Rub over the skin of the chicken with the squeezed lemon half, season with pepper, spread with a little butter or paint with vegetable oil and roast in foil for 1 hour 40 minutes. Remove foil for the last 20 minutes.

Chicken Biriani
Serves 4

Chicken Curry with Noodles
Serves 6-8

Ingredients

1.2l/2pt boiling water
450g/1lb desiccated coconut
450g/1lb egg noodles or rice noodles
1.5-kg/3-lb chicken, cut into quarters
salt to taste
450g/1lb onions, peeled
3 cloves garlic, peeled and crushed

4 fresh red chillies, seeded or 7g/2tsp chilli powder
5-10g/1-2tsp powdered turmeric
peanut oil for frying
45-60g/4-5tbsp chick-pea flour
15-30ml/1-2tbsp Worcestershire sauce
coriander leaves

Preparation First make coconut milk by pouring the boiling water over the coconut, leaving it to stand for 15 minutes, then squeezing out the liquid.

Break some of the rice noodles into 2.5-cm/1-in lengths and deep fry until crisp. Drain on absorbent kitchen paper.

Put the chicken joints in a pan. Add 2l/3½pt of water and some salt. Bring to the boil, then cover and simmer for 45-60 minutes or until the chicken is tender. Lift the chicken joints from the pan, cool and remove the meat and cut into small pieces. Discard the skin and bones. Strain the stock and reserve.

Meanwhile pound the onions, garlic and chillies, or chilli powder, to a paste in a food processor. Add turmeric. Fry in hot oil until it gives off a rich aroma. Stir in the coconut milk and 875ml/1½pt of the reserved chicken stock. Simmer for 15 minutes.

Blend the chick-pea flour with a little of the cold stock or water to make a cream. Slowly stir one ladleful of liquid from the pan into the cream, then pour this back into the pan. Simmer over a low heat, stirring until the soup thickens a little. Add the chicken pieces, salt and Worcestershire sauce. Turn into a serving tureen and scatter with fresh coriander leaves.

Cook the noodles in plenty of boiling water and spoon noodles into the bowls first then top with the curried chicken. Serve fried noodles separately.

Ingredients

225g/8oz long-grain rice, preferably basmati
15g/1tbsp salt
2 large onions, peeled
2 cloves garlic, crushed
2.5-cm/1-in piece root ginger, grated
50g/2oz slivered almonds
90ml/6tbsp vegetable oil
2-3 boned chicken portions

15g/1tbsp flour
¼tsp chilli powder
75ml/5tbsp yoghurt
15ml/1tbsp lemon juice
60ml/4tbsp water
5g/1tsp ground coriander
¼tsp ground cinnamon
2.5g/½tsp turmeric
1 hard-boiled egg
1 tomato, skinned

Preparation Wash the rice several times. Allow to soak in a large bowl of water and salt for at least 1 hour.

Slice half an onion finely into rings and reserve. Put the remaining onion, garlic, ginger, 15ml/1tbsp oil and some water in an electric grinder or food processor with a few slivered almonds. Grind to a paste.

Heat the remaining oil on a fairly high heat and fry the onion rings until golden brown. Remove with a slotted spoon and drain on kitchen paper.

Fry the remaining slivered almonds until golden on each side and drain with the onion rings.

Cut the chicken into small pieces and toss in seasoned flour mixed with the chilli powder. Fry until golden and drain on kitchen paper.

Fry the paste in the oil in the pan. Add the yoghurt, 15ml/1tbsp at a time, with the lemon juice. Add 60ml/4tbsp water and return the chicken to cook over a low heat for 15 minutes.

Add the coriander, cumin and cinnamon to the chicken after 5 minutes and stir well.

Meanwhile cook the rice in 1l/1¾pt boiling salted water with the turmeric for 10 minutes and drain.

Spread the drained rice on top of the chicken casserole. Add the almonds.

Cover the mixture with foil and then the casserole lid, and bake in the oven at 150°C/300°F/Gas 2 for 35 minutes.

To serve, mix the chicken and rice well with a fork and turn into a heated serving dish. Garnish with sliced hard-boiled eggs, tomato and browned onion rings.

Chicken Creole
Serves 6-8

Ingredients

8 chicken portions
100g/4oz peeled prawns
30ml/2tbsp olive oil
2.5g/¹⁄₂tsp dried tarragon
2 cloves of garlic, crushed
a few drops hot pepper
    sauce or cayenne

1 large onion, thinly sliced
1 red pepper, cored and
    thinly sliced
Concentrated Tomato
    Sauce

Preparation Score the chicken pieces and put them in a dish, with the prawns at one end. Pour over them a mixture of the oil, tarragon, garlic and hot pepper sauce or cayenne. Leave to marinate for at least an hour before cooking.

Drain the marinade into a frying pan. Remove the prawns and reserve until needed.

Fry the chicken in the heated marinade for 7 to 10 minutes, turning occasionally, until well-browned. Arrange in a roasting pan.

Fry the onion and sweet pepper in the oil left in the pan until the onion begins to brown, then arrange over the chicken.

Pour the Tomato Sauce over the vegetables and chicken, cover the pan with foil, and cook at 180°C/350°F/Gas 4 for 30 minutes.

Remove the foil, turn up the heat to 220°C/425°/Gas 7 and bake for another 20 minutes, adding the prawns 5 minutes before serving, to heat them through.

Chicken Casserole with Ginger
Serves 4-6

Ingredients

1.5-kg/3-lb chicken
2.5cm/1-in piece fresh
    ginger, scraped and
    chopped
1 large onion, peeled and
    sliced
2 cloves garlic, crushed
60-90ml/4-6 tbsp oil

600ml/1pt water or
    chicken stock
1 unripe papaya
30ml/2tbsp Worcestershire
    sauce
a good handful of washed
    spinach leaves
salt and pepper

Preparation Cut the chicken into eight or more pieces, dry on absorbent kitchen paper and set aside. Fry the ginger, onion and garlic in hot oil until soft and tender, but not coloured. Lift out and reserve.

Reheat the fat in the pan and fry the chicken pieces on all sides until golden, turning frequently. Add water or stock and seasoning. Stir in the onion, garlic and ginger. Cover and cook over a gentle heat until the chicken pieces are almost cooked — about 35-45 minutes depending on the size.

Wash and cut the papaya in half, remove the seeds and outer skin. Slice evenly and add to the chicken. Cover and cook until the papaya is tender — about 5 minutes.

Bring up to a rapid boil, add the Worcestershire sauce and spinach. Cover and cook for 1 minute. Taste for seasoning and serve.

Chicken Casserole with Coconut Milk
Serves 4

Ingredients

1.4kg/3lb chicken or 4 chicken quarters	450ml/³/₄pt boiling water
4 cloves garlic, crushed	450ml/³/₄pt chicken stock or water
175ml/7fl oz cider vinegar	oil for frying
2.5-5g/¹/₂-1 tsp black peppercorns, crushed	15ml/1tbsp soy sauce
225g/8oz dessiccated coconut	cucumber matchsticks and tomato slices to garnish

Preparation Wipe the chicken and cut into eight pieces, thigh and drumstick into two pieces and the breast and wing into a further two portions. Similarly cut each of the chicken quarters, if using, into two. Place in a glass or glazed bowl, add the garlic, vinegar and peppercorns. Mix well then leave to marinate for 1 hour.

Prepare coconut milk by putting the coconut in a bowl, pouring onto it the boiling water, leaving to stand for 15 minutes, then squeezing out the liquid.

Turn the marinaded chicken pieces into a pan with the stock or water. Bring to the boil, but do not cover, then simmer for 25-30 minutes adding a little extra water if necessary to keep the chicken moist. When the chicken is tender lift out and reduce the cooking liquid to 175ml/¹/₄pt and set aside.

Clean the pan, add oil and fry the chicken pieces until they are brown all over. Keep warm on a serving dish. Add the coconut milk to the reduced sauce in another pan. Add soy sauce and cook for 4-5 minutes.

Pour over the chicken pieces and garnish with cucumber matchsticks and tomato slices. Serve with freshly boiled rice.

Chicken Buried in Salt
Serves 4

The Chinese claim that this method of cooking ensures that the bird is full of vitamins and is especially good eaten on its own just before going to sleep!

Ingredients

1-kg/2-lb fresh chicken	3kg/7lb coarse salt (depending on size of casserole)
5-cm/2-in piece fresh ginger	
salt and pepper	

Preparation Preheat the oven to 200°C/400°F/Gas 6.

Remove the giblets from the chicken; dry inside and out with kitchen paper. Tie at the neck with a piece of string and tie up over a bowl so that the chicken will drain and dry.

Peel and bruise the ginger; place it inside the body cavity of the bird and wrap the chicken in a sheet of oiled greaseproof paper. Tie with a piece of string.

Cover the base of an ovenproof casserole with some of the salt. Place the chicken on the salt and spoon the remaining salt over it to completely cover. Cover with a tight fitting lid or foil.

Set in the preheated oven and cook for 1¹/₂ hours. Cool a little, then lift the chicken parcel out of the casserole carefully spooning out some of the salt first; it will be hot.

Unwrap the parcel and serve the chicken on a platter, cut up into small portions.

Chicken Curry
Serves 4

Ingredients

1 medium size chicken, cut into pieces and skinned	2 bay leaves
	cornflour
2 cloves garlic, chopped	4 bananas, green if possible
5ml/1tsp turmeric	
1 onion, finely chopped	2 slices ginger, finely chopped
15g/1tbsp curry powder	
450ml/15fl oz water	fresh lemon juice, to taste

Preparation Prick the chicken pieces with a fork and rub with a mixture of garlic and turmeric.

Fry half the onion until soft, add the chicken pieces and cook until tender and browned. Keep hot.

To make the curry sauce, fry the rest of the onion. When soft, add the curry powder and cook for 5 minutes, stirring. Add the water and one of the bay leaves. Cook until the sauce thickens, if necessary adding a little cornflour. Serve the curry sauce separately.

Split each banana into two. Sprinkle the bananas with chopped ginger and fry them in a non-stick pan with the other bay leaf.

Add the lemon juice to taste and serve with the cooked chicken.

Chicken Breasts with Sesame Seeds
Serves 6

Ingredients

2 eggs	1kg/2¹/₄lb chicken breasts (boneless), cut into small pieces
fresh rosemary, chopped	
black pepper, freshly ground	
	vegetable oil for frying
30g/2tbsp fine matzo meal	
45g/3tbsp sesame seeds	

Preparation Mix together the eggs, rosemary and black pepper.

Mix together the matzo meal and sesame seeds.

Dip pieces of the chicken into the egg then the sesame mixture.

When the oil is sizzling put in the chicken pieces.

When the chicken is golden-brown on one side, sprinkle generously with pepper and turn, sprinkling the other side when it has browned as well.

Drain on kitchen paper and serve.

Chicken Paprika
Serves 6-8

This delectable chicken dish is the perfect centrepiece for a holiday dinner. Although most cookbooks suggest serving it with egg noodles, for true authenticity it should be served on a bed of rice.

Ingredients

1.75-kg/4-lb chicken, cut into pieces	50g/2oz flour
225g/8oz margarine	12g/4tsp paprika
100g/4oz grated carrots	¼tsp salt
85g/3½oz chopped onions	pinch of black pepper
3 cloves garlic, quartered	100ml/4fl oz red wine
	900ml/1½pt chicken stock

Preparation Place all the ingredients except for half the chicken stock in a large soup pot. Simmer, covered, over a low heat for 1 hour.

Add the remaining stock, reduce the heat to very low and simmer, covered, for 1 hour longer.

Serve on a bed of rice.

Chicken Peanut Casserole
Serves 4

Ingredients

45ml/3tbsp vegetable oil	4 chicken drumsticks
25g/1oz butter	300ml/½pt chicken stock
2 onions, peeled and diced	30ml/2tbsp peanut butter
1 clove garlic, crushed	bouquet garni
30g/2tbsp flour	60ml/4 tbsp yoghurt
salt and freshly ground pepper	50g/2oz roasted peanuts, chopped
pinch of paprika	parsley or watercress
4 chicken thighs	

Preparation Heat the oil and butter in a frying pan, turn to low heat and cook the onions and garlic for 4 minutes.

Mix the flour with seasoning and paprika and toss the chicken pieces in flour.

Remove the onion to the casserole and, on a higher heat, brown the chicken pieces evenly. Remove, when golden brown, to the casserole dish.

Add any remaining flour to the juices in the pan, mix well and gradually add the stock and peanut butter. Mix and pour over the chicken in the casserole. Add bouquet garni. Cook on top of the cooker at a slow simmer for 40 minutes or in the oven at a temperature

of 180°C/350°F/Gas 4 for 50 minutes.

Arrange the chicken on a heated serving dish. Stir the yoghurt into the sauce and coat the chicken with the sauce.

Sprinkle with chopped peanuts and garnish with parsley or watercress.

Chicken with Kumquats
Serves 6

Kumquats look like miniature oranges. They are the only citrus fruit which are eaten whole, with the peel.

Ingredients

2×1.5kg/3lb chickens, cut into pieces	75g/3oz honey
350ml/12fl oz orange juice	5g/1tsp cayenne pepper
75g/3oz apricot jam	50ml/2fl oz lemon juice
75g/3oz peach jam	350g/12oz kumquats, boiled for 10 minutes, drained

Preparation Preheat the oven to 205°C/400°F/Gas 6. Arrange the chicken pieces in a large, lightly greased baking dish and bake for 30 minutes.

Combine the orange juice, apricot jam, peach jam, honey, cayenne pepper and lemon juice in a mixing bowl. Mix well.

After the chicken has baked for 30 minutes, brush the pieces with half the orange juice mixture. Reduce the oven temperature to 175°C/350°F/Gas 4 and bake for 15 minutes.

Turn the chicken pieces over and brush them with the remaining orange juice mixture. Arrange the kumquats in the pan with the chicken. Bake for 15 minutes longer.

Pour the pan juices over the chicken and kumquats before serving.

Chicken and Mushroom Lasagne
Serves 4-6

Ingredients

1 onion, peeled and diced	salt and freshly ground white pepper
25g/1oz butter	9 sheets "non cook" lasagne
100g/4oz mushrooms, washed and sliced	
350g/12oz cooked chicken, diced	20g/2tbsp fresh breadcrumbs
7g/1tbsp chopped parsley	25g/1oz grated Parmesan cheese
600ml/1pt Béchamel Sauce	

Preparation Cook the onion in the butter over a low heat for about 3 minutes. Add the mushrooms and cook for a further 2 minutes. Add the chicken to the mushroom and onions, season well and mix with chopped parsley. Make up the Béchamel Sauce, season well. Place about 60ml/4tbsp sauce in the bottom of an ovenproof dish. Cover with one-third of the chicken mixture. Put sheets of lasagne on top to cover. (If using fresh it can be cooked in boiling water for 3 minutes.)

Place a further 60ml/4tbsp sauce on top of the lasagne and a further third of the chicken mixture. Continue with third layer of lasagne, top with remaining Béchamel Sauce.

Mix the fresh crumbs with the cheese and sprinkle on top. Bake in the oven at a temperature of 180°C/350°F/Gas 4 for 25 minutes until golden brown.

Chicken Satay
Serves 4

Ingredients

Marinade

600ml/1pt boiling water
350g/12oz dessiccated
  coconut
1 spring onion, washed
  and chopped
2.5cm/1in fresh ginger,
  grated
grated rind of 1 lemon
pinch ground cinnamon
6 cardamom pods
5g/1tsp cumin
5g/1tsp ground coriander
7g/1tbsp parsley, chopped
675g/1½lb boneless
  chicken

Satay Sauce

100g/4oz peanuts
4 shallots, peeled and
  chopped
2 cloves garlic, peeled
6 macadamia, almond or
  cashew nuts
2 stems lemongrass
  (optional)
45ml/3tbsp coconut or
  peanut oil
7-10g/2-3tsp chilli powder
300ml/½pt coconut milk
tamarind water made from
  10g/1tbsp pulp or dried,
  soaked in 60ml/4tbsp
  water and squeezed out
15g/1tbsp brown sugar
salt to taste
chopped spring onion

Preparation Pour the boiling water over the coconut. Leave for 15 minutes, then squeeze out. Measure out 300ml/½pt of the liquid and reserve it. Mix the rest with the marinade ingredients. Cut chicken breasts and thighs into small pieces or use a whole chicken if liked. Cut meat from breasts and legs as needed. Marinate the chicken overnight in the refrigerator or at least for several hours. Remove from marinade and thread on to wooden or metal skewers.

To make the sauce, first toast the peanuts in a hot oven for about 20 minutes. Rub off the skins in a tea-towel and grind for just a few seconds in the liquidizer. Do not reduce the nuts to a powder — this would spoil the consistency of the sauce.

Grind or pound the onions and garlic and grind or pound the macadamia nuts and lemongrass.

Fry the onion mixture in hot oil, then add the nut and lemongrass paste. Reduce the heat, add the chilli powder and cook for 2 minutes.

Stir all the time while adding the reserved coconut milk. Allow to come to the boil, then reduce the heat and add tamarind water, sugar, salt to taste and peanuts. Cook for 2-3 minutes and stir frequently until the sauce thickens.

Grill the chicken skewers for 4 minutes each side under a high heat, then allow to cook for a further 4 minutes each side under a medium heat.

Serve with satay sauce dip and a green salad, the sauce garnished with spring onion.

Chicken Escalopes
Serves 4

Ingredients

4 chicken breasts, boned
salt and freshly ground
  pepper
60g/4tbsp bran
pinch paprika

1 egg, beaten
25g/1oz butter
45ml/3tbsp vegetable oil
lemon wedges to garnish

Preparation Cut the chicken breasts in half and place each half between a sheet of foil or cling film and beat to an escalope shape with a rolling pin. Season each side well. Mix the bran with the paprika. Dip chicken in beaten egg, and coat evenly with bran. Heat the butter and oil in a frying pan and, over a medium to high heat, fry the chicken breasts on both sides until golden. They will need about 5 minutes on each side. Turn the heat down after the first 5 minutes. Keep warm in a low oven. Garnish with lemon wedges.

Oriental Chicken and Mushroom Stew
Serves 4

Ingredients

300g/10oz boned chicken, with skin
4 large mushrooms, wiped
2 medium carrots
175g/7oz fresh or canned bean sprouts
4 small potatoes, scrubbed
5cm/2in square tofu (optional)
15-30ml/1-2tbsp vegetable oil
225ml/8fl oz well-flavoured chicken stock
30g/2tbsp sugar
30ml/2tbsp dry sherry
45ml/3tbsp soy sauce
50g/2oz mangetout
cress to garnish

Preparation Cut the chicken into 2-cm/³⁄₄-in cubes. Wash and trim the vegetables and cut into small chunks.

For the best flavour, the vegetables should then be parboiled separately in lightly salted water, rinsed and drained.

Heat the oil in a large saucepan over high heat.

Drop the chicken pieces into the oil and stir-fry to coat in oil. Add the carrots and tofu, if using, and then the mushrooms, bean sprouts and potatoes.

Stir-fry for 3 minutes, until the chicken and vegetables are lightly cooked and evenly coated with oil. Ladle the stock over them, add the sugar, dry sherry and soy sauce, and bring to a boil.

Cover and simmer for 15 minutes, until the simmering stock is glossy and reduced by one-third.

Trim the mangetout and slice diagonally into 2.5-cm/1-in slices. Parboil them in lightly salted water, and add to the chicken and vegetables just before serving.

Serve hot or at room temperature in individual bowls, arranging the vegetables attractively. Garnish with cress.

Chinese Chicken with Pineapple and Cashew Nuts
Serves 4-6

Serve with plain boiled rice and jasmine tea for a quick and tasty Chinese meal.

Ingredients

450g/1lb chicken breasts, skinned and boned
15g/1tbsp cornflour
240g/12oz can pineapple chunks in natural juice
30ml/2tbsp dry sherry
30ml/2tbsp oil
2.5-cm/1-in piece fresh root ginger, peeled and sliced
2 cloves garlic, peeled and sliced
75g/3oz cashew nuts
6 spring onions, trimmed and sliced
salt

Preparation Quarter the chicken breasts and chop roughly. Coat with 5g/1tsp of the cornflour, and set aside.

Drain the juice from the pineapple, and measure 200ml/7fl oz. Mix with the remaining cornflour and the sherry.

Heat the oil in a wok or large frying pan, and add the sliced ginger and garlic. Stir-fry for a few seconds, then add the chicken. Stir-fry over high heat, making sure the chicken pieces remain separate. When the chicken has become golden brown (after about 2 minutes), add the cashew nuts, and stir-fry for 1 minute. Add the pineapple and the juice mixture.

Bring to the boil, stirring constantly, and cook for another minute. Stir in the spring onions, and add salt to taste. Serve immediately.

Cold Chicken Millefoglie
Serves 4-6

Ingredients

350g/³⁄₄lb Puff Pastry dough
100ml/4fl oz Basic Garlic Dressing
8-10 canned artichoke hearts, quartered
7.5ml/¹⁄₂tbsp oil
1 clove of garlic, crushed
5g/1tsp ground coriander
2.5g/¹⁄₂tsp ground cumin
2.5g/¹⁄₂tsp turmeric
2.5g/¹⁄₂tsp paprika
2 pinches cayenne pepper
15ml/1tbsp lemon juice
100ml/4fl oz stiffly whipped cream
225g/8oz cold cooked chicken, cut or torn into bite-sized pieces
salt and pepper
30g/2tbsp finely chopped parsley
15ml/1tbsp Mayonnaise or Aïoli

Preparation Roll the pastry dough out thinly and cut into 3 strips approximately 10cm (4in) wide. Prick all over with a fork and bake for 7 to 10 minutes at 230°C/450°F/Gas 8 until well-risen and browned. Cool on a wire rack until needed.

Warm the Basic Garlic Dressing and pour over the artichoke hearts. Set aside for at least 1 hour.

To make the sauce for the chicken, heat the oil and add to it the garlic, coriander, cumin, turmeric, paprika, and cayenne. Stir over a moderate heat for several minutes. Remove from the heat and add the lemon juice, and either pour or strain the mixture into the cream. Fold the chicken into the sauce and season with salt and pepper to taste.

To assemble the Millefoglie, put one slice of cooked pastry on a serving dish and spread over it half the chicken mixture. Drain the dressing from the artichoke hearts, mix into them the parsley and put half of this on top of the chicken. Top with the second piece of pastry, the remaining chicken, and the rest of the artichoke mixture.

Spread the underside of the final pastry slice with the mayonnaise or Aïoli and press it gently, sticky side down, onto the artichoke and parsley mixture.

Chicken Stuffed with Fruit and Nuts
Serves 6

Ingredients

1.5-kg/3¹⁄₂-lb oven-ready chicken
salt and freshly ground pepper
2 medium onions, peeled
2 slices/50g/1oz crustless Granary bread, finely crumbled
100g/4oz butter
1 large cooking apple, peeled and cored
75g/3oz apricots, coarsely chopped
75g/3oz prunes, stoned and coarsely chopped
25g/1oz roasted almonds, roughly chopped
25g/1oz roasted hazelnuts, roughly chopped
25g/1oz pine nuts
15g/1tbsp raisins
225ml/¹⁄₂pt good chicken stock
7g/1tbsp fresh thyme

Preparation Wipe the chicken inside and out and season inside. Quarter one of the onions and put in a roasting pan.

Grate or grind the bread to form fine crumbs. Set aside. Finely chop the other onion. Heat half the butter in a frying pan and slowly cook the onion until soft and golden.

Add the apple, apricots and prunes to the onion and fry for 1 minute. Then add the chopped almonds, hazelnuts, pine nuts and raisins to the pan. Take the

pan off the heat and mix in the breadcrumbs. Add 15ml/1tbsp of the stock and season with salt and pepper. Cool, then use to stuff the chicken. Stand the chicken on the onion in the roasting pan. Rub with the remaining butter, sprinkle with salt and pepper and the thyme. Roast at a temperature of 200°C/400°F/Gas 6 in a preheated oven for about 1¹⁄₄ hours, basting frequently.

Remove the cooked chicken to a warmed serving dish, and keep warm. Add the stock to the pan, and bring to the boil on top of the stove, stirring to dislodge all the meat juices. Skim off any fat. Boil the gravy till reduced by a third. Season to taste, then strain and serve.

Variation This is a delicious way of cooking the Christmas turkey.

Chicken Garam Masala
Serves 4

Ingredients

225g/8oz onions, chopped
15g/1tbsp grated fresh ginger
2 cloves garlic
45ml/3tbsp Ghee (clarified butter) or butter
5g/1tsp cumin seeds
5g/1tsp ground coriander
5g/1tsp turmeric
5g/1tsp chilli powder
5g/1tsp salt
100g/4oz fresh tomatoes, skinned and chopped
1 medium chicken, jointed and skinned
20g/2tbsp coriander seeds, chopped
5g/1tsp garam masala
500ml/18fl oz water

Preparation Liquidize the onion, ginger and garlic to a smooth paste.

Heat the ghee or butter in a heavy-based saucepan. Add the onion mixture. Cook, stirring frequently, until golden brown. Add 15ml/1tbsp water to prevent the mixture from sticking to the pan, more if required.

Add the cumin seeds, ground coriander, turmeric, chilli powder and salt. Stir in well.

Add the tomatoes. Cook until the tomatoes are reduced to a pulp. Again, add a little water if the mixture is sticking to the pan.

Gently add the chicken pieces. Cook, still stirring, until the chicken turns golden brown and has absorbed the flavour of the spices.

Add the water to make the sauce.

Cover and cook on a low heat for 35 minutes, or until the chicken is tender. Do not let it fall off the bone.

Sprinkle with the chopped coriander and garam masala. Cover again and cook for a further 10 minutes.

Holiday Fried Chicken
Serves 8

This Italian version of fried chicken makes an excellent buffet dish.

Ingredients
5g/1 tsp salt	45ml/3tbsp lemon juice
2.5g/¹/₂tsp black pepper	225ml/8fl oz olive oil
pinch ground nutmeg	100g/4oz flour
pinch ground cinnamon	2 eggs, beaten
2.5g/¹/₂tsp finely chopped garlic	lemon wedges
2 small chickens, cut into small pieces	

Preparation In a small mixing bowl, combine the salt, pepper, nutmeg, cinnamon and garlic. Mix well. Rub the chicken pieces with the mixture and then sprinkle them with the lemon juice.

Heat the oil in a large heavy frying pan over a moderate heat until it is very hot.

Dip half the spiced chicken pieces in the flour and then in the egg. Sauté, turning frequently, for 20 minutes. Keep the pieces from the first batch in a warm oven while cooking the remainder.

Serve hot with lemon wedges.

Deep-fried Soy Chicken
Serves 4

Morsels of chicken marinated in soy sauce become a rich reddish brown. Fresh ginger gives a tang to the marinade and is frequently used to accompany chicken in Japanese cooking.

Ingredients
	Marinade
750g/1¹/₂lb boned chicken, skin attached	60ml/4tbsp soy sauce
90g/6tbsp cornflour	30ml/2tbsp dry sherry
vegetable oil for deep frying	5g/1tsp sugar
1 lemon, washed, dried and quartered	pinch of ginger
4 sprigs parsley, washed and patted dry	lemon quarters
	parsley sprigs

Preparation Cut the chicken into large bite-size chunks. Mix the marinade ingredients and pour over the chicken. Mix well so that the chicken is evenly covered. Set aside to marinate for 30 minutes.

Drain the chicken and coat with cornflour. Wait for a few minutes so that the coating can set.

In a small saucepan, heat oil for deep frying to 180°C/350°F. Carefully put the chicken in the oil, a few pieces at a time, and deep-fry for about 3 minutes, until crisp and brown.

Remove piece by piece and drain.

Serve garnished with lemon quarters and sprigs of parsley.

Glazed Chicken Wings
Serves 8

Ingredients
1.5kg/3lb chicken wings	pinch cayenne
60ml/4tbsp tomato sauce	100ml/4fl oz white wine
2.5g/¹/₂tsp garlic powder	60ml/4tbsp honey
2.5g/¹/₂tsp onion powder	60ml/4tbsp apricot jam
pinch ground ginger	30ml/2tbsp peach jam

Preparation Preheat the oven to 190°C/375°F/Gas 5. Cut the tips from the wings (discard or save them for stock). Spread the chicken wings in one layer in a large greased pan. Bake for 30 minutes.

Meanwhile, mix together the tomato sauce, garlic powder, onion powder, ginger, cayenne pepper and wine in a small bowl.

Spoon the mixture over the chicken wings and bake for a further 30 minutes. While the wings are cooking, mix together the honey, apricot and peach jams in a small bowl. Brush the glaze over the chicken wings. Raise the heat to 205°C/400°F/Gas 6 and bake for a further 10 to 15 minutes, or until the wings are golden and glazed.

Fried Chicken Wings
Serves 3-4

Ingredients
2 cloves garlic, crushed	5g/1tsp sugar
45ml/3tbsp oil	30ml/2tbsp white wine
3 pinches cayenne	salt and pepper
2.5g/¹/₂tsp oregano	10 chicken wings
5g/1tsp paprika	seasoned flour
10ml/2tsp vinegar	

Preparation Combine the garlic, half the oil, the cayenne, oregano, paprika, vinegar, sugar, white wine and plenty of salt and pepper. Cut a few slits in each chicken wing and put them in a large plastic bag. Pour over the marinade and knot the top of the bag. Put the bag in a bowl in case of leaks, and leave in a cool place for 2 to 4 hours. Drain the chicken wings of the marinade and toss them in the seasoned flour. Fry in the remaining oil for approximately 10 minutes, turning occasionally, until well browned. Drain on kitchen paper towels and serve hot with brown rice and salad.

Double Garlic Chicken
Serves 4

Ingredients

3 heads garlic (about 35 cloves)
1.5-2kg/3½-4lb roasting chicken
150g/6oz cream cheese or low fat soft cheese
15g/1tbsp chives, chopped
7g/1tbsp parsley, chopped
salt and pepper
225g/½lb seedless green grapes
1 sprig of rosemary
30g/1oz butter

Preparation Plunge the unpeeled garlic, except for 2 cloves, into a pan of boiling water for 30 seconds, drain and peel. Boil for a further 2 minutes, drain and set to one side.

Peel one of the remaining garlic cloves and cut it in half. Rub the cut side of the garlic over the breast and legs of the chicken, then slice it and its other half.

Peel and crush the last garlic clove and blend it with the cream or low fat cheese, chives and parsley. Season well with salt and pepper.

Work your fingers under the skin of the chicken breast, carefully freeing it from the meat without tearing it.

Pack the cheese mixture between the loosened skin and the meat, covering the breast completely.

Stuff the body of the chicken with the blanched garlic and the grapes, together with most of the rosemary.

Put the chicken in an oiled roasting pan and tuck slices of garlic and the remaining blades of rosemary between the legs and wings and the body of the chicken.

Sprinkle the breast with salt and dot it with the butter. Cover the breast and feet with foil.

Bake for approximately an hour and a half at 180°C/350°F/Gas 4, until the juice no longer runs pink, removing the foil for the last 20 minutes of cooking to crisp the skin.

Drunken Chicken
Serves 4-6

Ingredients

a 1.5-kg/3-lb fresh chicken
1cm/½in fresh ginger, scraped and sliced
2 spring onions
1.5l/3pt water or to cover
5g/1tsp salt
300ml/½pt dry sherry
brandy (optional)
spring onion curls to garnish

Preparation Wipe the chicken inside and out. Place the ginger and spring onion in the body cavity. Set the chicken in a large pan or flameproof casserole and cover with water. Bring to the boil, skim and cook for 15 minutes. Turn off the heat and allow the chicken to stay in the cooking liquid for 3-4 hours, by which time it will be cooked. Lift out and drain well. Reserve 300ml/½pt of the stock. Cool and skim.

First of all remove the leg joints — divide each into a drumstick and thigh. Now cut away the wings to include some of the breast. Cut away the breast still on the bone and divide it into two pieces. Arrange these chicken portions in a shallow glass or glazed dish (only use enamel if it is unchipped). Rub salt into the skin of the chicken, leave for several hours or overnight.

Next day mix the sherry and a few tablespoons of brandy, if you like, with an equal amount of chicken stock and pour over the chicken pieces. Cover with cling film or a lid and leave in a refrigerator or cool place for at least 2 or 3 days; turn over occasionally.

When ready to serve, cut into chunky pieces through the bone and arrange on a serving platter garnished with spring onion curls.

Add the coconut, chicken stock, seasoning and pineapple. Cover and cook in a preheated oven at a temperature of 180°C/350°F/Gas 4 for 1 hour.

Garnish with strips of blanched pepper and pineapple rings.

Jellied Chicken Salad
Serves 4

Ingredients
142g/5oz packet of lemon jelly	100g/4oz curd cheese
300ml/½pt boiling water	1 stick celery, chopped
juice of 1 lemon	4 thin slices of lemon
350g/12oz cooked chicken, diced	

Preparation Dissolve the jelly in the boiling water and add the lemon juice. Stir well and pour 75ml/3fl oz into a cup. Leave the jelly to cool.

Mix in the chicken, cheese and chopped celery and put the mixture into a serving dish. Refrigerate until set. If the reserved jelly in the cup has set, melt it by standing the cup in a pan of boiling water.

Put the lemon slices on top of the chicken mixture and carefully spoon over the reserved jelly. Leave to set before serving.

Malaysian Chicken
Serves 4

Ingredients
2 spring onions, washed	2.5g/½tsp paprika
2 stalks celery, washed	2.5g/½tsp cumin
1 onion, peeled	60ml/4tbsp oil
1 clove garlic	100g/4oz toasted
1 red pepper, seeded	dessiccated coconut
1 chilli pepper, seeded	600ml/1pt chicken stock
4 portions chicken	100g/4oz pineapple,
15g/1tbsp flour	chopped
salt and freshly ground pepper	8 strips of blanched red pepper
	4 pineapple rings

Preparation Prepare the vegetables and purée in a blender or food processor.

Toss the chicken portions in seasoned flour with paprika and cumin added.

Heat the oil in a casserole or frying pan and fry the chicken until golden. Turn the heat to low and add the puréed vegetables. Mix well with the chicken.

Poulet au Roquefort
Serves 4

Ingredients
4 chicken pieces	100g/4oz Roquefort or
15g/½oz butter	other blue cheese
salt and pepper	10g/2tsp cornflour
300ml/½pt yoghurt	15ml/1tbsp water

Preparation Brown the chicken in butter and remove it to a casserole. Season well. Blend the yoghurt and blue cheese together until the mixture is smooth.

Mix the cornflour and water and add to the yoghurt mixture. Pour over the chicken. Cover and bake at 180°C/350°F/Gas 4 for 50 minutes. Uncover and return to the oven for a further 10 minutes.

Lemon Chicken with Wholewheat Spaghetti
Serves 2

Ingredients
4 thick slices cooked chicken	175g/6oz wholewheat spaghetti
300ml/½pt Béchamel Sauce	oil
10ml/2tsp lime juice	parsley sprigs
juice of ½ lemon	lemon wedges

Preparation Heat the chicken in the Béchamel Sauce which has had the lime and lemon juice added.

Cook the pasta 2-3 minutes if fresh (12 minutes if dried) in boiling salted water with a few drops of oil added. Drain and toss in a little butter.

Serve with the chicken in sauce, garnished with parsley sprigs and lemon wedges.

Lemon Chicken with Wholewheat Spaghetti

Traditional Roast Chicken
Serves 6

Ingredients

1.75-2kg/3½-4lb roasting chicken, with liver
5g/1tsp salt
2 cloves garlic, finely chopped
15g/1tbsp ground ginger
5g/1tsp cayenne
90g/3½oz fresh breadcrumbs
65g/2½oz chopped celery
40g/1½oz chopped mushrooms
25g/1oz shredded carrots
7g/1tbsp chopped fresh parsley or 5g/1tsp dried
2.5g/½tsp dried thyme
2.5g/½tsp dried marjoram
50g/2oz butter or margarine, melted
225ml/8fl oz boiling water
1.5kg/3lb potatoes, cut into sixths
3 large onions, cut into sixths

Preparation Preheat the oven to 175°C/350°F/Gas 5. Place the cleaned chicken on a greased roasting pan. Reserve the chicken liver. Sprinkle the skin with 2.5g/½tsp each of the salt, garlic, ginger and cayenne pepper. Roast the chicken for 30 minutes.

While the chicken roasts, prepare the stuffing. In a mixing bowl, combine the breacrumbs with the celery, mushrooms, carrots, oil, and the remaining salt, garlic, ginger and cayenne pepper. Add the parsley, thyme and marjoram. Mix well.

Put the chicken liver in a small saucepan and add enough cold water to cover. Bring to the boil and cook until the liver is done, about 10 minutes. Drain well. Chop the liver coarsely. Add the chopped liver to the stuffing mixture. Add the melted butter or margarine and the boiling water. Mix well.

Remove the chicken from the oven and fill the cavity with the stuffing. Arrange the potato and onion pieces around the chicken in the roasting pan. Return the chicken to the oven and roast for 1½ to 2 hours basting with the pan drippings every 30 minutes.

Sprinkle the chicken, potatoes and onions with paprika after the final basting.

Penang Chicken Curry
Serves 4

Penang Chicken Curry doesn't look special under its mound of fried onions, but the smell really is special and the taste is out of this world.

Ingredients

1½-kg/3-lb fresh chicken, divided into 8 pieces
225g/8oz dessiccated coconut
just over 450ml/¾pt boiling water
10g/1tbsp tamarind, pulp or dried
150ml/¼pt water
5g/1tsp yeast extract
2-4 fresh chillies or 1-2 teaspoons chilli powder
2 macadamia nuts or almonds
2 stems lemongrass
2.5-cm/1-in piece fresh ginger
2 cloves garlic
4-8g/1-2tsp ground turmeric
60ml/4tbsp coconut or cooking oil
salt
piece cinnamon
6 green or white cardamom pods, bruised but left whole
2 large onions, finely sliced and deep fried or a handful of chopped coriander to garnish

Preparation Wipe the chicken and set aside. Make coconut milk by pouring the boiling water over the dessiccated coconut, leaving it to stand for 15 minutes, then squeezing out the liquid. Soak the tarmarind in the water for 10 minutes, squeeze out, and reserve the juice. Pound the prepared and chopped chillies, nuts, lemongrass, ginger and garlic into a paste with the yeast extract; if using dried chilli, add it to the paste. Stir in the turmeric.

Heat the oil and fry the spice mixture for a few minutes without browning. Stir in the chicken pieces until they are all coated with the spices. Add salt. Pour in the coconut milk and tamarind juice. Add the cinnamon and cardomom pods. Cook uncovered over a gentle heat for 35-45 minutes until almost all the sauce has cooked away. Taste for salt. Test the chicken pieces with a skewer. When tender, serve in a hot bowl. This is traditionally served with a topping of crispy fried onions, but you may prefer to use chopped coriander instead.

Ingredients

1.5-kg/3-lb chicken
45ml/3tbsp soy sauce
45ml/3tbsp dry sherry
salt
3 spring onions
25g/1oz seasoned
  cornflour
deep fat for frying
1-2 dried red peppers (or
  more if you like this dish
  hot), dry fried then
  crushed

2.5g/½tsp Szechuan
  peppercorns, crushed
1 piece dried tangerine
  peel, crushed
30ml/2tbsp wine vinegar
approx 125ml/¼pt chicken
  stock
salt to taste

Preparation Cut the chicken into eight pieces first and then each of these into a further two or three pieces. Marinate for 3-4 hours in soy sauce together with sherry, salt and one chopped spring onion. Chop the remaining spring onions and set aside for garnish.

Drain the chicken pieces and reserve the marinade. Dust the chicken with cornflour and deep fry in two or three lots for about 7 minutes or until golden and crisp. Lift out and keep warm.

In another pan, heat a little oil and fry the pepper, peppercorns and crushed tangerine rind for a minute. Add the cooked chicken pieces and toss all together. Pour in the vinegar and cook over a higher heat until the vinegar evaporates. Keep moving the chicken around in the pan. Add sufficient stock to the marinade to make up to 175ml/7fl oz. Pour into the pan. Do not cover.

Cook for 15 minutes or until the liquid evaporates, stirring occasionally. Serve at once sprinkled with spring onions.

Paper-Wrapped Chicken
Serves 3-4

Ingredients

2 chicken breasts, skinned
  and boned
45ml/3tbsp soy sauce
15ml/1tbsp dry sherry
15g/1tbsp caster sugar
pinch of freshly ground
  black pepper
3.5cm/1½in fresh ginger,
  scraped and sliced, then
  crushed in garlic press

1 small bunch spring
  onions, washed and
  dried
100g/4oz cooked ham
oil for deep frying
stir fried mangetout or
  broccoli to garnish

Preparation Cut the chicken into pieces the size of your little finger. Marinate in a mixture of soy sauce, wine or sherry, sugar, black pepper and ginger.

Meanwhile cut the spring onions into 5-cm (2½-in) lengths and the ham into small pieces. Prepare 18×18-cm(7-in) squares of greaseproof paper to make the parcels. Brush the paper with oil, then lay a piece of marinated chicken in the middle, top with a little spring onion, ham and another piece of chicken. Fold the paper up almost corner to corner to make a triangle. Fold sides to middle to make an envelope shape, then tuck the flap in to form a neat parcel. (Seal with a staple if your prefer, but do warn your guests when they open their parcels.) Repeat with the remaining ingredients.

Fry several parcels at a time in hot oil for 2-3 minutes. Do not overcook or let the paper turn brown. Serve hot, garnished with mangetout or broccoli and any remaining spring onions.

Salt-Grilled Chicken
Serves 4

Salt grilling accentuates the succulent taste of chicken.

Ingredients

8 small boned chicken
  thighs, skin intact
30ml/2tbsp sherry

salt
lemon wedges

Preparation Sprinkle the chicken thighs with sherry and leave to stand for 5 – 10 minutes to tenderize. Thread onto skewers.

Sprinkle both sides liberally with salt.

Grill over (or under) a hot flame for 10 minutes, turning occasionally, until the skin is golden and the flesh is cooked but still moist.

Serve hot or at room temperature, garnished with lemon wedges.

Chicken with Tangerine Peel
Serves 4-6

Szechuan peppercorns and dried tangerine peel are available at oriental grocers. If you cannot get them, use crushed whole allspice and dry your own tangerine peel in the oven.

Spicy Roast Chicken
Serves 4

Ingredients

1.75-kg/3½-lb chicken, cleaned	**Marinade**
Stuffing	100g/4oz onions, cut up
15ml/1tbsp oil	2-3 cloves garlic
50g/2oz onion, finely chopped	2.5-cm/1-in ginger root
1 large potato, boiled and diced	5g/½tsp ground turmeric
2 eggs, boiled and chopped	2.5g/½tsp chilli powder
50g/2oz peas, boiled	5g/½tsp garam masala
2.5g/½tsp salt	30g/2tbsp blanched almonds
pinch of pepper	100ml/4fl oz yoghurt
1–2 green chillies, chopped	5g/1tsp salt
7g/1tbsp coriander leaves, chopped	60ml/4tbsp oil
22.5g/1½tbsp ground almonds	

Preparation Heat the oil in a pan over a medium high heat. Fry the onion until lightly golden. Add all the remaining stuffing ingredients and fry for another 2-3 minutes. Pack into the body cavity of the chicken.

Blend together all the marinade ingredients except the oil. Stir the oil into the blended mixture. Rub the chicken all over with the marinade and set aside for 5-6 hours.

Roast the chicken in a preheated oven at 220°C/425°F/Gas 7 for 20 minutes. Cover with foil, lower heat to 190°C/375°F/Gas 5 and bake for a further 1½ hours. Remove the cover for the last 30 minutes of the cooking time.

To serve, place the chicken on a platter and offer the sauce separately in a bowl.

Red-Cooked Chicken
Serves 4-6

Ingredients

1.5-kg/3-lb fresh chicken	175ml/7fl oz each light and dark soy sauce
1 clove garlic, peeled and crushed	1 star anise
1.25cm/½in fresh ginger, scraped and chopped	15g/1tbsp sugar
175ml/7fl oz chicken stock	30ml/2tbsp sherry
	spring onions

Preparation Plunge the chicken into a pan of boiling water to completely cover it. Cook for 3-4 minutes. Carefully lift out and drain.

Put breast-side down in another large pan or flameproof casserole and add the garlic, ginger, chicken stock, soy sauces, star anise, sugar and sherry. Allow to come to the boil, cover and simmer for 45-60 minutes or until the chicken is tender, turning it over two or three times so that it is evenly cooked in the rich sauce. Turn by inserting a roasting fork into the body cavity to prevent damage to the skin or breast.

Allow to cool slightly, then lift out and chop into bite-size pieces to serve. Serve scattered with spring onions.

The sauce can be reserved and used again, several times in fact, with the flavour improving on each occasion as it gets stronger and matures.

Chicken in Mole Sauce
Serves 6

This Mexican dish is an ideal way of using up leftover turkey. Totally unsweetened chocolate is best for this dish; it can sometimes be found at Caribbean grocers.

Ingredients

1 large chicken, jointed	2.5g/½tsp coriander seeds
1 medium onion, coarsely chopped	30g/2tbsp whole almonds or pecans
6 tomatoes, peeled, or 375g/15oz tinned tomatoes	30g/2tbsp peanuts
3 red chillies, seeded and chopped	1.5-cm/½-in cinnamon stock, broken up
2 cloves garlic	2tbsp/30ml olive oil
30g/2tbsp sesame seeds	50g/2oz plain chocolate

Preparation Put the chicken pieces and onion in a pan. Season and add water to cover. Simmer, covered, for 20 minutes. Remove the chicken and drain on a paper towel. Reserve the stock.

To make the sauce, blend together the cooked onion, tomatoes, chillies and garlic. Grind the seeds, nuts and cinnamon. Heat the olive oil in a large, heavy-based saucepan and brown the chicken. Add the tomato mixture and the ground nut mixture. Cook for 5 minutes. Add half the chicken stock and the chocolate, broken into pieces. Stir over a low heat until the chocolate is dissolved.

Bring to the boil and simmer until the chicken is cooked, adding more stock if necessary.

Tandoori Chicken
Serves 4

This utterly delicious and extremely easy-to-make dish is good with *Nan* (Indian bread). Several points are worth noting. You need small pieces of chicken otherwise it is difficult to cook them thoroughly by grilling. Poussin, cut up, would be excellent, or ask your butcher to cut a larger bird into small pieces. You can use more marinade if you like. If using fresh chickens you can freeze the marinaded chicken uncooked. It freezes well but, as always with poultry, make sure it is thoroughly defrosted before cooking.

Ingredients
300ml/½pt yoghurt
2.5-cm/1-in piece root
  ginger, crushed
2 cloves garlic, crushed
salt and pepper
¼tsp garam masala
2.5g/½tsp red chilli pepper

15ml/1tbsp oil
5g/1tsp ground coriander
a few drops red colouring
  (optional)
1.75-2kg/3½-4lb roasting
  chicken, cut into 8 pieces
lemon wedges

Preparation Mix everything except the chicken and lemon together in a large bowl.

Remove the skin from the chicken and put the pieces into the yoghurt mixture to marinate for 24 hours. Turn the pieces from time to time.

Grill the marinaded chicken for at least 10 minutes on each side, basting with the juices. Serve with the lemon wedges.

Sesame Chicken
Serves 4

Ingredients
15g/1tbsp cornflour
45ml/3tbsp water
300ml/½pt yoghurt
45ml/3tbsp tahini

1 large clove garlic,
  crushed
salt and pepper
4 pieces of chicken
2tbsp sesame seeds

Preparation Mix the cornflour and water to make a smooth paste and add the yoghurt, tahini, garlic, salt and pepper.

Put the chicken pieces in a shallow ovenproof dish; prick the skin with a fork. Spread the yoghurt mixture over the chicken. Bake, uncovered at 180°C/350°F/Gas 4 for 50 minutes, basting from time to time.

Scatter the sesame seeds over the chicken and put under the grill for 5 minutes to brown.

Stuffed Poussins
Serves 4

Ingredients
450ml/¾pt yoghurt
15g/1tbsp cornflour
60ml/4tbsp water
7.5g/1½tsp ground cumin
7.5g/1½tsp ground
  cinnamon

salt and pepper
4 poussins, skin removed
100g/4oz rice, cooked
60g/6tbsp raisins
30g/4tbsp flaked almonds

Preparation First prepare the yoghurt sauce. Put the yoghurt into a saucepan. Mix together the flour and water. Stir into the yoghurt. Put on a medium heat, bring to the boil and then reduce the heat and simmer gently for 10 minutes, stirring from time to time. Remove from the heat and add the cumin, cinnamon, salt and pepper. Leave to cool while you stuff the poussins.

Mix the rice, raisins, almonds and salt and pepper together and stuff the mixture inside the poussins. Tie the legs together with string or thread. Place the poussins in a shallow oven dish. Spoon over the prepared yoghurt mixture. Bake at 180°C/350°F/Gas 4 for 1 hour. Baste with the sauce after 30 minutes. Remove from the oven dish and put them onto a serving dish. Spoon over the sauce.

Serve with a brightly coloured vegetable, such as carrots or peas.

Yakitori
Serves 4

Ingredients
90ml/6tbsp soy sauce
50ml/2fl oz sake
100ml/4fl oz mirin or
  sweet sherry
8 chicken livers (optional)

4 chicken thighs, boned
4 spring onions, or ½ green
  pepper, seeded and cut
  into 8 pieces

Preparation Heat the soy sauce, sake and mirin together, stirring all the time until it comes to the boil. Cook without a cover for 2-3 minutes until it has reduced to two-thirds, then cool.

Meanwhile clean the chicken livers, cutting away any threads with scissors. Cut the chicken thighs into even-sized pieces for grilling, about 2.5cm (1in). Cut the spring onions into the same size lengths. Thread the halved chicken livers, if you are using them, onto skewers with the chicken pieces and spring onion or green pepper.

Pour the marinade into a jam jar and dip each skewer of food into this. Set under a hot grill or over a barbecue. Dip in the marinade three or four times during the 10 minutes cooking period.

Serve at once to enjoy this succulent dish at its best.

Curry-fried Turkey
Serves 4

Ingredients

675g/1½lb turkey breasts, boned and skinned
2 cloves garlic, peeled
2.5-cm/1-in piece fresh root ginger, peeled
3 medium tomatoes, peeled
5g/1tsp tomato purée
2.5g/½tbsp fresh coriander leaves
2.5g/½tsp ground turmeric
2.5g/½tsp salt
5g/1tsp ground cumin
2.5g/½tsp ground fennel
pinch ground nutmeg
pinch ground cinnamon
2 drops Tabasco
30ml/2tbsp oil

Preparation Freeze the turkey until very firm. Slice very thinly, using a sharp knife or the slicing disc of a food processor, then turn into a shallow glass or china bowl. Using the metal blade, liquidize or process the garlic with the ginger.

Add all the remaining ingredients, except for the oil and blend for 20 seconds. Tip into the bowl and stir into the sliced turkey until well mixed. Cover and leave to marinate overnight in the fridge.

When ready to serve, heat the oil in a heavy sauté pan or heavy deep-frying pan. Add the meat and the marinade and fry over medium high heat for about 10 minutes, stirring frequently, until the turkey is golden brown and slightly crispy.

Serve hot with Nutty Rice Pilau or Spicy Potatoes or cold with a tossed green salad, and a rice salad.

Variation Replace the turkey with lean steak, chicken breasts, fillet of lamb or pork, or pheasant breasts.

Devilled Turkey Legs
Serves 4

Ingredients

4 cooked turkey legs or thighs
melted butter or margarine
breadcrumbs, browned
5g/1tsp mustard powder
pinch ground ginger
salt
black pepper
5g/1tsp cayenne pepper

Preparation Chop unsightly bits of bone off legs and thighs. Score the flesh deeply with a sharp knife and brush with melted butter.

Put breadcrumbs in a bowl and mix the rest of the ingredients with them.

Spread the breadcrumb mixture over the turkey pieces, pressing it well into the scored cuts, and leave them to stand for an hour.

Cook on a hot greased grill until crisp and brown. Serve at once with pats of butter.

Lemon Turkey
Serves 4

Ingredients

600g/1¼lb turkey fillet
juice and rind of 2 lemons
150ml/¼pt chicken stock
2.5g/½tsp sugar
salt and pepper
15g/1tbsp cornflour
15ml/1tbsp water
150ml/¼pt yoghurt

Preparation Cut the turkey fillets lengthwise into thin strips. Put them in a shallow pan and add the lemon juice and a little grated rind, the stock, sugar, salt and pepper. Poach the turkey on a gentle heat for 20 minutes.

Mix the cornflour and water to a smooth paste. Add this to the pan and stir around to thicken the poaching liquid. Add the yoghurt and cook for a further 5 minutes on a gentle heat. Adjust the seasoning.

Serve with a colourful vegetable — carrots or mangetout would go well.

Roast Turkey
Serves 6-8

Ingredients

4-kg/9-lb turkey
1 green pepper, finely chopped
10g/2tsp ginger
2 onions, finely chopped
350g/12oz half-cooked brown rice
30ml/2tbsp vinegar
10g/2tsp turmeric
10g/2tsp black pepper
10g/2tsp garam masala

Preparation Wash the turkey and remove its skin.

For the stuffing, mix together the green pepper, ginger, onions, rice and 2.5ml/½tsp vinegar and pack it into the bird.

Prepare a paste of turmeric, black pepper, garam masala, and the rest of the vinegar. Rub it onto the bird.

Cover with foil and bake in the oven at 170°C/325°F/ Gas 3 for 20 minutes for each 400g/lb.

Baste frequently with butter and the turkey's own fat.

Remove the foil to brown the turkey 20 minutes before taking it out of the oven.

Turkey Mole
Serves 8

This authentic Mexican dish uses unsweetened chocolate and has a rich, cinnamon taste that is quite unusual.

Ingredients

3.5-4.5kg/8-10lb turkey, cut into 8 serving pieces	2.5g/¹⁄₂tsp ground cinnamon
350g/12oz finely chopped onions	2.5g/¹⁄₂tsp ground cloves
3 tomatoes, skinned, seeded and coarsely chopped	100g/4oz finely chopped almonds
75g/3oz chopped seedless sultanas	2.5g/¹⁄₂tsp salt
2.5g/¹⁄₂tsp ground coriander	pinch black pepper
5g/1tsp cayenne pepper	450ml/16fl oz boiling chicken stock
2 cloves garlic, finely chopped	50g/2oz chicken fat
	450ml/16fl oz cold chicken stock
	40g/1¹⁄₂oz unsweetened chocolate

Preparation Put the turkey pieces in a large saucepan and cover with water. Cover the pan and cook over a high heat for 15 minutes. Reduce the heat to medium and cook for a further 45 minutes.

Meanwhile, combine the onions, tomatoes, sultanas, coriander, cayenne pepper, garlic, cinnamon, cloves, almonds, salt, pepper and boiling chicken stock in a large wooden mixing bowl. Mix to a paste.

In a large frying pan, melt the chicken fat over a low heat. Add the chopped vegetables and spice mixture. Fry for 5 minutes, stirring constantly.

Add the cold chicken stock and chocolate to the pan. Cook for 10 – 12 minutes over a moderate heat, or until the chocolate has completely melted. Stir constantly until the chocolate is evenly distributed throughout the sauce.

Preheat the oven to 230°C/450°F/Gas 8. Remove the turkey pieces from the frying pan and drain well. Pat the pieces dry with paper towels. Arrange the turkey pieces in a large baking dish in a single layer. Bake, uncovered, for 30 minutes.

Pour the sauce over the turkey pieces and lower the heat to 175°C/350°F/Gas 4. Cook for a further 30 minutes. You can sprinkle the dish with sesame seeds before serving.

Turkey Fillets in Wine Sauce
Serves 4

Ingredients

550g/1¹⁄₄lb turkey fillet	100g/4oz curd cheese
15g/1tbsp seasoned flour	100g/4oz button mushrooms, sliced
25g/1oz butter	grated nutmeg
150ml/¹⁄₄pt chicken stock	salt and pepper
150ml/¹⁄₄pt dry white wine	

Preparation Pass the turkey through the seasoned flour. Brown it lightly in the butter. Add the stock and wine and simmer it, covered, for 30 minutes.

Add the curd cheese, together with the mushrooms and nutmeg. Check the seasoning. Stir gently and cook for a further 10 minutes.

You could use turkey steaks for this but they would need longer cooking time – another 10 minutes before adding the curd cheese.

Peking Duck
Serves 8

Ingredients

2-kg/4-lb duckling	16 Mandarin Pancakes
45ml/3tbsp honey	50ml/2fl oz hoisin sauce
30ml/2tbsp water	a little thick soy sauce to taste
salt	
bunch spring onions	
¹⁄₂ cucumber, peeled and cut into thin, finger-like strips	

Preparation Bring a large pan of water to the boil and plunge in the duckling to scald the skin. Carefully lift out and drain thoroughly. Secure the legs with string and leave to drip over a bowl overnight in a cool dry place.

Blend the honey, water and salt together and use to brush over the duck skin. Hang up again and leave for 2-3 hours. Repeat and leave to dry completely for a further 3-4 hours.

Set the duck on a rack over a roasting tin and place in the centre of a hot oven (230°C/450°F/Gas 8). Immediately reduce the oven temperature to moderate (180°C/350°F/Gas 4) and cook for 1¹⁄₄

hours. Check that the skin is crisp (do not baste the duckling) and, if you think it necessary, increase the oven temperature for the last 15 minutes.

Meanwhile remove the root from the spring onions. Cut in half lengthwise and cut in half again. Pop in ice cold water. Prepare cucumber, drain and dry on paper towels. Prepare the mandarin pancakes and the sauce.

Carve the duckling at the table; traditionally only the skin was eaten, but these days most people carve the skin and meat togther into 4-cm (1½-in) pieces. This is then dipped into the prepared sauce and deftly rolled up in a pancake with some of the spring onions before eating.

Crispy Duck
Serves 4

Ingredients

First Marinade	Second Marinade
1.5-kg/3-lb duck	4 slices fresh ginger
6 spring onions	16 cloves
90ml/6tbsp wine	4 cloves star anise
30ml/2tbsp soy sauce	2 fennel bulbs

Preparation Wash and dry the duck. Crush the spring onions and add the remaining ingredients of the first marinade.

Put the spring onions only inside the duck, rub the marinade all over the outside of the duck and leave it for 2 hours.

Remove the spring onions and put in their place 2 slices of ginger.

Spread the spring onions, the other 2 slices of ginger and the other ingredients of the second marinade on and around the duck. Steam the duck for an hour, cool it and drain it.

Heat almost enough oil to cover the duck in a deep frying pan.

Once the oil is hot, remove the pan from the heat and place the duck gently in it, taking care not to burn yourself. Spoon the oil over the duck and fry until the duck is browned all over, returning it to the heat only if the oil cools down too much.

Serve with hoisin sauce.

Chinese Duck
Serves 4

Ingredients

2-kg/4-lb fresh duckling	15ml/1tbsp dark soy sauce
60ml/4tbsp cooking oil	15g/1tbsp sugar
2 cloves garlic, chopped	½tsp five spice powder
2.5-cm/1-in piece fresh	3 points star anise
ginger, thinly sliced	450ml/¾pt duck stock or
45ml/3tbsp bean paste	water
30ml/2tbsp light soy sauce	salt to taste

Preparation Use the duck giblets to make a duck stock; strain and reserve 450ml/¾pt. Heat the oil, fry the garlic without browning, then add the duck. Fry, turning frequently until the outside is slightly brown. Lift out the duck.

Add the ginger, then the bean paste to the pan. Cook to bring out the flavours. Add light and dark soy sauces, sugar and five spice powder.

Return the duck to the pan and fry it in this mixture to coat the outside of the duck. Add the star anise, duck stock and seasoning to taste. Cover and cook over a gentle heat until the duck is tender, stirring occasionally. Allow 2-2½ hours. Skim off any fat or oil, then leave in the sauce to cool.

Cut into serving portions. Skim the sauce and pour it over each helping, which will set like a jelly. Garnish with spring onion. Serve with rice.

Duck Breasts with Hazelnuts and Orange Potato Balls
Serves 4-6

This potato mixture can be made in advance, then fried just before serving. Duck breasts are now available from many supermarkets.

Ingredients

1kg/2lb potatoes, peeled	oil for deep-frying
rind and juice of 3 large	2 large duck breasts, boned
oranges	30ml/2tbsp oil
50g/2oz butter	½ small onion
3 egg yolks	150ml/¼pt duck or
3 small eggs	chicken stock
salt and freshly ground	1 large onion
pepper	5g/1tsp chunky
150g/6oz hazelnuts	marmalade
30g/2tbsp flour	

Preparation First make the potato balls. Halve the potatoes and cook in boiling salted water until tender. Drain well, then return to the pan and dry over low heat for 1 minute. Blend or process the potatoes, the juice of 2 oranges, egg yolks, and 2 of the eggs until smooth. Add salt and pepper to taste. Spoon on to a plate, cover and chill until firm.

Roll tablespoonfuls of the potato mixture into balls. Finely chop two-thirds of the nuts. Roll the potato balls in seasoned flour, then in the remaining egg, beaten, and finally roll in the nuts. Chill for 15 minutes or until ready to cook.

Heat the oil to 180°C/350°F and fry the balls a few at a time till golden brown. Drain on paper towels and keep warm.

Trim the duck breasts if necessary. Heat the 30ml/2tbsp oil in a frying pan and fry the duck for about 3 minutes on each side for rare meat, longer for medium and well done meat. Drain and keep warm.

Fry the remaining hazelnuts in the fat in the pan for a couple of minutes or until browned. Drain and remove. Finely chop the onion and add to the pan. Fry for a couple of minutes to soften then add the reserved flour. Fry for 1 minute stirring constantly, then stir in the stock. Bring to the boil, stirring, then simmer for 2 minutes.

Stir the remaining orange rind and juice into the sauce with the marmalade. Bring to the boil and season to taste. Thinly slice the duck, adding any juices to the sauce. Arrange the duck slices on a warmed serving dish with the potatoes. Stir the fried hazelnuts into the sauce and spoon over the meat. Serve immediately with the fried potato balls.

Roast Duck with Spaetzle
Serves 6

Spaetzle or spätzen are an extremely popular form of egg noodle. They go well with any sort of roast meat, but particularly with roast duck.

Ingredients

1kg-1.5kg/2-3lb duck, split	50ml/2fl oz lemon juice
and cleaned, with the fat	100ml/4fl oz orange juice
retained	45ml/3tbsp currant or
450g/1lb flour	blackberry jam
10g/2tsp salt	2.5g/½tsp black pepper
5 eggs	
450ml/16fl oz cold water	

Preparation Preheat the oven to 165°C/325°F/Gas 3. Put the duck halves, skin-side up, in a roasting pan. Roast the duck for 1 hour.

While the duck cooks, make the spaetzle. Place the flour in a large mixing bowl. Make a well in the centre of the mound. Sprinkle 5g/1tsp of salt in the well. Break the eggs into the well and mix them into the flour. Gradually add the water (more or less as needed) and mix to form a stiff dough.

Turn the dough out onto a lightly floured work surface and knead it vigorously until it is smooth and elastic. Roll or shape the dough into narrow strips. With a sharp knife, cut the strips into tiny pieces.

Bring 3l/5¼pt water to a furious boil in a very large pot. Drop the spaetzle into the water. (Since each spaetzle must be able to float to the top of the water as it cooks, you may prefer to cook them in batches in less boiling water.) After the spaetzle rises to the top, boil for a further 15 minutes. Drain the spaetzle well and set them aside.

After the duck has roasted for 1 hour, drain off the drippings, reserving ¼ cup.

In a small bowl, combine the lemon juice, orange juice, jam and pepper. Brush the skin of the duck with the mixture. Return the duck halves to the oven, skin-side up, and roast for 1 hour longer, draining off the drippings from the pan twice during the cooking time.

With a sharp knife, remove all the skin and meat from the duck halves and shred them coarsely. Discard the bones. Put the shredded meat and skin into a large serving bowl.

Bring 3l/5¼pt water to a furious boil in a large pot. Return the cooked spaetzle to the water for 1 minute. Drain the spaetzle well and add them to the shredded duck. Add the reserved duck drippings and salt to taste. Toss well and serve hot.

Duck with Pineapple
Serves 4

Ingredients

4 pieces of duck (or
  2.5-kg/5-lb duck cut into
  4)
salt and pepper
10g/2tsp cornflour

4 slices canned pineapple
  and juice from the can
10g/2tsp cornflour
150ml/¼pt sour cream
2.5g/½tsp paprika

Preparation Prick the duck and season well. Put the pieces on a wire rack in a roasting pan so that the fat runs off the duck. Roast at 220°C/425°F/Gas 7 for 10 minutes then reduce the heat to 180°C/350°F/Gas 4 for a further hour. Mix the cornflour with a little pineapple juice.

When the duck is cooked, remove the pieces from the pan and place each one on a piece of pineapple on a clean dish. Keep them warm while you make the sauce.

Remove as much fat as possible from the pan, leaving the juices. Mix the cornflour mixture into the juices over a gentle heat, cooking this for 2 minutes. Add the rest of the pineapple juice and warm the sauce through. Add the sour cream and stir it through.

Spoon the sauce over the duck. Sprinkle the paprika over the top and either serve it immediately or keep it warm in a low oven for up to 15 minutes.

Braised Coriander Duck
Serves 6

Ingredients

2.5-3-kg/5-6-lb duck, cut
  into 6 servings and
  trimmed of fat
50ml/2fl oz lemon juice
2.5g/½tsp ground cumin
2.5g/½tsp salt
2.5g/½tsp black pepper

50ml/2fl oz olive oil
900ml/1½pt lager
450g/1lb rice
150g/6oz cooked peas
75g/3oz finely chopped
  fresh coriander leaves

Preparation Brush the duck with a mixture of the lemon juice, cumin, salt and pepper. Put on a plate, cover and refrigerate for 4 – 5 hours.

In a large flameproof casserole, heat the olive oil over a medium heat. Add the duck pieces and brown them on all sides. Pour off all but 15ml/1tbsp of the fat.

Add the lager to the casserole and bring to a boil. Cover and reduce the heat to low. Simmer for 50 minutes.

Remove the duck pieces from the casserole. Set them aside and keep warm.

Remove 700ml/1⅖pt of the liquid from the casserole and bring it to a boil in a medium-sized saucepan over a high heat. Add the rice, stir, bring to a boil again and cover tightly. Reduce the heat to low and simmer for 18 minutes.

Stir the peas and coriander leaves into the rice. Cover, remove from the heat and allow to stand for 1 minute.

Arrange the duck pieces on a bed of rice and serve.

POULTRY AND GAME

Hot Game Pie with Fried Apples and Onions
Serves 4-6

Wild duck is particularly good cooked this way, although any sort of game can be used. Try to mix at least two types of game for the best flavour.

Ingredients

225g/8oz plain wholemeal flour	**Filling**
large pinch salt	240g/1lb cooked game, boned
25g/1oz white vegetable fat, diced	100g/4oz streaky bacon
75g/3oz butter or cooking margarine, diced	6 tart apples, quartered and cored
1 egg	2 large onions, peeled
15-30ml/1-2 tbsp milk	50g/2oz butter
	5g/1tsp caster sugar
	salt and freshly ground pepper
	mild paprika to taste
	125-175ml/5-7fl oz left-over game gravy
	1 beaten egg to glaze

Preparation Make the pastry first. Put the flour and salt in a bowl and rub in the fats until the mixture resembles fine crumbs. Mix the egg with 15ml/1tbsp of the milk and add to the mixture to form a soft but not sticky dough. If too dry add a little more milk. Wrap and chill while preparing the filling.

Cut or shred the game into bite-sized chunks. Coarsely chop the bacon, and slice the unpeeled apples. Slice the onions.

Heat half the butter in a frying pan, and fry the bacon till golden brown and crispy. Drain and remove. Fry the onions till soft and golden. Drain and remove. Heat the remaining butter and quickly fry the apple slices with the sugar till caramelized. Drain and remove.

Layer up the filling in a greased pie dish in this order: onion, bacon, apple, game, onion, apple, game, apple, onions and finally bacon. Add seasoning with each layer. Pour over enough of the gravy to come ⅔ the way up the dish.

Roll out the pastry on a floured board to an oval 5cm (2in) larger than the dish. Cut a strip the width of the rim of the dish. Brush the rim with a little of the beaten egg. Stick the pastry strip on to the rim then brush with egg. Cover the pie dish with the pastry. Seal well and flute the edges. Cut a small steam-hole in the top. Decorate the pie with any trimmings of pastry if wished. Glaze with beaten egg.

Bake in the preheated oven at 200°C/400°F/Gas 6 for 10 minutes, then reduce the heat to 190°C/375°F/Gas 5 and bake for a further 20 minutes or until the pastry is crisp and golden brown.

Serve hot.

Pheasant Pojarski Cutlets
Serves 6

Ingredients

225g/8oz pheasant breasts, boned and skinned	2 drops Tabasco
65g/2½oz fresh white bread crumbs	freshly ground black pepper
150ml/¼pt sour cream	6 slices Granary bread, toasted
15ml/1tbsp port	6 mushrooms
pinch of salt	25g/1oz butter
	6 sprigs parsley

Preparation Dice the pheasant and liquidize or process for 10 — 15 seconds, until finely chopped. Add the crumbs, cream, port and seasonings and blend for 30 seconds or until very smooth. Fry a teaspoonful of the mixture and taste for seasoning — it should not be too bland. Turn into a bowl and allow to chill until firm — about an hour.

Cut the toast into circles 7.5cm (3in) in diameter and put on a baking sheet.

Put the chilled pheasant mixture into a piping bag fitted with a star nozzle, and pipe the mixture neatly on the toast circles. Bake in the preheated oven (200°C/400°F/Gas 6) for 10 — 15 minutes until golden and firm to touch.

While they are cooking, fry the mushrooms using the butter and drain on kitchen paper.

Serve each cutlet capped with a mushroom and garnished with a sprig of parsley. Accompany with Mushroom Sauce and a green salad.

Variation The pheasant can be replaced with chicken, veal, scallops, or fillet of sole.

Pheasant Pojarski Cutlets

Jointing a Chicken

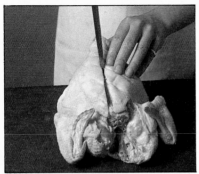

1 Turn the chicken over so that the backbone is uppermost. Cut through to the bone along the line of the spine.

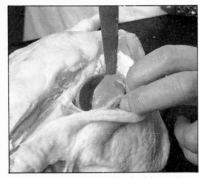

2 Where the thigh joins the backbone there is a fleshy 'oyster' on each side. Cut round them to loosen them from the carcass so that they come away when the legs are severed.

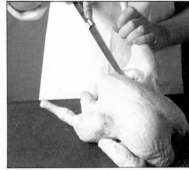

3 Turn the bird over and pull a leg away from the body. Cut through the skin only, as far round the leg as possible, close to the body.

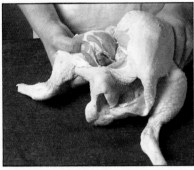

4 Pull the leg away from the body and twist it down so that the thigh bone pops out of its socket on the carcass and is exposed.

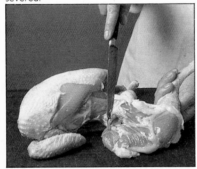

5 Cut the leg off, taking care to go between thigh, bone and carcass and to bring the 'oyster' away with the leg. (Turn over briefly to check.) Repeat the process for the other leg.

6 Now for the breast. Carefully cut down each side of the breast bone to free the breast flesh a little.

7 Use scissors to cut through the small bones close to the breast. Cut away the breast bone.

8 Open up the bird. Cut each wing and breast off the carcass with scissors, starting at the tail end and cutting up to and through the wing bone near the neck.

9 Cut the wing joint in two, leaving about one-third of the breast attached to the wing.

10 Cut off the almost meatless pinions (which can be used for stock, along with the carcass) from each wing.

11 Lay the legs skin-side down on the board and cut through where the thigh and lower leg bones meet.

12 With the heel end of a heavy knife (or a cleaver) chop the feet bones off the drumsticks.

Boning a Chicken

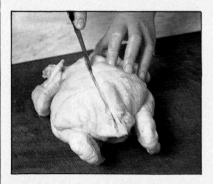

1 Put the chicken breast-side down on a board. Cut through to the backbone.

2 Feel for the fleshy 'oyster' at the top of each thigh and cut round it. Cut and scrape the flesh from the carcass with a sharp knife held as close as possible to the bone.

3 Continue along both sides of the backbone until the rib-cage is exposed. At the joint of the thigh and pelvis, cut between the bones at the socket so that the legs stay attached to the flesh and skin, and not to the body carcass.

4 Keep working right round the bird then use scissors to cut away most of the rib cage, leaving only the cartilaginous breast-bone in the centre.

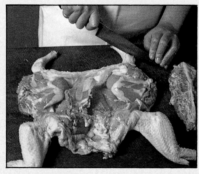

5 Using a heavy knife cut through the foot joints to remove the knuckle end of the drumsticks.

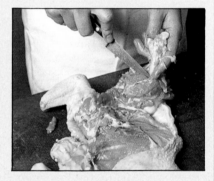

6 Working from the inside thigh end scrape one leg bone clean, pushing the flesh down towards the drumstick until you can feel the thigh bone. Repeat on the other leg.

7 Working from the drumstick ends, scrape the lower leg bones clean in the same way and remove them. Remove as many tendons as possible from the legs as you work.

8 Now for the wings. Cut off the pinions with a heavy knife.

9 Scrape the wing bones clean as you did the leg bones.

 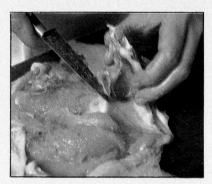 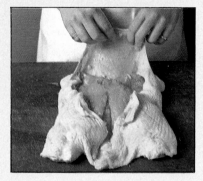

10 Carefully free the breastbone with the knife, working from the middle of the bird towards the tail.

11 Take great care not to puncture the skin, which has not flesh under it at this point so is easily torn.

12 You should now have a beautifully boned bird. Keep the neck flap of skin intact to fold over once the chicken is stuffed.

Mutton and Lamb

Baby Lamb 123
Capered Cutlets 123
Fragrant Lamb Stew 123
Crown Roast of Lamb with Apricot Rice Stuffing 124
Kashmiri Lamb with Fennel Seeds 124
Lamb Chops with Apricot Marsala Sauté 124
Lamb Biriyani 125
Lamb Chop Kebabs 125
Lamb Dhansak 126
Lamb Extravaganza 126
Lamb in Dill Sauce with Tagliolini 127
Lamb with Fennel and Lemon Sauce 127
Lamb Kidneys in Red Wine 128
Lamb Kebabs 128
Lamb Korma 128
Lamb and Okra Stew 129
Lamb and Lentil Meatballs 129
Lamb with Spinach 129
Lamb Tikka 130
Lamb-Stuffed Artichokes 130
Lamb with Onions 130

Hard-Boiled Eggs Wrapped in Spiced Meat 131
Marinated Lamb Chops 131
Light Lamb Curry 131
Rack of Lamb in a Garlic Crust 132
Persian Lamb Stew 132
Sauté of Lamb with Cranberries 132
Lamb with Almonds and Yoghurt 133
Simple Cassolet 133
Souvlakia 133
Wheat Grain Lamb 134
Spicy Lamb Rissoles 134
Spiced Lamb and Cheese Meatloaf 135
Stuffed Vine Leaves 135
Casseroled Leg of Lamb 135
Simple Lamb Curry 136
Orange Lamb Chops 136
Sweet and Sour Lamb 136
Tarragon Lamb 136

Preparing Lambs' Kidneys 137

Baby Lamb
Serves 8

This dish is traditionally made with chops from a young goat, but the recipe is often adapted to lamb, which is more readily available.

Ingredients

2kg/4lb lamb rib chops	*2 cloves garlic, finely*
45ml/3tbsp olive oil	*chopped*
2.5g/¹⁄₂tsp salt	*350ml/12fl oz cold water*
pinch black pepper	*2 egg yolks*
25g/1oz coarsely	*30ml/2tbsp lemon juice*
chopped parsley	

Preparation Put the lamb chops in a large heavy frying pan. Add the oil, salt, pepper, parsley and garlic. Pour the water over the meat and spices, cover, and simmer over a low heat for 1 hour.

In a small mixing bowl, combine the egg yolks and lemon juice. Pour over the lamb and cover. Simmer for another 3 minutes and serve.

Capered Cutlets
Serves 4

Ingredients

15-30ml/1-2tbsp oil	*15ml/1tbsp water*
1 medium onion, sliced	*150ml/¹⁄₄pt yoghurt*
8 lamb cutlets	*2 egg yolks*
salt and pepper	*15g/2tbsp capers*
300ml/¹⁄₂pt beef stock	*chopped parsley*
10g/2tsp cornflour	

Preparation Heat the oil, add the onion and cook until softened but not browned. Add the cutlets and brown them. Drain off excess fat and season well. Add the stock, bring to the boil and simmer for 30 minutes, or bake at 180°C/350°F/Gas 4.

Mix the cornflour with the water and add it to the pan. Stir over a gentle heat to thicken the sauce. Mix the yoghurt and egg yolks with the capers and add them to the pan. Warm through on a gentle heat. Sprinkle with the chopped parsley and serve immediately.

Fragrant Lamb Stew
Serves 6

Ingredients

150g/6oz creamed	*6 cloves*
coconut	*2 cardamom pods*
500ml/18fl oz hot water	*6-7 curry leaves*
1kg/2lb lamb, cut into	*7.5g/1¹⁄₂tsp salt*
2.5-cm (1-in) cubes	*30g/2tbsp Ghee (Clarified*
2-3 green chillies	*Butter)*
2.5cm (1in) ginger, cut	*1 small onion, finely*
into thin strips	*chopped*
2 large onions, diced	*2.5g/¹⁄₂tsp freshly milled*
5-cm (2-in) piece of stick	*pepper*
cinnamon	*15g/1tbsp flour*

Preparation Blend together the coconut and water until smooth.

In a large saucepan, put the lamb, chillies, ginger, onions, cinnamon, cloves, cardamom, curry leaves, salt and about 450ml/16fl oz of the coconut milk and bring to boil.

Cover, lower heat and simmer for 45 minutes. Add the remaining coconut milk and cook for a further 10 minutes. Remove from the heat.

In a small pan, heat the ghee and fry the onion until lightly browned. Add the pepper and the flour and, stirring constantly, mix the flour with the fried onion and ghee. Add a little of the meat gravy and mix until smooth.

Add this to the stew and, stirring constantly, bring to the boil. Serve hot with rice.

Fragrant Lamb Stew

Crown Roast of Lamb with Apricot Rice Stuffing
Serves 6

This is an excellent party dish as it can be prepared in advance.

Ingredients

2 best ends of neck (lamb)	2 stalks celery
45ml/1tbsp oil	100g/4oz dried apricots,
freshly ground pepper	steeped or 1 large can
Stuffing	apricots
100g/4oz long-grain or	10g/1tsbp sultanas
risotto rice	15g/1tbsp mixed nuts,
15g/1tbsp butter	chopped
1 onion, peeled and finely	1 egg, beaten
chopped	7g/1tbsp parsley, chopped
	salt and freshly ground
	pepper

Preparation Ask the butcher to prepare the crown roast, or, if this is not possible, have the best ends chined. Remove the skin from the fatty side of the joints. Cut along the fat about 3.5cm (1½in) from the top of the bone and remove fat and meat from the tops of the bones. Scrape the little end bones clean with a knife. Turn the meat over the cut between the cutlets to enable the joint to bend.

Stand the two pieces of meat up with the bones at the top. Turn fatty sides in and sew together at the top and bottom of the joints to make the crown roast. Paint over with oil and sprinkle with pepper.

For the stuffing, partially cook the rice for 10 minutes, rinse and allow to drain and cool. Heat the butter and oil and cook the onion for 4 minutes over a low heat. Add the chopped celery, chopped apricots (if using canned apricots retain 8 drained halves for garnish), sultanas and nuts. Lastly stir in the rice. Turn into a bowl and allow to cool. Mix with the egg yolk and parsley.

Fill the centre of the roast with the stuffing. Cover with a piece of foil.

Cover the individual tips of the bones with foil to prevent charring. Then completely cover with foil. Roast in the oven for 1½-2 hours at 180°C/350°F/Gas 4, depending on size of the cutlets.

Remove the crown roast to a heated plate and make gravy to accompany roast in the usual way. If using canned apricots, a little juice may be added to the gravy. Remove the string before carving.

Note Any excess stuffing may be used to stuff apricot halves which can be cooked brushed with oil for the last 30 minutes of cooking time.

Kashmiri Lamb with Fennel Seeds
Serves 6

Ingredients

8g/1¼tsp whole fennel	1kg/2lb lamb, cut into 2.5-
seeds	cm (1-in) cubes
90ml/6tbsp oil	10g/2tsp paprika
good pinch of asafetida	10g/2tsp chilli powder
(optional)	7.5g/1½tsp ground ginger
5-cm (2-in) piece of stick	5g/1tsp salt
cinnamon	500ml/18fl oz yoghurt,
4 cardamom pods	lightly beaten
4 cloves	

Preparation Put the fennel seeds in a grinder and grind until fine.

Heat oil in a large saucepan over a high heat. Add the asafetida (if used) and after 2 seconds add the cinnamon, cardamom and cloves and let them sizzle for 4-5 seconds.

Add the lamb and fry, stirring constantly, for about 5-7 minutes. Add the paprika, chilli, ginger and salt and fry for another 2-3 minutes.

Add the yoghurt, mix with the lamb, and cook for 10 minutes. Add the fennel, stir well to mix, cover, lower heat to very low and cook for about 1 hour, stirring occasionally, until the meat is tender and the gravy thickened. Serve with rice.

Lamb Chops with Apricot Marsala Sauce
Serves 4

Ingredients

225g/8oz dried apricots	1 onion, peeled and finely
300ml/½pt orange juice	chopped
60ml/4tbsp Marsala	15g/1tbsp flour
25g/1oz butter	300ml/½pt chicken stock
15ml/1tbsp oil	parsley sprigs
4 double lamb chops	

Preparation Cut the apricots in half and soak in the orange juice and Marsala for at least 4 hours.

Melt the butter and oil on a medium-high heat and brown the chops on each side. Transfer to an ovenproof dish.

Lower the heat and cook the finely chopped onion for 3 minutes. Sprinkle the flour on the onion and stir well with the juices in the pan.

Add the stock gradually and the strained liquid from the apricots. Stir continuously and bring to the boil. Season well. Stir in the apricots.

Pour the sauce over the chops and cook in the oven, covered with a lid or foil, for 45 minutes.

Serve garnished with parsley sprigs and boiled new potatoes in their skins with peas or French beans.

Lamb Biriyani
Serves 8

Ingredients

1kg/2lb lamb, cut into large pieces	6 cardamom pods, skinned
1kg/2lb basmati rice	90-120ml/6-8tbsp milk
2.5cm (1in) ginger	1tsp saffron threads
4 cloves garlic	150g/6oz Ghee (Clarified Butter)
28g/4tbsp coriander leaves	3 large onions, halved and finely sliced
7g/1tbsp mint leaves	
4 green chillies	10g/2tsp chilli powder
8 cloves	juice of 2 lemons
2×2.5-cm (1-in) pieces of stick cinnamon	450ml/16fl oz yoghurt
	15g/3tsp salt
5g/1tsp black cumin seeds	3l/5pt water
1/4 nutmeg	

Preparation Wash the meat and leave in a colander to allow all the water to drain out.

Wash the rice in several changes of water. Soak for 15 minutes in water and then leave in a sieve to drain.

Blend the ginger, garlic, coriander, mint and green chillies to a fine paste.

Grind together 4 cloves, 1 piece of stick cinnamon, 1/2tsp black cumin seeds, nutmeg and 3 cardamom pods to a fine powder.

Warm 30ml/2tbsp milk and soak the saffron in it. Put aside.

Heat the ghee and fry the onions until golden brown. Drain and put aside, reserving the ghee.

Put the meat in a large bowl, add the coriander paste and, with the back of a wooden spoon, beat the meat for 15-20 minutes, turning the meat frequently.

To the meat add the chilli powder, lemon juice, yoghurt, 10g/2tsp salt, the powdered spices and half the fried onions, mix and put aside for 3-4 hours.

In a saucepan, melt the ghee again over a medium high heat and add the meat and the marinade. When it starts to boil, lower the heat, cover and, stirring occasionally, cook for about 1 hour until the meat is tender and the gravy thickened.

While the meat is being cooked, bring the water to a boil in a large saucepan. Add the remaining spices and salt.

When the water is boiling rapidly, add the drained rice, bring it back to the boil and boil the rice for 3-4 minutes until the rice is nearly cooked. Remove and drain the rice.

Lightly grease a large casserole dish big enough to hold all the rice and meat, and put half the cooked rice evenly over the bottom. Put the meat and gravy on the rice and the remaining rice on top.

Sprinkle the saffron milk, the remaining milk and the rest of the fried onions on top. Cover tightly with aluminium foil and then the lid and put in a preheated oven at 190°C/375°F/Gas 5 for about 45 minutes until the rice is cooked.

Lamb Chop Kebabs
Serves 6

Ingredients

0.75kg/1 1/2lb lamb chops	4g/3/4tsp Garam Masala
450ml/16fl oz yoghurt	10g/1tbsp poppy seeds, ground
7.5g/1 1/2tsp salt	
2.5cm (1in) ginger, grated	2-3 green chillies, ground
8 cloves garlic, crushed	30ml/2tbsp oil

Preparation Remove excess fat from the chops. Wash and pat dry.

Lightly beat the yoghurt and mix in all the ingredients.

Add the lamb chops and marinate for at least 6 hours. You can marinate them for 24 hours, but the meat should be covered and refrigerated, then returned to room temperature before grilling.

Take the chops out of the marinade and place on a baking sheet. Cook under a preheated grill for 8-10 minutes on each side.

Lamb Chop Kebabs

Lamb Dhansak
Serves 4-6

Doddy is a vegetable widely available in Indian supermarkets and grocers' stores.

Ingredients

400g/14oz red lentils, washed
pumpkin, peeled and cut into 2.5-cm (1-in) pieces
350g/12oz doddy, peeled and cut into 2.5-cm (1-in) pieces
1 medium potato, peeled and diced
1 medium onion, chopped
5g/1tsp ground turmeric
10g/2tsp salt
3 medium tomatoes, chopped
675g/1½lb lamb, cut into 2.5-cm (1-in) cubes

50ml/2fl oz oil
2.5-cm (1-in) ginger, grated
3 cloves garlic, crushed
3 dried red chillies, ground
7g/1½tsp ground coriander
7g/1½tsp ground cumin
2.5g/½tsp ground mustard
2.5g/½tsp fenugreek seeds, ground
7g/1½tsp sambar powder (optional)

Preparation Put the lentils, pumpkin, doddy, potato, onion, turmeric and salt in a large saucepan, and add enough water to cover it by 3.75cm (1½in). Bring to the boil and simmer until tender. Add the tomatoes

and cook for a further 10 minutes. Pass the lentils and vegetables through a sieve and put aside.

Boil the meat in a little water for about 45 minutes until tender. Put aside.

Heat the oil in a large saucepan over a medium heat. Add all the spices and fry for 1-2 minutes, stirring constantly, so that they do not stick. If necessary, sprinkle on a few drops of water to prevent the spices from burning. Add the lentils and lamb and simmer on a low heat for about 30 minutes. (The lentils should be quite thick.)

Lamb Extravaganza
Serves 4-6

Ingredients

450g/1lb lamb fillet
30g/3tbsp paprika
20g/2tbsp chilli powder
15g/2tbsp fresh coriander, chopped
15g/2tbsp fresh parsley, chopped
70ml/6tbsp crème fraîche or thick yoghurt
45ml/3tbsp oil
2 cloves garlic
1 onion, finely chopped

100g/4oz mushrooms, sliced
1 red pepper, seeded and sliced
450g/16oz pineapple slices in own juice, quartered
275ml/½pt strong black coffee
20g/4tsp cornflour and water to mix
lime and coriander to garnish

Preparation Cut the meat into 2.5-cm (1-in) cubes. Mix together the paprika, chilli, coriander, parsley and Crème Fraîche in a bowl. Coat the meat with this mixture.

Heat the oil in a deep frying pan and lightly fry the garlic and vegetables for 2-3 minutes. Drain. Cook the meat for 10 minutes stirring occasionally, and mix in the vegetables.

Add the pineapple and coffee and simmer for 10 to 15 minutes. Blend the cornflour with a little cold water and add to the pan. Stir until the sauce thickens. Adjust the seasoning.

Garnish with slices of lime and sprigs of coriander. Serve with brown rice.

Lamb in Dill Sauce with Tagliolini
Serves 4

Ingredients

60ml/4tbsp oil
1 medium onion, peeled and diced
450g/1lb minced lamb
15g/2tbsp fresh white breadcrumbs
salt and freshly ground pepper
7g/1tbsp parsley, chopped
1 egg, beaten
2.5ml/½tsp Worcestershire sauce

450g/1lb fresh tagliolini verdi or fettucini
12.5g/½oz butter, melted
nutmeg
2 egg yolks
300ml/½pt sour cream
10g/2tsp dried dill
juice of 1 lemon
dill or parsley, freshly chopped

Preparation Heat half the oil in a frying pan and cook the onion over a low heat until soft and transparent. Drain from the pan with a slotted spoon and reserve the remaining oil. Put the onion in a mixing bowl and allow to cool.

Add the minced lamb to onion with the breadcrumbs, seasoning, beaten egg and Worcestershire sauce.

Mix well and with floured hands shape the mixture into balls 2.5cm (1in) in diameter. Roll them lightly in seasoned flour.

Add the remaining oil to the pan and brown the meatballs over a high heat for about 1 minute each side. Reduce heat and continue cooking for about 8 minutes.

Cook the fresh green tagliolini or fettucini for 2-3 minutes in boiling salted water with a few drops of oil. Drain the pasta and toss in a little melted butter with a shake of nutmeg. Arrange meatballs on the pasta and keep warm for a few minutes until the sauce is made.

To make the sauce, mix the egg yolks with a little cream and then add the dill. Add the remaining cream to the juices in the pan in which the meat was fried. Stir well, add some of the warm cream to the egg and return to the pan. Add lemon juice and warm through.

Pour the warmed sauce onto the meatballs, sprinkle with fresh dill or parsley and serve immediately. Do not boil the sauce if you are re-heating it.

Lamb with Fennel and Lemon Sauce
Serves 6

This dish comes from Greece. If you wish, you can replace the lamb with pork, chicken, veal or turkey.

Ingredients

2 bulbs fennel, trimmed and sliced
30ml/2tbsp oil
1kg/2lb lean, boneless lamb, cubed
2 medium onions, finely chopped
15g/2tbsp parsley, chopped
15g/1tbsp flour

150ml/¼pt red wine
600ml/1pt good lamb, veal or chicken stock
bouquet garni
salt and freshly ground pepper
2 eggs
60ml/4tbsp lemon juice

Preparation Blanch the fennel in boiling, salted water for 5 minutes. Drain, reserving the stock for soup and refresh the fennel with cold water. Drain thoroughly, and set aside.

Heat the oil in a heavy, flameproof casserole or pan and quickly brown the meat on all sides — this may have to be done in several batches. Drain well, remove and set aside on a plate.

Add the blanched fennel and the chopped onion and parsley to the casserole and cook over low heat for 10 minutes until soft and golden, stirring occasionally. Stir in the flour, cook for 1 minute, then stir in the wine, half the stock, and the bouquet garni, and bring to the boil, stirring constantly. Replace the meat, add a little salt and pepper, then cover and simmer gently for 1½ hours or until tender, stirring from time to time.

Make the sauce just before serving — whisk the eggs with the lemon juice.

Bring the remaining stock to the boil, remove from the heat and leave to cook for 1 minute. Then pour the hot stock onto the egg mixture whisking all the while. Remove the casserole from the heat, and stir in the sauce. Taste and adjust seasoning. Cover and leave to stand in a warm place, or on top of a hot plate for 10 minutes, for the flavours to blend. Serve with new potatoes or plain boiled rice.

Lamb Kidneys in Red Wine
Serves 4

Ingredients

12 lamb kidneys, skinned	150g/6oz mushrooms,
15g/1tbsp flour	washed and sliced
salt and freshly ground	2 tomatoes, skinned and
pepper	chopped
50g/2oz butter	150ml/¼pt red wine
1 onion, peeled and sliced	7g/1tbsp chopped parsley

Preparation Remove the core from each kidney and cut in half. Dredge with seasoned flour.

Heat the butter and gently cook the onion on a low heat. Remove from the pan into an ovenproof dish.

Sauté the kidneys for a few minutes on either side until golden brown. Add mushrooms and continue cooking for about 2 minutes.

Add the tomatoes and red wine. Spoon into the ovenproof dish, cover with foil and bake for 25 minutes at 180°C/350°F/Gas 4.

Serve individual portions in a ring of rice on the plate and garnish with parsley.

Lamb Kebabs
Serves 3

Ingredients

1 medium onion	450g/1lb lean, boneless
3 cloves garlic	lamb, cut into 2.5-cm
2.5cm (1-in) ginger	(1-in) cubes
2.5-cm (1-in) piece of stick	5g/1tsp salt
cinnamon	5g/1tsp chilli powder
2 cardamom pods, skinned	150 ml/¼pt yoghurt
5g/1tsp poppy seeds	Ghee (Clarified Butter) for
⅛ nutmeg	basting
1 clove	lemon wedges
2 peppercorns	

Preparation In a blender or food processor, blend together the onion, garlic and ginger, adding a little water if necessary.

Grind the cinnamon, cardamom, poppy seeds, nutmeg, clove and peppercorns to a fine powder.

Place the lamb in a large bowl, add the onion paste, powdered spices, salt, chilli powder and yoghurt, and mix thoroughly. Cover the bowl with plastic wrap and place in the refrigerator overnight to marinate.

Divide the meat between 6 skewers. Put under a hot grill and baste occasionally with the ghee. Turn once or twice and cook until tender — about 10 minutes.

Serve hot with wedges of lemon.

Lamb Korma
Serves 6

A korma is a mild curry, and because it is popular with everyone it is frequently served by Indian Muslims at the Festival of Id, which celebrates the end of Ramadan, the period of fasting. Chicken is often cooked in this manner and indeed this recipe can be adapted using chicken.

Ingredients

2 large onions, sliced	5g/1tsp ground turmeric
4 cloves garlic	1 tomato, peeled and
2.5-cm (1-in) piece root	chopped
ginger, finely chopped	pinch grated nutmeg
oil	pinch ground cinnamon
1kg/2lb boned shoulder of	pinch ground cloves
lamb, trimmed and	salt and pepper
cubed	150ml/¼pt water
15g/1tbsp ground	10g/2tsp cornflour
coriander	15ml/1tbsp water
10g/2tsp ground cumin	150ml/¼pt yoghurt

Preparation Put half the onions into a blender with the garlic and ginger and blend until smooth. Fry the remaining onion in oil until soft. Remove from the pan and reserve it. Brown the cubed meat, adding more oil if necessary. Remove the meat and keep it with the reserved onion. Add the blended mixture to the pan, stir well and fry for 5 minutes. Lower the heat and add the coriander, cumin and turmeric. Cook these for a further 3 minutes. Add the tomato and cook for 2 minutes. Add the remaining spices and cook them on a gentle heat for 5 minutes, stirring occasionally. Return the meat and onions to the pan with the 150ml/¼pt of water, bring to the boil, then cover and simmer for 30 minutes. Mix the cornflour with the tablespoon of water and add it to the yoghurt. Stir the yoghurt into the lamb and warm the sauce through.

Serve with rice, chapatis, poppadums and chutney.

Lamb Kebabs

Lamb and Okra Stew
Serves 6

The okra in this stew gives it a natural thickness and savoury taste. Be careful not to overcook the okra, or it will become stringy.

Ingredients

40g/1½oz butter or margarine	350ml/12fl oz Chicken Broth
1kg/2½lb boneless stewing lamb, cubed	2.5g/½tsp salt
100g/4oz chopped onion	2.5g/½tsp black pepper
2.5g/1tsp ground cumin	2.5g/½tsp sugar
225g/8oz canned tomatoes	450g/1lb fresh okra
60ml/4tbsp tomato purée	100ml/4fl oz water
	100ml/4fl oz white vinegar

Preparation Melt 25g/1oz of the butter or margarine in a large frying pan. Add the lamb cubes and sauté until they are browned on all sides. Add the onion, cumin, tomatoes, tomato purée, chicken broth, salt, pepper and sugar to the pan. Cook over a low heat, stirring frequently, for 5 minutes.

Preheat the oven to 165°C/325°F/Gas 3. Transfer the lamb mixture from the frying pan to a medium-sized casserole. Cover the dish and bake for 90 minutes.

Trim the okra and cut it into thin slices. Soak the slices in the water and vinegar for 20 minutes. Drain and pat the okra dry with paper towels.

Melt the remaining butter or margarine in a small frying pan. Add the okra slices and sauté for 6 minutes, stirring frequently.

After the casserole has baked for 90 minutes, add the okra slices to it. Stir well, cover the dish, and bake for a further 40 minutes. Serve hot.

Lamb and Lentil Meatballs
Serves 4

Ingredients

450g/1lb lean minced lamb	5g/1tsp salt
75g/3oz lentils, washed and drained	100ml/4fl oz water
2 large black cardamom pods, skinned	1 egg, lightly beaten
6 black peppercorns	**Filling**
1 medium onion, chopped	1 medium onion, finely chopped
3 cloves garlic, crushed	3 green chillies, chopped
2.5cm (1-in) ginger, grated	20g/3tbsp coriander leaves, chopped
2.5g/½tsp chilli powder	oil for frying
	lemon wedges

Preparation In a saucepan, put the minced lamb, lentils, cardamom, peppercorns, onions, garlic, ginger, chilli powder, salt and water. Bring to a boil over a medium high heat. Cover, lower the heat and simmer until the lentils are tender and all the water absorbed.

Place the mixture in a food processor or liquidizer and blend until smooth. Mix in the beaten egg, and divide into 16-18 small balls.

Combine the ingredients for the filling and put aside.

Take a minced lamb and lentil ball, and with your thumb, make a depression in the middle to form a cup shape. Fill the centre with a little filling and re-form into a smooth ball. Flatten slightly.

Heat the oil in a large frying pan and fry the meatballs, turning once until nicely browned. Drain.

Serve hot with wedges of lemon and a salad.

Lamb with Spinach
Serves 4-6

Ingredients

90ml/6tbsp oil	2cm (¾in) ginger, grated
4 cardamom pods	2.5g/½tsp ground turmeric
5-cm (2-in) piece of stick cinnamon	5g/1tsp chilli powder
3 bay leaves	675g/1½lb lamb, cut into 2.5-cm (2-in) cubes
2 medium onions, finely sliced	5g/1tsp salt
2 cloves garlic, crushed	675g/1½lb frozen spinach, chopped

Preparation Heat the oil in a large saucepan, add the cardamom, cinnamon and bay leaves and let them sizzle for 4-5 seconds.

Add the onions, garlic and ginger and fry until the onions are golden brown. Add the turmeric and chilli and fry for another minute. Add the lamb and salt and mix well with the spices.

Cover, lower heat to very low and cook for about 30 minutes, stirring occasionally.

Add the spinach and continue to cook until all the liquid has evaporated.

Lamb Tikka
Serves 4

Ingredients

550g/1¼lb leg of lamb (in a single thick slice)
300ml/½pt natural yoghurt
5g/1tsp chilli powder
5g/1tsp crushed coriander
5g/1tsp Garam Masala
2.5g/½tsp salt

juice of 1 fresh lime or lemon
8 lettuce leaves
2 tomatoes, sliced
12 slices of cucumber
1 small onion, peeled and finely sliced
1 lemon or lime, quartered

Preparation Leg of lamb sliced about 1.2cm (½in) thick is best for this dish. Remove any bone or gristle. Cut into 1.2-cm (½-in) cubes.

Mix yoghurt with the spices, salt and lime or lemon juice in a plastic bag or a flat dish. Add the meat to the marinade and allow to soak for several hours. Turn from time to time.

Divide the meat onto 4 skewers and cook under a hot grill, turning every two minutes.

Serve each portion off the skewer with Pilau Rice and a green salad. Garnish with the remaining ingredients and accompany with the sauce of your choice.

Lamb-Stuffed Artichokes
Serves 8

Ingredients

15ml/1tbsp olive oil
1 onion, finely chopped
25g/1oz pine nuts
450g/1lb minced lamb
15g/2tbsp chopped parsley
2.5g/½tsp black pepper
pinch salt

8 large artichokes, stems trimmed and outermost leaves removed
900ml/1½pt water
25g/1oz butter
50ml/2fl oz lemon juice

Preparation Heat the oil in a small saucepan. Add the onion and pine nuts and cook for 3-5 minutes over a low heat.

Combine the lamb with the onions and pine nuts in a small mixing bowl. Add the parsley, pepper and salt. Mix thoroughly.

Stuff the artichokes with the meat mixture, inserting small quantities between the leaves with a teaspoon.

Place the artichokes upright in 2 large saucepans, 4 in each pot. Fill each pot with half the water. Reduce the heat to low and cover the pots. Steam the artichokes for 45 minutes and then drain well.

In a small saucepan, melt the butter and add the lemon juice. Pour the mixture over the artichokes and simmer for 15 minutes. Serve warm.

Lamb with Onions
Serves 6

Ingredients

1kg/2lb lamb, cut into 2.5-cm (1-in) cubes
2.5g/½tsp ground turmeric
2.5g/½tsp chilli powder
5g/1tsp ground cumin seeds
5g/1tsp ground coriander seeds
2.5cm (1-in) ginger, grated

2 cloves garlic, crushed
350ml/12fl oz yoghurt
5g/1tsp salt
4 large onions
150ml/10tbsp oil
4 cardamom pods
5-cm (2-in) piece stick cinnamon
3 cloves

Preparation Marinate the lamb with the turmeric, chilli, cumin, coriander, ginger, garlic, yoghurt and salt and set aside for 3-4 hours.

Cut three of the onions in half and finely slice them. Chop the remaining onions.

Heat the oil in a large saucepan over a medium high heat and fry the sliced onions, stirring occasionally, until golden brown. Drain on paper towels and put aside.

In the remaining oil add the cardamom, cinnamon and cloves and let them sizzle for 4-5 seconds. Add the chopped onion and fry until lightly browned. Add the meat and spices and fry, stirring constantly, for about 5-7 minutes.

Cover, lower heat to very low and simmer for about 1 hour until tender. Add two thirds of the fried onions and mix with the meat and cook for another minute.

Serve garnished with the remaining onions.

Hard-Boiled Eggs Wrapped in Spiced Meat
Serves 4

Ingredients

350g/12oz lamb, finely
  minced
15g/2tbsp coriander
  leaves, finely chopped
5g/1tsp salt
2-3 green chillies, finely
  chopped

3 cloves garlic, crushed
30g/3tbsp onion, finely
  chopped
45ml/3tbsp lemon juice
1 egg, beaten
4 hard-boiled eggs
oil for deep frying

Preparation Mix the minced lamb well with the coriander, salt, chillies, garlic, onion, lemon juice and the beaten egg, and divide into 4 portions.

Wrap each portion round a hard-boiled egg, making sure the egg does not show through at any point.

Deep fry over a medium high heat for about 4-5 minutes until nicely browned.

Cut in half lengthwise to serve.

Marinated Lamb Chops
Serves 4

Ingredients

8 best end of neck chops
30ml/2tbsp oil
30ml/2tbsp soy sauce
5g/1tsp brown sugar
salt and freshly ground
  pepper
5ml/1tsp lemon juice

Sauce
1 onion, finely chopped
30ml/2tbsp sherry
30ml/2tbsp water
30g/2tbsp redcurrant jelly
5g/1tsp ground coriander
100g/4fl oz canned
  pineapple pieces
7g/1tbsp parsley

Preparation Put the chops in a plastic bag with the oil, soy sauce, brown sugar, seasoning and lemon juice. Leave to marinate for several hours. Turn the bag around on a dish to help the meat to contact the marinade.

Arrange the chops on a rack over a roasting pan and roast in a preheated oven at 200°C/400°F/Gas 6 for 15-20 minutes.

Make the sauce by cooking the onion in the oil for 3 minutes. Add the remainder of the marinade from the chops and simmer for a few minutes. Add the sherry, water, redcurrant jelly, coriander, seasoning and pineapple pieces. Simmer for 15 minutes. The sauce may be liquidized before serving. Alternatively mix 5g/1tsp cornflour with 15ml/1tbsp water, add a little warmed sauce and return to the saucepan. Stir until sauce is slightly thickened.

Serve the chops on a bed of rice, sprinkled with chopped parsley. Pour or pass the sauce as you like.

Light Lamb Curry
Serves 6

Ingredients

90ml/6tbsp oil
3 medium potatoes, peeled
  and halved
4 cardamom pods
5-cm (2-in) piece of stick
  cinnamon
2 bay leaves
1 large onion, finely sliced
2 cloves garlic, crushed

2.5cm (1in) ginger, grated
5g/1tsp ground turmeric
2.5g/½tsp chilli powder
5g/1tsp salt
good pinch sugar
15ml/1tbsp vinegar
1kg/2lb lamb, cut into
  2.5-cm (1-in) cubes
900ml/1½pt water

Preparation Heat the oil in a large saucepan over a medium high heat, and fry the pieces of potato until evenly browned. Put aside.

Put the cardamom, cinnamon and bay leaves in the hot oil and let them sizzle for 4-5 seconds. Add the onions, garlic and ginger and fry until the onions are golden brown.

Add the turmeric, chilli, salt, sugar and vinegar and fry for another minute.

Add the lamb, mix with the spices and fry, stirring constantly, for 10-15 minutes until all the meat juices have evaporated.

Add the water and bring to a boil. Cover, lower heat and cook for 40 minutes, stirring occasionally.

Add the potatoes, cover again and cook for a further 20 minutes until the meat and potatoes are tender. Serve with rice.

Marinated Lamb Chops

Rack of Lamb in a Garlic Crust
Serves 4-6

Ingredients

*2 racks of lamb of 6-8
  chops each, chined
3 cloves of garlic, peeled
sprig rosemary
15ml/1tbsp oil
30g/3tbsp fresh white
  breadcrumbs*

*30ml/2tbsp redcurrant or
  guava jelly, warmed
7g/1tbsp parsley, chopped
2.5g/½tsp French mustard
salt and pepper*

Preparation Turn the lamb racks bone side up and
cut a narrow slit between each chop at the meaty end.

Slice one clove of garlic and stuff each slit with a
sliver of garlic and a blade of rosemary.

Put the lamb racks, fat side up, into an oiled roasting
pan and cut several shallow diagonal slashes in the fat.

Crush the remaining garlic cloves and mix with the
breadcrumbs, warmed jelly, parsley and mustard, and
season well with salt and pepper.

Smear this mixture over the lamb racks and leave for
1-2 hours. Roast for 25-35 minutes at 230°C/450°F/Gas
8, until well browned but still pink in the centre.

Persian Lamb Stew
Serves 6-8

Lots of fresh parsley is crucial to this dish. Use the
flat-leaved kind for maximum flavour.

Ingredients

*75g/3oz butter
12 spring onions, finely
  chopped
180g/7oz finely chopped
  parsley
1.75kg/3½lb lean lamb,
  cubed
1.9l/3½pt water
65ml/2½fl oz fresh lemon
  juice*

*1 lemon, cut into small
  wedges
675g/1½lb cooked (or
  canned) red kidney
  beans, drained weight
scant 12g/1tbsp salt
10g/2tsp freshly ground
  black pepper*

Preparation Melt half the butter in a medium
stockpot. Add the spring onions and parsley and sauté
until the parsley turns a dark green.

Melt the remaining butter in a large frying pan. Add
the cubed lamb and sauté until the cubes are lightly
browned.

Add the lamb to the stockpot. Add the water, lemon
juice and lemon wedges. Stir well, cover and simmer
for 1 hour 15 minutes. Stir in the kidney beans, salt and
pepper. Cover and simmer for another 20 minutes, or
until the lamb is tender. Serve with rice.

Sauté of Lamb with Cranberries
Serves 4

Ingredients

*30ml/2tbsp oil
4 loin lamb chops,
  trimmed
450g/1lb onions, thinly
  sliced
2 medium carrots, peeled
  and thinly sliced or
  shredded*

*100g/4oz fresh cranberries
30ml/2tbsp port
30ml/2tbsp redcurrant
  jelly
30ml/2tbsp stock
salt and freshly ground
  pepper
7g/1tbsp parsley, chopped*

Preparation Heat the oil in a sauté pan or heavy deep
frying pan, and brown the chops on each side. Drain
and remove. Add the onions and cook slowly over low
heat for 10 minutes. Stir in the carrots and cook for a
further 5 minutes. Add the cranberries, port, redcurrant jelly and stock. Bring to the boil, then add the
chops. Shake the pan well, then cover and simmer for
20 minutes, turning the chops after 10 minutes.

When the chops are tender, taste for seasoning. The
sauce should not be too wet, however, if the
cranberries are particularly juicy, remove the chops
and keep warm, then boil the liquid rapidly to reduce
to a thick glaze. Spoon over the chops and serve
garnished with the parsley.

Lamb with Almonds and Yoghurt
Serves 6-8

Ingredients

1kg/2lb onions	10g/2tsp poppy seeds,
1kg/2lb lamb, cut into	ground
2.5-cm (1-in) cubes	7 cloves garlic, crushed
5g/1tsp ground coriander	2.5cm (1in) ginger, grated
5g/1tsp ground cumin	6 cardamom pods, slightly
5g/1tsp chilli powder	crushed
10g/1½tsp salt	75g/3oz almonds,
225ml/8fl oz oil	blanched and slivered
450ml/16fl oz yoghurt	225ml/8fl oz single cream
2.5g/½tsp Garam Masala	

Preparation Peel all the onions and finely chop half of them. Finely slice the other half.

Put the lamb in a large bowl, add the chopped onions, coriander, cumin, chilli and salt, mix with the meat and marinate for 4-5 hours.

Heat the oil in a large frying pan and fry the sliced onions until brown. Drain them on paper towels and blend to a fine paste in a liquidizer or food processor without adding any water. (Keep the oil for making the curry.)

Put the yoghurt, Garam Masala and poppy seeds in a bowl, add the onion paste, mix thoroughly and put aside.

Heat 90ml/6tbsp of the reserved oil in a large saucepan over a medium high heat. Add the garlic and ginger and fry until very lightly golden.

Add the lamb and the spices and mix with the oil. Lower the heat and, stirring occasionally, cook until all the water that came out of the lamb has been absorbed.

Add the yoghurt paste, cardamom and almonds and mix with the meat. Cover and cook for about 30 minutes until the lamb is tender and the gravy very thick.

Add the cream and stir gently to mix. Cook for a further 10 minutes.

After the gravy has thickened and the lamb is tender, it can be transferred to an ovenproof dish, the cream gently mixed in and then put in a preheated oven at 175°C/350°F/Gas 4 for 10 minutes.

Simple Cassoulet
Serves 6-8

Ingredients

450g/1lb white haricot	2 medium onions, sliced
beans	4 cloves garlic, crushed
225g/8oz raw, smoked	30ml/2tbsp tomato purée
bacon	5g/1tsp sugar
bay leaf	1kg/2lb boned shoulder or
225g/8oz Toulouse or	breast of lamb cut into
Polish sausage, cut into	3.5-cm (1½in) chunks
2.5-cm (1-in) chunks	2.5g/½tsp dried oregano
2.5g/½tsp dried thyme	300ml/½pt red wine
seasoned flour	salt and pepper
45ml/3tbsp olive oil	450ml/¾pt stock or water

Preparation Wash the haricot beans and soak them in cold water overnight.

Change the water, add the bacon and the bay leaf and simmer, covered, for an hour. Drain, discard the bayleaf and cut the bacon into 2.5-cm (1-in) chunks. Put the bacon, beans and Toulouse or Polish sausage into a large casserole.

Roll the meat in seasoned flour and brown in oil.

Transfer to the casserole.

Fry the onions and garlic in the remains of the oil until they begin to brown. Add the tomato purée, sugar, herbs, wine and plenty of salt and pepper. Simmer for a couple of minutes, then pour into the casserole together with the stock or water.

Put the casserole, uncovered, into a hot oven (200°C/400°F/Gas 6) for 20 minutes, stirring gently from time to time. Cover the casserole, turn down the heat to 160°C/325°F/Gas 3 for a further 2½ hours, stirring occasionally, until the lamb and beans are tender. (You may need to add a little more water if it looks like getting dry.)

Souvlakia
Serves 4

This dish is particularly delicious when cooked on a barbecue.

Ingredients

450g/1lb leg of lamb	salt and freshly ground
12 bay leaves	pepper
juice of ½ a lemon	5g/1tsp oregano
30ml/2tbsp olive oil	lemon quarters

Preparation Allow one skewer for each person. Cut the lamb into 2.5-cm (1-in) cubes and thread onto the skewers with pieces of bay leaf in between. Leave space at either end of the skewers to enable them to rest on the grill.

Beat the lemon juice into the olive oil, season with salt, pepper and oregano and leave the lamb to marinate in the mixture in a plastic bag for at least 1 hour.

Cook under a hot grill for about 10 minutes turning occasionally, so that the lamb becomes well seared on the outside and tender and juicy inside.

Serve immediately with quarters of lemon to squeeze over the meat, a tomato and cucumber salad and a dish of rice.

Souvlakia

Wheat Grain Lamb
Serves 6

Ingredients

450g/1lb wholewheat
  grains
5 cardamom pods
2.5-cm (1-in) piece of stick
  cinnamon
6 cloves
2.5cm (1in) ginger
4 cloves garlic
150g/6oz Ghee (Clarified
  Butter)
4 medium onions, finely
  sliced
675g/1½lb boneless lamb,
  cut into 2.5-cm (1-in)
  cubes

5g/1tsp ground turmeric
10g/2tsp chilli powder
15g/1tbsp ground poppy
  seeds
30g/3tbsp desiccated
  coconut
15g/2tbsp coriander
  leaves, chopped
7g/1tbsp mint leaves,
  chopped
10g/2tsp salt
150ml/¼pt yoghurt
juice of 2 limes

Preparation Soak the wheat in plenty of water overnight. Drain. Put the wheat and some water in a large saucepan and bring to a boil. Cook until tender and mushy.

Grind the cardamom, cinnamon and cloves to a fine powder and the ginger and garlic to a fine paste.

In a large saucepan, heat the ghee and fry the onions until golden. Remove one third of the fried onions and put aside.

Add the ginger and garlic paste, the lamb, turmeric, chilli powder, poppy seeds, coconut, coriander and mint leaves, the salt and half the ground spices and stir fry for 5-6 minutes.

Add the yoghurt and mix thoroughly. Lower the heat. Cover and cook for about 30 minutes.

Add the remaining ground spices and continue to cook for about another 30 minutes until the meat is tender. Remove from the heat.

Add the boiled wheat and beat with the back of a wooden spoon until the meat disintegrates.

Add the lime juice and stir well. Bring to a boil again and boil for 5 minutes.

Serve garnished with the remaining fried onions.

Spicy Lamb Rissoles
Serves 4

This is an excellent dish for using up leftover lamb from a joint. These rissoles are also well suited to being made in advance and frozen until needed.

Ingredients

225g/8oz cooked minced
  lamb
30ml/2tbsp vegetable oil
1 large onion, peeled and
  minced or finely
  chopped
2.5g/½tsp oregano
1 clove garlic, crushed
15ml/1tbsp lemon juice
225g/8oz cooked
  long-grain rice
30ml/2tbsp water

salt and freshly ground
  pepper
pinch ground cumin
2.5g/½tsp paprika
7g/1tbsp chopped parsley
30ml/2tbsp water
15g/1tbsp flour
100g/4oz dried
  breadcrumbs
oil for frying
300ml/½pt Spicy Tomato
  Sauce

Preparation Heat the oil in a large frying pan and cook the onion for 4 minutes. Push to one side of the pan and fry the lamb, separating the meat with a fork or spoon.

Mix the oregano, garlic, lemon juice and cooked riced and allow to cool in a mixing bowl.

Add the seasoning, cumin, paprika and parsley to the lamb mixture and mix well. Add a little beaten egg to bind the mixture together.

Mix the eggs with 2tbsp water.

With floured hands form rice and lamb mixture into 5-cm (2-in) rissole shapes. Dip into the egg and water, and then into the breadcrumbs. Arrange on a tray and chill for at least 15 minutes before frying.

Heat the oil in a deep fat pan and fry for 4-5 minutes. Serve hot with the sauce and crisp green salad.

Spicy Lamb Rissoles

Spiced Lamb and Cheese Meatloaf
Serves 4-6

Serve this meatloaf with Ratatouille (minus the cheese), or cold with relish or chutney and Rainbow Salad.

Ingredients

225g/8oz large spinach
  leaves, washed
100g/4oz crustless granary
  or wholemeal bread,
  finely crumbled
450g/1lb lean lamb,
  trimmed and coarsely
  minced
2 eggs, lightly beaten
30ml/2tbsp oil
1 medium onion, finely
  chopped

2 cloves garlic, crushed
1 green chilli, seeded and
  finely chopped
5g/1tsp ground coriander
2.5g/¹⁄₂tsp ground cumin
salt and freshly ground
  pepper
100g/4oz Gruyère cheese,
  sliced

Preparation Grease a 1-kg (2-lb) loaf tin, and line the base with a strip of greaseproof or waxed paper.

Remove the stalks from the spinach and blanch in boiling salted water for 1 minute. Drain and rinse with cold water. Drain well, pat dry with paper towels, then line the prepared tin with the spinach leaves so they completely cover the sides and base. Save any spinach leaves which are left over.

In a mixing bowl combine the breadcrumbs, lamb and eggs until thoroughly blended.

Heat the oil in a pan, add the onion, garlic and chilli and fry for 2 minutes. Stir in the spices and fry for 1 minute. Allow to cool, then add to the bowl with a little salt and pepper. Chop any remaining spinach and add to the lamb mixture. Mix all these ingredients together until smooth and well blended.

Pack half the meat mixture into the loaf tin. Cover with the sliced cheese, then with the remaining meat mixture. Press down firmly with the back of a spoon. Cover the tin with foil, then stand the tin in a roasting pan half-filled with hot water. Bake in the preheated oven at 190°C/375°F/Gas 5 for 1³⁄₄ to 2 hours. Turn out and serve sliced.

Stuffed Vine Leaves
Serves 4-6

This is a Bulgarian version of a dish which appears throughout the Middle East. Vine leaves can be bought at Greek or Turkish shops, either canned or salted in brine. If you have your own vines, it is gratifying to be able to make use of the leaves.

Ingredients

15ml/1tbsp oil
50g/2oz rice
10g/2tsp paprika
1 medium 100g/4oz
  tomato, peeled and
  chopped
500ml/³⁄₄pt beef stock
450g/1lb ground lamb
salt and pepper

parsley, finely chopped
5g/1tsp dried marjoram
225g/8oz vine leaves (if
  using preserved leaves,
  otherwise about 35 fresh
  leaves)
2 eggs
225ml/7fl oz yoghurt

Preparation Heat the oil, add the onion and cook until it has just softened but not browned. Add the rice and paprika and stir around well. Add the tomato and cook for 3 minutes. Add half the stock to the pan and bring the mixture to the boil. Add this sauce to the ground meat and season with salt and pepper, parsley and marjoram. Mix together very well to make a smooth mixture.

Rinse the leaves if using preserved leaves or blanch them if using fresh leaves. Remove the stems. Put a teaspoonful of the meat mixture into each leaf on the rough side and roll it up, tucking in the edges. Squeeze each roll to pack it firmly. Pack the rolls into a flameproof oven dish and pour over the remaining beef stock. Put a plate on the vine leaves (to keep them from rising up), cover and simmer for 45 minutes.

Mix the eggs and yoghurt and when the vine leaves are cooked, carefully drain off the liquid and mix it into the egg and yoghurt. Pour this back onto the vine leaves and either warm through on a very gentle heat or bake at 180°C/350°F/Gas 4 for 10 minutes.

Casseroled Leg of Lamb
Serves 6-8

Ingredients

3-3.5kg/7-8lb leg of lamb,
  boned and tied
5g/1tsp salt
3 bay leaves
225ml/8fl oz red wine
  vinegar
450ml/16fl oz water
300g/10oz diced onions

12g/¹⁄₂oz parsley, coarsely
  chopped
2.5g/¹⁄₂tsp dried thyme
2.5g/¹⁄₂tsp black pepper
4 large tomatoes, coarsely
  chopped
25g/1oz chicken fat or
  olive oil

Preparation Rub the leg of lamb with the salt. Put the lamb in a large casserole.

In a small saucepan combine the bay leaves, vinegar, water, onions, parsley, thyme, pepper and tomatoes. Bring the liquid to a boil over a high heat. Cook for 1 minute and remove the saucepan from the heat. Cool the mixture to room temperature and pour it over the lamb. Leave the lamb to marinate in the refrigerator for 6 hours, uncovered. Turn the lamb every 1¹⁄₂hours.

Preheat the oven to 190°C/375°F/Gas 5. Melt the chicken fat in a small saucepan over a medium heat. Remove the lamb from the refrigerator. Pour the chicken fat or olive oil over the lamb. Roast the lamb for 2 hours, basting every 30 minutes. (If the liquid in the casserole starts to boil too fast, reduce the heat to 175°C/350°F/Gas 4). Save the pan drippings for gravy.

Simple Lamb Curry
Serves 4

Ingredients

450g/1lb boneless lamb	7g/1½tsp ground cumin
3 onions	5g/1tsp chilli powder
4 cloves garlic	2.5g/½tsp Garam Masala
2.5cm (1in) ginger	5g/1tsp salt
3 tomatoes	50ml/2fl oz yoghurt, lightly
45g/3tbsp Ghee (Clarified	beaten
Butter)	225ml/8fl oz water
10g/2tsp ground coriander	

Preparation Wash and dry the meat. Cut into 2.5-cm (1-in) cubes.

In a blender or food processor, blend together the onion, garlic and ginger to a fine paste.

Plunge the tomatoes into boiling water for 10 seconds. Peel and chop them and put aside.

Heat the ghee in a large saucepan and fry the onion paste, stirring constantly, until golden brown.

Add the coriander, cumin, chilli, Garam Masala and salt and stir-fry for 1-2 minutes.

Add the meat and fry for a few minutes with the spices.

Add the yoghurt, mix well and fry for a further minute.

Add the water and, when it starts to boil, lower the heat. Cover and cook for about 40 minutes, stirring occasionally.

Add the tomatoes, stir well to mix, cover again and cook for a further 25-30 minutes until the meat is tender and the gravy slightly thickened.

Orange Lamb Chops
Serves 4

Ingredients

30ml/2tbsp oil	juice of 2 oranges
8 lamb chops	salt and pepper
5ml/1tsp ground	150ml/¼pt yoghurt
cinnamon	1 egg yolk

Preparation Heat the oil, add the chops and brown them. Remove them to a flameproof oven dish. Add the cinnamon to the pan and stir it around. Add the orange juice and bring it to the boil, scraping the sediment from the bottom of the pan. Pour the juice over the lamb, season well, cover and bake at 180°C/350°F/Gas 4 for 1 hour.

Mix the yoghurt with the egg yolk. Take the chops from the dish and keep them warm. Add the yoghurt mixture to the pan and warm it through on a gentle heat.

Return the chops to the sauce and serve immediately.

Sweet and Sour Lamb
Serves 6

Ingredients

125ml/4fl oz oil	3 medium tomatoes,
675g/1½lb onions, halved	chopped
and sliced	450ml/16fl oz water
2.5g/½tsp chilli powder	45ml/3tbsp vinegar
pinch ground turmeric	10g/2tsp sugar
2.5cm (1in) ginger, grated	5g/1tsp salt
675g/1½lb lamb, cut into	
2.5-cm (1-in) cubes	

Preparation Heat the oil in a saucepan over a medium high heat and fry the onions until golden brown. Add the chilli, turmeric and ginger and, stirring constantly, fry for 1-2 minutes. Add the lamb and tomatoes and continue to fry for another 8-10 minutes, until the meat is browned.

Add the water, stir well and bring to a boil. Lower heat, cover and cook for about 45 minutes. Add the vinegar, sugar and salt and cook for another 15 minutes.

Tarragon Lamb
Serves 6

Ingredients

1kg/2lb boned shoulder of	40g/1½oz butter or
lamb, trimmed and	margarine
cubed	25g/1oz flour
5g/1tsp salt	15ml/1tbsp tarragon
10g/1tbsp dried tarragon	vinegar
or 15g/2tbsp fresh,	1 egg yolk
chopped	150ml/¼pt sour cream
600ml/1pt water	pepper
1 medium onion, chopped	

Preparation Put the lamb into a large pan with the salt, tarragon, water and onion. Bring to the boil and then cover and simmer for about 1 hour, or until the meat is tender. At this stage you might care to cool the lamb overnight and skim off the fat before continuing.

In a clean pan melt the butter and stir in the flour off the heat. Add a little stock from the meat and stir it in well to make a smooth sauce. Return this mixture to the meat and add the vinegar. Cook for 5 minutes. Mix the egg yolk into the sour cream. Add several spoonsful of the hot liquid, a little at a time, and then return the mixture to the pan on a very gentle heat. Stir through well.

Variation Substitute dill for the tarragon if you prefer.

Preparing Lambs' Kidneys

 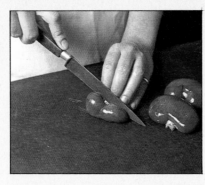 

1 Nick the membrane with a knife and pull it off.

2 Cut the kidneys lengthways through the core to give even halves.

3 Use scissors to remove all the white gristle and fat from the centre (the 'core'). Tuck the scissor points right in to snip out as much of the core as possible.

Beef and Veal

Beefburgers with Spicy Tomato Sauce   139
Cottabulla   139
Beef with Carrots   140
Indian Kebab   140
mediterranean Beef Casserole   140
Cholent   141
Little Meatballs   141
Beef Cobbler   141
Stuffed Peppers   142
Beef Patties   142
Corned Beef Stuffed Potatoes   143
Beef Goulash   143
Beouf Dijonnaise   143
Beef Satay   144
Korean Beef with Vegetable Noodles   145
Ground Beef Curry   145
Parsee Beef Curry   145
Ground Beef with Dill   145
Beef Stroganoff   146
Barbecued Ribs of Beef   147
Steak au Poivre Verte   147
Beef Strudel   147
Stir-Fried Beef with Baby Corn and Green Peppers   147

Beef Napoleon   148
Boiled Beef   148
Pickled Beef Tongue   148
Sauerbraten   149
Steak and Stout   149
Spiced Brisket I   150
Spiced Brisket II   150
Thai Beef with Spinach   150
Veal Paprika   151
Veal and Aubergine Casserole   151
Braised Veal Chops with Parsley Dressing   151
Veal Clou de Giroffe   151
Shoulder of Veal with Mushrooms and Spinach Fettucini   152
Sautéed Sherry Veal   152
Osso Buco   153
Veal Escalopes with Red Wine   153
Saltimbocca   153
Stuffed Veal Shoulder   154
Vitello Tonnato   154
Stuffed Cabbage Rolls   154

Preparing Veal or Beef Kidney and Veal Liver   155

Hamburgers with Spicy Tomato Sauce
Serves 4

Ingredients

450g/1lb lean minced beef	**Sauce**
1 onion, peeled and finely chopped	*5ml/1tsp oil*
	1 clove garlic, crushed
1 green pepper, seeded	*1 carrot, scraped and grated*
20g/2tbsp fresh breadcrumbs	*1 onion, peeled and finely chopped*
1 egg	
5ml/1tsp Worcestershire sauce	*1 chilli pepper seeded and chopped (optional)*
salt and freshly ground pepper	*200g/7oz canned peeled tomatoes*
	150ml/¼pt stock or water
	bay leaf
	2.5g/½tsp oregano

Preparation Put the meat in a bowl with the very finely chopped onion.

Chop the pepper into very small dice. If you prefer, both onion and pepper can be chopped in a blender.

Add the breadcrumbs. Mix with a beaten egg and add the Worcestershire sauce and seasoning.

Divided the mixture into 8 pieces and shape into rounds. A scone or pastry cutter is ideal for this purpose. Place on a tray in the refrigerator to chill while making the sauce.

To make the sauce heat the oil in a saucepan and cook over a low heat for 4 minutes. Add the garlic and grated carrot. Stir well and then add remaining ingredients. Season well. Simmer for at least 20 minutes on a low heat.

Brush the beefburgers over with oil and grill under a high heat for 4 minutes each side. If you like beef well cooked give the burgers a further 3 minutes.

Cottabulla
Jamaican Meatloaf
Serves 8

Ingredients

225g/½lb stale white bread, crusts removed	*5g/1tsp dried oregano*
	5g/1tsp paprika
1kg/2lb minced beef	*3 cloves of garlic, crushed*
2 medium onions, finely chopped	*pinch cayenne*
	5g/1tsp sugar
2 eggs	*salt and freshly ground black pepper*
5g/1tsp ground coriander	

Preparation Soak the bread in the water, squeeze out and crumble. Mix all the ingredients together thoroughly, seasoning with plenty of salt and pepper.

Pack into a large soufflé dish leaving a slight hollow in the middle. Cover with foil and bake for 40 to 50 minutes at 190°C/375°F/Gas 5 until cooked through, but still slightly pink in the middle.

While it is still hot, put a plate slightly smaller than the baking dish on top of the foil and weight it with some heavy cans. Leave until cold and firm, remove the weights and refrigerate until needed.

Slice into wedges and serve in its cooking dish.

Variation This can also be served hot. There is no need to weight it.

Shaped into patties, rolled in seasoned flour and fried, grilled or barbecued, this mixture makes sensational hamburgers!

Beef with Carrots
Serves 4-6

Ingredients

30ml/2tbsp oil	*5g/1tsp ground cumin*
1 large onion, chopped	*5g/1tsp sugar*
675g/1½lb stewing steak,	*300ml/½pt beef stock*
cubed	*salt and pepper*
450g/1lb carrots, sliced	*250ml/8fl oz yoghurt*

Preparation Heat the oil, add the onion and cook until it has just softened but not browned. Add the steak and brown it in the oil. Add the carrots, cumin and sugar, and stir well. Add the stock and seasoning. Bring to the boil, cover and bake at 140°C/275°F/Gas 1 for 3 hours.

Remove from the oven, stir in the yoghurt carefully and heat through gently before serving.

Indian Kebab
Serves 4

Ingredients

1 egg	*2 cloves garlic, crushed*
450g/1lb finely minced	*salt to taste*
beef	*1 onion, grated or*
5g/1tsp coriander seeds,	*liquidized*
ground	*breadcrumbs (optional)*
2.5g/½tsp chilli powder	*30ml/2tbsp oil*
2.5g/½tsp cumin	*1 lemon, sliced, pips*
2.5g/½tsp garam masala	*removed*
	1 onion, sliced into rings
	1 tomato, skinned and
	sliced

Preparation Mix the lightly beaten egg and beef in a bowl. Add the spices, salt and grated onion to the beef and use breadcrumbs to stiffen and bind the mixture if necessary.

Oil your fingers and the skewers. Wrap the meat around the skewers in cigar shapes. Brush the meat with oil and cook under a moderate grill until evenly browned.

Serve garnished with lemon, onion and tomato slices.

Mediterranean Beef Casserole
Serves 4

This is an excellent dish to prepare in advance as the flavour improves when the dish is re-heated.

Ingredients

675g/1½lb lean braising	*salt and freshly ground*
steak	*black pepper*
2 rashers bacon	*1-2 bay leaves*
30g/2tbsp seasoned flour	*1 bouquet garni*
60ml/4tbsp oil	*sprig of fresh or 5g/1tsp*
2 onions, peeled and diced	*dried thyme*
2 cloves garlic, crushed	*100g/4oz mushrooms*
2 stalks celery, washed	*350g/12oz penne pasta*
1 carrot, washed and sliced	*15g/½oz butter*
2 red peppers, seeded and	*pinch of nutmeg*
diced	*7g/1tbsp parsley, freshly*
425g/15oz canned	*chopped (optional)*
tomatoes	
300ml/½pt stock or water	
60ml/4tbsp red wine	

Preparation Trim the meat to remove excess fat or gristle, cut into small 1.5-cm (½-in) cubes. Toss the cubes in seasoned flour.

Heat half the oil in a frying pan on a high heat, turn down a little and fry the meat on all sides to seal. Drain on to a plate and leave the meat juices in the frying pan.

Put the remaining oil in an ovenproof casserole and cook the onion over a low heat for about 3 minutes. Add crushed garlic.

Remove the strings from the celery with a sharp knife and then cut into neat slices. Add to the onions. Add the carrot and diced peppers, toss all vegetables in the oil over a low heat for 2 minutes. Add the meat and tomatoes to the casserole.

Pour the stock into the frying pan and mix with the meat juices and the red wine over a low heat. Pour over the meat and vegetables. Add the herbs.

Bring to the boil and cook in the oven at 180°C/ 350°F/Gas 4 for 1 hour or until meat is tender. Add mushrooms either sliced or whole half way through the cooking time. The casserole may be cooked on top of the cooker but must only simmer gently for about 45 minutes.

Cook the pasta in boiling salted water with a few drops of oil added for approximately 12 minutes. Drain and toss in a little melted butter with a shake of pepper and nutmeg.

Serve the pasta with the casserole which may be garnished with chopped parsley.

Little Meatballs
Serves 8

Ingredients

1 kg/2 lb beef chuck steak, ground	*1 clove garlic, finely chopped*
55g/3½ tbsp tomato purée	*pinch dried oregano*
450ml/16fl oz chicken stock	*pinch dried rosemary*
60g/4 tbsp grape jelly	*25g/1oz chicken fat*
2.5g/½ tsp salt	*2.5g/½ tsp dried dill*
pinch ground white pepper	*2.5g/½ tsp dried basil*

Preparation In a large mixing bowl combine the ground beef, tomato purée, 100ml/4fl oz of the chicken stock, grape jelly, salt, white pepper, garlic, oregano and rosemary. Mix well. Shape the mixture into meatballs approximately 2.5cm (1in) in diameter.

In a large saucepan, melt the chicken fat over a low heat. Add the meatballs and brown for 5 minutes. Add the remaining chicken broth and the dill and basil. Simmer for 15 minutes over a very low heat. Serve warm.

Beef Cobbler
Serves 6-8

Ingredients

1 kg/2 lb stewing steak	*15g/1 tbsp paprika*
50g/2oz seasoned flour	*15ml/1 tbsp tomato purée*
60ml/4 tbsp oil	*300ml/½ pt red wine*
450g/1 lb onions, cut into 2.5-cm (1-in) chunks	*300ml/½ pt stock or water*
4-5 cloves garlic, crushed	*salt and pepper*
350g/12oz large carrots, cut into 1-cm (½-in) rounds	*225g/8oz plain flour*
	15g/2½ tsp baking powder
10g/2 tsp dried mixed herbs	*50g/2oz butter or shortening*
5g/1 tsp sugar	*150ml/¼ pt cold milk & water*

Preparation Trim the meat of fat and membrane and cut into 3-cm (1¼-in) chunks. Roll in the seasoned flour and fry rapidly in the oil in batches until browned all over. Transfer the meat to a large casserole and sprinkle with any remaining seasoned flour.

Fry the onions and garlic until they begin to brown and add to the casserole together with the carrots, herbs, sugar, paprika, tomato purée, wine, stock or water, and plenty of salt and pepper.

Stir gently and put the uncovered casserole into a hot oven for 20 minutes. Stir after 10 minutes.

Cover the casserole with foil, put its lid on and cook at 160°C/325°F/Gas 3 for a further 2 hours, stirring from time to time. Add more stock or water if it looks dry.

To make the scone topping, sift the flour and baking powder together and rub in the butter or shortening until the mixture resembles fine breadcrumbs.

Add plenty of salt and pepper and enough milk and water to make a soft dough.

Roll out to 1cm (½in) thick on a well-floured surface and stamp out circles 3.5-5cm (1½-2in) across.

Taste the stew and adjust the seasoning, adding a little more stock or water if necessary.

Arrange the scone circles on top of the stew and cook, uncovered, at 200°C/400°F/Gas 6 for 20 to 30 minutes, until the scones are puffy and well browned.

Cholent
Serves 8-10

Ingredients

225g/8oz dried baby butter beans	*2 cloves garlic, crushed*
225g/8oz dried red kidney beans	*5g/1 tsp black pepper*
	5g/1 tsp salt
225g/8oz dried yellow split peas	*10g/2 tsp paprika*
	2kg/4lb beef brisket
225g/8oz dried lentils	*700ml/1¼ pt white wine*
2oz butter or margarine	*675g/1½ lb potatoes, peeled and quartered*
4 large onions, quartered	

Preparation Preheat the oven to 230°C/450°F/Gas 8. Put the dried legumes in separate bowls. Add 700ml/1¼ pt of cold water to each bowl and leave the legumes to soak overnight. Drain well.

Melt the butter or margarine in a large heavy pot. Add the onions and brown them. Add the garlic, pepper, salt and paprika. Add the brisket and brown it.

Add the wine, 900ml/1½ pt cold water, all the legumes and the potatoes. Bring the liquid to a boil. Cover the pot tightly and place it in the oven. Bake for 1 hour, then reduce the heat to 150°C/300°F/Gas 2 and bake for a further 90 minutes.

Remove the brisket from the pot and let it rest for 10 minutes before slicing. Arrange the legumes and potatoes around the brisket and spoon over the broth.

Stuffed Peppers
Serves 4

Ingredients

4 large green peppers
450g/1lb ground beef
40g/1½oz cooked rice
1 small onion, finely
　chopped
pinch salt
2.5g/½tsp black pepper
1 egg yolk
50ml/2fl oz red wine
50g/2oz mushrooms,
　chopped

7.5ml/1½tsp raspberry or
　cider vinegar
1 medium tomato, seeded
　and chopped
50ml/2fl oz fresh lemon
　juice
30g/2tbsp sugar
pinch paprika
15ml/2tbsp brandy

Preparation Preheat the oven to 190°C/375°F/Gas 5. Cut the tops off the green peppers and carefully discard the seeds. Blanch the peppers in a large pot of boiling water for 3 minutes. Drain well and set aside.

In a large mixing bowl combine the minced beef, rice, onion, salt, pepper, egg yolk, wine and half the mushrooms. Mix well. Stuff the blanched peppers with the mixture.

Place the peppers on their sides in a large baking dish. Add the vinegar and enough water to fill the dish to a depth of 2 inches. Cover the dish and bake for 35 minutes.

Beef Patties

When the peppers have been in the oven for 30 minutes, combine the remaining mushrooms with the tomatoes, lemon juice, sugar, paprika and brandy in a small saucepan. Cover the saucepan and simmer over a very low heat for 5 minutes. Pour the mixture over the stuffed peppers.

Reduce the oven temperature to 150°C/300°F/Gas 2 and bake the stuffed peppers, uncovered, for a further 15 minutes. Serve warm.

Beef patties
Serves 4

Ingredients

450g/1lb minced beef
2 eggs
1 medium onion, chopped
1 large clove garlic, finely
　chopped
pinch ground rosemary

1 blade mace, broken
　between your fingers
dash soy sauce
pepper
fine matzo meal
vegetable oil for frying

Preparation Mix together all ingredients except for matzo meal and vegetable oil and shape into a dozen patties.

Coat both sides in matzo meal.

Heat vegetable oil until quite hot and fry the patties until brown on both sides.

Corned Beef Stuffed Potatoes
Serves 4

Children of all ages will love this meal in a potato.

Ingredients

4 large potatoes, scrubbed
5ml/1tsp oil
5g/1tsp salt
50g/2oz butter
1 medium onion, peeled and finely chopped
2 cloves garlic, peeled and crushed
1 stick celery, finely chopped

½ green pepper, cored, seeded and finely chopped
75g/3oz butter mushrooms, wiped and finely chopped
350-g/12-oz can corned beef, diced
salt and freshly ground pepper
75g/3oz Cheddar cheese, grated

Preparation Rub the potatoes with the oil and salt and bake in a preheated oven at 350°F/180°C/Gas 4 for about 1½ hours, or until tender.

Meanwhile, heat the butter in a frying pan, add the vegetables and stir-fry over medium heat for about 5 minutes or until slightly softened.

When the potatoes are ready, slice in half and scoop out the insides. Mash well and mix with the corned beef. Stir into the vegetables in the frying pan and reheat. Season to taste.

Heat the grill. Pile the mixture back into the potato skins. Sprinkle the cheese over the potatoes and grill until golden and bubbling. Serve immediately.

Beef Goulash
Serves 8

There is perhaps no dish so readily identifiable with Hungary than goulash. There are at least 80 standard variations calling for a variety of different ingredients. Below is a traditional beef goulash recipe.

Ingredients

65g/2½oz butter or margarine
1 large onion, coarsely chopped
1 large tomato, peeled, seeded and coarsely chopped
1 medium-sized green pepper, seeded and finely diced
2kg/4lb lean beef sirloin, cut into small pieces

700ml/1½pt beef stock
30g/2tbsp flour
30g/3tbsp poppy seeds
20g/2tbsp Hungarian sweet paprika
50ml/2fl oz dry red wine
225ml/8fl oz water
450g/1lb egg noodles
60ml/4tbsp sour cream

Preparation Melt the butter or margarine in a large saucepan over a low heat. Add the onion, tomato and green pepper and sauté for 5 minutes.

Add the beef, beef stock, flour, poppy seeds, paprika and red wine. Simmer for 30 minutes. Add the water, cover, and simmer for 90 minutes.

While the goulash simmers, cook the egg noodles in a large pan of boiling water. Drain well. Serve the goulash on a bed of noodles, and drizzle the cream over the dish.

Boeuf Dijonnaise
Serves 4-6

You may be able to buy fillet ends, which are much cheaper than the better end of the fillet and will do perfectly well for this type of dish.

Ingredients

30ml/2tbsp oil
1 large onion, sliced
675g/1½lb fillet of beef, cut into strips

15g/1tbsp seasoned flour
300ml/½pt beef stock
30ml/2tbsp Dijon mustard
150ml/¼pt yoghurt

Preparation Heat the oil, add the onion and cook until it has softened but not browned. Pass the beef strips through the seasoned flour and then brown them lightly. Add the stock and mustard to the pan, stirring well. Cover and simmer for 15 minutes. Stir the yoghurt in and gently warm it through.

Serve with rice and salad.

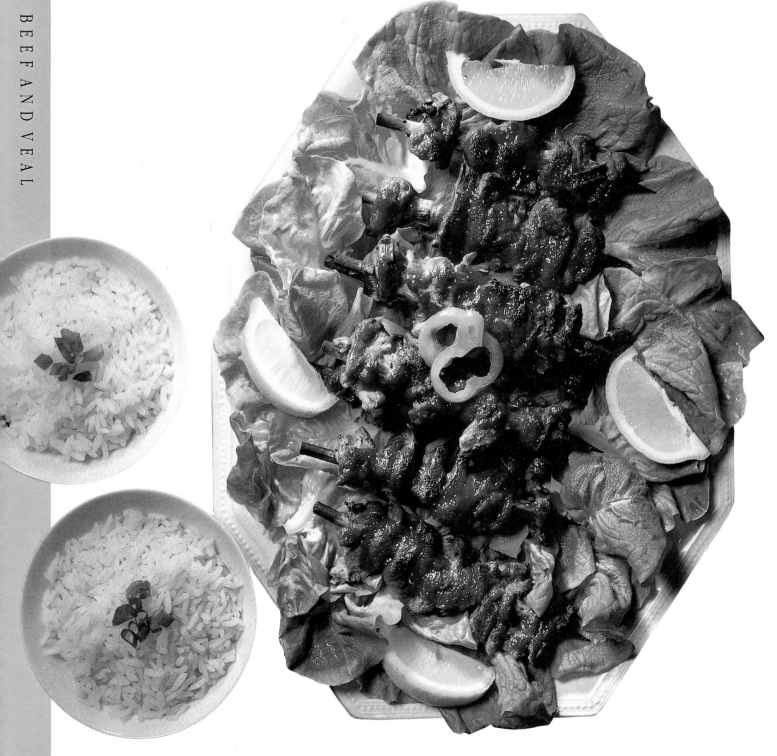

Beef Satay
Serves 4

Ingredients

2 spring onions, washed
2.5cm/1in fresh root
  ginger, grated
2 cloves garlic, crushed
8 cardamom pods
5g/1tsp cumin seeds
5g/1tsp coriander seeds
juice of 1 lemon
5g/1tsp grated or ground
  nutmeg
2 bay leaves
30ml/2tbsp oil
700g/1½lb rump steak

Sauce

90g/6tbsp peanut butter
15g/1tbsp brown sugar
2 chilli peppers, seeded
5g/1tsp sugar
150ml/¼pt beef stock
juice and rind of 1 lemon

Preparation Place all the ingredients except the meat in a blender to make a paste.

Trim the meat and cut into small squares. Mix with the paste and allow to marinate for several hours, then thread the meat onto skewers.

Make the sauce by mixing all the ingredients except the lemon juice together in a saucepan. Bring to the boil and simmer for about 20 minutes. Add the lemon juice.

While the sauce is cooking turn the grill onto a high heat and allow the skewered meat to cook. Turn every 2 minutes for the first 6 minutes, then lower the heat and continue cooking. The time will depend on whether you like your meat slightly rare or well cooked.

Accompany with boiled rice.

Korean Beef with Vegetable Noodles
Serves 4

Ingredients

225g/8oz rump or sirloin steak, thinly sliced
15g/1tbsp sugar
45ml/3tbsp soy sauce
4 spring onions
1 clove garlic, crushed
20g/2tbsp sesame seeds, roasted
100g/4oz transparent noodles, soaked in water for 20 minutes
40 Chinese mushrooms, soaked in water for 30 minutes
1 onion, peeled and sliced
1 carrot, peeled and cut into fine matchstick-like pieces
2 courgettes or ½ cucumber, trimmed and cut into sticks
½ red pepper, seeded and cut into strips
4 button mushrooms, sliced
75g/3oz bean sprouts, washed and drained
sesame oil for cooking
1-2 eggs, separated
salt and pepper

Preparation Chill the steak so that it is easier to slice finely and cut it into 5cm (2in) strips. Mix with the sugar, two thirds of the soy sauce, one of the spring onions, finely chopped, the garlic and a few crushed sesame seeds. Leave to marinate for an hour or two.

Cook the soaked and drained noodles in boiling water for 5 minutes. Drain well and separate by pulling apart. Drain the mushrooms and slice. Prepare the onion, carrot, courgettes or cucumber, red pepper, button mushrooms, bean sprouts and spring onions.

Heat a little oil in a frying pan or wok. Break the egg yolks and pour them into the pan. When they are set, remove them onto absorbent kitchen paper. Heat the pan again and pour in the egg whites. When these are set, drain, then cut up the yolk and white into strips or diamond shapes for the garnish.

Drain the marinade from the beef. Heat a little more sesame oil and stir-fry the beef until it changes colour. Add the carrot and onion next. Cook for 2 minutes then add all the other vegetables, tossing all the time until they are just cooked. Add noodles and soy sauce and taste for seasoning. Cook for 1 more minute.

Turn out onto a serving dish and garnish attractively with egg strips, the remaining spring onion, chopped and the rest of the sesame seeds.

Ground Beef Curry
Serves 4-6

Ingredients

15-30ml/1-2tbsp oil
1 large onion, sliced
1 clove garlic, crushed
675g/1½lb lean minced beef
10g/2tsp ground coriander
10g/2tsp ground cumin
5g/1tsp turmeric
2.5g/½tsp ground ginger
salt
15g/1tbsp cornflour
100ml/4fl oz water
300ml/½pt yogurt

Preparation Heat the oil, add the onion and garlic, and cook until they have just softened but not browned. Add the beef, a little at a time, and brown it well. Drain off any excess fat which may accumulate. Add the spices and salt and stir them in well. Cook for 5 minutes, stirring constantly.

Mix the cornflour with the water to a smooth paste. Add to the meat, together with the yoghurt. Stir well, cover and cook for 25 minutes on a gentle heat.

Serve with rice and usual curry accompaniments.

Parsee Beef Curry
Serves 6

Ingredients

400g/1lb lentils
400g/1lb lean beef
2 large onions, finely chopped
2 aubergines, coarsely chopped
1 green pepper, finely chopped
2 potatoes, peeled and coarsley chopped
450g/1lb spinach, washed and chopped
25g/5tsp ghee (clarified butter) or butter
5 cloves garlic, crushed
10g/1tbsp fenugreek seeds
15g/1tbsp cumin
5g/1tsp chilli
10g/1tbsp coriander seeds
5g/1tsp mint
salt

Preparation Wash the lentils and put them into a pan with the beef. Add the chopped vegetables and cover with water. Bring to the boil and simmer until the vegetables and meat are cooked.

Remove the meat and blend the vegetables and the lentils.

Heat up the ghee or butter and fry the garlic, fenugreek, cumin, chilli, coriander and mint. Add the lentils and meat, mix well and bring slowly to the boil, add salt to taste.

Serve with rice.

Ground Beef with Dill
Serves 4-6

Ingredients

15-30ml/1-2tbsp oil
1 large onion, chopped
675g/1½lb minced beef
15g/1tbsp dried dill
salt and pepper
125ml/¼pt yoghurt

Preparation Heat the oil, add the onion and cook until it has just softened but not browned. Add the beef and brown it. Drain off any excess fat. Add the dill, salt and pepper, cover and simmer for 30 minutes. Stir in the yoghurt and warm it through gently.

Serve with rice or pasta and a crisp salad.

Ground Beef Curry

Beef Stroganoff
Serves 4

Ingredients

350g/¾lb fillet or rump
   steak
25g/1oz butter
30ml/2tbsp vegetable oil
1 small onion, peeled and
   finely chopped
3 spring onions, washed
15g/1tbsp flour
pinch paprika
salt and freshly ground
   pepper

225g/8oz mushrooms,
   washed and sliced
15ml/1tbsp brandy
30ml/2tbsp madeira or
   sherry
150ml/¼pt beef stock
60ml/4tbsp sour cream
7g/1tbsp chopped parsley
onion rings

Preparation Trim the steak and cut into thin strips about 5cm (2in) long.

Heat the butter and oil in a frying pan and cook the onion for about 4 minutes over a low heat until translucent. Add the chopped spring onions, retaining a few rings of green for final garnish.

Meanwhile mix the flour with the paprika and seasoning and coat the meat strips evenly.

Add the sliced mushrooms to the onions and sauté gently for another 2 minutes. Remove the onions and mushrooms with a slotted spoon, leaving as much fat behind as possible.

Over a fairly high heat fry the meat for a few minutes; less for fillet steak than for rump. Heat the brandy in a ladle and ignite it with a match. Pour over the steak and allow to flame. Remove the meat and mix with the onion and mushrooms.

Add the madeira or sherry and any excess flour and paprika left over to the pan and stir well. Gradually add the stock, scraping all meat juices from the bottom of the pan. Add the meat, mushrooms and onions to the sauce and reheat for about 2-3 minutes. Turn the heat low. Add 2-3 tablespoons sour cream and mix well.

Serve in a ring of rice garnished with parsley, sour cream, onion rings, and a sprinkling of paprika. A crisp green salad or crisply cooked green vegetables, such as mangetout or french beans, makes an excellent accompaniment to this luxurious but quickly prepared dish.

Barbecued Ribs of Beef
Serves 6-8

Ingredients

15ml/1tbsp vegetable oil
1.5kg/3lb beef ribs, cut into
  2-in pieces
5g/1tsp salt
pinch pepper
5g/1tsp paprika
5g/1tsp dry mustard
15g/1tbsp sugar

15ml/1tbsp Worcestershire
  sauce
100ml/4fl oz tomato
  ketchup
100ml/4fl oz water
100ml/4fl oz cider vinegar
50g/2oz finely chopped
  onion
1 clove garlic, finely
  chopped

Preparation Preheat the oven to 175°C/350°F/Gas 4. Heat the vegetable oil in a flameproof casserole. Add the rib pieces and brown on all sides. Pour off the fat. Add the remaining ingredients to the casserole. Cover and bake for 2 hours. Remove the cover for the last 30 minutes. Arrange on a dish with parsley and serve.

Steak au Poivre Verte
Serves 4

Ingredients

50g/2oz unsalted butter
15g/1 full tbsp green
  peppercorns

15ml/1tbsp brandy
sea salt, freshly ground, to
  taste
4 steaks, 225g/8oz each

Preparation Liquidize the butter, peppercorns, brandy and salt until smooth.

Spread the flavoured butter on the steaks and grill under high heat until cooked the way you like them.

Beef Strudel
Serves 4-6

Ingredients

15ml/1tbsp oil
1 large onion, finely
  chopped
450g/1lb lean minced beef
75g/3oz rice, cooked
2 hard-boiled eggs,
  chopped

100g/4oz cottage cheese
salt and pepper
350g/12oz shortcrust
  pastry
egg for glazing
150ml/¼pt sour cream

Preparation Heat the oil, add the onion and cook until it has just softened but not browned. Add the meat, a little at a time, and brown it. Drain off excess fat. Add the cooked rice, chopped eggs, cottage cheese, salt and pepper. Mix thoroughly and leave it to cool.

Roll out the pastry until it is very thin. Spread the meat mixture over the pastry and carefully roll it up. Tuck the ends in well, sealing them with water. Glaze with the beaten egg (or just the white if preferred). Slide the roll carefully onto a greased baking sheet.

Bake at 180°C/350°F/Gas 4 for 30 minutes. Serve with the sour cream.

Stir-fried Beef with Baby Corn and Green Peppers

Stir-Fried Beef with Baby Corn and Green Peppers
Serves 4-6

Ingredients

450g/1lb piece of lean
  rump steak
15g/1tbsp cornflour
60ml/4tbsp oil
3 green peppers, cored,
  seeded, halved and
  thinly sliced
1 green chilli, seeded and
  thinly sliced
1 small onion, peeled,
  halved and thinly sliced

2 cloves garlic, sliced
2.5cm/1in piece root
  ginger, peeled and thinly
  sliced
2.5g/½tsp castor sugar
283g/10oz can baby corn,
  drained
15-30ml/1-2tbsp soy sauce,
  to taste
30ml/2tbsp sherry

Preparation Cut the meat into wafer-thin slices, either by hand, or by processor (it is best to semi-freeze the meat first if using this method). Coat with the cornflour, and set aside.

Heat 15ml/1tbsp of the oil in a wok or large frying pan. Add the sliced peppers, chilli and onion. Stir-fry over high heat for 2 minutes. Drain thoroughly and set aside.

Heat the remaining oil in the wok or pan, add the garlic and ginger and fry for a few seconds. Add the meat and sugar and stir-fry over high heat for 1 minute, add the corn and stir-fry for another minute. Season with the soy sauce and sherry, and stir-fry the whole mixture for 30 seconds.

Finally, add the pepper mixture and stir-fry for 1 or 2 minutes to heat through and blend the flavours. Serve immediately.

Beef Napoleon
Serves 6

Ingredients

2 heads garlic
45ml/3tbsp olive oil
60ml/4tbsp robust red wine
20g/2tl sp spring onions, finely chopped
15g/3tsp French mustard
6g/2½tsp fresh thyme or 2.5g/½tsp dried thyme
salt and pepper
1 beef fillet, weighing about 1kg/2lb
15g/2tbsp chopped parsley
450g/1lb puff pastry

Preparation To prepare the marinade, peel and crush 3 of the garlic cloves and mix with 30ml/2tbsp of the oil, the wine, spring onions, 5g/1tsp of the mustard, the thyme, and plenty of salt and pepper.

Lay the fillet at the bottom of a large plastic bag and pour the marinade over it. Seal the top of the bag, put it on a plate in case of leaks, and leave to marinate in a cool place for 6-8 hours.

Heat the remaining oil in a large frying pan until very hot.

Lift the meat out of its marinade and fry it quickly on all sides to seal in the juices; this should take no more than 2 minutes.

Cool the beef and return to its marinade. Freeze for an hour — more if you like your fillet really rare.

Simmer the remaining unpeeled garlic cloves for 20 to 25 minutes, until soft. Drain, peel and mash with a fork to a sticky paste.

Stir in the remaining mustard and the parsley, and season with salt and pepper to taste.

Take the beef out of the freezer and leave, to thaw the marinade. Roll out the pastry to a thickness of 0.5cm (¼in) — large enough to wrap the beef generously.

Drain the meat and add 15ml/1tbsp of its marinade to the garlic and parsley mixture.

Lay the beef in the middle of the pastry and spread the garlic and parsley mixture over it.

Wet the edges of the pastry with a little water, bring them up over the sides of the meat, and press them together. Seal the ends.

Put the pastry-wrapped beef, seam side down, on a well greased baking tray, brush the top with a little milk or egg yolk, and bake for 15 to 20 minutes at 230°C/450°F/Gas 8, until the pastry is cooked. If, after this time, the pastry is cooked but the fillet is too rare turn down the heat to 190°C/375°F/Gas 5 and cook for a further 7 to 10 minutes, and test again. Serve immediately.

Variation For Beef Garibaldi, spread the beef with half a cup of Pesto instead of the garlic and parsley paste.

Boiled Beef
Serves 8

This substantial dish is remarkably simple to prepare. The method is ideal for making less expensive beef cuts tender.

Ingredients

1.5kg/3lb beef flank or silverside
450ml/16fl oz beef broth
450ml/16fl oz chicken broth
450ml/16fl oz white wine
3 large onions, quartered
1 sprig parsley
2 bay leaves
6 potatoes, peeled and quartered
4 large carrots, peeled and halved
450g/1lb green beans, trimmed and halved
5 small beetroot, peeled and quartered
1 large turnip, peeled and cubed
1 clove garlic, crushed
2.5g/½tsp salt
2.5g/½tsp black pepper

Preparation Put all the ingredients into a large, heavy pan. Simmer, covered over a medium heat for 1 hour. Reduce the heat to low and simmer for 1 hour longer.

Remove the beef from the pan and leave to stand for 10 minutes before slicing.

Serve the beef slices in bowls with the vegetables and broth ladled over them.

Pickled Beef Tongue
Serves 8

Ingredients

2-2.5-kg/4-5-lb smoked beef tongue
450ml/16fl oz white wine vinegar
3 large onions, quartered
150g/6oz sugar
bay leaf
1 whole clove
pinch white pepper
30ml/2tbsp honey
pinch cinnamon
30g/2tbsp pickling spice, tied up in cheesecloth

Preparation In a large pot, cover the smoked beef tongue with water. Bring the water to a boil. Skim off the fat that rises to the surface. Reduce the heat to low and cover the pan. Simmer for 3 to 4 hours, or until tender, depending on the size of the tongue. Remove the pot from the heat and leave the tongue to cook in the liquid. Skim off the fat.

Put 700ml/1½pt of the cooking liquid into a saucepan. Discard the remaining cooking liquid or save it for stock. Add the vinegar, onions, sugar, bay leaf, clove, white pepper, honey and cinnamon. Bring the mixture to a boil and simmer for 5 minutes. Add the pickling spice. Remove the clove and simmer for a further 5 minutes. Remove the bay leaf and spice bag. Pour the liquid over the tongue. Chill for at least 90 minutes and serve.

Sauerbraten
Serves 8-10

There are as many different versions of Sauerbraten as there are localities in Germany and Austria. You need to begin this dish 5 days before you want to serve it.

Ingredients

2kg/4lb beef brisket
450ml/16fl oz red wine vinegar
450ml/16fl oz white wine
10g/2tsp whole cloves
5g/1tsp whole black peppercorns
2 bay leaves
2 small onions, coarsely chopped
3 cloves garlic, quartered
1 large seedless orange with peel, sliced
50ml/2fl oz lemon juice
225ml/8fl oz water
15g/1tbsp salt
30g/2tbsp butter
225g/8oz whole cooked (or tinned) tomatoes, drained weight
225ml/8oz tomato purée

Preparation Put the beef brisket in a large bowl or deep dish. Cover it with the vinegar, wine, cloves, peppercorns, bay leaves, onion, garlic, orange slices, lemon juice and water. Cover the bowl or dish tightly. Refrigerate for 4 days, turning the meat over daily.

On the fifth day, remove the meat from the marinade and pat dry with kitchen paper. Reserve the marinade. Melt the butter in a large casserole or heavy pot. Add the meat and brown well on all sides. Add the tomatoes, tomato purée and reserved marinade. Cover tightly and simmer for 2½ hours, or until the meat is tender.

Remove the meat from the casserole or pot and leave it to stand for ten minutes before slicing.

Strain 700ml/1½pt of the cooking liquid through a sieve into a saucepan. Bring the liquid to a boil and simmer for 5 minutes. Serve this as gravy with the sliced Sauerbraten.

Steak and Stout
Serves 6

Ingredients

900g/2lb rump steak (6 pieces)
Dijon mustard
freshly ground black pepper
vegetable oil for frying
12 black peppercorns
12 green peppercorns
8 whole allspice berries
100g/4oz mushrooms, sliced
225ml/8fl oz Guinness or stout
5ml/1tsp Worcestershire Sauce

Preparation Coat the steaks with a thin layer of Dijon mustard and lots of freshly ground pepper. Fry in oil as for rare steaks. Carefully lift out the meat and set aside.

Add to the pan juices the peppercorns, allspice and mushrooms. Cook for 2 minutes. Add the Guinness and cook on a high heat for a minute, then add the Worcestershire sauce.

Lay the steaks in an ovenproof dish and pour over them the Guinness mixture. Cover dish with foil and bake at 180°C/350°F/Gas 4 for an hour.

Steak and Stout

Spiced Brisket I
Serves 4

Ingredients
Marinade

salt, to taste
freshly ground black
  pepper
2 tbsp red and green
  peppercorns
3 garlic cloves, mashed
5ml/1tsp soy sauce
5g/1tsp paprika
10g/2tsp prepared mustard

1kg/2lb brisket of beef
1 onion, chopped
1 green pepper, chopped

Preparation Combine the ingredients for the marinade and spread generously over the brisket. Leave to stand for an hour at room temperature, turning every 15 minutes.

Sauté the diced onion and green pepper until soft and place at the bottom of a roasting tin. Place the brisket fat side up and baste well with the marinade. Cover and roast for 2 hours at 180°C/350°F/Gas 4.

Remove the roast and cool slightly until it can be sliced, then return to the oven and roast for another 20 minutes, until cooked.

Spiced Brisket II
Serves 6

Ingredients

1.5kg/3lb brisket beef
8 rashers bacon, rind
  removed
2 onions, coarsely chopped
2 cloves

1 blade mace
15g/1tbsp allspice berries
6 black peppercorns
water

Preparation Clean and dry the meat, trimming off excess fat if necessary.

Cover the bottom of a casserole dish with 4 rashers of bacon and the onion.

Put the meat on the bacon and onion and lay the remaining rashers of bacon on top. Add the spices and water so that the meat is nearly covered.

Cover the casserole and cook in a slow oven at 170°C/325°F/Gas 3 for 3 hours or until tender.

Thai Beef with Spinach
Serves 4

Ingredients

675g/1½lb chuck steak
300ml/1½pt unsweetened
  canned coconut milk
5g/1tsp brown sugar
15g/1tbsp mixed chopped
  nuts
15ml/1tbsp soy sauce
2 cloves garlic, crushed
1 onion, peeled

2.5cm/1in fresh root ginger
2 fresh chilli peppers,
  seeded
salt and freshly ground
  pepper
juice of ½ lemon
15g/1tbsp cornflour
450g/1lb frozen spinach or
  1kg/2lb fresh spinach
60ml/4tbsp yoghurt

Preparation Trim off excess fat from the meat, and cut into thin strips.

Put the coconut milk, sugar, nuts and soy sauce into a saucepan. Mix the beef with these ingredients and bring to the boil. Immediately the mixture bubbles, turn the heat down and allow to simmer for about 10 minutes.

In a blender or food processor make a paste with the garlic, onion, fresh ginger, chilli peppers, a little salt and lemon juice. Mix this paste with the cornflour and a little cold water. Add some of the hot liquid from the beef to the mixture before stirring into the beef. Cover and simmer gently for about 30-40 minutes until meat is cooked.

Cook the spinach as directed on the packet if using frozen. For fresh spinach wash and remove large stems and cook in a small amount of boiling salted water for about 5 minutes. Drain cooking water into a bowl and use to add to sauce if it has reduced too much. Arrange drained spinach in a hot serving dish. Put beef onto the spinach and trickle yoghurt on top.

Serve with plain boiled rice.

Veal Paprika
Serves 4-6

In Hungary, "paprika" in the title of the recipe usually means the dish will contain not only paprika but also sour cream. You could adapt this recipe using chicken or pork.

Ingredients

15ml/1tbsp oil
25g/1oz butter
450g/1lb onions, sliced
700g/1½lb braising veal, cubed
20g/2tbsp paprika
1 large clove garlic, crushed

2 green peppers, seeded and sliced
3 tomatoes, skinned and chopped
300ml/½pt veal or beef stock
salt and pepper
150ml/¼pt sour cream

Preparation Heat the oil and butter, add the onions and cook until they have just softened but not browned. Add the veal and let it colour slightly. Stir in the paprika and cook it for 2 minutes. Add the garlic, peppers and tomatoes and stir everything together well. Add the stock, salt and pepper, bring to the boil and simmer, covered, for 45 minutes. Stir in the sour cream and warm it through gently.

Serve this with green noodles — the contrasting colours make it a very pretty dish.

Veal and Aubergine Casserole
Serves 4

Ingredients

675g/1½lb veal, cubed
15g/1tbsp seasoned flour
30-45ml/2-3tbsp oil
10g/2tsp paprika
2 large aubergines
1 large onion, chopped

225g/8oz tomatoes, peeled and chopped
150ml/¼pt dry white wine
salt and pepper
2 eggs
300ml/½pt yoghurt

Preparation Lightly coat the veal in the seasoned flour. Heat the oil and brown the meat lightly. Add the paprika and stir. Remove the meat.

Cut the aubergines in half lengthwise and scoop out the flesh carefully, leaving the shells intact. Brown the shells in the hot oil (add more if necessary) and remove them from the pan. Add the onions and chopped aubergine flesh to the pan and brown everything lightly. Add the tomatoes and cook just to soften everything. Add the wine, browned meat, salt and pepper, cover and cook on a gentle heat for 30 minutes.

Put the browned aubergine shells in a shallow oven dish and fill them with the meat mixture. Spoon any extra meat around the shells. Cover and bake at 180°C/350°F/Gas 4 for 20 minutes.

Mix the eggs and yoghurt with a little salt and pepper and pour over the aubergines. Return to the oven uncovered, for a further 10 minutes, until the topping is set and lightly coloured.

Braised Veal Chops with Parsley Dressing
Serves 6-8

Ingredients

225g+15g/8oz+1tbsp butter or margarine
100g/4oz finely chopped onions
65g/2½oz finely chopped carrots
5g/1tsp dried basil
2.5g/½tsp salt
2.5g/½tsp black pepper
350ml/12fl oz white wine

225ml/8fl oz chicken stock
60ml/4tbsp vegetable oil
50g/2oz unflavoured breadcrumbs
100g/4oz minced ham
5ml/1tsp lemon juice
25g/3tbsp finely chopped parsley
8 loin veal chops, 2.5cm (1in) thick

Preparation In a medium-sized saucepan combine 225g/8oz butter or margarine with the onions, carrots, basil, salt, pepper, wine and chicken stock. Cover and simmer for 10 minutes over a medium heat.

Heat the vegetable oil in a small frying pan. Add the breadcrumbs and brown for 3 to 5 minutes over a low heat. Stir in the ham, lemon juice, parsley and the remaining butter or margarine. Cook over a low heat, stirring frequently, for 2 to 3 minutes.

In a large flameproof casserole, arrange the veal chops in a single layer. Pour the broth mixture over the chops, and then the seasoned breadcrumb mixture.

Cover and cook over a medium heat for 40 minutes, or until the veal is tender.

Veal Clou de Giroffe
Serves 4

Ingredients

800g/1¼lb leftover veal roast
freshly ground black pepper
225g/8oz Jarlsberg cheese, grated

10ml/2tsp French mustard
pinch ground cloves
100ml/4fl oz double cream

Preparation Cut the meat into slices 5mm (¼in) thick and arrange them in a well-greased roasting tin. Sprinkle with ground pepper to taste.

Mix cheese, mustard, cloves and double cream. Spread the mixture evenly over the meat. Bake for 6 minutes in the oven at 200°C/400°F/Gas 6, then grill until golden brown, taking care not to let the meat burn. Serve immediately.

Shoulder of Veal with Mushrooms and Spinach Fettucine
Serves 4

Ingredients

1.5kg/3-3½ boned rolled shoulder of veal
15ml/1tbsp oil
1 small onion, peeled and sliced
salt and freshly ground pepper
60ml/4tbsp dry white wine
600ml/1pt Béchamel Sauce
225g/8oz mushrooms, washed and sliced
7g/1tbsp freshly chopped parsley
675g/1½lb fresh spinach fettucine
2.5ml/½tsp oil
25g/1oz butter
nutmeg, freshly grated

Preparation Put the boned rolled shoulder in a roasting pan. Pour the oil over it, scatter the sliced onions on top and season well. Pour on the wine. Cook in the oven at 200°C/400°F/Gas 6 for 1½ hours turning the temperature down for the last hour to 180°C/350°F/Gas 4.

Make up the Béchamel Sauce, season well and add mushrooms, cook for 5 minutes.

Cook the fettucini in boiling salted water with a few drops of oil added. Fresh fettucini will take 2 minutes. Drain and toss in butter, arrange in a warm serving dish.

Slice the meat after allowing to stand for 10 minutes. Arrange sliced meat on the pasta and keep warm.

Drain the fat from the roasting pan, add 60ml/4tbsp water, boil, then add meat juices to the mushroom sauce and stir well. Coat the sliced veal, and serve hot.

Sautéed Sherry Veal
Serves 6

Ingredients

225ml/8fl oz olive oil
150g/6oz green olives, stoned and halved
100g/4oz mushrooms, coarsely chopped
225g/8oz finely chopped onions
2 green peppers, seeded and finely chopped
4 cloves garlic, finely chopped
4 ripe tomatoes, peeled, seeded and finely chopped
1.5kg/3lb thin veal escalopes
100g/4oz flour
pinch salt
pinch black pepper
100ml/4fl oz dry sherry
100ml/4fl oz water

Preparation Heat half the olive oil in a large heavy frying pan. Add the olives, mushrooms, onions, green pepper, garlic and tomatoes. Cook, stirring frequently, for 15 minutes over a low heat. Set aside.

Dredge the veal escalopes in a mixture of flour, salt and pepper.

In another pan, heat the remaining olive oil over a low heat. Add the veal escalopes, in batches if necessary, and cook for 3 to 4 minutes per side. As they are cooked, set them aside in a warm place.

Drain the oil and fat from the pan. Add the sherry, water and cooked vegetables. Cover and simmer for 8 minutes over a medium heat. Pour the sauce over the veal and serve hot.

Osso Buco
Serves 4

Ingredients

30ml/2tbsp vegetable oil
50g/2oz butter
1 onion, peeled and sliced
1 clove garlic, crushed
1kg/2lb shin of veal with bone
150ml/¼pt white wine

300ml/½pt chicken or veal stock
450g/1lb tomatoes or 425g/15oz canned peeled tomatoes
1 lemon, rind and juice
7-15g/1-2tbsp parsley

Preparation Heat the oil and butter in a heavy saucepan. Add the onion and garlic and cook for 3-4 minutes on a fairly low heat without browning. Remove onto a plate.

Brown the veal on all sides on a medium heat. Add white wine and stock. Allow to cook for a few minutes. Either add the onion to the saucepan, standing the veal upright to prevent the marrow coming out of the bone, or transfer all ingredients into an ovenproof casserole in the same way.

Add chopped tomatoes and simmer on top of the cooker or in the oven at 180°C/350°F/Gas 4 for about 1 hour or until the meat is tender. Add a few drops of lemon juice to the veal.

Mix the grated rind of a lemon with the chopped parsley and sprinkle over the Osso Buco. Serve with Risotto Milanese.

Veal Escalopes with Red Wine
Serves 8

Ingredients

50g/2oz flour
2.5g/½tsp salt
2.5g/½tsp ground white pepper
1.5kg/3lb thinly sliced veal escalopes
120ml/8tbsp olive oil
2 large onions, coarsely chopped

3 cloves garlic, finely chopped
15g/2tbsp coarsely chopped parsley
100ml/4fl oz red wine
100ml/4fl oz sweet sherry
450ml/16fl oz water
65g/2½oz tomato purée

Saltimbocca

Preparation On a large ceramic plate mix the flour, salt and pepper together. Lightly dredge the veal slices in the mixture.

Heat the olive oil in a large heavy frying pan. Add the veal, onions and garlic and cook over a medium heat for 3 to 5 minutes, or until both sides of the veal slices are browned. Remove the veal slices and keep warm.

Add the parsley, wine, sherry, water and tomato purée to the pan. Stir well and bring to a boil over a high heat. Cook for 3 minutes. Cover and simmer for 10 minutes longer. Serve the sauce spooned over the veal escalopes.

Saltimbocca
Serves 4

Ingredients

8 thin slices veal, about 7.5×10cm (3×4in)
8 thin slices cooked ham or proscuitto, about 7.5×10cm (3×4in)
8 thin slices mozzarella cheese
fresh or dried sage
30ml/2tbsp olive oil
2 cloves of garlic, crushed

juice of 1 large lemon
salt and pepper
50g/2oz butter
100ml/4fl oz white wine
10g/1tbsp finely chopped spring onions (green part only)
7g/1tbsp parsley, chopped
sprigs of parsley
lemon wedges

Preparation On each slice of veal lay a slice of ham, a slice of cheese and either a quarter of a well-bruised leaf of fresh sage or a tiny pinch of dried sage. Roll up and secure with a cocktail stick.

Mix the olive oil, garlic, and half the lemon juice, and season with salt, pepper and a little fresh or dried sage.

Pour over the veal rolls and leave in a cool place to marinate for 2 to 4 hours.

To cook, heat the butter in a large frying pan and gently sauté the veal rolls for about 10 minutes, turning occasionally.

Turn up the heat and add the wine, chopped spring onions, and the remaining lemon juice.

Allow the sauce to bubble and reduce for 5 minutes. Check the seasoning.

Sprinkle with the chopped parsley and serve immediately, garnished with parsley sprigs and lemon wedges.

Stuffed Veal Shoulder
Serves 6-8

Ingredients

450g/1lb minced veal	2 eggs
450g/1lb minced beef	5g/1tsp salt
225g/8oz minced chicken	2.5g/½tsp white pepper
50g/2oz finely chopped onion	2-2.5kg/4-5lb veal shoulder, boned
25g/1oz finely chopped spring onions	1 clove garlic, crushed
50g/2oz soft breadcrumbs	4 hard-boiled eggs
450ml/16fl oz cold water	75g/3oz butter or margarine

Preparation In a large mixing bowl, combine the minced veal, beef, chicken, onion, spring onions, breadcrumbs, water, eggs, salt and pepper. Mix thoroughly until the stuffing has an even consistency.

With a sharp knife, cut the veal shoulder almost in half horizontally, where it is thickest. The veal shoulder should lie flat on a large cutting board. Rub the cut surface of the veal with the garlic and then cover it with a large piece of waxed paper. Beat the veal with a meat pounder until the meat is flattened.

Remove the paper and spread half the flattened veal shoulder with half the stuffing mixture. Arrange the hard-boiled eggs on top of the stuffing. Spread the remaining stuffing mixture over the eggs.

Fold the veal over and tie with strong kitchen twine at 5cm (2in) intervals and put the veal in a shallow roasting pan filled with 5cm (2in) water. Roast for 2 hours at 190°C/375°F/Gas 5. Remove the veal from the oven. Remove the roast from the pan and put it on a carving board. Cut and remove the string. Let the roast stand for 10 minutes before slicing.

Melt the butter or margarine in a small saucepan. Add the drippings from the roasting pan. Stir well and simmer for 10 minutes, uncovered, until the gravy is slightly reduced and thickened. Serve separately.

Vitello Tonnato
Serves 6

This summery Italian dish of cold roast veal in a tuna fish sauce should be made a day or so in advance. Ask the butcher to bone the veal for you — you will need some bones for the sauce.

Ingredients

1-kg/2-lb piece boned leg or fillet of veal	**Sauce**
2 carrots, peeled and halved	3 egg yolks
	200ml/7fl oz olive oil
2 onions, peeled and halved	15-30ml/1-2tbsp lemon juice
25g/1oz butter	184g/6½oz can tuna fish
450g/1lb veal bones	salt and freshly ground pepper
	10g/1 tbsp capers
	lemon wedges

Preparation Trim the veal and tie into a neat cylinder if necessary. Coarsely chop the carrots and onions. Put half the vegetables in a roasting pan and set the meat on top. Rub with the butter and roast in the heated oven at 200°C/400°F/Gas 6 for 1½ to 1¾ hours, basting frequently. Remove from the tin and allow to cool completely.

Put the remaining vegetables and the veal bones into a large saucepan, and add the vegetables and meat juices from the roasting tin. Barely cover with water and bring to the boil, skimming frequently. Simmer for 1½ to 2 hours. Strain, discarding the bones and vegetables. Boil the stock rapidly to reduce to 300ml/½pt. Cool.

In the meantime prepare the sauce. With the egg yolks and oil make a thick mayonnaise. Add 15ml/ 1tbsp of the lemon juice. Drain and flake the tuna fish, and gradually process or liquidize with the sauce. Add enough stock to make a sauce of coating consistency. Season to taste, adding more lemon juice if necessary.

Remove the string from the meat and slice it thinly. Put the sliced veal into a terrine and spoon over the sauce. Cover and chill overnight for the flavours to blend.

Garnish with the capers and lemon wedges. Serve with crusty bread, and a crisp salad.

Stuffed Cabbage Rolls
Serves 8

This is the Hungarian version of stuffed cabbage. It is unique in the that the sauce is neither red nor sweet.

Ingredients

10 large white cabbage leaves	pinch salt
	pinch white pepper
50g/2oz chicken fat	5g/1tsp Hungarian sweet paprika
1kg/2lb minced veal	
150g/6oz cooked rice	225ml/8fl oz cold water
3 cloves garlic, quartered	
100g/4oz finely chopped onion	

Preparation Cook the cabbage leaves in a large pot of boiling water for 5 to 8 minutes or until they are soft. Drain well and set aside.

In a large saucepan, melt the chicken fat. Add the veal, rice, garlic, onions, salt and pepper. Cook over a low heat, stirring often, until the veal loses its raw look. Cover and simmer for 20 minutes, stirring frequently.

Add the paprika to the veal mixture and cook, stirring frequently, for 2 minutes.

Spoon 45g/3tbsp of the veal mixture on to the centre of each cabbage leaf. Roll up the cabbage leaves, tucking in the edges of the leaves as you roll.

Place the cabbage rolls in a large saucepan. Add the water and cover. Simmer over a low heat for 50 minutes. Serve warm.

Preparing Veal or Beef Kidney

1 Remove as much of the white 'core' as possible with scissors.

2 Slice the kidney thinly. Veal kidney (which is smaller and pale) is usually cooked at this stage. Beef kidney is chopped smaller for mixing with other meats.

Preparing Veal Liver

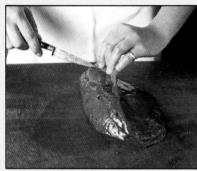

1 With a small sharp knife remove the fine membrane that covers the liver. Hold the knife aginst the liver and gently pull away the skin.

2 Cut into very fine slices with a long, thin knife. Remove any 'tubes' carefully — they are unpleasantly tough when cooked.

Pork and Ham

Sausage and Bacon Kebabs   157
Bacon and Potato Supper   157
Sausage and Bacon Rolls with Tomato Rice   158
Pork Dijonnaise   158
Stuffed Pork Chops with Pasta Bows   158
Fried Pork with Mushrooms and Water Chestnuts   159
Stir Fry Pork   159
Pork Fillet en Croûte   160
Pork Satay   160
Peppery Pork   161
Pork Fillets in Brandy Cream Sauce   161
Baked Ham and Broccoli   161
Ham in Sour Cream I   162
Ham in Sour Cream II   162
Burmese Pork Curry   162
Lion's Head Meatballs   162
Deep fried Wonton with Apricot Sauce   163

Pork Baked Beans   163
Pork and Bean Casserole   164
Pork Curry   164
Pork and Garlic Satay   164
Steamed Pork Buns   165
Crispy Pork Knuckle   165
Transylvanian Goulash   166
Long Cook Pork Leg Stew   166
Sweet and Sour Pork   166
Spiced Pork in Coconut Milk   167
Twice Cooked Pork   167
Coffee Spare Ribs   168
Canton Barbecued Spare Ribs   168
Pork Spare Ribs in Barbecued Sauce   168

Stretching Bacon and Scoring for Crackling   169

Sausage and Bacon Kebabs
Serves 4

Ingredients

16 cocktail sausages
8 rashers bacon
8 mushrooms
1 green pepper, seeded
1 red pepper, seeded
4 bay leaves

4 tomatoes
30ml/2tbsp vegetable oil
salt and freshly ground
   pepper
300ml/¹/₂pt Spicy Tomato
   Sauce

Preparation You will need 4 large or 8 small skewers to prepare the kebabs. If cocktail sausages are not easily available simply twist the longer chipolata-type sausage into two.

Roll the bacon after flattening each rasher with a knife. Each rasher will make 2 small rolls.

Remove the mushroom stalks and cut the peppers into squares.

Thread sausages, bacon, mushrooms, peppers and bay leaves alternately onto the skewers. Lay in a flat dish and pour the oil over. Season well. Turn in the oil for 5 minutes until well coated.

Prepare the Tomato Sauce.

Put the kebabs under a high grill and turn the skewers round every 2 minutes until the food is evenly browned on all sides. When it is golden brown turn the heat to medium and cook for 3-4 minutes each side. Lay the tomatoes on the grill for the last few minutes of cooking. (Tomatoes are best cooked separately as they tend to fall off skewers when cooked.)

Lay the kebabs on a bed of rice and serve with the Spicy Tomato Sauce. If you wish to remove the skewers use a fork to slide the food off.

Bacon and Potato Supper
Serves 4-6

Ingredients

175g/6oz back bacon
1kg/2lb potatoes, peeled
2 cloves garlic, peeled and
   crushed
300ml/¹/₂pt sour cream
3 eggs

6 spring onions, trimmed
   and finely chopped
7g/1 tbsp parsley, chopped
100g/4oz Cheddar cheese
salt and freshly ground
   pepper

Preparation Heat then grill, the grill the bacon until crisp. Drain on paper towels.

Coarsely grate the potatoes. This is much quicker if you have a food processor. Remove the excess water from the potatoes by squeezing well, then draining on paper towels.

Mix the garlic, cream, eggs, spring onions and parsley. Crumble the bacon and add. Mix the grated potatoes with the grated cheese in a bowl, then stir in the egg and cream mixture. Season to taste, then pour into a greased shallow ovenproof baking dish.

Place in the heated oven and bake at 200°C/400°F/Gas 6 for 30 to 40 minutes until golden brown and crispy.

Serve with a crisp green salad.

Sausage and Bacon Kebabs

Sausage and Bacon Rolls with Tomato Rice
Serves 4

Ingredients

225g/8oz long-grain rice
600ml/1pt beef stock
10ml/2tsp tomato purée
1 small onion, peeled and
  chopped

2.5g/¹/₂tsp salt
8 sausages
8 rashers bacon
300ml/¹/₂pt Spicy Tomato
  Sauce

Preparation Wash the rice several times and drain.

Mix the beef stock, tomato purée and onion with the salt and bring to the boil. Pour over the rice and fork through to stop grains sticking together. Cover and simmer until all liquid is absorbed, about 15 minutes.

Turn the grill on high and brown the sausages on each side for 3 minutes. Allow to cool slightly and then wrap bacon rashers around the sausages.

Grill for a further 5 minutes under a medium heat. Alternatively bake in the oven at 180°C/350°F/Gas 4 in the tomato sauce for 15 minutes after browning under the grill.

Arrange the sausage and bacon rolls on the tomato rice and pour the sauce on top.

Pork Dijonnaise
Serves 4

Serve noodles tossed in butter and black pepper or creamy mashed potatoes to complement the rich piquant sauce.

Ingredients

4 pork chops
30ml/2tbsp oil
2 shallots, peeled and
  finely chopped
300ml/¹/₂pt dry white wine
bouquet garni

salt and freshly ground
  pepper
2 egg yolks
30ml/2tbsp Dijon mustard
7g/1tbsp parsley, finely
  chopped
60ml/4tbsp sour cream

Preparation Trim the chops and pat dry.

Heat the oil in a heavy saute or frying pan, and brown the chops on both sides. Stir in the shallots and cook for 1 minute. Add the wine, bouquet garni and a little salt and pepper. Stir well, bring to the boil, then cover and cook very gently for 20 minutes, or until the chops are tender.

Combine the yolks with the mustard and parsley. Drain the juices from the meat and skim off the fat then, whisking all the while, pour the hot juices on to the egg yolk mixture. Beat well, then add the cream.

Taste the sauce for seasoning then pour over the chops. Reheat without boiling and serve immediately.

Variation Replace the chops with boneless chicken breasts or veal chops.

Stuffed Pork Chops with Pasta Bows
Serves 4

Ingredients

15ml/1tbsp oil
1 small onion, peeled and
  finely diced
50g/2oz mushrooms,
  washed and finely
  chopped
2.5g/¹/₂tsp dried or 2g/1tsp
  chopped fresh sage
2g/1tsp freshly chopped
  parsley
2.5g/¹/₂tsp grated lemon
  rind

salt and freshly ground
  pepper
15g/1tbsp fresh white
  breadcrumbs
4 thick pork chops
450ml/³/₄pt Concentrated
  Tomato Sauce
225g/8oz pasta bows
25g/1oz butter
freshly grated nutmeg
bunch watercress

Preparation Heat the oil and cook the finely diced onion over a low heat for 4 minutes, add finely chopped mushrooms and cook for a further 2 minutes.

Add sage, parsley, lemon rind, salt and pepper to the breadcrumbs in a small mixing bowl. Tip the onion and mushrooms into the bowl and mix well.

Cut a slit in each chop at the fat end. Fill the slit with the onion and mushroom stuffing. Put the chops under the grill for 4 minutes each side. Dry on kitchen paper to remove excess fat.

Arrange the chops in an ovenproof dish, pour over the tomato sauce, cover with foil and bake for 25 minutes at 180°C/350°F/Gas 4.

Cook the pasta bows for about 10 minutes, drain and toss in melted butter. Add a shake of pepper and nutmeg.

Serve the bows and chops garnished with watercress.

Stuffed Pork Chops with Pasta Bows

and all the vegetables.

Stir-fry for 2 minutes, then transfer to a serving dish and serve immediately sprinkled with sesame seeds.

Fried Pork with Mushrooms and Water Chestnuts
Serves 4-6

The pork can be replaced with lean steak, or boneless, skinned chicken breasts for a change of flavour.

Ingredients
450g/1lb pork fillet, roughly chopped
5g/1tsp cornflour
60ml/4tbsp oil
1 small onion, peeled and finely chopped
2.5cm/1in ginger, peeled and finely chopped
225g/8oz button mushrooms, sliced
225-g/8-oz can water chestnuts, drained and sliced
15ml/1tbsp soy sauce, or to taste
30ml/2tbsp sherry
15ml/1tbsp hoisin sauce, or to taste
10g/1tbsp sesame seeds

Preparation Coat the pork with cornflour and set aside.

Heat half the oil in a wok or large frying pan, and add the onion and ginger. Stir-fry for 1 minute, then add the mushrooms and water chestnuts and stir-fry for another minute. Add half of the soy sauce, fry for 30 seconds, then remove the vegetables to a plate.

Wipe out the wok or pan, add the remaining oil and heat. Add the meat, and stir-fry over high heat to separate the pieces and brown evenly. After 2 minutes, add the remaining soy sauce, the sherry, hoisin sauce

Stir Fry Pork
Serves 4-6

Ingredients
450g/1lb pork fillet
a piece of pork fat or oil
1 onion, peeled and chopped
1 clove garlic, peeled and crushed
2 green chillies, seeded and pounded
225g/½lb green beans, cut into 2.5-cm/1-in lengths
7.5ml/1½tsp Worcestershire sauce
salt and sugar to taste
coriander leaves to garnish
plain boiled rice to serve

Preparation Trim the pork and cut into small pieces. Render the fat from the pork. When all the fat is in the pan, discard it and heat the oil, if preferred.

Fry the onion, garlic and chilli until it gives off a rich aroma; do not allow to brown. Push to the side of the pan and stir in the pork fillet pieces. Turn all the time until the meat changes colour. Cook for 2-3 minutes.

Now add the beans and toss all the ingredients well. Add the Worcestershire sauce, if used, sugar and salt to taste.

Garnish with fresh coriander leaves and serve with plain rice.

Pork Fillet en Croûte
Serves 4-6

Ingredients

3 medium-size or 2 large pork fillets

Stuffing
30ml/2tbsp oil
1 small onion, peeled
100g/4oz rice, uncooked
300ml/¹⁄₂pt stock or water
1 small apple, peeled and diced
15g/1tbsp sultanas
15g/1tbsp mixed nuts

rind and juice of 1 lemon
1 egg, beaten
225g/8oz Puff Pastry

Gravy
15g/1tbsp flour
5g/1tsp dried sage or 7g/1tbsp chopped fresh sage
salt and freshly ground pepper
30-45ml/2-3tbsp white wine
150ml/¹⁄₄pt stock

Preparation Trim the fat and gristle from the fillets. Cut into 15-cm/6-in lengths.

For the stuffing, heat the oil in a frying pan and cook the onion for 2 minutes. Add the rice and stir well for a further 2 minutes. Pour in the stock or water with a pinch of salt. Cover and cook for 5 minutes. Remove the lid and fork through the rice, then add the diced apple, sultanas, nuts, lemon rind and juice. Mix through with a fork, cover and continue cooking for 5 minutes. When all the stock has been absorbed the rice should be slightly undercooked. Put the mixture into a bowl and allow to cool. Mix in most of the egg, leaving a little for glazing the pastry.

Put 2-3 lengths of fillets, slightly flattened, on a board. Cover with rice stuffing. Top with the remaining lengths of fillets and tie neatly into a cylinder with string.

Brush over with oil and wrap loosely in foil. Roast at 200°C/400°F/Gas 6 for 35 minutes. Allow to cool and retain any meat juices for use in the gravy.

Roll the thawed pastry into an even shape, about 25cm/10in square. Put the cooled meat, with string removed, in the centre. Fold the pastry over the meat and damp the edges with cold water. Turn the pastry parcel over so that the fold is underneath. Fold the ends neatly, cutting a square out and placing flaps over like a parcel. Put on a baking sheet.

Roll out any scraps of pastry and cut out leaves. Alternatively, cut out decorative shapes with a cocktail cutter. Wet the shapes and arrange them on the croûte. Make sure there are several slits to allow steam to escape.

Brush over with the remaining egg. Cook in the oven at 210°C/425°F/Gas 7 for a further 10 minutes.

For a gravy, scrape the meat juices into a saucepan. Add the flour, seasoning, white wine and stock. Whisk well and serve in a heated sauceboat when thickened.

Pork Satay
Serves 2-3

Ingredients

225g/8oz desiccated coconut
425ml/³⁄₄pt water
450g/1lb pork fillet
15g/1tbsp brown sugar
1-cm/¹⁄₂-in cube blanchan (optional)
2 medium-sized onions, peeled
3-6 red chillies, seeded

10g/2tsp coriander seeds
6 blanched almonds
1-2 stems lemongrass peeled and sliced
2.5g/¹⁄₂tsp ground turmeric (optional)
30ml/2tbsp coconut or peanut oil
cucumber cubes

Preparation Soak 8-12 bamboo skewers in water for at least an hour to prevent them from burning under the grill.

Make the coconut milk by putting the desiccated coconut in a bowl, pouring over it the boiling water and leaving to stand for 15 minutes. Squeeze out the liquid and refrigerate it until needed.

Cut the pork into even-sized pieces, about the size of your thumb nail, and sprinkle with sugar to help release the juices. If using blanchan fry it in a foil parcel in a dry frying pan or on a skewer over the gas flame. Make the onions and chillies into a paste in the food processor.

Pound the coriander seeds, then add the nuts and the bulb part of the lemongrass and grind using a pestle and mortar. Add turmeric and salt and then stir this into the onion mixture in the food processor.

Pour in the coconut milk and oil. Switch the machine on and then off. Pour the contents into a shallow bowl containing the pork. Marinate for an hour or two.

Thread five or six pieces of pork onto each skewer. Grill or cook over charcoal for an even more authentic flavour. Baste with the marinade.

When tender, serve hot with cubes of cucumber.

Peppery Pork
Serves 4

Ingredients

15ml/1tbsp oil
4 pork steaks (or
equivalent amount of
fillet)
pinch chilli powder
300g/10oz canned
tomatoes

10g/2tsp cornflour
15ml/1tbsp water
150ml/¼pt yoghurt
salt

Preparation Heat the oil, add the pork and lightly brown it. Drain off excess fat. Sprinkle over the chilli powder and stir it around. Add the tomatoes and bring the liquid to the boil, breaking up the tomatoes a little.

Mix the cornflour with the water to a smooth paste and add to the pan. Stir until the sauce has thickened. Add the yoghurt and mix it in well. Season with salt. Bake at 180°C/350°F/Gas 4 for 1 hour.

Serve with rice or noodles. You may prefer more or less chilli powder.

Pork Fillets in Brandy Cream Sauce
Serves 4

Ingredients

675g/1½lb pork fillet
15g/1tbsp flour
salt and freshly ground
pepper
25g/1oz butter
30ml/2tbsp oil
1 onion, peeled and finely
chopped

250g/8oz Herbed Rice
30ml/2tbsp brandy
pinch nutmeg
150ml/¼pt single cream
4 lemon wedges
bunch watercress

Preparation Trim the pork fillets. Remove any gristle and excess fat. Cut into diagonal slices. Beat out to about 1cm/½in thick.

Mix the flour with the seasoning and coat each slice evenly.

Heat the butter and oil in a frying pan and cook the onions for 4 minutes. Remove onto a plate with a slotted spoon.

Prepare and cook the Herbed Rice.

On a medium heat sauté the pork fillet slices for about 4 minutes each side until golden brown. Heat the brandy in a ladle and set alight. Pour onto the pork and allow to flambé.

Serve the Herbed Rice on a warmed serving dish. Arrange the pork slices on top and keep warm in a low oven.

Add nutmeg and single cream to the frying pan and stir over a low heat to combine the meat juices and cream. Pour the sauce over the meat.

Garnish with the lemon wedges and watercress and accompany with a crisp green salad.

Baked Ham and Broccoli
Serves 4

Ingredients

8 slices cooked ham
8 florets fresh or frozen
broccoli
600ml/1pt Mornay Sauce
5g/1tsp dried mustard

50g/2oz grated cheese
350g/12oz cooked pasta
shapes
salt and freshly ground
pepper
5g/1tsp ground nutmeg

Preparation Lay out slices of ham on a board.

Wash and drain fresh broccoli. If using frozen, blanch in boiling water for 3 minutes, drain well.

Roll the broccoli florets neatly in the ham.

When making up the Mornay sauce, grated Cheddar may be used or a mixture of Parmesan cheese. Add the dried mustard and mix well.

Butter an ovenproof dish, spread the pasta over the bottom, season with a shake of pepper and nutmeg. Arrange the filled ham on top.

Pour over the sauce and finish with sprinkled grated cheese. Cook for 20 minutes at 180°C/350°F/Gas 4 or until cheese is golden on top.

Baked Ham and Broccoli

Ham in Sour Cream I
Serves 4

Ingredients

15ml/1tbsp oil or butter
1 onion, sliced
10g/2tsp flour
225g/8oz canned
   tomatoes

150ml/¼pt dry white wine
450g/1lb cooked ham,
   sliced
150ml/¼pt sour cream
freshly ground pepper

Preparation Heat the oil, add the onion and cook until it has softened but not browned. Add the flour and stir it off the heat until smooth. Add the tomatoes and wine. Break the tomatoes up a little and cook gently for a minute. Add the ham and let it warm through. Stir in the sour cream and season with pepper to taste.

Variation Serve on a bed of noodles, with 45g/3tbsp grated Parmesan sprinkled over the top and flash it under a hot grill just to brown the top.

Ham in Sour Cream II
Serves 6-8

Ingredients

1.5kg/3lb ham
450ml/¾pt chicken stock
grated lemon rind
bay leaf
225g/8oz carrots, sliced

2 large onions, sliced
100g/4oz button
   mushrooms
30g/2tbsp cornflour
30ml/2tbsp water
300ml/½pt sour cream
pepper

Preparation Put the ham into a large pan with water to cover. Bring to the boil and then reduce the heat, cover and simmer for 45 minutes. Pour off the cooking liquid (reserve it to use as stock for a lentil soup).

Remove the skin from the ham and return it to the pan with the stock, lemon rind, bay leaf, carrots, and onions. Bring to the boil and then cover and simmer for a further 45 minutes. Add the mushrooms, whole.

Mix the cornflour with the water and stir in the sour cream. Add to the pan and stir in well. Add some pepper (it shouldn't need any salt), cover and simmer for 20 minutes.

Slice the ham and serve it with the sauce spooned over.

Burmese Pork Curry
Serves 6

Ingredients

900g/2lb lean pork, cut
   into 2.5-cm/1-in pieces
450g/1lb onions, peeled
8 cloves garlic, peeled and
   crushed
5cm/2in piece fresh ginger,
   scraped and chopped
10g/2½tsp chilli powder

4 stems lemongrass, peeled
2.5cm/1in ngapi or
   blachan (optional)
5g/1tsp turmeric
60ml/4tbsp peanut oil for
   frying
300ml/½pt stock or water
coriander leaves to garnish

Preparation Put the pork pieces on a dish. Slice half the onions and put the remainder into a food processor with the garlic, ginger, chillies, the lower 6cm/2½in of the lemongrass (bruise and reserve the top of the stem), ngapi if used and turmeric. Make these ingredients into a coarse paste.

Fry the pork pieces in the hot oil until they change colour, then increase the heat and add the paste. Fry for 2 minutes, then add the remaining onion slices. When the pork is well coated with the spice mixture, pour on the stock or water. Add salt and the lemongrass tops. Cover and cook for 1½ hours or until the pork is tender.

Cook uncovered for a further 15 minutes, if liked, to reduce the liquid. Remove the lemongrass. Add more chilli if a hotter curry is preferred.

Sprinkle with fresh coriander and eat with rice.

Lion's Head Meatballs
Serves 2-3

Ingredients

450g/1lb lean pork, finely
   minced with a little fat
4-6 canned water
   chestnuts, finely chopped
5g/1tsp finely chopped
   ginger
10g/1tbsp finely chopped
   onion
30ml/2tbsp soy sauce
seasoning to taste

beaten egg to bind
30g/2tbsp cornflour
peanut oil for frying
300ml/½pt chicken stock
a little sugar
seasoning
100g/4oz each Chinese
   leaves and spinach
   leaves, washed, dried
   and shredded

Preparation Mix the pork, water chestnuts, ginger, onion, 15ml/1tbsp of the soy sauce and the seasoning together. Bind with sufficient beaten egg to form into eight balls. Toss in a little seasoned cornflour and make a paste with the remaining cornflour and water.

Fry the balls in the hot oil to brown all over then transfer them to another pan or flameproof casserole. Add stock, sugar, seasoning and the remaining soy sauce. Cover and simmer for 20-25 minutes, then increase the heat and add the Chinese leaves and spinach. Cook for 3-4 minutes.

Lift out the vegetables with a draining spoon onto a serving platter. Arrange the meatballs on top and keep warm.

Thicken the gravy with the cornflour paste and pour over just before serving.

Deep Fried Wonton with Apricot Sauce
Makes 40-50

Ingredients

1 packet wonton wrappers
(40-50 approx.), thawed
175g/6oz pork meat with a
little fat
100g/4oz raw prawns
2 spring onions, finely
chopped
5-10ml/1-2tsp oyster sauce
(optional)

salt and freshly ground
black pepper
flour and water paste
oil for deep frying
Apricot sauce
450g/1lb apricot jam
45-60ml/3-4tbsp light
vinegar
30-45ml/2-3 tbsp hot
water

Preparation If the wrappers are frozen leave them on a worktop to thaw. When thawed remove them from the packet. Gently ease up the top one at a corner and slowly lift, pushing your finger between this and the next one to prevent tearing. Place each one on top of the other in a pile on the worktop, covered with a sheet of greaseproof paper and a slightly damp cloth to prevent drying out. Any torn wrappers can be used for patches, should you accidently damage any while filling them.

Prepare the filling by blending meat and prawns in a food processor. Add spring onions, oyster sauce, if used, and seasoning to taste. Now you are ready to fill the wrappers.

Put the wrappers singly on a worktop, say 10 at a time (leave the rest covered). Place a tiny spoonful of the filling onto the centre of each wrapper. Damp two edges with flour and water paste and fold over to form a triangle which is slightly off centre. Now put two minute pieces of filling onto each side of the centre mound. Draw the mid points of the triangle over the filling and press down. The wings will then fall back.

Deep fry for 1-2 minutes. Drain well.

To prepare the sauce, warm the jam, vinegar and water together, sieve and pour into a bowl.

To serve, put the sauce in a bowl surrounded by the wonton puffs.

Pork Baked Beans
Serves 6

Ingredients

25g/1oz butter
450g/1lb salt pork, cubed
2 onions, finely chopped
2 cloves garlic, crushed
450g/1lb dried haricot
beans, soaked in cold
water overnight

4 small leeks, sliced
100g/4oz carrots, chopped
4 raw potatoes, washed
and cubed
150ml/¼pt tomato juice
150ml/¼pt red wine
300ml/½pt strong black
coffee

Preparation Melt the butter and add the pork, onions and garlic. Cook gently until the onion is soft and transparent. Season to taste.

Put the beans in a large casserole, add the pork and onion mixture and stir in the leeks, carrots, potatoes, tomato juice, red wine and coffee. Mix well. Put the covered casserole in the oven and bake for 2½ to 3 hours at 180°C/350°F/Gas 4 until the beans are tender and most of the liquid absorbed. If the beans are still firm and all the liquid has been absorbed, add extra coffee and continue to cook until tender.

Check the seasoning and serve hot with fresh crusty bread.

Pork Baked Beans

Pork and Bean Casserole
Serves 4

Ingredients

225g/8oz red kidney beans, soaked	1 large onion, sliced
100g/4oz bacon	450-g/15-oz can tomatoes
225g/8oz loin or leg of pork	5g/1tsp chilli powder
100g/4oz bacon hock	2.5g/¹/₂tsp cumin
15g/1tbsp flour	bay leaf
salt and freshly ground pepper	bouquet garni
	150ml/¹/₄pt beer
	300ml/¹/₂pt stock
	7g/1tbsp parsley, chopped

Preparation Cook the red kidney beans for 15 minutes in cold water that has been brought to the boil.

Remove the rind from the bacon. Cut it into small pieces and cook in a frying pan.

Trim fat and gristle from pork and bacon hock, cut into small cubes, toss in seasoned flour.

Remove bacon to a casserole, fry the pork and the fat left in the pan over a medium heat.

Add sliced onion and cook over a low heat for 3 minutes.

Transfer to the casserole, add all other ingredients including the beans. Cover and cook in the oven for 1¹/₂ hours at 180°C/350°F/Gas 4.

Serve sprinkled with chopped parsley.

Pork Curry
Serves 4

Ingredients

15ml/1tbsp tamarind pulp	15ml/1tbsp vinegar
225ml/8fl oz water	450g/1lb pork, cut into cubes
50g/2oz ghee (Clarified Butter) or oil	3g/¹/₂tsp curry powder
2 medium onions, finely sliced	5g/1tsp salt, or to taste
3 cloves garlic, crushed	

Preparation Soak the tamarind in half the water for 10 minutes, then squeeze and strain off the juice.

Heat the fat and fry the onions. Add the tamarind, garlic and vinegar. Fry. Add the meat and cook until well browned.

Add the curry powder and cook for a further 3 minutes. Add the water and salt and simmer gently until the pork is tender.

Pork and Garlic Satay
Serves 6

Ingredients

1 head of garlic, unpeeled (about 15 cloves)	4 spring onions, chopped
2.5g/¹/₂tsp ground cumin	30ml/2tbsp oil
5g/1tsp ground coriander	1kg/2lb lean pork, cubed
2.5g/¹/₂tsp ground cinnamon	a small Spanish onion, finely chopped
5g/1tsp turmeric	2.5cm/1in root ginger, grated
75g/3oz sugar	chilli powder to taste
75ml/3fl oz lime juice	175g/6oz raw peanuts, roasted and ground
sprigs of lemon verbena or lemon balm, well bruised (optional)	salt to taste

Preparation To make the marinade, peel and crush 3 of the garlic cloves and combine with the cumin, coriander, cinnamon, turmeric, 10g/2tsp of the sugar, 30ml/1fl oz of the lime juice, the lemon verbena and lemon balm, the spring onions and 15ml/1tbsp of the oil.

Put the cubed pork into a plastic bag and pour in the marinade. Tie up the top of the bag and put it on a plate in case it leaks, and leave in a cool place for 2 to 4 hours.

Plunge the remaining unpeeled garlic cloves into boiling water and simmer for 10 minutes or until just tender. Drain, peel and cut each clove lengthwise into 3 or 4 pieces.

To make the sauce, fry the onion in the remaining oil with the grated ginger and the chilli powder — don't put in too much — you can always add more later — until transparent.

Preparation Dissolve the sugar in half the water then sprinkle into the yeast. Stir and leave for 10-15 minutes until the mixture is frothy.,

Meanwhile sift the flour and salt together in a bowl and leave in a warm place or put into a food processor. Stir in the yeast mixture with sufficient of the remaining water to make a soft but not sticky dough. Knead for 1 minute in a food processor, or on a floured board by hand for 10 minutes.

Pop into a large, oiled plastic bag, seal the top and leave in a warm place until it doubles in size. Knock out the air bubbles and knead again for 5 minutes or 30 seconds in the food processor.

Put the pork on a plate. Heat the oil and fry the garlic, then add pork, spring onions and crushed bean sauce (this can be done in a pestle and mortar). Add sugar and thicken slightly with the cornflour paste. Draw from the heat and cool.

Divide the dough into 16 pieces; roll each out into 7.5-10-cm/3-4-in rounds. Place a spoonful of filling into the centre of each and gather up the sides and cover the filling. Twist the top to seal. Set on cheesecloth or baking parchment in a steamer and leave to double in size.

Cook over fast-boiling water for 30-35 minutes or until done.

Drain the marinade from the pork, remove the lemon verbena or lemon balm, and add to the onion. Simmer for several minutes.

Add the remaining lime juice, sugar, and the peanuts. Season with salt, extra chilli if necessary, and simmer until thickened.

Thread the marinaded pork cubes and garlic slices alternately onto thin skewers — wooden ones are traditional — 5 to 7 pork cubes to each, and either grill for about 10 minutes, turning once, or barbecue, basting with a little oil, until glistening brown and cooked.

Steamed Pork Buns
Makes 16

Ingredients
15g/1tbsp sugar
approx. 300ml/¹/₂pt warm
   water
20g/1¹/₂tbsp dried yeast
450g/1lb strong or plain
   flour
5g/1tsp salt
15g/1oz lard, for greasing

Filling
225g/8oz roast pork, very
   finely chopped
a little oil for frying
1 clove garlic, peeled and
   crushed
20g/2tbsp chopped spring
   onion
20ml/1¹/₂tbsp canned
   baked beans, mashed
7.5g/¹/₂tbsp sugar
5g/1tsp cornflour, mixed to
   a paste with a little water

Crispy Pork Knuckle
Serves 1-2

Ingredients
1-2 pieces pork knuckle
salt to taste
oil for frying

Sauce
100ml/3¹/₂fl oz vinegar
1¹/₂ cloves garlic
salt and black pepper to
   taste
5-7 pieces chilli, sliced

Preparation Allow 400-500g/13-17oz raw weight pork knuckle per person. Cook the pork knuckle in salted water over a low heat until tender (1-1¹/₂ hours, depending on their size). Remove and pat dry with kitchen towel.

Fry in medium hot oil for 15 minutes until they have acquired a crispy consistency.

Mix together the vinegar sauce ingredients and serve as an accompaniment.

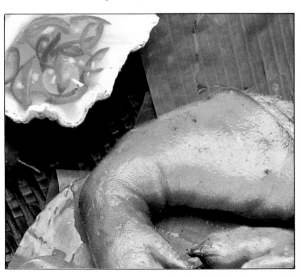

one whole chilli aside for garnish and pound the remainder with the garlic and onions. Fry in oil for 2-3 minutes. Stir in the bean paste, then turn the trotters in this mixture to coat them on all sides. Add the soy sauces, tamarind juice, star anise, ginger, sugar and water. Add salt if necessary, but go carefully as the bean paste is quite salty.

Cover and cook gently for at least 2 hours or until the pork is tender. Cool and leave overnight. Skim away any excess fat. Cover and bake in an ovenproof casserole in a moderately hot oven (160 C/325 F/Gas 3) for an hour or until the pork is cooked through and the sauce is bubbling.

Serve scattered with fresh coriander leaves or spring onions and the reserved chilli, cut into rings.

Transylvanian Goulash
Serves 6

Ingredients

30-45ml/2-3tbsp oil	10g/2tsp dried dill
1 large onion, finely chopped	10g/2tsp caraway seeds
20g/2tbsp paprika	300ml/¹/₂pt water
675g/1¹/₂lb pork, cubed	675g/1¹/₂lb sauerkraut
salt	150ml/¹/₄pt sour cream
1 large clove garlic, crushed	

Preparation Heat the oil, add the onion and cook until it has just softened but not browned. Add the paprika and stir well. Add the pork, garlic, dill and caraway seeds. Stir well. Add the water and sauerkraut. Cook on a low heat for 1¹/₄ hours. Stir in the sour cream and warm through gently.

Variation This is equally tasty with veal, which needs less cooking (1 hour). Fresh sauerkraut is most delicious but canned or bottled is very acceptable.

Long Cook Pork Leg Stew
Serves 4

Cook this stew the day before you wish to serve it, as this gives the dish a richer blend of flavours and a chance to skim off any excess fat which may collect. The trotters have a large proportion of bone so you will require this quantity for four people. It would be advisable to order them from the butcher in advance.

Ingredients

1.3-1.75kg/3¹/₂-4lb meaty pig's trotters	30ml/2tbsp dark soy sauce
15ml/1tbsp tamarind pulp	1 star anise
150ml/¹/₄pt water	1cm/¹/₂in fresh ginger, finely shredded
6 red chillies, seeded (use red for good colour)	10g/2¹/₂tsp dark brown sugar
6 cloves garlic, crushed	just under 600ml/1pt water
2-3 medium-sized onions, peeled	salt
120ml/8tbsp oil	fresh coriander leaves or shredded spring onion to garnish
20ml/2tbsp soya bean paste	
30ml/2tbsp light soy sauce	

Preparation Ask the butcher to cut the trotters into chunky pieces through the bone. Soak the tamarind pulp in the water for 10 minutes, then squeeze out. Set

Sweet and Sour Pork
Serves 4

Ingredients

450g/1lb leg of pork, cut in a thick slice	**Sauce**
1 small onion, peeled and sliced	1 small red pepper, seeded
2.5cm/1in fresh root ginger, finely chopped	1 small green pepper, seeded
1 clove garlic	2 spring onions, washed
15ml/1tbsp dry sherry	150ml/¹/₄pt chicken stock
30ml/2tbsp soy sauce	15ml/1tbsp white wine vinegar
salt and freshly ground pepper	10g/2tsp brown sugar
	15ml/1tbsp tomato purée
	10g/2tsp cornflour
	30ml/2tbsp cold water
	Batter
	45g/3tbsp cornflour
	10ml/2tsp water
	1 egg
	oil for frying

Preparation Cut the pork into 2.5-cm/1-in cubes after trimming away any fat or gristle.

Mix up the marinade of onion, ginger, garlic, sherry, soy sauce and seasoning and allow the pork to stand in this for at least 1 hour, turning from time to time.

Cut the peppers into 1-cm/¼-in cubes and chop the spring onions into thick rings

Put all other ingredients for the sauce, apart from the cornflour and the cold water into a saucepan with the peppers and spring onions. Mix the cornflour with the cold water and then mix into the saucepan. Fry the meat before heating the sauce.

Make up the batter in a deep plate, mixing the cornflour, water and egg together until thick.

Drop the drained marinated meat into the batter. Make sure the fat is very hot before dropping the meat in to it, either with tongs or a slotted spoon. Cook for about 2-4 minutes until golden. Drain on kitchen paper.

Heat the sweet and sour sauce and, when thickened and hot, add the fried pork.

Serve with plain boiled rice.

Spiced Pork In Coconut Milk
Serves 3

Ingredients
450ml/¾pt boiling water
225g/8oz desiccated
  coconut
2 medium-sized red
  onions, peeled and
  chopped
5g/1tsp yeast extract
5-7.5g/1½-2tsp chilli
  powder

45ml/3tbsp vegetable oil
450g/1lb lean pork, cut
  into cubes
1 stem lemongrass
salt to taste
juice ½ lemon
pinch sugar

Preparation First make the coconut milk by pouring the boiling water over the coconut, leaving to stand for 15 minutes, and then squeezing out the liquid. Discard the coconut, and refrigerate the milk until required.

Pound the onions with the yeast extract and chilli powder. Fry in oil without browning. Add the pork and fry until the meat changes colour and is well covered with the spices.

Stir in the prepared coconut milk over a gentle heat and the bruised stem of lemongrass. Slowly bring to the boil, stirring to prevent curdling. Add salt to taste. Simmer until the pork is tender.

Remove the lemongrass stem. Add lemon juice and sugar to taste.

Serve with plain boiled rice.

Twice Cooked Pork
Serves 6

Ingredients
900g/2lb belly of pork,
  rind and bones removed
  after weighing
60g/4tbsp canned black
  beans
15g/1tbsp soya bean paste
30ml/2tbsp soy sauce
15ml/1tbsp tomato purée
15ml/1tbsp hoisin sauce
5ml/1tsp Tabasco
7.5-15g/½-1tbsp sugar

a little oil for frying
2 cloves garlic, peeled and
  crushed
1cm/½in ginger, peeled
  and finely chopped
50ml/2fl oz chicken stock
50g/2oz bean sprouts
30ml/2tbsp sherry
few drops sesame oil
spring onion curls to
  garnish

Preparation Put the pork in a pan of boiling water and cook for just over 30 minutes or until tender. Lift out, drain, cool a little and cut into finger-width slices, and then each slice into four pieces, and set aside.

Drain the beans. Blend the soya bean paste with soy sauce, tomato purée, hoisin and Tabasco sauces. Stir in a little sugar to taste. Mash the black beans to a paste.

Heat the oil in a wok and fry the garlic and ginger. Add the mashed beans, stir well, then add the meat and the mixture of sauces. Toss the meat well to coat each piece with the sauce. Add stock and extra water if the sauce is too thick. Cook for 5 minutes. Increase the heat, add the bean sprouts, sherry and sesame oil.

Serve on a warm platter garnished with spring onion curls.

Baste again if desired, then reduce the heat to 175°C/350°F/Gas 4 for a further 35-45 minutes or until the ribs are cooked.

Cool for a few minutes then divide into separate ribs and arrange attractively on a hot platter garnished with spring onion curls. You can serve these ribs with an accompaniment of salad and rice.

Coffee Spare Ribs
Serves 6

Ingredients

6 pork spare rib chops cut into individual ribs	45ml/3tbsp honey
45ml/3tbsp olive oil	salt and freshly ground black pepper
2 cloves garlic, crushed	grated rind and juice of 1 lime
15g/2tbsp parsley, chopped	
150ml/¼pt red wine	
150ml/¼pt strong black coffee	

Preparation Put the spare ribs in a large shallow pan. Mix all the remaining ingredients together and pour over the spare ribs. Leave to marinate overnight, turning occasionally.

Remove the ribs from the marinade. Put under a preheated grill, turning until evenly browned.

Put ribs back into the marinade and bake for 30 minutes at 180°C/350°F/Gas 4.

Remove the ribs and skim the fat off the sauce. Serve with rice.

Canton Barbecued Spare Ribs
Serves 4

Ingredients

1kg/2lb pork spare ribs	45ml/3tbsp sherry
10g/2tsp salt	30ml/2tbsp honey
good pinch five spice powder	15ml/1tbsp hoisin sauce
freshly ground black pepper	2 cloves garlic, peeled and crushed
15ml/1tbsp soy sauce	45ml/3tbsp oil
15ml/1tbsp light soy sauce	spring onion curls to garnish

Preparation Wipe the spare ribs and leave them in sections of several ribs as you bought them. Rub with salt, dust lightly with five spice powder and pepper; leave for 1 hour.

Blend the soy sauces with sherry, honey, hoisin sauce and garlic. Finally stir in the oil. Pour this marinade over the ribs and spoon onto the surface. Leave for 2-4 hours, turning occasionally.

Put on a wire rack above a roasting tin containing 5mm/¼in of water to catch the drips of marinade from the ribs. Cook at 200°C/400°F/Gas 6 for 20 minutes.

Pork Spare Ribs in Barbecue Sauce
Serves 4

Ingredients

	Sauce
2kg/4½lb spare ribs	2 cloves garlic, finely chopped
30ml/2tbsp soy sauce	3 spring onions, washed and chopped
30ml/2tbsp sherry	2.5g/½tsp fennel seeds
45ml/3tbsp red wine vinegar	2.5g/½tsp cinnamon
1 clove garlic, crushed	2.5g/½tsp basil
1 small onion, peeled and sliced	2 cloves
salt and freshly ground pepper	10g/2tsp brown sugar
1 small piece root ginger, grated	juice of ½ lemon
	juice of ½ orange
	30ml/2tbsp red wine vinegar
	300ml/½pt stock
	30ml/2tbsp soy sauce
	425g/15oz canned peeled tomatoes
	150ml/¼pt chicken stock

Preparation If possible ask the butcher to trim the spare ribs to good handling size, about 10cm/4in long.

In a clean screw-top jar, put all the marinade ingredients together and mix well by shaking. Pour the marinade over the pork and turn from time to time for about ½-1 hour, or longer if you wish.

Deep fry the spare ribs for about 5 minutes and drain on kitchen paper.

Mix the ingredients for the sauce in a saucepan, wok or frying pan and bring to the boil.

Add the spare ribs and simmer in the sauce for about 30 minutes. Add a little water and the remaining marinade to prevent it going dry.

Variation Cook the marinated ribs on a wire rack over a roasting pan in a hot oven at 210°C/425°F/Gas 7. Pour the sauce over the roasted meat.

Stretching Bacon

Cut off rind then use the flat of a knife to 'stretch' the slice.

Scoring for Crackling.

Use a very sharp knife to score through pork rind and fat. Score evenly and thoroughly for crisp crackling.

Pasta, Rice and Dumplings

Curry Noodles   171
Celebration Noodles   171
Crisp Fried Noodles   172
Prawn and Noodle Balls   172
Noodles with Peanut Sauce   172
Noodles with Cottage Cheese   172
Macaroni Cheese with Bacon and Tomato   173
Fettucine alla Romana   173
Lasagne Al Forno   173
Vegetable Lasagne   174
Pasta with Aubergine and Apple   174
Chilli Pasta   174
Pasta Trio   175
Pasta with Spinach Sauce   175
Pasta with Mushroom Sauce   175
Pasta Wheels with Salami   176
Spaghetti con Vongole   176
Spaghetti alla Carbonara   177
Spinach Tagliatelle with Asparagus   177
Spinach with Ricotta Cannelloni   177
Jambalaya   178
Coconut Rice   178
Rice with Chicken   178
Herbed Rice   179
Curried Fried Rice   179
Fried Rice   179
Chop Suey   180

Paella   180
Kedgeree with Cherries   181
Kedgeree   181
Rice à la Provençale   182
Pamplona Rice   182
Milanese Risotto   183
Risotto   183
Pilaf   183
Pilau Rice   184
Nutty Rice Pilau   184
Savoury Spinach Rice   185
Rice Cubes   185
Spanish Rice   185
Thai Steamed Rice   186
Spiced Rice Salad   186
Kaska   187
Couscous   187
Cornmeal Pudding   188
Curd Cheese Dumplings   188
Ravioli   188
Pasta Bows with Buckwheat   188
Polenta   189
Matza Balls   189
Potato Gnocchi I   190
Potato Gnocchi II   190

Making Pasta Dough by Hand   191

Curry Noodles
Serves 4-6

This is a truly international dish combining Indian, Chinese and Western ingredients.

Ingredients
450g/1lb fresh yellow noodles
60-90ml/4-6tbsp oil
1 square bean curd, well drained, cut into dice
2 beaten eggs, seasoned
1 medium onion, peeled and sliced
1 clove garlic, crushed
15ml/1tbsp soy sauce
30-45ml/2-3tbsp tomato ketchup
15ml/1tbsp chilli sauce (or to taste)
1 large cooked potato, diced
4 spring onions
1-2 green chillies, seeded and shredded

Preparation Cook the noodles in boiling water in a large pan for just 2-3 minutes. Do not overcook. Drain and rinse with cold water to halt cooking; set on one side.

Heat 30ml/2tbsp of the oil in a pan and fry the bean curd until brown. Drain and set aside.

Pour the beaten eggs into the pan. When it has set like an omelette roll it up on a board and chop finely.

Spoon the remaining oil into a frying pan or wok and fry the onion and garlic for 2-3 minutes. Add the drained noodles, soy sauce, ketchup and chilli sauce. Toss well over a medium heat.

Add the potato dice, most of the spring onion, some of the chilli and all the bean curd. Keep tossing. When hot, add pieces of the cooked egg.

Serve on a hot platter garnished with the remaining spring onion and chilli.

Celebration Noodles
Serves 8

Chinese fish sauce is a bottled condiment, similar in flavour to anchovy essence which could be used instead.

Ingredients
450-675g/1-1½lb egg noodles, fresh or dried
450g/1lb whole, fresh prawns, or 225g/8oz thawed, frozen prawns
225g/8oz cooked chicken breast
225g/8oz cooked ham or lean pork
50g/2oz lard or 60-90ml/4-6tbsp cooking oil
1 medium onion, peeled and chopped
2 cloves garlic, peeled and crushed
½ small Chinese cabbage, finely shredded or 225g/8oz bean sprouts
150ml/¼pt fish stock from prawns or chicken stock
30ml/2tbsp Chinese fish sauce (optional)
seasoning
chopped spring onions
lemon or lime wedges

Preparation Cook fresh noodles in boiling water for 1-2 minutes, rinse with cold water and drain thoroughly, or dried noodles according to packet directions and drain in the same way.

Cover the fresh prawns, if using, with cold water. Bring to the boil and cook gently for 5 minutes. Lift out with a draining spoon, remove the heads and shells and reserve the prawns. Discard the shells. Strain the cooking liquid. If using frozen prawns, thaw well. You will need to substitute the prawn stock with chicken stock later in the recipe.

Using a very sharp knife, finely slice the chicken meat and ham or pork.

Heat half the oil in a wok and fry the drained noodles for 2-3 minutes, stirring. Lift out of the pan onto a platter and keep warm.

Heat the remaining oil in the pan, fry the onion and garlic until soft and just beginning to turn golden. Add the cabbage or bean sprouts, cook for 1-2 minutes, mix well, then stir in most of the chicken, ham or pork and prawns, reserved fish or prepared chicken stock and fish sauce. Turn the mixture all the time.

Return the noodles to pan, taste for seasoning and serve on a hot platter garnished with the reserved prawns, the chicken, ham or pork and the spring onions, and accompany with wedges of lemon or lime.

Curry Noodles

Crisp Fried Noodles
Serves 6-8

Ingredients

6 shallots, peeled and chopped
2 cloves garlic, peeled and crushed
oil for frying
100g/4oz finely chopped raw chicken breast
50g/2oz cooked pork, sliced
100g/4oz cooked, shelled prawns
1 square tofu
150g/6oz canned salted soya beans, drained
4 beaten eggs
25ml/1fl oz cider or wine vinegar
15-30g/1-2tbsp icing sugar

fish sauce to taste (optional)
350g/12oz rice vermicelli
deep fat for frying
pinch chilli powder
spring onions
2-3 red chillies, seeded and finely sliced
fresh coriander leaves
chopped, pickled garlic or fried garlic flakes
rind of lime or a strip of grapefruit peel, cut into fine shreds
175g/6oz bean sprouts, tails removed for best effect

Preparation For the sauce, fry the shallots and garlic in hot oil in a wok; do not colour. Add the chicken and stir for 3-4 minutes, then stir in the pork and prawns. Turn the ingredients all the time. Add the tofu cubes and salted soya beans and cook for 2-3 minutes. Then add the beaten eggs little by little, stirring throughout and adding extra oil if necessary to the sauce. At this stage stir in the vinegar, icing sugar and fish sauce if used. Toss in the pan for 1-2 minutes, then check the flavour. It should have a sweet, salty taste. Set aside.

Heat fat in a large pan and deep fry the noodles for just a few seconds. This is best done in several stages in a frying basket or wok. The noodles will become puffy and crisp. Remove them from the fat, drain and keep warm.

Just before serving, put half the sauce and a sprinkling of the chilli powder in a large wok or pan with half the noodles. Toss together without breaking up the noodles too much. Repeat with the remaining sauce, chilli powder and noodles.

Pile onto a large serving platter and garnish attractively with spring onions, chillies, coriander leaves, garlic and lime rind or grapefruit shreds. Arrange the bean sprouts all around the base.

Prawn and Noodle Balls
Makes 15

Ingredients

100g/4oz vermicelli
225g/8oz peeled prawns
2.5g/½tsp sugar
50g/2oz pork fat

few slices fresh ginger
salt and pepper
a little lightly beaten egg white
oil for deep frying

Preparation Crush the vermicelli finely and leave in a dry place. Mince the prawns in a food processor and sprinkle with sugar. Mince the pork fat with the fresh ginger, add the prawns with seasoning and bind with a little egg white.

Use wetted hands to form into even bite-size balls. Chill well, and roll in the crushed vermicelli just before frying in hot oil. Cook for about 3-4 minutes until cooked through, or steam in a bamboo steamer over hot water for 30 minutes.

Noodles with Peanut Sauce
Serves 6

Ingredients

450g/1lb egg noodles, cooked according to packet directions
45g/3tbsp crunchy peanut butter
15ml/1tbsp hot oil
5ml/1tsp sesame oil
60ml/4tbsp oil for frying

Garnishes
handful dry-fried peanuts, lightly crushed
2 spring onions, shredded
100g/4oz bean sprouts, blanched in boiling water for 1 minute, rinsed in cold water and drained
¼-½ cucumber, cut into small chunks
a few radishes

Preparation Plunge the cooked noodles into boiling water for 1 minute. Rinse with cold water and leave on one side to dry.

Meanwhile prepare the sauce by blending the peanut butter with the hot oil and sesame oil to a smooth paste. Prepare the garnishes.

Fry the noodles in two or three lots in hot oil. Flatten out on one side and, when hot, turn over and fry on the other side. Keep warm while cooking the other noodles.

Pile onto a large platter and pour over the sauce — mix lightly then scatter with peanuts and spring onions. Arrange the bean sprouts, cucumber and radishes either around the noodles or in separate bowls.

Noodles with Cottage Cheese
Serves 4-6

Ingredients

175g/6oz bacon, diced
350g/12oz noodles, cooked and drained
50g/2oz butter

225g/8oz cottage cheese
150ml/¼pt sour cream or thick yoghurt
salt and pepper

Preparation Fry the bacon until it is crisp. Drain it and reserve.

Put the cooked noodles into a large dish. Add the butter, cottage cheese, sour cream, salt and pepper, and mix everything into the noodles.

Scatter the fried bacon on top and serve immediately.

Add more bacon if you want to make a more substantial dish.

Macaroni Cheese with Bacon and Tomato
Serves 4

Ingredients
175g/6oz short cut
  macaroni
salt and freshly ground
  pepper
2.5ml/¹/₂tsp oil
25g/1oz butter
600ml/1pt Mornay Sauce

50g/2oz grated cheese
10g/1tbsp fresh
  breadcrumbs
4 slices back bacon
2 tomatoes, sliced

Preparation Cook the macaroni for 7 minutes in boiling salted water to which the oil has been added. Drain well.

Butter an ovenproof dish and prepare the sauce.

Mix the macaroni with the sauce and pour into the dish.

Sprinkle with the grated cheese mixed with the breadcrumbs.

Arrange the bacon slices on top of the macaroni alternately with tomato slices. Cook at 200°C/400°F/Gas 6 for 15-20 minutes until the bacon is done.

Fettuccine alla Romana
Serves 4

Ingredients
450g/1lb fettucini
50g/2oz butter
2.5g/¹/₂tsp ground nutmeg
150ml/¹/₄pt cream

salt and freshly ground
  pepper
100g/4oz Parmesan cheese,
  grated

Preparation Bring a well-filled saucepan of salted water to boil; add a few drops of oil and salt. Feed in the fettucini and cook until *al dente* — fresh pasta will only take about 2 minutes. Drain in a colander.

Melt the butter in the saucepan, add the nutmeg, pour in half the cream and stir until shiny and bubbles start to appear.

Add the fettucini and stir around in the pan. Pour in the remaining cream and cheese alternately, forking the pasta as it is mixed. Serve immediately.

Note This is a real pasta-lovers' dish. To obtain best results use freshly grated Parmesan cheese rather than the commercially grated variety.

Lasagne al Forno
Serves 4-6

Ingredients
9 sheets cooked lasagne
450ml/³/₄pt Bolognese
  Sauce
600ml/1pt Béchamel
  Sauce

10g/1tbsp dried
  breadcrumbs
15g/1tbsp Parmesan cheese
salt and pepper

Preparation Place 4 tbsp of the Bolognese sauce on the bottom of a 25×20cm (10×8in) dish. Top with 3 tbsp of the Béchamel sauce and three strips of cooked lasagne. Season the pasta with salt and pepper.

Start the layers of sauce again as shown in the picture. Use another 3 tbsp Bolognese sauce and 3 tbsp Béchamel.

Top with another 3 strips of lasagne, a further 3 tbsp Bolognese sauce and 3 tbsp Béchamel. Add remaining strips of lasagne, season and spread the meat sauce on top of the final topping of white sauce.

Spread the Béchamel over the surface and sprinkle it with grated Parmesan cheese or Parmesan cheese mixed with dried breadcrumbs to give a crunchy topping when cooked. Bake the lasagne in a preheated oven 180°C/350°F/Gas 4 for 25 minutes until golden brown. For a really crisp topping, put the dish under the grill for 3 minutes.

Vegetable Lasagne
Serves 4

Ingredients

60ml/4tbsp oil
1 aubergine, sliced
1 red pepper, seeded and sliced
1 courgette, sliced
salt and freshly ground pepper

100g/4oz mushrooms, sliced
425ml/³/₄pt Concentrated Tomato Sauce
600ml/1pt Béchamel Sauce
9 sheets cooked lasagne

Preparation Heat the oil and fry the vegetables over a low heat filling the pan and turning in the oil for about 3 minutes each batch. You will need to allow 15 minutes for preparing and frying the vegetables.

Start with the Concentrated Tomato Sauce and one third of the vegetables. Top with Béchamel Sauce and lasagne. Season and start layering as in Lasagne al Forno, ending with Béchamel and cheese.

When all the ingredients are used, bake in a preheated 180°C/350°F/Gas 4 oven until golden brown, about 25 minutes.

Pasta with Aubergine and Apple
Serves 2-3

Ingredients

1 large aubergine
1 large cooking apple
1 egg, beaten
seasoned white flour
60ml/4tbsp walnut oil

2 cloves garlic, crushed
225g/8oz wholewheat or spinach pasta shapes
salt and freshly ground black pepper

Preparation Slice the aubergine, sprinkle liberally with salt and leave in a colander for 30 minutes. Rinse and dry on kitchen paper and cut into strips. Peel, core and dice the apple.

Toss aubergine and apple in the beaten egg, and then in the seasoned flour to give a light coating. Heat some oil in a pan and fry the aubergine, apple and garlic, stirring, until crisp.

Meanwhile, cook pasta shells in plenty of salted water at a full rolling boil, until *al dente*. Add a few drops of oil to the water to prevent the pasta from sticking. Drain well, season with black pepper and toss in a little walnut oil. Stir in the aubergine mixture and serve with Parmesan cheese.

Pasta Trio

Chilli Pasta
Serves 4

Ingredients

30ml/2tbsp oil
2 cloves garlic, crushed
450g/1lb lean minced beef
2 small onions, peeled
1 red pepper, seeded
1 green pepper, seeded
1 small chilli pepper
425g/15oz canned tomatoes
pinch chilli powder

150ml/¹/₄pt beef stock
1 small can kidney beans or 100g/4oz dried beans, soaked and cooked
350g/12oz pasta shells, cooked
salt and freshly ground pepper
25g/1oz butter
shake of grated nutmeg

Preparation Heat the oil in a pan, add the crushed garlic and the meat, turn over with a fork until the meat is brown and separated into particles. Break down lumps with a fork. Add the diced onion and continue cooking over a low heat until the onions are slightly transparent.

Cut the peppers into bite-size strips and add to the meat.

Seed the chilli pepper, taking care the seeds do not touch your skin or eyes. Chop into small pieces and add to the meat mixture which is still cooking slowly over a low heat.

Add the canned tomatoes, chilli powder and beef stock and bring to the boil, then simmer for 45 minutes. Add canned beans 15 minutes before serving.

Pasta with Spinach Sauce
Serves 4

Ingredients

1kg/2lb fresh spinach
30ml/2tbsp oil
1 onion, chopped
2 cloves garlic, chopped
175g/6oz mushrooms,
* sliced*
225g/8oz curd, ricotta or
* cream cheese*

15-30ml/1-2tbsp pine
* kernels*
salt and freshly ground
* black pepper*
300g/10oz wholewheat or
* spinach pasta shapes*
Parmesan cheese, grated

Preparation Wash spinach and discard tough stalks. Pack into a large pan, cover and cook over a low heat until soft, stirring occasionally. Drain and chop.

Heat oil in a pan and fry the onion and garlic until soft. Stir in the mushrooms. Cover and cook over a low heat until soft.

Mix the vegetables with the cheese and pine kernels and season to taste. Keep warm.

Cook the pasta in plenty of boiling salted water until *al dente*. Drain. Stir sauce into pasta and serve with Parmesan cheese.

Pasta with Mushroom Sauce
Serves 1

Ingredients

2-4 handfuls green pasta
* spirals*
5ml/1tsp oil
50g/2oz mushrooms
milk
salt and freshly ground
* black pepper*

yolk of 1 egg
15ml/1tbsp cream
as much parsley as you
* like, chopped*
Parmesan cheese, grated

Preparation Cook the pasta in plenty of boiling salted water with the oil, until *al dente*.

Meanwhile, wipe and slice the mushrooms. Put in a pan with a little milk, season well and poach gently, stirring, until soft and very black and the liquid has almost gone.

Beat the egg yolk with the cream and stir in the mushrooms.

Drain the pasta and stir in the mushroom mixture with plenty of parsley. Serve at once with Parmesan and a tender lettuce salad.

Dried beans must be soaked and boiled for 30 minutes before being added to the chilli for 30 minutes of cooking time. Taste for seasoning and add salt and pepper if necessary.

Serve with the cooked hot pasta which has been tossed in butter with a shake of nutmeg.

Pasta Trio
Serves 4

Ingredients

225g/8oz stuffed ravioli or
* tortellini*
225g/8oz tagliatelli
225g/8oz wholewheat
* pasta spirals*

300ml/¹/₂pt Béchamel Sauce
300ml/1/2pt Bolognese
* Sauce*
100g/4oz Parmesan cheese

Preparation Cook the pasta. Drain the cooking water into a bowl and return the pasta to the saucepan and keep it warm.

Warm the sauces.

Serve the pasta on individual dishes and the sauces in bowls, accompanied by a bowl of Parmesan cheese and green salad.

Variation Other combinations of pastas and sauces can be used.

Pasta Wheels with Salami
Serves 4

Ingredients

2 stalks celery
1 eating apple, peeled
juice of 1 lemon
1 small lettuce
225g/8oz cooked pasta
    wheels

150ml/¼pt Mayonnaise
8 slices salami
2 tomatoes
celery leaves

Preparation Remove the strings from the celery stalks with a sharp knife and cut into thin slices. Dice the apple and mix with the celery.

Sprinkle the lemon juice on the celery and apple and arrange on the bottom of a dish lined with lettuce.

Mix the pasta wheels with the mayonnaise, arrange on top of the apples and celery.

Roll up slices of salami and arrange in a wheel pattern on the pasta wheels.

Garnish with tomato wedges and some celery leaves in the centre.

Spaghetti con Vongole
Serves 4

Ingredients

1 onion, peeled
2 cloves garlic, crushed
60ml/4tbsp olive oil
6 beef tomatoes, peeled
    and diced or 425g/15oz
    canned tomatoes
60ml/4tbsp white wine

salt and freshly ground
    pepper
1 small can clams, drained
350g/12oz spaghetti
15g/½oz butter
pinch of nutmeg
15g/2tbsp freshly chopped
    parsley

Preparation Dice the onion finely, peel and crush the garlic. Heat the oil in a saucepan or large frying pan and cook over a low heat until the onion is transparent.

Add the tomatoes, white wine and seasoning. Simmer for 10 minutes. Add the clams and heat gently for a further 6 minutes.

Meanwhile cook the spaghetti in plenty of boiling salted water for about 12 minutes. Drain and toss in a little melted butter. Add a shake of pepper and nutmeg.

Add the parsley to the spaghetti and stir well. Combine with the clam sauce and serve at once on heated plates.

If you are using fresh clams scrub the shells and wash well in several batches of cold water to remove sand and grit. Place them in a frying pan with half the white wine and cook over a high heat until the shells open. Strain and use the juice in the sauce. Remove the fish from the shells and heat through in the sauce as above.

Variation Add 45ml/3tbsp single cream to the sauce before serving.

Spaghetti con Vongole

Spaghetti alla Carbonara
Serves 4

Ingredients

450g/1lb spaghetti	50g/2oz butter
salt and freshly ground pepper	50g/2oz Parmesan cheese
2.5ml/½tsp oil	5 eggs, beaten
1 onion, peeled and finely sliced	7g/1tbsp freshly chopped parsley
5 slices of back bacon	
100g/4oz mushrooms, washed and sliced	

Preparation Cook the spaghetti in a large saucepan of boiling salted water with the oil added, for 12 minutes. Drain well.

Meanwhile prepare the other ingredients, slice the onion, and dice the bacon. Wash and slice the mushrooms.

Melt half the butter in a large pan and cook the onion and bacon for 5 minutes over a low heat. Add the mushrooms and cook for a further 3 minutes.

Toss the drained spaghetti in the other half of the melted butter over a medium heat for a few seconds. Season with pepper, add cheese.

Toss the spaghetti into the pan with the onion, bacon and mushrooms and mix well. Add the seasoned beaten egg and stir vigorously into the mixture. Cook over the heat for a few minutes until thick and creamy.

Serve on warmed plates or serving dish, sprinkled with chopped parsley.

Spinach Tagliatelle with Asparagus
Serves 2

Ingredients

225g/8oz asparagus	225g/8oz green tagliatelle
15g/1oz butter	10ml/2tsp oil
60ml/4tbsp single cream	Parmesan cheese, grated
salt and freshly ground black pepper	

Preparation If you are using fresh asparagus, clean it under cold running water, tie it in a bundle and stand upright in a tall saucepan containing about 7cm (3in) boiling salted water. Cover with foil so that the asparagus tips cook by steaming. Alternatively, use a double boiler, inverting the inner saucepan over the bottom one. The asparagus will take 10-20 minutes to cook, depending on its thickness. Test by piercing half-way up the stalk with a sharp knife — if you can insert the knife easily, the asparagus is done. Drain it. Cut off and discard the woody lower pieces. Cut the asparagus into bite-size pieces

Melt the butter in a saucepan and toss the asparagus in it. Add half the cream, season and leave for a few minutes over a very low heat to thicken.

Meanwhile, cook the pasta until *al dente* in plenty of boiling salted water to which you have added 2tsp oil.

Drain the pasta, toss in the remaining cream and pour over the asparagus sauce. Serve and offer Parmesan cheese.

Spinach and Ricotta Cannelloni
Serves 4

Ingredients

175g/6oz chopped spinach, cooked	pinch marjoram
100g/4oz Ricotta cheese	pinch nutmeg
salt and freshly ground pepper	6 strips fresh pasta
10g/1tbsp fresh breadcrumbs	150ml/¼pt Concentrated Tomato Sauce
50g/2oz Parmesan cheese	300ml/½pt Béchamel Sauce

Preparation Mix the cooked spinach, which can be fresh, frozen or canned, with the Ricotta cheese in a bowl. Season and add the breadcrumbs, marjoram and nutmeg and 1 tsp Parmesan cheese. Cream to a smooth paste.

Put the spinach and Ricotta cheese mixture into a piping bag with a 1.25-cm (½-in) plain nozzle.If you do not want to use a piping bag, spoon the mixture with a teaspoon. Lay the uncooked pasta strips (7.5cm/2½in wide) on a board. Pipe the mixture along the width of the pasta, roll into a tube, cut with a sharp knife.

Put the Concentrated Tomato Sauce in the bottom of the dish, arrrange the tubes on top and season the cannelloni.

When all the pasta tubes are arranged in the sauce pour the Béchamel on top covering the pasta completely.

Sprinkle with the remaining Parmesan cheese and bake in a preheated 180°C/350°F/Gas 4 oven for 30 minutes. For a crisper topping, finish under the grill.

Jambalaya
Serves 4

Ingredients

25g/1oz butter
30ml/2tbsp oil
1 onion, peeled and finely chopped
4 stalks celery
1 green pepper, seeded
2 aubergines
225g/8oz long-grain rice
5g/1tsp salt
freshly ground black pepper

15ml/1tbsp Worcestershire sauce
5ml/1tsp soy sauce
600ml/1pt chicken stock
100g/4oz cooked ham, diced
225g/8oz peeled prawns
15g/3tbsp chopped parsley
whole prawns to garnish (optional)

Preparation Heat the butter and oil in a frying pan and cook the onion over a low heat until translucent.

Wash the celery and peel the strings from the rounded side with a sharp knife. Cut into small pieces. Add to the onions.

Dice the pepper and aubergines. Add to the celery and onion and stir for a few minutes to mix well. Add the rice and stir if there is room in the pan. If there is not, put the vegetables and rice into a large casserole and mix well.

Add the salt and pepper, Worcestershire and soy sauces to the stock.

Transfer the vegetables and rice into the casserole if not already there. Add the stock over a medium heat. When the liquid comes to the boil cover with a lid and bake at 180°C/350°F/Gas 4.

Remove from the oven. Stir in the prawns and ham. Replace the lid and cook for a further 10-15 minutes until the rice is cooked. Taste for seasoning.

Mix in the chopped parsley before serving. Garnish with whole prawns if you like.

Rice with Chicken
Serves 4

Chicken stock enriched with sherry gives a rich flavour to the rice which is mixed with small pieces of chicken and dried mushrooms.

Ingredients

400g/14oz short-grain rice
100g/4oz boned chicken breast or thigh
30ml/2tbsp soy sauce
4 dried mushrooms, soaked in hot water

450ml/¾pt chicken stock
20ml/4tsp sherry
4 sprigs fresh coriander

Preparation Wash the rice thoroughly and put in a strainer to drain for at least 30 minutes. Cut the chicken into short, 1.25-cm (½-in) strips, sprinkle with the soy sauce and set aside to marinate for 30 minutes. Discard the mushroom stems and slice the caps finely.

Put the rice in a saucepan and pour the chicken stock and sherry over it. Add the chicken and mushroom pieces. Bring to the boil over high heat, stirring occasionally. Cover tightly and reduce the heat to very low. Simmer for 8-10 minutes, then turn off the heat and leave, still covered, to steam for 15 minutes. Mix well and serve, garnishing each bowl with a coriander sprig.

Coconut Rice
Serves 4

Rice cooked in coconut milk is a wonderful accompaniment to chicken and pork dishes and curries.

Ingredients

225g/8oz desiccated coconut
600ml/1pt boiling water
175g/6oz long-grain rice
2.5g/½tsp ground coriander

1 stick cinnamon
1 stem lemongrass, bruised
bay leaf (optional)
salt
fried onions

Preparation First make the coconut milk by pouring the boiling water over the desicated coconut, leaving to stand for 15 minutes, then squeezing out the liquid.

Put the coconut milk in a pan with the rice, washed if necessary, coriander, cinnamon stick, lemongrass and bay leaf if used. Add salt. Bring to the boil over a medium heat, stirring a few times. Cook over the lowest heat for 12-15 minutes or until all the coconut milk has been absorbed.

Fork through carefully and remove the cinnamon, lemongrass and leaf. Cover with a tight-fitting lid, then cook over the lowest heat for a further 10 minutes.

Serve garnished with crispy fried onions.

Herbed Rice
Serves 4

Serve this with grilled poultry or meat. Vegetarians can simply add grated cheese instead.

Ingredients
225-275g/8-10oz long-grain rice	1 clove garlic, crushed
5g/1tsp salt	8 spring onions, washed
50g/2oz butter	25g/1oz freshly chopped parsley
1 onion, peeled and finely chopped	8 basil leaves, chopped black pepper

Preparation Cook the rice in 1l/1¾pt boiling water with the salt added. Leave the pan uncovered and fork the rice occasionally for first 10 minutes.

Heat the butter in a frying pan and cook the onion and garlic over a low heat for 3 minutes. Add the finely chopped spring onions.

Mix the onion mixture and the rice well. There should still be a little water left.

Cover with a lid and allow the remaining water to be absorbed. This will take another 5-7 minutes over a low heat.

Remove the lid and taste to make sure rice is tender. Add the parsley and basil leaves. Season with freshly ground black pepper and extra salt if necessary.

Fried Rice

Curried Fried Rice
Serves 4-6

Ingredients
225g/8oz cooked chicken, pork and/or prawns	6 shallots, peeled and chopped finely
450g/1lb cold, cooked rice	2 cloves garlic, peeled and chopped
100g/4oz runner beans or French haricot beans, cut into 5cm (2in) lengths and blanched	2 stems lemongrass, use bottom part of bulb, sliced
3-5 dried red chillies, seeded and pounded or 5-10g/1-2tsp chilli powder	4 stems coriander, chopped, leaves reserved for garnish
	60-90ml/6-8tbsp vegetable oil

Preparation Cut the meats into fine slices and leave the prawns, if using, whole. Set the rice on one side. Prepare and blanch the beans.

Pound the chillies with shallots, garlic, lemongrass and coriander stems and peel. This can be done in a food processor. If using the chilli powder add it to these pounded ingredients.

Heat the oil and fry this paste until it gives off a fragrant aroma. Add the cooked meats then the rice, stirring all the time until the fried rice is well mixed. Add more oil if necessary. Season with salt, fish sauce and sugar, if liked, to taste. Finally, add the green beans.

Serve garnished with the coriander leaves.

Fried Rice
Serves 4

This is a useful way to make a delicious savoury rice dish with leftovers.

Ingredients
45ml/3tbsp vegetable oil	salt and freshly ground pepper
1 large onion, peeled and finely chopped	15ml/1tbsp soy sauce
225g/8oz cooked long-grain rice	50g/2oz cooked ham, chopped
	25g/1oz bamboo shoots
	50g/2oz cooked shrimps

Preparation Heat the oil in a large frying pan. Cook the onion over a medium heat until it is a pale golden colour.

Add the long-grain rice and stir in with the onion. Season well.

Stir in the soy sauce, ham, bamboo shoots and shrimps. Cook until golden brown. Taste for flavour. Add more soy sauce, vegetables, meat or fish if necessary.

Chop Suey
Serves 4

Ingredients

450g/1lb long-grain rice	100g/4oz cooked prawns
salt	225g/8oz cooked chicken
90ml/6tbsp oil	100g/4oz cooked ham
2 medium onions, peeled	2 eggs (or 4 if making the
2 cloves garlic, crushed	omelette)
2 fresh chilli peppers,	salt and freshly ground
seeded	pepper
5g/1tsp Garam Masala	10g/1tbsp chopped spring
30ml/2tbsp soy sauce	onions
2.5ml/½tsp Worcestershire	
sauce	

Preparation Cook the long-grain rice in 1200ml/2pt boiling water with 5g/1tsp salt until the liquid is absorbed and the rice is done, about 15 minutes. Fork through the grains to make sure they are separated before putting on the lid.

Heat one-third of the oil in a frying pan. Add 1 onion, finely chopped and the garlic, and cook until translucent. Remove with a slotted spoon.

In a blender or food processor whizz together the other onion, chopped, the chilli peppers, Garam Masala, and the soy and Worcestershire sauces to make a paste.

Add the remaining oil and fry the paste over a medium heat for 3 minutes.

Add the prawns, chicken and ham and stir for a few minutes. Beat the eggs with salt and pepper. Turn the heat up fairly high and add the egg mixture, stirring continuously until the egg begins to set.

Add the cooked rice and blend with the other ingredients on a lower heat.

Decorate the rice mixture with omelette strips (see below) if liked, sprinkle with chopped spring onion and serve immediately.

Variation To garnish with omelette strips, use 4 eggs. Add 2 to the meat and prawn mixture and make a small omelette with the rest.

Mix them vigorously with a fork. Add seasoning. Melt a knob of butter in an omelette pan over a high heat. Pour in the egg mixture and pull the cooked edges back from the sides of the pan to the centre (do not mix as if you were making scrambled egg). When the mixture is almost set, put the pan under a hot grill for about 1 minute. Turn onto a board and cut into thin strips.

Paella
Serves 6

Ingredients

120ml/8tbsp oil	1 green pepper, seeded
2 large onions, peeled and	225g/8oz white fish, boned
finely chopped	150ml/¼pt white wine
2-3 cloves garlic, crushed	1 bay leaf
275g/10oz long-grain rice	4-8 chicken drumsticks
salt and freshly ground	450g/1lb mussels
pepper	100g/4oz peeled prawns
pinch turmeric	7g/1tbsp parsley, chopped
600ml/1pt chicken stock	
1 red pepper, seeded	

Preparation Heat three quarters of the oil in a large frying pan or casserole. Over a low heat cook the onions until they become translucent. Add the garlic.

Gradually add the rice and stir around in the onions and oil until the grains are coated with oil.

Add seasoning and turmeric to the hot stock and pour on the rice gradually, stirring as the rice is brought to the boil. Cover with a lid or with foil, and simmer gently for 10 minutes.

Meanwhile dice the green and red peppers and blanch for 1 minute in boiling water.

Poach the white fish in water with a little of the wine and the bay leaf for about 5 minutes.

Fry the drumsticks in another pan in the remaining oil until golden brown and cooked through.

Clean the mussels by removing the beards and rinsing several times in cold water. Any which remain open when tapped should be discarded. Pour the wine into the saucepan with a little fish stock from the poached fish. Add the mussels and shake the pan from time to time until the mussels open. This will take about 8 minutes. Keep warm.

Remove the lid from the rice and separate the grains with a fork. Stirring gently, add the peppers, the white fish, prawns, about 150ml/¼pt mussel stock and then the chicken. Cover and cook until rice is separate and liquid is absorbed.

Decorate with parsley before serving.

Kedgeree with Cherries
Serves 6

Ingredients

50g/2oz clarified butter
1 onion, finely chopped
450g/1lb firm white fish
  fillets, cut into small
  pieces
2.5g/¹/₂tsp ground
  cinnamon
350g/12oz fresh or canned
  (drained weight) sour
  cherries, stoned

75g/3oz unsalted
  almonds, chopped
75g/3oz currants, or
  raisins
50g/2oz dried apricots
7.5g/1¹/₂tsp salt
2.5g/¹/₂tsp black pepper
600g/1¹/₄lb long grain rice,
  rinsed and drained
1.2l/2pt water

Preparation Heat the butter in a large skillet. Add the onion and fish pieces and sauté over a low heat for 10 minutes. Stir constantly.

Add the cinnamon, cherries, almonds, currants, apricots, salt and pepper to the skillet. Stir and simmer for 3 to 4 minutes.

Add the rice and water. Stir gently but well. Cover tightly and simmer over a very low heat for 55 minutes.

Kedgeree
Serves 4

This makes an excellent breakfast dish for guests as it can be prepared in advance and heated through just before serving.

Ingredients

100g/4oz long-grain rice
300ml/¹/₂pt boiling water
2.5g/¹/₂tsp salt
3 hard-boiled eggs, shelled
salt and freshly ground
  pepper
225g/8oz smoked haddock
150ml/¹/₄pt milk

1 bay leaf
1 slice of peeled onion
Garnish
7g/1 tbsp parsley, chopped
2.5g/¹/₂tsp paprika
1 lemon, quartered

Preparation Cook the rice in the boiling water with the salt added until the water has been absorbed and the rice is done, about 15 minutes.

Chop 2 of the hard-boiled eggs. Sieve the white and yolk of the third egg separately to decorate the kedgeree.

Add the chopped eggs to the rice, with the salt and pepper.

Put the smoked haddock in a saucepan with the milk, bay leaf, onion and a little pepper. Bring to the boil and simmer for 5 minutes. Allow to cool slightly in the milk. Remove and flake the fish from the skin. Add to the rice.

Heat all the ingredients together and pile onto a heated serving dish. Garnish with rows of egg yolk, egg white and chopped parsley with a little paprika. Serve with lemon quarters.

Rice à la Provençale
Serves 4

This is a useful recipe to serve with many main dishes as there is no need to cook separate vegetables.

Ingredients

225g/8oz long-grain rice
600ml/1pt water
2.5g/½tsp salt
60ml/4tbsp oil
25g/1oz butter
2 onions, peeled and finely
  chopped
2 cloves garlic, crushed
salt and freshly ground
  black pepper
2 red peppers, seeded and
  blanched

4 courgettes, washed and
  thinly sliced
2.5g/½tsp basil
60ml/4tbsp white wine
8 tomatoes, skinned and
  chopped
7g/1tbsp capers, chopped
2 hard-boiled eggs
8 green olives, stoned
15g/2tbsp chopped parsley
  or chervil

Preparation Cook the rice in the water with the salt, by bringing the water to the boil, adding the rice and stirring to separate the grains. Cover and simmer gently until the water has all been absorbed, which will take about 15 minutes.

Heat the oil and butter and cook the onions over a low heat for about 4 minutes. Add the garlic.

Dice the blanched peppers and add with the sliced courgettes, the basil and white wine. Stir gently until cooked for about 5 minutes. Lastly stir in the tomatoes. Gently fold in the cooked rice and season well.

Add the chopped capers and turn into a heated serving dish.

Serve decorated with hard-boiled eggs, green olives and chopped herbs.

Rice à la Provençale

Pamplona Rice
Serves 4

Ingredients

90ml/6tbsp vegetable oil
1 large onion, peeled and
  finely sliced
1 red pepper, seeded
1 green or yellow pepper,
  seeded
2 chilli peppers, seeded
350g/12oz cod, boned and
  skinned
425g/15oz canned, peeled
  tomatoes

275g/10oz long-grain rice
750ml/1¼pt water
freshly ground pepper
4g/¾tsp salt
2.5g/½tsp turmeric or a
  few drops of yellow
  colouring
1 tomato, sliced
1 lemon, quartered

Preparation Heat the oil in a large pan. Cook the onion for 4 minutes over a low heat.

Slice the peppers into strips. Add to the onion with the chopped chilli peppers, and cook for a further 2 minutes. Push to one side of the pan. Raise the heat a little and add the chunks of fish. Fry on each side. Season well.

Add the tomatoes. Stir well. Add the rice. Stir round in the mixture.

Add 3.5g/¾tsp salt and the turmeric or yellow colouring to the water. Gradually pour over the rice. After the water has come to the boil, turn the heat down and simmer gently for 10 minutes.

Turn into an ovenproof dish and allow to dry off in the oven at 180°C/350°F/Gas 4. Fork through the mixture after 5 minutes.

Variation A can of anchovies can be used with 12 green olives to garnish the dish. Arrange and allow rice to heat through again in the oven for 5 minutes. All tomato sauces go well with this.

Milanese Risotto
Serves 4

Ingredients

25g/1oz beef bone marrow
1 small onion, thinly sliced
125g/5oz butter
400g/14oz rice
200ml/⅓pt dry white wine

1l/2pt meat stock, well
  skimmed of fat
good pinch saffron
60g/5tbsp Parmesan cheese

Preparation Scrape the marrow with a knife to remove any bits of bone, then chop and put in a pan with the onion and half the butter. Fry until the onion is soft but not brown. Add the rice and fry for 2 or 3 minutes. Add the wine and cook until absorbed. Add the stock with a ladle, waiting between each addition until it has been absorbed. Cook the rice for 30 minutes. 10 minutes before the end of the cooking time, dissolve the saffron in a few tablespoons of boiling stock and add to the rice. Finally, add the remaining butter and stir in the Parmesan. Let it stand, covered, for 2 minutes before serving.

Risotto
Serves 4

Ingredients

15ml/1tbsp olive oil
25g/1oz butter
1 medium onion, peeled
  and finely chopped
350g/12oz Italian risotto
  rice

900ml/1½pt chicken stock
5g/1tsp salt
freshly ground pepper
7g/1tbsp freshly chopped
  parsley (optional)

Preparation Using a heavy-bottomed saucepan, heat the oil and butter. Add the onion and cook over a low heat for about 3-4 minutes without browning.

Add the risotto rice dry and stir-fry for about 2 minutes over a medium heat.

Add half the hot chicken stock. Stir from the bottom to avoid sticking and continue to do so until the grains are separate and the stock is absorbed.

Continue adding the remaining stock with the salt bit by bit, stirring all the time, until it is all absorbed. The risotto should have cooked to a creamy consistency in about 25 minutes without becoming mushy.

Add the freshly ground pepper and, if you wish, a little freshly chopped parsley for colour, and serve hot.
Variation For Risotto Milanese cook as above but substitute 150ml/¼pt white wine for the equivalent stock. Add 25g/1oz butter and 25g/1oz Parmesan cheese at the end of the cooking time just before serving. Serve with Ossobuco. Can be garnished with mushrooms.

Pilaf
Serves 4

Ingredients

50g/2oz butter
1 medium onion, peeled
  and thinly sliced
225g/8oz long-grain rice
salt and freshly ground
  pepper

pinch of saffron threads or
  a few drops of yellow
  food colouring
450ml/¾pt stock

Preparation Heat 40g/1½oz of the butter in an ovenproof casserole and cook the onion over a low heat for 4 minutes. Add the rice and continue stirring for another 3 minutes.

Season well. Add the saffron or colouring to the stock. Then pour the stock on to the rice and mix well with a fork. Bring to the boil. Cover and cook in the oven at 180°C/350°F/Gas 4 for about 15 minutes until stock is absorbed and rice grains are separate.

Add the remaining butter together with, if you like, 15g/1tbsp grated cheese, and serve hot.

Variation Another version of this savoury rice can be made by adding mushrooms, peppers or grated carrot to the onion. Alternatively add small strips of meat or ham to the rice, or even flaked fish or prawns.

Pilau Rice
Serves 4

Ingredients

225g/8oz long-grain rice
30ml/2tbsp vegetable oil
1 onion, peeled and finely
   chopped
1 clove garlic, crushed
2.5g/½tsp cumin
pinch of turmeric

½ fresh chilli pepper,
   crushed or finely
   chopped (optional)
pinch ground coriander
5g/1tsp salt
600ml/1pt stock or boiling
   water

Preparation Wash the rice and allow it to soak for 20-30 minutes. Drain in a sieve, shaking from time to time.

Heat the oil in a pan on a medium heat and fry the onions and garlic until golden brown.

Add the drained rice, turn the heat down and stir in well. Add the cumin, turmeric, chilli pepper and coriander.

Add the salt with the boiling liquid and gradually mix with the rice. Bring to the boil and simmer, covered, over a low heat for 15-20 minutes, until the rice is cooked. Fluff with a fork.

Variation Vegetable Pilau can be made by adding peas, beans, carrots, peppers, potatoes or a combination of any favourite vegetables. It is advisable to cut the potatoes and carrots into small dice, and blanch them for 4 minutes to ensure that they become cooked through. Add the chopped vegetables to the onion and garlic, and cook all together in 90ml/6tbsp oil over a low heat before adding the rice.

A further 2.5g/½tsp salt should be added to the stock, and 2.5g/½tsp Garam Masala and 30g/2tbsp chopped coriander will add extra flavour.

Spanish Rice

Nutty Rice Pilau
Serves 6

This is a complete main dish, but can also be served as a first course or as an accompaniment.

Ingredients

30ml/2tbsp oil
1 large onion, peeled and
   chopped
175g/6oz mushrooms,
   chopped
450g/1lb long-grain
   American rice
298g/10½oz can
   condensed clear soup
600ml/1pt water
bouquet garni

75g/3oz hazelnuts
50g/2oz almonds
50g/2oz walnuts
25g/1oz pine nuts
10g/1tbsp sunflower seeds
50g/2oz butter
salt and freshly ground
   pepper
7g/1tbsp snipped chives
10g/1tbsp sesame seeds

Preparation Heat the oil in an oven-proof casserole, add the onion and mushrooms and fry over medium heat for a couple of minutes. Add the rice and fry for a minute or until golden. Stir in the clear soup, water and bouquet garni. Bring to the boil then stir well, cover, and put in the oven. Cook for 20 to 25 minutes, without stirring at 180°C/350°F/Gas 4.

While the rice is cooking, toast the hazelnuts and almonds in the oven until golden brown. Put into a grinder or processor with the walnuts, pine nuts and sunflower seeds to chop coarsely.

When the rice is tender and all the liquid has been absorbed, remove the bouquet garni and stir in the nuts, butter and seasonings. Sprinkle with the chives and sesame seeds, and serve hot.

Variation Replace half the quantity of nuts with grated cheese, or substitute condensed tomato soup for the clear soup.

Savoury Spinach Rice
Serves 4

This goes well with meats or fish or it can be served simply as a vegetarian main dish.

Ingredients

450g/1lb frozen leaf spinach or 1kg/2lb fresh spinach, washed	*salt and freshly ground pepper*
25g/1oz butter	*225g/8oz long-grain rice*
15ml/1tbsp oil	*600ml/1pt water or stock*
1 medium onion, peeled	*2.5g/½tsp salt*
1 leek, washed and trimmed	*pinch of nutmeg*
juice of ½ lemon	*7g/1tbsp parsley, chopped*
	15ml/1tbsp natural yoghurt (optional)

Preparation Cook the frozen spinach as directed on the packet or, if thawed, simmer for a few minutes in 60ml/4tbsp water. Drain well in a colander, squeezing out excess moisture with the back of a wooden spoon. If using fresh spinach remove thick stems, tear into manageable pieces and cook in 1.2cm (½in) boiling water for 4 minutes. Drain well.

Heat the butter and oil over a low heat in a large saucepan. Slice the onion and leek finely and cook in the fat for 4-5 minutes. Sprinkle with lemon juice and seasoning.

Add the long-grain rice and stir in with the vegetables. Pour on boiling water or stock with the salt added. Cover with a tight-fitting lid and simmer for 15 minutes.

Fluff the rice with a fork and add the spinach, nutmeg and chopped parsley. Mix with a fork, cover and reheat for 5 minutes.

Serve topped with the yoghurt if you like.

Rice cubes

Ingredients

1×100g/4oz packet boil-in-the-bag rice	*boiling, salted water*

Preparation Put the boil-in-the-bag rice in the water and boil for 1¼ hours or until the whole bag is puffy and firm and rice fills the whole of it. The bag must be covered in water all the time. You can put a sauce or plate on top to weight it down if necessary.

Allow to cool completely before stripping off the bag, leaving a cushion of rice which can then be cut into neat cubes and served with spiced and deep fried chicken or with satay.

Variation Alternatively use 225g/8oz short-grain rice (pudding rice). Wash the rice and put in a pan with 450ml/¾pt salted water. Bring to the boil, stir, cover and simmer for 30-35 minutes over the gentlest heat until the rice is tender. Cool, then turn into a 2.5cm/1in deep dish. Press down, cover with foil, a plate and a weight. Leave until firm. Remove the weights and foil and cut into cubes or diamond shapes.

Spanish Rice
Serves 4

Ingredients

225g/8oz long-grain rice	*6 tomatoes, peeled and chopped or 425g/15oz canned peeled tomatoes*
600ml/1pt stock or water	
5g/1tsp salt	
2.5g/½tsp turmeric	*salt and freshly ground pepper*
30ml/2tbsp vegetable oil	
125g/4oz chicken livers, trimmed and chopped	*pinch of sugar*
1 onion, peeled and finely chopped	*2 red peppers, seeded, chopped and blanched*
	125g/4oz peas
	125g/4oz cooked prawns
	7g/1tbsp parsley, chopped

Preparation Cook the long-grain rice with boiling water or stock to which the salt and turmeric has been added, until the liquid is absorbed and the rice is done, about 15 minutes.

Meanwhile heat the oil in a frying pan, and over a medium heat fry the chopped chicken livers until golden brown. Turn the heat down and add the onion. Cook, stirring well, for 4 minutes. Add the tomatoes, salt, pepper, sugar and chopped peppers. Stir gently.

Add the thawed peas and prawns. Heat through in the vegetable mixture and mix in the warmed rice.

Turn out into a dish and serve hot sprinkled with the parsley. A little butter may be added if you like.

Thai Steamed Rice
Serves 4

Steaming rice after boiling separates out each grain, making it very light and fluffy. It is delicious served with any type of curry.

Ingredients
225g/8oz long-grain rice   *600ml/1pt cold water*

Preparation Rinse the rice in a sieve then put it in a pan with the water. Bring to the boil, lower the heat and cook uncovered until the water has been absorbed and a series of holes appears in the surface of the rice.

Line the base of a steamer within 1.25cm (½in) of the edges with foil and raise the edges into a shallow, bowl-like shape. Puncture all over base with a skewer. Turn the rice into the foil in the steamer and place over a pan of fairly fast-bubbling water. Cover and cook for 30 minutes until the rice is just tender and fluffy. Refill the base pan with boiling water if necessary.

No salt is necessary for this recipe as real Thai rice is of such excellent quality, with a fragrant flavour, that salt detracts from this.

Spiced Rice Salad
Serves 4

Ingredients
225g/8oz rice	*1 clove garlic, crushed*
5g/1tsp salt	*1 onion, peeled and diced*
5g/1tsp Garam Masala	*50g/2oz sultanas*
5g/1tsp turmeric	*1 green pepper, seeded,*
1 bay leaf	*blanched and diced*
25g/1oz butter	*90ml/6tbsp low-fat yoghurt*
	2 spring onions, washed

Preparation Cook the rice in boiling salted water with the Garam Masala, turmeric and bay leaf for about 15 minutes until tender.

Meanwhile melt the butter and gently sweat the garlic and onion without browning for 5 minutes.

Add the garlic and onion to the rice when it is cooked and allow it to cool.

Stir in the sultanas and pepper.

Stir in the yoghurt and serve garnished with chopped spring onions.

Kasha
Buckwheat Groats with Mushrooms
Serves 8-10

Packaged, roasted buckwheat groats are available in many wholefood shops. This dish can be made with just fresh mushrooms, but the rich aroma imparted by the dried mushrooms should not be missed.

Ingredients

225g/8oz dried	*225g/8oz butter*
mushrooms (ceps)	*225g/8oz fresh*
350g/12oz kasha (coarse	*mushrooms, quartered*
buckwheat groats)	*350g/12oz small onions,*
2 eggs, beaten	*quartered*
7.5g/1½tsp salt	*30g/3tbsp finely chopped*
1.2l/2pt boiling water	*spring onions*

Preparation Put the dried mushrooms into a small bowl and add enough warm water to cover. Let the mushrooms soak for 1 hour. Drain well. Trim away any tough stems and cut any large mushrooms in half.

Put the kasha into a medium-sized mixing bowl. Fold the beaten eggs into the kasha.

In a large, heavy frying pan, sauté the kasha and egg mixture over a medium heat, until the kasha begins to become dry. Add the salt, 900ml/1½pt of the boiling water and half the butter. Cover the pan tightly and reduce the heat to low. Simmer for 20 minutes, stirring at 5-minute intervals.

Add the remaining boiling water to the pan. Cover and simmer for a further 5 minutes. Turn the heat off. Leave to stand for 15 minutes.

Turn the heat on again and add the onions, dried mushrooms, fresh mushrooms and spring onion. Stir briefly. Reduce the heat to medium and add the remaining butter. Cook, stirring constantly, until the mushrooms are done and the kasha is dry again, about 3 to 5 minutes.

Couscous
Serves 4-6

Ingredients

100-175g/4-6oz couscous	*4 courgettes, sliced*
5g/1tsp salt	*6 tomatoes, sliced*
300ml/½pt boiling water	*100g/4oz peas*
15ml/1tbsp oil	*100g/4oz kidney beans*
2 large onions, chopped	*presoaked and cooked*
2 leeks, sliced	*100g/4oz chick peas,*
4 carrots, sliced	*presoaked and cooked*
1l/2pts stock	*a few strands of saffron*
salt and freshly ground	*40g/1½oz butter*
black pepper	*Spicy Tomato Sauce*

Preparation Put the couscous in a bowl, add the salt and pour over the boiling water. Let it soak for 20 minutes until the water has been absorbed. Break up any grains that are sticking together.

Meanwhile, make the vegetable topping. Heat the oil in a large saucepan and stir-fry the onions and leeks. Add the carrots and stock and season well. Bring to the boil.

Put the couscous in a vegetable steamer (or a sieve or colander) lined with muslin, and put this over the saucepan. Put on the lid and simmer for 30 minutes.

Remove the steamer and add the remaining vegetables and the saffron to the stock. Stir the couscous with a fork to break up any lumps. Replace steamer, covered, and continue cooking for 10 minutes.

Turn couscous into a bowl and stir in the butter. Serve vegetables separately in a tureen. Offer Spicy Tomato Sauce and pitta bread.

Cornmeal Pudding
Serves 6-8

Ingredients
180g/6½oz cornmeal
22.5g/1½tbsp chicken fat
400ml/¾pt boiling water
2.5g/½tsp salt
pinch black pepper

2 eggs, separated
400ml/¾pt buttermilk
6g/1¼tsp baking soda
50g/2oz butter or
   margarine, melted

Preparation In a large pot, combine the cornmeal with the chicken fat and boiling water. Mix until the consistency of the dough is even. Add the salt, pepper, egg yolks, buttermilk and baking soda. Combine thoroughly.

Beat the egg whites until they are stiff. Fold them into the cornmeal mixture.

Grease a large casserole dish with 15ml/1tbsp of the melted butter or margarine. Preheat the oven to 165°C/325°F/Gas 3. Scrape the cornmeal mixture into the casserole with a spatula. Bake for 1 hour 15 minutes. Pour the remaining melted butter or margarine over the pudding before serving. Serve with a casserole or stew.

Curd Cheese Dumplings
Serves 4

Ingredients
225g/8oz curd cheese
75g/3oz butter or
   margarine
75g/3oz semolina

1 egg
salt and pepper

Preparation Mix everything together well and let the mixture rest for 30 minutes. Lightly flour a board and form the mixture into a roll. Cut off slices and roll them into balls the size of new potatoes.

Drop them into boiling salted water. When they rise to the top they are cooked. Drain them well and serve with meat.

Variation Add some chopped herbs to the mixture if you like and you can roll them in breadcrumbs or finely chopped nuts which have been fried in butter before serving them.

Ravioli
Makes about 50

These meat dumplings are traditionally served in chicken soup.

Ingredients
1kg/2lb boneless chuck
   steak, coarsely minced
4 small onions, coarsely
   chopped
75ml/5tbsp vegetable oil

2.5g/½tsp salt
2.5g/½tsp black pepper
225g/8oz fine wholemeal
   flour
2 eggs
350ml/12fl oz warm water

Preparation In a large saucepan, brown the meat and onions in the oil over a low heat for 8 to 10 minutes. Add half the salt and the black pepper. Stir well. Remove from the heat and set aside.

In a large mixing bowl, make the flour into a mound. Make a well in the flour. Sprinkle the remaining salt over the flour and break the eggs into the well. Beat with a whisk, gradually adding the warm water, until the consistency of the dough is smooth and even. Roll the dough into a ball.

Cut the dough into approximately 15 equal pieces. One by one, roll each piece out into a thin sheet. Cut 3×7.5cm (3-in) rounds from each sheet with a biscuit cutter. Repeat the process until all the dough is used up.

Put 5g/1tsp of the meat and onion filling in the centre of each dough round. Fold the dough over and seal the edges together with the blunt end of a spoon.

Bring a very large pot of water to the boil. Drop in the ravioli, about 8 to 15 at a time, depending on the size of the pot. When the water returns to the boil, cook them for 3 to 5 minutes, or until they float to the top. Remove with a slotted spoon and set aside. If the Ravioli are not being served within 30 minutes, refrigerate them. Add them to the soup for 4 minutes before serving.

Pasta Bows with Buckwheat
Serves 6

Ingredients
1 egg
150g/6oz medium-grain
   kasha (buckwheat
   groats)
50g/2oz butter, margarine
   or chicken fat

2 onions, diced
40g/1½oz mushrooms,
   sliced
boiling water
salt to taste
225g/8oz pasta bows

Preparation Beat the egg in a bowl and add the kasha. Stir well to coat the kasha.

Heat a large heavy pot on the stove top. Add the kasha and cook, stirring until each kasha grain is dry and separate. Make sure this is done thoroughly or the kasha will be soggy and lumpy.

Melt 15g/1tbsp of the fat in a small frying pan. Add the onions and mushrooms, and sauté until soft.

Add the cooked vegetables, boiling water, remaining fat and salt to taste to the kasha. Cover tightly and cook over a medium heat until all the water has been absorbed, about 40 minutes.

Cook the pasta in a large pot of boiling water until *al dente*. Drain well. Mix the pasta with the kasha and serve.

Polenta
Serves 4-6

Ingredients

225g/8oz wholewheat
  flour
50g/2oz fine cornmeal
salt and freshly ground
  black pepper
750ml/1¼pt water

150g/5oz butter
100g/4oz Mozzarella
  cheese, cut into thin
  strips
grated Parmesan cheese

Preparation Put the flour in a bowl and stir in the cornmeal and seasoning.

Bring water to the boil and sprinkle in the mixture, stirring with a wooden spoon. Cook over a low heat, stirring occasionally, for about 45 minutes until the mixture is very thick and comes away easily from the sides of the pan.

Stir in the cheese. Keep stirring until it melts. Serve hot with Tomato Sauce and offer Parmesan.

Matzo Balls
Serves 8

Ingredients

4 eggs, separated
350g/12oz matzo meal
2.5g/½tsp ground ginger
2.5g/½tsp ground white
  pepper

2.5g/½tsp salt
65ml/2½fl oz chicken fat
225ml/8fl oz hot chicken
  stock
1.9l/3½pt water

Preparation Beat the egg whites in a medium-sized mixing bowl until stiff. Set aside.

In a large mixing bowl, combine the matzo meal, ginger, pepper, and salt. Add the fat, stock and egg yolks. Fold in the egg whites and chill for 90 minutes.

In a large soup pot, bring the water to a boil. Form the matzo meal dough into balls with a diameter of about 3.75cm (1½in) and drop them into the pot. Cover tightly and cook for 25 to 30 minutes. Do not remove the cover during this time. If the matzo balls are not being used within 30 minutes, refrigerate them and add them to the liquid 5 minutes before serving.

Potato Gnocchi I
Serves 4-6

Ingredients
450g/1lb cooked potatoes, sliced
225g/8oz plain flour, sifted
salt and pepper
25g/1oz butter, melted

Preparation Force the cooked boiled potatoes through a large sieve or potato ricer. Add the flour with some seasoning and the melted butter. Mix together.

Turn onto a floured board and knead lightly until you have an elastic dough. Divide into 2.5-cm (1-in) pieces and make into little rolls. Shape by pulling the end pieces towards you.

Cook in boiling, salted water for about 10 minutes. Serve with a piquant, well-flavoured sauce and cheese.

Variation Alternately, dot the gnocchi with butter and sprinkled cheese and bake at 205°C/400°F/Gas 6 until golden brown.

(Above) Twisting the dough for Potato Gnocchi.

Potato Gnocchi II
Serves 4

Ingredients
1kg/2lb potatoes
225g/8oz wholemeal flour
salt
1 egg
50g/2oz butter
100g/4oz Mozzarella cheese, thinly sliced

Tomato Sauce
1-2tbsp oil
1 onion, chopped
2 cloves garlic, chopped
400-g/15-oz can tomatoes, mashed
30ml/2tbsp tomato purée
salt and freshly ground black pepper
7g/1tbsp fresh oregano, chopped

Preparation Preheat the oven to 190°C/375°F/Gas 5.

Peel the potatoes and boil until soft. Mash well. Mash in the flour, salt, egg and half the butter. Shape into balls.

Make the tomato sauce. Heat the oil and fry the onion and garlic until soft. Add the tomatoes, tomato purée, seasoning and herbs and simmer, stirring occasionally, for 5 minutes.

Layer the gnocchi in an ovenproof dish with the cheese, dotted with butter, and the tomato sauce. Finish with a cheese layer.

Bake in the oven for about 20 minutes until the dish has heated through and the cheese has melted.

Making Pasta Dough by Hand

1 Sieve the flour on to a clean surface, make a well in the centre of the flour large enough to hold the eggs. Add the eggs and a little oil.

2 Sprinkle flour over the eggs and stir with a spatula. Add the water gradually, stirring the mixture around with some added flour. Pull a little flour from the sides to cover the egg mixture.

3 Start to mix the dough by pulling the flour on to the egg mixture gradually until it is all mixed in. If the mixture is too stiff, add a few drops of water to take up all the flour. Take care not to make the mixture too wet.

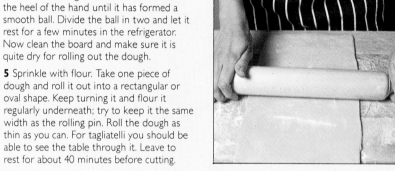

4 Knead the dough for several minutes with the heel of the hand until it has formed a smooth ball. Divide the ball in two and let it rest for a few minutes in the refrigerator. Now clean the board and make sure it is quite dry for rolling out the dough.

5 Sprinkle with flour. Take one piece of dough and roll it out into a rectangular or oval shape. Keep turning it and flour it regularly underneath; try to keep it the same width as the rolling pin. Roll the dough as thin as you can. For tagliatelli you should be able to see the table through it. Leave to rest for about 40 minutes before cutting.

Vegetable Dishes

Mushroom-Stuffed Artichokes   193
Asparagus with Hollandaise Sauce   193
Bean, Mushroom and Asparagus Purée   193
Green Beans Paprika   193
Spicy Green Bean and Tomato Pasties   194
Brussels Sprouts with Garlic and Mushrooms   194
Brussels Sprouts with Hazelnuts   194
Stuffed Cabbage   194
Caraway Cabbage   195
Crispy Fried Cabbage   195
Indian Cabbage with Peas   195
Red Cabbage with Apples   195
Crispy "Seaweed"   196
Shredded Carrot and Cabbage   196
Braised Carrots and Onions   197
Holiday Carrots   197
Carrots with Yoghurt   197
Celery Mousse   198
Corn Croquettes   198
Courgettes with Almonds   198
Courgettes au Gratin   198
Fennel Mornay   199
Stewed Fennel   199
Lentil Purée   199
Stuffed Marrow or Courgettes   200
Marrow or Courgettes in Cream Sauce   200
Okra with Mustard   201
Stuffed Mushrooms   201
Paprika Mushrooms   201

Petits Pois à la Française   201
Spiced Potatoes   202
Baked Potatoes with Eggs   203
Spicy Potato Cakes   203
Russian Potatoes   202
Sour Potatoes with Pickles   204
Crispy Potato Cakes   204
Curry Potatoes   204
Spinach Ring   205
Creamed Spinach   205
Cheesy Ratatouille   205
Vegetable Cutlets   206
Chestnuts and Vegetables   206
Vegetables in Aspic   206
Vegetable Chop Suey   207
Curried Vegetables   207
Oriental Stir-Fry Vegetables with Noodles   208
Summer Vegetable Pasties   209
Vegetables in Vinaigrette   209
Vegetable and Rice Hotch Potch   209
Purée of Root Vegetables   210
Five Vegetable Gratin   210

Chopping and Slicing Onions   211
Preparing Tomatoes   211
Preparing Globe Artichokes   212
Preparing Fennel   212
Chopping Parsley   213

Mushroom-Stuffed Artichokes
Serves 4

Ingredients

4 globe artichokes	15g/1 tbsp pine kernels
juice of 1 lemon	15g/2tbsp chopped parsley
25g/1oz butter	salt and freshly ground
1 clove garlic, crushed	black pepper
225g/8oz mushrooms,	
chopped	

Preparation Remove the artichokes' tough outer leaves and snip 2cm (1in) off the rest. Dip the cut edges of the leaves in most of the lemon juice. Trim off the stalks and stand the artichokes upright in a large pan of boiling salted water. Simmer for 15 minutes. Drain upside down and allow to cool.

Meanwhile, make the filling. Heat the butter in a pan and cook the garlic until soft. Add the mushrooms. Cook gently until very black and juicy. Mix in the pine kernels and parsley and season with salt and pepper and a dash of lemon juice.

When the artichokes are cool, pull out the tiny leaves from the middle and the hairy inedible "chokes" beneath them.

Spoon the filling into each artichoke, closing the leaves over it. Put the artichokes in a greased ovenproof dish and heat through before serving.

Asparagus with Hollandaise Sauce
Serves 6

When making Hollandaise sauce, never let the sauce boil, or it will curdle. Use the thinnest, freshest asparagus you can find.

Ingredients

1kg/2lb asparagus,	15ml/1tbsp lemon juice
trimmed	15ml/1tbsp double cream
150g/6oz butter	pinch salt
3 egg yolks	pinch ground white pepper

Preparation Fill a medium-sized saucepan to a depth of 7.5cm (3in) with water.

Add the asparagus, cover and simmer over a medium heat for 12 minutes.

Meanwhile, melt the butter in a small saucepan and set aside, keeping the butter warm over a very low heat.

In a small mixing bowl, beat the egg yolks and lemon juice together for 3 to 4 minutes, or until the mixture thickens.

Beat the egg yolk mixture into the melted butter over a very low heat. Beat in the cream, salt and white pepper. Remove from the heat and let the sauce thicken for 5 minutes, stirring gently but frequently.

Drain the cooked asparagus well and place in a large deep serving dish. Top with the Hollandaise sauce. Serve warm.

Bean, Mushroom and Asparagus Purée
Serves 6

Ingredients

450g/1lb fresh green beans	2.5g/½tsp nutmeg
225g/8oz mushrooms	2.5g/½tsp white pepper
450g/1lb fresh asparagus	2.5g/½tsp salt
15ml/1tbsp clarified butter	1 egg yolk
or oil	croûtons

Preparation Fill a large pot to the depth of 3.5cm (1½in) with cold water. Add the green beans, mushrooms and asparagus. Cook over a low heat for 5 minutes. Add the clarified butter or oil, nutmeg, pepper and salt. Cook for a further 1 minute.

Put the vegetables, along with the egg yolk and 100ml/4fl oz of the cooking liquid, in a blender or food processor. Purée in bursts of 30 seconds until the vegetable mixture is smooth and well blended.

Serve hot with croûtons.

Green Beans Paprika
Serves 6

Ingredients

1kg/2lb fresh green beans,	10g/1tbsp paprika
trimmed and halved	15g/1tbsp flour
100g/4oz butter	425ml/¾pt sour cream
225g/8oz spring onions,	2.5g/½tsp salt
coarsely chopped	

Preparation Cook the green beans in a large pot of boiling water until they are tender but still crisp, about 7 minutes. Drain well.

Melt the butter in a medium-sized saucepan over a low heat. Add the spring onions and cook, stirring frequently, for 4 to 5 minutes, or until they are translucent. Remove the saucepan from the heat and stir in the paprika. Set aside.

Combine the flour and sour cream in a small bowl until they are well mixed. Add the mixture to the spring onions. Add the salt. Simmer the mixture over a low heat for 5 minutes. Add the beans and simmer for 5 minutes longer. Serve hot.

Spicy Green Bean and Tomato Pasties
Makes 4

Ingredients

350g/12oz Shortcrust Pastry	100g/4oz French beans, parboiled, trimmed and sliced
1.5-3ml/1-2tbsp oil	
5g/1tsp fennel seeds	400-g/15-oz can tomatoes, mashed
1 slice fresh ginger	
2 cloves garlic, crushed	5g/1tsp Garam Masala
1 small onion, chopped	salt and freshly ground black pepper
75g/3oz potatoes, parboiled and diced	beaten egg to glaze

Preparation Make the pastry and chill for 30 minutes. Preheat the oven to 180°C/350°F/Gas 4.

Heat oil in a pan and when hot, add fennel seeds. Stir in ginger, garlic and onion. Cook, stirring, until lightly browned.

Stir in potatoes and beans. Add enough tomatoes and juice to prevent the mixture sticking. Add garam masala, salt and pepper and simmer for about 5 minutes, stirring occasionally and adding more tomato juice as necessary. Do not make the mixture too wet.

Divide the pastry into 4 balls and roll out. Share the mixture between the pastry rounds, crimp together to form pasties and brush with beaten egg. Put pasties on a baking tray and bake for 30 minutes or until pastry has cooked.

Brussels Sprouts with Garlic and Mushrooms
Serves 4

Ingredients

30-45ml/2-3tbsp oil	450g/1lb Brussels sprouts, thinly sliced
4 cloves garlic, chopped	100g/4oz mushrooms, sliced

Preparation Heat the oil in a wok or deep-sided frying pan. Add the garlic and fry quickly, stirring, until crisp and brown.

Add the sprouts and mushrooms and stir until coated with garlic and oil. Stir-fry for 1-2 minutes and eat while crisp and hot. This is particularly good with bean dishes.

Brussels Sprouts with Hazelnuts
Serves 4

Ingredients

450g/1lb small Brussels sprouts, fresh or frozen	pinch of nutmeg
salt and freshly ground pepper	600ml/1pt Cheese Sauce
	100g/4oz hazelnuts, chopped

Preparation Cook Brussels sprouts in boiling salted water for 10 minutes. Drain and season with salt, pepper and nutmeg. Place in a buttered ovenproof dish.

Coat them with the cheese sauce. Add the hazelnuts and cook for 2-3 minutes.

Bake at 190°C/375°F/Gas 5 for 10 minutes.

Variation Use walnuts instead of hazelnuts.

Stuffed Cabbage
Serves 6

Ingredients

medium-sized green cabbage, cored and trimmed	2.5g/½tsp salt
	5g/1tsp black pepper
60ml/4tbsp vegetable oil	25g/1oz butter or margarine
2 large onions, chopped	75g/3oz seedless white grapes, halved
350g/12oz cooked rice	
4 eggs, beaten	50g/2oz shredded red cabbage
50g/2oz sultanas	6 canned tomatoes, chopped

Preparation Separate the leaves from the cabbage. Blanch the leaves in a large pot of boiling water for 5 minutes. Drain well.

Heat the oil in a saucepan. Add the onions and brown over a low heat. Add the rice, eggs and sultanas. Cook, stirring frequently, for 30 seconds. Add the salt, pepper, butter or margarine and grapes. Cook, stirring frequently, for 90 seconds.

Put 2 to 3 tablespoons of the rice filling at the edge of a cabbage leaf. Roll the leaf up, tucking the ends under. Repeat with the remaining cabbage leaves until the rice filling is used up. Coarsely chop the remaining cabbage leaves.

Heat the remaining oil in a large heavy frying pan over a moderate heat. Add the chopped green cabbage and the red cabbage. Sauté for 3 to 4 minutes. Add the stuffed cabbage leaves and tomatoes. Cover and cook gently for 12 minutes.

Caraway Cabbage

Caraway Cabbage
Serves 4-6

Ingredients
25g/1oz butter
675g/1½lb white or green
  cabbage, finely sliced
10g/1tbsp caraway seeds
salt and pepper
10g/2tsp flour
150ml/¼pt sour cream

Preparation Melt the butter and add the cabbage. Stir well. Add the caraway seeds, salt and pepper. Cover and cook, stirring occasionally, until the cabbage is cooked but still crisp.

Add the flour and stir it in well. Cook for a further 2 minutes, stirring constantly.

Add the sour cream, warm it through and serve.

Crispy Fried Cabbage
Serves 4-6

Even children will eat cabbage cooked this way. Serve with grilled or fried meat, sausages or bacon.

Ingredients
1 small, firm green or white
  cabbage
1 medium onion, peeled
30ml/2tbsp oil
50g/2oz butter
15g/1tbsp caraway seeds
sea salt and freshly ground
  pepper

Preparation Trim the cabbage, removing the outer leaves and core. Quarter and shred it. Wash in icy water, then drain. Slice the onion.

Heat the oil and butter in a heavy sauté pan, large frying pan, or wok. When very hot, stir in the cabbage, onion and caraway seeds. Stir-fry for 2 to 3 minutes until crisp and brown. Add salt and pepper to taste. Turn out into a warmed serving dish and serve immediately.

Indian Cabbage with Peas
Serves 4

Ingredients
45ml/3tbsp oil
2 bay leaves
3.5g/¾tsp whole cumin
  seeds
700g/1½lb cabbage, finely
  shredded
5g/1tsp ground turmeric
2.5g/½tsp chilli powder
7.5g/1½tsp ground cumin
5g/1tsp ground coriander
2 tomatoes, chopped
3.5g/¾tsp salt
2.5g/½tsp sugar
100g/4oz peas

Preparation Heat the oil over medium high heat and add the bay leaves and the cumin seeds. Let them sizzle for a few seconds.

Add the cabbage and stir for 2-3 minutes. Add the turmeric, chilli, cumin, coriander, tomatoes, salt and sugar and mix with the cabbage.

Lower heat, cover and cook for 15 minutes. Add the peas and cover again. Continue to cook for a further 15 minutes, stirring occasionally.

Remove the cover, turn heat up to medium high and, stirring continuously, cook until dry.

Red Cabbage with Apples
Serves 6

Ingredients
1 large red cabbage,
  shredded
30g/2tbsp sugar
5g/1tsp salt
100ml/4fl oz raspberry, red
  wine or herb vinegar
50g/2oz butter
3 large cooking apples,
  peeled, cored and diced
2 spring onions, chopped
bay leaf
whole clove
1.2l/2½pt boiling water
60ml/4tbsp blackberry jam
50ml/2fl oz dry red wine

Preparation In a large bowl, combine the shredded cabbage with the sugar, salt and vinegar. Toss until the cabbage is evenly coated with the vinegar mixture.

In a large casserole, melt the butter. Add the apples and spring onions and cook over a very low heat for 8 minutes, stirring frequently. Add the cabbage and vinegar mixture, the bay leaf and the clove. Stir in the boiling water. Cover and simmer over a low heat for 90 minutes.

Add the blackberry jam and red wine. Simmer for a further 30 minutes.

Serve hot or cold, in a large glass or procelain bowl.

Crispy "Seaweed"
Serves 6

The very popular "seaweed" served in Chinese restaurants is, in fact, green cabbage. Choose fresh, young spring greens with pointed heads. Even the deep green outer leaves should be tender. This recipe also makes an ideal garnish for a number of dishes, particularly cold starters and buffet dishes.

Ingredients

675g/1½lb spring greens	5g/1tsp sugar
600ml/1pt oil for deep frying	50g/2oz blanched split almonds
5g/1tsp salt	

Preparation Wash and dry the spring green leaves and shred them with a sharp knife into the thinnest possible shavings. Spread them out on absorbent paper or put in a large colander to dry thoroughly.

Heat the oil in a wok or deep-fryer. Before the oil gets too hot, turn off the heat for 30 seconds. Add the spring green shavings in several batches and turn the heat up to medium high. Stir with a pair of cooking chopsticks.

When the shavings start to float to the surface, scoop them out gently with a slotted spoon and drain on absorbent paper to remove as much of the oil as possible. Sprinkle the salt and sugar evenly on top and mix gently. Serve cold. Deep fry or toast the split almonds until crisp and add to the "seaweed" as a garnish.

Shredded Carrot and Cabbage
Serves 4

Ingredients

30ml/2tbsp oil	450g/1lb carrots, grated
5g/1tsp mustard seeds	a little honey
1 tight head spring greens, finely shredded	salt and freshly ground pepper

Preparation Heat oil in a heavy pan with a lid. When it is hot, add the mustard seeds.

As soon as the mustard seeds begin to pop, pile in the shredded vegetables, drizzle over the honey and stir well. Turn down the heat, put on the lid and cook for about 3 minutes until just tender. Season and serve.

Add the carrots, salt and white pepper, coriander and parsley. Reduce the heat to low. Cook for 1 to 2 minutes stirring constantly. Cover the saucepan and reduce the heat to very low. Simmer for 5 minutes and serve.

Braised Carrots and Onions
Serves 6

Ingredients

50g/2oz butter or margarine
1 medium onion, sliced into rings
2 spring onions, finely chopped
2 large tomatoes, cut into eighths and seeded
16 baby carrots, scraped and cut into quarters
pinch salt
pinch ground white pepper
7g/1tbsp chopped fresh coriander
15g/2tbsp chopped fresh parsley

Preparation Melt the margarine in a large saucepan over a low heat. Add the onion and spring onions. Sauté, stirring constantly, for 5 minutes. Add the tomatoes and raise the heat to medium. Sauté, stirring constantly, for a further 3 to 4 minutes.

Holiday Carrots
Serves 6

Ingredients

25g/1oz butter or margarine
675g/1½lb baby carrots, finely chopped
225g/8oz canned mandarin orange segments, drained and finely chopped
50ml/2fl oz water
50ml/2fl oz fresh lime juice
¼tsp salt

Preparation Melt the butter or margarine in a medium-sized saucepan.

Add the remaining ingredients and simmer over a low heat for 20 minutes. Serve hot.

Carrots with Yoghurt
Serves 4

Ingredients

450g/1lb carrots, sliced
5g/1tsp sugar
2.5g/½tsp ground cumin
1 small onion, finely chopped
juice of ½ lemon
150ml/¼pt yoghurt
salt and pepper

Preparation Cook the carrots with the sugar in boiling water just until they are *al dente*. Drain them and add the cumin and onion. Stir around.

Mix the lemon juice into the yoghurt, season to taste and spoon it over the carrots.

Serve immediately or leave it to cook and serve as a salad or an accompaniment to curry.

Celery Mousse
Serves 4 approx.

Ingredients

5ml/1tsp gelatine
30ml/2tbsp boiling water
1 medium head of celery
  with leaves
175ml/7fl oz yoghurt
5ml/1tsp lemon juice

1 small onion
about 30g/1oz chopped
  parsley
salt and pepper
140g/5oz curd cheese

Preparation Dissolve the gelatine in the boiling water. Blend all the remaining ingredients, except the curd cheese, feeding them into the liquidizer or food processor a little at a time. Add the dissolved gelatine and curd cheese and blend it into the mixture. Turn into a moistened mould (a small ring mould looks nice). Refrigerate until set.

Unmould and serve as a part of a cold buffet, or as an accompaniment to cold meat or chicken or fish.

Variation For a richer mousse, substitute mayonnaise for the yoghurt.

Corn Croquettes
Serves 4-6

Ingredients

45g/3tbsp butter
45g/3tbsp flour
300ml/¹/₂pt milk
salt and freshly ground
  black pepper
7-15g/1-2tbsp finely
  chopped parsley

400g/14oz tinned
  sweetcorn
2 egg yolks
Coating
2 eggs, beaten
seasoned flour
fine stale breadcrumbs
oil for frying

Preparation Cut the butter into small pieces and melt in a heavy-bottomed pan. Stir in the flour and cook for a few minutes until the mixture is pale gold.

Remove from the heat and gradually stir in the milk. Return to the heat and stir until the sauce has thickened. Season with salt and plenty of pepper. Stir the parsley, sweetcorn and egg yolks into the mixture. Chill. The mixture should have a heavy dropping consistency. Form it into croquettes. Dip in the beaten egg, then roll it in the seasoned flour and breadcrumbs, coating each croquette firmly. Fry the croquettes in oil until heated through and crisp on the outside.

Courgettes with Almonds
Serves 6

Ingredients

675g/1¹/₂lb courgettes,
  sliced lengthwise
1 medium onion, finely
  chopped
15ml/1tbsp olive oil

salt and pepper
50g/2oz flaked almonds
1tsp cornflour
15ml/1tbsp water
225ml/8fl oz yoghurt

Preparation Put the courgettes in a shallow ovenproof dish. Mix the onions, oil, salt and pepper and spoon the mixture over them. Bake uncovered at 180°C/350°F/Gas 4 for 40 minutes, or until tender.

Meanwhile toast the almonds: put them into a heavy frying pan over a high heat and shake the pan from time to time. Take care that they do not burn.

Mix the cornflour with the water and add it to the yoghurt with seasoning to taste. Warm the mixture over a gentle heat, stirring constantly, for 3 minutes. Spoon it over the courgettes and scatter the almonds on top.

Courgettes au Gratin
Serves 4

Ingredients

15-30ml/1-2tbsp oil
450g/1lb courgettes, sliced
1 large onion, chopped
400g/14oz tinned
  tomatoes
chopped basil, thyme or
  marjoram

a sliver of lemon peel
salt and pepper
225g/8oz uncooked
  macaroni
2 eggs
150ml/¹/₄pt plain yoghurt
75g/3oz grated Cheddar
  cheese

Preparation Heat the oil and fry the courgettes until they are lightly coloured. Remove them from the pan and reserve. Fry the onion until golden, adding more oil if necessary. Add the tomatoes, herbs, lemon peel, salt and pepper and simmer for 10 minutes, breaking up the tomatoes and stirring from time to time.

Meanwhile cook the macaroni in boiling, salted water and drain it well. Put it into an ovenproof dish. Pour the sauce over the macaroni and mix it through well. Lay the cooked courgettes on top.

Mix the eggs, yoghurt and half the cheese and pour the mixture over the courgettes. Scatter the remaining cheese on top. Bake at 190°C/375°F/Gas 5 for 30 minutes.

Variation You could use aubergines instead of courgettes, in which case slice and salt them, leave them to drain for 20 minutes, rinse and dry them and proceed as above.

Fennel Mornay
Serves 6

Ingredients

3 bulbs fennel	100g/4oz Cheddar cheese,
1 bay leaf	grated
25g/1oz butter	salt and freshly ground
25g/1oz plain flour	black pepper
300ml/½pt milk	25-50g/1-2oz
150ml/¼pt single cream	breadcrumbs

Preparation Trim the fennel and simmer in salted water with the bay leaf for about 30 minutes until tender.

Meanwhile, make the sauce. Melt the butter in a pan and stir in the flour. Cook, stirring, for a couple of minutes and then gradually stir in the milk. Add the cream and most of the cheese and cook gently until the cheese has melted. Season well and keep warm.

Drain the fennel and cut each bulb in half. Lay the halves in a flameproof dish and pour the sauce over them. Sprinkle with the remaining cheese and the breadcrumbs. Put under a hot grill to brown and melt the cheese.

Variation For a tangier sauce, add a little powdered mustard to taste.

Stewed Fennel
Serves 6

Ingredients

3 large bulbs fennel	425ml/¾pt water
90ml/6tbsp olive oil	2.5g/½tsp salt
1 medium onion, chopped	pinch black pepper

Preparation Trim the fronds from the fennel bulbs and reserve. Cut the bulbs in half vertically, then slice each half horizontally.

Heat the olive oil in a large heavy pan. Add the fennel slices and onion and sauté over a low heat for 6 to 8 minutes. Stir frequently.

Add the water, salt and pepper and raise the heat to medium. Cook for 25 to 30 minutes.

Serve with the cooking liquid in a deep dish, garnished with fennel fronds.

Lentil Purée
Serves 4

This German dish goes well with ham, pork, or game.

Ingredients

225g/8oz lentils	
600ml/1pt vegetable or	bouquet garni
chicken stock	50g/2oz butter
100g/4oz Polish-style	60ml/4tbsp double cream
sausage or smoked	15g/2tbsp fresh herbs,
sausage	parsley, chives, chervil or
1 large onion, peeled	savoury
2 cloves garlic, peeled	salt and freshly ground
	pepper

Preparation Rinse the lentils and pick them over. Put them in a pan with the stock. Skin the sausage if necessary, and add to the pan. Slice the onion and add to the pan with the garlic and bouquet garni. Cover, bring to a boil, and simmer for about 40 minutes, until reduced to a thick purée.

Remove the bouquet garni and discard. Remove the sausage and chop roughly. Liquidize or process the lentils and sausage until smooth. With the machine running, gradually add the butter, cream and herbs. Taste for seasoning, then spoon into a warmed serving dish.

Stuffed Marrow or Courgettes
Serves 4-6

Ingredients

1 marrow or 4 courgettes
salt and freshly ground
*   black pepper*
75g/3oz brown rice
2 small carrots, diced
50g/2oz peas
15-30ml/1-2tbsp oil
1 onion, chopped
1 clove garlic, chopped
1 stalk celery, chopped
handful of parsley, chopped
30g/2tbsp hazelnuts,
*   chopped*

Tomato sauce
15-30ml/1-2tbsp oil
1 onion, chopped
2 cloves garlic, chopped
425-g/15-oz can tomatoes,
*   mashed*
15ml/1tbsp tomato purée
salt and freshly ground
*   black pepper*

Preparation Preheat the oven to 180°C/350°F/Gas 4. Cut the marrow or courgettes in half lengthwise and scoop out the pith and seeds. Sprinkle the flesh with salt and leave the halves upside down to drain.

Meanwhile, make the filling. Simmer the rice in a covered pan of salted water until just tender (about 30 minutes). Drain.

Parboil the carrots and peas and drain. Heat the oil in a pan and fry the onion and garlic until translucent. Add celery, carrots and peas. Stir in the rice, parsley and hazelnuts and season well. Dry the marrow or courgettes and pile filling into one half. Top with second half.

Make the tomato sauce. Heat oil in a pan and add onion and garlic. Fry, stirring, until soft. Add tomatoes and tomato purée. Simmer for 5 minutes, stirring occasionally, and season well.

Put the marrow or courgettes in a baking dish with a lid, if you have one big enough, otherwise use foil to cover. Surround with the sauce. Cover and cook for 45 minutes until marrow or courgettes are tender. Serve hot or cold with a crisp green salad.

Marrow or Courgettes in Cream Sauce
Serves 4

Ingredients

1 medium to large marrow
*   or 6 courgettes*
25g/1oz butter
10g/2tsp cornflour

15ml/1tbsp water
15g/1tbsp dried dill weed
salt and pepper
150ml/¼pt sour cream

Preparation Peel the marrow or courgettes and either finely chop or grate them. Cook them with the butter, stirring from time to time, just until it begins to soften.

Mix the cornflour with the water until smooth and add. Stir and cook for a further 3 minutes.

Add the dill, salt and pepper and finally stir in the sour cream. Warm through gently and serve hot, with roast meat, chicken or fish.

Okra with Mustard
Serves 4

Okra, also known as Ladies Fingers, can be bought at any Indian or Caribbean greengrocers.

Ingredients

7.5g/1½tsp ground mustard	*450g/1lb okra*
2.5g/½tsp ground turmeric	*60ml/4tbsp oil*
pinch chilli powder	*2-3 fresh green chillies, cut lengthwise*
3.5g/¾tsp salt	*25ml/1½tbsp yoghurt*
30ml/2tbsp hot water	*75ml/3fl oz water*

Preparation Mix the mustard, turmeric, chilli and salt with the hot water, cover and set aside for 20 minutes. Wash the okra, pat dry with paper towels. Cut off the stems and leave whole. Heat oil over medium high heat, add the green chillies and let them sizzle for a few seconds. Add the okra and, stirring gently, fry for 5 minutes.

Add the spice mixture and yoghurt and mix with the okra; add the water and bring it to boil. Lower heat, cover and simmer till the okra is tender.

Stuffed Mushrooms
Serves 6-8

An excellent side dish, these mushrooms can also be served as an appetizer.

Ingredients

45 to 50 medium mushrooms, stems removed and reserved	*15g/2tbsp chopped parsley*
2 spring onions, finely chopped	*50g/2oz butter or margarine*
2 shallots, finely chopped	*30g/2tbsp flour*
140g/5oz fresh spinach, finely chopped	*50ml/2fl oz white wine*
	45ml/3tbsp olive oil

Preparation Preheat the oven to 175°C/350°F/Gas 4. Finely chop the mushroom stems. In a small saucepan, combine the spring onions, shallots, spinach, parsley, butter or margarine, flour, white wine and olive oil.

Mix thoroughly and cook over a low heat until the fat melts. Cover and simmer for 2 minutes.

Add the mushroom stems. Mix thoroughly and cover. Simmer the filling over a low heat for a further 5 minutes.

Put approximately 1tsp of the filling in each mushroom cap. Arrange the filled caps on greased baking sheets and bake for 15 minutes. Serve hot.

Paprika Mushrooms
Serves 4

Ingredients

25g/1oz butter or margarine	*10g/1tbsp paprika*
1 medium onion, finely chopped	*350g/12oz mushrooms, sliced*
½ green pepper, seeded and finely chopped	*150ml/¼pt sour cream*
	salt and pepper
	chopped parsley

Preparation Heat the butter, add the onion and cook until it has just softened but not browned. Add the green pepper and paprika and cook on a low heat for 3 minutes. Add the mushrooms, stir well and cook for a further 5 minutes until they are soft. Stir in the sour cream, season to taste and warm through gently.

Serve, sprinkled with parsley, as a vegetable accompaniment, as an hors d'oeuvre with hot French bread, as a filling for vol-au-vent, or on fried bread or with a crisp salad, as a light supper.

Petits Pois à la Française
Serves 4

Ingredients

50g/2oz butter
1 lettuce, washed and
    shredded
12 small pearl onions,
    peeled
2 rashers bacon, chopped
    (optional)

5g/1tsp flour
salt and freshly ground
    pepper
600ml/1pt salted water
pinch of sugar
450g/1lb fresh or frozen
    peas
3 sprigs parsley

Preparation Heat the butter in a saucepan, add shredded lettuce (retain some outside leaves for garnish if liked), the pearl onions and chopped bacon. Cook for 2 minutes. Stir in the flour and season.

Add the salted water and sugar. Bring to the boil, add the fresh peas, if using, and parsley. Simmer for 20-30 minutes until peas and onions are tender.

Most of the liquid should be absorbed and the consistency should be creamy. Check seasoning. Serve on lettuce leaves, if liked. If you are using frozen peas, reduce cooking time to 10 minutes, but cook the lettuce, onion and bacon for 10 minutes before adding peas. One chopped onion or 4 spring onions can be substituted for the pearl onions.

Spiced Potatoes
Serves 6

Ingredients

30ml/2tbsp vegetable oil
2.5g/¹⁄₂tsp mustard powder
1 tomato, seeded and
    finely chopped
60g/4tbsp green pepper,
    seeded and diced
pinch cayenne
pinch ground turmeric

pinch ground allspice
2.5g/¹⁄₂tsp ground ginger
pinch salt
2.5g/¹⁄₂tsp sugar
pinch ground coriander
5 large boiled potatoes, cut
    into chunks

Preparation Heat the oil in a large, heavy frying pan over a moderate heat. Add the mustard, tomato, green pepper, cayenne pepper, turmeric, allspice, ginger, salt, sugar and coriander. Cook, stirring constantly, for 2 minutes.

Add the potatoes and cook, stirring constantly, until the potatoes are coated with the spices and heated through, about 5 minutes.

Baked Potatoes with Eggs
Serves 6

Ingredients

1kg/2lb large potatoes, peeled
salt to taste
10g/2tsp paprika

4 eggs, hard-cooked and sliced
150ml/¹/₄pt sour cream
30ml/2tbsp milk
15g/¹/₂oz butter

Preparation Boil the potatoes until they are cooked but still firm. Drain off the water and slice them. Put a layer of potatoes in the bottom of a greased ovenproof dish. Season with salt and paprika. Lay the sliced eggs over the potatoes.

Mix the sour cream with the milk until smooth. Spoon over the eggs. Season again. Add the remaining potatoes. Dot with butter and bake at 180°C/350°F/Gas 4 for 25 minutes, until lightly browned.

Variation To make this a more substantial dish, you could add slices of salami over the sliced eggs.

Spicy Potato Cakes
Serves 4

Ingredients

450g/1lb potatoes, boiled and mashed
1-2 fresh green chillies, seeded and chopped
2.5g/¹/₂tsp salt

7g/1tbsp coriander leaves, chopped
30g/2tbsp chopped onions
oil for frying

Preparation Mix the mashed potatoes with the chillies, salt, coriander leaves and onions. Form into small balls and flatten. Heat oil for shallow frying till hot and fry the potato cakes for a few minutes each side till golden. Drain and serve hot.

Spicy Potato Cakes

Russian Potatoes
Serves 6

Ingredients

1kg/2lb potatoes
salt and freshly ground black pepper
approx. 50g/2oz butter

1 large onion, sliced
100g/4oz mushrooms, sliced
175ml/6fl oz sour cream
20g/3tbsp chopped chives

Preparation Scrub the potatoes and cook in salted water until barely tender. Drain, peel and slice. Heat some of the butter in a flameproof casserole and fry the onion until translucent. Add the mushrooms and cook gently until the juices run. Add the rest of the butter as necessary and stir in the potatoes. Let them gently brown on one side, season, turn over and add the cream. When most of the cream has been absorbed, sprinkle over the chopped chives and a little more pepper and serve.

Sour Potatoes with Pickles
Serves 6-8

This unusual hot potato dish should be made on the day the meal is served. The sourer the pickles, the better the dish.

Ingredients

6 large potatoes	2.5g/½tsp salt
30ml/2tbsp lemon juice	2.5g/½tsp black pepper
100g/4oz steak	2.5g/½tsp dried parsley
425ml/¾pt beef stock	pinch of dried thyme
50g/2oz Spanish onion,	1 large bay leaf
diced	3 large pickled cucumbers,
30g/2tbsp flour	finely chopped
pinch of dried marjoram	

Preparation Scrub the potatoes and parboil them in a large pot of boiling water for 15 minutes, or until they are tender but not mushy. Drain well. Cut the potatoes into medium-sized chunks and put them into a serving bowl. Sprinkle the potatoes with the lemon juice and set aside.

In a medium-sized heavy frying pan brown the steak in a third of a cup of the beef stock for about 2 minutes. Add the onions and flour and brown over a low heat for 10 minutes. Turn off the heat.

Remove the steak and cut it into small pieces. Return the steak pieces to the pan. Add the remaining beef stock and the marjoram, salt, pepper, parsley, thyme, bay leaf, and pickled cucumbers. Cover the pan and simmer for 30 minutes

Pour the mixture over the potatoes. Toss well and serve.

Crispy Potato Cakes
Serves 4

These potato cakes can be served as an accompaniment or as a meal in themselves when topped with puréed spinach and a poached egg. You can vary the mixture by adding some grated onion or some grated cheese, or a bit of both.

Ingredients

450g/1lb waxy potatoes	salt and freshly ground
2 eggs	black pepper
15g/1tbsp potato flour	60ml/4tbsp oil

Preparation Peel the potatoes and grate them into a bowl of cold water. Drain. Squeeze the potato shreds dry in a cloth. Mix with the eggs, flour and seasoning.

Heat 15ml/1tbsp of the oil in a frying pan and make your first potato cake using a quarter of the mixture. Spread it out in the pan and flatten it. When the underside is crisp and golden, turn it over and brown the top. Keep it warm while you make the other three.

Curry Potatoes
Serves 4-6

This potato dish goes well with sausages and chops.

Ingredients

1kg/2lb large potatoes,	7.5g/1½tsp chilli powder
peeled and thinly sliced	7.5g/1½tsp coarse sea salt
120ml/6tbsp oil	freshly ground black
50g/2oz butter	pepper
3 cloves garlic, peeled	2.5g/½tsp ground
2.5-cm/1-in piece root	coriander
ginger, peeled and sliced	7-14/1-2tbsp fresh
15g/3tsp mustard seeds	coriander or mint
2.5g/½tsp turmeric	leaves, chopped

Preparation Heat the oil and butter in a large heavy frying pan. Add the garlic and ginger and fry for 2 minutes or until brown. Remove using a slotted spoon.

Add the mustard seeds and fry for a couple of minutes. When the seeds being to pop, add the potatoes and carefully stir-fry for 1 minute.

Sprinkle with the turmeric, chilli powder, sea salt, pepper and ground coriander. Mix well, then fry the potatoes over medium-high heat, turning frequently, for about 10 minutes, until crisp and golden brown.

When the potatoes are ready to serve, stir in the herbs, taste for seasoning and spoon into a warmed serving dish.

Spinach Ring
Serves 4

Ingredients

1kg/2lb spinach	**Sauce**
75g/3oz butter	15-30ml/1-2tbsp oil
salt and freshly ground	1 onion, finely chopped
black pepper	2 cloves garlic, crushed
50g/2oz plain flour	425-g/15-oz can tomatoes,
300ml/½pt milk	mashed
50g/2oz Parmesan cheese	15ml/1tbsp tomato purée
3 eggs	salt and freshly ground
	black pepper

Preparation Pre-heat the oven to 190°C/375°F/Gas 5. Grease a 1.7-l/3-pt ring mould.

Wash the spinach and discard tough stalks. Pack spinach into a large pan with 15g/1oz of the butter and seasoning and cover tightly. Cook over a low heat for about 5 minutes, stirring occasionally, until spinach is soft. Drain and purée in a blender.

Melt the rest of the butter in a heavy-bottomed pan and add the flour, stirring. Gradually add the milk, stirring continuously. Stir in the cheese and season. Stir until sauce bubbles and thickens, then turn down the heat and cook for a further minute. Mix thoroughly with the spinach.

Separate the eggs. Beat the yolks into the spinach mixture. Whisk the whites until soft peaks have formed and fold into the mixture. Pour the mixture into the ring mould and bake for 30-40 minutes until risen and lightly set.

Meanwhile, make the tomato sauce. Heat the oil in a frying pan and add the onion and garlic. Fry, stirring, until transparent. Add the tomatoes, reserving the juice. Add the tomato purée and season. Simmer for 5 minutes adding more juice and adjusting seasoning if necessary.

To turn out the spinach ring, dip the mould into ice-cold water for a few seconds. Run a knife blade round edges of mould. Invert onto a warmed plate. Spoon over the sauce and serve with wholewheat bread or new potatoes and a crunchy salad.

Creamed Spinach
Serves 4

Ingredients

675g/1½lb fresh spinach,	grated nutmeg
washed and picked over	salt and pepper
1 egg yolk	150ml/¼pt yoghurt

Preparation Cook the spinach without an excess water (the water adhering to it is sufficient) and a little salt. Drain the cooked spinach very well (press it between two plates for most effective drainage). Add the yogurt and mix it into the spinach. Warm through gently.

If you prefer to use frozen spinach, use leaf, not chopped spinach, and follow the cooking directions on the packet.

Cheesy Ratatouille
Serves 4-6

This lovely, colourful dish can also be served as a first course, or as a main course dish with baked potatoes.

Ingredients

60ml/4tbsp olive oil	3 cloves garlic, crushed
3 medium onions, peeled	450g/1lb ripe tomatoes,
and sliced	quartered
2 medium aubergines	5g/1tsp thyme
salt and freshly ground	ground coriander to taste
pepper	200g/8oz Cheddar cheese,
450g/1lb courgettes,	grated
trimmed and sliced	**Topping**
1 large red pepper, cored,	30g/2tbsp breadcrumbs
seeded and sliced	30g/2tbsp grated
1 large green pepper,	Parmesan cheese
cored, seeded and sliced	
1 large yellow pepper,	
cored, seeded and sliced	

Preparation Heat the oil in a large, deep, heavy pan. Add the onions, and cook over a medium heat for 5 minutes.

While the onions are cooking, slice the aubergines. Sprinkle with a little salt, mix well, and place in a colander to drain for 5 minutes. Rinse well and pat dry with paper towels.

Add the sliced vegetables, garlic and quartered tomatoes to the pan with the onion. Stir well over high heat for a minute then stir in salt, pepper, thyme and ground coriander to taste. Cook, stirring frequently, over medium high heat for 20 minutes or until the vegetables are just tender. If there is too much liquid, turn up the heat, and boil rapidly till reduced — the ratatouille should be fairly dry. Taste the ratatouille, it should be well-seasoned.

Heat the grill. Stir half the Cheddar cheese into the vegetable mixture, and transfer to a greased ovenproof baking dish. Mix the ingredients for the topping together with the remaining Cheddar cheese and sprinkle over the ratatouille. Grill until golden brown and bubbling.

Vegetable Cutlets
Makes 6

Ingredients

25g/1oz butter
1 medium onion, chopped
65g/2½oz chopped celery
100g/4oz grated carrots
90g/3½oz cooked green
   beans, coarsely chopped

75g/3oz cooked peas
3 eggs
5g/1tsp salt
2.5g/½tsp black pepper
45g/3tbsp matzo meal or
   fine oatmeal
vegetable oil for frying

Preparation Melt the butter in a frying pan. Add the onion, celery and carrots and sauté for 10 minutes. Remove from the heat. Add the green beans, peas, two of the eggs, and the salt, pepper and matzo meal. Mix well. Shape the mixture into 6 cutlets.

Beat the remaining egg in a bowl. Dip the cutlets in the egg.

Heat the vegetable oil in a frying pan. Add the cutlets and sauté until both sides are browned.

Chestnuts and Vegetables
Serves 6

Ingredients

450g/1lb chestnuts
60ml/4tbsp olive oil
2 fat cloves garlic, chopped
150g/6oz mushrooms,
   sliced

350g/12oz Brussels sprouts
350g/12oz red cabbage
salt and freshly ground
   black pepper
small glass red wine

Preparation Preheat the oven to 200°C/400°F/Gas 6.

Make a nick in the top of the chestnuts with a sharp knife and boil them for 10 minutes. Plunge them in cold water and peel.

Heat the olive oil in a flameproof casserole and fry the garlic. Add the mushrooms, sprouts and red cabbage and season. Cook, stirring occasionally, for about 5 minutes until coated with oil and beginning to soften.

Stir in the chestnuts and red wine. Cover and bake for 40 minutes.

Vegetables in Aspic
Serves 6

Ingredients

300ml/10fl oz aspic or
   equivalent (see Note)
150g/6oz peeled and diced
   carrot
150g/6oz trimmed and
   sliced green beans

15ml/1tbsp walnut oil
75g/3oz sliced button
   mushrooms
15g/1tbsp stuffed olives,
   sliced
150ml/¼pt thick
   Mayonnaise

Preparation Prepare the aspic or equivalent and allow it to cool. Chill a mould. Wet the mould and when the aspic is almost set, line the mould with some of it. Put in the fridge to set.

Meanwhile cook the carrot and green beans in salted water until tender. Refresh in cold water. Heat the walnut oil in a pan and gently sauté the mushrooms. Allow to cool.

Mix the vegetables together with the olives, mayonnaise and the remaining aspic, remelted, then cooked almost to setting point, and fill the mould. Chill until set.

To serve, dip the mould into hot water, turn out onto a plate and cut into wedges.

Note Commerical gelatine and aspic powders are made from the bones of animals and fish. Vegetarians who prefer not to use them can set foods in carageen or Irish moss, an edible seaweed available in powder form from health food shops. Another vegetable substitute for gelatine is agar-agar. Like gelatine, caregeen and agar-agar come in varying strengths and you should follow the instructions on the pack when making them up. Neither imparts a taste to the finished dish.

Vegetable Chop Suey
Serves 4

Ingredients

2 large carrots, peeled
1 medium leek, trimmed
2 medium onions
225-g/8-oz can bamboo
  shoots
2.5-cm/1-in piece root
  ginger, peeled
100g/4oz button
  mushrooms
175g/6oz beansprouts
600ml/1pt boiling water

30ml/2tbsp oil for frying
5g/1tsp cornflour
150ml/¼pt vegetable stock
45ml/3tbsp tomato
  ketchup
7.5-15ml/½-1tbsp soy
  sauce, to taste
salt to taste
6 spring onions, trimmed
  and sliced

Preparation First prepare all the vegetables for cooking. Either grate or shred the carrots. Set aside. Halve the leek, rinse well and slice. Halve and slice the onions. Set aside. Drain the bamboo shoots and slice in the same way. Set aside. Grate the ginger. Quarter the mushrooms. Put the beansprouts in a colander and pour the boiling water over them. Drain thoroughly.

Heat the oil in a wok or large, deep, frying pan. Add the ginger, carrots and onions. Stir-fry for 2 minutes then stir in the leeks, bamboo shoots and mushrooms. Stir-fry over high heat for 2 minutes, then stir in the beansprouts, and fry for 1 minute.

Mix the cornflour with the stock, ketchup and soy sauce. Stir into the vegetables and bring to the boil, stirring constantly. When the mixture has thickened taste for seasoning, adding more soy sauce, ketchup or salt if necessary. Transfer the chop suey to a warmed serving dish and sprinkle with the spring onions.

Variation For a non-vegetarian chop suey, add 100-225g/4-8oz shelled shrimps or diced cooked chicken to the chop suey with the bamboo shoots or mushrooms.

Curried Vegetables
Serves 4

Ingredients

225g/8oz aubergine, cut
  in chunks
30ml/2tbsp oil
50g/2oz cashew nuts
1 medium onion, chopped
1 clove garlic, crushed
10g/2tsp curry powder
1 large potato, peeled and
  parboiled
100g/4oz green beans,
  trimmed

150ml/¼pt water
100g/4oz tomatoes,
  quartered
10g/1tbsp Garam Masala
150ml/¼pt yoghurt
10g/2tsp cornflour
30ml/2tbsp water
salt

Preparation Salt the aubergines and leave for 30 minutes. Rinse and pat dry.

Heat the oil and fry the cashews to a golden brown. Remove them from the pan and put them to one side. Fry the onions and garlic and cook until they begin to soften. Add the curry powder and stir in. Add the aubergines and cook on a low heat for about five minutes, stirring from time to time. Add a little more oil if necessary.

Add the potato, cut into large chunks, together with the green beans. Pour on the water, cover and leave to cook until the potatoes are ready. Add the tomatoes and the garam masala, stir round carefully and continue cooking for a few more minutes.

Mix the cornflour with the water to a smooth paste, stir into the contents of the pan and warm through for three minutes.

Serve hot, with the browned cashew nuts sprinkled on top.

Vegetable Chop Suey

Oriental Stir-Fry Vegetables with Noodles
Serves 4

Ingredients

1 onion, peeled
1 red pepper, seeded
1 green pepper, seeded
1 small chilli pepper,
  seeded
1 clove garlic, crushed
150g/6oz mushrooms,
  washed and sliced

1 small cauliflower
2 courgettes, washed
100g/4oz French beans
60ml/4tbsp olive oil
2.5ml/½tsp oil
salt and freshly ground
  pepper
30ml/2tbsp soy sauce
350g/12oz noodles

Preparation Prepare the vegetables by thinly slicing the onions and the peppers, dice the chilli finely, crush the garlic and slice the mushrooms. Divide the cauliflower into small florets and slice the courgettes and beans.

Heat the oil in a large casserole or wok, throw in the onions and other vegetables a few at a time and stir-fry for about 5 minutes turning the vegetables over to obtain an even distribution of heat. Stir in the seasoning and soy sauce.

Cook the noodles in boiling salted water for about 6 minutes, drain well and toss in a little butter. Serve with the vegetables.

Summer Vegetable Pasties
Makes 4

Ingredients

350g/12oz Shortcrust Pastry	**Cheese sauce**
beaten egg to glaze	25g/1oz butter
100g/4oz potatoes, diced	25g/1oz plain flour
4 baby carrots, sliced	up to 300ml/¹/₂pt milk
50g/2oz shelled peas	50g/2oz Cheddar cheese, grated
2 courgettes, sliced	salt and freshly ground black pepper
2 sticks celery, sliced	
¹/₂ green pepper, diced	

Preparation Make the pastry. Preheat the oven to 180°C/350°F/Gas 4.

Boil the potatoes and carrots in salted water until just tender. In another pan, boil the remaining vegetables for about 2 minutes. Drain. To make the cheese sauce, melt the butter in a heavy-bottomed pan, stir in the flour and gradually add half the milk, stirring. Add the cheese. Stir until melted. Add a little more milk and season to taste. Don't make the sauce too thin or it will pour out of the pastry shells. Mix sauce into vegetables to coat them generously. Divided the pastry into 4 balls and roll out. Share the mixture between the pastry rounds. Crimp together to form pasties and brush with beaten egg. Put the pasties on a baking tray and bake in the oven for 30 minutes or until the pastry is cooked.

Vegetables in Vinaigrette
Serves 8

Ingredients

450g/1lb fresh asparagus	30ml/2tbsp Dijon mustard
1 large head fresh broccoli, cut into florets	2.5g/¹/₂tsp dried chives
1 large can artichoke hearts, drained	30ml/2tbsp honey
100ml/4fl oz red wine vinegar	2.5g/¹/₂tsp celery salt
100ml/4fl oz olive oil	pinch of black pepper
20g/2tbsp chopped spring onions	pinch of ground white pepper
	1 clove garlic, finely chopped

Preparation Cook the asparagus in a large, covered pot of boiling water until they are tender, about 10 to 12 minutes. Cook the broccoli florets in a large pot of boiling water until they are tender but still crisp, about 7 minutes. Drain well.

Put the asparagus, broccoli and artichoke hearts into a large bowl, cover and chill for 40 minutes.

In another bowl, make the dressing. Combine the vinegar, olive oil, spring onions, mustard, chives, honey, salt, black pepper, white pepper and garlic. Mix well. Chill for 40 minutes.

Stir the dressing well and pour it over the vegetables.

Vegetable and Rice Hotch Potch
Serves 4

Ingredients

90ml/6tbsp oil	5g/1tsp paprika
350g/12oz onions, sliced	400g/14oz canned tomatoes
225g/8oz rice	150ml/¹/₄pt water
1 large green or red pepper, chopped	600ml/1pt yoghurt
salt and pepper	4 eggs

Preparation Heat a third of the oil, add the onions and cook until they have just softened but not browned. Add the rice and peppers and stir them round to colour them a little. Season well with salt, pepper and paprika. Layer the rice mixture with the tomatoes in an ovenproof dish. Pour over the remaining oil, mixed with the water. Cover and bake at 190°C/375°F/Gas 5 for 30 minutes (or on top of a medium heat).

Mix the yoghurt with the eggs. Pour over the vegetables and return the dish, uncovered, to the oven for a further 20 minutes.

Variation This dish adapts to endless variations — add some more vegetables, such as aubergines, courgettes, mushrooms, fennel. Salami, sausages or cooked meat can be added before the yoghurt topping.

Purée of Root Vegetables
Serves 4

Ingredients

150g/6oz carrots
150g/6oz swede
1 turnip
1 parsnip

25-50g/1-2oz butter
salt and freshly ground
  black pepper

Preparation Trim and peel the vegetables and simmer in salted water until tender. Drain and mash to a fluffy purée with butter. Season with salt and plenty of black pepper.

Five Vegetable Gratin
Serves 4-6

This is a nutritious and hearty main dish, that can be prepared in advance. It makes a lovely winter supper.

Ingredients

450g/1lb leeks, trimmed
50g/2oz butter or
  margarine
1kg/2lb onions, peeled and
  sliced
40g/1½oz flour
450ml/¾pt milk
200g/8oz Gruyère or
  strong Cheddar cheese,
  grated

salt and freshly ground
  pepper
pinch nutmeg
6 eggs
300g/10oz each carrots,
  parsnips, potatoes, all
  peeled and roughly
  chopped
50g/2oz butter
7g/1tbsp chopped chives
  or parsley (optional)

Preparation Rinse and slice the leeks, then steam or boil them until just tender. Drain and set aside.

Melt the butter or margarine in a large pan. Stir in the onions and cook slowly till soft and golden, about 15 to 20 minutes. Take the pan off the heat, stir in the flour, then gradually stir in the milk. Return to the heat and stir continuously until the mixture comes to the boil. Simmer for 2 minutes.

Stir the leeks and 100g/4oz of the grated cheese into the sauce, and season to taste. Spoon into a large shallow, greased baking dish. Make 6 hollows in the mixture for the eggs, and allow to cool. Break an egg into each hollow, and sprinkle 50g/2oz of the grated cheese over the eggs.

While the base is cooling, steam or boil the carrots, parsnips and potatoes until tender. Drain if necessary, then mash, process or liquidize with the butter, herbs and seasoning until very smooth and creamy. You may have to do this in two batches. Taste for seasoning.

If you are preparing the dish in advance, allow the vegetable purée to cool before spooning carefully over the eggs and onion mixture in the baking dish. Smooth the top.

When ready to cook — sprinkle on the remaining 50g/2oz grated cheese. Bake in a preheated oven at 200°C/400°F/Gas 6 for 15 to 20 minutes until brown and bubbling. The exact timing will depend on how you like your eggs cooked, and whether the gratin has come straight from the fridge, or has been prepared immediately beforehand.

Chopping Onions	**Slicing Onions**	**Preparing Tomatoes**

1 Slice the unpeeled onion lengthwise through the core, then peel both halves. Do not remove the root-end, which will serve to hold the 'leaves' together when chopping.

2 Put one half of the onion flat on the board. Using a thin, sharp knive make horizontal parallel cuts towards the root, without cutting through to the root-end.

3 Make a series of parallel, vertical cuts down to the board, again, avoiding the root-end.

4 Finally, slice the onion, making the cuts at right angles to the previous two sets of cuts. Use the root-end for stock or chop it separately like parsley.

1 Split the unskinned onion in half through the top and tail.

2 Pull away the onion skin from the pointed top, leaving the root-end intact. This will prevent the 'leaves' of onion slipping while being sliced. Repeat with the second half-onion.

3 Put each onion-half, cut-side down, on the board and slice widthways, from tip to root. Use the knuckles as a guide, moving them back a little after each cut. Use a downwards and forwards cutting action, keep the knife-tip touching the board.

1 Make a small cross in the skin of each tomato where the stem was attached to the fruit.

2 Dip in boiling water for 10 seconds (more if under-ripe, less if very soft) and immediately transfer to cold water to stop further cooking. Peel off the skins, starting at the 'nicked' point near the stem. They should come away easily.

3 Cut the tomatoes from top to bottom in quarters and push out the seeds and fleshy core with your thumbs.

4 Cut each quarter into even halves or into finer julienne slices if preferred.

Preparing an Artichoke

1 Cut off the tips of the artichoke's leaves with a kitchen knife. Use scissors to trim the lower leaves.

2 Make a shallow cut around the stem about 2.5cm/1in from the head. The idea is just to score the stem, not sever it.

3 Place the artichoke at the edge of the worktop and grip the stem firmly, steadying the head with your other hand. Twist and pull the stem down and away. The fibrous centre of the stem should come away too.

4 Trim off the rest of the stem with a kitchen knife.

5 When cooked, gently separate the tops of the outer leaves and pull out the central bud of small leaves.

6 Use a teaspoon to scrape out the fibrous 'choke' from the heart.

Preparing Fennel

1 Remove discoloured or leathery outer leaves. Split the head in half lengthwise.

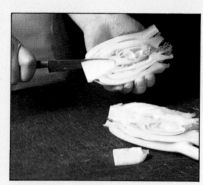

2 Remove inner thick core. It may be sliced thinly if liked, or discarded.

Chopping Parsley

1 Hold the tip of a large, heavy knife down with one hand and firmly move the handle up and down with the other, using a sharp cutting action.

2 Use the blade to scrape the parsley into a pile every now and then so that each chop cuts the maximum amount of parsley. Continue until the leaves are finely and evenly chopped.

Salads

Cabbage Salad   215
Stir-Fried Cabbage Salad   215
Spicy Potato Salad   215
Indian Potato Salad   215
Potato Salad with Horseradish I   216
Potato Salad with Horseradish II   216
Oriental Cucumber Salad   216
Cucumber Salad I   216
Cucumber Salad II   217
Hot and Spicy Cucumber Salad   217
Yoghurt with Cucumbers   217
Curried Coleslaw   217
Coleslaw   218
Tortellini Coleslaw   218
Tomato Salad   219
Tomato Salad with Olives   219
Spinach and Chickpea Salad   219
French Bean Salad in Mustard Sauce   219
Spicy Bean Salad   219
Red Bean Salad   220
Salad of Broad Beans   220
Haricot Bean Salad   220
Kidney Bean, Chick Pea and Corn Salad   221
Butter Bean Salad   221
Haricot Bean and Cottage Cheese   221
Kidney Bean Salad   221
Mixed Bean Salad   222
Strawberry and Avocado Salad   222
Vegetable Salad with Hot Peanut Sauce   222
Fennel Salad   222
Lentil and Feta Salad   223
Chicory and Walnut Salad   223
Salad of Broadsprouts and Bean Curd   223
Spinach and Orange Salad   224

Russian Salad   224
Onion Salad   224
Rainbow Salad   225
Egg and Pasta Salad   225
Chicory Orange Walnut Salad   225
Green Salad with Coconut Dressing   225
Mangetout and Carrot Salad   226
Tabouleh   226
Green Bean Salad   226
Wholefood Pasta Salad   226
Beetroot, Apple, Roquefort and Walnut Salad   227
Waldorf Salad   227
Tsatziki   227
La Lechuga   227
Greek Salad   228
Cauliflower, Blue Cheese and Yoghurt Salad   228
Caesar Salad   228
Feta Garlic Salad   228/229
Hot Pasta Salad   229
Double Gloucester Salad   229
Provencal Rice Salad   230
Seafood Salad   230
Prawn and Pasta Salad   230
Smoked Fish Salad   230
Salad Nicoise   231
Savoury Fruit Salad   231
Warm Potato and Bacon Salad   231
Avocado, Grapefruit and Prawn or Shrimp   231
Warm Chicken Liver Salad with Garlic   232
Vietnamese Salad   232
Pasta Salad   232

Oil Hints   233

Cabbage Salad
Serves 8

Ingredients
600g/1¼lb white cabbage, shredded
1 small onion, diced
2 spring onions, chopped
2 fresh green chillies, seeded and diced
2.5g/½tsp salt

20g/4tbsp fresh coriander, coarsely chopped
45ml/3tbsp olive oil
100ml/4fl oz lime juice
15ml/1tbsp Dijon mustard
15ml/1tbsp honey

Preparation Combine all the ingredients in a large serving bowl and toss well. Chill for 20-30 minutes before serving.

Stir-Fried Cabbage Salad
Serves 4

Ingredients
450g/1lb green cabbage
5ml/1tsp oil
2 green chillies, chopped
2.5g/½tsp mustard seeds
salt to taste

10g/1tbsp coconut, grated or desicated
7g/1tbsp coriander leaves, chopped

Preparation Cut the cabbage very finely into long strips. Wash and dry them.

Heat the oil in a large saucepan over a medium high heat. Add the chillies and fry for 3-4 seconds, then add the mustard seeds and fry for a further 2-3 seconds.

Add the cabbage and salt and, stirring constantly, cook for 3-4 minutes.

Serve immediately, garnished with the coconut and coriander leaves.

Spicy Potato Salad
Serves 6

Ingredients
425ml/¾pt yoghurt
450g/1lb boiled potatoes, diced into 0.5-cm/¼-in cubes
1 small onion, finely chopped
2.5g/½tsp salt

ground black pepper to taste
2.5g/½tsp ground cumin
1 green chilli, chopped
7g/1tbsp chopped coriander leaves

Preparation Whisk the yoghurt in a bowl until smooth, then add the potatoes, onions, salt, pepper and cumin. Mix gently and chill.

Serve sprinkled with the chopped chilli and coriander leaves.

Indian Potato Salad
Serves 3-4

Ingredients
15g/1tbsp tamarind, pulp or dried
75ml/5tbsp hot water
325g/12oz potatoes, boiled and peeled
1 small onion, finely chopped

1-2 fresh green chillies, seeded and finely chopped
2.5g/½tsp salt
2.5g/½tsp chilli powder
7g/1tbsp coriander leaves, chopped

Preparation Soak the tamarind in the hot water for 20 minutes. Squeeze out and reserve liquid.

Cut the potatoes into 0.5cm (¼in) slices and cool thoroughly.

Gently mix in all the ingredients. Serve cold.

Potato Salad with Horseradish I
Serves 4

Ingredients

1kg/2lb potatoes | a litle milk
Horseradish Mayonnaise | parsley

Preparation Peel the potatoes and boil in salted water, allow to cool, then cut into chunky slices.

Cover the potato slices with mayonnaise (you may need to thin it with milk), taking care not to break the potatoes.

Serve garnished with parsley.

Potato Salad with Horseradish II
Serves 4

Ingredients

675g/1½lb new potatoes | salt and freshly ground
150ml/¼pt sour cream | black pepper
25g/3tbsp finely grated | bunch spring onions or
horseradish | chives
pinch paprika | handful parsley, chopped
2.5ml/½tsp honey

Preparation Wash the potatoes, but do not peel. Boil in salted water until tender.

Meanwhile, make the dressing. Combine the cream with the horseradish, paprika and honey. Mix well and season with salt and pepper.

Trim the spring onions and slit down the stalks so that they curl outwards. Chop the chives.

When the potatoes are done, slice them while still hot and mix into the dressing with parsley. Toss in the onions and chives.

Serve immediately, or chill the salad and serve cold.

Oriental Cucumber Salad
Serves 4-6

Ingredients

1 large cucumber | 5g/1tsp chilli powder
10g/2tsp salt | 30ml/2tbsp soy sauce
3 spring onions, finely | sugar to taste
chopped | 15g/1tbsp roasted sesame
15ml/1tbsp sesame oil | seeds, lightly crushed

Preparation Halve the cucumber, trim the ends, cut it into 5cm (2in) lengths, then into stick-like pieces. Sprinkle with salt and after 30 minutes squeeze to drain off any excess liquid.

Fry the cucumber and two-thirds of the onion in hot sesame oil without browning. Add chilli powder and cook for 1 minute. Stir in the soy sauce, sugar to taste and the sesame seeds.

Turn onto a serving dish and leave for 2-3 hours so that the flavours blend.

Serve sprinkled with the remaining spring onions.

Cucumber Salad I
Serves 4

Ingredients

one large cucumber | 1 large clove garlic,
5g/1tsp salt | crushed
300ml/½pt yoghurt | dill or chopped mint
15ml/1tbsp oil (optional) | pepper
5ml/1tsp vinegar
(optional)

Preparation First prepare the cucumber: leave the peel on if preferred. Grate, dice finely or thinly slice it. Add the salt and leave for 15 minutes.

Rinse off the salt and drain the cucumber very well. Add the remaining ingredients, with pepper to taste, mix well and chill before serving.

The amount of herbs you add is purely a matter of individual taste and you may prefer your cucumber salad without oil and vinegar.

Variation To make Raita add 2.5g/½tsp ground cumin (preferably made from freshly roasted seeds), a pinch of cayenne and some pepper to the cucumber and yoghurt.

Dry Tarator is a Bulgarian variation — drain the yoghurt for 2 hours and add it to the finely chopped cucumber, with 50g/2oz chopped walnuts, 15ml/1tsp oil, dill, and salt and pepper to taste.

Cucumber Salad II
Serves 8

Ingredients

3 large cucumbers, peeled
  and thinly sliced
300ml/^{1}/$_2$pt red wine
  vinegar
2.5g/^{1}/$_2$tsp celery salt
^{1}/$_2$ head lettuce, shredded

15ml/1tbsp honey
good pinch black pepper
2.5g/^{1}/$_2$tsp fresh dill,
  chopped
60ml/4tbsp olive oil
5ml/1tsp Dijon mustard

Preparation Toss all the ingredients thoroughly in a large salad bowl. Chill for 2 hours before serving.

Hot and Spicy Cucumber Salad
Serves 3-4

Ingredients

30g/2tbsp unsalted
  peanuts
^{1}/$_2$ cucumber, peeled and
  cut into fine strips
20g/2tbsp grated or
  desiccated coconut
30ml/2tbsp lemon juice

2.5g/^{1}/$_2$tsp salt
15g/^{1}/$_2$oz butter
2.5g/^{1}/$_2$tsp cumin seeds
2 fresh green chillies,
  chopped
7g/1tbsp chopped
  coriander leaves

Preparation Dry-roast the peanuts and grind them to a fine powder.

Gently squeeze the cucumber to get rid of excess water.

Put the cucumber, coconut, ground peanuts, lemon juice and salt in a bowl and mix gently.

In a small saucepan, heat the butter. Add the cumin seeds and let them sizzle for 3-4 seconds. Add the green chillies and fry for 5-6 seconds. Pour this over the cucumber mixture and mix well.

Serve immediately garnished with the coriander leaves.

Hot and Spicy Cucumber Salad

Yoghurt with Cucumbers
Serves 6

Ingredients

750ml/1^1/$_4$pt yoghurt
2 large cucumbers, peeled,
  thickly sliced and then
  quartered
2 large onions, finely
  chopped

100g/4oz walnuts,
  chopped
2.5g/^{1}/$_2$tsp salt
2.5g/^{1}/$_2$tsp white pepper
15g/2tbsp chopped fresh
  mint

Preparation Combine all the ingredients in a large mixing bowl, and mix thoroughly, taking care not to bruise the cucumber slices.

Curried Coleslaw
Serves 4

This crisp salad is a refreshing change from the usual coleslaw.

Ingredients

225g/8oz white cabbage,
  trimmed, cored and
  shredded
2 medium carrots, peeled
  and grated
1 large green-skinned
  apple, cored and sliced
4 spring onions, trimmed
  and sliced

150ml/^{1}/$_4$pt Curry
  Mayonnaise
50g/2oz cashew nuts or
  dry-roasted peanuts
salt and freshly ground
  pepper
coriander leaves

Preparation Put the cabbage, carrots, apples and onions into a mixing bowl. Add the Mayonnaise and nuts and toss well. Taste for seasoning.

Spoon into a salad bowl and serve garnished with coriander leaves.

Variation Add shredded chicken, diced ham, prawns or shrimps to the salad for a main dish.

Coleslaw
Serves 6

Ingredients

1 small crisp head white
  cabbage
225g/8oz carrots
15g/2tbsp chopped chives

50g/2oz sultanas
15g/1tbsp sesame seeds
Mayonnaise

Preparation Shred the cabbage finely, discarding the stalk. Grate the carrots.

Toss all the ingredients together in sufficient mayonnaise to coat and mix well. Taste and adjust seasoning. Chill overnight in the fridge.

Mix well again before serving.

Tortellini Coleslaw
Serves 4-6

Ingredients

225g/8oz stuffed tortellini,
  cooked
45ml/3tbsp olive oil
15ml/1tbsp white wine
  vinegar
5ml/1tsp French mustard
salt and freshly ground
  pepper
½ whole cabbage (approx.
  450g/1lb)

1 carrot, scraped and
  grated
25g/1oz raisins
2 spring onions, washed
  and chopped
25g/1oz raisins
2 stalks celery, washed
150ml/¼pt Mayonnaise
black olives

Preparation Put the cooked tortellini (after rinsing in cold water and draining) in a bowl.

Mix the dressing by putting the oil, vinegar, mustard and seasoning in a screw-top jar. Shake well and pour over the pasta.

Wash, drain and shred the cabbage. Mix in a separate bowl with the grated carrot and raisins.

After washing the celery remove the strings with a sharp knife and then chop them into thin slices, add to the cabbage and season well. Mix in the mayonnaise.

On a serving dish arrange rows of coleslaw with alternating rows of tortellini. Garnish with the olives.

Tomato Salad
Serves 4

Ingredients

6 tomatoes, thickly sliced	45ml/3tbsp olive oil
freshly ground black	freshly chopped herbs
pepper (lots!)	6 peppercorns

Preparation Lay tomato slices on a large plate and dust them liberally with black pepper. Turn over and dust the other side.

Pour over the olive oil. Sprinkle with the herbs and decorate with the peppercorns.

Tomato Salad with Olives
Serves 6

Ingredients

4 large ripe tomatoes, thinly sliced	50ml/2fl oz lemon juice
2 cucumbers, peeled and thinly sliced	30ml/2tbsp tarragon vinegar
1 cup black olives, pitted	50ml/2fl oz olive oil
15g/2tbsp finely chopped parsley	good pinch salt
7g/1tbsp finely chopped mint	2.5g/½tsp black pepper

Preparation Arrange the tomato and cucumber slices on a serving platter, with the olives around them.

To make the dressing, combine the parsley, mint, lemon juice, vinegar, oil, salt and pepper in a small bowl. Mix well with a fork or small whisk until well blended.

Pour the dressing over the salad. Chill for 30 minutes and serve cold.

Spinach and Chick Pea Salad
Serves 4

Ingredients

150g/6oz chick peas	freshly ground white pepper
450g/1lb spinach, washed	salt to taste
15g/½oz butter	1 onion, cut into rings
90ml/6tbsp olive oil	125ml/4fl oz yoghurt
30ml/2tbsp white wine vinegar	parsley, chopped

Preparation Soak the chick peas in water overnight and then cook them in unsalted water for an hour or until tender.

Cook the spinach in a saucepan with a small amount of butter, but no water. Drain and chop.

Add the chick peas to the cooled spinach. Mix in the olive oil, vinegar, pepper and salt, taking care not to crush the chick peas. Add the onion rings.

Serve the salad with the yoghurt spooned on top, and sprinkled with parsley.

French Bean Salad in Mustard Sauce
Serves 4

Ingredients

45ml/3tbsp olive oil	black pepper, freshly ground, to taste
15ml/1tsp white wine vinegar	450g/1lb French beans, cooked
5g/1tsp turmeric powder	
pinch chilli powder	
10g/1tbsp dry mustard powder	

Preparation Stir together olive oil, white wine vinegar and spices.

Toss in the cooked French beans and mix gently.

Chill slightly, but not too much — too long in the refrigerator will dull the flavour.

Spicy Bean Salad
Serves 6

Ingredients

75ml/3fl oz olive oil	2 pinches chilli powder
40ml/1½fl oz wine vinegar	1 clove garlic, crushed
2.5g/½tsp freshly ground coriander seeds	225g/8oz cooked red kidney beans
2.5g/½tsp freshly ground cumin	½ cucumber, peeled and cut into chunks

Preparation Blend the olive oil, vinegar and spices together, and pour the mixture over warm, freshly cooked kidney beans.

Add the cucumber and combine well. Let the vegetables marinate in the dressing.

Before serving, drain off any excess liquid.

Red Bean Salad
Serves 4-6

Ingredients

225g/8oz red kidney
  beans, soaked overnight
45ml/3tbsp Vinaigrette
1 small onion, finely
  chopped
3 hard-cooked eggs,
  chopped
1 small head celery,
  chopped or 1 small
  cauliflower, chopped

45ml/3tbsp brown or
  mustard pickle
5 anchovy fillets, chopped
  (optional)
150ml/¼pt sour cream or
  yoghurt
salt and pepper

Preparation Bring the soaked beans to the boil in fresh water and boil rapidly for 10 minutes, then cook for 1 to 1½ hours, until they are tender but not soft.

Drain them and pour over the vinaigrette and onion while the beans are still warm.

When the beans are cold, add the remaining ingredients, mixing everything together well. Refrigerate and serve cold.

Salad of Broad Beans
Serves 4

A magnificent and very simple summer salad made with fresh young beans and peas.

Ingredients

350g/12oz unshelled
  broad beans
350g/12oz unshelled peas
4 small fresh Jerusalem
  artichokes
15-30ml/1-2tbsp walnut
  oil or olive oil

15-30ml/1-2tbsp lemon
  juice
fresh mint
salt and freshly ground
  black pepper

Preparation Shell the beans and pod the peas. If they are not quite tender enough to eat raw, put them in a pan of boiling salted water for a minute, then refresh in cold water.

Clean the artichokes, cut each into 6 and cook in boiling salted water for 5 minutes. Drain and refresh.

Make the dressing by blending the oil and lemon juice and adding chopped mint and seasoning to taste.

Toss the vegetables in the dressing and garnish with a few sprigs of mint. Serve with good crusty bread.

Variation Use drained, canned artichoke hearts instead of the Jerusualem artichokes. There is no need to cook them.

Haricot Bean Salad
Serves 4

Ingredients

225g/½lb dried white
  haricot beans
175ml/6fl oz Basic Garlic
  Dressing
2 cloves garlic, crushed
1 large red pepper, seeded
  and thinly sliced

2 small leeks, thinly sliced
7g/1tbsp finely chopped
  spring onions (green
  part only)

Preparation Cover the beans with boiling water and leave to soak overnight.

Pour off the soaking water. Cover with fresh water and boil for 1½-2 hours, until tender. You may need to add more water from time to time to prevent them sticking.

Drain the beans and, while still hot, pour over the Basic Garlic Dressing. Stir in the crushed garlic and cool until needed.

Before serving, stir in the pepper and leeks and sprinkle with the chopped spring onions.

Variation Omit the spring onions, and stir in 15g/ 2tbsp of coarsely chopped fresh mint just before serving.

Kidney Bean, Chick Pea and Corn Salad
Serves 4

Ingredients

175g/6oz kidney beans
175g/6oz chick peas
6 spring onions
2 large tomatoes

175g/6oz corn kernels,
    cooked
Vinaigrette

Preparation Soak the kidney beans and the chick peas separately overnight, then simmer in water until cooked. Drain and cool.

Chop the spring onions and slice the tomatoes.

Toss all the ingredients in sufficient vinaigrette to coat and serve at room temperature with hot pitta bread.

Butter Bean Salad
Serves 4-6

Ingredients

225g/8oz butter beans,
    soaked
4 spring onions, washed
    and finely chopped
1 clove garlic, crushed
1 red or green pepper,
    seeded and finely diced
300ml/¹⁄₂pt Mayonnaise or
    Vinaigrette

salt and freshly ground
    pepper
1 lettuce
12 stuffed olives
15g/2tbsp chopped parsley

Preparation Cook the soaked butter beans for about 45 minutes or until tender but not mushy. Drain and allow to cool.

Mix all the ingredients in a bowl with mayonnaise or vinaigrette.

Arrange in a dish lined with lettuce. Garnish with olives and chopped parsley.

Haricot Bean and Cottage Cheese
Serves 4-8

Ingredients

225g/8oz haricot beans
2 pinches bicarbonate of
    soda
150ml/¹⁄₄pt Vinaigrette
4 spring onions, washed
    and sliced
1 green pepper, seeded and
    cut into thin strips

1 red pepper, seeded and
    cut into thin strips
¹⁄₂ shredded iceberg lettuce
225g/8oz cottage cheese
20 stuffed olives

Preparation Soak the haricot beans in cold water for at least 8 hours. Drain and pour into a saucepan, cover with cold water, add the bicarbonate of soda and bring to the boil. Simmer for 30 minutes or until just cooked. Drain and allow to cool in a bowl.

Add the dressing to the cooked beans, then stir in the spring onions and pepper.

Arrange the shredded lettuce on a round dish. Inside the lettuce ring, arrange a ring of cottage cheese.

Tip the dressed bean salad into the centre of the cottage cheese ring. Garnish with whole stuffed olives and serve with sliced wholewheat bread.

Kidney Bean Salad
Serves 4

Ingredients

225g/8oz cooked kidney
    beans
2 spring onions, washed
    and chopped

150ml/¹⁄₄pt Vinaigrette
7g/1tbsp chopped
    parsley

Preparation Combine the beans, onions, vinaigrette and parsley. Chill for 30 minutes before serving.

Mixed Bean Salad
Serves 4

Ingredients

100g/4oz butter beans	8 slices salami, diced
100g/4oz kidney beans	150ml/¼pt Vinaigrette
3 spring onions, washed and chopped	15g/2tbsp chopped parsley
	2 heads chicory, sliced
3 small peppers, yellow, green and red, seeded and cut into thin strips	2 tomatoes, cut into wedges
	¼ cucumber, thinly sliced

Preparation Soak the butter and kidney beans in separate bowls overnight. Cook in separate saucepans just covered with water, bring to the boil and simmer for 30-40 minutes until the beans are just tender. Allow to cool.

Put the onions, peppers and salami in a bowl with the cold beans and vinaigrette and mix well. Add the chopped parsley and mix again.

Arrange the sliced chicory around a shallow salad bowl and surround with tomato wedges and cucumber. Pile the bean salad in the centre.

Strawberry and Avocado Salad
Serves 4

Serve this as an accompaniment to white fish, meat or egg dishes, or as a first course.

Ingredients

2 avocados	30ml/2tbsp oil
225g/8oz strawberries	5ml/1tsp honey
30ml/2tbsp vinegar, preferably strawberry	salt and freshly ground black pepper

Preparation Slice the avocados in half, remove the stones and scoop flesh out of shells in one piece if possible, using a palette knife. Slice.

Hull and slice the strawberries. Arrange the avocado halves and strawberries on 4 side plates.

Mix together the vinegar, oil and honey and season. Pour dressing over salad.

Vegetable Salad with Hot Peanut Sauce
Serves 4-6

Ingredients

100g/4oz salted peanuts	**Salad**
300ml/½pt coconut milk (see note)	2 medium potatoes, cooked and diced
1 clove garlic, crushed	100g/4oz bean sprouts, blanched, rinsed and drained
3 shallots or 1 small red onion, peeled	100g/4oz cabbage, shredded, blanched and rinsed
30ml/2tbsp oil	
5g/1tsp chilli powder	100g/4oz each green beans and cauliflower florets, boiled until just tender and drained
60ml/4tbsp lemon juice	
15g/1tbsp brown sugar	
5ml/1tsp soy sauce	
salt to taste	5-cm/2-in piece cucumber, sliced
	1 small carrot, cut into matchsticks
	Chinese leaves, shredded
	watercress (optional)
	2 hard-boiled eggs

Preparation Grind the salted peanuts until gritty but not a paste; set aside. Prepare the coconut milk.

Pound the garlic with the shallots or onion and fry in the oil without browning. Stir in the chilli powder and cook for 1 minute. Add the coconut milk and allow to come to the boil. Stir in the lemon juice, sugar, soy sauce, and the ground peanuts, which will thicken the sauce. Taste for seasoning. Allow to simmer until creamy in consistency. Set aside.

Arrange the vegetables in piles on a large platter with egg quarters. Serve the reheated sauce separately.

Note To make coconut milk, grate the flesh of 1 coconut and blend with 425ml/¾pt very hot water. Sieve, and squeeze the pulp to draw out the liquid. The milk can be thinned by adding more hot water before blending.

A quick method of making coconut milk is to blend together 125g/4oz creamed coconut (widely available in supermarkets) with 400ml/⅔pt hot water.

Fennel Salad
Serves 6

A sharp, tangy salad, refreshing with cold meat pies, or rich mousses.

Ingredients

3 heads fennel, trimmed	good pinch mustard powder
2 medium courgettes	
100g/4oz beansprouts	salt and freshly ground black pepper
100g/4oz watercress	
grated rind of ½ lemon	7g/1tbsp snipped chives or parsley
45ml/3tbsp lemon juice	
60ml/4tbsp olive oil	

Preparation Slice the fennel and plunge into a bowl of icy water. Leave for 5 minutes, or until crisp, then drain thoroughly.

Meanwhile, slice the courgettes and pick over the beansprouts and watercress.

Mix the fennel with the courgettes, beansprouts and watercress.

For the dressing, combine the remaining ingredients until emulsified. Taste for seasoning, then pour over the salad and toss well.

Lentil and Feta Salad
Serves 6

This hearty salad is a meal in itself. Serve it with pitta bread.

Ingredients
350g/12oz brown lentils   *100g/4oz chopped fresh*
750ml/1¼pt cold water   *chives*
bay leaf   *90ml/6tbsp olive oil*
2.5g/½tsp dried basil   *45ml/3tbsp wine vinegar*
2 cloves garlic   *pinch dried oregano*
75g/3oz diced celery   *2.5g/½tsp salt*
1 small onion, chopped   *2.5g/½tsp freshly ground*
150g/6oz feta cheese,   *black pepper*
   crumbled

Preparation Soak the lentils in water for 2 hours. Drain. Put the lentils into a saucepan and add enough cold water to cover them completely. Add the bay leaf, basil and one of the garlic cloves. Bring to the boil and then reduce the heat. Simmer, covered, for 20 minutes.

Add the celery and onion. Add enough extra water to cover the lentils. Cover the saucepan and simmer for 10 minutes.

Drain the lentils, discarding the bay leaf and garlic cloves and put them into a serving bowl. Add the feta cheese and chives. Toss.

Put the olive oil, vinegar, oregano, remaining garlic clove, crushed, salt and pepper into a jar with a tightly fitting lid. Cover tightly and shake until well blended.

Pour the dressing over the lentil salad and toss. Let the salad stand at room temperature for 2 hours, tossing occasionally, before serving.

Salad of Beansprouts and Bean Curd

Chicory and Walnut Salad
Serves 4

Ingredients
3 heads chicory   *1 box mustard/cress*
1 head celery   *seedlings*
3 onions, finely chopped   *50g/2oz chopped walnuts*
25g/1oz sprouted   *150ml/¼pt Vinaigrette*
   fenugreek seeds

Preparation Wash and slice the chicory and the celery. Mix them with the onions and the other ingredients.

Pour on the vinaigrette at the last moment, toss and serve.

Salad of Beansprouts and Bean Curd
Serves 4

Ingredients
225g/8oz can beansprouts   *2.5g/½tsp chilli powder*
1 square bean curd, cut   *30ml/2tbsp oil*
   into small dice   *juice 1 lemon*
fat for frying   *onion, crisply fried*

Preparation Soak the beansprouts in cold water. Toss into boiling water for 1 minute, then drain and rinse with cold water. Fry the bean curd in fat until it is crisp; drain.

Put the beansprouts, chilli powder and oil in a bowl and toss together. Squeeze over the lemon juice. Taste for seasoning.

Just before serving, add the crisp bean curds and top with fried onion.

Russian Salad
Serves 6

Ingredients

1 large potato, peeled
1 small cauliflower
1 piece broccoli
2 medium carrots, diced
1 aubergine, diced
100g/4oz French beans,
   diced

20g/2tbsp green peas
4 stalks celery, diced
6 spring onions, finely
   chopped
7g/1tbsp chives, chopped
125ml/4fl oz Mustard
   Mayonnaise

Preparation Bring the potato to the boil and simmer until just cooked. Drain and dice when cool.

   Break the florets off the cauliflower and the broccoli. Cook separately in salted water until crisp-tender.

   Cook the carrots, aubergines and beans separately in salted boiling water until crisp-tender. Cook the peas until just tender.

   Drain all vegetables immediately and cool under cold running water, then drain again. It is important to cook each batch separately.

   Combine the vegetables. Add the celery, spring onions, chives and mayonnaise and gently toss.

Spinach and Orange Salad
Serves 2-4

Ingredients

450g/1lb young spinach
   leaves
1 bunch watercress
1 large juicy orange
crispy bacon pieces
   (optional)

15-30ml/1-2 tbsp olive oil
salt and freshly ground
   black pepper

Preparation Use only young tender spinach for this salad. Outside leaves are too bitter and tough to be enjoyed raw. Wash the spinach thoroughly, discarding any discoloured leaves and tough stalks. Tear into manageable pieces.

   Wash the watercress, discarding tough stalks and yellow leaves. Shake water off the spinach and watercress in a lettuce basket.

   Peel the orange. Remove the pith and pips and slice as finely as possible. Cut the slices into quarters.

   Toss the ingredients together in a large bowl with the oil and season well.

Onion Salad
Serves 4

Just what you need to brighten your cold cuts.

Ingredients

4 large onions, finely
   chopped
1 small hot green chilli,
   finely chopped
1 slice fresh ginger, finely
   chopped

15g/½oz coconut, grated
juice of ½ lemon
salt to taste

Preparation Mix the onion and chilli together. Add the ginger, coconut, lemon juice and mix well.

Rainbow Salad
Serves 6-8

A colourful salad to cheer up a winter's day.

Ingredients

225g/8oz red cabbage, trimmed, cored and shredded
225g/8oz white cabbage, trimmed, cored and shredded
2 medium courgettes, trimmed and chopped
2 large carrots, peeled and grated
1 medium onion, peeled and finely chopped
2 green-skinned apples, quartered, cored and sliced
300ml/½pt Yoghurt Mayonnaise
salt and freshly ground pepper
10g/1tbsp pomegranate seeds (optional)

Preparation Put the cabbage, courgettes, carrots, onions and apples into a large bowl and toss well with the mayonnaise. Taste, and add salt and pepper if necessary.

Spoon into a salad bowl and serve sprinkled, if you like, with pomegranate seeds.

Egg and Pasta Salad
Serves 4

Ingredients

225g/8oz green or wholewheat pasta shapes
10ml/2tsp oil
4 eggs
100g/4oz green beans
2 stalks celery
1 dessert apple
50g/2oz walnuts
Mayonnaise
salt and freshly ground black pepper
7-15ml/1-2tbsp fresh dill

Preparation Cook the pasta in plenty of boiling salted water, to which you have added 10ml/2tsp oil, until *al dente*. Drain and allow to cool

Hard-boil the eggs, peel under cold running water and allow to cool. Cut into quarters.

Top and tail the beans and cut into manageable lengths. Simmer in salted water until cooked but not soft. Drain and allow to cool.

Chop the celery. Peel, core and dice the apple.

Toss all the ingredients except the eggs together in sufficient mayonnaise to coat. Season and garnish with eggs and dill.

Chicory Orange Walnut Salad
Serves 4-6

Ingredients

4 plump heads chicory
2 large sweet oranges
75g/3oz walnut halves
45ml/3tbsp olive or walnut oil
15ml/1tbsp lemon juice
1 clove garlic, finely crushed
2.5g/½tsp sugar

Preparation Cut the chicory into 1.25-cm (½-in) slices.

Peel and slice the oranges — or divide them into segments — removing the skin and pith from each.

Coarsely chop the walnuts, reserving a few for decoration.

Mix the olive or walnut oil, lemon juice, garlic and sugar, and pour this dressing over the combined chicory, orange and walnuts.

Decorate with the reserved walnuts and serve chilled.

Green Salad with Coconut Dressing
Serves 4

Ingredients

450g/1lb (prepared weight) mixed green vegetables such as: beans, Chinese cabbage, beansprouts and cucumber
100g/4oz desiccated coconut
150ml/5fl oz water
1 clove garlic, crushed
1 green chilli
salt
juice ½ lemon
sugar to taste
mint sprigs

Preparation Trim ends from the beans and blanch in boiling water for 2-3 minutes until just cooked. Rinse in cold water to retain the colour. Wash the cabbage and shred, not too finely. Plunge the beansprouts into cold water for a few minutes and drain. Cut the cucumber in 2.5cm (1in) lengths and each chunk into 10 pieces.

Cook the coconut and water together for 5 minutes. Cool. Pound the garlic and chilli to a paste. Add to the coconut, with salt, lemon juice and sugar to taste. Transfer to a large bowl then add the prepared vegetables.

Toss well and serve garnished with mint leaves. Do not keep overnight.

Mangetout and Carrot Salad
Serves 4

Ingredients

3 carrots, scraped and
  sliced
good pinch salt
450g/1lb mangetout
1 large leek, washed

30ml/2tbsp vegetable oil
salt and freshly ground
  pepper
15g/2tbsp chopped parsley
150ml/¼pt Vinaigrette

Preparation Cook the carrots in a small amount of
cold water with the salt. Bring to boil simmer for 10
minutes, drain. Prepare the mangetout by removing
the small stalks at the end. Cook in a small amount of
boiling salted water for 4 minutes, test for tenderness.
(The peas should still be slightly crunchy.) Drain.

Wash the leek thoroughly and cut a cross through
the centre, wash again to make sure all the mud is
removed from the inside. Slice thinly.

Heat the oil in a frying pan and cook the leek over a
low heat for 4 minutes. At this stage if you want to serve
a hot vegetable salad, add the carrots and mangetout,
season well and stir over a low heat. Serve in a heated
vegetable dish, sprinkled with chopped parsley.

To serve cold, allow all the vegetables to cool, mix
together, season well and toss in the vinaigrette.
Sprinkle with chopped parsley.

Tabouleh
Serves 6

Ingredients

150g/6oz bulgur wheat
450ml/¾pt boiling water
4 spring onions, chopped
35g/5tbsp chopped fresh
  mint
2 medium tomatoes,
  seeded and chopped
60g/2½oz chopped fresh
  parsley

75ml/5tbsp olive oil
90ml/6tbsp fresh lemon
  juice
2.5g/½tsp salt
2.5g/½tsp freshly ground
  black pepper
10 large lettuce leaves

Preparation Put the bulgur into a bowl and add the
boiling water. Stir, cover the bowl, and leave to stand
for 35 minutes.

Drain the bulgur, squeezing out any remaining
water between the palms of your hands. Put the bulgur
into a serving bowl. Add the onions, mint, tomatoes
and parsley. Toss gently. Add the olive oil. Stir until well
mixed. Add the lemon juice, salt and pepper. Stir until
well mixed.

Serve the tabouleh in its bowl or on individual
plates. Use the lettuce leaves as scoops to eat the
tabouleh.

Green Bean Salad
Serves 6

Ingredients

675g/1½lb fresh green
  beans, trimmed and
  halved
60ml/4tbsp olive oil
30ml/2tbsp white wine
  vinegar
50ml/2fl oz vegetable stock
  or water

2.5g/½tsp salt
5g/1tsp cayenne pepper
7g/1tbsp finely chopped
  fresh dill or 5g/1tsp
  dried dill
5g/2tsp chopped fresh
  parsley
15ml/1tbsp Dijon mustard

Preparation Cook the green beans in a large pot of
boiling water until they are tender but still crisp. Drain
well. Put the green beans into a large serving bowl.

In a mixing bowl combine the olive oil, vinegar,
stock or water, salt, cayenne pepper, dill, parsley and
mustard. Mix well.

Pour the dressing over the green beans and toss
well. Chill for 1 hour before serving.

Wholefood Pasta Salad
Serves 4

Ingredients

225g/8oz wholewheat
  pasta spirals
150ml/¼pt yoghurt
2.5g/½tsp cumin
½ clove garlic, crushed
salt and freshly ground
  pepper

juice of 1 lemon
1 small lettuce, washed
1 bunch watercress,
  washed
15g/1tbsp bran (optional)

Preparation Cook the pasta spirals for 10-12 minutes,
drain, then rinse in cold water. Allow to drain well in a
colander.

Put the yoghurt into a bowl and mix in the cumin,
crushed garlic and seasoning. Add a few drops of
lemon juice.

Toss the pasta in the yoghurt dressing.

Arrange the drained lettuce and watercress in a salad
bowl, sprinkle with lemon juice. Arrange the pasta in
the centre of the bowl and sprinkle with the bran, if
liked.

Variation Cucumber and tomatoes can be added.

Beetroot, Apple, Roquefort and Walnut Salad
Serves 4

A very attractive salad to serve with cold meats and baked jacket potatoes on a chilly day.

Ingredients
450g/1lb beetroot boiled, peeled and shredded
75ml/5tbsp Vinaigrette
2 crisp green apples, quartered, cored and thinly sliced
½ crisp lettuce, rinsed
75g/3oz Roquefort cheese
50g/2oz walnut halves

Preparation Put the beetroot into a bowl and mix with half the vinaigrette.

Toss the apples with the remaining dressing in another bowl.

Tear the lettuce and arrange in a salad bowl, and top with the beetroot, then the apple slices. Crumble the cheese over the whole salad and decorate with walnut halves.

Waldorf Salad
Serves 2-4

Ingredients
8 stalks crisp celery
2 rosy-skinned dessert apples
lemon juice
50g/2oz walnuts
90ml/6tbsp Mayonnaise
salt and freshly ground black pepper

Preparation If the celery is not crisp, immerse it in ice-cold water. It will soon freshen up. Pat dry and slice.

Core the apples but do not peel — the pink skin will give colour contrast to the salad. Slice and sprinkle with lemon juice to prevent discolouring.

Toss all the ingredients in the mayonnaise and season well.

Variation This salad also tastes good with blue cheese dressing. Blend the mayonnaise with 15g/1tbsp blue cheese before adding the salt.

Tsatziki
Serves 4

Ingredients
1 large cucumber, unpeeled
2.5g/½tsp salt
2 cloves garlic, finely chopped
450ml/¾pt thick Greek yoghurt
pepper
a little lemon juice

Preparation Coarsely grate the cucumber into a colander. Sprinkle with the salt and leave to drain for about 1 hour.

Stir in the drained cucumber and garlic into the yoghurt and add pepper and lemon juice to taste.

Serve chilled.

La Lechuga
Serves 4

Ingredients
1 tight head crisp lettuce, preferably iceberg
60ml/4tbsp olive oil
4 cloves garlic, finely chopped

Preparation Discard looser outer leaves of the lettuce. With a very sharp knife, cut lettuce in half from stalk to tip. Cut each half into 3. Keep cold.

Heat the oil in frying pan and when hot, add garlic. Fry, stirring, until brown. Pour over the lettuce and serve immediately.

This is best eaten with the fingers if you don't mind the mess. Offer plenty of paper napkins.

Greek Salad

Ingredients

1 head crunchy lettuce, shredded
2 large beef tomatoes, sliced
½ cucumber, thinly sliced
1 onion, coarsely chopped

handful black olives
150g/6oz feta cheese, cubed
olive oil
salt and plenty of freshly ground black pepper

Preparation Combine the vegetables and cheese in a large bowl. Pour over enough olive oil to just coat the salad. Season well and toss.

Chill for an hour. Toss again, check seasoning and serve.

Cauliflower, Blue Cheese and Yoghurt Salad
Serves 4

Ingredients

1 head cauliflower
60ml/4tbsp yoghurt
30g/2tbsp blue cheese, softened

30g/4tbsp parsley, chopped
salt and freshly ground black pepper

Preparation Cut the cauliflower into tiny florets — reserve the stalks for use in a soup.

Cream the yoghurt and blue cheese together. Toss cauliflower and parsley in the dressing and season well.

Caesar Salad
Serves 4

Ingredients

30ml/2tbsp olive oil
30ml/2tbsp white wine vinegar
1 clove garlic, crushed
salt and freshly ground black pepper
½ crisp iceberg lettuce
4 eggs

4 anchovy fillets
100g/4oz Roquefort cheese, crumbled
Croûtons
2 slices brown bread, crusts removed
30ml/2tbsp olive oil
1 clove garlic, crushed

Preparation Make the dressing by combining the olive oil, vinegar, garlic and seasoning.

Break up the lettuce and divide between four salad plates. Soft boil the eggs and shell them under cold running water. Roll up the anchovy fillets. Put an egg and an anchovy fillet on each plate. Sprinkle the cheese over the top and pour the dressing over all.

To make the croûtons, cut the bread into small squares. Heat the oil in a pan, add the garlic and, when cooked, add the bread squares. Fry till golden. Divide between the plates.

Cut into each egg so that the yolk can run out and serve straight away.

Feta Garlic Salad
Serves 4

With fresh crusty bread, this aromatic and refreshing salad is virtually a meal in itself.

Ingredients

450g/1lb ripe tomatoes, skinned and cut into 2.5-cm (1-in) chunks
225g/8oz feta cheese, cut into 2.5-cm (1-in) chunks
50g/2oz black olives, stoned
45ml/3tbsp good olive oil

1-2 cloves of garlic, finely chopped
15g/2tbsp fresh basil leaves, coarsely chopped
2.5g/½tsp sugar
freshly ground black pepper

Preparation First make the dressing. Chop the garlic and put it in a mortar. Pour in a little of the olive oil and pound it to a pulp. Gradually add the basil and cheese with the rest of the oil, pounding all the time. You should have a thick paste.

Dice the Mozzarella. Peel the tomatoes by immersing them in boiling water until their skins burst. Chop them roughly. Mix the cheese, tomatoes and olives together and season.

Cook the pasta in boiling salted water, to which you have added a little olive oil, until *al dente*. Drain. Toss the pasta in the dressing. Pile it into four warmed serving bowls and top with the tomato mixture.

Preparation Combine the tomatoes, feta and olives in a glass serving bowl, and add the oil, garlic, basil and sugar.

Sprinkle with plenty of freshly ground black pepper and stir gently.

Leave in a cool place for at least an hour for the flavours to combine before serving.

Variation For Mozzarella Garlic Salad, slice the tomatoes and arrange alternately with 225g/8oz of sliced Mozzarella cheese in overlapping concentric circles. Pour over the oil and sprinkle on the garlic, basil, sugar and pepper. Decorate with the olives.

Double Gloucester Salad
Serves 2

Hot Pasta Salad
Serves 6

Ingredients

2 cloves garlic	450g/1lb Mediterranean
45ml/3tbsp olive oil	tomatoes
handful fresh basil	75g/3oz black olives
15g/1tbsp grated Parmesan	salt and freshly ground
cheese	black pepper
100g/4oz Mozzarella	350g/12oz spinach leaves
cheese	a little extra olive oil

Ingredients

2 handfuls young spinach	15ml/1tbsp wine vinegar
leaves	5-10g/1-2tsp mustard
1 bunch watercress	powder
2 large beef tomatoes	salt and freshly ground
50g/2oz mushrooms	black pepper
6-8 spring onions	100g/4oz Double
30ml/2tbsp olive oil	Gloucester cheese, cubed

Preparation Wash the spinach and watercress, discarding stalks and any tough or yellow leaves. Immerse the tomatoes in boiling water until their skins split, then refresh with cold water, peel and roughly chop. Slice the mushrooms. Trim the spring onions; make several lengthwise cuts into each onion and splay out the layers in a decorative fashion.

Make the dressing by combining the oil, vinegar, mustard and seasoning.

Combine the watercress, spinach, tomatoes and mushrooms in a salad bowl, add the dressing and toss. Top with the cheese and onions.

Provençal Rice Salad
Serves 4

A meal in itself, serve this with red wine and crusty French bread for a taste of the Mediterranean.

Ingredients

225g/8oz long grain rice, cooked
8 spring onions, trimmed and sliced
225g/8oz French beans, cooked and coarsely chopped
3 hard-boiled eggs, shelled and quartered
185g/6½oz can tuna, drained and flaked
50g/2oz black olives, stoned

Dressing
2-3 cloves garlic, peeled and crushed
4 anchovy fillets, mashed
1 egg yolk
175ml/6fl oz Vinaigrette
salt and freshly ground pepper
fresh coriander leaves

Preparation Put the rice in a large bowl and toss with a fork to separate the grains. Add the spring onions, French beans, hard-boiled eggs, tuna and olives.

For the dressing, blend or process the garlic, anchovies and egg yolk. With the machine running, pour in the vinaigrette through the feed tube. Process until smooth and emulsified.

Pour the dressing over the rice mixture and toss well. Taste for seasoning, adding more salt and pepper if necessary.

Leave to stand for 20-30 minutes, then spoon into a salad bowl and garnish with the coriander leaves.

Seafood Salad
Serves 4-6

Serve as a first course or with thinly sliced brown bread for a light lunch.

Ingredients

100g/4oz smoked salmon, coarsely chopped
100g/4oz frozen prawns, thawed
225g/8oz cold, cooked monkfish, white fish or salmon, flaked
300ml/½pt Avocado Mayonnaise

Tabasco
lemon juice
1 hard green apple, quartered, cored and coarsely chopped
3 sticks celery, quartered and sliced
1 small green pepper, cored, seeded and sliced

Preparation Combine the smoked salmon, prawns, flaked fish and mayonnaise. Season to taste with Tabasco and lemon juice.

Stir in the apple, celery and pepper. Serve immediately.

Prawn and Pasta Salad
Serves 4

Ingredients

300ml/½pt Mayonnaise
10ml/2tsp tomato purée
2-3 drops Tabasco sauce
juice of ½ lemon
100g/4oz cooked peeled prawns
½ lettuce, washed

1 bunch watercress, washed
225g/8oz cooked pasta shells
large prawns in shells (optional)

Preparation Mix into the Mayonnaise the tomato purée and Tabasco. Sprinkle the lemon juice over the prawns.

Line a salad bowl with the lettuce and watercress sprigs.

Add the mayonnaise to the pasta shells and prawns and mix well.

Pile the prawns and pasta in the centre of the lined salad bowl. Garnish, if you like, with large prawns.

Smoked Fish Salad
Serves 4

Ingredients

350g/12oz smoked mackerel fillets, skinned
225g/8oz pasta bows
5ml/1tsp curry paste
5ml/1tsp tomato purée
300ml/½pt Yoghurt Mayonnaise
salt and freshly ground pepper

100g/4oz firm white button mushrooms, sliced
1 medium courgette, sliced
2 sticks celery, sliced
½ crisp lettuce
cherry tomatoes

Preparation Flake the fish into a mixing bowl. Cook the pasta in boiling salted water until just tender. Drain and refresh in cold water. Dry thoroughly, then add the fish.

Mix the curry paste and the tomato purée into the dressing. Season to taste. Add to the fish and pasta, with the mushrooms, courgette and celery and adjust the seasoning.

Arrange the salad on a bed of lettuce leaves, garnish with cherry tomatoes and serve with garlic bread.

Salad Niçoise
Serves 4

This makes a delicious lunch, dinner party appetizer or buffet salad, with crispy French bread.

Ingredients
450g/1lb potatoes, boiled	¼ cucumber
250g/8oz green beans, fresh or frozen	2 hard-boiled eggs
200-g/7-oz can tuna fish, drained	12 black or green olives, stones removed
150ml/¼pt Vinaigrette	6 anchovy fillets, cut into thin slices
4 tomatoes, skinned and sliced	small cherry tomatoes to garnish

Preparation Cook the potatoes in their skins until tender. Remove the skins and dice finely. Cook the beans in a small amount of boiling water for about 6 minutes. Frozen beans can be used; cook as directed on the packet.

Mix the potatoes, beans and half the tuna fish with three-quarters of the Vinaigrette.

Arrange the sliced tomatoes on the bottom and around the bowl, arrange thinly sliced cucumber on top, and sprinkle with a little Vinaigrette. Place a few chunks of tuna fish on the tomato and cucumber.

The eggs may be cut into slices or wedges and can be used on top as a garnish or arranged to make a bed for the beans, potatoes and tuna fish mixture.

Arrange the fish mixture in the middle and arrange the anchovies in a diamond-shaped pattern on the beans, decorating each space with an olive. Pour over any remaining dressing.

Savoury Fruit Salad
Serves 4-6

Ingredients
2 green apples	50g/2oz cooked prawns
2 green mangoes	30-45ml/2-3tbsp lemon juice
½ small pineapple	10g/2tsp sugar
100g/4oz cooked pork, cut into strips	mint or coriander

Preparation Peel and cut the apples and mangoes into even-sized pieces. Peel and quarter the pineapple, remove the core and cut the flesh into bite-sized pieces. Arrange these attractively with the pork and prawns on a serving dish.

Blend the dressing ingredients together and pour over the salad.

Serve garnished with mint or coriander leaves.

Warm Potato and Bacon Salad
Serves 4

This is good with cold poultry or quiches, or on its own as a first course.

Ingredients
450g/1lb small new potatoes, scrubbed	75ml/5tbsp chicken or beef stock
45ml/3tbsp olive oil	salt and freshly ground pepper
225g/8oz streaky bacon, chopped	sugar to taste
1 medium onion, peeled and chopped	2 egg yolks, beaten
60ml/4tbsp wine vinegar	7g/1tbsp snipped fresh dill

Preparation Cook the potatoes in boiling salted water for about 20 minutes or until tender. Drain and turn into an ovenproof serving dish.

Heat the oil in a deep frying pan. Add the bacon and onion and fry gently for 5 minutes to soften the onion. Turn up the heat and fry until the bacon becomes crispy.

Remove from the heat, and add the vinegar and stock. Bring to the boil then taste, and season. Remove from the heat and stir in the egg yolks and dill. Pour over the potatoes and toss well. Serve immediately.

Avocado, Grapefruit and Prawn or Shrimp Salad
Serves 4

Ingredients
2 grapefruit	225g/8oz prawns or shrimps
2 avocados	150ml/¼pt Vinaigrette

Preparation To make the grapefruit sections, place the fruit in a bowl and pour boiling water on top to cover. Leave for 2 minutes, then remove and allow to cool. Cut a slice from the top of the fruit, then cut the peel and pith off in strips to reveal the flesh. It is essential to use a small sharp knife.

When all the pith has been cut away, remove each section by cutting between the membranes of each segment. At the end only the tough outer skin should be left and each section of fruit is separate without skin.

Peel the avocados, cut in half lengthways and remove the stones. Cut the flesh into slices.

Arrange the avocado slices, grapefruit segments and prawns or shrimps in the dishes and serve with Vinaigrette or Mayonnaise as preferred. The dressing may be poured over the salad or served separately.

Warm Chicken Liver Salad with Garlic Croûtons
Serves 4-6

Ingredients
45ml/3tbsp olive oil
2 cloves garlic, crushed
1 cos or iceberg lettuce, torn into bite-size pieces
225g/½lb fresh young spinach leaves, torn into bite-sized pieces
6 rashers streaky bacon, cut into 1.25-cm (½-in) pieces
300g/12oz chicken livers
3 slices white bread cut into 1.25/½in cubes
10g/2tsp sugar
15ml/1tbsp Garlic Vinegar or wine vinegar
10g/1tbsp chives, finely chopped

Preparation Put the oil and garlic into a frying pan and leave to infuse.

Combine the lettuce and spinach in a salad bowl or individual serving bowls and leave to one side.

In another pan, fry the bacon until crisp, drain on a paper towel and keep warm.

Fry the chicken livers in the bacon fat for about 5 minutes or until firm and well browned on the outside, but still slightly pink in the middle. Drain and keep warm.

Fry the bread cubes in the garlicky oil until golden and crisp. Drain and keep warm.

Heat the bacon fat and add the sugar and vinegar. Cook gently until the sugar dissolves.

Arrange the chicken livers and bacon on top of the lettuce and spinach. Pour over the warm dressing, and serve immediately, topped with the garlic croûtons and chives.

Vietnamese Salad
Serves 4

Ingredients
225g/½lb Chinese leaves
2 carrots
½ cucumber
salt
2 red chillies, seeded and finely sliced
1 small onion, sliced into fine rings
4 pickled gherkins, sliced, plus 45ml/3tbsp of the liquid
1 clove garlic, crushed
5g/1tsp sugar
30ml/2tbsp cider or white vinegar
50g/2oz peanuts, lightly pounded
225g/8oz chicken, cooked and shredded
fresh coriander

Preparation Wash and shred the Chinese leaves finely. Peel and cut the carrots into matchstick-like strips.

Trim the ends from the cucumber, cut in half lengthwise and scoop out the seeds. Cut in pieces the same size as the carrot, sprinkle with salt and leave for 15 minutes.

Put the chillies, onion and gherkin slices in a bowl. Blend the gherkin liquid with the garlic, sugar and vinegar.

Rinse and dry the cabbage, carrot and cucumber, then add these to the liquid ingredients with the nuts and chicken, toss altogether to taste. Add more vinegar, if you wish, for a sharper taste.

Serve garnished with coriander leaves.

Pasta Salad
Serves 4

Ingredients
225g/8oz dry pasta: bows, shells or spirals
7.5ml/½tbsp oil
15ml/1tbsp Garlic Purée or 2 cloves of garlic, crushed
150ml/¼pt Mayonnaise
15ml/1tbsp single cream
150g/6oz button mushrooms, quartered
150g/6oz thinly sliced French garlic sausage, cut into strips and fried till crisp
15g/1½tbsp spring onions, finely chopped
salt and pepper to taste

Preparation Cook the pasta with the oil in lots of salted boiling water for 15-20 minutes, until just tender. Drain well, and while still warm stir in the remaining ingredients.

Serve warm or chilled.

Variation Vary the dressing by using half mayonnaise and half Pesto.

Use Aïoli instead of the mayonnaise. You will probably not need the extra garlic.

Lots of other vegetables and nuts can be added, singly or in combination: chopped or sliced sweet pepper, thinly sliced or grated baby courgettes, cubed avocado pear, toasted peanuts, blanched almonds, walnuts or pine nuts.

Pasta salad is also very good with 100ml/4fl oz of Basic Garlic Dressing instead of the mayonnaise and cream. This dressing goes particularly well with quartered artichoke hearts and browned cashew nuts.

Oil Hints

Olive oil is not the only oil used in salad dressings, but it is the most common. The price of olive oil has much to do with which pressing you purchase. Extra virgin olive oil is about twice as costly as pure olive oil. French oils, light and golden, are considered by many to be the best in the world. Greek and Italian oils are less expensive, more robust and aromatic.

1 Pure olive oil: an inexpensive grade oil. Produced from the treated olive mash left over from the first two pressings of the olives.

2 Fine olive oil: not to be used for salads. Good for frying, however.

3 Extra virgin olive oil: rare, expensive and heavy. Product of the first cold pressing.

4 Peanut oil: used in South-East Asian cooking. The peanut taste is not very pronounced.

5 Grape seed oil: full-bodied. Usually found in combination with pepper or herbs.

7 Walnut oil: aromatic, expensive. Refrigerate to maintain freshness.

8 Hazelnut oil: delicate, for delicate salad greens.

9 Sesame oil: pungent, exotic.

Cold Desserts and Sweets

Easy Ice Cream 235
Bombe 235
Luxury Mocha Ice Cream 236
Elderflower Water Ice 236
Mocha Bombe 237
Mississippi Mud Pie 237
Raspberry Ice Cream 237
Snowball Pie 238
Chocolate Ice Cream 238
Tea Granita 239
Strawberry Granita 239
Orange Granita 239
Chocolate Granita 239
Easy Ice Cream Loaf 240
Kulfi (Indian Ice Cream) 240
Ginger Ice Cream 241
Maple Walnut Ice Cream 241
Pineapple Ice Cream 241
Caramel Ice Cream 242
Avocado Ice Cream 242
Apricot Ice Cream 242
Chestnut Mousse 243
Fruit Surprise 243
Dutch Apple Special 243
Sundae Supreme 244
Red Fruit Soufflé 244
Kamla Khir 244
Chilled Orange Soufflé 244
Ginger and Rhubarb Fool 245
Stuffed Pears 245
Orange Pudding 245
Quince Sherbet 245
Nut Pudding 245
Fruit Kisel 246
Apple Charlotte 246
Cherries Jubilee 246
Banana Split 247
Pears Hélène 247
Strawberry Shortcake 248
Flans aux Fruits 248
Blueberry Tart 249
Chocolate Fondue 250
Chocolate Chiffon Pie 250
Chocolate Mousse 251
Chocolate Orange Pots 251
Chocolate and Coffee Bavarois 252
Chocolate Hazelnut Bombe 252

Choc-Chestnut Mont blanc 253
Mohr Im Hemd 253
Choc Nut Slice 254
Chocolate Terrine 254
Frozen Chocolate Sandwiches 255
Ricotta al Café 255
Coffee Coconut Soufflé 256
Coffee Charlotte 256
Coffee and Raspberry Frou Frou 257
Iced Chocolate Praline Mousse 257
Coffee Meringue Pyramid 258
Coffee Apricot Condé 258
Coffee Fruit Flans 259
Coffee and Vanilla Jelly 259
Weight Watchers' Cheesecake 260
Topfen Kuchen 260
Italian Cheesecake 260
Chilled Sultana and Orange Cheesecake 261
Curd Cheesecake 261
Cottage Cheesecake 262
Raisin Cheesecake 263
Pineapple Coconut Cheesecake 263
Chocolate Cheesecake Cups 263
Summer Pudding 264
Sailors' Delight 264
Semolina Pudding 264
Rice Flour Dessert 265
Marshmallow Crunch 265
Charlotte Louise 265
Crème Caramel 266
Payodhi 266
Shrikhand 266
Vanilla Cream 267
Charlotte Russe 267
Crème Brûlée 268
Strawberry Peach Sherbet 268
Yorkshire Curd Tart 268
Pâté à Choux 269
Rice and Raisin Pudding 269
Cream Puffs 270
Meringue Torte 271
Baklava 271
Tortoni 272
Millefeuilles 272
Basic Yoghurt 272

Preparing Pineapples and Avocados 273

Easy Ice Cream
Serves 8

Ingredients

4 eggs, separated   100g/4oz icing sugar
2.5ml/¹/₂tsp vanilla essence   300ml/¹/₂pt double cream

Preparation Beat the egg yolks with the vanilla and sifted sugar until the mixture is very thick and almost white. Lightly whip the cream until it is just beginning to thicken. Gently fold into the yolks.

Whisk the egg whites until they are stiff but not dry. Gently fold one spoonful into the ice cream mixture. Gradually add the remaining egg whites.

If you are adding flavouring, blend in carefully at this stage.

Turn the cream into a large freezer tray or plastic box and cover. Stir occasionally during freezing.

Bombe
Serves 8

Ingredients

600 ml /1pt ice cream   125ml/4fl oz double cream
300ml/¹/₂pt sorbet   pieces of crystallized fruit

Preparation Remove half of the ice cream from the freezer and leave until slightly softened. Press over the base and up the sides of a medium sized mould or pudding bowl. Cover and return to the freezer until firm.

Remove the sorbet from the freezer and leave until slightly softened. Press into the middle of the mould, cover and return to the freezer.

Remove the remaining ice cream, which should be a different flavour, and leave to soften. Spread over the surface of the sorbet, cover and refreeze.

To serve, run a warm cloth over the surface of the mould, invert and turn out onto an attractive dish. Smooth with a knife. Decorate with piped, whipped cream and pieces of crystallized fruit.

Variations Beat into slightly softened vanilla ice cream an assortment of dried fruit which has been soaked in rum or sherry and some chopped crystallized fruit. Fill the mould and freeze until firm.

Soak fresh or dried fruit in liqueur and pour into the bombe before adding the sorbet. Alternatively, replace the sorbet with a Chocolate or Chestnut Mousse.

Luxury Mocha Ice Cream

Ingredients

140g/5oz plain chocolate
4 eggs, separated
60ml/4tbsp strong coffee
300ml/½pt double cream
15ml/1tbsp coffee liqueur
100g/4oz sugar
chocolate curls

Preparation Place the chocolate in a bowl over a pan of hot water. When melted, remove from the heat and beat in the egg yolks and coffee.

In a large bowl, whip the cream until stiff and fold in the coffee liqueur.

In another bowl whisk the egg whites until they form stiff peaks, gradually adding the sugar.

Whisk the mocha mixture into the cream and then fold it gently into the egg whites.

Spoon into a 1.75l/3pt freeze-proof container. Freeze for at least 5 hours. It is not necessary to stir the ice cream during the freezing time. This ice cream is quite soft so you can serve straight from the freezer.

To serve, scoop into sundae glasses and decorate with chocolate curls.

An alternative serving suggestion is to scoop the ice cream into individual biscuit base tartlets.

Elderflower Water Ice
Serves 6

A water ice like this refreshes the palate between courses. It can also be served as a very light dessert.

Ingredients

600ml/1pt water
250g/8oz fruit sugar
6 heads elderflowers
juice of 1 lemon
2 egg whites

Preparation Heat the water and add the sugar, stirring until dissolved. Add the elderflowers and lemon juice and bring to the boil.

Strain the syrup through a jelly bag. Allow it to cool, then freeze.

When the syrup is half frozen, beat the egg whites until stiff and fold into the syrup. Freeze in individual dishes.

Mocha Bombe
Serves 6-8

Ingredients

Cream Layer
450ml/¾pt whipping cream
25g/1oz Vanilla Sugar (see note to recipe for Le Succès)
25g/1oz vanilla essence

Mocha filling
1 full quantity Luxury Mocha Ice Cream

Coffee Cream
450ml/¾pt whipping cream
5g/1tsp instant powdered coffee dissolved in 15ml/ 1tbsp hot water
15g/1tbsp Vanilla Sugar
50g/2oz toasted almonds

Preparation Chill a 2l/3½pt pudding bowl or bombe mould. Whisk the cream, sugar and essence together until stiff, then spread in the pudding basin to line it evenly. Freeze until firm.

Pour the luxury mocha ice cream into the cream lined basin, cover and freeze for 24 hours.

To serve place the bowl briefly into a larger bowl of hot water then turn out onto a large serving plate.

Whisk the cream, instant coffee and sugar until firm. Pile a decoration over the bombe and decorate with the toasted almonds.

Return to the freezer until hard, and serve.

Mississippi Mud Pie
Serves 8

Ingredients

175g/6oz digestive biscuits
large knob butter, melted
100g/4oz plain chocolate, melted
1l/2pt coffee ice cream
1l/2pt chocolate ice cream

30ml/2tbsp Tia Maria
30ml/2tbsp brandy
whipped cream
grated chocolate

Preparation Crush the biscuits or wafers in a food processor or in a polythene bag with a rolling pin. Stir in the butter and chocolate and mix well together.

Press the crumbs firmly and evenly over the bottom and sides of a greased 23cm/9in flan dish. Chill.

Allow the ice creams to soften slightly. Put in a bowl and add the liqueur and brandy. Blend well together.

Spoon the ice cream into the chocolate case and put in the freezer until solid.

To serve remove pie from freezer about 15 minutes before serving. Decorate with whipping cream and grated chocolate.

Raspberry Ice Cream
Serves 4-6

Ingredients

200g/7oz raspberries
15ml/1tbsp dried milk powder
30ml/2tbsp yoghurt

30ml/2tbsp honey
250ml/8fl oz whipping cream

Preparation Purée the raspberries with the milk powder, yoghurt and honey in a blender. Freeze.

When the raspberries have frozen into a mush, whip the cream and mix in well. Return to the freezer.

Snowball Pie
Serves 6

Ingredients

225g/8oz plain chocolate
50g/2oz butter
75g/3oz crisp rice cereal
  (Rice Krispies)
400ml/¾pt vanilla ice
  cream

400ml/¾pt chocolate ice
  cream
400ml/¾pt strawberry ice
  cream
Chocolate or Fudge Sauce
long shred coconut, toasted

Preparation Melt the chocolate and butter together. Stir in the crisp rice cereal and mix well together.

Press the mixture over the base and up the sides of a 20cm/8in flan dish. Place in the freezer until firm.

Arrange alternate scoops of the ice cream. Pour over the sauce and sprinkle with the coconut. Serve immediately.

Chocolate Ice Cream
Serves 4-6

Ingredients

175g/6oz sugar
150ml/¼pt water
450g/1lb plain or milk
  chocolate

4 egg yolks
900ml/1½pt double cream

Preparation Put sugar and water into a saucepan and stir over a gentle heat until dissolved. Bring to the boil and simmer gently for 7 minutes.

Break the chocolate into small pieces and stir into the hot syrup. Stir until dissolved. Whisk in the egg yolks and cool.

Whip the cream until thick, but not stiff. Fold into the chocolate mixture.

Freeze in an electric ice cream maker according to manufacturer's instructions. Alternatively, pour into a freezer tray and freeze. Beat the mixture twice, at hourly intervals. Cover, seal and freeze.

Remove ice cream from freezer to refrigerator and allow to 'come to' about 30 minutes before serving.

Tea Granita
Serves 4

Ingredients

20g/2tbsp tea leaves (Orange Pekoe, Darjeeling, Ceylon, rosehip or any other kind)	45g/3tbsp sugar 30ml/2tbsp lemon or lime juice 600ml/1pt boiling water

Preparation Combine the tea leaves, sugar and juice. Pour over the boiling water, mix well and leave until cold. Strain and freeze as for granita.

Variation Infuse mint leaves or lemon balm in the tea while it is cooling. Strain before freezing. Pour a measure of Crème de Menthe over the granita before serving.

Strawberry Granita
Serves 4

Ingredients

100g/4oz sugar	450g/1lb fresh strawberries
175ml/6fl oz water	15ml/1tbsp lemon juice

Preparation Heat the sugar with the water over a medium heat, stirring constantly until it has dissolved. Boil for 5 minutes. Leave to cool.

Purée the strawberries and sieve to remove any seeds. Mix in the lemon juice.

Stir the syrup into the strawberry purée.

Pour the granita mixture into a very shallow freezer-proof dish and freeze until nearly firm. Stir the ice crystals at the edge of the dish into the centre several times but take care not to break them up — the granita should be fairly coarse.

Variations Flavour the granita with Grand Marnier, orange flower water or the juice of 1 orange.

Omit the sugar syrup. Purée and sieve the strawberries. Sweeten with icing sugar, add orange and/or lemon juice to taste and freeze.

Mix half frozen granita with partly defrosted concentrated orange juice.

Use half strawberries and half raspberries.

Frozen fruit can be used instead of fresh fruit but use half the amount of sugar.

Orange Granita
Serves 4

Ingredients

175g/6oz sugar	2-3 oranges
450ml/16fl oz water	15ml/1tbsp orange flower water (optional)
1 lemon	

Preparation Heat the sugar in the water over a medium heat, stirring constantly until the sugar has dissolved. Boil for 5 minutes.

Add the finely grated peel and the lemon and both oranges to the syrup. Leave until completely cold.

Stir the juice of the lemon and oranges into the syrup. Add the orange flower water if you are using it.

Pour the granita mixture into a very shallow freezer-proof dish and freeze until nearly firm. Stir the ice crystals at the edge of the dish into the centre several times but take care not to break them up — the granita should be fairly coarse.

Variations Use tangerines instead of oranges.

Do not use the peel of the oranges. Squeeze the juice from the fruit carefully, keeping the shells intact, and spoon the frozen granita back into the shells for serving.

Chocolate Granita
Serves 4

Ingredients

75g/3oz unsweetened cocoa	45g/3tbsp sugar 575ml/1pt boiling water

Preparation Combine the cocoa and sugar. Pour over the boiling water, mix well and leave until cold. Freeze as for orange granita.

Orange Granita

Easy Ice Cream Loaf
Serves 8

Ingredients

24 Boudoir biscuits (ladies fingers or sponge fingers)
30ml/2tbsp Marsala, sherry, brandy, rum, liqueur or fruit juice
600ml/1pt ice cream
225ml/8fl oz double cream
30ml/2tbsp Coffee, Chocolate, Butterscotch or Fruit sauce
50g/2oz toasted flaked almonds

Preparation Arrange half the biscuits in the base of a loaf tin. Sprinkle with wine, spirit or juice. Soften the ice cream and spread half of it over the biscuits. Repeat with a second layer each of biscuits and ice cream. Cover and freeze for 1 hour or more.

Whisk the cream until it is thick. Unmould the ice cream loaf onto a serving dish. Cover with cream and drizzle the sauce over it. Garnish with flaked almonds

Variation Use two different kinds of ice cream or sorbet.

Alternatively, use more ice cream, of several different kinds, and freeze in 20cm/8in sandwich cake tins. Assemble the ice cream cake by piling the layers on top of each other. Press boudoir biscuits or langues de chat gently around the outside. Top with cream and sauce as above.

Kulfi (Indian Ice Cream)
Serves 8

Ingredients

950ml/32fl oz milk
10g/1tbsp arrowroot
3 cardamom pods
50g/2oz sugar
10g/1tbsp almonds or pistachios, chopped
125ml/4fl oz double cream
few drops rose water

Preparation Bring a quarter of the milk to the boil in a wide, shallow pan. Keep it on the boil, stirring constantly, until it is very thick. Most of it will evaporate but this is as it should be. The length of time it takes for the milk to thicken depends on the surface area of your pan — the wider the pan, the faster the milk will thicken. Set aside until it is completely cold.

Mix some of the remaining milk with the arrowroot to make a paste. Add one of the cardamom pods to the rest of the milk and bring to the boil. Keep boiling, stirring constantly, for 10 minutes. Remove the cardamom pod. Add the arrowroot paste and continue stirring until the milk has thickened.

Stir the sugar into the hot milk until it has dissolved. Remove the seeds from the remaining cardamom pods, crush them and stir into the milk.

Stir in the chopped nuts. Leave the milk to cool, stirring occasionally.

Whisk the cream until it is stiff enough to hold its shape. Gently fold into the cooled milk, starting with just one spoonful and gradually adding the remainder. Stir in the cooled thickened milk which was made earlier and add the few drops of rose water.

Pour the Kulfi into a freezer tray or plastic box, cover and freeze for 1-2 hours. Beat well and return to the freezer. Beat again every 2 hours until the ice cream is firm.

Ginger Ice Cream
Serves 6

Ingredients

3 egg yolks	15ml/1tbsp ginger syrup
50g/2oz sugar	300ml/½pt milk
100g/4oz stem ginger	150ml/¼pt double cream

Preparation Whisk the egg yolks with the sugar until very light and thick. Then drain and dice the stem ginger. Stir into the eggs along with the ginger syrup.

Scald the milk and slowly pour over the eggs, whisking constantly. Pour the custard into the top of a double boiler and heat, stirring constantly, until it is thick enough to coat the back of the spoon. Leave to cool.

Pour the custard into a freezer tray or plastic box, cover and freeze for 1-2 hours. Transfer to a bowl and whisk until it is smooth and all the ice crystals have been mixed in.

Whisk the cream until it is just beginning to thicken. Gently fold into the custard. Pour into the freezer tray again, cover and freeze until firm.

Variation Omit the stem ginger and flavour the custard with 5g/1tsp ground ginger or 7g/1tbsp grated fresh ginger and 10g/1tbsp crystalized ginger pieces.

Following the method described above, a liqueur may be added to the custard mixture. For extra variation, omit the ginger and divide the custard into separate containers and add a different liqueur — Benedictine, Crème de Menthe, Kahlua, Tia Maria, Cassis — to each batch. Serve a tiny scoop of each kind in either glass dishes, or as a filling for miniature meringues, or in a pie shell made from biscuit crumbs in *tulipes*. Alternatively, freeze the flavours in small sandwich pans and assemble a multi-coloured gâteau.

Maple Walnut Ice Cream
Serves 8

Ingredients

150ml/5fl oz maple syrup
4 egg yolks
300ml/½pt double cream
100g/4oz chopped walnuts

Preparation Boil the maple syrup until it is very thick.

Beat the egg yolks until they are very thick and light. Pour into the top of a double boiler and slowly add the hot syrup, whisking constantly. Continue beating the yolks and syrup in a double boiler until it thickens to the consistency of whipped cream.

Remove the top of the double boiler from the heat and stand in a bowl full of ice cubes. Continue beating the yolks until they are completely cold.

Whisk the cream until it is thick enough to hold its shape. Carefully fold into the yolk mixture, starting with just one spoonful and gradually adding the remainder. Stir in the walnuts.

Pour the ice cream mixture into a plastic tray or mould, cover and freeze. This ice cream does not need stirring while it is freezing and one can therefore unmould it. Serve in slices or scoops, decorated with glazed walnut halves and a rum, brandy or coffee sauce.

Pineapple Ice Cream
Serves 8

Ingredients

175g/6oz sugar	300ml/½pt double cream
450ml/16fl oz water	2 egg whites (optional)
1 lemon	
450g/1lb crushed, fresh pineapple	

Preparation Stir the sugar in the water over a medium heat until it has dissolved. Add the finely grated lemon rind and boil rapidly for 5 minutes. Leave until thoroughly cooled.

Combine the crushed pineapple and lemon juice. Measure and mix with an equal amount of syrup.

Whisk the cream until it is just beginning to thicken. Carefully fold into the fruit purée.

Whisk the egg whites until they are stiff but not dry. Gently fold into the fruit.

Pour the ice cream mixture into a freezer tray or plastic box, cover and freeze for 1-2 hours. Whisk well so that all the ice crystals are mixed in. Return to the freezer until firm.

Tinned pineapple can be used very successfully for this ice cream. If you are using fresh pineapple, save the shell and pile the ice cream into it before serving.

Caramel Ice Cream
Serves 4

Ingredients

60g/4tbsp sugar	2 egg yolks
90ml/6tbsp water	300ml/¹/₂pt double cream

Preparation Place the sugar and a third of the water in a heavy-based pan. Stir over a medium heat until the sugar has dissolved. Raise the heat, boil rapidly until brown in colour and add the remaining water.

Whisk the egg yolks until they are thick and light. Slowly pour on the hot caramel and continue whisking until the mixture is thick and cold.

Whisk the cream until it is just beginning to thicken. Carefully fold into the eggs and caramel.

Pour the ice cream mixture into a freezer tray or plastic box, cover and freeze for 1-2 hours. Whisk well and return to the freezer until firm.

Avocado Ice Cream
Serves 4

Ingredients

1 avocado	30ml/2tbsp single cream
15ml/1tbsp lime juice	1 egg white

Preparation Peel the avocado, cut in half and remove the stone. Mash or purée it until it is smooth. Stir in the lime juice and cream, beating well to ensure that the mixture is well blended and completely smooth.

Whisk the egg white until it is stiff but not dry. Gently fold into the avocado mixture, starting with just one spoonful and gradually adding the remainder.

Pour into a freezer tray or plastic box, cover and freeze for 1-2 hours.

Beat well so that all the ice crystals are mixed in. Return to the freezer until firm.

Apricot Ice Cream
Serves 6

Ingredients

130g/4¹/₂oz dried apricots	2 egg whites
125ml/4fl oz dry white wine	150ml/¹/₄pt whipping cream
100g/4oz sugar	few drops almond essence (optional)
150ml/5fl oz water	

Preparation Dice the apricots and cook in an uncovered tin with the white wine for 15-20 minutes or until they are soft. If the liquid evaporates, add some apple juice.

Cool the apricots and then sieve or liquidize them to make a smooth purée. If you have less than 150ml/5oz when you are finished, make up to that quantity with unsweetened apple juice.

Stir the sugar into the water over a medium heat until it has dissolved. Boil rapidly for 5 minutes.

Whisk the egg whites until they are stiff but not dry. Slowly pour in the hot syrup, whisking constantly. Beat until the meringue is very thick.

Whisk the cream until it is just beginning to thicken. Carefully fold the fruit purée into the egg whites and then add the whipped cream, starting with one spoonful and gradually adding the remainder. Stir in the almond essence.

Turn the ice cream mixture into a loaf tin, ring mould or cake tin. Cover and freezer until firm. This ice cream does not need to be stirred while freezing. Unmould and serve garnished with slices of fresh or tinned apricots or a puréed sauce made from fresh fruit or poached dried fruit. Toasted almonds can also be sprinkled on top.

Variation Replace the dried apricots with fresh (skinned), bottled or tinned apricots. Drain well, purée and add 15ml/1tbsp white wine.

Other fruits can be used according to availability with equal success. Firm fruits such as plums, greengages (small green plums) or pears should be cooked in syrup, apple juice or wine if they are fresh. Dried fruit such as prunes need to be poached. Soft fruits such as strawberries, or pineapple need only be liquidized or sieved before adding to the egg whites.

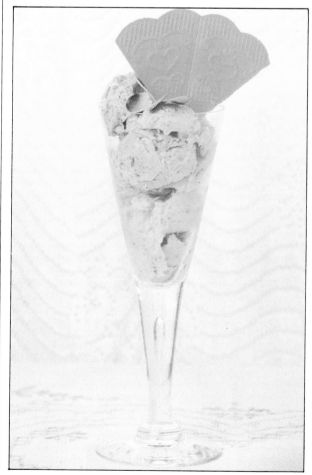

Chestnut Mousse
Serves 4-6

Ingredients

90g/6tbsp butter	25g/1oz ground almonds
225g/8oz unsweetened chestnut purée	22ml/1½tbsp brandy
2 eggs, separated	125ml/4fl oz double cream
30g/2tbsp sugar	8-10 blanched almonds
25g/1oz unsweetened cocoa	15g/1tbsp chocolate strands

Preparation Melt the butter and leave to cool.

Beat the chestnut purée until it is smooth. Add the butter, egg yolks, sugar, cocoa, almonds and brandy. Mix well.

Whisk the egg whites until they are stiff but not dry. Gently fold into the chestnut mixture, starting with one spoonful and gradually adding the remainder.

Decorate the mousse with lightly whipped cream, almonds and chocolate strands and chill for at least 2 hours before serving.

Fruit Surprise
Serves 8

Ingredients

600ml/1pt ice cream or sorbet	8 oranges or lemons, or 1 pineapple

Preparation Remove the ice cream or sorbet from the freezer and leave to slightly soften for approximately 30 minutes. Use any flavour you think will go well with the fruit you have chosen.

Cut the top off the orange or lemon, or cut the pineapple in half. Carefully remove the fruit from its shell, leaving enough to keep the shape of the fruit. Chop coarsely and mix into the softened ice cream or sorbet.

Spoon the mixture back into the fruit shell and return to the freezer. Remove 15 minutes before serving.

Variation After removing the fruit from its shell, mix with alcohol of virtually any sort — brandy, gin, liqueur — and leave to soak for 1 hour. Put the fruit back in its shell and top with the ice cream or sorbet. Freeze until firm.

Dutch Apple Special
Serves 4

Ingredients

450g/1lb apples, cored and sliced	50g/2oz raisins
30ml/2tbsp water	5g/1tsp cinnamon
50g/2oz brown sugar	2.5g/½tsp nutmeg
	600ml/1pt ice cream

Preparation Place the apples in a pan with the water. Cook over a low heat until the apples are soft.

Purée the apples and stir in the sugar until it has melted. Add the raisins, cinnamon and nutmeg.

To serve, arrange two scoops of ice cream in each serving dish. Spoon the warm apple sauce over the top and serve immediately.

Sundae Supreme
Serves 4

Ingredients
600ml/1pt ice cream
8 wafers or cookies
450ml/16oz Chocolate or
    Fruit Sauce
250ml/8fl oz whipped
    cream

50g/2oz toasted nuts,
    chopped
4 glacé or maraschino
    cherries

Preparation Arrange two scoops of ice cream in each serving dish, preferably two flavours.

Crumble the wafers or cookies and sprinkle over the ice cream. Pour on the sauce. Top with whipped cream, piled as high as you can, and scatter chopped nuts on top. Crown each sundae with a cherry.

Red Fruit Soufflé
Serves 4

Ingredients
225g/8oz raspberries,
    strawberries, red or
    black currants
100g/4oz sugar
15ml/1tbsp Kirsch, Cassis,
    or Framboise

30g/2tbsp cornflour
300ml/1/2pt milk
2 eggs
175ml/6fl oz double cream
extra fruit to garnish
    (optional)

Preparation If using raspberries or strawberries, sieve or purée the fruit and mix with the sugar. If using red or black currants, sprinkle with sugar and heat in a heavy-bottomed pan until the berries are soft. Cool slightly and sieve or purée. Stir in the liqueur.

Mix the cornflour with enough of the milk to make a smooth paste. Heat the remaining milk until it just reaches boiling point. Pour over the cornflour and mix well.

Lightly beat the eggs and stir into the hot milk. Return to the heat and cook, stirring constantly, until the mixture begins to thicken. Leave to cool.

Combine the fruit purée with the sauce.

Whisk the cream until it is just thick enough to hold its shape. Gently fold into the fruit sauce.

Tie a paper collar around the outside of a 600ml/1pt soufflé dish so that it extends 5cm/2in above the top of the dish. Pour the soufflé mixture into the dish and chill overnight or until firm.

Serve the soufflé garnished if you like with fresh fruit.

Kamla Khir
Khir with Oranges

Ingredients
1.5l/2pt milk
40g/1½oz sugar

2 oranges, peeled

Preparation Boil the milk in a large saucepan, stirring constantly. Add the sugar and stir. Reduce heat and, stirring occasionally, simmer until it is reduced to 425ml/¾pt. Cool

Remove all the pith from the oranges and slice. Add to the cooled milk. Serve chilled.

Chilled Orange Soufflé
Serves 4

Ingredients
2 eggs
100g/4oz sugar
150ml/¼pt double cream

1 orange
15ml/1tbsp Cointreau or
    Grand Marnier

Preparation Whisk one of the eggs and the yolk from the second with the sugar until very light and frothy.

Whisk the cream until it is just firm enough to hold its shape. Stir in the finely grated rind of the orange, 30ml/2tbsp of its juice and the liqueur.

Combine the yolk and cream mixtures.

Whisk the remaining egg white until it is stiff but not dry. Gently fold into the soufflé starting with just one spoonful and gradually adding the remainder. Spoon into individual soufflé dishes and chill until set, overnight is fine.

Ginger and Rhubarb Fool

Ingredients

25g/1oz butter
450g/1lb rhubarb, cut into chunks
10ml/2tbsp brown sugar
5g/1tsp ground ginger
125ml/4fl oz double cream

Preparation Melt the butter in a saucepan. Add the rhubarb, sugar and ginger. Simmer until the rhubarb is soft.

Add the cream and liquidize. Chill and serve.

Stuffed Pears
Serves 6

This recipe uses dates and walnuts to create a simple and delightful dessert.

Ingredients

50g/2oz dates, pitted and chopped
225g/8oz ground walnuts
5g/1tsp cinnamon
12 canned pear halves, drained
125ml/4fl oz water
75g/3oz sugar
250g/8fl oz white wine
2 whole cloves
30ml/2tbsp lemon juice

Preparation Preheat the oven to 350°F/180°C/Gas 4. In a small mixing bowl, combine the dates, walnuts and cinnamon. Mix well. Fill the cavities of the pear halves with the mixture. Place the pears in a shallow baking dish.

In a small saucepan, bring the water, sugar, wine, cloves and lemon juice to a boil over a medium heat. Stir frequently until the sugar is dissolved. Reduce the heat to low and simmer for 2 minutes.

Pour the wine sauce over the pears in the baking dish. Bake for 20 minutes. Chill for 1 hour before serving.

Orange Pudding
Serves 6

Ingredients

rind from 2 oranges, finely grated
225g/8oz sugar
75g/3oz cornflour
pinch salt
4 eggs, separated
1l/2pt orange juice

Preparation In a large mixing bowl combine the orange rind, sugar, cornflour and salt.

In a separate bowl beat the egg yolks into the orange juice. Gradually add the cornflour mixture and stir until smooth.

Put the mixture into a medium-sized saucepan. Cook over a medium heat, stirring constantly, until the custard mixture thickens, about 12 minutes.

Remove the saucepan from the heat and plunge it into a large pan of cold water. Leave it for 2-3 minutes.

Beat the egg whites in a small mixing bowl until they are stiff. Fold the egg whites into the custard until the mixture is smooth.

Spoon the pudding into tulip glasses or dessert dishes and chill before serving.

Quince Sherbet
Serves 6

This is a distinctive Middle Eastern sherbet. Serve it in tulip or dessert glasses.

Ingredients

3 large ripe quinces, peeled, cored and cut into small pieces.
200ml/7fl oz water
575g/1¼lb sugar
75ml/3fl oz lemon juice

Preparation Put the fruit and water into a large saucepan. Bring the mixture to a boil over a high heat. Reduce the heat to low and simmer for 40 minutes.

Strain the mixture through a sieve into another saucepan. Discard any solids that remain in the sieve. Add the sugar and lemon juice and bring the mixture to a boil over a high heat. Boil for 10 minutes, stirring frequently to dissolve the sugar.

Remove the saucepan from the heat and let the mixture cool for 5 minutes.

Pour the sherbet mixture into a large bowl and put it in the ice compartment of the refrigerator or the freezer for 2 hours.

Stir the mixture every 10-15 minutes to break up the ice crystals and make a smooth texture.

Nut Pudding
Serves 8

This is a traditional Syrian nut pudding. Use white, not green, pistachio nuts.

Ingredients

1l/1¼pt single cream
130g/4½oz ground rice
pinch salt
100g/4oz sugar
50g/2oz ground unsalted almonds
50g/2oz ground unsalted pistachio nuts
30ml/2tbsp grenadine syrup

Preparation In a medium-sized saucepan, bring the cream to the boil. Add the ground rice, salt and sugar. Simmer over a medium heat for 5 minutes, stirring constantly.

Stir in the ground almonds, ground pistachios and grenadine syrup. Reduce the heat to low and simmer for 2 minutes, stirring constantly.

Remove the saucepan from the heat and let the mixture cool until it is warm. Spoon the pudding into small individual dessert dishes and chill. Serve cold.

Fruit Kisel
Serves 8-10

Kisel is a cold, thick liquid dessert very popular in Russia. There are many different recipes, and there are no hard and fast rules about ingredients. Try different combinations of fruit, making sure to mash the fruit into a smooth purée. More potato starch may be needed to thicken the kisel if very juicy fresh fruits are used.

Ingredients

225g/8oz tart red apples, peeled, cored and cut into small chunks	60ml/4tbsp jellied cranberry sauce
100g/4oz dried apricots	225g/8oz sugar
675g/1½lb fresh or thawed frozen strawberries	15g/1½tbsp potato starch, dissolved in 30ml/2tbsp cold water
300ml/½pt cold water	

Preparation Place the apples, apricots and strawberries in a large saucepan. Add the cranberry sauce and cold water and bring the mixture to a boil over a high heat.

Reduce the heat to low and simmer uncovered for 15 minutes, stirring occasionally.

With the back of a spoon, press the fruit mixture through a fine sieve into a large mixing bowl. Discard any solids that remain in the sieve. Stir in the sugar.

Put the fruit and sugar mixture into a large saucepan and bring it to a boil. Reduce the heat to medium and stir in the potato starch mixture.

Cook until the purée returns to a boil. Remove the saucepan from the heat and let the purée cool to room temperature.

Spoon the purée into pudding or tulip glasses. Chill for 4 hours before serving.

Apple Charlotte
Serves 8

There are many kinds of Charlotte. Apple Charlotte, one of the simpler versions is popular as a lunchtime dish.

Ingredients

15g/½oz unsalted butter, softened	375g/13oz sugar
350g/12oz unsalted butter, clarified	125ml/4fl oz water
12 large slices white bread, halved, crusts removed	30ml/2tbsp lime juice
	30ml/2tbsp lemon juice
1.4kg/3lb tart apples, peeled, cored and chopped	5g/1tsp cinnamon
	250ml/8fl oz apricot preserves
1.4kg/3lb sweet apples, peeled, cored and chopped	50ml/2fl oz apricot brandy
	50ml/2fl oz orange juice
	2-3 drops pure vanilla essence

Preparation Rub the softened butter over the inside surface of a pudding mould.

Put the clarified butter into a large mixing bowl. Dip the bread into the butter and line the sides and bottom of the pudding mould with them.

Combine the apples, sugar, water, lemon juice and lime juice in a large flameproof casserole. Bring the mixture to a boil, cover and simmer for 40 minutes over a low heat.

Add the cinnamon and cook, uncovered, over a medium heat for a further 15 minutes. Chill the mixture

for 1 hour.

Gently pour the chilled apple mixture into the prepared pudding mould.

Preheat the oven to 400°F/200°C/Gas 6. Bake the pudding for 1 hour. Cool for 30 minutes at room temperature.

Invert the pudding on a large flat plate. Gently shake the mould to loosen the apple charlotte. Carefully pull the pudding mould away.

In a small mixing bowl, combine the apricot preserves, apricot brandy, orange juice and vanilla essence. Spoon over the apple charlotte before serving.

Cherries Jubilee
Serves 4

Ingredients

450ml/16fl oz ice cream	225ml/8fl oz fruit juice or water
225g/8oz black cherries	
15ml/1tbsp sugar	50ml/2fl oz brandy
15ml/1tbsp cornflour	

Preparation Use vanilla, cherry or orange ice cream or cherry, orange or lemon sorbet. A yoghurt-based ice cream can also be used — its tart flavour makes a superb contrast with the fruit sauce.

Arrange scoops of ice cream or sorbet in a large glass serving dish.

Drain and stone the cherries.

Combine the sugar and cornflour. Stir in the fruit juice or water and heat gently until the sauce has thickened. Add the cherries and heat for 3-4 minutes.

Warm the brandy, pour it over the cherry sauce and set alight. Pour the sauce over the ice cream and serve immediately.

Variation Substitute red wine for the fruit juice and sharpen with a spoonful of lemon juice. Use Kirsch instead of brandy.

Banana Split
Serves 4

Ingredients

4 medium bananas
450ml/16fl oz ice cream
130g/4½oz crushed
  pineapple
130g/4½oz crushed
  raspberries
125ml/4fl oz Chocolate
  Sauce

125ml/4fl oz double or
  whipping cream
8 Maraschino or glacé
  cherries
50g/2oz flaked or chopped
  nuts

Preparation Cut the bananas in half lengthways and place two halves on opposite sides of each serving dish.

The ice cream can be any flavour you choose, and a Banana Split is all the better for having two or three flavours of ice cream. Place three scoops of ice cream on each dish, between the banana halves.

Carefully spoon the fruit over two of the scoops of ice cream and the chocolate sauce over the remaining scoop.

Whisk the cream until it is stiff and pile or pipe it on top of the Banana Split. Decorate with chopped cherries and toasted or chopped nuts.

Variation The pineapple and raspberries can be left out or replaced by any other fruit you prefer.

Pears Hélène
Serves 4

Ingredients

175g/6oz sugar
250ml/8fl oz water
1 vanilla pod (optional)
2 large pears
225g/8oz plain chocolate
  pieces

250ml/8fl oz water
100g/4oz butter
450ml/16fl oz vanilla ice
  cream

Preparation Stir the sugar into the water over a medium heat until it has dissolved.

Add the split vanilla pod if you are using it.

Alternatively, use sugar that has been stored with a vanilla pod in it.

Peel the pears, cut in half and carefully remove the core. Place the pears in the syrup and simmer gently until they are tender. Cool in the syrup.

Melt the chocolate and 250ml/8fl oz of water together, mixing occasionally, until smooth and thoroughly blended. Cut the butter into small pieces and stir in until the sauce is smooth.

To assemble the pears Hélène, drain the fruit well and place one half in each serving dish. Top with a scoop of ice cream and carefully pour the hot chocolate sauce over the top.

Variation Substitute 50ml/2fl oz single cream for half of the butter in the chocolate sauce.

Strawberry Shortcake

This mouth-watering dessert should be eaten while it is still warm. The shortcake dough may be prepared 1-2 hours ahead of time and kept in a cool place. Have the butter, fruits and the cream ready too, so that the warm cake can be assembled in just a few minutes.

Ingredients

350g/12oz strawberries, redcurrants or raspberies	65g/2½oz unsalted butter, chilled and cubed
45g/3tbsp sugar	1 egg
30ml/2tbsp kirsch or Grand Marnier	150ml/¼pt double cream or ½ cream and ½ milk
250g/9oz plain flour	130g/4½oz unsalted butter, softened for spreading on cooked layers
10g/2tsp baking powder	
2.5g/½tsp salt	
pinch nutmeg	
50g/2oz caster sugar	250ml/9fl oz double or whipping cream

Preparation Reserve a few fruits for decoration. Slice 75g/3oz strawberries but leave other fruits whole. Crush the rest of the fruit and stir in 2tbsp sugar and 1tbsp of the liqueur. Fold in the sliced fruit and set aside.

Sift together the flour, baking powder, salt, nutmeg and caster sugar into a bowl. Drop in the butter pieces and quickly rub to a crumb texture. Lightly whisk the egg into the cream and pour on to the dry mixture.

Combine quickly into a smooth dough. Butter and flour a 22cm/8½in spring-form tin and press in the dough. Bake at 230°C/450°F/Gas 8 for 20 minutes on a wire rack.

Split the shortcake in two and spread half the butter on the bottom layer and the rest on the underside of the top layer. Spread the fruit filling over the bottom cake and sandwich with the top layer. It does not matter if the fruit oozes out.

Whisk the cream until softly peaked and beat in the rest of the sugar and liqueur. Spoon the cream on to the shortcake and decorate with reserved fruits.

Flans aux Fruits

In former times, puff pastry was used as a base for fruit flans, but now sweet shortcrust pastry is preferred as it gives a crisper base. Choose seasonal fruits; they should be unblemished and fully ripe. Most of all be generous with the quantities as the fruit shrinks as it bakes.

Ingredients

Sweet Shortcrust Pastry for a 22cm/8½in flan tin or spring-form tin	lemon juice
	45g/3tbsp icing sugar, sifted
¼-1kg/1½-2lb ripe fruit	45ml/3tbsp apricot jam

Preparation Line the base and 2.5cm/1in up the

Blueberry Tart

Ingredients

Sweet Shortcrust Pastry for a 22cm/8½in flan tin
50g/2oz ground almonds

100g/4oz butter
3 eggs
30g/2tbsp cornflour or potato flour, sifted

Filling

400g/14oz blueberries or bilberries, fresh or frozen
140g/5oz caster sugar
30ml/2tbsp Grand Marnier or Cointreau

65ml/2½fl oz double cream
10g/2tsp orange zest
30ml/2tbsp lemon juice
50g/2oz icing sugar

Preparation Defrost the fruit and drain off the surplus juice. Line the base and 2cm/1in up the sides of a greased flan tin with shortcrust pastry, prick all over with a fork. Chill.

Make the filling. Drop the blueberries, 3tbsp sugar, liqueur and 15g/½oz butter into a pan, heat and stir gently until the fruit has slightly caramelized. Leave to cool.

Beat together the remaining butter and caster sugar until pale and fluffy; whisk in the eggs one at a time, add the flour and cream.

Mix in the orange zest and lemon juice, then fold in the blueberry mixture. Scatter the ground almonds over the base of the pastry shell and pour in the prepared filling.

Dredge with icing sugar and bake in the preheated oven at 180°C/350°F/Gas 4 for 1 hour. Leave to cool in the tin.

Serve with whipped cream on the side.

Above, Fresh Fruit Tarts of strawberries, mirabelle plums; apricots cooked on a base of crème pâtissière, gooseberries and black muscat grapes; raspberry and gooseberry tartlets. Right, Blueberry Tart.

sides of the flan tin with the pastry. Prick all over with a fork and chill. Wash and dry the fruit carefully; stone cherries and mirabelle plums but leave whole. Cut other fruits in half and remove the stones. Cut peaches into thick slices and rub them with lemon juice to stop them going brown.

Arrange the whole fruits, the fruit halves or slices in circles, cut sides up and each overlapping the preceding one a little; reverse the direction of the fruit for each new circle. Bake in the preheated oven at 190°C/375°F/Gas 5 for 50-60 minutes.

Meanwhile, heat the apricot jam with 2tbsp water until slightly thick; strain.

Remove the flan from the oven and leave in the tin on a wire rack to cool for 10 minutes. Lift off the outer rim of the tin and slide the flan off the base on to the rack. Dust with icing sugar all over, then brush the whole fruited surface with the warm jam, which will cool into a glossy jelly.

Serve when cold with whipped cream on the side.

Melt the chocolate with the butter and cream in the top of a double boiler. Stir occasionally.

Remove the melted chocolate from the heat. Gradually stir in the sweetened water and mix well Stir in the rum, brandy or Grand Marnier.

To eat the fondue, your guests each dip fruit pieces into the warm sauce.

Chocolate Fondue
Serves 6

Ingredients

300g/10oz sugar
150ml/¹/₄pt water
100g/4oz plain chocolate in small pieces
100g/4oz milk chocolate in small pieces
65g/2¹/₂oz butter

40ml/2¹/₂tbsp double cream
75ml/5tbsp rum, brandy or Grand Marnier
approx. 675g/1¹/₂lb prepared mixed fruit in bite-sized pieces

Preparation Heat the sugar and water over a low heat, stirring constantly, until the sugar has dissolved. Leave to cool.

Chocolate Chiffon Pie
Serves 6

Ingredients

1 portion Shortcrust Pastry
150ml/¹/₄pt milk
75g/3oz sugar
100g/4oz plain chocolate, chopped
2 small eggs, separated

10g/2tsp powdered gelatine
30ml/2tbsp hot water
150ml/¹/₄pt double cream whipped cream
chocolate curls

Preparation Roll out the pastry and use to line a 20cm/8in flan tin. Bake "blind" (lined with greaseproof paper and baking beans) for 20-25 minutes at 190°C/375°F/Gas 5. Remove the greaseproof paper and baking beans and return to oven for a further 5-10 minutes until crisp and lightly browned. Leave to cool.

Put the milk, sugar and chocolate into a saucepan and melt over a gentle heat, stirring continuously. Cool slightly.

Whisk the egg yolks into the chocolate mixture.

Dissolve the gelatine in the water and stir into chocolate. Leave until the mixture is beginning to thicken and set.

Whisk egg whites until stiff. Whisk in the remaining sugar.

Whisk the cream until it stands in soft peaks.

Fold the egg whites and cream thoroughly into the chocolate mixture. Pour into the pastry case.

Chill until set, then decorate with piped whipped cream and chocolate curls.

Chocolate Mousse
Serves 4-6

Ingredients

175g/6oz plain chocolate	*45ml/3tbsp hot water*
30ml/2tbsp honey	*150ml/¹/₄pt double cream*
3 eggs, separated	*whipped cream*
12.5g/¹/₂oz powdered gelatine	*sliced bananas*

Preparation Melt the chocolate and honey into a bowl over a pan of hot water.

Stir in the egg yolks and beat until smooth. Remove from the heat.

Dissolve the gelatine in the water. Stir into the chocolate mixture. Chill until the mixture is the consistency of unbeaten egg white.

Whip the double cream until thick, but not stiff. Fold into the chocolate mixture.

Whisk the egg whites until stiff and fold them into the chocolate mixture.

Pour into an 8-in/1-l/1³/₄-pt mould and chill until set.

Unmould onto a serving dish and decorate with whipped cream and banana slices.

Chocolate Orange Pots
Serves 8

Ingredients

175g/6oz plain chocolate	*250ml/8fl oz double cream*
rind of 1 small orange, finely grated	*whipped cream*
3 eggs, separated	*orange rind spirals*
30-45ml/2-3tbsp orange Curaçao	*chocolate orange sticks*

Preparation Melt the chocolate into a bowl over a pan of hot water. Remove from heat and stir in the orange rind, egg yolks and liqueur. Stir well and leave to cool.

Whip the double cream until thick. Whisk the egg whites until stiff. Fold cream and egg whites into the chocolate mixture.

Pour into 8 individual pots (e.g. custard cups) and chill.

Serve each topped with a spoonful of softly whipped cream and decorated with orange rind spirals and chocolate sticks.

Chocolate and Coffee Bavarois
Serves 6-8

Ingredients

4 egg yolks
50g/2oz sugar
5ml/1tsp vanilla essence
600ml/1pt milk
175g/6oz plain chocolate, grated
15ml/1tbsp coffee essence
15g/½oz powdered gelatine

60ml/4tbsp cold water
150ml/¼pt double cream
150ml/¼pt single cream
2 egg whites

Decoration
whipped cream
Chocolate Caraque

Preparation Beat together the egg yolks, sugar and vanilla essence until pale and fluffy.

Warm the milk. Stir into the egg yolk mixture. Put into a double saucepan or a bowl over a pan of hot water. Stir gently until the mixture thickens.

Stir the chocolate and coffee essence into the custard. Stir until completely dissolved. Remove from heat.

Put water into a bowl and add the gelatine. Place over a pan of hot water and stir until dissolved. Cool slightly.

Stir the gelatine into the chocolate custard. Leave until the mixture begins to thicken.

Whisk the creams together until thick. Whisk the egg whites until stiff.

Fold the cream into the chocolate mixture and then fold in the egg whites thoroughly.

Pour into a lightly-oiled approx. 8in/1.5l/2½pt mould. Chill until set.

Turn Bavarois out on to a serving plate. Decorate with piped whipped cream and Chocolate Caraque.

Chocolate Hazelnut Bombe
Serves 6-8

Ingredients

600ml/1pt vanilla ice cream
50g/2oz hazelnuts, finely chopped and toasted
600ml/1pt Chocolate Ice Cream
30ml/2tbsp dark rum

Decoration
300ml/½pt double cream, whipped
whole hazelnuts

Preparation Put an 8 or 9in/1.2l/2pt bombe mould or pudding basin into the freezer overnight.

Soften the vanilla ice cream and mix in the hazelnuts. Line the bombe mould with the ice cream and freeze.

Soften the chocolate ice cream and blend in the rum. Fill the centre of the bombe. Cover with oiled greaseproof or waxed paper and freeze.

Turn out the bombe on to a plate. Pipe with whipped cream and decorate with whole hazelnuts. Serve cut into wedges.

Choc-Chestnut Mont Blanc
Serves 6-8

Ingredients

50g/2oz unsalted butter	**Decoration**
25g/1oz sugar	*whipped cream*
175g/6oz plain chocolate,	*ratafias*
melted	*glacé chestnuts*
350g/12oz chestnut purée	*grated chocolate*
15-30ml/1-2tbsp sherry	

Preparation Cream the butter and sugar together until light and fluffy. Beat in the melted chocolate and blend in the chestnut purée and sherry.

Pile the mixture into the centre of individual dessert dishes and form into mountain shapes and chill.

Spoon or pipe a capping of whipped cream on the summit. Decorate the base with ratafia biscuits and glacé chestnuts. Sprinkle with grated chocolate if you wish.

Mohr Im Hemd
Moor In His Nightshirt
Makes 6-8

Ingredients

100g/4oz butter	**Sauce**
100g/4oz sugar	*175g/6oz plain chocolate*
6 eggs, separated	*175ml/6fl oz water*
100g/4oz plain chocolate,	*75g/3oz unsalted butter*
grated	**Cream**
100g/4oz ground almonds	*150ml/¼pt single cream*
5ml/1tsp coffee essence	*150ml/¼pt double cream*
	15-30ml/1-2tbsp icing
	sugar
	few drops vanilla essence

Preparation Cream together the butter and sugar until light and fluffy. Beat in the egg yolks one at a time. Mix in the chocolate, almonds and essence.

Whisk the egg whites until stiff and fold gently into the chocolate mixture. Butter and dust with caster sugar 6-8 individual soufflé dishes. Pour in the chocolate mixture.

Place in a roasting tin, half filled with hot water. Bake in the oven at 180°C/350°F/Gas 4 for 30-40 minutes until puffed and just firm. Leave to cool for a few minutes.

To make the sauce put the chocolate and water into a pan. Stir over a low heat until the mixture is smooth. Remove from the heat and stir in the butter.

Whisk the single and double creams together until light and fluffy. Stir in the icing sugar and vanilla essence.

Spoon a little sauce on to each serving plate. Invert the puddings onto the sauce. Cover puddings with whipped cream.

Choc Nut Slice
Serves 8-10

Ingredients

175g/6oz plain chocolate in small pieces
100g/4oz icing sugar
100g/4oz peanut butter
15g/1tbsp butter
pinch salt

10g/2tsp instant coffee granules
50ml/2fl oz boiling water
1 egg
5ml/1tsp vanilla essence
300g/10oz biscuit crumbs

Preparation Melt the chocolate in the top of a double boiler.

Sift the icing sugar. Mix together the melted chocolate, sugar, peanut butter, butter and salt.

Dissolve the instant coffee granules in boiling water and lightly beat the egg. Add the coffee, egg, vanilla and crumbs to the chocolate. Mix well so that the crumbs are well coated.

Line a loaf tin with foil. Spoon the chocolate mixture in the tin. Smooth the surface and cover with foil. Freeze for at least 4 hours.

Remove from the freezer one hour before you are ready to serve. Slice and arrange on serving dishes. Decorate with whipped cream to serve.

Chocolate Terrine
Serves 6-8

Ingredients

one purchased 450g/1lb Madeira or other loaf cake
175g/6oz plain chocolate
140g/5oz sugar
60ml/4tbsp water
100g/4oz cocoa
175g/6oz unsalted butter
1 egg

2 egg yolks
50g/2oz glacé cherries, chopped
50g/2oz raisins
50g/2oz pistachios, chopped
300ml/¹/₂pt whipping cream

Preparation Line a 1.4-kg/3-lb loaf tin with non-stick paper.

Cut the loaf cake into thin slices. Line the bottom and sides of the pan with some slices. Melt the chocolate.

Put the sugar and water into a small pan and heat gently over a low heat until the sugar is dissolved.

Beat together the cocoa and butter. Beat in the sugar syrup, melted chocolate and eggs. Stir in the cherries, raisins and pistachios.

Spread one third of the chocolate mixture in the lined tin. Top with slices of cake. Trim cake level. Cover and chill overnight.

Unmould terrine onto a serving plate and spread the whipped cream over the top and sides of terrine.

Frozen Chocolate Sandwiches
Makes about 20

Ingredients
100g/4oz butter
100g/4oz sugar
30ml/2tbsp beaten egg
a few drops vanilla essence
25g/1oz unsweetened
  cocoa powder
200g/7oz plain flour

15ml/1tbsp unsweetened
  cocoa powder
few drops vanilla essence
Coating
Chopped toasted almonds,
  alternatively toasted
  desiccated coconut or
  crushed digestive biscuits

Filling
1 large egg white
90ml/6tbsp sugar
250ml/8fl oz double
  cream

Preparation Beat the butter and sugar until pale and creamy. Beat in the egg and vanilla essence. Stir in the flour and cocoa, which have been sieved together, to give a firm dough.

Knead lightly until smooth. Roll out on a lightly floured surface to a thickness of about 0.5cm/¼in. Using a 6.5cm/2½in round fluted cutter, stamp out circles. Put on a baking sheet and cook in the oven at 180°C/350°F/Gas 4 for 15 minutes. Cool on a wire rack.

To make the filling, whisk the egg white until stiff. Whisk in 30g/2tbsp of the sugar. Put cream, remaining sugar, cocoa and vanilla essence into another bowl and whisk until stiff. Fold egg white into chocolate mixture.

Put a spoonful of the mixture on to half the chocolate biscuits. Top with remaining biscuits. Press lightly so filling reaches the edges. Arrange on a baking sheet and freeze until firm.

Spread the chosen coating on a baking sheet. Run each sandwich through the coating like a wheel, so that the sides are covered. Wrap individually in foil and freeze overnight.

Frozen Chocolate Sandwiches

Ricotta al Café
Serves 4

This delicious dessert is an Italian favourite. Eat it by dipping a spoonful of the cheese first into the coffee, then into the sugar.

Ingredients
225g/8oz ricotta cheese
30g/2tbsp fruit sugar
  (fructose) or caster
  sugar

60g/4tbsp finely ground
  fresh coffee
30ml/2tbsp brandy

Preparation Choose really moist ricotta cheese, or use fresh curd cheese as a substitute. Press the cheese with half the sugar through a sieve to make it light and fluffy. Form into mounds on four individual dessert plates.

Sprinkle half the coffee over the cheese mounds. Spoon the remaining coffee and sugar onto the plates in two separate heaps on either side of the cheese and pour the brandy over the sweetened cheese.

Prepare a soufflé dish by cutting a band of paper 7.5cm/3in deeper than the dish from a double layer of nonstick paper. Fold over 2.5cm/1in along one of the long edges. Wrap the band around the dish, the folded edge level with the base and the upper edge extending beyond the rim 5cm/2in. Secure firmly with string or paper clips.

Spoon the mixture into the dish until it almost reaches the top of the paper band. Chill.

Remove the paper and decorate with the remaining coconut, before serving.

Coffee Charlotte
Serves 6

Ingredients

32 sponge fingers (boudoir biscuits)	25g/1oz plain flour
60ml/4tbsp water	50g/2oz ground almonds
60ml/4tbsp coffee liqueur	1 whole egg
250ml/8fl oz milky coffee	1 egg yolk
50g/2oz Vanilla Sugar (see note to recipe for Le Succès)	100g/4oz milk chocolate, coarsely grated

Preparation Dip the sponge fingers lightly in the mixture of water and liqueur, and line the base and sides of a 15-18cm/6-7in charlotte mould.

Heat the milky coffee. Mix the sugar, flour and ground almonds together. Add the eggs and gradually pour into the coffee saucepan, beating thoroughly. Bring to the boil stirring constantly. Remove from the heat and leave to cool.

Spoon a layer of the coffee cream into the mould and sprinkle over it a layer of grated chocolate. Repeat until all the cream is used. Trim the sponge fingers lining the mould level with the filling and arrange the trimmings on top.

Press down well and leave to stand for 4-6 hours in a refrigerator until firm, then unmould to serve.

Coffee Coconut Soufflé
Serves 4-6

Ingredients

3 eggs, separated	75g/3oz desiccated or flaked coconut
60ml/4tbsp strong black coffee	15g/¹⁄₂oz powdered gelatine
15ml/1tbsp Crème de Cacao	30ml/2tbsp cold water
75g/3oz sugar	150ml/¹⁄₄pt double cream

Preparation Beat the egg yolks, coffee, Crème de Cacao and sugar in a bowl until thick. Stir in most of the coconut.

Melt the gelatine in a bowl of water over a pan of hot water. When clear, pour slowly into the coffee mixture, stirring all the time.

Beat the cream until it just holds its shape and fold into the mixture. Whisk the egg whites until nearly stiff and fold them carefully into the mixture when nearly set.

Coffee and Raspberry Frou Frou
Serves 6-8

Ingredients

600ml/1pt double cream
600ml/1pt single cream
225g/8oz meringue
20g/4tsp powdered instant coffee dissolved in 15ml/ 1tbsp hot water, cooled
100g/4oz frozen or fresh raspberries
5ml/1tsp lemon juice

40g/1½oz Vanilla Sugar (see note to recipe for Le Succès)
grated rind of one orange
15ml/1tbsp water
a selection of fruit e.g. strawberries, raspberries, peaches, washed and sliced

Preparation Whip the two creams together until they just hold soft peaks. Break the meringue into small pieces and fold into the cream. Divide the mixture between three bowls. Add the coffee to one bowl and fold in.

For the raspberry sauce, combine all the remaining ingredients, except the mixed fruit, in a saucepan and heat gently until the raspberries are soft. Stir well to break up the berries and mix with one of the bowls of cream and meringue mixture.

Grease a 1.8l/3pt ring mould and put alternate spoonfuls from the 3 bowls into it. Repeat until all the mixture is used. Gently smooth the surface and cover. Freeze for at least 6 hours.

Move to a refrigerator 30 minutes before serving. Unmould onto a serving plate and fill the centre with the mixed fruit.

Iced Coffee Praline Mousse
Serves 6

Ingredients

100g/4oz whole hazelnuts
45g/3tbsp sugar
4 large eggs, separated
90g/6tbsp Vanilla Sugar (see note to recipe for Le Succès) or caster sugar

30g/2tbsp powdered instant coffee
300ml/½pt double cream

Preparation Brown the hazelnuts in a frying pan over a medium heat. When the skins begin to loosen, remove from heat. Put in a dish cloth and rub gently to remove the skins. Chop roughly.

Add the sugar to the pan. When the sugar has melted and is slightly brown, stir in the hazelnuts. Pour the mixture onto a lightly oiled tray. When cool, break the praline into pieces and blend briefly in a liquidizer or food processor.

Beat the egg yolks with 60g/4tbsp of the sugar until pale and light. Put the bowl over a pan of hot water and continue beating until the mixture leaves a trail. Stir in the coffee and allow to cool.

Whip the cream to soft peaks and gently stir in the coffee mixture. Fold in the praline. Whisk the egg whites until stiff and beat in the remaining sugar. Gently fold the egg whites into the cream mixture.

Pour the mixture either into a glass serving bowl or individual glasses. Cover and freeze for at least 1-2 hours.

Remove from the freezer 20 minutes before serving.

Preparation Whisk the egg whites until they form very stiff peaks. Mix the coffee with the sugar and add a little at a time, beating well after each addition.

Put the mixture in a piping bag fitted with a star nozzle and pipe small meringues 2.5cm/1in in diameter onto a baking tray lined with non-stick paper. Bake for 2-3 hours at 120°C/250°F/Gas ¼ until crisp and dry.

To assemble put a layer of meringues closely together on a serving plate and cover with some of the cream, grapes and almonds. Continue with layers of meringue, cream and grapes to form a pyramid.

Decorate with almonds, cream, grapes and, if you likes, chocolate coffee beans.

Coffee Meringue Pyramid
Serves 8-10

Ingredients

8 egg whites
60g/4tbsp instant coffee
   powder
450g/1lb sugar
600ml/1pt double cream,
   whipped
225g/8oz black grapes,
   halved and seeded

225g/8oz green grapes,
   halved and seeded
100g/4oz flaked almonds
chocolate coffee beans
   (optional)

Coffee Apricot Condé
Serves 8

Ingredients

100g/4oz short-grain rice
900ml/1½pt milk
60g/4tbsp powdered
   instant coffee
12.5g/½oz powdered
   gelatine
juice of 1 orange

60g/4tbsp sugar
300ml/½pt double cream,
   whipped
8 ripe apricots, peeled,
   stoned and chopped
100g/4oz raspberries

Preparation Put the rice, milk and coffee into a pan and bring to the boil, stirring occasionally. Simmer for 30-40 minutes, or until the rice is cooked, adding extra milk if necessary.

Dissolve the gelatine in the orange juice over a pan of hot water. Stir into the rice mixture and add the sugar. Leave to cool.

Fold half the cream and half the apricots, chopped, into the rice mixture. Spoon into a greased 1.2l/2pt mould. Chill until set.

Turn out onto a serving plate, arrange some raspberries around the base, pipe the remaining whipped cream onto the top of the mould and decorate with the rest of the apricots, sliced, and the raspberries.

Coffee Fruit Flans
Makes 8

Ingredients

100g/4oz butter	**Filling**
100g/4oz vanilla sugar or	*225g/8oz selected fruit, eg*
caster sugar	*peaches, apricots, green*
2 eggs	*grapes, strawberries, etc.*
grated rind of one lemon	*12.5g/¹⁄₂oz powdered*
100g/4oz self-raising flour	*gelatine*
5g/1tsp baking powder	*150ml/¹⁄₄pt orange juice*
15g/1tbsp instant coffee	
powder	

Preparation Cream the butter and sugar together until light and fluffy. Gradually beat in the eggs and lemon rind. Sift together the flour, baking powder and instant coffee and gently fold into the mixture with a metal spoon.

Grease eight individual muffin or cupcake tins and divide the mixture between them. Bake for 15 minutes at 190°C/375°F/Gas 5 until cooked through, then remove from the tins and cool on a wire rack.

Slice or halve the fruit, as required. Fill the sponge cases, make little domes of fruit.

Over a gentle heat, melt the gelatine in two tablespoons of the juice, then add the remaining liquid. Cool until just on the point of setting.

Spoon over the fruit in the sponge cases and leave to set.

Coffee and Vanilla Jelly
Serves 6

Ingredients

25g/1oz vanilla sugar or	**Vanilla Jelly**
caster sugar	*1 egg yolk*
300ml/¹⁄₂pt hot strong	*25g/1oz caster sugar*
coffee	*300ml/¹⁄₂pt milk*
12.5g/¹⁄₂oz powdered	*vanilla essence*
gelatine	*12.5g/¹⁄₂oz powdered*
45ml/3tbsp water	*gelatine*
	45ml/3tbsp water

Preparation Add the sugar to the hot coffee. Dissolve the gelatine in the water over a saucepan of hot water. Add to the coffee mixture and stir well to make sure the jelly is clear.

Pour half the mixture into a greased ³⁄₄l/1¹⁄₂pt decorative jelly mould. Leave to set but keep the rest of the mixture warm.

Mix the egg yolk with the sugar, pour on the milk in a saucepan and heat, stirring all the time. When thickened, add vanilla essence to taste. Strain and cool.

Melt the gelatine in the water and add to the vanilla cream. Pour half this mixture onto the set coffee jelly and leave this to set. Repeat the layers.

Refrigerate until completely set and then turn out onto a serving plate.

Weight Watchers' Cheesecake
Serves 6

Ingredients

Base
75g/3oz margarine
75g/3oz sugar
75g/3oz plain flour
30g/2tbsp cornflour

Filling
1 egg, separated
1 lemon
30ml/2tbsp milk
40g/1½oz sugar
100g/4oz skimmed milk cheese
100g/4oz cottage cheese
150ml/¼pt whipping cream

Preparation To make the shortbread base, rub the margarine into the combined sugar, flour and cornflour until it resembles coarse crumbs. Bind lightly and press over the base of a 20cm/8in tin. Prick and bake for 40 minutes at 160°C/325°F/Gas 3.

Combine the egg yolk, grated lemon rind, milk and sugar for the filling. Heat, stirring, until thick. Leave to cool.

Beat the skimmed milk cheese until it is smooth. Strain the cottage cheese before adding to the skimmed milk cheese. Stir in the lemon juice.

Whip the cream and gently fold into the cheese mixture.

Whisk the egg white until it is stiff but not dry. Fold into the filling mixture, starting with just one spoonful and gradually adding the remainder.

Pour the filling over the cool shortbread and chill until set. Serve with fresh fruit or a fruit topping.

Topfen Kuchen
Cheesecake

Ingredients

1 portion Sweet Shortcrust Pastry for a 22cm/8½in spring-form tin
140g/5oz caster sugar
75g/3oz butter
1tsp lemon zest

4 eggs, separated
300g/11oz curd cheese, sieved
50g/2oz raisins
60ml/4tbsp double cream

Preparation Par-bake a pastry case for 15 minutes. Leave to cool. Beat the sugar and butter until thick, pale and fluffy. Mix in the lemon zest and egg yolks, one at a time. Blend in the cheese and raisins.

Whisk the egg whites until they form soft peaks and fold them into the cheese mixture. Fold in the double cream.

Pour the filling into the pastry case and bake in the warmed oven at 180°C/350°F/Gas 4 for 1 hour, until well risen and golden. Cool in the tin on a wire rack. The cake will collapse and crack as it cools, which is typical of cheesecakes. Dredge with icing sugar to serve.

The cake freezes successfully for up to 2 months. Defrost at room temperature for 3-4 hours.

Italian Cheesecake
Serves 10-12

Ingredients

Base
75g/3oz butter
2 egg yolks
25g/2tbsp sugar
15ml/1tbsp Marsala
2.5g/½tsp lemon rind
pinch salt
100g/4oz plain flour

Filling
450g/1lb curd cheese
50g/2oz sugar
5g/1tsp plain flour
pinch salt
2.5ml/½tsp vanilla essence
2.5g/½tsp orange rind
2 egg yolks
15g/1tbsp sultanas
15g/1tbsp candied peel
15g/1tbsp chopped almonds

Preparation Mix all the base ingredients together until a dough has formed. Handle as little as possible while blending. Gently roll or press into shape and line the base and sides of a 23cm/9in loose-bottomed tin.

Beat the cheese until it is smooth. Mix well with all the other ingredients, adding the fruit and nuts last of all. Pour into the pastry case.

Bake at 180°C/350°F/Gas 4 for 45-50 minutes. Cool and dust with icing sugar before serving.

Chilled Sultana and Orange Cheesecake

Ingredients

75g/3oz candied orange
  and lemon peel, chopped
100g/3½oz sultanas
45ml/3tbsp Grand
  Marnier or Cointreau
25g/1oz gelatine powder
300g/11oz curd cheese,
  sieved
75g/3oz caster sugar
250g/9oz lemon curd
20g/2tbsp orange zest
375ml/13fl oz double
  cream, softly whipped

35g/5tbsp pistachios,
  chopped
Syrup
75g/3oz granulated sugar
25ml/1fl oz water
45ml/3tbsp Grand
  Marnier or Cointreau
1 cooked fat-free sponge
  24cm/9½in diameter
  (see note)

Preparation Soak the orange and lemon peel and the sultanas in Grand Marnier or Cointreau for at least 30 minutes. Make a syrup with the sugar and water boiled to 'thread stage', when the syrup will form a thread between the opened blade points of a pair of scissors. Mix in the liqueur. Cool.

Slice the sponge cake horizontally into two layers, of one-third and two-thirds thicknesses. Lightly oil a 24cm/9½in spring-form tin and line the base with greaseproof paper. Drop the thicker cake layer into the tin and brush all over with the flavoured syrup.

Sprinkle the gelatine powder on to 75ml/3fl oz very hot, but not boiling, water in a cup and stir to dissolve. Leave to cool. The mixture should be transparent and lump-free, if it is not, place the cup in a pan of warm water and heat gently. Cool to room temperature before using.

Meanwhile, beat the curd cheese with the sugar, lemon curd and orange zest until well blended. Gently trickle over the gelatine liquid, beating all the time.

Set aside until the cream is on the point of setting. Using a large metal spoon, lightly fold in the soaked peel and sultanas, the liqueur, whipped cream and the pistachios.

Pour the cream cheese filling on to the sponge cake in the prepared tin and smooth it out. Carefully cut half of the remaining sponge layer into six triangular pieces and evenly space them on top of the filling to create a fan effect.

Flavour 140ml/5fl oz sweetened whipped cream with 30ml/2tbsp of orange liqueur and pipe rosettes of cream on the cake. Decorate with candied peels and pistachios. Chill for 5-6 hours. The cake may be prepared 2-3 days ahead of time and kept in the refrigerator.

Note To make a fat-free sponge of the size needed here, lightly whisk 4 whole eggs and 100g/4oz caster sugar in a bowl set over a pan a quarter filled with simmering water, for 5-10 minutes, until the mixture is rich and creamy. Remove from the heat and beat for another 20 minutes by hand, or 10 minutes with an electric mixer. Blend in the seeds of a 5cm/2in vanilla pod.

Fold in 100g/4oz sifted plain flour using a large metal spoon. Work in a figure-of-eight movement, avoiding stirring the mixture, which will lose all the air and make the sponge heavy and damp.

Pour the batter into a prepared spring-form tin and bake immediately in a preheated oven at 180°C/350°F/ Gas 4 for 30-35 minutes for a deep cake, 20 minutes for a shallow cake.

Curd Cheese Cake

Curd cheese, like sour cream is an important ingredient in Hungarian cooking. The airy, mousse-like filling of this cake has a lemony tang, which is enhanced by the sour-cream pastry.

Ingredients

130g/4½oz plain flour
65g/2½oz butter
5g/1tsp caster sugar
1 egg yolk
150ml/¼pt sour cream

Filling
7 egg yolks
250g/9oz caster sugar
20g/2tbsp lemon zest
275g/10oz curd cheese
8 egg whites

Preparation Sift the flour into a bowl and drop in the butter, cut in pieces. Rub together to make fine crumbs. Mix in the sugar. Add the egg and sour cream and blend and knead into a firm paste. Roll into a ball, wrap in plastic film and chill for 30 minutes.

Divide the dough in two and roll each piece to fit a 26cm/10½in spring-form tin. Line the greased base of the tin with one sheet of pastry. Make pastry leaves or flowers with any remaining scraps of dough.

Whisk together the egg yolks and caster sugar until pale and creamy and well expanded. Beat in the lemon zest and the sieved cheese.

In another bowl whip up the egg whites until they are firm and well peaked. Lightly fold them into the cheese mixture using a large metal spoon and taking care not to lose any air. Pour the filling into the cake tin. Smooth gently, then lay the remaining sheet of pastry on top and press it down lightly.

Place the pastry leaves or flowers quickly on the pastry top, using a little whipped egg white. Bake immediately in the preheated oven at 170°C/325°F/ Gas 3 for 50-60 minutes.

The cake will colour only slightly and rise quite high out of the tin. As it cools it will drop quite dramatically — most cheesecakes do — but it will not crack because of the pastry covering. Dredge with icing sugar to serve.

Cottage Cheesecake
Serves 6-8

Ingredients

Base	Filling
100g/4oz soft margarine	3 eggs, separated
175g/6oz plain flour	100g/4oz sugar
2.5g/½tsp baking powder	350g/12oz cottage cheese
50g/2oz sugar	150ml/¼pt sour cream
1 lemon	

Preparation Beat together all the base ingredients to form a dough. Roll out gently to line the base and sides of a 20cm/8in tin.

Beat the egg yolks with the sugar until they are nearly white. Strain the cheese and add to the egg yolks along with the sour cream. Mix well.

Whisk the egg whites until they are stiff but not dry. Gently fold into the filling mixture starting with just one spoonful and gradually adding the remainder. Pour into the pastry case.

Bake for 50 minutes at 160°C/325°F/Gas 3. Cool in the oven with the door slightly open. Chill before serving.

Raisin Cheesecake

Raisin Cheesecake
Serves 6-8

Ingredients

Base
100g/4oz digestive biscuits
40g/1½oz butter
15g/1tbsp sugar
5g/1tsp cinnamon

Filling
225g/8oz cottage cheese
225g/8oz curd cheese
2 eggs, separated
50g/2oz sugar
5g/1tsp lemon rind
50g/2oz raisins
50g/2oz sultanas

Preparation Crush the biscuits and mix with melted butter, sugar and cinnamon. Press over the base of a 20cm/8in tin.

Strain the cottage cheese so that the lumps are as small as possible. Beat with the curd cheese until smooth. Mix the egg yolks with the cheese. Beat in the sugar and grated lemon rind and stir in the fruit.

Beat the egg whites until they are stiff but not dry. Gently fold into the cheese mixture. Pour the filling onto the base and bake for 40 minutes at 170°C/325°F/ Gas 3. Cool in the oven with the door slightly open.

Pineapple Coconut Cheesecake
Serves 8

Ingredients

Base
50g/2oz butter
15g/1tbsp sugar
50g/2oz desiccated coconut
50g/2oz ground hazelnuts

Filling
450g/1lb curd cheese
30ml/2tbsp lemon juice
1 egg
30g/2tbsp sugar

Topping
130g/4½oz pineapple pieces
12.5g/2½tsp cornflour
125ml/4fl oz pineapple juice
12.5ml/2½tsp rum
125ml/4fl oz water
15g/1tbsp desiccated coconut

Preparation Melt the butter and stir into the other base ingredients. Press over the bottom and up the sides of a greased 20cm/8in tin. Bake for 5 minutes at 180°C/350°F/Gas 4.

Beat together all the filling ingredients. Pour onto the base. Bake for 20 minutes at 190°C/375°F/Gas 4.

Leave the cake to cool slightly before adding the topping. Arrange the pineapple pieces on top of the cake.

Combine the cornflour, pineapple juice and rum. Heat, stirring constantly, until the glaze thickens and clears. Gently spoon the glaze over the fruit.

To serve, garnish the cheesecake by sprinkling with coconut.

Chocolate Cheesecake Cups
Serves 6

Ingredients

450g/1lb cream cheese
3 eggs, separated
100g/4oz sugar
150ml/¼pt sour cream
12.5g/½oz powdered gelatine
60ml/4tbsp water

175g/6oz plain or milk chocolate, chopped
175g/6oz plain chocolate
6 individual Shortcrust Pastry cases approx. 7.5cm/3in diameter
Chocolate Caraque

Preparation Put the cheese and egg yolks into a bowl. Add half the sugar and beat well, then stir in the sour cream.

Dissolve the gelatine in the water.

Whisk the egg whites until stiff. Whisk in the remaining sugar.

Stir the gelatine into the cheese mixture.

Fold the meringue and the chopped chocolate into the cheese mixture.

Pour into six individual moulds and chill until set.

Melt the chocolate and spread over the underneath and outsides of the pastry cases. Put upside down over small glasses to set.

Turn out the cheesecakes and put one in each chocolate cup.

Serve decorated with chocolate caraque.

Summer Pudding
Serves 6-8

Ingredients
6-8 slices white bread
675g/1½lb soft fruit
100g/4oz sugar
30ml/2tbsp water

Preparation Remove the crusts from the bread and cut into fingers. Cover the base and sides of a 1l/2pt soufflé dish or pudding bowl, saving enough pieces of bread to make a lid for the pudding.

Put the fruit in a heavy-bottomed pan. Sprinkle with sugar and water. Cook over a very low heat until the sugar has dissolved and the fruit is soft but not mushy. The juices should be running freely.

Strain the fruit, reserving the juice. Pour two spoonfuls of juice over the bread in the base of the bowl. Spoon the fruit into the bread case. Pour over all but 6 spoonfuls of the juice.

Arrange the remaining bread fingers over the top of the fruit. Pour over the remaining juice.

Put a dish, small enough to fit inside the rim of the bowl, on top of the pudding. Press down with heavy cans or weights. Put the Summer Pudding into the refrigerator and leave for at least 8 hours.

Just before you are ready to eat the pudding, remove the weights and the dish. Put a serving dish over the pudding and turn upside down to unmould.

Serve with cream, whipped or pouring.

Sailors' Delight
Serves 4

Ingredients
225ml/8oz mincemeat
50ml/2fl oz rum
600ml/1pt ice cream

Preparation Gently heat the mincemeat with the rum. Spoon over the ice cream.

Semolina Pudding
Serves 4

Ingredients
350ml/12fl oz white wine
300ml/½pt water
½ lemon
1 orange
pinch salt
100g/4oz semolina (or farina)
100g/4oz sugar
3 eggs, separated

Preparation Combine the wine, water, finely grated rinds of the lemon and orange, and the salt. Bring to the boil.

Add the semolina to the pan, stirring constantly. Reduce the heat and simmer gently for approximately 5 minutes, or until the mixture is thick and smooth.

Stir the sugar and juice of the orange into the semolina, and continue to cook, stirring, until the pudding boils again.

Remove the pan from the heat and stir in 2 egg yolks. Save the remaining yolk to use for another recipe.

Whisk the egg whites until they are stiff but not dry. Fold gently into the semolina, starting with just one spoonful and gradually adding the remainder.

Pour the pudding into one large or several small, wetted moulds.

Serve with fresh or poached fruit or with a warm or cold fruit purée.

Variation For a hot semolina pudding, put the mould in a roasting tin containing enough hot water to come halfway up the side of dish. Cover the mould loosely with foil. Bake for 50-60 minutes at 170°C/325°F/Gas 3 until the pudding has set. Serve from the dish or unmoulded.

Rice Flour Dessert
Serves 6-8

The unusual flavour of this dessert comes in part from the rose water, which can be bought at some chemists and speciality shops.

Ingredients
45ml/3tbsp sesame oil
45ml/3tbsp vegetable oil
175g/6oz rice flour
900ml/1½pt milk
30ml/2tbsp rose water
15ml/1tbsp almond
  essence
100g/4oz caster sugar
5g/1tsp ground cardamom
  seeds
good pinch ground
  cinnamon
60g/2½oz icing sugar
100g/4oz pistachio nuts,
  chopped

Preparation Heat the sesame and vegetable oils together in a saucepan over a moderate heat. Stir in the rice flour and cook until a light golden brown.

Reduce the heat to low and stir in the milk. Continue stirring until the milk and flour mixture is smooth. Add the rose water, almond essence, sugar, cardamom and cinnamon. Cook the mixture over a low heat, stirring constantly, until it thickens. Add the icing sugar and stir until it dissolves.

Pour the mixture into a lightly greased shallow rectangular pan, sprinkle the top with the pistachio nuts, and allow it to cool and become firm.

Serve cut into rectangles or squares.

Marshmallow Crunch
Serves 4

Ingredients
8 small meringues
600ml/1pt ice cream
8 small marshmallows
450ml/16oz Chocolate or
  Fruit Sauce

Charlotte Louise

Preparation Crush the meringues coarsely and arrange at the bottom of each serving dish. Top with two scoops of ice cream. Add the marshmallows and spoon over the sauce.

As an alternative, the meringues can be left whole and sandwiched together with the ice cream. The marshmallows and sauce are arranged on top. If you like your sundaes gooey, melt the marshmallows!

Charlotte Louise
Serves 8

Ingredients
18-20 sponge fingers
  (boudoir biscuits)
150g/6oz unsalted butter
75g/3oz sugar
150g/6oz plain chocolate
100g/4oz ground almonds
300ml/½pt double cream
2.5ml/½tsp almond
  essence
Decoration
whipped cream
pistachio nuts
crystallized violets or roses
satin ribbon

Preparation Cut a round of greaseproof (waxed) paper to fit the base of an 8 or 9in/1.4l/2½pt Charlotte mould. Oil it lightly and put in the mould. Line the sides of the mould with the sponge fingers.

Cream the butter and sugar together until light and fluffy.

Melt the chocolate. Cool slightly, then beat into the butter, together with the ground almonds.

Whip the cream until thick, but not stiff. Add the almond essence. Fold into the chocolate mixture and mix well.

Spoon the mixture into the lined mould. Press in firmly. Chill.

Turn the Charlotte onto a serving plate. Remove the paper and pipe with whipped cream. Decorate with pistachio nuts and violets. Tie a satin ribbon round it for the finishing touch.

Crème Caramel
Serves 6

Ingredients

60g/4tbsp fruit sugar
(fructose) or caster
sugar
60ml/4tbsp water

Custard
600ml/1pt milk
few drops vanilla essence
4 eggs
45g/3tbsp fruit sugar
(fructose) or caster
sugar

Preparation For the caramel, put the sugar and the water in a heavy saucepan and stir over a low heat until the sugar has dissolved. Bring to the boil and boil until the syrup is golden. Pour the caramel into 6 individual moulds (or one large one) and swirl it around so that it coats the bottom and sides.

Bring the milk and vanilla essence to the boil in a saucepan. Remove from the heat.

Beat the eggs and sugar together in a bowl. Gradually add the hot milk, stirring all the while.

Strain or ladle the custard into the moulds. Stand them in a roasting tin half-filled with hot water and bake for 45 minutes at 180°C/350°F/Gas 4 until set.

Allow to cool and then chill. Don't turn out the Crème Caramel until you are ready to serve or it will lose its gloss.

Payodhi
Baked Yoghurt

Ingredients

425ml/14fl oz evaporated
milk
425ml/14fl oz condensed
milk

550ml/18fl oz yoghurt
15g/1tbsp pistachio nuts,
skinned and chopped

Preparation Preheat oven to 450°F/225°C/Gas 5.

Whisk the evaporated milk, condensed milk and yoghurt together for 1 minute. Pour into an ovenproof dish and place in the preheated oven.

Turn the oven off after 6 minutes and leave the dish in the oven overnight. Chill. Serve garnished with chopped pistachio nuts.

Shrikhand
Yoghurt with Saffron

Ingredients

600ml/1pt yoghurt
¼tsp saffron
15ml/1tbsp warm milk

100g/4oz castor sugar
20g/2tbsp pistachio nuts,
skinned and chopped

Preparation Put the yoghurt in a muslin bag and hang it up for 4-5 hours to get rid of the excess water.

Soak the saffron in the milk for 30 minutes.

Whisk together the drained yoghurt, sugar and saffron milk till smooth and creamy. Put in a dish and garnish with the nuts. Chill until set. Any seasonal fruit may be added while whisking.

Vanilla Cream

Vanilla Cream

Ingredients

3 eggs
50g/2oz vanilla sugar
250ml/8fl oz milk
12.5g/¹⁄₂oz gelatine

50ml/2fl oz water
10ml/2tsp vanilla essence
250ml/8fl oz double cream

Preparation Beat the eggs and sugar until pale and frothy. Heat the milk to almost boiling point and pour over the egg mixture.

Strain the mixture back into the saucepan. Simmer over a very low heat or in a double boiler until thick, stirring all the time. Allow to cool.

Soak the gelatine in water for 5 minutes, then heat to dissolve. Stir the vanilla essence into the cooled custard, followed by the gelatine.

Whip the cream and fold into the mixture before it sets. Pour into a dish and refrigerate.

Charlotte Russe
Serves 8

The great French chef Antoine Carême created this celebrated dessert after visiting Russia in the mid-nineteenth century.

Ingredients

16 ladyfingers, halved lengthwise
4 egg yolks
130g/4¹⁄₂oz sugar
225ml/8fl oz milk
15ml/1tbsp pure vanilla essence
30ml/2tbsp unflavored gelatin, dissolved in 50ml/2fl oz cold water

125ml/4fl oz sour cream
125ml/4fl oz double cream, chilled
15ml/1tbsp Triple Sec liqueur
575g/20oz frozen raspberries, thawed and drained
45g/3tbsp caster sugar
30ml/2tbsp blackberry brandy

Preparation Set 16 ladyfinger halves aside. Take the remaining ladyfingers and cut diagonal slices from each side of one end, so that one end of each is still curved and the other comes to a point.

In a pudding mould, arrange the trimmed ladyfinger halves at the bottom so that their points touch and their diagonal edges are side by side. The pattern on the bottom of the pudding mould should resemble a doily with beveled edges.

Place the remaining untrimmed ladyfinger halves against the side of the mould, standing them straight up. Try not to leave any gaps between the untrimmed ladyfinger halves.

In a mixing bowl, beat the egg yolks. Gradually beat in the sugar. Continue beating until the sugar is fully incorporated into the egg yolks.

Warm the milk and vanilla essence in a small saucepan over a low heat. When the milk starts to bubble, beat it into the egg mixture.

Pour the egg and milk mixture back into the saucepan. Cook over a low heat, stirring all the time, until the mixture becomes a thick custard. Do not let the mixture boil.

Stir in the dissolved gelatin. When the mixture has an even consistency throughout, strain it through a fine sieve into a mixing bowl.

In another bowl, whip the sour cream and double cream together until the mixture begins to stiffen.

Place the bowl containing the custard mixture inside a larger bowl. Put ice cubes and cold water into the larger bowl until it comes halfway up the sides of the custard bowl. Stir the custard with a metal spoon until it begins to thicken noticeably.

Fold the whipped cream mixture into the custard, breaking up any lumps with a whisk or fork. Stir in the Triple Sec liqueur.

Pour the contents of the custard bowl into the mould lined with ladyfingers. Chill for 5-6 hours before serving.

Blend the strained raspberries, caster sugar and blackberry brandy together in a small bowl. Spoon the sauce over slices of the Charlotte Russe just before serving.

Crème Brûlée
Serves 6

Ingredients
750ml/1¼pt single cream   22ml/1½tbsp vanilla
6 egg yolks   essence
45g/3tbsp white sugar   30g/2tbsp Demerara sugar

Preparation Put the cream in a bowl over a pan of simmering water. Beat the egg yolks, add the sugar and essence, and gently stir into the warmed cream. Continue cooking, stirring all the time, until the sauce is thick enough to coat the back of the wooden spoon.

Strain the mixture through a fine sieve into either a large soufflé dish or individual custard dishes.

Put the dish or dishes into a large shallow pan and place on the middle rack of the oven. Fill the pan with hot water until it reaches the level of the custard in the serving dishes. Bake for 35-45 minutes depending on size at 150°C/300°F/Gas 2 until the centre of the custard is firm. Cool, cover and chill

Sprinkle the Demerara sugar on top of the chilled custard. Put under a preheated hot grill, as close to the heat as possible, until the sugar has caramelized. Watch closely.

Chill for 2-3 hours before serving.

Variation For Coffee Brûlée, add 60g/4tbsp instant powdered coffee and 30ml/2tbsp coffee liqueur to the egg yolks and sugar instead of the vanilla essence.

Strawberry Peach Sherbet
Serves 6-8

Ingredients
4 large peaches   140g/5oz superfine sugar
225g/8oz fresh
  strawberries, chopped
75ml/3fl oz fresh lemon
  juice

Preparation Add the peaches to boiling water and cook for 2 minutes.

Remove the peaches from the pot and drain well. When the peaches are cool enough to handle, remove the skins and stones. Mash the peaches into a pulp in a large mixing bowl.

Purée the peach pulp, strawberries and lemon juice in a liquidizer or food processor.

Stir the sugar into the fruit mixture and purée for another 10-15 seconds. Pour the mixture into a large, shallow dish and freeze until hard. Remove the dish from the freezer 1 hour before serving and let the sherbet soften in the refrigerator.

Yorkshire Curd Tart

Ingredients
1 portion Sweet Shortcrust   2 eggs, separated
  Pastry for a 22cm/8½in   100g/4oz raisins
  loose-based flan tin   pinch salt
100g/4oz butter   2.5g/½tsp ground nutmeg
50g/2oz caster sugar   7g/1tbsp ground almond
5g/1tsp lemon zest   or toasted breadcrumbs
250g/9oz curd cheese,
  sieved

Preparation Butter the tin and line with the pastry; prick all over with a fork. Chill.

Cream the butter and sugar until light and fluffy, mix in the lemon zest, curd cheese, egg yolks and raisins. Add the salt and nutmeg.

Whisk the egg whites separately until they are firm and lightly fold them into the mixture. Scatter the almonds or breadcrumbs over the pastry base. Pour the cheese filling into the pastry case, and bake at 200°C/400°F/Gas 6 for 30 minutes, reducing the temperature after the first 15 minutes to 170°C/325°F/Gas 3 until golden and the pastry is brown. Leave to cool on a wire rack in the tin.

The tart will freeze well for up to 2 months.

Pâte à Choux
Choux Pastry
Makes 22 buns

Choux pastry is thought to have originated in the mid-sixteenth century, and it was especially popular made in deep-fried fritter or beignet form.

The preparation of choux pastry takes very little time and is quite unlike any other baking technique. The basic ingredients of butter, flour and water are cooked together to make a type of white sauce, or roux, before the eggs are beaten in. During baking the paste expands and puffs into a crisp hollow shell, almost three times it original size.

Uncooked choux pastry freezes very well for up to 2 months. For small buns pipe or spoon the mixture on to greaseproof paper and open-freeze before packing in air-tight bags. Bake from the freezer 5 minutes longer than the normal time.

Ingredients

130g/4½oz strong plain flour, sifted
10g/2tsp caster sugar
125ml/4fl oz water
125ml/4fl oz milk
100g/4oz lightly salted butter, diced

4 eggs
5ml/1tsp brandy, rum or orange-flower water (optional)

Preparation Sift the flour and sugar two or three times, finally on to a sheet of greaseproof paper. Set aside. Measure the water and milk into a deep pan, and drop in the butter pieces.

Set the pan over heat and warm gently until all the butter has melted, then raise the temperature and bring the liquid to a rolling boil. Draw the pan aside and shoot in the flour mixture all at once. Beat vigorously with a wooden spoon and quickly replace the pan on a low heat.

Continue beating and cook the paste for just a few seconds more so that the flour is properly combined. The paste should have an ungrained, smooth appearance and roll cleanly off the bottom and sides of the pan into a ball (a floury film is left on the base of the pan). Avoid over-cooking the paste or the finished buns will be heavy.

The mixture may now be beaten in the bowl of an electric mixer as the eggs are added. Care must be taken here as too much egg can spoil the paste, making it too runny, so add a little at a time.

Lightly whisk the eggs together in a separate bowl, and pour about a quarter on the flour paste, beat vigorously until well combined; add more egg and beat again. Continue adding egg and beating, until the paste is quite firm but elastic — it will drop from a spoon reluctantly when jerked slightly. You may not need quite all of the egg, although if the weather conditions are dry, you may need a little more. Beat the paste well until it is shiny and smooth; finally add the spirit or flour water.

The paste is now ready for use and may be kept for an hour or two if covered with a damp cloth.

Choux pastry must be cooked until all the surfaces are completely browned, otherwise it will collapse and go soggy as it cools. It is, however, inclined to burn rather easily underneath and needs additional protection in the oven. Either use a second large baking sheet, warmed in the oven beforehand, or line the one that you are using with a thick layer of aluminium foil.

To bake choux pastry buns hold a large, flat baking sheet under cold running water for a few seconds to chill it; shake off the excess water but leave it damp. Place teaspoonfuls of the mixture, about 2.5cm/1in high and 5cm/2in apart on the baking sheet. Remember that they expand to two or three times their size during baking. Lightly brush a little beaten egg on each one and scatter over a pinch of granulated sugar to give sparkle; chopped or flaked almonds are also nice. Bake in the preheated oven at 200°C/400°F/Gas 6.

Choux buns take about 20 minutes to cook. Never open the oven door until at least 15 minutes have elapsed, as the delicate structure will collapse immediately if it is not cooked sufficiently.

The baked pastries will be light, hollow and golden brown. Lift the tray out of the oven and transfer the buns to a wire rack. Pierce each one with a skewer or knife to release the steam inside and leave them to cool.

Choux pastries are best eaten on the day they are baked, but they can be stored for a day or two in an air-tight tin, then reheated in a low oven for about 10 minutes to crisp them up again. They should be filled no more than 1 hour before serving.

Rice and Raisin Pudding
Serves 8

Ingredients

100g/4oz rice
225ml/8fl oz wter
pinch salt
100g/4oz sugar

5g/1tsp ground cinnamon
900ml/1½pt milk
2 eggs
50g/2oz raisins

Preparation Wash the rice in running water until the water is clear. Put it in a bowl with enough hot water to cover and leave to soak for 15 minutes.

Drain the rice and put in a heavy-bottomed pan with the water and salt. Cover the pan, bring to the boil and then cook on a low heat until the water has been absorbed.

Stir most of the sugar and half of the cinnamon into the cooked rice. Add the milk and mix well. Cook, uncovered, over a low heat until most of milk has been absorbed. Stir occasionally.

Lightly beat the eggs and mix into the rice. Continue to cook for 5 minutes.

Stir in the raisins and turn the rice pudding into a serving dish. Combine the remaining cinnamon with the remaining sugar and sprinkle over the pudding.

Cool and chill before serving, perhaps with fresh raspberries and single cream.

Cream Puffs
Makes 24

Ingredients

65g/2½oz plain flour	**Crème Patisserie**
pinch salt	45ml/1½oz sugar
50g/2oz butter	10g/2tsp cornflour
150ml/¼pt water	15g/1tbsp plain flour
2 eggs	2 eggs
	300ml/½pt milk

Preparation Sift the flour and salt.

Heat the butter and water together until the butter has melted and the water is just about to boil.

Add the flour and stir with a wooden spoon until the mixture forms a ball which leaves the sides of the pan clean. Remove from the heat and leave to cool for 2-3 minutes.

Lightly beat the eggs and stir into the dough. Mix well. It should be just firm enough to hold its shape.

Drop small spoonfuls of dough onto a greased baking sheet and bake for 15 minutes at 220°C/425°F/Gas 7 until well risen and golden brown. Transfer to a wire rack to cool.

Combine the sugar, cornflour and flour. Add one whole egg plus the yolk of the second and mix well.

Heat the milk until it is just about to boil. Pour over the egg mixture and blend well. Return to the pan and cook over a low heat, stirring consantly, until thick.

Leave to cool, stirring occasionally, to prevent a skin forming. To assemble the cream puffs, cut the choux buns nearly in half and place a spoonful of filling in each.

To serve, sprinkle with icing sugar or spread with chocolate icing. Serve immediately.

Variation To make éclairs, pipe the choux pastry onto baking sheets in 8cm/3in lengths. Bake for 20 minutes then cool and fill as above.

To make profiteroles, pile cream puffs in a pyramid and pour chocolate sauce over the top.

Meringue Torte
Serves 8-10

Ingredients

4 egg whites
225g/8oz sugar
600ml/1pt ice cream

*225ml/8fl oz double
cream*
*16 glazed pecans or
walnut halves*

Preparation Whisk the egg whites until they are stiff. Add the sugar, a spoonful at a time, and continue whisking until the meringue is stiff again. Spoon carefully into a piping bag.

Line two flat baking trays with greaseproof paper. Trace a 22cm/9in circle on each. On one tray, pipe the meringue in rings to fill the entire circle. Smooth the surface with a pallette knife (metal spatula).

On the second tray, pipe the meringue in one ring around the inside edge of the circle and then make three parallel lines in each direction to form a lattice.

Bake the meringues in a preheated oven for 30 minutes at 160°C/300°F/Gas 2. Transfer to a wire cooling rack. When the meringues are completely cold, carefully peel off the lining paper. If you are not using them immediately, store in an airtight container.

Several hours before serving the torte, prepare the ice cream and freeze in a 22cm/9in cake tin. If the ice cream is already made, soften slightly, press into a cake and re-freeze until firm.

To assemble the torte, place the meringue circle on a serving dish. Top with a layer of ice cream or several layers of different kinds of ice cream.

Whisk the cream until it is stiff and pile on top of the ice cream. Carefully place the lattice meringue on top of the whipped cream. Press down gently so that the cream oozes through the gaps. Place a nut in each gap and serve immediately.

Variation Add instant coffee, unsweetened cocoa or ground nuts to the unbaked meringue mixture.

Baklava

To make a vacherin, make one solid layer of meringue only and pipe the remaining mixture onto individual baking trays or sheets to make several rings. When they have been baked, place the solid layer at the bottom and pile the rings on top of each other to make a basket.

Make a Swiss meringue and pipe between the layers to seal them and then in vertical lines all around the basket, topping it with a row of rosettes. Bake for 1½ hours until firm. Cool and store until ready for use, then fill with ice cream and top with fresh fruit. Garnish with a fruit sauce.

Baklava
Serves 8-12

Ingredients

225g/8oz sugar
150ml/¼pt water
15ml/1tbsp lemon juice
225g/8oz butter, melted

*24 sheets filo pastry
(bought)*
225g/8oz chopped nuts

Preparation Place the sugar, water and lemon juice in a heavy-bottomed pan. Heat, stirring constantly, until the sugar has dissolved. Increase the heat and boil the syrup for 5 minutes. Leave to cool.

Brush melted butter over the base and sides of a 23×28cm/9×11in roasting tin.

Arrange a layer of pastry over the base of the pan, overlapping to cover the entire surface. Brush with butter and sprinkle with nuts.

Cover with another layer of pastry and repeat the process until you have used all the nuts and pastry. Brush each layer of pastry well with the butter and finish with a layer of pastry.

Cut into diamond-shaped pieces. Bake for 30 minutes at 180°C/350°F/Gas 4 and then increase to 230°C/450°F/Gas 8 for another 15 minutes or until golden. Pour over the syrup and leave to cool before serving.

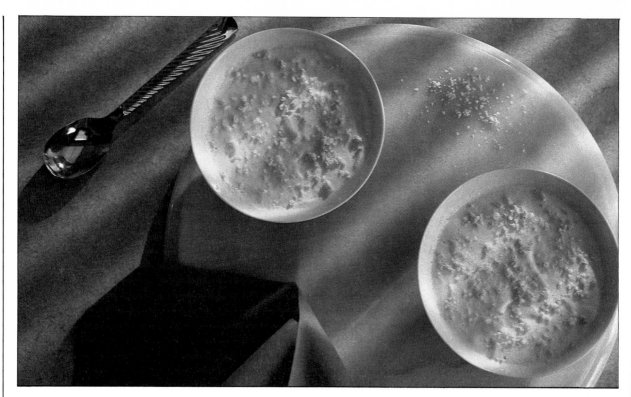

Tortoni
Serves 8

Ingredients
5 eggs, separated
75g/3oz sugar
600ml/1pt double cream

175g/6oz macaroon or
   ratafia crumbs
75ml/3fl oz Marsala or
   sweet sherry

Preparation Beat the egg yolks with the sugar until thick and almost white.

Whisk the cream until it is just starting to thicken. Stir into the eggs. Stir in ¾ of the crumbs and the wine.

Whisk the egg whites until they are stiff but not dry. Gently fold one spoonful into the cream mixture then gradually add the remainder.

Pour the cream into a soufflé dish or individual serving dishes and freeze, stirring occasionally. Remove 15 minutes before serving. Gently pan the remaining crumbs over the surface and press onto the top.

Millefeuilles

One thousand leaves is the literal translation, and it is almost true! For by the time the puff pastry has been rolled, folded and turned half a dozen times, there are more than 700 layers of trapped air and butter dough. This feather-like assemblage needs only the simplest embellishment, and it makes a sumptuous and impressive after-dinner dessert.

Ingredients
450g/1lb Puff Pastry chilled
   (or use a ready-made
   fresh or frozen pastry)

Preparation Roll out the pastry on a chilled, floured surface to 2mm/⅛in thick, and use a sharp knife to cut it into three equal rectangles, 17.5×30cm/7×12in. Leave to chill for at least 1 hour, or overnight if possible.

Heat the oven to 220°C/425°F/Gas 7. Chill a baking sheet under running cold waer and shake off the excess moisture. Transfer one of the pastries to the wet tray, prick all over with a fork to prevent it from puffing too much and bake it in the hot oven for 20 minutes until well puffed and golden. Cool on a wire rack. Prepare and bake the other pastries in the same way.

The uncooked, prepared pastry rectangles may be frozen for up to 2 months. Bake from frozen and allow 5 minutes more baking time.

Basic Yoghurt

Ingredients
1l/2pt milk
30ml/2tbsp unflavoured
   commercial yoghurt at
   room temperature

Preparation Yoghurt can be made in any sterile container with a tightly fitting lid inside any sort of incubator, such as an oven with the pilot light on or a styrofoam box, but because the secret of successful yoghurt-making is a constant lukewarm temperature, it is best to use a special yoghurt maker. Don't put incubating yoghurt near a heat source regulated by a thermostat that switches on and off. Use 30ml/2tbsp of the home-made yoghurt to start the next batch. The cost of making yoghurt at home is minimal and the method is easy.

Scald the milk. Heat it until it is ready to boil. Just before boiling point, remove the pan from the heat and allow to cool until lukewarm. Test by dripping a little milk on your wrist. It should feel warm, not hot.

Put the yoghurt in the chosen container and stir in a little milk until smooth. Now stir in the remaining milk.

Cover and place container in the incubator. Be careful not to disturb the yoghurt for about 4 hours. When the consistency is right, chill in the fridge to set before using.

Preparing Pineapple

The best pineapples available in Europe or North America are not picked until ripe, when they are flown to their destination. They have the central core of leaves intact. Pineapples that ripen on a long sea voyage have their central leaves removed to prevent sprouting during storage.

1 Cut off the top and bottom with a sharp knife. Cut these end slices thickly so what is left is not barrel-shaped but cylindrical.

2 Cut round inside the skin, working first from one end, then the other, until you can push the fruit out in one piece. Try to cut as close to the skin as possible.

3 Slice the fruit and remove the central core with an apple corer if at all woody.

To Pit and Peel Avocado

1 Split the avocado and carefully twist to separate the two halves. Pierce the avocado pit with a sharp knife and twist to extract it.

2 Turn each half of the avocado face down and cut just through the skin from top to tail.

3 Carefully peel back the skin using the knife blade. Gripped firmly with the thumb, the skin should come away without tearing.

Hot Desserts

Baked Alaska   275
Baked Apples with Almonds   275
Baked Bananas   276
Baked Pineapple Rings   276
Hot Curd Cheesecake   276
Crunchy Apple Crumble   276
Fruit Crumble   277
Cinnamon Chocolate Pain Perdu   277
Banana Custard   277
Prune and Noodle Custard   277
Blueberry Buckwheat Pancakes   278
Sweet Rice Fritters   278
Apple Parcels with Coffee Sauce   278
Rich Chocolate Meringue Pie   279
Lemon Meringue Pie   279
Matzo Omelette   279
Sweet Potato Pie   279
Apple Sponge Pudding   280
Banana Choc-Chip Pudding   280
Bread Pudding   280
Brown Rice Pudding   281
Chocolate Semolina Pudding   281
Chocolate Upside-Down Pudding   281
Coffee Bread Pudding   282

Indian Rice Pudding   282
Magic Chocolate Pudding   282
Queen of Puddings   283
Steamed Fruit Pudding   283
Steamed Coffee Pudding   284
Sussex Pond Pudding   284
Upside Down Lemon Pudding   285
Fritters in Syrup   285
Hot Fruit Soufflé   286
Pear Soufflé   286
Chocolate Soufflé   286
Coffee Orange Soufflés   287
Orange Soufflé   287
Lemon and Almond Strudel   288
Apple Strudel   288
Curd Cheese Strudel   288
Apple Tart with Cinnamon Sticks   289
Mincemeat Open Tart   289
Chocolate Syrup Tart   289
Morello Cherry Tart   290
Spiced Apple Tart   290
Switzen Plum Tart   290

Handling Steamed Puddings   291

Baked Alaska
Serves 6-8

Ingredients

900ml/1½pt vanilla or
  chocolate ice cream
3 eggs
75g/3oz sugar
65g/2½oz plain flour
30g/2tbsp unsweetened
  cocoa powder

approx 225g/½lb fruit
  (strawberries, bananas,
  raspberries, or cherries,
  or a mixture)
60ml/4tbsp Marsala or
  sweet sherry
4 egg whites
225g/8oz sugar

Preparation Pack the ice cream into a 450-g/1-lb loaf tin lined with non-stick paper or foil. Freeze overnight.

Put the eggs and sugar into a bowl and whisk until thick and creamy, and the whisk leaves a trail.

Sieve the flour and cocoa together and fold gently into the mixture.

Turn into a greased and lined 23-cm/9-in tin. Bake at 200°C/400°F/Gas 6 for 12-15 minutes. Cook and remove paper.

Prepare the fruit by slicing and removing stones if necessary. Put into a bowl with the Marsala or sherry.

Whisk the egg whites until stiff. Whisk in the sugar a little at a time. Spoon the meringue into a piping bag fitted with a large star nozzle.

Trim the edges of the sponge, then cut 2.5-cm/1-in strips from each of two sides of the cake to make an oblong slightly larger than the ice cream block.

Put sponge on an ovenproof serving dish. Spoon the fruit and juices over the sponge.

Remove the ice cream from the freezer and turn it onto the sponge. Remove the paper or foil.

Quickly pipe the meringue decoratively over the ice cream, covering it completely.

Bake at 230°C/450°F/Gas 8 for 3-5 minutes until lightly browned. Serve immediately.

Baked Apples with Almonds
Serves 4

Ingredients

4 large cooking apples
30g/2tbsp sultanas
5g/1tsp cinnamon
15g/1tbsp ground almonds
10ml/2tsp lemon juice

15ml/1tbsp syrup
25g/1oz butter
4 slices brown bread
4 glacé cherries
24 almond flakes

Preparation Wash the apples and remove the cores, leaving the apples whole. Slit the skins shallowly around the equator to prevent splitting when cooking.

Mix the sultanas, cinnamon, ground almonds, lemon juice and syrup together in a bowl.

Stuff the mixture into the centre of each apple, top with a knob of butter. Cook in the oven at 200°C/400°F/Gas 6 for 40-60 minutes, depending on size.

Toast the brown bread. Arrange on 4 plates with an apple each. Decorate the tops with a glacé cherry and flaked almonds and serve warm. The toast soaks up all the delicious juice.

Baked Bananas
Serves 4

Ingredients
4 bananas, peeled   *20g/4tsp dark brown sugar*
20g/4tsp butter   *20ml/4tsp rum*

Preparation Put each banana on a large square of foil.
Dot with butter and sprinkle with sugar and rum

Fold the foil not too tightly, but seal it well. Bake at
200°C/400°F/Gas 6 for 15 minutes.

Unwrap each banana and arrange on a serving dish.
Top with a scoop of ice cream.

Variation Bake or barbecue the bananas in their skins
and let everyone pour on their own rum.

Alternatively, scatter chocolate buttons over them
before wrapping in foil.

Baked Pineapple Rings
Serves 8

Ingredients
1 large pineapple, sliced in   *30ml/2tbsp Kirsch*
8 rings   *(optional)*
60ml/4tbsp apricot jam

Preparation Arrange the pineapple rings on a large
baking tray. Spread with apricot jam and sprinkle over
the Kirsch.

Bake for 5-10 minutes at 200°C/400°F/Gas 6.

Variation As with Baked Bananas, pineapple rings
can be cooked to perfection on a barbecue. In this
case, spread both sides of the pineapple with jam and
grill for 3-4 minutes on each side.

Hot Curd Cheesecake
Serves

This traditional cake has a yeasty pastry base and is
baked in a rectangular tin. Because the cheese layer is
thin, the flavour is much more concentrated than the
familiar deep cheesecakes.

Ingredients
yeast dough for 2   *2 eggs*
rectangular cake tins   *pinch salt*
21×30×3cm/8×12×   *5g/1tsp lemon zest*
1½in   *65g/2½oz raisins*
100ml/4fl oz double cream   *25g/1oz melted butter,*
50g/2oz caster sugar   *cooled*
375g/13oz curd cheese,
sieved

Preparation Prepare the dough and line the tins.
Leave to rise a second time while you prepare the
filling.

Mix the filling by hand. Stir the cream and caster
sugar into the cheese. Mix in the lightly beaten eggs
one at a time, the salt and lemon zest, and, lastly the
raisins.

Divide the filling evenly between the two tins and
smooth out. Trickle the butter over both surfaces and
bake in the heated oven at 200°C/400°F/Gas 6 till risen
and golden, about 35 minutes. Cut in slices to serve.

This will keep fresh for 2 days. Freeze while still
slightly warm, wrapped in aluminium foil.

Crunchy Apple Crumble
Serves 4

Ingredients
675g/1½lb apples, peeled,   *30-60g/2-4tbsp sugar*
quartered, cored and   *lemon juice*
sliced   *225g/8oz crunchy muesli*
150ml/¼pt water   *25g/1oz butter*

Preparation Poach the apples in a pan with the water,
sugar and lemon juice to taste until just tender. Drain.

Arrange half the cooked apple slices in the bottom
of the baking dish.

Sprinkle on a layer of crunchy muesli, arrange the
remaining apples on top and cover with the muesli.

Dot with butter and bake at 180°C/350°F/Gas 4 for
25 minutes.

Fruit Crumble
Serves 4

Ingredients
675g/1½lb stewed, fresh or poached fruit
150g/6oz wholewheat flour
75g/3oz margarine or butter
15g/1tbsp bran

Preparation Arrange the fruit in the pie dish.

Sprinkle the flour into a bowl, rub the fat into the flour until the mixture resembles fine breadcrumbs. Add the sugar and bran, mixing well.

Sprinkle on top of the fruit and bake at 200°C/400°F/Gas 6 until golden brown, about 30 minutes.

Cinnamon Chocolate Pain Perdu
Serves 4-6

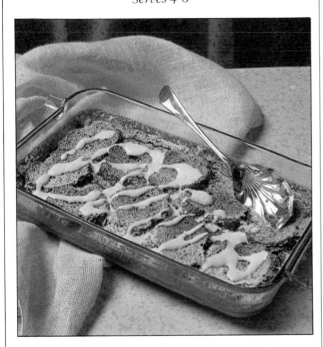

Ingredients
75-100g/3-4 oz butter
12-14 slices French bread
150g/6oz plain chocolate
600ml/1pt milk
2 eggs
2 egg yolks
5g/1tsp ground cinnamon
50g/2oz sugar
icing sugar

Preparation Butter the slices of bread on both sides. Arrange on a baking tray and bake in the oven at 190°C/375°F/Gas 5 for about 5 minutes or until lightly golden. Turn over and bake on the other side until golden.

Melt the chocolate.

Bring the milk almost to boiling point. Remove from the heat and whisk into the chocolate.

Beat together the eggs, egg yolks, cinnamon and sugar. Pour on the chocolate milk and whisk well.

Arrange the baked French bread in a large shallow baking dish. Strain the chocolate custard over the bread.

Put the dish into a roasting pan and pour in boiling water to come half-way up the side of the baking dish.

Cook in the oven for 30-40 minutes until lightly set.

Dredge with icing sugar and serve hot or warm with single cream.

Banana Custard
Serves 6

Ingredients
6 ripe bananas
150g/6oz Demerara sugar
5g/1tsp freshly grated nutmeg
15ml/1tbsp lime juice
125g/5oz fresh breadcrumbs
4 eggs
750ml/1¼pt milk

Preparation Peel and mash the bananas, add half the sugar, nutmeg and lime juice and mix well.

Put the mixture in a buttered dish and top with the breadcrumbs.

Beat the eggs and add the remaining sugar, beating well.

Warm the milk and pour into the egg mixture, stirring all the time. Pour over the banana and crumbs and sprinkle nutmeg on top.

Bake in the oven at 180°C/350°F/Gas 4 until the custard is set and the top golden brown, approximately 35 minutes.

Prune and Noodle Custard
Serves 4-6

Ingredients
300ml/½pt boiling water
150g/6oz dried prunes, stoned
225g/8oz wholewheat macaroni
few drops oil
3 eggs
300ml/½pt milk
30ml/2tbsp honey
5ml/1tsp vanilla essence
pinch nutmeg

Preparation Pour the boiling water over the prunes and leave to plump up overnight.

Cook the macaroni in boiling salted water with the oil, until tender.

In a bowl, beat together the eggs, milk, honey and vanilla with a fork.

Grease an ovenproof casserole and mix the prunes and noodles together in it. Pour over the custard and sprinkle the top with nutmeg.

Bake for half an hour in a preheated oven at 160°C/375°F/Gas 3 and serve hot. This dish is also good chilled.

Blueberry Buckwheat Pancakes
Serves 4

Ingredients

40g/1½oz wholewheat
 flour
40g/1½oz buckwheat flour
pinch salt
1 egg
150ml/¼pt milk
15ml/1tbsp melted butter

Filling
450g/1lb blueberries
60ml/4tbsp honey
whipped cream

Preparation To make the pancake batter, sift the flour and salt into a bowl. Make a well in the middle of it and add the egg.

Gradually beat in the milk. When half of the milk has been added, beat in the melted butter. Continue beating in the milk until you have a thin batter. Allow the batter to stand for half an hour.

Meanwhile, prepare the filling. Wash and pick over the blueberries. Put them in a heavy-bottomed pan over a very low flame. It is best to add no water at all. When the fruit is submerged in its own juice, add the honey and stir until dissolved. The syrup should be thick and fruity.

To cook the pancakes, oil a heavy-bottomed pan 18cm (7in) in diameter. When it is very hot, add 30ml/2tbsp of the batter. Tilt the pan so that the batter covers the base. Cook until the pancake is beginning to brown on the underside and then turn over and cook the other side. You may have to throw the first pancake away, as it will absorb the excess oil in the pan.

Continue making the pancakes, keeping them warm, until all the batter has been used up. Divide the filling between them and roll the pancakes into cigar shapes.

Serve warm, each pancake topped with a dollop of whipped cream.

Sweet Rice Fritters
Makes 25

Ingredients

100g/4oz long grain rice
2 eggs, beaten
50g/2oz caster sugar
few drops vanilla essence
75g/3oz plain flour
15g/1tbsp baking powder

salt
pinch ground cinnamon
50g/2oz desiccated
 coconut
oil for deep frying
icing sugar for dredging

Preparation Cook the rice and cool. Turn it into a bowl, add the beaten eggs, sugar and flavouring. Mix well. Sift in the flour, baking powder, salt and cinnamon with the coconut. Mix thoroughly.

Drop tsps of the mixture into hot oil and cook until golden brown. Cook three or four fritters at a time, draining them on absorbent kitchen paper.

Dredge with icing sugar and serve hot.

Apple Parcels with Coffee Sauce
Serves 4

Ingredients

350g/12oz plain flour
pinch salt
75g/3oz sugar
150g/6oz butter
2 egg, beaten
1 banana, mashed
2 rings pineapple, finely
 chopped
rind of one orange
4 apples, peeled and cored

Sauce
25g/1oz butter
25g/1oz plain flour
150ml/¼pt milk
50ml/2fl oz cooled extra
 strong coffee
150ml/¼pt single cream

Preparation Sift the flour, salt and 50g/2oz of the sugar into a bowl. Rub in the butter until the mixture resembles fine breadcrumbs. Mix to a stiff pastry with the eggs.

Mix together the bananas, pineapple, remaining sugar and orange rind.

Into a saucepan, put all the sauce ingredients, except the single cream, and heat, whisking all the time. When thick, remove from the heat and use a little of the sauce to moisten the fruit filling.

Roll out the pastry to a square. Cut out four circles. Put an apple in the centre of each square and fill with the banana and pineapple mixture.

Brush the edges with water and completely enclose the apple, pressing the joins neatly together.

Put the apple parcels, join side down, on a baking sheet and make a small hole in the centre of each. Decorate with pastry trimmings.

Bake for 30 to 35 minutes on the centre shelf at 220°C/425°F/Gas 7 until golden.

Gently heat the coffee sauce and add the single cream. Do not boil. Serve with the hot apples.

Rich Chocolate Meringue Pie
Serves 6

Ingredients

225g/8oz digestive biscuits
100g/4oz butter

Filling
25g/1oz sugar
25g/1oz plain flour
10g/2tsp cornflour
2 large eggs, separated

300ml/½pt milk
25g/1oz butter
4 oz plain chocolate, finely chopped
10ml/2tsp rum (optional)
100g/4oz caster sugar
ground cinnamon

Preparation Crush the biscuits until they resemble fine breadcrumbs.

Melt the butter and stir into the biscuits. Press the biscuits over the base and sides of a 20-cm/8-in ovenproof flan dish.

Blend together the sugar, flour, cornflour, egg yolks and a little of the milk. Heat the remaining milk.

Stir the hot milk on to the flour mixture and whisk well. Return the mixture to the pan. Heat gently, stirring until the mixture thickens.

Stir in the butter, chocolate and rum if used. Stir until smooth. Pour into the biscuit pie shell. Chill.

About ½ hour before serving, making the meringue topping. Whisk the egg whites until stiff. Whisk in half the sugar, a teaspoonful at a time. Add the remaining sugar and whisk well.

Spread the meringue over the chocolate flan. Swirl decoratively with a teaspoon.

Bake in the oven at 200°C/400°F/Gas 6 for 5-7 minutes, until the meringue is golden brown.

Sprinkle with a little ground cinnamon, and serve hot or warm.

Lemon Meringue Pie
Serves 4-6

Ingredients

zest and juice of 3 lemons
165g/5½oz granulated sugar
75g/3oz unsalted butter, softened and cubed
2 large eggs

22-cm/8½-in square Sweet Shortcrust Pastry, baked blind

Meringue
2 egg whites
100g/4oz caster sugar

Preparation Using a wooden spoon, crush the lemon zest and sugar in a heat-proof bowl. Strain in the lemon juice and add the butter cubes. Set the bowl over a pan of simmering water and leave the butter to melt and the sugar to dissolve.

Meanwhile whisk the eggs in a separate bowl until frothy and strain them into the lemon mixture. Blend all the ingredients carefully and cook slowly, stirring often, until the mixture thickens to a creamy consistency. Draw off the heat, lightly rub a little butter over the surface to prevent a skin forming and set aside to cool.

Pour the lemon curd into the cooled pastry shell and level out. Bake flan at 180°C/350°F/Gas 4 for 10 minutes to set the filling.

Make the meringue. Lift the flan out of the oven and reduce the temperature. Quickly spoon the meringue on to the lemon filling and dredge with caster sugar. Replace the pie in the oven and bake for about 45 minutes at 150°C/300°F/Gas 2 until the meringue peaks are crisp and have turned a golden colour.

Serve warm or cold.

Matzo Omelette
Serves 8

Ingredients

8 plain matzos
12 eggs, beaten
2.5g/½tsp salt
40g/1½pz pine kernels
75g/3oz sultanas
finely grated rind of 1 lemon

25g/1oz butter
100g/4oz sugar
8g/1½tsp ground cinnamon

Preparation Soak the matzos in water for 3-5 minutes or until soft. Drain well.

In a large mixing bowl, combine the softened matzos, eggs, salt, pine kernels, sultanas and lemon rind. Mix well.

Heat the butter in a large heavy frying pan over a low heat. Pour in the omelette mixture and cover.

Cook for 5 minutes or until the omelette is just set. Sprinkle with the sugar and cinnamon.

Fold the omelette in half and serve immediately.

Sweet Potato Pie
Serves 4-6

This recipe is from the Caribbean, so sweet potatoes from a West Indian store should be perfect. The yellower sweet potatoes from the Middle East will work just as well.

Ingredients

1kg/2lb sweet potatoes, peeled and thickly sliced
1 egg, beaten
45g/1½oz margarine
150g/6oz dark soft brown sugar

4g/1 level tsp salt
5g/1tsp ground cinnamon or cinnamon quill, crushed

Preparation Boil the peeled sweet potatoes in lightly salted water until cooked through.

Add the beaten egg and stir well while mixing in all the other ingredients.

Spoon the mixture into a greased shallow baking tin and bake at 180°C/350°F/Gas 4 for an hour.

Cut into squares and serve warm.

Apple Sponge Pudding
Serves 4-6

Ingredients

100g/4oz caster sugar
100g/4oz butter, softened
2 eggs
30ml/2tbsp milk
150g/6oz plain flour
5g/1tsp baking powder

450g/1lb cooking apples or
  Cox's, cut into 5-mm (¼-
  in) slices
30g/2tbsp caster sugar for
  dredging

Preparation Beat the sugar and butter until pale and fluffy. Beat in the eggs one at a time and the milk and blend well. Sift the flour with the baking powder to aerate well, then combine lightly with the main mixture without over-beating.

Pour the mixture into a 20-cm/8-in spring-form tin, greased and lined with silicone paper, and smooth the top. Press the prepared apples into the surface of the mixture in an even pattern.

Bake in a preheated oven at 180°C/350°F/Gas 4 until well risen and golden, about an hour. Test for readiness. Lift the tin out of the oven and dredge the surface with caster sugar.

Remove the cake from the tin, peel off the paper and serve warm or cold with whipped cream on the side.

Banana Choc-Chip Pudding
Serves 4

Ingredients

100g/4oz butter or
  margarine, softened
100g/4oz sugar
2 eggs, beaten
125g/5oz self-raising flour
25g/1oz unsweetened
  cocoa powder
approx 30ml/2tbsp milk
1 small banana, peeled
  and chopped
50g/2oz chocolate chips

Sauce
150g/6oz soft brown sugar
25g/1oz butter
30ml/2tbsp golden syrup
60ml/4tbsp single cream

Preparation Cream the butter or margarine and sugar together until light and fluffy.

Gradually add the eggs, beating well between each addition.

Sieve together the flour and cocoa, and fold into the egg mixture. Add enough milk to give a soft dropping consistency. Stir the banana and chocolate chips.

Turn mixture into a greased 900-ml/1½-pt pudding basin. Cover with greased greaseproof paper and foil, with a central pleat in each. Secure with string. Steam for about 1½ hours.

To make the sauce, put all the ingredients into a saucepan and bring to the boil, stirring.

Turn out pudding and serve with the hot sauce.

Bread Pudding
Serves 8

Ingredients

1 small loaf white bread
225ml/8fl oz milk
150g/6oz sugar
100g/4oz butter or
  margarine, softened
150ml/6fl oz evaporated
  milk

10ml/2tsp vanilla essence
5g/1tsp mixed spice
5g/1tsp cinnamon or
  nutmeg
50g/2oz raisins
30g/2tbsp mixed peel

Preparation Remove the crust from the bread and cut the loaf into chunks. Pour over the milk, stir to make sure all the bread is moist and leave to soak for 20 minutes.

Cream the sugar and butter or margarine until they are light and fluffy.

Add the soaked bread, along with any milk remaining. Beat well.

Stir in the evaporated milk, vanilla and spices and fold in the raisins and mixed peel.

Pour the pudding mixture into a well greased roasting tin or baking dish and bake at 170°C/325°F/Gas 3 for 1 hour and 10 minutes, or until firm to the touch and golden brown.

Serve warm or cold.

Brown Rice Pudding
Serves 4

Ingredients
100g/4oz brown rice	50g/2oz dried apricots,
500ml/1pt China tea	chopped
1 stick cinnamon	50g/2oz almonds
50g/2oz sultanas	sliced fresh fruit (optional)

Preparation Wash the rice thoroughly under running water. Put it in a heavy pan with the tea and cinnamon and simmer gently for about an hour.

Preheat the oven to 180°C/350°F/Gas 4. Remove the cinnamon and transfer the rice to an ovenproof dish. Stir in the remaining ingredients and bake for about 25 minutes. Serve hot or chilled, garnished, if you like, with sliced fresh fruit.

Chocolate Semolina Pudding
Serves 4

Ingredients
600ml/1pt milk	60g/4tbsp semolina (or
30g/2tbsp butter	farina)
30g/2tbsp sugar	
50g/2oz chocolate, plain	
or milk	

Preparation Heat the milk with the butter, sugar and chocolate until the chocolate has melted and the milk has reached boiling point.

Sprinkle in the semolina and cook, stirring constantly, until the pudding thickens.

Pour into one large or several small serving dishes and eat hot or cold.

Variation For Butterscotch Pudding, use brown sugar instead of white, omit the chocolate and add 15ml/1tbsp golden syrup or corn syrup.

For Holyrood Pudding, omit the chocolate and add 10g/2tsp orange marmalade. Sift in 30g/2tbsp ratafia or macaroon crumbs.

To make semolina puddings particularly light, cool slightly and fold in 2 beaten egg whites. The pudding should then be baked for 30 minutes at 150°C/300°F/Gas 2 or steamed for 1¼ hours.

Chocolate Upside-Down Pudding
Serves 6

Ingredients
100g/4oz Demerara sugar	25g/1oz butter, melted
50g/2oz butter, softened	100g/4oz soft brown sugar
4 pineapple rings, fresh or	100g/4oz self-raising flour
tinned	25g/1oz unsweetened
6 walnut halves	cocoa powder
2 eggs, separated	

Preparation Cream together the sugar and butter and spread over the base of a greased 20-cm/8-in cake tin. Arrange the pineapple rings on top, with a walnut in the centre of each.

Beat together the egg yolks and melted butter until creamy.

Whisk the egg whites until stiff. Fold in the sugar and egg yolks mixture.

Sieve together the flour and cocoa and fold in carefully. Pour the mixture over the fruit and spread evenly.

Bake at 180°C/350°F/Gas 4 for about 30 minutes.

Carefully turn out onto a serving dish and serve with pouring custard or single cream.

Coffee Bread Pudding
Serves 6

Ingredients

20 slices day-old bread (crusts removed)
300ml/½pt orange juice
300ml/½pt strong black coffee
2 large eggs
50g/2oz sugar

75g/3oz sultanas
75g/3oz candied orange peel
100ml/¼pt Tia Maria
5g/1tsp ground cinnamon
5g/1tsp ground allspice
25g/1oz butter

Preparation Soak the bread in the orange juice and coffee, then mash to a pulp.

Beat the egg yolks and add them to the mashed bread. Stir in the sugar, sultanas, orange peel, Tia Maria and spices.

Whisk the egg whites until they form stiff peaks and fold into the mixture.

Butter a 1.5-l/3-pt ovenproof dish, pour the mixture into it and dot with knobs of butter.

Bake for 30 minutes at 170°C/325°F/Gas 3 until golden brown.

Indian Rice Pudding
Serves 4

Ingredients

1.2l/2pt milk
90g/3½oz basmati rice, washed
30g/2tbsp sugar
15g/1tbsp raisins

2.5g/½tsp ground cardamom seeds
25g/1½tbsp pistachio nuts, skinned and chopped

Preparation Bring the milk to the boil in a large pan, stirring continuously.

Lower the heat and simmer for 20 minutes. Add the rice and sugar and continue simmering for another 35-40 minutes until the mixture has thickened and reduced to 600ml/1pt. During the cooking time stir occasionally to stop the milk sticking to the bottom of the pan.

Add the raisins and cardamoms and, stirring constantly, cook for a further 3-4 minutes.

Serve hot or cold, garnished with the nuts.

Magic Chocolate Pudding
Serves 4

Ingredients

100g/4oz self-raising flour, sieved
50g/2oz sugar
30ml/2 level tbsp unsweetened cocoa powder, sieved
50g/2oz walnuts, chopped

50g/2oz butter, melted
150ml/¼pt milk
few drops vanilla essence
Sauce
125g/5oz soft brown sugar
30g/2tbsp unsweetened cocoa powder, sieved
210ml/¼pt+4tbsp boiling water

Preparation To make the sponge, put the dry ingredients into a bowl. Add the butter, milk and essence and mix to form a thick batter.

Pour the mixture into a buttered 900ml/1½ pt ovenproof dish.

To make the sauce, mix together the brown sugar, cocoa and boiling water. Pour this sauce over the batter.

Bake in the oven at 180°C/350°F/Gas 4 for about 40 minutes. During cooking the chocolate sponge rises to the top, and a chocolate fudge sauce forms underneath.

Serve hot with vanilla ice cream.

Queen of Puddings
Serves 4

Ingredients

600ml/1pt milk	100g/4oz sugar
50g/2oz butter	100g/4oz fresh
4 eggs, separated	breadcrumbs
1 lemon	60ml/4tbsp jam

Preparation Heat the milk with the butter over a gentle heat until the butter is melted.

Combine the egg yolks with the finely grated rind of the lemon and half of the sugar. Mix well.

Pour the warm milk over the yolks and mix well. Stir in the breadcrumbs.

Pour the pudding mixture into a well greased baking or pie dish. Bake at 180°C/350°F/Gas 4 for approximately 20 minutes, or until the custard has set.

Warm the jam over a very low heat until it has melted. Spread carefully over the baked pudding.

Whisk the egg whites until they are stiff but not dry. Gently fold in the remaining sugar. Spoon or pipe the meringue over the pudding. Be sure that all the edges are well sealed.

Return the pudding to the oven and bake at 150°C/300°F/Gas 2 for 20-25 minutes or until the meringue is brown and crisp.

Steamed Fruit Pudding
Serves 6

Ingredients

50g/2oz plain flour	150g/6oz dates, stoned
5g/1tsp baking powder	and chopped
175g/6oz fresh	150g/6oz dried figs,
breadcrumbs	chopped
100g/4oz shredded suet	150g/6oz raisins
1 orange	2 eggs
2.5g/½tsp mixed spice	30ml/2tbsp rum or brandy
pinch nutmeg	

Preparation Combine the sifted flour and baking powder with the breadcrumbs, suet and finely grated orange rind.

Stir in the mixed spice, nutmeg, dates, figs and raisins.

Lightly beat the eggs with the juice of the orange and the rum or brandy. Add to the flour and fruit mixture. Mix thoroughly so that the whole pudding is moist.

Grease a 900ml/1½pt pudding basin. Put a circle of greaseproof paper in the base. Spoon the pudding into the bowl, but make sure that it is no more than ¾ full. Cover with a buttered circle of greasproof paper, pleated in the middle — this allows the pudding room to rise during cooking. Cover the top of the bowl with a circle of pleated foil and tie securely.

Put the bowl on a trivet or saucer in a pan of boiling water. There should be just enough water to come halfway up the bowl.

Steam the pudding for 4 hours, topping up the water from time to time.

Turn out the pudding and serve with custard, cream or the sauce of your choice.

Steamed Coffee Pudding
Serves 6

Ingredients

125g/5oz dry coffee sponge
   cake
75g/3oz plain chocolate
150ml/¼pt milky coffee
50g/2oz butter
30g/2tbsp vanilla sugar or
   white sugar

2 large eggs, separated
30g/2tbsp powdered
   instant coffee dissolved
   in 15ml/1tbsp hot water
sugar

Preparation Crumble the cake into fine crumbs. Melt the chocolate in a bowl over a pan of gently simmering water. When melted, pour over the cake crumbs. Leave to stand for 30 minutes.

Cream the butter and sugar together until light and fluffy. Beat in the egg yolks. Stir in the soaked crumbs and coffee.

Beat the egg whites until stiff and gently fold into the chocolate and coffee mixture. Spoon into a large buttered pudding bowl — the mixture should only half fill it. Cover with greased foil or double thickness of greasproof paper. Steam for 1½ hours.

Turn out the pudding onto a serving dish, dust with sugar and serve with custard, cream or chocolate sauce.

Sussex Pond Pudding
Serves 8

Ingredients

350g/12oz plain flour
10g/2tsp baking powder
pinch salt
150g/6oz suet or butter
150ml/¼pt milk or water

1 large lemon
100g/4oz unsalted butter
100g/4oz soft brown or
   Demerara sugar

Preparation Sift the flour with the baking powder and salt.

Add the suet or butter and rub together until the mixture resembles coarse breadcrumbs.

Bind the dough with milk or water and knead lightly until smooth but not sticky. Cut into two pieces, one twice as large as the other.

Roll the larger piece of dough until it is big enough to line the base and sides of a 1-l/1-pt pudding bowl. Gently press the dough into the basin.

Cut the butter into small pieces and put half in the bottom of the lined basin. Sprinkle with half of the sugar.

Prick the surface of the lemon all over with a fork so that the juice can flow as the pudding is cooked. Put it on top of the butter and sugar. Sprinkle with the remaining butter and sugar.

Roll out the smaller piece of dough. Lay on top of the pudding and seal well.

Cover the basin with a piece of greaseproof paper and then a large piece of foil. Put in a pan containing enough boiling water to come halfway up the sides of the pudding basin.

Steam for approximately 4 hours. Check the water occasionally and top up — it must not be allowed to boil dry.

Unmould the pudding and serve immediately, either on its own or with custard.

Upside Down Lemon Pudding
Serves 6

Ingredients

75g/3oz butter or
  margarine, softened
100g/4oz sugar
3 lemons

3 eggs, separated
75g/3oz flour
5g/1tsp baking powder
225ml/8fl oz milk

Preparation Cream the butter or margarine with the sugar and finely grated lemon rind until very smooth. Beat in the egg yolks.

Sift the flour and baking powder. Fold into the sugar mixture, alternating with the milk and juice of the lemons.

Whisk the egg whites until they are stiff but not dry. Carefully fold into the pudding batter, starting with one spoonful and gradually adding the remainder.

Grease a deep pie dish, approximately 900ml/1½pt in capacity. Pour the pudding into the dish and bake at 180°C/350°F/Gas 4 for 30 minutes or until firm and golden.

Serve warm or cold with single cream.

Fritters in Syrup
Serves 4-6

Ingredients

200g/7oz plain flour
7.5g/1½tsp baking powder
150ml/¼pt yoghurt
approx. 225ml/8fl oz milk

225g/8oz sugar
450ml/¾pt water
oil for deep frying

Preparation Sieve together the flour and baking powder. Mix in the yoghurt. Add enough milk to make a thick batter.

Boil the sugar and water together for 10 minutes.

Heat the oil in a pan over medium high heat. Drop in 15ml/1tbsp of the batter at a time and fry until crisp and brown. Drain on paper towels, and keep warm.

Soak the fried malpoa in the syrup for 5 minutes. Serve in a little syrup, hot, warm or cold.

Hot Fruit Soufflé
Serves 4

Ingredients

225g/8oz prepared soft fruit
100g/4oz sugar

15ml/1tbsp liqueur
5 egg whites
icing sugar

Preparation Sieve and purée the fruit with the sugar and stir in the liqueur.

Whisk the egg whites until they are stiff but not dry. Fold them into the fruit purée, starting with just one spoonful and gradually adding the remainder.

Turn the soufflé into a greased 1½-2½-pt dish which has been sprinkled with sugar. Bake at 180°C/350°F/Gas 4 for 30 minutes or until well risen.

Sprinkle with icing sugar just before serving.

Variation Substitute chestnut purée for the fruit and use whole eggs. Beat the yolks into the sweetened purée and then fold in the stiffly whisked whites. Bake as described above.

Pear Soufflé
Serves 4

Ingredients

450g/1lb pears
15-30g/1-2tbsp butter
honey

pinch ground cinnamon
3 large eggs, separated

Preparation Preheat the oven to 200°C/400°F/Gas 6.

Peel, halve and core the pears. Cut them into slices.

Chocolate Soufflé

Heat the butter in a pan and add the pear slices. When the fruit has softened, raise the heat a little, break up the fruit with a wooden spoon and cook until mushy.

Put the contents of the pan into a blender. Blend until smooth and add honey and cinnamon to taste. Pour into a bowl and beat in the egg yolks.

Butter a 1.75-l/3-pt soufflé dish. Whisk the egg whites until they form soft peaks and fold into the mixture. Pour into the soufflé dish and bake in the preheated oven for 20-25 minutes until just golden brown and nearly set.

Chocolate Soufflé
Serves 4-6

Ingredients

50g/2oz butter
50g/2oz flour
300ml/½pt milk
75g/3oz plain chocolate, grated

3 eggs, separated
1 egg white
50g/2oz sugar
icing sugar

Preparation Melt the butter in a pan and stir in the flour. Remove from heat and stir in the milk. Return to heat and bring to the boil, stirring. Cook gently for 2 minutes, stirring all the time.

Remove from the heat and stir in the chocolate and egg yolks.

Whisk all the egg whites until stiff. Whisk in the sugar a little at a time.

Fold the chocolate sauce into the egg whites.

Pour the mixture into a greased 1.2-l/2-pt soufflé dish.

Bake for about 40 minutes until well risen and firm. Serve immediately, dredged with icing sugar.

Coffee Orange Soufflés
Serves 6

Ingredients

6 large thick-skinned
  oranges
3 eggs, separated
100g/4oz sugar

15g/1tbsp powdered
  instant coffee
30g/2tbsp cornflour
15ml/1tbsp Cointreau

Preparation With a sharp knife, cut the top from each orange and a thin slice from the base so that they stand upright.

Using a teaspoon or grapefruit knife, gently remove the flesh from the inside. Squeeze the flesh to extract the juice and strain it.

Beat together the egg yolks, sugar, coffee and cornflour. Dilute the orange juice. Put over a low heat and, stirring constantly, bring to the boil. When the mixture has thickened, remove the pan from the heat and stir in the orange liqueur. Cover and leave to cool.

Thirty minutes before serving, whisk the egg whites until they form really stiff peaks and gently fold into the coffee cream.

Spoon the filling into the shells until level. Transfer to an ovenproof dish and bake for 10 to 15 minutes at 220°C/425°F/Gas 7 or until well risen and set.

Serve immediately.

Orange Soufflé
Serves 4

Ingredients

4 large oranges
1 lemon
30g/2tbsp butter
30g/2tbsp plain flour

4 eggs, separated
45g/3tbsp sugar
icing sugar

Preparation Cut the oranges in half crossways and carefully remove the flesh. Squeeze to extract the juice.

Add the juice of the lemon to the juice of the oranges.

Carefully cut strips of peel off half of each orange. Blanch in boiling water for 5 minutes.

Melt the butter in a heavy-bottomed pan. Add the flour and cook, stirring constantly, until all the butter

has been absorbed.

Slowly add in the fruit and juice and peel, stirring constantly, and cook until the sauce thickens and comes to the boil. Simmer gently for 2 minutes.

Whisk the egg yolks with the sugar until they are thick and frothy. Stir into the sauce, off the heat.

Whisk the egg whites until they are stiff but not dry. Gently fold them into the sauce, starting with just one spoonful and gradually adding the remainder.

Grease a 600-ml/1-pt soufflé dish and sprinkle the base with sugar. Pour in the soufflé mixture and bake at 200°C/400°F/Gas 6 for approximately 25 minutes or until well risen.

Sprinkle with icing sugar before serving.

Variations Bake the soufflé in the orange shells allowing 20 minutes to cook.

Stir 1tbsp/15ml of Cointreau or Grand Marnier into the soufflé mixture before adding the egg whites.

To glaze the soufflé sprinkle with icing sugar 2-3 minutes before it has finished cooking.

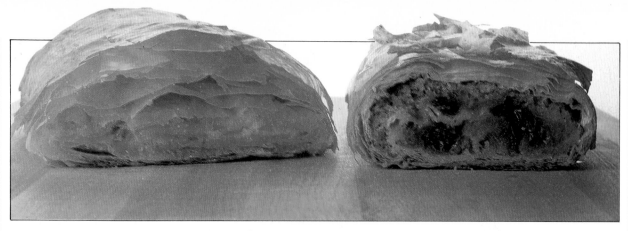

Lemon and Almond Strudel
Serves 8

Ingredients

50g/2oz butter
2 egg yolks
1 whole egg
125g/5oz caster sugar
grated zest of 2 lemons
20ml/1½tbsp lemon juice, strained
2 egg whites
75g/3oz ground almonds
1 recipe Strudel Dough
25g/1oz butter, melted

Preparation Beat two thirds of the butter until pale and creamy. Whisk in the egg yolks one at a time and the whole egg. Beat in 75g/3oz of the sugar and mix in the lemon zest. Set aside.

Beat together the lemon juice and 50g/2oz sugar.

Whisk the egg whites until they stand in firm, snowy peaks and beat the lemon juice and sugar mixture into them until they are thick and glossy.

Melt the remaining butter and brush the strudel dough with some of it. Cover two-thirds with the butter and egg yolk filling. Scatter the ground almonds all over and cover with the lemon and egg white mixture. Roll up the strudel lightly. Brush with melted butter and finish as before.

Bake in a preheated oven at 200°C/400°F/Gas 6 for 30 minutes and serve warm.

Apple Strudel
Serves 8-10

Ingredients

225g/8oz bread flour
1 small egg, lightly beaten
5g/1tsp sugar
pinch salt
15ml/1tbsp melted butter or oil
50ml/2fl oz warm water

Filling

50g/2oz breadcrumbs
50g/2oz butter, melted
450g/1lb cooking apples, peeled and thinly sliced
75g/3oz sugar
50g/2oz sultanas
50g/2oz chopped almonds or hazelnuts

Preparation Sift the flour into a large mixing bowl and make a well in the centre. Add the egg, sugar, salt, and butter or oil. Gradually draw the flour into the centre as you mix.

Gradually add the water to make a soft, sticky dough. Knead the dough until it is smooth and no longer sticky.

Leave the dough to rest for 30 minutes, covered with a bowl or clean cloth.

Sprinkle a cloth-covered table with flour and roll the dough out very thinly to a large circle. Lightly brush with oil or melted butter.

Lift and stretch gently until nearly transparent. Trim off any edges that may still be thick or hard.

Brush the centre of the pastry with melted butter,

Left, Lemon and Almond Strudel; right, Apple Strudel.

leaving a margin of approximately 2.5cm (1in) all the way around.

Brown the breadcrumbs in most of the melted butter remaining and sprinkle over the strudel pastry.

Arrange the apples over the breadcrumbs and sprinkle with sugar. Scatter the sultanas and nuts over the top.

Fold the top, bottom and one long side of the pastry over the filling. Brush the fourth side with the end of the melted butter and place a sheet of greaseproof paper under it.

Roll the strudel towards the unfolded edge. Lift the paper onto a greased baking sheet.

Brush the surface with melted butter and bake at 190°C/375°F/Gas 5 for 30 minutes or until the pastry is crisp and golden.

Serve the strudel warm, sprinkled with icing sugar and accompanied by a bowl of cream.

Curd Cheese Strudel
Serves 4-6

Ingredients

50g/2oz sultanas
15ml/1tbsp rum
100g/4oz butter, softened
75g/3oz caster sugar
4 egg yolks
325g/11oz curd cheese, sieved
50ml/2fl oz sour cream
5g/1tsp lemon zest
1 recipe Strudel Dough or 12 sheets filo pastry
25g/1oz butter, melted

Preparation Soak the sultanas in the rum for 30 minutes to plump them. Beat three quarters of the butter and the sugar until light and fluffy. Beat in the egg yolks one at a time. Mix in the cheese, sour cream and zest.

Brush the dough with some of the melted butter. Spread the filling over two-thirds of the pastry and sprinkle with sultanas and rum. Using the cloth to help, roll the pastry loosely over the filling; tuck in the ends carefully, so that the filling cannot leak out, and transfer to a large, greased baking sheet, seam side down.

Brush with more melted butter and bake in the preheated oven at 200°C/400°F/Gas 6 for 30 minutes until crisp and well-browned. Serve warm or cold dredged with icing sugar.

If using filo pastry, use six sheets at a time. Brush one sheet with melted butter and cover with a second sheet of pastry; brush with more melted butter and continue layering and brushing with butter with the remaining layers. Place half the cheese filling in the middle and roll up in the same way as for strudel. Finish with the rest of the filo sheets in the same way.

Apple Tart with Cinnamon Sticks
Serves 4-6

Ingredients

75g/3oz butter or margarine	**Filling**
150g/6oz plain flour, sifted	5 eating apples, sliced
15g/1tbsp sugar	25g/1oz butter
approx 50ml/2fl oz cold water	20g/1½tbsp Demerara sugar
	7.5-cm/3-in cinnamon stick, broken
	1 egg
	50ml/2fl oz double cream

Preparation First make the pastry by rubbing the margarine into the flour and sugar, then add enough water to form a ball.

Line a 20-cm/8-in flan dish with the pastry. Cover with a piece of greaseproof paper or foil. Fill with baking beans and bake at 200°C/400°F/Gas 6 for 20 minutes.

Cook the apples, butter, sugar and cinnamon until the apples are soft.

Drain the apples, reserving the juice. Lay the apples in the baked pastry case.

Mix together the egg, cream and reserved juice. Pour the mixture over the apples.

Bake for 20 minutes, until just set.

Mincemeat Open Tart
Serves 4

Ingredients

1 recipe Wholewheat Shortcrust Pastry	60-90g/4-6tbsp mincemeat
	8 glacé cherries

Preparation Make the pastry and allow to rest in the refrigerator before using.

Roll it out about 0.75cm (⅛in) thick to fint a 20cm/8in ovenproof plate.

Lift the pastry on to the plate and press into the sides. Do not stretch. Trim leftover pastry with a sharp knife, cutting at an angle of 45° away from the edge of the plate. If you cut edges angled into the plate, the edge will shrink.

Cut diagonally across the edge of the plate every 2.5cm (1in). Fold the pastry back to form a triangle. Remove folded pastry.

Roll remaining pastry to make six even strips.

Spoon in the mincemeat and twist the pastry strips across the tart decoratively. Decorate each square with a halved glacé cherry and bake for 20-25 minutes.

Serve hot with cream or custard.

Chocolate Syrup Tart
Serves 8

Ingredients

225g/8oz plain flour	45ml/3tbsp golden syrup
30g/2tbsp icing sugar	(or corn syrup)
225g/8oz butter	225g/8oz sugar
a little water	5ml/1tsp vanilla essence
100g/4oz plain chocolate	
3 eggs	

Preparation Sieve the flour and icing sugar into a bowl. Rub in 125g/5oz of the butter until the mixture resembles fine crumbs.

Add enough water to mix to a stiff dough, then roll out pastry and use to line a 23-cm/9-in pie tin.

Put the remaining butter and the chocolate into a saucepan. Stir over gentle heat until melted and blended.

Beat the eggs, syrup, sugar and essence together. Stir in the chocolate mixture.

Pour the filling into the pastry case. Bake in the oven at 180°C/350°F/Gas 4 for about 40 minutes, until the top is crunchy and the filling just set. (It should still be slightly sticky inside.)

Serve warm with scoops of vanilla ice cream.

and two-thirds and roll out the smaller piece to fit a 20-cm (8in) tart plate or dish, leaving it to rest for a few minutes. Lift up the pastry using the rolling pin as an aid, and line the plate with it. Trim the edge and prick all over with a fork.

Spoon the cold apple mixture into the shell, mounding it high in the middle and leaving a wide border of pastry all round the rim of the dish. Moisten the pastry rim with water. Roll out the remainder of the pastry and lay it on top of the apple filling. Pinch and crimp the two pastry edges well together, trim the sides and decorate with leftover scraps of pastry. Make two small cuts in the middle of the crust to allow the steam to escape.

Put the tart plate on a hot baking sheet in the oven and bake at 200°C/400°F/Gas 6 for 10 minutes then reduce the heat to 180°C/350°F/Gas 4 and bake until golden, about 40 minutes. Dredge the top generously with the mixed sugar and ground cinnamon.

Serve hot or cold with whipped cream or custard on the side.

Variations Other fillings are made with rhubarb, gooseberries, blueberries, blackberries — they also taste splendid mixed with apples — and blackcurrants. These soft fruit do not need pre-cooking.

Morello Cherry Tart
Serves 6

If morello cherries are unavailable, bitter or well-flavoured dark cherries will do.

Ingredients

150g/6oz plain flour, sifted	*675g/1½lb fresh or bottled*
pinch salt	*morello cherries*
65g/2½oz butter, cut in	*75g/3oz walnuts, ground*
pieces	*5g/1tsp lemon zest, grated*
10g/2tsp caster sugar	*25g/1oz vanilla sugar*
1 egg yolk	*50g/2oz caster sugar*
50ml/2fl oz sour cream	*1 egg white, lightly beaten*
20g/2tbsp toasted	*30g/2tbsp walnuts,*
breadcrumbs	*chopped*

Preparation Sift the flour and salt into a bowl, drop in the butter pieces and blend to a crumb texture. Mix in the sugar. Add the egg yolk and enough sour cream to make a firm paste. Knead well, divide in two and wrap in plastic film. Chill.

Roll out each piece large enough to fit a 24-cm/9½-in spring-form tin. Line the base and sides of the tin with silicone paper, grease well and lay a sheet of pastry on the bottom; scatter over half the breadcrumbs.

Wash and dry the cherries and remove the stones. If using bottled fruit, drain well and dry on paper towels. Mix the fruit in a bowl with the ground walnuts, lemon zest and vanilla sugar, and spread the mixture on the breadcrumb base in the tin.

Sprinkle with the rest of the breadcrumbs and the caster sugar and cover with the remaining piece of pastry. Brush with egg white and scatter the chopped walnuts all over the top. Bake in a preheated oven at 180°C/350°F/Gas 4 for an hour until slightly coloured.

Serve either warm or cold, with whipped cream on the side.

Spiced Apple Tart
Serves 4-6

Ingredients

Sweet Shortcrust pastry for	*90ml/6tbsp water*
a 20-cm (8in) tart plate	*5cm/2in cinnamon stick*
or dish	*2.5g/½tsp ground nutmeg*
Filling	*75g/3oz castor sugar*
450g/1lb Bramley, Cox's or	*15g/1tbsp sugar*
Golden Delicious apples	*2.5g/½tsp ground*
15g/½oz butter	*cinnamon*

Preparation Peel, core and slice the apples thickly. Put them in a pan with the cinnamon stick, butter and the water. Bring to a simmer then stew until tender. Draw off the heat, stir in the sugar and nutmeg and leave to cool. Remove the cinnamon stick.

Meanwhile make the pastry. Divide it into one-third

Switzen Plum Tart
Serves 6

Switzen plums usually appear in mid-autumn. They have deep purple skins and firm green flesh, and their slightly tart taste blends exceptionally well with the sweet-and-sour pastry. No other plum will really replace them, but if you cannot obtain them, be sure to choose a variety that has a good strong flavour.

Ingredients

125g/5oz plain flour, sifted	*450g/1lb Switzen plums,*
85g/3½ oz butter, cut in	*stoned*
pieces	*25g/1oz caster sugar*
15g/1tbsp caster sugar	**Topping**
1 egg yolk	*1 egg yolk*
pinch salt	*40g/1½oz caster sugar*
approx 15ml/1tbsp sour	*75ml/3fl oz sour cream*
cream	*2 egg whites*
10g/1tbsp toasted	*25g/1oz plain flour*
breadcrumbs	
10g/2tsp ground	
cinnamon	

Preparation Combine the flour with the butter pieces and rub to a fine crumb texture. Toss in the sugar. Mix in the egg yolk, salt and enough sour cream to blend it all to a firm smooth paste. Roll into a ball, wrap in plastic film and chill in the refrigerator for 1 hour.

Roll out the pastry and line the base of a 24-cm/9½-in spring-form tin. Prick all over with a fork. Scatter the mixture of breadcrumbs and cinnamon over the pastry and cover with a close layer of plums. Dredge with sugar.

To prepare the topping, beat the egg yolk and half the sugar until creamy and pale, and mix in the sour cream. Whisk the egg whites until firm, then beat in the rest of the sugar until the mixture is satiny and smooth. Fold the egg snow and spoonfuls of sifted flour alternately into the main mixture. Spoon over the top of the plums and level out. Bake until well risen and golden.

Dredge with icing sugar to serve and eat either warm or cold.

Handling Steamed Puddings

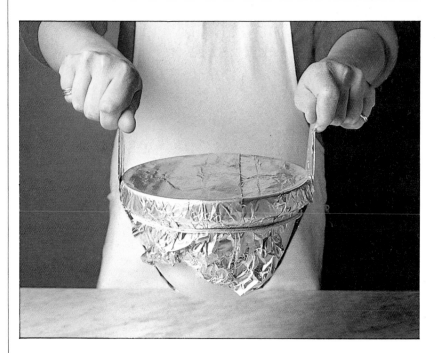

Traditional English sweet and savoury puddings (particularly suet puddings) are cooked by steaming. The food is cooked in a container heated by steam. This gives the suet mixture its distinctive soft, open texture. The easiest way to cook the pudding is to put its container in a saucepan with hot water that comes half way up the sides of the container. The pan is covered and cooked over a low heat to steam gently for a long time, and water is added to the pan as necessary. Take care to put a band of folded foil under the basin with ends projecting up the sides to act as handles.

Cakes, Biscuits, Pastries and Breads

Puff Pastry   293
Sweet Shortcrust Pastry   293
Shortcrust Pastry   293
Yoghurt Pastry   294
Soured Cream Pastry   294
Cheese Pastry   294
Fondant Icing   294
Glacé Icing   294
Thick Chocolate Icing   295
Soft Chocolate Icing   295
Whipped Chocolate Cream   295
Crème Pâtissière   295
Cooked Egg Yolk and Buttercream   295
Basic Buttercream   296
Basic Classic Meringue   296
Italian Meringue   296
Strudel Dough   297
Yeast Dough and Yeast Sponge Batter   297
Chocolate Caraque   297
Buttermilk Spice Cake   297
Spice Cake   298
Engadiner Nusstorte   298
Gâteau Pithiviers   298
Orange, Mousseline Gâteau   299
Le Succès   300
A Light Pound Cake   300
Gàteau des Rois   301
Banana, Peach and Almond Loaf   301
Simnel Cake   302
Sandtorte   302
'Plumb Cake'   303
Coffee Sponge with Rum   304
Dark Almond Cake   304
Walnut Torte   304
Linzetorte   304
Punschtorte   305
Orangen Torte   305
Habsburger Torte   306
Dobostorta   307
Acacia Honey Cake   308
Hazelnut Torte   308
Hunyady Chestnut Torta   308
Russian Cream Cake   309
Sachertorte   309
Black Forest Kirschtorte   310
Baumkuchen   310
Bienenstich   311
Hobelspänne   311
Schraderpuffer   312
Mohrenkopf   312
Truffel Torte   312
Carrot Cake 313
Raisin Chocolate Fudge Cake   313
Poppy Seed or Walnut Roll   314
Streusselkuchen   314
Frankfurter Kranz   35
Sunshine Cake   315
Chocolate Roulade   316

Mushroom Cake   322
Chequerboard Cake   322
Banana Cake   322
Chocolate Meringue Gâteau   323
Family Chocolate Cake   323
Lemon and Clove Cake   323
Russian Seedcake   323
Coffee Knots   324
Yeasted Crescents   324
Eliza Leslie's Ginger Cup Cakes   324
Doughnuts   325
Chocolate Ring Doughnuts   326
Spiced Buttermilk Scones   326
Muesli Scones   326
Blueberry Muffins   327
Bran and Sultana Muffins   327
Madeleines   327
Raspberry Chocolate Eclairs   328
Maids of Honour   328
Brownies   329
Triple Decker Squares   329
Chocolate Meringues   330
Butterfly Cakes   330
Jaffa Cakes   330
Chocolate Chip Cookies   331
Chocolate Malties   331
"Christmas Pudding" Cakes   331
Danish Pastries   332
Chocolate Boxes   332
Sweetheart Cookies   333
Chocolate Spiced Biscuits   333
Cinnamon Stars   333
Coffee Macaroons   334
Nun's Pretzels   334
Vanilla Crescents   335
Flapjacks   335
Scottish Shortbread   335
Ginger Snaps   335
Florentines   336
Cheese Shortbreads   336
Sesame Snaps   336
Oatcakes   336
Rye Biscuits   337
Hazelnut and Apricot Crunch   337
Coffee Slices   337
Cherry Chocolate Crunch   337
Anise Cookies   338
Langues de Chat   338
Chocolate Pinwheels   338
Viennese Chocolate Biscuits   339
Birnbrot   339
Bishop's Bread   340
Cornish Saffron Bread   340
Poori   340
Naan   341
Wholewheat Bread   341
Almond Loaf   341
Garlic Milk Loaf   341

Gugelhupf 316
Lardy Cake 316
Red Velvet Cake 317
Chocolate Chip Cake 318
Coffee Almond Slice 318
Chocolate Rum Cake 319
Coffee Carrot Cake 319
Chocolate and Sour Cream Marble Cake 320
Mocha Hazelnut Cake 320
Coffee Fruit Loaf 321
Refrigerator Biscuit Cake 321

Pitta Bread 342
Yom Kippur Bread 342
Austrian Bagels 342
Challah 342

Making a Flan Case 343
Beating Strudel Paste and Making Apple Strudel 344
Making Processor Pastry 345

Puff Pastry
For 450g/1lb pastry

Always use unsalted butter for puff pastry, *never margarine.*

Ingredients
200g/7oz strong plain flour, sifted
2.5g/½tsp salt
25g/1oz unsalted butter, softened
2.5ml/½tsp lemon juice
75-125ml/3-4fl oz chilled water
175g/6oz unsalted butter, chilled

Basic dough Sift the flour and salt into a large bowl. Cut in 25g/1oz softened butter and work together with the flour to a fine crumbed texture. Add the lemon juice and most of the water, and knead lightly into a firm dough; if it is too stiff, add more water. Gather into a ball and flatten slightly. Score the top crosswise with a knife. Close cover and leave to chill in the refrigerator for 2 hours.

Wrapping in the butter The work-surface must be chilled to the same temperature as the ingredients. Use a marble slab or place a bag of ice-cubes on the work-top beforehand. Lay the cold butter between two large sheets of plastic film and lightly bat it with a rolling pin into a flattened, pliable 15cm/6in square.

Lightly flour the work-top and the rolling pin. Unwrap the chilled pastry and bat it two or three times to soften it slightly, then roll it out on the floured top into a 30cm/12in square. Place the square of butter in the centre of the pastry square and wrap over the pastry sides to envelop it completely. Make sure that all the seams are well sealed by pressing gently with the rolling pin.

Rolling and folding the dough Always keep the work-top and rolling pin lightly dusted with flour, but brush away any excess. Always roll away from you.

Lay the rolling pin across the dough about 2cm/1in from the edge; never roll over the ends as the butter and trapped air may be squeezed out. Lightly roll the dough into a rectangle about 15×30cm/6×12in. Fold over and overlap each end into a square. This is the first fold. Turn the pastry by making a quarter turn to the right, so that the open ends are parallel to the rolling pin. Roll the pastry away from you as before and fold again into a square. This is the second fold. Turn the pastry another quarter turn and make a slight indentation in the side that is to be rolled next.

Carefully wrap the dough in plastic film and chill for 15-20 minutes. It is essential to allow the dough to rest so that it may relax and stretch when it is rolled. Lightly bat the dough two or three times to start it moving, then roll, fold and turn it twice more. Indent, wrap and chill again. Repeat this sequence once more and chill for 30 minutes.

In all, you have made six folds and turns. The dough is now ready for use.

Raw puff pastry keeps in the freezer for up to 6 months. Defrost in the refrigerator overnight. If it has been finished for baking there is no need to defrost it; simply increase the basic baking time by about 5 minutes.

Raw puff pastry can be kept in the refrigerator, closely wrapped, for 3-4 days.

Sweet Shortcrust Pastry
For a 20-22-cm/8-8½-in tin

Ingredients
100g/4oz plain flour, sifted
pinch salt
40g/1½oz caster sugar
2.5g/½tsp baking powder
1 egg yolk
90g/3½oz butter, softened

Preparation by hand Sift the flour and salt into a mound on the work-surface. Make a well in the centre and drop in the sugar, lemon zest and egg yolks. Working with the tips of the fingers, lightly and quickly draw in a little flour from the edges and toss to combine until the sugar is absorbed. Add the butter pieces and blend all the ingredients together into a crumbly texture. Gather the pastry into a ball, it does not matter if butter pieces are still visible, and blend it on the work-surface by pushing away small portions of dough at a time, using the heel of the hand. Form the dough into a ball, wrap it in plastic film or aluminium foil and chill for at least 30 minutes before using.

Shortcrust Pastry

Ingredients
100g/4oz flour
pinch of salt
50g/2oz butter or a mixture of butter and margarine
approx. 30ml/2tbsp cold water

Preparation Sift the flour and salt into a bowl. Cut up the butter and crumble it into the flour. Mix in just enough water with a knife to make a firm dough and gather it into a ball. On a floured surface, knead the dough gently until smooth. Wrap it in plastic wrap and refrigerate for a short while to firm.

To line a pie plate, roll out the pastry on a floured surface to a thickness of 3-6mm/⅛-¼in and about 5cm/2in bigger than the pie plate. Grease the pie plate and lay the pastry gently in it, pressing it down to fit the bottom and sides. Prick the bottom lightly and leave to rest in a cool place for 30 minutes.

Using an electric food processor The butter should be chilled before use so that the pastry is less likely to be overworked and lose elasticity, which makes it tough.

Drop the flour, salt, lemon zest and chilled butter cubes into the processor bowl. Blend for 10-15 seconds to a fine crumb texture; coarse lumps mean that it has been over-blended. Drop in the egg yolk and blend for a further 10 seconds until it forms a compact ball. Wrap and chill overnight.

Yoghurt Pastry

Ingredients

100g/4oz butter or   *175g/6oz flour*
    margarine, cut into   *5g/1tsp baking powder*
    small pieces   *75ml/3fl oz yoghurt*

Preparation Combine the butter, flour and baking powder, rubbing them together until the mixture is like fine breadcrumbs. Add the yoghurt and stir it in well. Gather the pastry together and knead it gently. Refrigerate it for an hour or more. Use as required.

This recipe makes a nice shortcrust pastry, suitable for sweet or savoury pies.

Soured Cream Pastry

Ingredients

300g/10oz flour   *15ml/1tbsp rum (optional)*
200g/7oz butter or   *30ml/2tbsp sour cream*
    margarine   *75g/3oz caster sugar*
1 egg

Preparation Rub the flour and butter together. Mix in the remaining ingredients to make a firm dough. Knead well and let it rest for half an hour before using.

This is excellent for any pie or tart that requires a sweet pastry. You can make delicious cookies from any trimmings when using the pastry (or make some specially for cookies).

Cheese Pastry

Ingredients

225g/8oz curd cheese   *225g/8oz flour*
100g/4oz butter   *5g/1tsp baking powder*
100g/4oz margarine

Preparation Mix the cheese and fats together and rub them into the flour and baking powder. Refrigerate for a minimum of 3 hours.

This pastry can be used to make sweet tarts, Danish pastries, strudels.

For a strudel, roll out and spread with chopped apples, jam, raisins, crushed cornflakes and sugar. Roll up and bake.

For individual pastries, cut pastry into squares measuring about 5cm/2in. Fill with apricot jam, finely chopped apples with raisins, or cheese filling. Either fold over to make a triangle or bring the corners together in the middle. Brush with beaten egg and bake at 180°C/350°F/Gas 4 for 30 minutes.

It may seem surprising that curd cheese can make a light pastry, but it does.

Fondant Icing
For 450g/1lb icing

This is not as complicated to prepare as it first seems, and it does keep fresh for several months. If you make a large quantity it will always be on hand when you need it. Half the quantity is enough to cover a 22-24cm/8½-9½in cake.

Ingredients

450g/1lb granulated sugar   *2.5ml/½tsp lemon juice,*
140ml/5fl oz water   *strained*

Preparation Pour the water into a heavy-based pan, or unlined copper sugar boiler; add the sugar and lemon juice. Heat gently until the sugar has all dissolved, then bring to the boil and cook briskly until the syrup reaches the 'soft ball stage' (115°C/240°F), when ½tsp of the mixture dropped into a cup of cold water will form a soft ball; 2-3 minutes of boiling. Pour the syrup straight on to a cold wet marble slab or wet work-top and leave to cool for 1 minute.

Using a wooden spatula or metal scraper, work all round the syrup, lifting it from the edges and slapping and folding it over into the middle. It will change from a clear, transparent syrup to a dense, creamy mass.

The syrup will now be cool enough to handle. Continue working — it will set hard otherwise — kneading and punching by hand, and folding in the same way as one handles dough. After about 10 minutes it should look matt white and feel smooth and firm.

Wrap in plastic film and leave to rest for 1 hour; or store in the refrigerator.

The fondant must be softened before use. Place the amount you need in a heat-proof bowl and stir it over a pan half-filled with simmering water; in this instance the water may come up the sides of the bowl. Warm very gently and add just a little tepid water (about 30ml/2tbsp is enough for 250g/9oz fondant), for an unperfumed flavour. When the fondant mixture has the texture of thick cream it is ready for instant use.

To colour the fondant, add a drop of vegetable colouring. For a spirituous flavour, use kirsch, dark rum or Grand Marnier instead of the water.

Strained lemon juice or orange juice gives a good citrus tang, while 10ml/2tsp coffee essence or 15g/1tbsp coffee powder dissolved in 1tsp boiling water gives coffee flavouring. For chocolate flavour add 30g/2tbsp cocoa powder, or melt 40g/1½oz chocolate and mix it with the thinned fondant. Fondant handles in much the same way as Glacé Icing.

Glacé Icing
Makes enough vanilla icing for a 20-22cm/8-8½in cake

This simple icing is easy to prepare but a little tricky to handle. You have to work fast as it dries very quickly.

Glacé icing starts to crack after about 4 days.

Ingredients

200g/7oz icing sugar,   *4 drops vanilla essence*
    sifted
30-45ml/2-3tbsp water,
    almost boiling

Preparation Sieve the icing sugar into a small, heat-proof bowl; make a well in the middle and gently and gradually stir in the water and vanilla essence using a wooden spoon. Avoid adding too much liquid at once or the icing will be too thin and runny. It should be smooth and thick, and creamy enough to coat the back of the spoon. If too thin, add more sugar; if too thick, add more liquid.

Set the bowl over a pan of simmering water, making sure that the base does not touch the water, and gently warm the icing so that it runs more easily when it is poured on the cake. Use straight away.

Flavourings Use the liquid flavourings instead of water.
Orange 15-30ml/1-2tbsp orange juice, strained.
Lemon 30-45ml/2-3tbsp lemon juice, strained.
Punch 15ml/1tbsp orange juice, 2.5ml/½tsp lemon juice, 30ml/2tbsp rum.
Rum 45ml/3tbsp rum, 15ml/1tbsp water.
Coffee 10g/2tsp coffee powder dissolved in 40ml/2½tbsp water.
Chocolate 10g/2tsp cocoa powder dissolved in 40ml/2½tbsp water.
Liqueur 30ml/2tbsp liqueur (kirsch, Grand Marnier, Tia Maria, etc), 15ml/1tbsp water.

Thick Chocolate Icing
Makes enough for a 22-24cm/8½-9½in cake

Ingredients
100g/4oz plain chocolate
7.5g/½tbsp unsalted butter
165ml/5¼fl oz water
90g/3½oz granulated sugar

Preparation Melt the chocolate and butter together with 1tbsp of boiling water in a heat-proof bowl set over simmering water. Draw off the heat and stir to blend. Put the water in an unlined copper sugar boiler or heavy-based pan, add the sugar and boil to the 'thread stage'; dip a pair of scissors into the mixture and when the blades are opened, the syrup will form a thin thread between the points. Stir the chocolate liquid straight into the syrup and replace the pan on the heat. Boil gently for 5 minutes when the icing will have thickened. Test a few drops on a plate — it should feel sticky. Pour the icing straight over the apricot-glazed cake, tipping the wire rack back and forth so that the icing runs all over the top. Do not use a spatula on the surface, but smooth more on the sides. Decorate with fruits and nuts immediately, although piped decorations should be applied when the chocolate icing has cooled completely. The icing will set with a high gloss but will dull a little after 24 hours. The cake may then be stored in the refrigerator without spoiling.

Soft Chocolate Icing
Makes enough for a 22-24cm/8½-9½in cake

Ingredients
100g/4oz plain chocolate
40g/1½oz unsalted butter, cut in pieces
30ml/2tbsp water
75g/3oz icing sugar, sifted

Preparation Melt the chocolate in a bowl set over simmering water. Stir in the icing sugar and the butter and continue stirring until the butter has melted and the mixture is smooth. Remove from the heat and add the water, 1tbsp at a time. Use while lukewarm.

Whipped Chocolate Cream

Ingredients
250g/9oz plain, dessert chocolate
225ml/8fl oz double cream
5cm/2in vanilla pod, split
15ml/1tbsp coffee liqueur or dark rum

Preparation Break the chocolate into small pieces and drop them in a pan with the cream and vanilla seeds. Set the pan on a low heat and, stirring all the time, melt the chocolate and bring the mixture to the boil. Draw off the heat immediately. Pour the mixture into a large bowl and leave to cool, stirring from time to time to prevent a skin forming. When cool, add the liqueur or rum and beat vigorously until the mixture lightens and doubles in volume. Use immediately as the filling hardens very quickly.

Crème Pâtissière

Ingredients
250ml/9fl oz milk
4cm/1½in vanilla pod, split
30g/2tbsp cornflour
2 egg yolks
100g/4oz unsalted butter, softened
50g/2oz icing sugar, sifted
15ml/1tbsp rum or kirsch (optional)

Preparation Reserve 45ml/3tbsp of milk. Bring the rest of the milk and the vanilla pod to the boil, draw off the heat and leave to infuse for 10 minutes. Whisk the cornflour and egg yolks with the cold reserved milk. Remove the vanilla pod from the hot milk and stir the milk into the egg mixture. Pour the batter back into the pan and reheat the custard until it has thickened. Set aside to cool. Beat the unsalted butter and the icing sugar until light and fluffy, then whip in the cold custard a tablespoon at a time. Mix in the spirit or kirsch if used. Chill for at least 30 minutes. The custard may be kept in the refrigerator for 2-3 days or frozen for up to 1 month.
Chocolate and coffee flavour Melt 100g/4oz plain chocolate with 5g/1tbsp instant coffee powder and 15ml/1tbsp water. Leave to cool. Blend into the finished custard.

Cooked Egg Yolk and Buttercream

Ingredients
100g/4oz granulated sugar
100ml/3½oz water
225g/8oz unsalted butter
5 egg yolks
5cm/2in vanilla pod, split

Preparation Dissolve the sugar in the water in a heavy-based pan over gentle heat, then boil briskly to the thread stage (110°C/225°F: see Thick Chocolate Icing). Lightly beat the egg yolks in a bowl and slowly pour on the sugar syrup; continue whisking until the mixture has cooled and is light and fluffy. Mix in the seeds of the vanilla. Beat the butter in another bowl and beat in the egg mixture a spoonful at a time. Leave to cool before before beating in the flavour of your choice.
Chocolate and coffee flavour Melt and cool 100g/4oz plain chocolate. Dissolve 5g/1tsp coffee powder in ½tsp boiling water. Stir together well before blending with the finished cream.

Mocha flavour Replace the water in the main recipe with very strong, fresh black coffee. Proceed as above. Add 15ml/1tbsp rum.

Rum, kirsch or Grand Marnier flavour Adding 30ml/2tbsp of any one of these liqueurs will give a good strong punch!

Basic Buttercream

Ingredients

3 egg yolks
75g/3oz icing sugar, sifted
200g/7oz unsalted butter, softened

Preparation Combine all the ingredients and the chosen flavour together and beat until well blended and smooth. Chill for a short time.

Flavourings 40ml/2½tbsp fresh lemon or orange juice, strained *or* 2½tbsp liqueur, spirit or eau de vie (Grand Marnier, rum or kirsch); *or* 5g/1tbsp coffee powder dissolved in ½tsp boiling water; *or* 100g/3½oz plain chocolate, melted and cooled; *or* 15g/1tbsp cocoa powder.

Basic Classic Meringue
Makes a 20cm/8½in flat disc of meringue

Ingredients

2 eggs
100g/4oz caster sugar

Preparation Carefully separate the egg whites from the yolks, and drop them into a large spotlessly clean bowl.

Lightly whisk the egg whites until they are foamy. Continue whisking more vigorously until the egg whites have expanded into firm creamy peaks about three times their original volume.

Sift half the sugar into the mixture and beat until it is smooth and shiny.

Gently fold in the rest of the sugar in two stages, using a large metal spoon.

Tip the meringue onto silicone paper and lightly smooth it out. Using a metal spatula, gently coax it into a circular disc about 2cm/¼in deep, taking care not to flatten it or lose the air that has been beaten into it. Smooth the surface lightly. Dry out immediately in a low oven (140°C/275°F/Gas 1). It will take anything from 1½to 3 hours to dry, depending on the size, and it will turn a very pale coffee colour.

Test for readiness by gently tapping the underside of the meringue. If it sounds slightly hollow, it is ready; if not, leave to bake a little longer.

Meringues may be kept for several weeks wrapped in aluminium foil and stored in a dry, cool place.

Variation Gently fold unsweetened cocoa, instant coffee or ground nuts into the meringue before baking.

Italian Meringue

Ingredients

100g/4oz caster sugar
65ml/2½fl oz water
2 egg whites

Preparation Stir the sugar in the water over a medium heat until it has dissolved. Boil for 5 minutes. Whisk the egg whites until they are stiff but not dry.

Slowly pour the hot syrup over the egg whites, whisking constantly, until the meringue is thick and has cooled completely.

Spoon or pipe the meringue onto greased baking sheets lined with greaseproof paper.

The mixture is somewhat easier to make than Classic Meringue, goes further because the syrup makes it expand, and produces a slightly softer meringue.

Bake in a preheated oven at 120°C/250°F/Gas ½ for 1 hour. If the meringues are not completely dried out, continue baking for 30 minutes longer.

Variation Gently fold unsweetened cocoa, instant coffee or ground nuts into the meringue before baking.

Italian Meringue can also be mixed with whipped cream or pastry cream and served as a topping/filling for baked meringues or cream puffs.

Strudel Dough

Ingredients

25g/1oz butter or 45ml/	*pinch salt*
3tbsp vegetable oil	*1 egg*
200ml/7fl oz water	
300g/11oz strong plain	
flour	

Preparation Place the butter or oil and water in a small pan and heat gently until the butter has melted. Set aside.

Sift the flour and salt two or three times and finally on to a pastry board. Make a well in the centre, drop in the egg and the lukewarm butter and water. Blend in the flour and knead gently at first, for the dough will be rather sticky, but continue kneading until it comes cleanly off the fingers and the board. Wash your hands in between and dust with more flour if necessary. Continue working and kneading the dough for about 15 minutes until it is smooth and elastic and air bubbles start to develop. Roll it into a ball, place on a freshly floured corner of the board and brush with melted butter. Cover with a warm bowl and leave to rest for 15-20 minutes.

It is simplest to roll out and stretch the dough on a table so that you can work round all the sides.

Cover the table with a large, clean cloth dusted heavily with flour. Place the dough in the centre, pat it into a square and roll it out thinly. Brush with more melted butter if it starts to dry out.

Flour your hands and place them under the pastry, backs uppermost and thumbs tucked out of the way. If two people can work, so much the better, otherwise lay the rolling pin on the other end of the pastry to stop it slipping. Working from the middle outwards, gently pull the pastry and stretch it evenly until it is paper thin and almost transparent. Gently drop the dough down on the floured cloth, move around and start working on the next side; continue until the whole piece of pastry is evenly stretched. Cut away the thicker edges. Leave to dry for a few minutes, then brush with melted butter before filling.

Yeast Dough and Yeast Sponge Batter

Yeast pastries are usually prepared in three stages: an initial batter sponge, followed by two rising or proving periods. The dough is covered at these times and set in a warm, draught-free place. An airing cupboard is ideal, or above the oven. The dough should be left to rise in a large mixing bowl; remember it must increase to about double the volume. A large, lightly oiled plastic bag may also be used.

To make a yeast sponge batter Warm the liquid to blood heat (80°F/25°C) as stated in the recipe and pour it into a jug or bowl. Crumble over the fresh yeast and stir. Add 5g/1tsp of sugar and about a quarter of the flour in the recipe and beat until smooth. Cover and leave to ferment for about 10 minutes. It should bubble and expand in volume to about twice the size. Make sure that the yeast has completely dissolved. If there is little or no action after about 20 minutes, the yeast is old. Throw it away and start with a new batch.

Note When the yeast has been incorporated with the other ingredients, the dough needs considerable beating and kneading to encourage the yeast activity and to give lightness and a fine texture. At first it will be rather sticky and difficult to handle, but the more it is worked the less sticky it will become. Finally it will detach itself entirely and roll off the sides of the bowl into a smooth, silky and elastic mass, showing large bubbles of air. At this point the dough is covered and left for its first proving.

When the dough has doubled in bulk it is knocked back — the air is punched out of it and it is kneaded for a minute or two longer. The remaining enriching ingredients, such as nuts, dried and crystallized fruits, are usually added at this stage. The dough is finished and placed in the warmed, buttered and floured baking utensil, and left for a further, shorter period of proving. It is then baked in a hot oven. See the individual recipes for temperatures.

Chocolate Caraque

Melt and spread some cooking or plain chocolate on a cool work surface to a thickness of about 3mm/⅛in. Using a sharp pointed, long-bladed knife, place it on the surface of the chocolate. Hold the tip of the knife securely in one place. Holding the knife at a slight angle, scrape in a quarter circle movement to produce long, thin slightly cone-shaped curls.

Buttermilk Spice Cake

Ingredients

300g/10oz flour	*5g/1tsp ground cinnamon*
225g/8oz sugar	*2.5g/½tsp ground cloves*
8g/1½tsp bicarbonate of	*100g/4oz butter, melted*
soda	*350ml/12fl oz buttermilk*
5g/1tsp baking powder	*2 eggs*
pinch salt	

Preparation Sift the dry ingredients together. Add the butter and buttermilk and beat the mixture until it is smooth.

Pour the batter into a greased and floured 20cm/8in cake tin and bake in a preheated oven 180°C/350°F/Gas 4 for 40 minutes.

Spice Cake

Ingredients

225g/8oz butter or soft
  margarine
140g/5oz white sugar
140g/5oz dark soft brown
  sugar
4 eggs, separated
350g/12oz plain flour

15g/1tbsp baking powder
10g/2tsp ground allspice
10g/2tsp ground
  cinnamon
5g/1tsp ground nutmeg
225ml/8fl oz water

Preparation Cream the butter or margarine with the sugars, then beat in the egg yolks, one at a time.

Sieve together the dry ingredients and gradually add to the creamed mixture, alternating with the water.

Beat the egg whites until stiff and gently fold them into the mixture.

Turn the mixture into a well-greased 22.5-cm/9-in square pan and bake in a preheated oven at 190°C/375°F/Gas 5 for 40 minutes.

Cook the cake for 10 minutes then turn out onto a wire rack.

Engadiner Nusstorte

This Swiss cake orginates in the Engadin, a region famous for its pastry chefs.

Ingredients

Sweet Shortcrust Pastry for
  a 24cm/9½in spring-
  form tin
Filling
250g/9oz granulated
  sugar
225g/8oz walnuts,
  coarsely chopped

300ml/½pt double cream
15ml/1tbsp honey
50g/2oz candied orange
  and lemon peel, chopped
1 egg white, lightly beaten

Preparation Make the pastry and chill it while you prepare the filling. Cook the sugar in a large heavy-based frying pan over low heat, and stir until it turns to a pale golden caramel.

Drop in the walnuts, stir and coat them well with the syrup for 2-3 minutes. Pour on the cream. Combine well and mix in the honey and candied fruits. Set aside to cool.

Roll out two-thirds of the pastry and line the base and 5cm/2in up the sides of the greased cake tin. Brush with the egg white. Spread the cooled filling evenly over the base and lift up and fold the surplus edge of pastry over the top of the filling all round the edges. Brush with water.

Roll out the rest of the pastry to cover the walnut filling and lay it on top of the filling, making sure that the sides stick well. Prick the pastry lid all over with a fork, which is traditional.

Bake at 180°C/350°F/Gas 4 for 1 hour, until just coloured; if necessary, cover with foil towards the end of the cooking time. Allow to mature for 3-4 days before cutting. Keeps well for at least 1 month.

Gâteau Pithiviers

Pithiviers is a small town, some 80 kilometres south of Paris, which has gained world renown for the delicious pastry named after it.

Ingredients

450g/1lb Puff Pastry or
  ready-made fresh or
  frozen pastry
1 egg, lightly beaten

Almond Paste
65g/2½oz ground almonds
65g/2½oz caster sugar
50g/2oz butter, softened
1 egg yolk, lightly beaten
30ml/2tbsp dark rum

Preparation First make the almond paste, a day ahead if possible. Mix together the ground almonds and sugar and beat to a smooth paste with the butter and egg. Beat in the rum. Cover and leave to chill and harden.

Reserve two-thirds of the puff pastry, wrap in plastic film and leave in the refrigerator. Roll the remainder on a floured board, into a 20cm/8in circle. Trim the edge cleanly with a sharp knife. Run cold water over a large, flat baking sheet to moisten it and shake off the excess. Transfer the pastry circle to it, cover and chill for 30 minutes.

Smooth the hardened lump of almond paste over the pastry to within 2.5cm/1in of the edge, and lightly brush water on the border. Roll out the remainder of the pastry to twice the thickness of the base, and trim the edges cleanly, as before. Carefully fold the pastry circle over the rolling pin and lay it on top of the almond filling.

Press all round the edge firmly to seal the two layers together. Using a sharp, pointed knife dipped in hot water, cut a scalloped border. Cover and chill for 30 minutes.

Brush all over the tart top with beaten egg, cut a hole in the centre and insert a small, buttered aluminium foil chimney in it. Brush a second coat of egg glaze all over.

The decoration is distinctive and traditional. Using a pointed knife, cut into the pastry about 2mm/⅛in deep. Inscribe lines radiating from the middle to the scalloped edge in a curved half-moon shape. Prick right through the pastry to the baking sheet in about six places.

Bake in the preheated oven at 230°C/450°F/Gas 8 for 15 minutes then reduce the temperature to 200°C/400°F/Gas 6 and bake for a further 30-40 minutes.

About 10 minutes before the cooking time is complete, sprinkle the top of the cake generously with sifted icing sugar and return the cake to the oven for it to caramelize.

The cooked cake should have puffed right up into a dome and be golden in colour. Lift out of the oven, remove the foil chimney and leave to cool on the baking sheet set on a wire rack.

Gâteau Pithiviers

Orange Mousseline Gâteau

Orange Mousseline Gâteau

This sponge, known as *biscuit de savoie*, has a light, airy texture. The method of beating egg whites separately before folding them into the main mixture helps give air, and the potato flour gives a fine nutty flavour.

Ingredients

130g/4½oz icing sugar, sifted
15g/1tbsp orange zest
6 egg yolks
50g/2oz plain flour
50g/2oz potato flour

3 egg whites
45ml/3tbsp Grand Marnier or Curaçao
Orange Fondant Icing
candied orange peel for decoration

Preparation Whisk the sifted sugar and orange zest with the egg yolks until light and foamy. Sift together the two flours to aerate them well. Whisk the egg whites in a separate bowl until they stand in firm peaks. Alternatively fold in the egg whites and sift the flours into the yolk mixture in three separate stages. Fold in 30g/2tbsp of the liqueur.

Grease and line a 22cm/8½in springform tin with wax paper. Butter, then dust the paper with sugar and flour, pour in cake mixture and bake at 170°C/325°F/ Gas 3 for 40 minutes.

When the cake has risen well and is springy to the touch, place on a wire rack.

Weigh out 225g/½lb fondant icing and flavour with 15ml/1tbsp liqueur.

Decorate with candied orange peel while still soft. Leave to set overnight.

Le Succès

Grind the hazelnuts for this recipe yourself, as the flavour is far better and they should be a little coarse.

Ingredients

260g/9½oz ground toasted hazelnuts
275g/10oz caster sugar
30g/2tbsp plain flour
6 egg whites
30g/2tbsp Vanilla Sugar (see note)

1 portion Cooked Egg Yolk and Buttercream Filling flavoured with chocolate
1 whole toasted hazelnut for decoration

Preparation Cover three baking sheets with greaseproof paper. Draw the chosen shape on each.

Mix together 165g/5½oz hazelnuts, 140g/5oz sugar and the flour; set aside. Whisk the egg whites in a large, spotlessly clean bowl until they hold firm, snowy peaks. Beat in the rest of the sugar and vanilla sugar until the mixture is firm and glossy. Using a large metal spoon, lightly fold in the nut, sugar and flour mixture. Divide the mixture evenly between the three baking sheets and level out, taking care not to break down the delicate aerated structure. Because of the nut content the succès bases rise little.

Bake them in the preheated oven at 150°C/300°F/Gas 2 for about 1 hour until lightly coloured; they will feel slightly soft to the touch while warm but become crisp and brittle as they cool. Leave on the papers to cool on wire racks.

Prepare the chocolate buttercream filling. (If it has been previously chilled, bring to room temperature for an hour before it is needed.)

To assemble the cake trim the meringue bases to the same size. Place one on a wire rack. Spread one-third of the buttercream over it and cover with the second layer. Smooth over half the remaining cream and place the last meringue on top.

Cover the top and sides of the cake with the remaining cream. Press the last of the hazelnuts all round the side of the cake. Place one whole hazelnut in the centre.

Transfer to a serving dish and chill for at least 3-4 hours or, if possible, overnight. The top may be piped with a chocolate buttercream decoration if wished.

Note To make vanilla sugar, put a whole vanilla pod cut into pieces into a close-stoppered jar filled with caster sugar. Top up the jar with more sugar as it is used. The pod will keep fresh for up to a year.

A Light Pound Cake

Pound cake is an equal-weight cake, in which each of the main dry ingredients weighs the same as the eggs. It originated centuries ago and was highly spiced, flavoured and perfumed, and filled with seeds or dried fruits.

Ingredients

250g/9oz butter
250g/9oz caster sugar
5cm/2in vanilla pod, split
5g/1tsp lemon zest
4 large eggs (250g/9oz)

130g/4½oz plain flour
130g/4½oz potato flour
5g/1tsp baking powder
5ml/1tsp orange-flower water
15ml/1tbsp dark rum

Preparation Cream the butter and half the sugar until light and fluffy. Beat in the seeds of vanilla pod and the lemon zest. Beat in, one at a time, one whole egg and the three yolks.

Sift together two or three times the flours and baking powder; then lightly beat 45g/3tbsp at a time into the butter and sugar mixture, taking care not to over-beat.

Whisk the egg whites in a separate bowl until they are firm, and beat in the rest of the sugar until the mixture looks satiny and smooth. Lighten the main mixture by beating in 2-3 spoonfuls of the meringue, then tip the rest and gently fold in using a large metal spoon.

Use a deep 20-22cm/8-8½in cake tin, a gugelhupf mould, a guttered mould or a 1kg/2lb loaf tin. Butter well and dust with flour. Pour in the cake mixture and smooth level. Make a slight hollow in the middle. Bake in the warmed oven at 180°C/350°F/Gas 4 for 1¼ hours until well risen and golden brown. Leave to cool in the tin for 10 minutes before turning out on to a wire rack. Dredge with icing sugar before serving.

Pound cake keeps fresh for at least a week.

Variations This basic pound cake is quite simple, but it may be enriched in a variety of exciting ways.

Try a mixture of dried fruits — apricots (soaked in water for 2-3 hours, then dried and chopped), sultanas and raisins weighing 275g/10oz altogether; you need two 1-kg/2-lb loaf tins for this.

Mixed candied orange, citron and lemon peel also tastes good. Chocolate and ginger make the cake rich and spicy. Pour half the cake mixture into a gugelhupf mould, and to the remaining mixture add 30g/2tbsp cocoa powder, 5g/1tsp ginger powder and 50g/2oz preserved ginger chopped small. Blend the mixture well and spoon it on to the first quantity in the tin; gently drag a fork through it to give a marbled effect.

A favourite version is one incorporating fresh fruits. Choose any seasonal firm fruits, but avoid soft or citrus ones: plums, grapes, apples, cherries, rhubarb, apricots and pears are all good. You will need about 750g/1½lb stone fruits, 500g/1lb others.

Wash, dry, peel and core or remove the stones. Pour half of the cake mixture into the tin and cover with a layer of fruit; spoon over the rest of the cake batter and cover with the remaining fruit. The baking time will be a little longer, and the cake will not keep for more than about 5 days.

Gâteau des Rois
Twelfth Night Cake

In France, where it originated, there is a charming custom connected with the Twelfth Night cake, for each one contains either a small porcelain figure, a silver coin or, in the past, a bean. The intention is that, when the cake is cut, the person whose slice contains the token is crowned king or queen for the night. It then falls to him or her to entertain the guests in their own home and offer in turn, yet another gâteau des rois. In this way the entire month of January becomes a merry extension of the Christmas festivities.

Ingredients

330g/11½oz strong, plain flour	1 egg, lightly beaten
75g/3oz caster sugar	45g/3tbsp coffee sugar crystals or preserving sugar
100ml/3½fl oz water heated to blood heat	
15g/1tbsp fresh yeast	15ml/1tbsp strained apricot jam
75g/3oz butter, softened	
3 eggs	50g/2oz candied angelica, lemon and orange peel, cut in strips
10g/2tsp lemon zest	
5g/1tsp salt	
1 dried haricot bean or silver coin	50g/2oz glacé cherries

Preparation Make a Yeast Sponge Batter with 65g/2½oz flour and 5g/1tsp sugar taken from the main recipe and the water and yeast. Beat well, cover and set aside to rise.

Beat the butter and the rest of the sugar until pale and creamy, beat in the eggs one at a time and the lemon zest.

Sift the flour and salt two or three times and finally into a large bowl. Make a well in the middle and drop in the butter mixture. Draw in a little flour from the sides and add the yeast batter. Mix all the ingredients thoroughly and beat hard; it should be quite a limp dough but elastic and shiny with large bubbles of air.

Cover the bowl with a clean towel and leave it overnight in the cool kitchen or larder to rise and at least double in bulk.

Next day, turn out the dough on to a floured surface, knock it back and knead in the dried bean or silver coin for a few moments. Pinch off pieces of dough and make six hazelnut-sized balls; set them aside.

Cut off two-thirds of the remaining dough and roll it into a rope about 55cm/22in long; curve it round into a circle and pinch the ends firmly together. Transfer to a large (26cm/10½in), well-buttered ring mould and carefully brush the top only with beaten egg.

Divide the remaining dough into two and roll each piece into a rope a little longer than the first one. Lightly twist the two together into a braid and carefully lay it in a circle on top of the egg-washed ring. Pinch the ends well to secure them.

Brush a dab of egg on the base of each reserved dough ball and space them equally apart on the braided ring. Lightly cover the crown with a floured cloth and leave to rise for 45-60 minutes until risen to about double in bulk.

Brush all the surfaces lightly with egg and scatter over the sugar crystals. Bake in the preheated oven at 190°C/375°F/Gas 5 for 20-30 minutes until golden brown.

While the cake is still warm, brush the top with strained apricot jam and stick the candied fruits and cherries on the surface to resemble jewels in a crown.

Banana, Peach and Almond Loaf
Makes 1 loaf

Ingredients

225g/8oz wholewheat flour	5g/1tsp bicarbonate of soda
50g/2oz wheatgerm	pinch salt
50g/2oz dried peaches, chopped	30ml/2tbsp honey
40g/1½oz almonds, chopped	30g/2tbsp molasses or dark soft brown sugar
10g/2tsp baking powder	2.5ml/½tsp vanilla essence
	3 small bananas, mashed
	1 egg, beaten

Preparation Preheat oven to 180°C/350°F/Gas 4.

Mix the dry ingredients together in a large bowl. Mix the remaining ingredients together thoroughly in another bowl, then combine the two and stir well.

Tip into a greased and floured loaf tin, 22×10cm (9×4in), and bake for about 50 minutes, or until a toothpick inserted in the middle of the loaf comes out cleanly.

Allow to cool for 15 minutes, then tip out of the tin and cool completely on a wire rack before cutting.

Eat it on its own or spread with butter or cream cheese.

Simnel Cake

The richly fruited simnel cake that we know today originated in the late 1600s. It was baked for Mothering Sunday, which falls in mid-Lent and gave a welcome break from the Lenten fast.

Ingredients

175g/6oz butter	**Marzipan layer**
175g/6oz light, muscavado sugar	350g/12oz ground almonds
4 large eggs, separated	350g/12oz icing sugar, sifted
40g/1½oz ground almonds	10ml/2tsp orange-flower water
15ml/1tbsp dark rum	3 drops bitter almond essence
200g/7oz plain flour	3 egg yolks
10g/2tsp mixed spice	30ml/2tbsp apricot jam
250g/9oz currants	1 egg yolk for finishing
165g/5½oz sultanas	
130g/4½oz candied orange and lemon peel	

Preparation Make the marzipan first. Combine the almonds and icing sugar in a bowl, add the flower water, almond essence and egg yolks, and knead to a smooth firm paste. Roll into a ball, wrap and chill.

Prepare a deep 20cm/8in loose-bottomed cake tin, line with greaseproof paper and butter.

Beat the butter and sugar until light and fluffy, beat in the eggs one at a time, add the almonds and rum. Sift the flour and spices together, then lightly mix about one-third of it into the egg batter. Combine the dried fruits and candied peels.

Whisk the egg whites in a clean bowl, until they stand in firm peaks and lightly fold them into the main mixture, alternating with siftings of flour and portions of dried fruits and peels. Pour half the mixture into the prepared baking tin.

On a board dusted with sifted icing sugar roll one-third of the marzipan into a circle 18cm/7in in diameter. Lay it on top of the cake mixture in the tin and press down lightly. Pour on the remainder of the batter, smooth level and make a small hollow in the centre.

Set the cake tin on a baking tray and bake in the preheated oven at 170°C/325°F/Gas 3, reducing the heat to 150°C/300°F/Gas 2 after 2 hours. Cover the cake with two sheets of greaseproof paper to prevent the top from browning too much. Bake for a further ½ hour until it starts to shrink away slightly from the sides of the tin. Test with a skewer for readiness. Leave in the tin to settle for 15 minutes then turn out on to a wire rack to cool.

To finish the cake heat 30ml/2tbsp apricot jam with the same amount of water until thickened. Strain and cool. Brush the apricot on the top of the cake only.

Roll out the remaining marzipan to fit the top of the cake, and trim neatly. Make 12 small balls with the left-over scraps. Lightly press the squared mesh of a wire rack into the marzipan layer; fix the marzipan balls on the edge of the cake with a dab of beaten egg yolk. Brush the whole of the surface with egg yolk.

Push the cake under a hot grill and toast the marzipan for 3-4 minutes to a golden colour but watching all the time so that it does not burn.

The cake keeps fresh in an airtight tin for up to 2 months. Dredge a little icing sugar over just before serving. Serve on Easter Day with a glass of sweet white wine or a hock; or on Mothering Sunday in the traditional manner.

Simnel Cake

Sandtorte
Sandcake

Sandtorte is related to pound cake but the method of preparation is quite different. The mixture has to be beaten for a considerable time so that when it has been baked the texture is fine and sand-like. Potato flour gives added refinement with a powdery dense texture and a sweet, nutty flavour.

Ingredients

165g/5½oz butter	2.5g/½tsp lemon zest
165g/5½oz caster sugar	165g/5½oz potato flour, sifted
1 egg	pinch baking powder
3 egg yolks	2 egg whites
15ml/1tbsp rum	

Preparation Gently melt the butter in a small pan, taking care not to let it brown. As it starts to bubble, draw the pan off the heat and carefully pour the clear liquid into a small mixing bowl, leaving the thick sediment in the bottom of the pan. Allow to cool.

As it starts to solidify, set the bowl on a bed of ice-cubes and beat the clarified butter for 10 minutes by machine (20 minutes by hand) until it is very thick and almost white. Transfer the butter to a large bowl.

Add the sugar, egg and egg yolks a little at a time, making sure that the mixture never becomes runny, and beat for a further 15 minutes. Slowly add the rum, beating all the time, then the zest.

Sift the flour and baking powder and fold in half but do not over-blend. Whisk the egg whites until they are stiff and fold them into the main mixture in three stages, alternating with siftings of flour.

Pour into a greased and floured 1kg/2lb loaf tin and smooth out. Bake in the preheated oven at 170°C/325°F/Gas 3 for 1 hour. Turn out of the tin to cool on a wire rack. Dredge with icing sugar to serve. Keeps fresh for up to a week.

'Plumb Cake'
A Rich Fruit Cake for Christmas

Ingredients

300g/11oz currants
300g/11oz raisins
140g/5oz orange and lemon candied peels, chopped
60ml/4tbsp sherry or madeira wine
60ml/4tbsp brandy
350g/12oz unsalted butter
225g/8oz soft brown sugar, light or dark
5 large egg yolks
140g/5oz ground almonds
5ml/1tsp orange-flower water
285g/10½oz plain flour
10g/2tsp baking powder
5g/1tsp ground cloves
5g/1tsp ground nutmeg
5g/1tsp ground cinnamon
pinch ginger powder
3 large egg whites

Decoration

90ml/6tbsp apricot jam
250g/9oz pecan or walnut halves
140g/5oz glacé cherries
50g/2oz crystallized angelica or other candied fruits of your choice

Preparation Mix the dried fruits and peel with the sherry and brandy and leave to soak for 1 hour while you prepare the other ingredients.

Line the base and sides of a deep, loose-based 20-22cm/8-8½in cake tin with two layers of brown or greaseproof paper, and finish with a third sheet of greaseproof standing with a 5cm/2in high collar above the side of the tin. Grease well with butter.

Beat the butter and sugar until light and fluffy. Beat in the egg yolks one at a time, mixing well between each addition. Beat in the ground almonds and orange-flower water.

Sift the flour with the ground spices and baking powder and set aside. Whisk the egg whites in a clean bowl until they stand in firm, snowy peaks, then fold about one-third into the main mixture with alternate siftings of the flour and spices. Continue until all is incorporated, but avoid over-beating.

Mix in the dried fruits and liquids until well blended.

Pour the mixture into the prepared cake tin; smooth the surface and make a hollow in the middle so that it will bake flat.

Place the tin on a flat baking sheet that has been lined with two sheets of brown paper to give added protection, and bake in the preheated oven at 150°C/300°F/Gas 2 for 1½ hours. Reduce the temperature to 140°C/275°F/Gas 1 and bake for a further 3-3½ hours. If the top appears to be browning too much, cover it with a sheet of brown paper. Test the cake for readiness.

Leave the cake to cool in the tin, set on a wire rack. Strip off the papers the following day and wrap in clean paper before storing in an airtight tin.

For a strong spirituous flavour, the cake may be un-wrapped and fed with 10ml/2tbsp of brandy weekly.

Variation It is traditional to cover a Christmas cake with a layer of marzipan (see Simnel Cake recipe) and decorate it with a coating of white royal icing. The following decoration is more unusual – you may lay it on a base of marzipan too if you like.

Heat the apricot jam with 45ml/3tbsp water and cook until thickened. Strain.

Place the cake on a wire rack. Brush apricot jam all over the top of the cake. Embed the prepared fruits and nuts in a random pattern. Finish by brushing more apricot jam over all the fruits and nuts, to give a high sheen.

When the apricot coating has set, tie a wide ribbon or paper frill around the cake and place it on an elegant plate or silver board to serve.

The cake should be stored in an airtight tin and will keep fresh for several weeks.

cinnamon, makes it quite special. The secret of its success lies in the long but essential period of beating during preparation.

Ingredients

65g/2½oz butter	5ml/1tsp lemon juice
4 hard-boiled egg yolks	1 whole egg
250g/9oz unblanched almonds, ground slightly coarse	1 egg yolk
	2.5g/½tsp cinnamon powder
250g/9oz caster sugar	25g/1oz plain flour
5ml/1tsp lemon zest	

Preparation Cream the butter and mix in the hard-boiled egg yolks; beat well. Add the remaining ingredients and beat the mixture very thoroughly for about 15 minutes by machine (30 minutes by hand). Pour into a greased and floured 22cm/8½in spring-form tin and bake in the preheated oven at 180°C/350°F/Gas 4 for 1 hour until risen and well browned. Place the tin on a wire rack and unmould after 10 minutes to finish cooling. The cake will keep fresh for several weeks. Serve it in small slices as it is very rich and delicious.

Walnut Torte

Ingredients

4 eggs, separated	10g/1tbsp toasted breadcrumbs
100g/4oz caster sugar	15g/1tbsp cocoa powder
225g/8oz ground walnuts	5g/1tsp coffee powder
50g/2oz ground almonds, unblanched	

Preparation Beat the egg yolks and sugar until pale, creamy and well expanded. Mix the walnuts with the almonds, breadcrumbs and cocoa and coffee powders and blend well with the egg yolk mixture. Whisk the egg whites until they are firm and beat 60g/4tbsp into the main mixture to lighten it. Carefully fold in the rest of the egg snow. Pour the batter into a buttered and breadcrumbed 22cm/8½in spring-form tin and bake immediately at 180°C/350°F/Gas 4 for 50 minutes. Leave to cool in the tin for 10 minutes before turning out on to a wire rack.

Dredge with icing sugar to serve. For a more elaborate occasion, brush with warm strained apricot jam and cover with a coffee or chocolate flavoured Fondant or Glacé Icing. Decorate with a few walnut halves while the icing is still warm.

Linzertorte
Jam Tart

Until the Sachertorte ousted it from popularity, Linzertorte was a favourite Austrian cake for festivals and celebrations during the eighteenth and nineteenth centuries. Almonds, the main ingredient, were coveted in early times and brought as valuable trading cargo from the east along with spices.

Ingredients

160g/5½oz plain flour, sifted	5g/1tsp ground cinnamon
200g/7oz butter	10g/2tsp lemon zest
200g/7oz caster sugar	3 egg yolks
200g/7oz unblanched almonds or toasted hazelnuts, ground slightly coarse	15ml/1tbsp lemon juice
	250g/9oz raspberry or redcurrant jam
	egg yolk for brushing on top

Coffee Sponge with Rum

An airy, light coffee sponge with a rich alcoholic tang.

Ingredients

25g/5tsp instant coffee powder	140ml/5fl oz double or whipping cream
4 eggs, separated	30ml/2tbsp single cream
65g/2½oz caster sugar	30g/2tbsp caster sugar
5cm/2in vanilla pod, split	30-45ml/2-3tbsp Tia Maria or dark rum
50g/2oz ground almonds	
30g/2tbsp plain flour, sifted	

Preparation Dissolve the coffee powder in 1½tsp boiling water and leave to cool. Beat the egg yolks and sugar until thick, pale and creamy. Beat in the seeds of vanilla, ground almonds and about two-thirds of the coffee liquid.

Whisk the egg whites until they stand in firm, snowy peaks and fold them into the main mixture in two stages, alternating with siftings of flour.

Pour the batter into a buttered, flour- and sugar-dusted 22cm/8½in spring-form tin and bake at 180°C/350°F/Gas 4 for 30 minutes until well risen and brown. Leave to settle in the tin for 10 minutes before turning out to cool on a wire rack.

Whip the cream to hold soft peaks and beat in the sugar, remaining coffee liquid and liqueur.

Split the cooled cake in half and spread half the cream on the base. Cover with the top layer and smooth over the rest of the cream. Decorate with chocolate coffee beans and grated chocolate. Chill before serving.

Dark Almond Cake

The unusual proportions in the blend of ingredients give this cake a rather crunchy, chewy texture, and the flavour of the raw almonds, combined with lemon and

Linzertorte

Preparation Sift the flour on to the work-top and make a well in the middle. Cut in the butter and blend together to a fine crumb texture. Mix in the sugar, ground nuts, cinnamon and lemon zest. Combine to a smooth pastry with the egg yolks and lemon juice.

Blend the dough, roll into a ball, wrap in plastic film and chill for 1 hour.

Roll out half the pastry on a floured board and line the base and 1cm/½in up the sides of an ungreased 24cm/9½in spring-form tin or flan tin.

Prick the base all over with a fork and spread a thick, even layer of jam over the base. Roll out the rest of the pastry 3mm/⅛in thick, and use a fluted pastry wheel to cut long narrow strips about 1cm/½in wide.

Start making the trellis by laying the pastry strips across the jam surface. Lay one piece straight down the middle and evenly space four more strips on either side. Lay further strips in the same way across at right angles. Reserve some for the edges.

Brush all the pastry strips with beaten egg and, to give a neat finish, lay a long strip of pastry all around the side of the tin over the edges of the trellis. The egg helps seal the joints. Brush the edge with egg.

Bake the Linzertorte in the preheated oven at 200°C/ 400°F/Gas 6 for 30-40 minutes. Dot a little more jam into each lattice hole and leave to cool in the tin on a wire rack. Dredge with icing sugar and serve.

Punschtorte

Ingredients

175g/6oz caster sugar	**Punsch syrup**
4 egg yolks	100g/4oz granulated sugar
5g/1tsp orange zest	50ml/2fl oz water
5g/1tsp lemon zest	45ml/3tbsp lemon juice,
60g/2½oz butter, melted	strained
and cooled	45ml/3tbsp orange juice,
3 egg whites	strained
85g/3½oz potato flour,	60ml/4tbsp dark rum
sifted	30ml/2tbsp apricot jam
	strained
	Punch Icing

Preparation Butter and line two 20cm/8in spring-form tins.

Beat the caster sugar and egg yolks until thick, pale and creamy. Beat in the citrus zests. Slowly pour on the butter while still beating, taking care to leave the creamy sediment in the bottom of the pan.

Whisk the egg whites into firm peaks and lightly fold them into the mixture, in three stages, alternating with siftings of potato flour.

Divide the mixture equally between the two baking tins. Bake at 180°C/350°F/Gas 4 for 30 minutes until golden and shrinking slightly from the sides of the tin. Leave to cool on wire racks.

Meanwhile, prepare the syrup. Dissolve the sugar in the water over gentle heat and boil to a 'thread stage', that is, when the syrup will form thin threads across the opened blade points of a pair of scissors, at 102°C/ 215°F/. Draw off the heat, stir in the lemon and orange juice, and finally the rum. Leave to cool.

As soon as the cake layers have cooled, prick them all over with a fork and brush liberally with the rum syrup. Place one layer on a wire rack and spread the apricot jam all over, sandwich with the other cake layer.

Make the punch icing and pour it straight over the cake. Smooth the sides using a palette knife but avoid touching the top. While still warm decorate with small pieces of candied orange and lemon peel.

Leave to mature for a day before cutting.

Orangen Torte

The Punschtorte may be adapted to have a strong orange flavour. Leave out the rum in the syrup and fill and cover the layers with orange cream.

Ingredients

Orange cream	30g/2tbsp orange zest
4 egg yolks	165g/5½oz unsalted butter
100g/3½oz caster sugar	125ml/4fl oz double cream
100ml/3½fl oz orange	
juice, strained	

Preparation Prepare the sponge as for Punschtorte and leave to cool. Make the syrup using 75ml/5tbsp each of orange and lemon juice. Brush the cooled syrup over the cake layers.

For the orange cream, whisk the egg yolks, sugar, orange juice and zest in a heat-proof bowl. Set the bowl on a pan a quarter filled with simmering water and cook until the mixture has thickened, stirring all the time. Draw off the heat and beat until cool.

Beat the butter separately until creamy, then beat the cool cream into it, a spoonful at a time. Whisk the double cream until it is stiff and gently fold into the main mixture. Chill before using.

Split the cake in half and spread one-third of the cream over the bottom layer. Sandwich with the top sponge layer. Smooth the rest of the cream round the sides and over the top of the cake.

Decorate with slices of candied orange and lemon peel and angelica. Chill before serving.

Habsburger Torte
Serves about 40

This is an elaborate cake that takes quite some time to prepare, but it is ideal for a special function or celebration.

The moist texture and unusual taste of the unpeeled hazelnuts are a perfect foil for the sweeter fillings. Make it 2-3 days ahead of time so that the flavours may develop.

Ingredients

Hazelnut sponge
100g/4oz caster sugar
6 eggs, separated
5cm/2in vanilla pod, split
100g/4oz unpeeled, ground hazelnuts
50g/2oz toasted breadcrumbs

Chocolate sponge
85g/3¹/₂oz caster sugar
5 eggs, separated
85g/3¹/₂oz unpeeled, ground hazelnuts
100g/4oz dark, dessert chocolate, melted and cooled
25g/1oz toasted breadcrumbs

Chocolate filling
140g/5oz unsalted butter
140g/5oz icing sugar, sifted
130g/4¹/₂oz dark dessert chocolate, melted and cooled
45ml/3tbsp dark rum or Tia Maria

Pistachio and almond filling
100g/4oz unsalted butter
100g/4oz icing sugar, sifted
2.5cm/1in vanilla pod, split
130g/4¹/₂oz pistachios, ground
130g/4¹/₂oz ground almonds
45ml/3tbsp apricot jam
1¹/₂portions Thick Chocolate Icing

Preparation Butter base, line and butter again two 26cm/10¹/₂in spring-form tins. Dust with a mixture of caster sugar and flour and shake off the excess.

Make the hazelnut sponge by beating the caster sugar and egg yolks until pale, thick and fluffy. Add the seeds of vanilla and blend well. Mix in the nuts and breadcrumbs and combine well.

Whisk the egg whites until they are firm and lightly fold them into the mixture. Pour the batter into one of the tins, level it out and tap the tin sharply on the work-top to pop any bubbles of air. Bake at 180°C/350°F/Gas 4 for 30 minutes and cool.

After about 15 minutes of cooking time has elapsed make the chocolate sponge. Follow the same method as above, but before whisking the egg whites, beat the melted chocolate into the nut mixture. Proceed as before; bake and cool.

Chocolate filling Beat the butter and icing sugar until pale and fluffy. Mix in the cooled chocolate and the rum. Cover and chill.

Pistachio and almond filling Beat the butter and icing sugar with the vanilla seeds until pale and fluffy. Mix in the nuts. Cover and chill.

Trim the cake sides, then split the hazelnut sponge in two and place the base on a wire rack. Reserve one-third of the chocolate filling for piping decoration later and smooth the remainder on the sponge. Cover with the chocolate cake layer.

On sifted icing sugar roll out the pistachio paste to fit the cake and lay it on top; sandwich with the remaining hazelnut layer.

Heat the apricot jam with 30ml/2tbsp water and strain. Brush the slightly cooled jam on the sides and top of the cake. Prepare the chocolate icing and pour it straight over the top and down the sides of the cake, smoothing with a palette knife as necessary. Avoid touching the top or it will lose its sheen. Leave to set.

Fit a piping bag with a small, star-shaped nozzle and fill with the reserved chocolate cream. Pipe stars around the edge of the cake and in the middle. Stud with hazelnuts and pistachios and serve.

Dobostorta
Drum Cake

Ingredients

Sponge
6 egg yolks
130g/4½oz caster sugar
5g/1tsp orange zest
70g/2½oz plain flour
70g/2½oz potato flour
6 egg whites

1 portion cooked
　Buttercream with Egg
　Yolks flavoured with
　chocolate and rum
Caramel glaze
165g/5½oz granulated
　sugar

Preparation Beat the egg yolks and sugar until pale and creamy. Mix in the orange zest. Sift together both

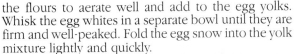

the flours to aerate well and add to the egg yolks. Whisk the egg whites in a separate bowl until they are firm and well-peaked. Fold the egg snow into the yolk mixture lightly and quickly.

This quantity makes six layers. Spread a thin coating of mixture in the bottom of a greased and floured 24cm/9½in spring-form tin and smooth carefully. Bake immediately in the preheated oven at 180°C/350°F/Gas 4 for 5-8 minutes each layer. (Bake two layers at a time if you have the tins.)

When it is coloured light gold, remove the cake from the oven and turn out of the tin straight on to a wire rack to cool. Make the remaining layers in the same way.

Assemble the cake as soon as the layers have cooled so that they do not dry out and become crisp.

Set aside the best-looking cake layer and sandwich the rest together with the chocolate filling, spreading it over the top and the sides.

Prepare the top layer. Brush any loose crumbs off the cake and lay it on a large sheet of greaseproof paper. Take two long knives, lightly greasing the blade of one with oil or butter.

Make the caramel glaze by gently heating 65g/2½oz granulated sugar in a copper sugar boiler until golden, then add the rest of the sugar and cook until it has thickened. Quickly pour the caramel straight over the cake layer and smooth it out using the clean knife.

Using the greased knife, immediately mark the cake out into 10 sections and cut through the sugar glaze. Leave to cool. Lay the caramel disc on top of the filled cake layers.

Do not store in the refrigerator as this spoils the caramel surface.

Acacia Honey Cake

Honey cakes are among the earliest to be found throughout the world. They were usually prepared for festivals and celebrations.

Ingredients

320ml/11½fl oz acacia
  honey
3 whole eggs, lightly beaten
300g/11oz rye flour
100g/4oz unblanched
  almonds or hazelnuts,
  ground coarse
5g/1tsp ground cinnamon

large pinch crushed cloves
30ml/2tbsp dark rum
2.5g/½tsp bicarbonate of
  soda
15ml/1tbsp milk
blanched almond halves to
  decorate

Preparation Warm the honey in the jar set in a pan of hot water, then pour it into a large mixing bowl and whisk until it is frothy, thick and white. Beat in the eggs and add the flour a spoonful at a time.

Mix together the spices and nuts and stir in the rum, and combine with the honey and egg mixture. Dissolve the bicarbonate of soda with the milk and beat it into the mixture. Leave to mature in a covered bowl overnight as this helps to lighten the mixture.

Press the paste into a greased and floured deep rectangular baking tin 36×24cm/12½×8½in. Stud with almond halves and bake at 180°C/350°F/Gas 4 for 30-35 minutes. Avoid letting it brown too much as this gives a bitter taste. When the cake has cooled in the tin, cut it into rectangular pieces and store for at least a week in an airtight tin before serving.

Hazelnut Torta

Almonds or walnuts can be substituted in this basic recipe.

Ingredients

130g/4½oz caster sugar
4 egg yolks
130g/4½oz toasted
  hazelnuts, ground

8g/1tbsp toasted
  breadcrumbs
20ml/1½tbsp dark rum
3 egg whites

Preparation Beat the egg yolks and 100g/3½oz of the sugar until pale and creamy. Whisk in the nuts, breadcrumbs and rum. Whip the egg whites in a separate bowl until they stand in firm, snowy peaks. Beat in the rest of the sugar. Lightly fold the egg snow

into the main mixture in three stages, taking care not to stir it and break down the pockets of air.

Pour the mixture into a greased and floured 22cm/8½in spring-form tin and bake in the preheated oven at 180°C/350°F/Gas 4 for 1 hour until well risen and brown. Leave in the tin for 10 minutes before turning out on to a wire rack to finish cooling.

The cake may be dressed up in several ways. Dredge it with icing sugar and offer whipped cream on the side. Glaze it with rum icing decorated with whole caramelized nuts. It can also be divided into three layers and filled with strained apricot jam and a layer of whipped cream, then finished with chocolate icing.

A chocolate cream filling is especially good: use half a portion of Basic Buttercream flavoured with 15g/1tbsp coffee powder and 15ml/1tbsp coffee liqueur. Chill overnight before cutting. Dredge with icing sugar to serve.

Hunyady Chestnut Torta

Ingredients

75g/3oz dark, dessert
  chocolate
15ml/1tbsp rum
130g/4½oz caster sugar
4 eggs, separated
250g/9oz cooked
  chestnuts, sieved (350g/
  12oz raw)
30g/2tbsp potato flour
Hazelnut filling
75g/3oz toasted hazelnuts,
  ground

3 egg yolks
75g/3oz unsalted butter
75g/3oz icing sugar
15ml/2tbsp coffee liqueur
  (Tia Maria) or rum
apricot jam, strained
Thick Chocolate Icing or
  140ml/5fl oz double or
  whipping cream,
  whipped
30g/2tbsp caster sugar

Preparation Carefully melt the chocolate in 1tbsp water and stir in the rum. Leave to cool.

Beat together the sugar and egg yolks until pale and creamy. Whisk in the chocolate and stir in the sieved chestnuts.

Whip the egg whites in a separate bowl, until they hold firm peaks, and lightly fold them into the chestnut mixture using a large metal spoon.

Sift over and fold in the potato flour. Pour the mixture into two 22cm/8½in base-lined, greased and floured spring-form tins and bake at 180°C/350°F/Gas 4 for 50 minutes until well risen, leave to cool in the tins before turning out on to wire racks. Strip off the paper carefully.

To make the filling, mix the hazelnuts and one egg yolk to a smooth paste. Cream the butter and sugar until light and fluffy and beat in the remaining egg yolks one at a time. Mix in the hazelnut paste and Tia Maria.

Split both sponge layers in two and fill with the hazelnut cream. Sandwich both cakes with 30ml/2tbsp strained and warmed apricot jam. Cover the cake and leave to chill for a day.

Brush the top and sides of the cake with strained apricot jam. Make the icing. Pour the warm icing straight over the cake, smooth out and decorate. Do not leave the cake in a cold place as it will spoil the gloss of the icing.

For a whipped cream filling sweeten the cream with the sugar and blend in 30ml/2tbsp rum or Tia Maria. Sandwich the two cakes with cream, reserving some for the top and sides.

Smooth the rest of the cream all over the cake and decorate with candied chestnut pieces, toasted hazelnuts and chocolate curls. This should be assembled 3-4 hours before it is to be eaten.

Russian Cream Cake

Ingredients

4 eggs, separated
75g/3oz caster sugar
5g/1tsp orange zest
50g/2oz plain flour
50g/2oz potato flour

Filling
25g/1oz candied orange
  and lemon peel, chopped
25g/1oz sultanas

100g/4oz glacé cherries,
  pineapple, plum, pear,
  angelica, etc
20ml/1½tbsp dark rum
100ml/3½fl oz milk
vanilla pod
50g/2oz caster sugar
3 egg yolks
15g/1tbsp gelatine powder
140ml/5fl oz double cream

Preparation To make the sponge whisk the egg whites in a large, clean bowl, until they stand in firm, snowy peaks. Gradually sift and beat in the sugar until the mixture is satiny and smooth; mix in the zest. Lightly whisk the egg yolks separately, then beat them into the meringue a spoonful at a time and continue to blend them in well.

Sift over one-third of the flour and gently fold it in using a large metal spoon; fold in the rest of the flour in two stages.

Pour the mixture into a greased and floured 22cm/8½in spring-form tin and bake at 180°C/350°F/Gas 4 for 40 minutes until well risen and golden. Cool on a wire rack.

Meanwhile make the filling. Steep the candied peels, sultanas and candied fruits in a bowl with the rum for 1 hour, mixing it every now and then. Bring the milk to the boil with a split piece of vanilla pod, draw off the heat and leave to infuse and cool. Remove the pod.

Whisk together the caster sugar and the egg yolks in a heat-proof bowl, sprinkle over the gelatine powder and gradually pour on the cooled milk, whisking all the time. Place the bowl over a pan, a quarter filled with simmering water, and stir gently while the custard cooks and thickens. Set aside to cool.

Whip the cream until softly peaked. Beat the vanilla custard until smooth and creamy, then fold it into the whipped cream together with the soaked fruits and rum. Leave to chill for 1 hour.

Cut the sponge into three layers. Reserve about one-third of the cream for the top and the sides of the cake and use the rest to fill the two layers. Cover the top and sides of cake with the rest of the cream, then decorate with pieces of fruit. Chill for 3-4 hours before serving.

Sachertorte
Chocolate Cake

Sachertorte was invented in Vienna in the mid-nineteenth century by the chef Franz Sacher for his employer Prince Lothar Metternich.

Ingredients

130g/4½oz butter
100g/4oz caster sugar
4 egg yolks
175g/6oz plain dessert
  chocolate, melted and
  cooled
15g/1tbsp Vanilla Sugar

2 drops bitter almond
  essence
75g/3oz plain flour, sifted
3 egg whites
apricot jam
Thick Chocolate Icing or
  chocolate fondant

Preparation Cream the butter with the sugar until pale and fluffy. Beat in the egg yolks, one at a time, and the cooled chocolate. Beat in the vanilla sugar and bitter almond essence and continue beating for 15 minutes by machine (25 minutes by hand).

Sift the flour over the mixture and quickly but lightly blend it in without over-beating. Whisk the egg whites until they stand in stiff, creamy peaks and fold them into the mixture. Pour it into a buttered 24cm/9½in spring-form tin — the mixture should be no more than 4cm/1¼in deep. Bake in the warmed oven at 170°C/325°F/Gas 3 for 1 hour until slightly shrinking from the sides of the tin. Cool on a wire rack.

Brush the cake with strained apricot jam and glaze with the chocolate icing.

Black Forest Kirschtorte

Black cherries combined wth chocolate or nuts in cakes were very popular in south Germany, Austria and Switzerland during the last century. Occasionally the cakes were built in layers, but mostly a layer of fresh fruit was covered with the uncooked cake mixture or blended with it and, typical of those regions, nuts were often included. Kirsch was not evident although rum was very common.

Ingredients

75g/3oz unblanched almonds, coarsely ground
50g/2oz toasted breadcrumbs
5g/1tsp ground cinnamon
5g/1tsp ground cloves
30ml/2tbsp kirsch
130g/4½oz caster sugar
9 egg yolks
10g/2tsp orange zest
100g/4oz plain dessert chocolate, melted and cooled
6 egg whites

Filling
1kg/2lb morello, sour or black cherries, washed and stoned or 850g/1lb 12oz tinned pitted cherries
250ml/9fl oz red wine
250ml/9fl oz water
100g/4oz granulated sugar
cinnamon stick
10g/2tsp orange zest
140ml/5fl oz kirsch
425ml/15fl oz double or whipping cream
45g/3tbsp caster sugar
40g/4tbsp grated chocolate and chocolate curls for decoration

Preparation Prepare two 22cm/8½in spring-form tins: butter, line the base with paper, butter again, dredge with sugar and flour. Mix together the almonds, breadcrumbs, cinnamon and cloves and moisten with kirsch.

In a separate bowl beat the sugar and egg yolks until thick, pale and creamy. Mix in the orange zest and chocolate. Lightly combine with the first mixture. Whisk the egg whites separately until they hold firm snowy peaks. Lightly and quickly fold them into the main mixture until just combined.

Divide the mixture equally between the two tins. Smooth the top and tap each tin once to disperse any air pockets. Bake in the preheated oven at 180°C/350°F/Gas 4 for 30 minutes until well risen and slightly shrinking away from the sides of the tin. Cool on wire racks.

To cook the fresh cherries for the filling, combine the wine, water and sugar in a pan and heat gently until the sugar has dissolved. Add the cinnamon stick and orange zest, and simmer for about 20 minutes. Drop in the cleaned fruits and poach lightly for 10 minutes. Lift the fruits carefully out of the syrup and drain in a colander. Boil the syrup on a high heat for two minutes to reduce and thicken it slightly. Draw off the heat and leave to cool.

Mix 75ml/3fl oz cherry syrup with 125ml/4fl oz kirsch. Dry the cherries with absorbent kitchen paper. Whisk the cream until softly peaked and beat in the sugar until firm; fold in the remaining kirsch. Cut both chocolate sponges across the middle. Reserve 45-60ml/3-4tbsp cream and a few cherries for decoration.

Place a sponge base on an elegant serving platter and sprinkle over about one-third of the kirsch syrup. Smooth over a quarter of the cream and press in half the cherries. Cover with a second sponge, sprinkle with more syrup, a layer of cream and the rest of the fruit. Place the third sponge on top, sprinkle with the remaining syrup and a layer of whipped cream. Cover with the last sponge layer and coat the top and sides of the whole cake with the rest of the cream. Dust the cake sides with chocolate.

Pipe the reserved cream in large rosettes on the cake surface and dot with cherries. Place a few chocolate curls in the middle to finish. Chill for 3-4 hours. Just before serving dredge a little icing sugar on the chocolate curls.

Baumkuchen
Tree Cake

Spit cooking was the usual method of roasting in early times, and a tree cake was quite popular. It was baked on a hand-turned, tapered, wooden spit, set in front of an open fire, and it was made of a thin batter, ladled on slowly as it cooked. Each wafer-thin layer was toasted to a golden brown colour, and then another coating of fresh batter was poured on, to be coated in its turn. The tree effect was achieved by varying the rotating speed of the spit as fresh batter was poured over.

Today, we have to adapt the technique, and the modern grill is most suitable. You can use a plain baking tin or spring-form tin for a basic cake, or you could try experimenting with different forms such as a gugelhupf or angel cake mould or with shapes that can be assembled later with apricot jam before being iced.

Ingredients

250g/9oz butter
250g/9oz caster sugar
7 eggs, separated
10g/2tsp lemon zest
15ml/1tbsp rum

50g/2oz ground almonds
130g/4½oz plain flour, sifted
130g/4½oz potato flour, sifted

Preparation Beat the butter and caster sugar until pale and creamy, beat in the egg yolks one at a time, mix in the lemon zest, rum and almonds. Sift together the flours, and beat two spoonfuls at a time into the egg mixture.

Whisk the egg whites in a spotlessly clean bowl until firm, then lightly fold them into the main mixture. Lightly oil the chosen cake tin (24cm/9½in diameter). Smooth 1-2 tbsp of cake batter on the base and place under the grill. Grill at 180-200°C/350-400°F/Gas 4-6 for 4-5 minutes until golden brown. Remove from the heat and smooth over another thin layer of mixture. Cook again. Continue toasting the layers until all the mixture is used (about 16-18 layers). Leave to cool in the tin. Unmould; brush with warm apricot jam and glaze with lemon-flavoured Glacé Icing.

The cake keeps fresh for 2-3 weeks.

Bienenstich
Beesting

Although Bienenstich is usually made with a yeast pastry base, the fine butter pastry in this recipe tastes just as good with a vanilla cream filling.

Ingredients

130g/4½oz butter, melted
   and cooled
100g/4oz caster sugar
2 eggs
5g/1tsp lemon zest
130g/4½oz plain flour
60g/2½oz (generous)
   potato flour
2.5g/½tsp baking powder

Almond toffee
50g/2oz butter, diced
250g/9oz caster sugar
75g/3oz flaked almonds
approx. 100ml/3½fl oz
   milk

Vanilla cream (crème St
   Honoré)
250ml/9fl oz milk
2cm/1in vanilla pod
1 egg yolk
25g/1oz cornflour, sifted
110g/4oz caster sugar
2 egg whites

Preparation Make the almond toffee first. Melt the butter over a low heat, then stir in the sugar and mix until it has completely dissolved. Toss in the flaked almonds and beat the mixture, adding enough milk to give a firm but spreading consistency. Leave to cool.

Prepare the vanilla cream by heating the milk with the vanilla pod, leaving it to infuse for a few minutes. Remove the pod. Beat the egg yolk with the flour and 40g/1½oz caster sugar in a heat-proof bowl, then slowly pour the hot milk over the mixture, beating all the time.

Set the bowl over a pan a quarter filled with simmering water, and heat and stir the mixture until it thickens. It must not boil. Draw off the heat and pour into a bowl.

Whisk the egg whites until they are stiff and well peaked, beat in half the remaining sugar and fold in the rest. Lightly fold the meringue mixture into the hot cream. Cool and chill.

To make the pastry beat the cool butter and caster sugar until pale and fluffy; beat in the eggs one at a time blending well between each addition. Mix in the

lemon zest. Sift together the flours and baking powder and blend them into the mixture 30g/2tbsp at a time, taking care not to overbeat.

Spread the mixture on a buttered 34×24×3cm/ 13½in×9½×1½in cake tray and smooth even.

Cover with the almond toffee layer and bake at 170°C/325°F/Gas 3 for 1 hour in the preheated oven. Cut the cake into slices while it is still warm; leave in the tin to cool. Lift the slices out of the tin and cut each in half; sandwich together with some of the vanilla cream.

Hobelspänne
Wood Shavings
Makes 24 pieces

Ingredients

165g/5½oz plain flour
2.5g/½tsp baking powder
40g/1½oz butter, cubed
25g/1oz caster sugar

5g/1tsp lemon zest
1 egg
30ml/2tbsp milk
icing sugar to dredge

Preparation Sift together the flour and baking powder until well aerated and finally into a bowl. Drop in the butter pieces and rub to a fine crumb texture. Stir in the sugar and lemon zest. Mix in the egg and the milk and blend to a fine dough.

Roll out the pastry to a thickness of 2mm/⅛in and cut into rectangular strips 8×2.5cm/3½×1in. Cut a slit about 3cm/1½in in the centre of the length. Lift each pastry and carefully draw one end through the slit, gently easing it back to give a looped effect.

Heat the oil to the correct temperature and deep fry three or four pastries at a time until golden, turning them if necessary with a perforated spoon. They take about 1½ minutes each side.

Lift out the pastries and drain them on absorbent paper. Roll them in icing sugar while they are still warm and leave to dry on a wire rack.

Schraderpuffer
Sponge Cushion

This is a speciality of Schleswig-Holstein, the most northerly point of Germany almost on the Danish border. The method of preparation and baking is quite unusual and gives a not too sweet, light and airy cake that is ideal for tea or coffee time.

Ingredients

75g/3oz butter
75g/3oz plain flour, sifted
75g/3oz raisins
5g/1tsp lemon zest
4 eggs, separated
75g/3oz caster sugar

Preparation Cut the butter into the flour and rub to a fine crumb texture. Toss in the raisins and lemon zest, making sure that they are well coated with flour. Set aside.

Whisk the egg whites in a large clean bowl until they stand in firm, snowy peaks and beat in half the sugar until the mixture is firm and glossy. Using a large metal spoon fold in the rest of the sugar and lightly beaten egg yolks.

Very carefully and lightly, fold in the flour and butter mixture in three portions. Pour the mixture into a greased and floured 22cm/8½in ring or savarin mould.

Level out and bake immediately in the preheated oven at 240°C/475°F/Gas 9 for a total of 45 minutes, reducing the temperature after the first five minutes to 220°C/425°F/Gas 7 and then again after a further ten minutes to 180°C/350°F/Gas 4. The cake puffs up high and turns a rich, golden brown. Lift out of the oven and turn out on a wire rack after 10 minutes to cool. Dust with icing sugar to serve.

Mohrenkopf
Othello's or Moor's Heads
Makes 25 pieces

Ingredients

4 egg yolks
50g/2oz caster sugar
50g/2oz plain flour, sifted
6 egg whites
pinch salt
50g/2oz potato flour, sifted
150ml/¼pt double or
  whipping cream
30g/2tbsp caster sugar
30ml/2tbsp Grand
  Marnier or Cointreau
Soft Chocolate Icing

Preparation Whisk the egg yolks and half the sugar until pale and creamy. Beat in the plain flour. Whip up the egg whites with the salt until firm, then beat in the remaining sugar until satiny and smooth. Fold the egg snow into the first mixture, then sift over the potato flour in two stages and fold it in lightly.

Line a baking sheet with greaseproof paper.

Fit a large piping bag with a plain nozzle and spoon some of the mixture into it. Pipe rounds of paste about 1cm/½in across at 5cm/2in intervals. Dust with a little flour. Bake in the preheated oven at 200°C/400°F/Gas 6 for 20-30 minutes until puffed and golden. Remove from the paper and cool on a wire rack. Split the cakes and scoop out a little of the pastry from the base. Whip the cream into soft peaks and whisk in the rest of the sugar and the liqueur. Place a spoonful of cream in the hollow of each split pastry and close. Prepare the soft chocolate icing and coat the top of each pastry with it; stand on the wire rack to set.

Variations: Desdemonas Fill with vanilla-flavoured whipped cream, brush the top with strained apricot purée, and mask with kirsch-flavoured Glacé Icing.
Iagos Fill the base with coffee-flavoured Crème Pâtissière, brush with apricot purée, and ice with Coffee Glacé Icing.
Chocolate beans Fill with rum-flavoured chocolate cream (see Basic Buttercream), cover the top with the same cream, and decorate with chocolate vermicelli.

Truffle Torte
Chocolate Truffle Cake

Ingredients

165g/5½oz dark dessert
  chocolate, melted and
  cooled
10g/2tsp coffee powder
100g/4oz butter, softened
130g/4½oz caster sugar
4 eggs, separated
100g/4oz toasted
  hazelnuts, ground
1½ portions Whipped
  Chocolate Cream
  flavoured with coffee
  liqueur
mimosa balls or whole
  caramelized hazelnuts
  to decorate

Preparation Break the chocolate into pieces and place them in a small heat-proof bowl with the coffee powder and 90ml/6tbsp boiling water. Set the bowl over a pan of simmering water to melt the chocolate. Stir gently to blend, then set aside to cool.

Mix the butter and sugar until pale and creamy. Beat in the egg yolks one at a time and continue beating until the mixture is very thick and pale in colour. Beat in the cool chocolate liquid and hazelnuts.

Whisk the egg whites separately until they are stiff, and fold them lightly and carefully into the chocolate mixture. Pour into a buttered 22cm/8½in base-lined spring-form tin and bake immediately at 170°C/325°F/Gas 3 for 1 hour 15 minutes. Leave to settle in the tin for 10 minutes before turning out to cool.

The cake should feel quite moist. When cold, wrap in plastic film and chill for 2 days. Assemble the cake a day before it is needed.

Make the whipped chocolate cream. Split the cake into three layers. Reserve about one-third of the cream for the top and sides of the cake and use the rest to sandwich the three layers.

Fit a piping bag with a large plain nozzle and spoon about 75ml/5tbsp cream into the bag. Smooth the rest of the cream on the sides and top of the cake. Pipe five thick, straight and parallel lines across the top of the cake and dredge generously all over with cocoa powder.

Stud the mimosa balls or hazelnuts along the piped lines. Cover and chill overnight before serving.

Carrot Cake

Ingredients

6 egg yolks	25g/1oz potato flour
75g/3oz icing sugar, sifted	5g/1tsp baking powder
5g/1tsp lemon zest	5g/1tsp ground cinnamon
pinch salt	pinch ground cloves
200g/7oz peeled carrots	30ml/2tbsp kirsch
100g/4oz roasted	4 egg whites
hazelnuts, ground	75g/3oz caster sugar
100g/4oz ground almonds	

Preparation Beat the egg yolks with the icing sugar, lemon zest and salt until pale and creamy. Grate the carrots, drain any liquid and pat dry with paper towel. Stir into the egg and sugar with the hazelnuts and almonds. Sift the flour with the baking powder and spices and blend with the mixture. Mix in the kirsch.

Whip the egg whites until softly peaked; sift in the caster sugar and beat until the mixture looks satiny and smooth. Fold the meringue into the carrot mixture lightly and carefully. Pour into a greased and floured 24cm/9½in spring-form tin and bake at 180°/350°F/Gas 4 for 1 hour. Cool on a wire rack.

Dredge with icing sugar before serving. Do not cut the cake for at least 3 days, so that the flavours may mature. Offer whipped cream on the side.

In Switzerland, where this cake originates, it is the custom to finish the cake with a white Glacé or Fondant Icing and to decorate it with marzipan carrots.

Brush the warm cake with strained apricot jam and coat with Fondant Icing. Tint a little marzipan with orange food colouring and make 13 small carrot shapes. Use angelica for the stems. Lay the carrots on the icing before it has set; one for each slice of the cake is fun. Lay three in the middle of the cake and the other ten around the outside.

Raisin Chocolate Fudge Cake

Ingredients

65g/2½oz butter	pinch ground cloves
200g/7oz brown sugar	75g/3oz raisins
1 whole egg	50g/2oz flaked almonds
30ml/2tbsp orange juice,	**Filling**
sieved	1 portion Buttercream with
10g/2tsp orange zest	Cooked Egg Yolks
50g/2oz chocolate, melted	75g/3oz pecan nuts,
and cooled	chopped
60ml/2fl oz milk	50g/2oz grated coconut
pinch bicarbonate of soda	75g/3oz raisins, cut in half
130g/4½oz plain flour	pecan halves and flaked
sifted	almonds to decorate
2.5g/½tsp baking powder	
2.5g/½tsp ground	
cinnamon	

Preparation Cream the butter and half the sugar. Beat in the egg, blend well. Add the orange juice and zest. Beat in the rest of the sugar and the chocolate. Combine well. Mix the milk with 60ml/2fl oz water and blend in the bicarbonate of soda. Sieve together the flour and baking powder with the cinnamon and cloves. Dust the almonds and raisins with some of the flour and set aside.

Beat one-third of the liquid into the mixture followed by one-third of the dry ingredients. Repeat in two further stages. Mix in the raisins and almonds. Turn into a deep, ready-greased and fully lined 22cm/8½in loose-based tin. Level the surface. Bake in the preheated oven at 180°C/350°F/Gas 4 for 1 hour until risen and shrinking away slightly from the edges of the tin. Cool on a wire rack.

Make the filling. Into the cooled cream mix the pecan nuts, coconut and raisins.

To assemble, split the cake into three layers. Reserve just over one-third of the filling for the outside and use the remainder to sandwich the three chocolate layers together. Smooth the rest on the top and sides of the cake. Decorate with pecans and almond flakes.

The cake should settle for at least a day before it is cut. It will stay fresh for up to a week.

Poppy Seed or Walnut Roll
Makes 2 rolls

This yeasted roll is served all the year round in Hungary as a coffee-time pastry.

Ingredients

Yeast pastry
75ml/3fl oz milk
25g/1oz fresh yeast
450g/1lb strong plain
*   flour, sifted*
100g/4oz caster sugar
pinch salt
225g/8oz butter
2 egg yolks
50ml/2fl oz soured cream
1 whole egg for brushing

Poppy seed filling
100ml/3½fl oz milk
200g/7oz poppy seeds,
*   ground*
140g/5oz granulated sugar
10g/2tsp lemon zest
1 large Cox's apple, peeled
*   and grated*

Walnut filling
140g/5oz granulated sugar
45ml/3tbsp milk
200g/7oz ground walnuts
5g/1tsp lemon zest
2 Cox's apples, peeled and
*   grated*

Preparation Prepare a sponge batter. Warm the milk to blood heat and sprinkle over the crumbled yeast; mix in 100g/4oz flour taken from the recipe and 5g/1tsp caster sugar. Beat well. Cover and leave to rise until at least double in bulk.

Meanwhile, sift the flour and salt into a large bowl, cut in the butter and rub to a crumb texture. Mix in the sugar and egg yolks, then pour on the sponge batter. Beat in enough soured cream to make a not too soft dough.

Knead thoroughly until the dough becomes elastic and throws large air bubbles. Leave in the bowl closely covered with a cloth, or place the dough in a large, lightly oiled polythene bag and seal. Set in a warm place to rise for about 3 hours until it has at least doubled in bulk. While the dough is rising make the filling.

Poppy seed filling Boil the milk and pour it over the ground poppy seeds; leave to infuse and swell. Gently dissolve the granulated sugar in 30ml/2tbsp water, sieve the seed and stir into the syrup; draw off the heat. Stir in the lemon zest and grated apple. Cool before using.

Walnut filling Dissolve the sugar in the milk to make a syrup. Stir in the walnuts, and draw off the heat. Mix in the lemon zest and grated apple. Cool before using.

For a very simple filling sprinkle a mixture of 140g/5oz granulated sugar, 2tsp ground cinnamon and ½tsp ground clove over the dough before rolling it up.

Turn the risen dough on to a floured pastry board, knock it back for a moment or two, then divide it into two, replacing the unused piece in the covered bowl or bag.

Roll out the dough into a rectangle 0.5cm/¼in thick. Spread generously with the chosen filling to within 2cm/¾in of the edge and roll up carefully, tucking in both ends so that the filling cannot leak out. Transfer the roll to a lightly greased baking sheet, with the open seam underneath. Brush lightly with beaten egg and leave to rise for a further 30 minutes. Brush again with beaten egg and prick all over with a fork. Bake in the preheated oven at 180°C/350°F/Gas 4 for 1 hour. Finish the reserve dough in the same way.

Serve cut in slices. The pastries keep well for at least a week.

Streusselkuchen
Crumb Cake

This is a German classic. Here the yeast dough base is covered with a thick cinnamon and almond crumb covering. Streussel is made like pastry, and here are two simple ways of making it.

Ingredients

Yeast Dough
Almond streussel
250g/9oz unsalted butter
300g/11oz plain flour,
*   sifted*

100g/4oz ground almonds
10g/2tsp cinnamon
*   powder*
5g/1tsp lemon zest
165g/5½oz granulated
*   sugar*

Preparation Prepare the yeast dough and line two baking tins. Leave to rise.

Using a food processor Gently melt the butter and leave to cool. Drop the flour, almonds, cinnamon, lemon zest and sugar into the processor bowl and switch on for 2-3 seconds to mix well. Then quickly pour the cooled butter through the tube on to the mixture with the machine switched on. Stop the motor as soon as a crumb texture is reached.

By hand Cut the chilled butter pieces into the sifted flour and rub to fine crumbs. Use a knife to blend in the rest of the ingredients and make a coarse crumb texture. Roll into a ball, wrap and chill for 1 hour until hardened. Rub the dough through a coarse grater and dust lightly with flour to prevent it from sticking together.

Finish the cakes by brushing the risen dough with melted butter; scatter the crumb mixture generously on top. Bake in the preheated oven at 200°C/400°F/Gas 6 for 35 minutes until well risen and golden. Cool in the tins, set on a wire rack. Dust with icing sugar before serving and cut in slices.

Frankfurter Kranz

This is baked in a plain ring or savarin mould.

Ingredients

130g/4½oz butter
140g/5oz caster sugar
4 eggs, lightly beaten
10g/2tsp lemon zest
10ml/2tsp rum
100g/3½oz plain flour
100g/3½oz potato flour
5g/1tsp baking powder
2 portions vanilla
    Buttercream (cooled)
    plus 50g/2oz unsalted
    butter

Praline croquant
50g/2oz granulated sugar
15ml/1tbsp water
50g/2oz flaked or chopped
    toasted almonds
90ml/6tbsp rum, kirsch or
    Grand Marnier
glacé cherries and
    pistachio nuts for
    decoration

Preparation Beat the butter and sugar until light, pale and fluffy. Whisk in the egg a little at a time, beating well between each addition. Mix in the lemon zest and rum. Sift together the flours with the baking powder two or three times, then beat them into the egg mixture in three stages. The mixture should be quite firm but not stiff.

Turn it into the buttered ring mould and smooth level. Bake in the preheated oven at 180°C/350°F/Gas 4 for 45 minutes until well risen and brown and shrinking slightly from the edges of the tin. Turn out on to a wire rack to cool. Let the cake rest overnight if possible.

Prepare the buttercream and beat in the additional butter before combining it with the cooked buttercream.

To make the praline croquant boil the water and sugar to form a caramel. Drop in the almonds and stir lightly to coat them with the sugar. When the mixture starts to boil, pour on to an oiled baking sheet, smooth out and leave to cool. Break the praline into pieces and chop or pound into a coarse powder.

Assemble the cake. Split the cake into four layers and brush a little alcohol on each. Reserve 45ml/3tbsp buttercream and sandwich all the layers together with the buttercream covering the top and sides also. Sprinkle the crushed croquant all over the cake. Pipe a few rosettes on the top and decorate with cherries and pistachios.

Sunshine Cake

Ingredients

165g/5½oz plain flour,
    sifted
pinch salt
6 eggs, separated

5cm/2in vanilla pod
5ml/1tsp cream of tartar
250g/9oz caster sugar

Preparation Carefully wash and dry a 24cm/9½in angel cake tin and dust with flour.

Sift the flour and salt several times to aerate well. Whisk the egg yolks until thick and frothy, then mix in the seeds of the vanilla pod. Set aside. Lightly whip the egg whites in a spotlessly clean bowl until they are foamy, add the cream of tartar and continue whisking until they have expanded into firm white peaks. Sift 75g/3oz of sugar over the egg whites and beat in until glossy and smooth. Continue by hand.

Using a large metal spoon, carefully fold in the beaten egg yolks and lemon juice. Sift over one-third of the flour and gently fold it in; repeat in two more stages.

Pour the sponge batter into the floured mould. Drag a knife through it to break any pockets of air. Bake at 180°C/350°F/Gas 4 for 45 minutes. When well risen and springy to the touch, turn over to balance on a small inverted funnel or a wire rack to cool, leaving the cake tin in place.

Dredge with icing sugar to serve.

Chocolate Roulade

Ingredients
175g/6oz plain chocolate
5 eggs, separated
175g/6oz sugar
45ml/3tbsp hot water
icing sugar, sieved

25g/1oz unsweetened
    cocoa powder
10ml/2tsp instant coffee
2.5ml/¹/₂tsp vanilla extract

Decoration
whipped cream
crystallized violets
angelica leaves

Filling
450ml/³/₄pt double cream
50g/2oz icing sugar, sieved

Preparation Melt the chocolate in a bowl over a pan of hot water.

Put egg yolks into a large bowl. Add the sugar and beat well until pale and fluffy.

Add the hot water to the chocolate and stir until smooth. Whisk into the egg mixture.

Whisk the egg whites until stiff. Lightly fold into the chocolate mixture. Pour into a greased and lined 39×24cm/15¹/₂×9¹/₂in Swiss roll pan. Cook in the oven at 180°C/350°F/Gas 4 for 15-20 minutes, until firm.

Remove from the oven. Cover with a sheet of greaseproof or waxed paper and a damp tea-towel. Leave until completely cold.

To make the filling put all the ingredients into a bowl. Whisk until thick. Chill.

Turn roulade on to a sheet of greaseproof paper dusted with icing sugar. Peel away lining paper.

Spread the filling over the cake to within 2.5cm/1in of the edge. Roll up like a Swiss roll, using the greaseproof paper to help.

Put seam side down on a serving plate and chill for an hour before serving.

To serve, dredge the roulade with icing sugar. Pipe whipped cream down the centre and decorate with crystallized violets and angelica leaves.

Gugelhupf

It is difficult to attribute Gugelhupf to any one country as it has remained popular throughout the Teutonic lands for centuries. The name comes from the mould in which the cake is baked: an unusual utensil, with sloping and moulded, patterned sides and a central funnel. Simple, early models were made of tin, but more elaborate embossed ones of fired clay or copper were used for special occasions. Today they are usually made of aluminium or copper and are available in many specialist kitchen shops.

Ingredients
50ml/2fl oz milk, warmed
    to blood heat
10g/¹/₂oz fresh yeast
130g/4¹/₂oz strong plain
    flour, sifted
50g/2oz caster sugar
75g/3oz butter
5g/1tsp grated lemon zest

6 egg yolks
100g/4oz raisins
30ml/2tbsp kirsch
5ml/1tsp corn oil
2 egg whites
25g/1oz pine nuts
    (optional)

Preparation Carefully brush with melted butter a 23cm/9in gugelhupf mould and dust with flour; drop the pine nuts, if used, in the bottom.

Make a Yeast Sponge Batter with the warm milk, yeast, 30g/2tbsp flour and 5g/1tsp sugar taken from the main mixture; beat well. Cover and set aside for about 10 minutes to rise and double in bulk.

Cream the butter with the sugar and lemon zest until thick and fluffy. Whisk in the egg yolks one at a time, beating thoroughly between each addition. Mix in the sponge batter and a quarter of the remaining flour and continue beating for about 10 minutes by machine (20 minutes by hand). The mixture should be well aerated and have thickened.

Dust the raisins with a little flour and blend them into the mixture. Stir in the kirsch and the oil. Whisk the egg whites in a separate, clean bowl until they hold firm, glossy peaks. Lightly fold them into the main mixture, with alternate siftings of flour, until all is well combined.

Pour the yeast dough into the prepared tin and set it in a warm place to rise and at least double in bulk; it should rise to almost the top of the tin and this takes about 1¹/₂ hours.

Bake in the preheated oven at 190°C/375°F/Gas 5 for 30 minutes until well browned and turn out onto a wire rack to cool. Dredge with icing sugar to serve. Freeze while still warm. Defrost at room temperature for 3-4 hours.

Lardy Cake

Lardy cake is based on a plain bread dough, enriched with a delicious sticky-sweet mixture of lard and sugar as well as dried fruits and mixed spices, and it is prepared in much the same way as puff pastry. In early times, when sugar was scarce, this was a treat reserved for harvest days and special celebrations, and, like gingerbread, was sold at local fairs. Later, when sugar dropped in price, lardy cake became very popular and could be bought from the bakery every week.

Home-make pork lard has the best flavour if you are able to obtain it.

Ingredients
Bread dough
475g/17oz strong plain
    flour
250ml/9fl oz milk,
    warmed to blood heat
10g/1tbsp fresh yeast
15g/1tbsp lard

Filling
185g/6¹/₂oz lard, well
    chilled
100g/4oz light muscavado
    sugar
250g/9oz mixed fruit and
    peel
5g/1tsp ground mixed
    spice

Preparation Make a Yeast Sponge Batter with 100g/4oz flour, 125ml/4½fl oz milk and the yeast, beat well, cover and set aside to rise and double in bulk. Sift the remaining flour and salt together into a large bowl. Rub in 15g/1tbsp lard and make a crumb texture.

Make a well in the centre, pour in the risen sponge batter and most of the remaining milk. Blend well, then work and knead the dough mixture until it starts to roll off the sides of the bowl.

Turn the dough out on to a lightly floured work-surface and knead hard for about 10 minutes until it is elastic, looks shiny and throws large pockets of air. Roll it into a ball, drop it back into the mixing bowl and cover with a floured cloth. Set aside to rise in a warm place until it has doubled in bulk.

Roll the dough out on a floured work-top into a rectangle about 6mm/¼in thick. Dot about one-third of the chilled lard across the dough, to within 1cm/½in of the edges.

Scatter over one-third each of the sugar and dried fruits, and a little spice. Fold one-third of the dough over from the short side into the middle, and cover with the top third of the dough. Press the sides firmly together so that the filling is completely sealed and make a quarter turn to the right; indent with two fingers. Chill in the refrigerator for 15 minutes.

Roll the dough into a rectangle as before on the indented edge, dot with half the remaining lard, sugar, fruits and spice, fold, seal and turn again; indent and chill. Repeat with the rest of the ingredients.

Finish by rolling and folding the dough to fit snugly into a deep, 20×25cm/8×10in greased baking tin. Press down well in the corners. Cover the tin with the floured cloth and leave to rise or prove and double in bulk.

Remove the cloth and brush the surface with a little milk and beaten egg, and sprinkle with granulated sugar. Score a criss-cross pattern in the surface with a sharp knife from one side to the other and bake in the preheated oven at 220°C/425°F/Gas 7 for 30-40 minutes. Turn out of the tin to cool upside down on a wire rack. Serve cut in slices when tepid or cold.

Red Velvet Cake
Serves 10-12

Ingredients

100g/4oz margarine
350g/12oz sugar
2 eggs
50ml/2fl oz red food colouring
30g/2tbsp unsweetened cocoa
250g/9oz plain flour
5g/1tsp salt
225ml/8fl oz buttermilk
5ml/1tsp vanilla essence

5g/1tsp bicarbonate of soda
5ml/1tsp white wine vinegar

Icing
45g/3tbsp flour
225g/8oz sugar
225ml/8fl oz milk
225g/8oz butter
5ml/1tsp vanilla essence

Preparation Cream the margarine and sugar until fluffy, then beat in the eggs.

Make a paste of the food colouring and cocoa. Add to the butter mixture and blend well.

Sift the flour and salt. Gradually add to the butter mixture, alternating with the buttermilk and vanilla.

Stir the bicarbonate of soda into the vinegar in a large spoon, holding it over the mixing bowl as it foams. Add to the cake mixture stirring well.

Grease two 20cm/8in cake tins. Divide the mixture between them and bake for 30 minutes at 180°C/350°F/Gas 4. Cool.

To make the icing, stir the flour, sugar and milk over a very low heat until thick.

Cream the butter with the vanilla until it is very light.

Beat the cooked mixture into the butter until the icing has the texture of whipped cream.

To assemble the cake, put one layer, upside down, on a serving dish. Spread with one-third of the icing. Gently place the second layer, right side up on top. Spread the sides of the cake with icing, and finally the top.

Red Velvet Cake

Chocolate Chip Cake
Serves 8-12

Ingredients

100g/4oz margarine	*5g/1tsp baking powder*
75g/3oz soft brown sugar	*3 eggs, separated*
100g/4oz ground	*1 orange*
hazelnuts	*50g/2oz chocolate pieces*
75g/3oz plain flour	

Preparation Cream the margarine and sugar until they are light and fluffy. Add the nuts, flour, baking powder, egg yolks and the grated rind and juice of the orange. Mix well. Fold in the chocolate pieces.

Whisk the egg whites until they are stiff but not dry. Gently fold into the cake mixture, starting with just one spoonful and gradually adding the remainder.

Grease an 18cm/7in square cake tin and line with greaseproof paper. Turn the mixture into it and bake for 45 minutes at 170°C/325°F/Gas 3.

For a large cake double all the ingredients and use a roasting pan, 23×28cm/9×11in.

Coffee Almond Slice
Serves 8-10

Ingredients

100g/4oz butter	*25g/1oz plain chocolate*
100g/4oz sugar	*300ml/¹/₂pt double cream*
2 eggs	*20g/4tsp instant powdered*
100g/4oz self-raising flour	*coffee dissolved in 15ml/*
15g/1tbsp baking powder	*1tbsp hot water*
50g/2oz ground almonds	*45g/3tbsp icing sugar*
2 drops almond essence	*50g/2oz chocolate*
15ml/1tbsp water	*vermicelli*

Preparation Grease and line an 18×28cm/7×11in tin with non-stick paper.

Put the first 8 ingredients in a bowl. Mix together and beat until smooth.

Pour the batter into the prepared pan. Bake for 25-30 minutes at 180°C/350°F/Gas 4 until firm to the touch. Turn out, remove paper and cool.

Melt the chocolate until runny and keep warm. Whisk the cream with the dissolved coffee and icing sugar until it forms soft peaks.

Trim the edges of the cake and cut into three even-sized pieces.

Spread a layer of cream on one piece, top with a second layer and spread with more cream. Top with the final layer of sponge cake.

Spread the sides with cream and coat with the chocolate vermicelli. Spread the remaining cream on the top.

Spoon the chocolate into a piping bag with a fine nozzle. Pipe straight lines along the length of the cake and with the point of a knife draw lines backwards and forwards across the chocolate lines creating a chevron effect.

Chill for at least an hour before serving.

Chocolate Rum Cake
Serves 6

Ingredients

15ml/1tbsp water
25g/1oz sugar
100g/4oz plain chocolate in small pieces
15ml/1tbsp rum, brandy or Grand Marnier

300ml/½pt double cream
20 sponge fingers (Boudoir biscuits)
100ml/4fl oz strong black coffee
25g/1oz grated chocolate

Preparation Heat the water and sugar, stirring constantly, until the sugar has dissolved. Leave to cool.

Melt the chocolate in the top of a double boiler. Add the cooled syrup, stirring constantly. Stir in the rum, brandy or Grand Marnier and 45ml/3tbsp cream.

Arrange half of the sponge fingers in the bottom of a serving dish. Carefully sprinkle some of the coffee over the sponge fingers, enough to just moisten them. Spread half of the chocolate mixture over the top.

Arrange a second layer of sponge fingers gently over the chocolate. Sprinkle with coffee and spread with chocolate as before.

Whisk the remaining cream until it is just firm. Spread over the top and sides of the cake and chill for 1 hour.

Serve decorated with grated chocolate.

Coffee Carrot Cake
Serves 8-10

Ingredients

100g/4oz butter, softened
150g/6oz sugar
1 egg
2.5g/½tsp mixed spice
60ml/4tbsp marmalade
30ml/2tbsp orange juice
60ml/4tbsp strong black coffee
225g/8oz carrots, grated
50g/2oz walnuts
225g/8oz self-raising flour

Topping
100g/4oz soft cream cheese
50g/2oz unsalted butter
75g/3oz icing sugar
5ml/1tsp vanilla essence
juice of ½ lemon

Preparation Cream the butter and sugar together until light and fluffy. Beat in the egg, mixed spice, marmalade, orange rind, juice and coffee. Mix well. Toss the carrots and walnuts in the flour and gradually stir them into the beaten mixture.

Turn into a lined and greased 20cm/8in cake tin and bake for 1½ hours at 180°C/350°F/Gas 4.

Cool the cake in the pan for one hour. Remove and finish cooling on a wire rack.

Cream the cream cheese and butter together. Slowly sift in the icing sugar and continue beating until the mixture is quite smooth. Stir in the vanilla and lemon juice.

Spread two-thirds of the mixture on top of the carrot cake. Put the remainder in a piping bag and pipe rosettes around the cake.

Chocolate & Sour Cream Marble Cake

Ingredients

175g/6oz plain chocolate
225g/8oz butter, softened
225g/8oz sugar
4 eggs
350g/12oz self-raising
  flour

150ml/¼pt sour cream
10ml/2tsp vanilla essence
2.5ml/½tsp almond
  essence
icing sugar

Preparation Melt the chocolate and allow to cool slightly.

Cream together the butter and sugar until light and fluffy. Beat in the eggs one at a time. Add the vanilla and almond essence, and fold in the flour.

Divide the mixture into two. Add the sour cream to one half and the melted chocolate to the other.

In a buttered and thickly sugared 9-10-in/2.6-l/4½-pt gugelhupf or ring pan, put alternate spoonfuls of the mixtures. Using a teaspoon, cut down into the mixture and swirl together. Bake at 180°C/350°F/Gas 4 for about 1 hour.

Serve warm or cold, dredged with icing sugar.

Mocha Hazelnut Cake
Serves 6

Ingredients

100g/4oz hazelnuts, shelled
3 egg whites
15g/1tbsp instant coffee
  powder
100g/4oz granulated sugar
15ml/1tbsp white vinegar
25g/1oz grated chocolate

Filling
75g/3oz plain chocolate
30ml/2tbsp coffee liqueur
300ml/½pt double cream,
  whipped
100g/4oz chocolate
  shavings

Preparation Roast the hazelnuts in a hot oven until well browned. Put inside a dry dish cloth and rub off the skins. Cool and chop roughly.

Whisk the egg whites until they form stiff peaks. Mix the coffee powder with 15g/1tbsp sugar and whisk in. Fold in the remaining sugar and vinegar. Lastly, fold in the nuts with the grated chocolate.

Line two baking trays with non-stick paper. Mark out two 20cm/8in circles and spread the mixture out to cover them.

Bake for 1¾ hours at 100°C/200°F/Gas ¼ until the meringue has dried out. Cool on wire racks.

For the filling, melt the chocolate with the coffee liqueur. Leave until cool but not set, then fold the chocolate mixture into the cream.

Sandwich the meringue rounds together with the chocolate cream and decorate with the chocolate shavings.

Coffee Fruit Loaf

Ingredients

225g/8oz strong flour
5g/1tsp salt
5g/1tsp sugar
small knob lard
15g/½oz fresh yeast
150ml/¼pt tepid black
  coffee
50g/2oz vanilla sugar
50g/2oz dried apricots,
  chopped

50g/2oz dried figs,
  chopped
50g/2oz almonds, roughly
  chopped

Topping

25g/1oz butter
40g/1½oz plain flour
25g/1oz vanilla sugar
15g/1tbsp instant coffee

Preparation Mix the flour, salt and sugar in a bowl and rub in the lard. Blend the yeast with the coffee and add to the flour, mixing to a soft dough that leaves the bowl clean. Cover with lightly greased polythene and leave to rise in a warm place until doubled in size.

Line and grease a 450g/1lb loaf pan. Gently knead in the sugar, apricots, figs and almonds, place in the prepared pan and cover with lighly oiled polythene. Leave to prove in a warm place until the mixture comes to the top of the pan.

For the topping, rub the butter into the flour until the mixture resembles breadcrumbs. Stir in the sugar and coffee and spoon over the loaf. Bake for 40-45 minutes at 200°C/400°F/Gas 6.

Cool in the tin for 10 minutes and then turn out onto a wire rack.

Serve warm or cold, sliced and spread with butter.

Refrigerator Biscuit Cake

Ingredients

225g/8oz milk or plain
  chocolate
100g/4oz butter
50g/2oz golden syrup (or
  corn syrup)
50g/2oz raisins, soaked
  overnight in a little rum
50g/2oz Brazil nuts,
  roughly chopped

50g/2oz glacé cherries,
  roughly chopped
225g/8oz digestive biscuits,
  crushed
glacé cherries
whole Brazil nuts

Preparation Put chocolate, butter and golden syrup into a bowl over a pan of hot water.

When the chocolate has melted, stir in the raisins, nuts and cherries. Add the biscuits and mix well together.

Press the mixture into a lined 450g/1lb loaf tin and chill for at least 4 hours, preferably overnight.

Turn out and decorate with glacé cherries and Brazil nuts.

Mushroom Cake

Ingredients

25g/1oz unsweetened
  cocoa powder
15ml/1tbsp boiling water
100g/4oz butter or
  margarine
100g/4oz light, soft brown
  sugar
2 eggs, beaten
100g/4oz self-raising flour

Icing
100g/4oz butter or
  margarine
225g/8oz icing sugar
50g/2oz plain chocolate,
  melted
225g/8oz marzipan
apricot jam, sieved
icing sugar or drinking
  chocolate

Preparation Mix together the cocoa powder and water to form a paste. Put butter, sugar and chocolate paste into a bowl and beat until light and fluffy. Beat in the eggs a little at a time. Fold in the flour.

Spread the mixture into one greased and base-lined, 20cm/8in sandwich tin. Bake in the oven at 180°C/350°F/Gas 4 for about 25 minutes. Turn out and cool.

To make the icing, cream together the butter or margarine and icing sugar. Stir in the melted chocolate and beat well. Cool. Using a piping bag fitted with a star nozzle, pipe lines of icing from the edge of the cake to the centre, to represent the underside of a mushroom.

Reserve a small piece of marzipan for the stalk. Roll the remaining marzipan out to a strip about 60cm/24in long and wide enough to stand just above the sides of the cake. Brush the sides of the cake with apricot jam. Press the marzipan strip round the edge of the cake. Curve the top of the marzipan over the piped ridges.

Shape the reserved marzipan into a stalk and place in the centre of the cake. Sieve a little icing sugar or drinking chocolate over the icing on the cake.

Chequerboard Cake

Ingredients

175g/6oz butter or
  margarine
175g/6oz sugar
3 eggs, beaten
175g/6oz self-raising flour
15ml/1tbsp milk
25g/1oz unsweetened
  cocoa powder

15ml/1tbsp boiling water
ginger marmalade
350g/12oz marzipan
175g/6oz plain chocolate
15g/½oz butter
crystallized ginger

Preparation Divide a 20cm/8in square cake tin in half by base-lining with foil with a pleat, supported by cardboard, down the centre. Grease well.

Cream together the butter or margarine and sugar. Gradually beat in the eggs. Fold in the flour. Divide the mixture in half.

Blend the cocoa powder and boiling water together. Stir the milk into one portion and the chocolate paste into the other. Spoon one flavour into each side of the pan. Bake for about 30 minutes at 190°C/375°F/Gas 5. Turn out. Cool.

Trim each piece of cake and divide in half lengthwise. Sandwich alternately together with marmalade and place one pair of cakes on top of the other to form an oblong with square ends.

Cut a sheet of greaseproof paper big enough to wrap around the cake. Roll the marzipan on top to fit it. Brush the cake with jam. Wrap the marzipan around the cake.

Melt the chocolate with the butter. Spread over the surface of the cake. Decorate with crystallized ginger and leave until set.

Banana Cake

Ingredients

100g/4oz butter or
  margarine
130g/4½oz dark soft
  brown sugar
3 eggs
4 bananas

10g/2tsp ground cassia or
  cinnamon
5g/1tsp baking powder
30ml/2tbsp boiling milk
170g/6oz plain flour
5g/1tsp baking powder

Preparation Melt the butter and sugar together, then beat in the eggs.

Mash the bananas with the cassia or cinnamon. Add to the egg mixture.

Mix the baking powder with the boiling milk and add to the mixture.

Stir in the flour and the second quantity of baking powder, sieved together.

Put into a greased 20×20cm/8×8in square tin and bake in a preheated oven at 190°C/375°F/Gas 5 for an hour.

Chocolate Meringue Gâteau
Serves 6

Ingredients

3 egg whites
pinch cream of tartar
140g/5oz caster sugar
75g/3oz ground hazelnuts

Sponge
50g/2oz plain flour
50g/2oz unsweetened
   cocoa powder
4 eggs, separated
100g/4oz sugar

Filling
225g/8oz plain chocolate
2 egg yolks
30ml/2tbsp water
300ml/½pt double cream
50g/2oz sugar
red jam

Decoration
mixed chopped nuts
chocolate curls
icing sugar

Preparation Line two baking trays with greaseproof paper. Draw an 18cm/7in circle on each one. Put the egg whites and cream of tartar into a bowl and whisk until stiff. Whisk in the sugar a little at a time until mixture is thick and glossy. Fold in the nuts.

Spread or pipe the meringue in the circles marked on the paper. Bake in the oven for 1 hour at 150°C/300°F/Gas 2. Turn off heat and leave to dry in closed oven for a further ½ hour, or until crisp. Remove and cool. Carefully peel away the paper.

To make the cake, sieve together the flour and cocoa. Whisk together the egg yolks and sugar until the mixture is thick and pale. Whisk the egg whites until thick, but not stiff. Fold the flour and egg whites alternately into the egg yolk mixture.

Pour into a greased and lined 18cm/7in cake tin. Bake for about 40 minutes at 180°C/350°F/Gas 4. Remove and cool.

To make the chocolate cream, melt the chocolate. Cool slightly. Beat together the eggs and water. Stir the melted chocolate into the egg yolks, mixing well. Put in a pan and cook very gently for a minute. Cool. Beat together the cream and sugar until soft peaks form. Fold into the chocolate mixture. Cover and chill.

To assemble the gâteau, cut the cake into two layers and spread each with a little red jam. Put a meringue round on a plate and spread with a little chocolate cream. Top with a layer of sponge, spread with cream and place on the second meringue round. Spread with cream and place on the second layer of sponge. Spread remaining chocolate cream over top and sides of cake. To decorate, put chopped nuts round side of cake. Top with chocolate curls and sprinkle with icing sugar.

Family Chocolate Cake

Ingredients

75g/3oz plain chocolate
50g/2oz clear honey
100g/4oz butter or
   margarine
75g/3oz sugar
2 eggs
140g/5oz self-raising flour
25g/1oz unsweetened
   cocoa powder
5g/1½ level tsp baking
   powder

2-3 drops vanilla essence
150ml/¼pt milk

Icing
50g/2oz plain chocolate
45ml/3tbsp water
25g/1oz butter
200g/7oz icing sugar,
   sieved

Preparation Put the chocolate and honey into a small bowl over a pan of hot water. Stir until the chocolate has melted. Cool.

Cream together the butter or margarine and sugar until light and fluffy. Beat in the chocolate mixture, then the eggs.

Sieve together the flour, cocoa powder and baking powder. Stir in the flour mixture a little at a time, alternately with the vanilla essence and milk. Pour mixture into a lined 19cm/7½in round cake pan.

Bake in the oven at 180°C/350°F/Gas 4 for about 45 minutes. Turn on to a wire rack, leaving the lining paper on the cake to form a collar.

When the cake is cool, make the icing. Put the chocolate and water into a small saucepan and melt over a gentle heat. Remove from the heat and stir in the butter. When the butter has melted, beat in the icing sugar.

Spread the icing over the top of the cake and swirl with a palette knife. When icing is firm, remove the lining paper from the cake.

Lemon and Clove Cake

Ingredients

100g/4oz butter
75g/3oz demerara sugar
2 eggs
130g/4½oz fine
   wholewheat flour
5g/1tsp baking powder

juice and grated rind of 1
   lemon
pinch cloves, powdered
30ml/2tbsp lemon curd
50g/2tbsp granulated
   sugar

Preparation Cream the butter and sugar. Beat the eggs together. Sift the flour and baking powder together and mix. Add the beaten egg and lemon rind, mix gradually into the creamed butter and sugar. Sprinkle the cloves in. Add the lemon curd and mix thoroughly.

Put the mixture into a greased and floured loaf tin and bake in the oven at 180°C/350°F/Gas 4 for an hour.

Dissolve the sugar in the lemon juice and pour it over the cake when you remove the cake from the oven. Take the cake out of the tin when it is cool.

Russian Seedcake

This simple yet deliciously aromatic cake is the perfect ending to any meal. Serve it with Russian-style tea — stir a spoonful of preserves or rum, or both, into each glass of tea.

Ingredients

450g/1lb sugar
450g/1lb unsalted butter
10 eggs
450g/1lb flour
5g/1tsp salt
10g/2tsp baking powder
15ml/3tsp vanilla extract

10g/2tbsp sesame seeds
10g/2tbsp caraway seeds
125ml/4fl oz orange juice
2.5g/½tsp cinnamon
raspberry or plum
   preserves to decorate

Preparation Preheat the oven to 180°C/350°F/Gas 4. Cream the sugar and butter together in a large mixing bowl. Add the eggs, two at a time, beating well after each addition. Add the flour, salt, baking powder, vanilla extract, sesame seeds, caraway seeds, orange juice and cinnamon. Beat for 7 minutes. Butter and four a 30-cm (12-in) diameter cake tin. Pour in the batter and bake for 1 hour or until a cocktail stick inserted in the center of the cake comes out clean.

Remove the cake from the oven and leave it to cool to room temperature. Spread the top of the cake with raspberry or plum preserves and serve.

Coffee Knots
Serves 8-10

Ingredients
15g/½oz fresh yeast
60ml/4tbsp tepid strong
  milky coffee
5g/1tsp vanilla sugar
225g/8oz strong white
  flour

2.5g/½tsp salt
25g/1oz butter
1 egg, beaten
vegetable oil for deep frying
5g/1tsp sugar
5g/1tsp cocoa

Preparation Blend the yeast with the coffee and sugar. Leave in a warm place until frothy. Sift the flour and salt into a large bowl and rub in the butter. Add the egg and yeast liquid to the dry ingredients and beat for five minutes.

Divide the dough into 8-10 pieces and shape into an 18-cm/7-in long roll. Tie each into a knot.

Heat the oil to 180°C/350°F and fry the doughnuts for 5-10 minutes, until golden brown.

Drain on kitchen towels. Stir sugar and cocoa together and toss the warm doughnuts in it.

Yeasted Crescents
Makes 15 crescents

Yeasted Crescents, or Kipfel, are a traditional favourite pastry in Austria. A charming legend attached to them suggests that they were first baked in Vienna, in 1683, during the Turkish siege of the city. The crescent, in imitation of their invaders' emblem, was the Austrian gesture of defiance.

Ingredients
15g/½oz fresh yeast
50ml/2fl oz milk, warmed
  to blood heat
20g/1½tbsp caster sugar
130g/4½oz strong plain
  flour, sifted
pinch salt
2 small egg yolks
75g/3oz butter

Walnut filling
50g/2oz granulated sugar
15ml/1tbsp milk
130g/4½oz ground
  walnuts
1tsp lemon zest
1 small Cox's apple, peeled
  and grated

Preparation Prepare the Yeast Sponge with the yeast, warm milk, 5g/1 tsp sugar and 30g/2tbsp flour taken from the main quantity; blend and beat well. Cover and set aside to rise.

Sift the rest of the flour with the salt into a large warm bowl and make a well in the centre. Drop in the lightly beaten egg yolks, the butter cut in pieces and the sugar. Draw a little flour in from the sides and pour in the sponge batter.

Combine all the ingredients by beating at first, then kneading, until the dough is very elastic and large bubbles of air start to form. Cover with a cloth and leave in a warm place for 1-2 hours to rise and double in volume.

Knock the dough back and roll it out on a floured board to 3mm/⅛in thick. Cut into 10cm/4in triangles and place a spoonful of filling (see below) in the centre of each. Roll the pastry up starting from the base line, bending it into a crescent shape. Lay the pastries on a greased and floured baking sheet and brush them with lightly beaten egg.

Cover the pastries with a lightly floured cloth and leave to rise for a further 30-40 minutes until they have doubled in size. Brush again with beaten egg and bake in the warmed oven at 190°C/375°F/Gas 5 until risen and golden. Cool on a wire rack and dredge with icing sugar to serve.

Prepare the filling following the instructions for Poppy Seed or Walnut Roll.

Eliza Leslie's Ginger Cup Cakes
Makes 28 cup cakes

This is a modern interpretation of a recipe in Eliza Leslie's *Seventy-Five Recipes for Pastry, Cakes and Sweetmeats. By a Lady of Philadelphia*, published in 1828.

Ingredients

100g/4oz butter	2.5g/½tsp ground allspice
100g/4oz light muscavado sugar	5g/1tsp ground cloves
175ml/6fl oz molasses or treacle and syrup, mixed	10g/2tsp ground ginger
200g/7oz plain flour	1 egg
5g/1tsp bicarbonate of soda	1 egg yolk
	60ml/4tbsp milk

Preparation Gently heat the butter, sugar and molasses in a pan until the butter has melted and the sugar dissolved. (Do not boil or the cakes will be hard.) Draw off the heat to cool.

Sift together two or three times, the flour, bicarbonate, allspice, cloves and ginger, finally into a large bowl. Make a well in the middle.

Whisk the egg and egg yolk with about half the milk and pour the mixture into the flour with the cooled syrup. Beat to a smooth batter, adding more milk if necessary.

Use waxed paper cases and fill each no more than half full with the mixture, which rises a lot during baking. Bake at 170°C/325°F/Gas 3 for 30 minutes, until well risen. The cakes should feel slightly soft to the touch. Leave to cool on wire racks.

Doughnuts
Makes 27 doughnuts

The Rhinelanders of Germany began emigrating to Pennsylvania in the seventeenth century when the religious persecution and deprivation in their native land had become intolerable. The Pennsylvania Dutch, as they were known, brought *Fastnachts* with them from the Old World, delicious yeasted doughnuts, which were baked for Shrovetide and Christmas.

All the ingredients should be at room temperature before baking commences and the flour warmed.

Ingredients

250ml/9fl oz milk, warmed to blood heat	100g/4oz butter
25g/1oz fresh yeast	2.5g/½tsp salt
400g/14oz strong plain flour, sifted	15ml/1tbsp brandy
30g/2tbsp sugar	5ml/1tsp rose water
8 egg yolks, lightly beaten	rose conserve or raspberry jam for the filling
	caster sugar for dredging

Preparation Prepare the Yeast Batter with 75ml/3fl oz milk, the yeast, 100g/3½oz flour and 1tsp of sugar. Beat well. Set aside to ferment. Mix half the remaining milk with the egg yolks and set aside. Melt the butter in the rest of the milk. Cool to lukewarm.

Sift together the rest of the flour with the salt into a large bowl and make a well in the centre. Stir in the rest of the sugar, the fermented yeast and the milk mixture. Blend all together and beat well until the dough thickens. Add the brandy and rose water and continue beating until the dough texture is smooth, shiny and will drop off a spoon.

Take out half the mixture and cover the bowl with a warm tea-cloth while you prepare the first batch of doughnuts.

Dust the work-top well with flour and drop the mixture on to it. Dredge with just a little flour and gently roll it out to about 1cm/½in thick. Using a floured glass or biscuit cutter about 5cm/2in in diameter, lightly press circles into half the dough, but do not actually cut it.

Place a small teaspoonful of jam in the centre of each. Cut out the same number of circles from the other half of the dough, and turn the top, unfloured sides over onto the jam circles.

Stick the doughnut edges well together (the jam must not leak out as they cook) and gently press around the edges with the end of a teaspoon handle. Cut out each pastry with a slightly smaller cutter. Turn over the finished doughnuts and place them well apart on a floured board, covered lightly with a tea-cloth.

Set the doughnuts to rise in a warm place and turn them over when they have risen on one side so that the other side may rise. Assemble the left-over scraps and beat them into the remaining dough with 2 spoonfuls of warm milk and finish in the same way.

A light and well-risen doughnut should have a pale ring around its middle, and the wider the ring, the lighter the pastry will be. Cook only four or five pastries at a time and always start by cooking the side that has risen first.

Heat the vegetable oil to 170-175°C/330-350°F. Using a large slotted spoon, gently lower each pastry into the hot oil at 4-second intervals. Watch them all the time for they brown very quickly. As soon as they have coloured well, which takes about 2 minutes, flip each one over and cook the other side until it is golden brown.

Lift the doughnuts out of the oil, drain on kitchen paper for a minute or two and roll them in caster sugar. Serve the doughnuts while they are still warm.

Chocolate Ring Doughnuts
Makes about 12

Ingredients

225g/8oz plain flour
2.5g/½tsp bicarbonate of soda
5ml/1tsp cream of tartar
25g/1oz butter
50g/2oz soft brown sugar
50g/2oz plain chocolate
5ml/1tsp vanilla essence
1 egg, beaten
milk

oil for deep frying
caster sugar mixed with ground cinnamon
Icing
100g/4oz plain chocolate
60ml/4tbsp milk and water mixed
225g/8oz icing sugar, sieved

Preparation Sieve the flour, bicarbonate of soda and cream of tartar into a bowl. Rub in the butter and stir in the sugar.

Melt the vanilla essence and chocolate together. Pour the beaten egg and chocolate into the dry ingredients and mix to a stiff dough, adding a little milk if necessary.

Knead very lightly and roll out until about 1cm/½in thick. Using a floured ring cutter (or a large and small round pastry cutter) stamp out doughnuts. Reserve the centres.

Heat the oil to 182°C/360°F/Gas 4 and fry the doughnuts a few at a time until golden brown. Drain and cool. Cook the doughnut centres (called doughnut 'holes'). Drain. While still warm toss in caster sugar which has cinnamon added to it. Serve doughnut 'holes' warm.

To make the icing, melt the chocolate and liquid together. Add the icing sugar and beat well.

Spread icing over cooled doughnut rings. These are always best eaten on the day they are made.

Spiced Buttermilk Scones
Makes 8

Ingredients

225g/8oz plain flour
225g/8oz wholewheat flour
10g/2tsp bicarbonate of soda
10ml/2tsp cream of tartar
15g/1tbsp fruit sugar (fructose) or 30g/2tbsp white sugar

5g/1tsp mixed spice
100g/4oz butter, diced
300ml/½pt buttermilk
15g/3tsp baking powder

Preparation Preheat the oven to 220°C/425°F/Gas 7.

Sift the flours together and mix thoroughly with the other dry ingredients. Rub the butter in well with your fingertips.

Stir in the buttermilk and mix to form a soft dough. Knead the dough lightly on a floured board. Divide in half, form each half into a round and cut each round into four wedges.

Arrange the wedges on a greased baking sheet, dust with flour and bake for about 12 minutes. Cool on a wire rack.

These scones are best eaten while still warm, split and filled with butter and jam, or jam and clotted cream.

Muesli Scones
Makes 10-12

These scones have a lovely nutty flavour, and crunchy texture.

Ingredients

175g/6oz wholemeal flour
50g/2oz sugar-free muesli
20g/4tsp baking powder

40g/1½oz butter, diced
40g/1½oz demerara sugar
1 egg
175ml/6fl oz single cream

Preparation Rub together the flour, muesli, baking powder, butter and sugar until well-mixed.

Add the egg and enough cream to make a soft, but not sticky dough.

Turn this out onto a well-floured board and roll out to 2.5cm/1in thick. Cut into 3cm/1½in rounds with a plain biscuit cutter.

Arrange the scones on well-greased baking sheets and cook in a preheated oven at 220°C/425°F/Gas 7 for 10 minutes till well-risen and golden.

Serve warm, split and buttered.

Blueberry Muffins
Makes about 36 breakfast muffins

Ingredients

450g/1lb blueberries,
 washed and thoroughly
 dried
300g/10oz plain flour
60g/2oz butter
75g/3oz sugar

2 eggs, beaten
300ml/½pt milk
15g/½oz grated lemon
 rind
8g/2tsp baking powder
5g/1tsp salt

Preparation Preheat the oven to 200°C/400°F/Gas 6. Put the berries into a sieve and add a few spoonfuls of flour. Shake sieve to dust berries lightly. Cream together the butter and sugar. Stir in the eggs, then the milk and lemon rind. Sift together flour, baking powder and salt and gradually stir into the moist ingredients to make a lumpy batter (do not overstir). Gently stir in berries. Fill greased bun tin hollows two-thirds full with batter. Bake muffins for about 25 minutes until firm and golden.

Bran and Sultana Muffins
Makes 12

Ingredients

30ml/2tbsp oil
30ml/2tbsp honey
1 egg
150ml/¼pt milk
140g/5oz wholewheat flour

75g/3oz bran
10g/2tsp baking powder
pinch salt
50g/2oz sultanas

Preparation Preheat the oven to 190°C/375°F/Gas 5.

Beat together the oil and honey. Beat in the egg. Gradually beat in the milk until smooth.

Combine the dry ingredients and stir these into the liquid ones. When the bran has soaked up the liquid, you should have a soft dough.

Spoon into oiled muffin tins and bake for about 20 minutes.

Madeleines
Makes 36 cakes

When Madeleines are mentioned one immediately thinks of Marcel Proust. In his *Remembrance of Things Past* the French author recalls his childhood and Sunday mornings taking lime tea and Madeleines with his aunt in Combray. He found 'the taste of the crumb of Madeleine soaked in her decoction of lime-flowers ... an exquisite pleasure [that] invaded my senses'.

Ingredients

130g/4½oz unsalted butter
15ml/1tbsp honey
100g/3½oz caster sugar
15g/1tbsp soft brown sugar
3 eggs

pinch salt
5cm/2in vanilla pod, split
130g/4½oz plain flour,
 sifted
flaked almonds

Preparation Gently melt the butter in the honey and set aside to cool. Beat the caster and moist sugars with the eggs and salt until the 'ribbon stage', that is, when the volume has trebled and a thick ribbon of batter will drop off the whisk and leave a trail in the mixture for at least 5 seconds. Beat in the vanilla seeds.

Lightly fold in the flour in three stages and finally fold in the cooled butter and honey mixture, taking care not to mix in any of the sediment in the bottom of the pan.

Half fill each of the buttered and floured madeleine moulds and sprinkle a few flaked almonds on top of each.

Bake at 180°C/350°F/Gas 4 for 20 minutes until risen and golden. Leave to cool on a wire rack before storing in an airtight tin.

Madeleines

Raspberry Chocolate Eclairs
Makes approx. 10

Ingredients

50g/2oz butter or	**Filling**
margarine, cut in pieces	150ml/¼pt double cream
150ml/¼pt water	225g/8oz fresh raspberries
65g/2½oz plain flour,	a little sugar
sifted	**Topping**
2 eggs, beaten	175g/6oz plain chocolate
	25g/1oz butter

Preparation Put the butter or margarine and water into a pan and bring to the boil.

Remove from the heat and tip all the flour into the pan at once. Beat with a wooden spoon until the paste forms a ball. Cool.

Whisk the eggs into the paste, a little at a time. Continue beating until mixture is glossy.

Put pastry into a piping bag fitted with a large plain nozzle. Pipe 7.5cm/3in lengths onto greased baking trays and bake at 200°C/400°F/Gas 6 for about 25 minutes, until golden brown.

Remove from the oven and make a couple of slits in the sides of each one to allow steam to escape. Return to the oven for a few minutes to dry. Cool on a wire rack.

To make the filling, whisk the cream until stiff. Fold in the raspberries and sugar to taste.

Split one side of each eclair and fill with the cream mixture.

Melt together the chocolate and butter. Dip the tops of the eclairs into the chocolate and leave to set.

Maids of Honour
Makes 8

Ingredients

225g/8oz Puff Pastry	40g/1½oz sugar
30ml/2tbsp apricot jam	rind of 1 lemon
225g/8oz curd cheese	30g/2tbsp ground almonds
1 egg	15g/1tbsp currants
1 egg yolk	icing sugar

Preparation Roll out the pastry and line 8 tart tins. Put a little jam into each.

Beat the cheese until it is smooth. Add the egg and extra yolk and mix well.

Stir in the lemon rind and ground almonds and fold in the currants.

Carefully spoon the filling into the prepared pastry cases.

Bake for 25 minutes at 200°C/400°F/Gas 6. Serve cool but not chilled, dredged with a little icing sugar.

Brownies
Makes 8-12

Ingredients

65g/2½oz butter
2 eggs
225g/8oz sugar
75g/3oz plain flour
5g/1tsp baking powder

45g/3tbsp unsweetened
   cocoa
100g/4oz walnuts,
   chopped

Preparation Melt the butter and leave to cool slightly.

Beat the eggs and sugar until they are very light and fluffy.

Sift together the flour and baking powder.

Stir the flour, baking powder, cocoa, walnuts and melted butter into the egg mixture. Mix well.

Spoon the brownie mixture into a greased 20cm/8in square baking tray and bake for 30 minutes at 180°C/375°F/Gas 4.

Cut the brownies into squares while they are warm, but leave in their pan until they have cooled completely.

Triple Decker Squares
Makes 16

Ingredients

100g/4oz butter or
   margarine, softened
50g/2oz sugar
150g/6oz plain flour
Filling
100g/4oz butter or
   margarine
75g/3oz sugar

30ml/2tbsp golden syrup
   (or corn syrup)
196-g/6-oz can condensed
   milk
Topping
175g/6oz plain chocolate
30ml/2tbsp milk

Preparation Cream together the butter or margarine and sugar until light and fluffy. Stir in the flour. Work the dough with your hands and knead well together.

Roll out and press into a shallow 20cm/8in square pan. Prick well with a fork. Bake at 180°C/350°F/Gas 4 for 25-30 minutes. Cool in the pan.

To make the filling, put all the ingredients into a pan and heat gently, stirring until the sugar has dissolved. Bring to the boil and cook, stirring for 5-7 minutes until golden.

Pour the caramel over the shortbread base and leave to set.

Melt the chocolate and milk together. Spread it evenly over the caramel. Leave until quite cold before cutting into squares.

Chocolate Meringues
Makes 6-8

Ingredients

3 egg whites
75g/3oz caster sugar
75g/3oz icing sugar, sieved
25g/1oz unsweetened
  cocoa powder, sieved

Filling
150ml/¼pt double cream
15g/1tbsp soft brown
  sugar
10ml/2tsp unsweetened
  cocoa powder

Preparation Beat the egg whites until they form stiff peaks. Gradually whisk in the caster sugar, a little at a time. Whisk in the icing sugar. Fold in the cocoa powder.

Put the mixture into a piping bag fitted with a large star nozzle and pipe into spirals on baking trays lined with non-stick paper.

Bake in the oven at 110°C/225°F/Gas ¼ for 2-3 hours or until the meringues are dry. Cool on a wire rack.

Whip the cream until stiff. Stir in the sugar and cocoa. Sandwich the meringues together, two at a time, with the chocolate cream.

Butterfly Cakes
Makes 12-14

Ingredients

100g/4oz butter, softened
100g/4oz sugar
2 eggs
5ml/1tsp grated orange
  rind
50g/2oz plain chocolate,
  finely grated
100g/4oz self-raising flour

Icing
75g/3oz butter or
  margarine
175g/6oz icing sugar,
  sieved
75g/3oz plain chocolate,
  melted

Decoration
icing sugar
seedless raspberry jam or
  glacé cherries

Preparation Cream the butter and sugar together until light and fluffy, then beat in the eggs, a little at a time. Stir in the orange rind and chocolate, and finally fold in the flour.

Arrange paper cases in a metal bun tin. Divide the mixture between the cases and bake at 180°C/350°F/Gas 4 for about 15-20 minutes. Cool.

To make the icing, cream together the butter and icing sugar. Gradually beat in the cooled, melted chocolate.

Starting 6mm/¼in from the edge, remove the top of each cake by cutting in and slightly down to form a cavity.

Pipe a little icing in the cavity of each cake.

Sprinkle the reserved cake tops with a little icing sugar and cut each one in half. Position each half on the icing to form wings.

Pipe small rosettes of icing in the centre of each cake, and top with a small blob of raspberry jam or half a glacé cherry.

Jaffa Cakes
Makes 18

Ingredients

2 eggs
50g/2oz sugar
65g/2½oz self-raising flour,
  sieved
approx. 60ml/4tbsp
  marmalade, sieved

100g/4oz plain chocolate
rind of ¼ orange, finely
  grated
10ml/2tsp corn oil
15ml/1tbsp water

Preparation Whisk the eggs and sugar until thick and creamy; when the whisk is lifted the mixture leaves a trail. If using a hand whisk put the bowl over a pan of hot water, then fold in the flour.

Spoon the mixture into 18 well-greased, round-bottomed patty tins. Bake for about 10 minutes at 200°C/400°F/Gas 6 until golden brown. Cool on a wire rack.

Spread a little marmalade over each cake.

Put the chocolate, orange rind, oil and water into a bowl over a pan of hot water. Stir well until melted. Cool until the chocolate starts to thicken and then spoon over the marmalade. Leave to set.

Chocolate Chip Cookies
Makes about 30

Ingredients
100g/4oz self-raising flour
25g/1oz unsweetened
  cocoa powder
2.5ml/¹/₂tsp baking powder
100g/4oz butter or
  margarine

75g/3oz brown sugar
50g/2oz sugar
2 eggs
2.5ml/¹/₂tsp vanilla essence
175g/6oz chocolate chips
75g/3oz chopped walnuts

Preparation Sieve together the flour, cocoa and baking powder. Beat together the butter or margarine and sugars until light and fluffy. Beat in the eggs one at a time and then add the vanilla. Add the dry ingredients and beat until well combined. Stir in the chocolate chips and the nuts.

Drop the dough in heaped teaspoonfuls onto a baking tray. Bake in the oven at 190°C/375°F/Gas 5 for about 10 minutes. Cool for a minute then remove from baking tray and cool on a wire rack.

Chocolate Malties
Makes 20-24

Ingredients
75g/3oz plain chocolate
75g/3oz cream cheese
75g/3oz butter or
  margarine, softened
25g/1oz instant malted
  milk powder
few drops vanilla essence
350g/12oz icing sugar,
  sieved

60ml/4tbsp milk
200g/7oz self-raising flour
2.5ml/¹/₂tsp baking powder
2 eggs
45ml/3tbsp milk
chocolate buttons
  (optional)

Preparation Melt the chocolate and cool slightly.
Beat together the cream cheese, two-thirds of the butter or margarine, malted milk powder and vanilla essence. Beat in the icing sugar and milk alternately, and finally the melted chocolate.

Remove 225g/8oz of the chocolate mixture. Cover and reserve for the icing.

Sieve together the flour and baking powder.

Beat the remaining softened butter or margarine into the chocolate mixture, then the eggs and the flour alternately with the milk.

Put paper cases into patty tins and fill two-thirds full with the mixture.

Bake at 180°C/350°F/Gas 4 for about 20 minutes. Cool.

Ice the cakes with the reserved chocolate mixture and decorate, if you like, with chocolate buttons.

"Christmas Pudding" Cakes
Makes 4-6

Ingredients
100g/4oz plain chocolate
30g/2tbsp butter
30ml/2tbsp orange juice
30ml/2tbsp icing sugar
20g/2tbsp cake crumbs
  (preferably a plain
  sponge)
15ml/1tbsp ground
  almonds

Decoration
grated chocolate
a little thick white Glacé
  Icing
glacé cherries
angelica leaves

Preparation Melt the chocolate in a bowl over a pan of hot water. Stir in the butter until melted. Remove from heat.

Stir in the orange juice, icing sugar, cake crumbs and ground almonds. Mix well. Chill for about 1 hour until firm.

Roll into balls and coat in grated chocolate.

Put into small paper cake cases. Top with a little thick glacé icing and decorate with pieces of glacé cherry and angelica leaves.

Danish Pastries
Makes about 16

Ingredients
25g/1oz fresh yeast
150ml/¹/₄pt tepid water
450g/1lb plain flour
pinch salt
50g/2oz lard
30ml/2tbsp sugar
2 eggs, beaten
275g/10oz butter
Filling
50g/2oz butter
100g/4oz icing sugar, sieved

75g/3oz plain chocolate, melted
25g/1oz toasted almonds, finely chopped
a few drops almond essence
Glaze
1 egg, beaten
honey

Preparation Blend the yeast and water together. Sieve flour and salt into a bowl and rub in the lard. Stir in the sugar.

Add the yeast liquid and eggs to the flour and mix to a smooth elastic dough. Knead lightly. Put into a lightly oiled bowl and cover with cling film. Chill for 10 minutes.

Soften the butter and shape into a flat oblong on greaseproof paper.

Roll out the dough on a floured surface to a rectangle three times the size of the butter. Place the butter in the centre of the dough and fold the dough over to enclose it. Press the rolling pin firmly along the open sides. Give the dough a quarter turn and roll out to a rectangle three times as long as it is wide.

Fold into three. Wrap in cling film and chill for 10 minutes. Repeat the rolling and folding three more times.

To make the filling, beat together the butter and icing sugar. Beat in the chocolate, almonds and essence. Chill. Roll out the dough thinly and cut into 7.5cm/3in squares.

Put a rounded teaspoonful of filling on to the centre of each square. Bring opposite corners of the dough to the centre. Either seal with beaten egg or insert a wooden cocktail stick through.

Place on a greased baking sheet. Cover with greased cling film and leave to prove for about 30 minutes. Brush with beaten egg. Bake for about 20 minutes at 220°C/425°F/Gas 7. Brush with a little honey whilst warm.

Chocolate Boxes
Makes 9

Ingredients
1 egg
25g/1oz sugar
25g/1oz plain flour
Filling
150ml/¹/₄pt water
140g/5oz tangerine jelly
225g/8oz curd cheese
300ml/¹/₂pt double cream

30ml/2tbsp apricot jam, sieved
Decoration
Chocolate Squares (see note)
whipped cream
9 mandarin orange segments
quartered walnuts

Preparation Whisk the egg and sugar together until the mixture is thick and creamy and the whisk leaves a trail when lifted. Using a metal spoon, gently fold in the flour. Pour into a shallow greased and base-lined, 18cm/7in square tin. Bake for 10-12 minutes at 200°C/400°F/Gas 6. Turn out and cool.

Heat the water. Add the jelly and stir until dissolved. Chill until the mixture begins to turn syrupy.

Beat the cheese and gradually add the jelly. Whip the cream until thick and fold into the cheese mixture. Pour into an 18cm/7in square cake tin, lined with greaseproof paper. Chill until set.

Spread the sponge with apricot jam. Unmould the cheese mixture onto the sponge. Trim edges.

Cut the cake into nine squares. Press a chocolate square onto each side of each cake. To serve, pipe whipped cream on top of each chocolate box. Top with mandarins and walnuts.

Variation Use cherry jelly, cherry jam and top with canned or fresh cherries.

Use strawberry/raspberry jelly, strawberry/raspberry jam and top with fresh strawberries/raspberries.

Use lemon jelly, lemon curd and top with pieces of canned or fresh pineapple.

Use lime jelly, lime marmalade and top with halved slices of kiwi fruit.

Note To make Chocolate Squares, melt plain chocolate and spread evenly onto greaseproof paper. Leave to set. Using a ruler, mark into squares and cut.

Sweetheart Cookies
Serves 10-12

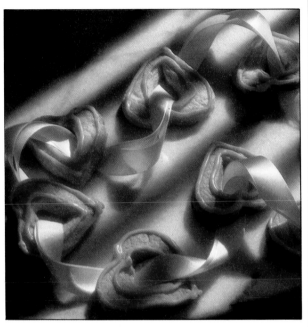

Ingredients
100g/4oz butter
100g/4oz sugar
30ml/2tbsp coffee essence
1 egg
275g/10oz plain flour

Decoration
100g/4oz icing sugar,
    sieved
1-2tbsp/15-30ml warm
    water
a few drops of red food
    colouring
pink and cream ribbons
    12mm/½in wide

Preparation Cream the butter and sugar together until pale and fluffy. Stir in the coffee essence and egg, and mix thoroughly. Fold in the flour and turn the mixture onto a board dusted with icing sugar.

Knead gently and roll out to 6mm/¼in thickness and cut into heart shapes. Cut a smaller heart shape in the centre for the ribbon. Place on a baking tray and bake for approximately 15 minutes at 180°C/350°F/Gas 4 and leave to cool.

Put the decoration ingredients into a bowl and mix until smooth. Spoon into a piping bag with a fine plain nozzle and pipe around the edges of the cookies and round the shape in the centre.

Allow to dry and thread the ribbons through the cookies and tie.

Chocolate Spiced Biscuits
Makes 60 pieces

In Austria it is customary to hang Chocolate Spiced Biscuits on the Christmas tree. Pierce a hole in each biscuit while it is still warm.

Ingredients
165g/5½oz unblanched
    almonds, ground
50g/2oz plain chocolate,
    grated
40g/1½oz candied orange
    and lemon peel, chopped
    small
5g/1tsp ground cinnamon

5g/1tsp ground cloves
3 egg whites
185g/6½oz icing sugar,
    sifted
ice-cream wafers
Icing
50g/2oz plain chocolate
50g/2oz icing sugar, sifted

Preparation Mix together in a bowl the almonds, chocolate, candied peels and spices. Make sure that the peels are separated and coated with nuts. Set aside.

Whisk the egg whites until they stand in firm, snowy peaks. Sift over and beat in the icing sugar in three stages and continue beating for about 7 minutes by machine (15 minutes by hand) until the mixture is thick, satiny and very smooth. Tip the nut mixture on to the meringue and use a large metal spoon to fold it in lightly.

Prepare the wafers by cutting them with sharp biscuit cutters into diamonds, squares or heart shapes. Pile a little of the nut meringue mixture on each of the wafers and taper it up from the sides into the middle in a dome about 12mm/½in high. Cover and leave to dry overnight in the kitchen.

Place the biscuits close together on a baking sheet — they do not rise — and bake in a preheated oven at 180°C/350°F/Gas 4 for 25 minutes or until pale golden brown. Lay them to cool on a wire rack.

To make the icing, melt the chocolate with 1½tbsp of water in a small bowl set over a pan of simmering water. Stir to combine. Sift the icing sugar into another bowl and stir in 1tbsp hot water, then blend in the chocolate mixture and stir until smooth. Cover the bowl with a damp cloth to keep it moist. As soon as the biscuits are cool enough to handle, dip each one into the chocolate icing, holding it by the base.

Cinnamon Stars
Makes 30 pieces

A Christmas speciality. Cinnamon Stars are often used as Christmas tree decorations. Use a cocktail stick or skewer to pierce a hole in the top of each biscuit before baking.

Ingredients
2 egg whites
250g/9oz caster sugar
250g/9oz unblanched
    almonds, coarsely
    ground

15g/1tbsp ground
    cinnamon
22.5ml/1½tbsp kirsch

Preparation Beat the egg whites until stiff, then mix in the sugar and beat for about 10 minutes by machine (20 minutes by hand) until the mixture is very thick, white and highly glossed. Reserve about 6tbsp of the mixture.

Mix the almonds, spice and kirsch into the rest of the snow. Gather into a ball, cover and chill for 30 minutes. Roll the paste out on a sugared board to 7mm/⅜in thick, and cut out star shapes with a pastry cutter.

Transfer the biscuits to a highly buttered greaseproof paper-lined baking sheet and smooth some of the reserved meringue on top of each. Bake at 200°C/400°F/Gas 6 for 15 minutes. Cool on a wire rack. These biscuits keep for several weeks stored in an airtight tin.

Coffee Macaroons

Ingredients

rice paper
100g/4oz ground almonds
175g/6oz sugar
2 egg whites

1tbsp/15g cornflour
2-3 drops vanilla essence
15ml/1tbsp coffee essence
12 chocolate coffee beans

Preparation Line two or three baking trays with rice paper. Mix the ground almonds, sugar and all but one tbsp of the egg white together. Stir until all the ingredients are evenly blended. Stir in the cornflour, vanilla essence and coffee essence.

Spoon into a piping bag fitted with a 1.2cm/½in plain nozzle. Pipe the mixture onto the rice paper in large round circles. Top each one with a chocolate coffee bean. Brush with the remaining egg white.

Bake the coffee macaroons at 190°C/375°F/Gas 5 for 15 minutes or until lightly browned, risen and slightly cracked. Cut the rice paper to fit round each coffee macaroon and leave to cool on a wire rack.

Nun's Pretzels
Makes 25-30 pieces

Ingredients

25g/1oz butter
1 small egg
50g/2oz icing sugar
100ml/3½fl oz double
  cream

175g/6oz plain flour, sifted
coarse sugar

Preparation Beat the butter and egg until creamy. Mix in the sugar and cream. Sieve most of the flour on to the work-top, make a well in the centre and drop in the mixture. Combine the ingredients to make a smooth pastry.

Roll into a ball, wrap in plastic film and chill for at least 30 minutes. Divide the dough into two and leave half in the refrigerator while you work with the other.

Pinch off walnut-sized pieces of dough, and lightly roll each into a rope about 6mm/¼in thick and 22cm/9in long, slightly tapered at the ends.

To shape the pretzel, lift up both ends and cross them over in the centre by pressing both the ends lightly on the top of the roll. Place on a greased and floured baking sheet. Finish the rest of the dough in

the same way.

Brush the pastries with lightly beaten egg white and sprinkle with a little coarse sugar. Bake in the preheated oven at 200°C/400°F/Gas 6 for 20 minutes until only just coloured. Cool on a wire rack. Serve with coffee. Stored in an airtight tin, pretzels will keep fresh for several weeks.

Vanilla Crescents
Makes 20 pieces

Ingredients

130g/4½oz plain flour,
  sifted
100g/3½oz unsalted butter,
  chilled

50g/2oz ground almonds
40g/1½oz caster sugar
vanilla flavoured, sifted
  icing sugar for dredging

Preparation Sift the flour on to the work-top and cut in the cold butter. Blend together into a fine crumb texture and fork in the almonds and sugar. Knead into a smooth pastry. Pinch off walnut-sized pieces and roll each into a cylindrical rope with tapered ends; curve gently into a crescent or quarter-moon shape. Transfer to a buttered and floured baking sheet and bake in the warmed oven at 150°C/300°F/Gas 2 for about 30 minutes or until lightly coloured.

Prepare a large sheet of greaseproof paper and dredge generously with vanilla icing sugar. Remove the crescents from the oven and leave to cool for 1-2 minutes. While they are still warm, lift the pastries one at a time, between two forks, and roll them in the icing sugar so that they are completely coated. Leave to cool on a clean sheet of greaseproof paper on a wire rack.

The crescents will keep fresh for several weeks stored in an airtight tin.

Vanilla Crescents and Nun's Pretzels

Flapjacks

Ingredients
100g/4oz butter
75g/3oz light muscavado
  sugar
75ml/3fl oz golden syrup
3g/¼tsp ground ginger
175g/6oz porridge oats
50g/2oz flaked almonds

Preparation Heat gently the butter, sugar and syrup in a small pan until the butter has melted and the sugar dissolved. Stir until smooth. Draw off the heat and stir in the ginger, oats and almonds. Spread the mixture out in a buttered 34×24cm/13½×9½in Swiss roll tin. Bake until golden at 180°C/350°F/Gas 4 (about 15-20 minutes), taking care that it does not scorch; it should still feel quite soft to the touch. Cut into fingers in the tin with a buttered knife while still hot. Flapjacks harden and crisp as they cool. Leave to cool in the tin. They keep well in an airtight tin.

Scottish Shortbread
Makes 60 pieces

Butter shortbread originated in Scotland as a festive confection particularly for Christmas and Hogmanay.

Ingredients
225g/8oz unsalted butter
100g/4oz icing sugar, sifted
2cm/1in vanilla pod, split
2tsp hot water
100g/4oz plain flour
100g/4oz potato flour

Preparation Cream the butter, add the icing sugar and blend well. Work the ingredients by hand in a chilled bowl as little and as quickly as possible. Do not use an electric mixer, which tends to over-beat, and make the pastry heavy.

Mix in the seeds of vanilla and stir in the hot water. Sift the flours together two or three times and combine lightly with the butter and sugar mixture. Gather the pastry into a ball, divide and roll into two long ropes about 2cm/¾in in diameter. Wrap closely in plastic film and chill for at least 1 hour. (The pastry may be frozen at this stage for up to 2 months.)

Cut 1cm/½in slices with a sharp knife and space 2-3cm/1-1½in apart on a greased and floured baking sheet. Bake at 170°C/325°F/Gas 3 for 25 minutes until slightly coloured. Cool on a wire rack. Dredge with icing sugar and store between sheets of greaseproof paper in an airtight tin.

Ginger Snaps
Makes 30 snaps

Ginger snap dough spreads out to about five times its original size when baked. Bake only two or three at a time so that the cooked, toffee-like snap can be rolled as soon as it is lifted off the tray and before it hardens.

Ingredients
140g/5oz plain flour
2.5g/½tsp ground ginger
pinch allspice
130g/4½oz butter, chilled
140g/5oz caster sugar
140ml/5fl oz golden syrup
1tbsp brandy

Preparation Sift the flour and spices together two or three times. Cut in the butter and rub to a fine crumb texture. Mix in the sugar. Add the syrup and brandy and blend into a smooth dough. The dough may be used straight away or chilled for a day so that the flavours develop.

Roll the dough into thick ropes, and pinch off walnut-sized pieces. Space two or three at a time, well apart, on a greased baking sheet and flatten a little. Bake at 170°C/325°F/Gas 3 for about 6-7 minutes, but watch carefully so that they do not burn. Cool for a minute or two, then lightly roll each one around the greased and oiled handle of a wooden spoon or a wooden dowel. Slide the snaps off the handle as soon as they have set and lay them on a wire rack to finish cooling.

Store between sheets of greaseproof paper in an airtight tin for up to a week. They taste good unfilled, served with ice cream or a creamy pudding; and for tea or coffee-time a filling of brandy-flavoured whipped cream studded with candied peels is a special treat.

Florentines
Makes 40

Ingredients

100g/4oz butter	**Icing**
100g/4oz sugar	225g/8oz icing sugar
15ml/1tbsp double cream	90g/6tbsp unsweetened
100g/4oz almonds,	cocoa
chopped	50g/2oz butter
50g/2oz glacé cherries	90ml/6tbsp milk
50g/2oz sultanas	5ml/1tsp vanilla essence

Preparation Place the butter, sugar and cream in a heavy-bottomed pan. Heat over a low flame, stirring constantly, until the sugar has dissolved. Remove the butter from the heat and stir in the chopped nuts and fruit.

Grease flat baking trays and line with rice paper. Drop small spoonfuls of the mixture onto the baking trays. Be sure to leave as much space as possible between them as they spread while they are baking. Bake for 10 minutes at 180°C/350°F/Gas 4 and leave to cool on the trays for at least 5 minutes. Move to a cooling rack and trim extra paper.

To make the icing, sift together the sugar and cocoa. Combine half of the sugar with the butter and beat well. Gradually add the remaining sugar, alternating with the combined milk and vanilla. When the Florentines have cooled completely, turn them upside down and spread with the icing. Leave to set before serving.

Cheese Shortbreads
Makes 30-40

Ingredients

175g/6oz Parmesan cheese	pinch mustard powder
or dry, strong Cheddar	pinch ground pepper
250g/9oz plain flour	beaten egg to glaze
200g/7oz butter, diced	

Preparation Grease several baking sheets. Grate the cheese. Mix the cheese with the flour, butter and seasonings till the mixture forms a stiff dough. Turn out on to a floured board and roll out 6mm/¼in thick and cut into fingers 7.5cm/3in long and 1cm/½in wide. Or cut into circles 5cm/2in in diameter.

Place on baking sheets, and prick well. Chill for 20 minutes then brush with the egg and bake in the heated oven at 200°C/400°F/Gas 6 for 10 minutes till crisp and golden. Cool on a wire rack.

Sesame Snaps
Makes about 20

Ingredients

100g/4oz wholewheat flour	10ml/2tbsp tahini (sesame)
50g/2oz sesame seeds	paste
5g/1tsp baking powder	15ml/1tbsp olive oil
5-10g/1-2tsp salt	50-75ml/2-3fl oz tepid water

Preparation Preheat the oven to 220°C/425°F/Gas 7. Combine the dry ingredients in a bowl. Add the tahini paste and olive oil and mix with the fingertips until crumbly. Gradually add enough water to form a soft dough.

Knead gently on a floured board and then roll out thinly. Press out rounds with a biscuit cutter and arrange on a greased baking sheet. Bake in the oven for 15 minutes until crisp and golden.

Cool on a wire rack, store in a tin and serve with cheese.

Oatcakes
Makes approx. 20

Ingredients

100g/4oz soft brown sugar	pinch bicarbonate of soda
50g/2oz plain flour	pinch salt
100g/4oz wholewheat flour	100g/4oz butter
100g/4oz porridge oats	1 egg yolk

Preparation Preheat the oven to 180°C/350°F/Gas 4.

Mix the dry ingredients together in a bowl. Cut the butter into small pieces in the bowl and rub in with your fingertips.

Mix in the egg yolk and form into a dough. Knead for a few minutes and then roll out thinly on a lightly floured surface and cut into 5cm/2in rounds with a biscuit cutter.

Leaving plenty of space between each one, arrange the rounds on a greased baking sheet and bake for 10-15 minutes until crisp and golden. Allow to cool slightly before transferring to a wire rack.

When cool, store in an airtight tin. Serve with cheese.

Rye Biscuits
Makes approx. 20

Ingredients
25g/1oz butter
100g/4oz rye flour
pinch salt
a little milk, heated

Preparation Preheat the oven to 180°C/350°F/Gas 4.
Rub the butter into the flour with the salt, and bind with enough milk to make a dough. Knead for about 7 minutes.
Form the dough into about 20 balls and roll flat on a floured surface.
Cook on a baking tray for about 10 minutes, until the edges are just beginning to brown. Cool on a wire rack.
Store in a tin and serve with butter and cheese.

Hazelnut and Apricot Crunch
Makes about 16 bars

Ingredients
100g/4oz butter
50g/2oz soft brown sugar
30ml/2tbsp maple syrup
100g/4oz porridge oats
50g/2oz chopped
  hazelnuts
50g/2oz dried apricots,
  chopped

Preparation Preheat the oven to 180°C/350°F/Gas 4.
Put the butter, sugar and syrup in a heavy-bottomed pan and stir over a low heat until combined. Stir in the remaining ingredients. Press into a Swiss roll tin lined with greaseproof paper.
Bake for about 45 minutes, until golden. Cut into bars in the pan using an oiled knife. Cool in the tin.

Coffee Slices
Makes 18

Ingredients
100g/4oz butter, softened
50g/2oz sugar
100g/4oz self-raising flour
15ml/1tbsp coffee essence

Icing
60g/4tbsp icing sugar
15g/1tbsp instant coffee
50g/2oz butter

Preparation Cream together the butter and sugar until light and fluffy. Fold in the flour and coffee essence.
Press into a greased Swiss roll tin and bake for 15-20 minutes at 180°C/350°F/Gas 4.
Put all the icing ingredients into a saucepan and over a moderate heat stir for 2-3 minutes until the mixture looks like fudge.
Pour the mixture on top of the shortbread. Leave to set and cut into slices.

Cherry Chocolate Crunch
Serves 8-10

Ingredients
100g/4oz plain chocolate
  in small pieces
100g/4oz butter
1 egg, lightly beaten
100g/4oz digestive biscuit
  crumbs
50g/2oz glacé cherries,
  chopped
50ml/2fl oz rum
30g/2tbsp chopped nuts

Preparation Melt the chocolate with the butter in the top of a double boiler. Off the heat, beat the egg.
Add the remaining ingredients and mix well so that the biscuit crumbs are well coated with chocolate.
Turn the chocolate mixture into a well greased 20cm/8in cake tin and chill for at least 8 hours before serving.

Anise Cookies

Ingredients

100g/4oz demerara sugar
150g/6oz wholewheat flour

5ml/1tsp baking powder
30g/1½oz finely ground
  aniseed

Preparation Beat the eggs until pale yellow. Add the sugar and beat for 3 minutes. Mix the dry ingredients together and fold into the mixture.

Drop the mixture a teaspoonful at a time onto a well-greased baking sheet, allowing an inch between each. Leave to stand at room temperature for 18 hours.

Bake in a preheated oven at 170°C/325°F/Gas 3 for approximately 12 minutes, or until cookies begin to colour.

Langues de Chat

Ingredients

90g/3½oz unsalted butter
100g/4oz sugar
3 egg whites

5ml/1tbsp vanilla essence
30ml/2tbsp single cream
100g/4oz flour

Preparation Cream the butter and sugar until very light and fluffy. Lightly whisk the egg whites. Stir into the butter mixture along with the vanilla and cream. Gently fold in the sieved flour.

Spoon or pipe the batter onto a well greased tray, allowing enough space for the biscuits to spread while they are baking. Langues de chat are traditionally finger shaped, but if you are planning to make baskets, spread the mixture into 10cm/4in circles.

Bake in a preheated oven at 200°C/425°F/Gas 7 for 5 minutes. Leave the biscuits to cool on the tray for a few minutes before transferring to a wire rack.

Variation When the langues de chat have cooled, their ends can be dipped into melted chocolate. Place the biscuits on a sheet of greaseproof paper for the chocolate to set.

To make baskets (*tulipes*) which can be filled with scoops of sorbet or ice cream, quickly lift the hot, soft biscuits with a spatula and gently press over upturned cups or moulds or slightly greased oranges. Leave to cool.

Baskets or *tulipes* can be made from batter flavoured with almond paste, orange or lemon rind or the mixture usually used for brandy snaps. Be sure to work quickly and shape the freshly baked biscuits before they have time to cool and firm.

Chocolate Pinwheels
Makes about 40

Ingredients

175g/6oz butter or
  margarine
175g/6oz sugar
1 large egg, beaten
5ml/1tsp vanilla essence

350g/12oz self-raising
  flour
45ml/3tbsp unsweetened
  cocoa powder
a little beaten egg white

Preparation Put the butter or margarine and sugar into a bowl and cream together until light and fluffy. Beat in the egg and vanilla essence.

Work the flour into the creamed mixture. Divide the mixture in half and knead the cocoa into one half. Shape into two smooth balls. Wrap in cling film and chill.

To make pinwheel biscuits, roll out the plain and chocolate doughs separately into equal rectangles. Brush the plain dough with egg white and place the chocolate mixture on top. Brush the chocolate mixture with egg white.

Roll up like a Swiss roll. Wrap in foil and chill. Cut into 5mm/¼in thick slices. Place on a baking tray and bake for about 8 minutes at 190°C/375°F/Gas 5.

Variations To make chequerboard biscuits reserve about a quarter of the plain dough. Shape the remaining plain and chocolate doughs each into two long thin rolls. Brush with egg white.

Put a chocolate roll next to a plain roll. Place the other two rolls on top, reversing the colours. Press lightly together.

Roll out the reserved plain dough to a large rectangle. Brush with egg white and roll it around the four thin rolls. Chill, slice and cook as in recipe above.

To make owl biscuits roll out the plain mixture to a rectangle. Form the chocolate mixture into a roll. Brush with egg white and roll up in the plain mixture. Wrap and chill.

Cut into 5mm/¼in slices. To form the owl's head, put two circles side by side. Brush join with egg white and press lightly together. Pinch the top corners of each head to form ears.

Place almond halves in the centre of each head for a beak. Put two chocolate dots for the eyes. Cook as in main recipe.

Viennese Chocolate Biscuits
Makes about 20

Ingredients
225g/8oz butter or
 margarine
50g/2oz icing sugar, sieved
225g/8oz plain flour
50g/2oz drinking
 chocolate powder
25g/1oz cornflour
100g/4oz plain chocolate
a little icing sugar

Preparation Cream together the butter or margarine and sugar until light and fluffy. Work in the flour, drinking chocolate powder and cornflour.

Put the mixture into a piping bag fitted with a large star nozzle. Pipe in fingers, or shells, or 's' shapes on to greased baking trays. Bake in the oven at 180°C/350°F/Gas 4 for 20-25 minutes. Cool on a wire rack.

Melt the chocolate. Dip half of each biscuit into the chocolate and leave to set on greaseproof paper.

Dust the uncoated halves of the biscuit with icing sugar.

Variation To make chocolate gems pipe the mixture into small individual star shapes. Bake for about half the time. Place a chocolate button in the centre of each one while still hot.

Birnbrot
Christmas Pear and Nut Bread

Bake the Birnbrot 3-4 weeks before Christmas. Wrap closely in foil and store in a cool place.

Ingredients
250g/9oz dried pears
100g/4oz dried prunes
100g/4oz dried figs,
 chopped small
100g/4oz dried or fresh
 dates, without stones
75g/3oz candied orange
 and lemon peel, chopped
100g/4oz raisins
100g/4oz sultanas
7g/1tbsp pine kernels
75g/3oz hazelnuts, toasted
 and chopped coarsely
75g/3oz walnuts, chopped
 coarsely
5g/1tsp lemon zest
10g/2tsp orange zest
25ml/1fl oz kirsch or rum

Bread dough
250g/9oz strong plain
 flour
20g/¾oz fresh yeast
60g/2½oz caster sugar
pinch salt
7.5g/1½tsp cinnamon
large pinch clove
2.5g/½tsp star aniseed or
 allspice
5cm/2in vanilla pod, split

30g/2tbsp granulated
 sugar
15g/1tbsp cornflour
30ml/2tbsp kirsh or rum

Preparation Carefully wash the pears and prunes. Place them in a pan and just cover with water. Leave to soften for 2-3 hours. Set the pan on the heat, bring to the boil and simmer gently for about 20 minutes. Drain the fruits but reserve the juice and leave to cool. Chop up the figs.

Place the figs, dates, orange and lemon peels, raisins, sultanas, the pine nuts, hazelnuts, walnuts, and the lemon and orange zests in a large bowl. Toss well together to mix and pour on the kirsch. Chop up the cooled fruit roughly and remove the stones. Add to the fruit and nut mixture.

Make a sponge batter with 50ml/2fl oz of the reserved fruit syrup, warmed to blood heat, yeast, 50g/2oz flour and 5g/1tsp sugar taken from the main quantity. Cover and set aside to rise and double in bulk.

Meanwhile, sift the remaining flour with the salt and spices in a large bowl. Make a well in the centre, pour in the sponge batter and draw in a little of the flour. Scoop in the seeds of the split vanilla pod and sugar. Combine well together and moisten with about 100ml/4fl oz of the fruit syrup.

Knead the dough very thoroughly until it becomes less sticky and starts to roll off the sides of the bowl. When it is very elastic and large air bubbles have started to form, gather into a large ball and place on the flour-dusted work-top.

Pull the dough out and gradually knead in the fruit and nut mixture until all has been used. Roll into a large ball and lay in the large flour-dusted bowl. Dredge with a little more flour and cover with a clean tea-towel. Set aside in a cool place to rise overnight.

Next day, break off pieces of dough and form into hand-sized 4-5cm/1½-2in rolls, or make two larger loaves (for 550g/1lb loaf tins), according to your choice. Lay small rolls, well apart, on greased baking sheets. Leave to rest and rise a little for 15-20 minutes, then bake in the preheated oven at 180°C/350°F/Gas 4 for 1 hour until golden and well risen.

Kirsch glaze for the warm loaves: heat 250ml/9fl oz fruit syrup with 30g/2tbsp granulated sugar, bring to the boil. Stir in 15g/1tbsp cornflour and cook until thickened. Draw off the heat and stir in 30ml/2tbsp kirsch. Brush on the warm loaves, press in a few almond halves for decoration, and leave to cool.

Bishop's Bread

A simple bread to serve with tea or coffee.

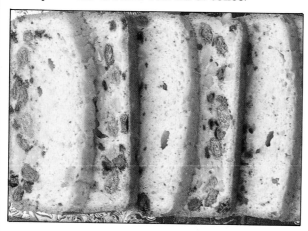

Ingredients

75g/3oz butter	25g/1oz raisins
75g/3oz caster sugar	25g/1oz sultanas
5 egg yolks	25g/1oz dark dessert
75g/3oz plain flour, sifted	chocolate, cut in small
5g/1tsp orange zest	pieces
25g/1oz pine nuts	4 egg whites

Preparation Beat the butter and sugar until pale and fluffy. Beat in the egg yolks one at a time, adding 5g/1tsp flour if necessary to prevent the mixture from curdling. Mix in the orange zest and pine kernels.

Dust the raisins and sultanas with a little flour, taken from the main quantity, and combine them with the mixture. Mix in the chocolate pieces.

Whip up the egg whites until they stand in firm snowy peaks and lightly fold them into the mixture. Lastly sift in the flour in three stages and combine gently.

Pour the mixture into a buttered gutter mould or a 1k/2lb loaf tin lined with greaseproof paper.

Bake at 180°C/350°F/Gas 4 for 1 hour until well risen and golden. Turn out of the tin to cool on a wire rack. Keep for 2 days before cutting. The loaf will stay fresh for about 10 days.

Cornish Saffron Bread
Makes two 1kg/2lb loaves

Saffron has always been the most expensive spice in the world, and it was especially favoured in Middle Eastern dishes for both its pungent and exotic flavour and its colour. The spicy cake has a yeasted, lightly fruited dough usually made without eggs.

Always buy whole saffron stamens rather than powder, which may be adulterated.

Ingredients

½tsp whole saffron	20g/1oz (scant) fresh yeast
filaments	375g/13oz strong plain
150ml/1¼pt water,	flour
warmed to blood heat	5g/1tsp salt
300g/11oz currants	pinch ground nutmeg
100g/4oz sultanas	pinch ground cinnamon
65g/2½oz candied orange	pinch mixed spice
and lemon peel, chopped	75g/3oz butter
140g/5oz plain flour, sifted	75g/3oz lard
50g/2oz caster sugar	**Glaze**
150ml/¼pt milk,	30g/2tbsp sugar
warmed to blood heat	15ml/1tbsp milk

Preparation Dry the saffron filaments in a hot oven for 5 minutes, then crumble them into a cup filled with the hot water and leave to infuse while you prepare the other ingredients.

Place the dried fruits and peel in a large bowl and set it in the warm, switched-off oven to heat through.

Make a Yeast Sponge Batter with 140g/5oz plain flour, 10g/2tsp sugar, the milk and yeast; beat well, cover and leave to rise and double in bulk.

Sift the strong flour with the salt and spices into a large bowl. Cut in the butter and lard and rub to a crumb texture. Mix in the rest of the sugar. Make a well in the centre and pour in the yeast batter and saffron liquid. Draw in the flour mixture and beat into a soft dough. Mix in the warmed fruits and blend thoroughly until the dough is shiny and shows large air bubbles.

Cover the bowl with a floured cloth, stand it in a warm place and leave to rise until it doubles in bulk, which may take as long as 2 hours.

Knock back the dough and knead for a moment or two, then divide it equally between two lightly greased 1kg/2lb loaf tins. Pat into shape and leave to rise for up to 1 hour more until risen almost to the top of the tin. Bake immediately in the hot oven at 220°C/425°F/Gas 7 for 30 minutes.

As soon as they are removed from the oven brush the loaves with a warmed mixture of 30ml/2tbsp milk and 15g/1tbsp sugar. Leave in the tins for 15 minutes before turning out to cool on a wire rack.

Serve saffron bread as soon as it has cooled. You may like to freeze one loaf while it is still warm.

Poori
Deep Fried Bread
Makes 20

Ingredients

225g/8oz plain flour	approx. 100ml/3½fl oz hot
2.5g/½tsp salt	water
30ml/2tbsp oil	oil for deep frying

Preparation Sieve together the flour and salt. Rub in the oil, and add enough water to make a stiff dough. Put the dough on a floured surface and knead for about 10 minutes till soft and smooth. Divide the mixture into 20 balls.

Taking one ball at a time, flatten on a slightly oiled surface and roll into a round of 10cm/4in across. (Do not stack the rolled pooris on one another as they will stick together.)

Heat the frying oil until very hot, add a poori, pressing the middle with a slotted spoon so that it puffs up. Quickly turn and cook the other side for a few seconds. Drain and keep warm while you make the rest. Serve hot.

Naan
Makes 12

Ingredients

5g/1tsp dried yeast	2.5g/¹/₂tsp salt
5g/1tsp sugar	4g/¹/₄tsp baking powder
75ml/3fl oz lukewarm	15ml/1tbsp oil
water	approx. 45ml/3tbsp plain
300g/10oz plain flour	yoghurt

Preparation Stir the yeast and sugar into the water and set aside for 15-20 minutes until the liquid is frothy.

Sieve together the flour, salt and baking powder. Make a well in the middle, add the yeast liquid, oil and yoghurt and knead for about 10 minutes till soft and no longer sticky.

Put the dough in an oiled plastic bag and set aside in a warm place for 2-3 hours until doubled in size.

Knead again for 1-2 minutes and divide into 12 balls. Roll into 18-cm/7-in rounds.

Arrange as many as possible on a baking sheet and put in a preheated oven at 200°C/400°F/Gas 6 for 4-5 minutes each side until brown spots appear. Put them under a hot grill for a few seconds until slightly browned.

Wrap the cooked ones in foil while cooking the others.

Wholewheat Bread
Makes 1 loaf

Ingredients

450g/1lb wholewheat flour	2.5g/¹/₂tsp molasses or dark
15g/1¹/₂tbsp sesame,	soft brown sugar
caraway or poppy seeds	15ml/1tbsp oil
10g/2tsp salt	15ml/1tbsp malt extract
300ml/¹/₂pt warm water	beaten egg to glaze
25g/1oz fresh yeast or 10g/	
¹/₂oz dried yeast	

Preparation Preheat the oven to 200°C/400°F/Gas 6. Mix the flour, most of the seeds and the salt together in a warm bowl.

Pour a little of the water into a small bowl and add the yeast and molasses or sugar. Put in a warm place for 10 minutes. If using dried yeast, make up according to manufacturer's instructions.

Add the oil, the malt extract and the molasses to the rest of the water in the jug.

Pour the yeast mixture into the flour and stir. Add enough of the other liquid to make a soft dough, but don't allow it to get too sticky. As different brands of flour absorb different amounts, it may not be necessary to add all this liquid, so don't add it all at once.

Knead the dough for 20 minutes, then put it in a greased plastic bag to rise. Leave in a warm place, such as the airing cupboard or a sunny window sill, for an hour.

Punch down the dough with the heel of your hand to redistribute the raising agent and knead it for a minute. Put it in an oiled loaf tin, 22×12cm/8¹/₂× 4¹/₂inches. Brush the top with beaten egg and sprinkle over the remaining seeds. Cover the loaf with a clean damp tea towel and leave it to rise in a warm place for a further half hour.

Bake for 35 minutes. Turn it out of the tin and tap the bottom of the loaf with your fingertips. It should sound hollow. The sides of the loaf should spring back when pressed. Allow it to cool on a wire rack.

Variation For Walnut Bread, add 50-75g/2-3oz roughly chopped walnuts and use walnut oil.

For a more savoury loaf, replace the malt extract with a yeast extract spread, such as Marmite.

Almond Loaf
Makes 1 loaf

A deliciously light bread, almond loaf is wonderful with morning coffee or afternoon tea.

Ingredients

4 eggs	2.5g/¹/₂tsp ground
225g/8oz sugar	cinnamon
few drops pure almond	100g/4oz flour
extract	15g/¹/₂oz butter, melted
5g/1tsp baking powder	225g/8oz unsalted, roasted
good pinch salt	almonds, finely chopped

Preparation Preheat the oven to 175°C/350°F/Gas 4.

Beat the eggs in a mixing bowl. Gradually beat in the sugar. Add the almond extract, baking powder, salt and cinnamon. Add the flour, melted butter and almonds. Stir until the batter is well blended. Pour the batter into a lightly greased 22cm/9in loaf tin and bake for 40 minutes.

Invert the pan over a wire rack and turn the loaf out. Let the almond loaf cool. When it is cool, cut it into quarters. Cut the quarters into 1cm/¹/₂in slices. Re-form the slices into a loaf shape in the pan and bake at 165°C/125°F/Gas 3 for 10 minutes. Turn off the heat and leave the loaf in the oven for 15 minutes, before cooling and serving.

Garlic Milk Loaf

Ingredients

1 head garlic, about 12	15g/¹/₂oz fresh yeast
cloves	2.5g/¹/₂tsp sugar
300ml/¹/₂pt milk	1 egg, well-beaten
450g/1lb flour, warmed	rock salt
5g/1tsp salt	a little garlic, finely
25g/1oz butter, melted	chopped (optional)

Preparation Blanch the separated, unpeeled garlic cloves in boiling water for 5 minutes. Drain and peel them, and simmer in the milk for about 10-15 minutes, until tender.

Sieve the flour with the salt and make a well in it.

Either sieve or blend the milk and garlic until smooth, and add the melted butter.

Cream the yeast with the sugar and add to the warm garlic milk with the beaten egg, and pour onto the flour.

Mix the ingredients thoroughly and knead lightly until smooth. The dough should be soft. Leave to rise, covered, in a warm place for approximately 1 hour.

Shape the dough into one large or two small loaves and place on a greased baking sheet. Cut several parallel slashes from end to end of each loaf, and leave to prove for 15 minutes.

Sprinkle each loaf with rock salt and a little chopped garlic, and bake at 230°C/450°F/Gas 8 for 20-30 minutes until well browned and hollow-sounding when tapped underneath.

Variations Leave the garlic cloves whole or add 50g/ 2oz pine nuts, browned in a little oil, to the dough before leaving to rise.

Pitta Bread
Makes 8

Preparation Follow Wholewheat Bread recipe. Preheat the oven to 230°C/450°F/Gas 8.

Divide the dough into 8 and roll out into thin ovals. Place on baking sheets and cover with clean damp cloths. Leave on top of the stove for 20 minutes.

Bake for 5-7 minutes. Allow to cool. These pitta breads freeze very successfully.

Yom Kippur Bread
Serves 8

This traditional Jewish loaf is served immediately after the holy day ends, to break the fast.

Ingredients

650g/1lb 6oz flour	125ml/4fl oz olive oil
2 packages active dry yeast	20g/2tbsp anise seeds
225ml/7½fl oz tepid water	15ml/1tbsp vanilla essence
350g/12oz sugar	7.5g/1½tsp salt
3 eggs	2 egg yolks

Preparation In a large mixing bowl, combine 200g/8oz of the flour with the yeast, water, and 30g/2tbsp of the sugar. Mix with a whisk into a smooth dough. Sprinkle with 50g/2oz of the flour and cover the bowl with a clean tea-towel. Set aside for 2½ hours.

Add the 3 whole eggs, remaining sugar, olive oil, anise seeds, vanilla essence, salt and remaining flour. Mix into an even dough. Knead the dough until stiff on a floured surface. Divide the dough in half and knead each half for an additional 5 minutes. Let the dough rest for 5 minutes.

Shape the dough halves into two 25cm/10in loaves and place them on a greased and floured baking sheet. Cover with a clean tea-towel and leave for 1½ hours. In a small mixing bowl, beat the egg yolks with 10ml/2tsp of water and brush the mixture over the tops of the loaves. Bake for 30 minutes at 190°C/375°F/Gas 5. Remove and leave them to cool on wire racks.

Austrian Bagels
Makes 12 bagels

Historians of the bagel recount that in 1683 an anonymous Viennese baker decided to honour the King of Poland's favorite pastime, riding, by making a bread roll in the shape of a stirrup. The German word for stirrup is *beugel* — hence the modern bagel. The controversy over what makes a proper bagel continues to rage. But there is no dispute that the true bagel is boiled first and them baked, giving it a dense texture.

Ingredients

1 packet active dried yeast	pinch salt
450ml/15fl oz warm water	475g/17oz flour
25g/1oz sugar	4.5l/8pts water

Preparation Dissolve the yeast in the warm water in a large bowl. Add the sugar, salt and flour and stir to form a soft dough.

Turn the dough out on to a floured surface and knead until smooth and elastic, about 10 minutes. Cover the dough with a tea-towel and leave to rise for 15 minutes.

Flatten the dough and roll out to a thickness of 2.5cm/1in. Cut the dough into strips 30cm/12in long and 2.5cm/1in wide. Roll each strip into a cylinder with a diameter of 1cm/½in. Cut each cylinder in half. Pinch together the ends of the strips to form circles.

Cover the bagels with a tea-towel and leave them to rise for 20 minutes. Bring the water to a boil in a large pot. Add the bagels in batches of 4 to the boiling water, reduce the heat, and simmer for 7 minutes. Remove the bagels, drain well, and place them on baking sheets. Bake for 30 minutes at 180°C/375°F/Gas 4.

Challah
Makes 2 loaves

Ingredients

225ml/7½fl oz lukewarm water	8g/1½tsp salt
3 packets active dry yeast	3 eggs
25g/1oz sugar	60ml/2fl oz vegetable oil
675g/1½lb flour	1 egg yolk

Preparation In a small bowl combine the water, yeast and 5g/1tsp of the sugar. Leave it to stand for 3 minutes and then stir until the yeast is dissolved. Leave it for a further 5 minutes.

Combine 400g/16oz of the flour with the salt and remaining sugar in a large, deep mixing bowl. Make a well in the centre of the flour and pour in the yeast mixture. Add the eggs and vegetable oil. Gently stir until the ingredients are blended together. Stirring more vigorously, blend in the remaining flour.

Turn the dough out onto a lightly floured surface and knead for 20 minutes with a rolling pin, flattening the dough with the rolling pin, gathering it back into a ball and flattening again. Place the dough ball into a bowl, cover with a clean cloth, and leave it to stand for 45 minutes or until it is nearly doubled in bulk. Turn the dough out and knead for 5 minutes. Leave to rest for 5 minutes.

Cut the dough in half with a sharp knife. Cut each half into thirds. Roll each piece of dough into a cylinder that tapers at each end. Pinch the ends of the 3 dough cylinders together. Braid the cylinders and pinch the other ends together. Repeat with the remaining dough. Place the challahs on a lightly greased baking sheet and leave them to stand for 30 minutes.

In a small bowl, beat the egg yolk with 30ml/2tbsp cold water. Brush the tops of the challahs with the egg yolk and bake for 20 minutes at 200°C/400°F/Gas 6. Reduce the temperature to 190°C/375°F/Gas 5 and bake for 40 minutes longer, or until the challahs are lightly browned. Cool on a rack.

Making a Flan Case

1 Roll out the pastry on a floured surface to a round 6cm/2½in larger than the flan ring. Lay the rolling pin gently on the pastry and fold one side over it.

2 Lift up the pastry on the rolling pin. Brush off excess flour.

3 Drape the pastry carefully over the flan ring by turning the pin slowly to allow it to fall gently over the ring. Do not let the pin touch the ring or it may cut through the pastry. Do not stretch the pastry or it will shrink back once in the oven.

4 Ease the pastry into the corners with the back of a finger.

5 Alternatively, you can use a small ball of paste to push it well into the corners.

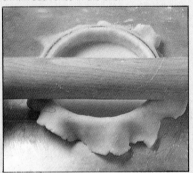

6 Roll the pin over the top of the flan ring to cut off the excess pastry.

7 Gently dislodge the pastry edge with a fingernail if it sticks to the flan ring — this will prevent it sticking in the oven.

8 To bake blind, prick the bottom of the flan case to prevent bubbling up while baking.

9 Line with waxed paper (crumpling the paper first will ensure that you do not damage the pastry) and fill with 'blind beans' (here a mixture of dry rice and pasta). 'Blind beans' may be re-used indefinitely. Remove the paper and beans when the case is half-baked.

10 Remove the flan ring once the case is almost cooked and return to the oven to allow the sides to brown.

Beating Strudel Paste

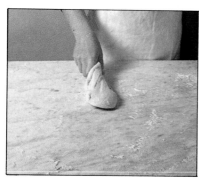

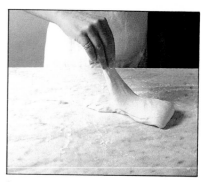

1 Lift the dough up in one hand and with a flick of the wrist throw it onto a lightly floured marbled slab or board without letting go of it.

2 Gather it up again and repeat the flinging down. Keep doing this for a few minutes. The paste will gradually become more elastic and less sticky.

3 Keep folding and flicking until the paste is smooth, shiny and elastic. Cover and leave in a warm place for 15 minutes.

Making Apple Strudel

1 On a table covered by a large floured cloth, roll the paste out as thinly as possible.

2 Now put your hands, lightly floured, under the paste and gently pull and stretch it keeping your hands fairly flat. Carefully work all round the table, gently pulling the paste until it is evenly paper-thin.

3 Trim the thick edges. Do not worry about the odd tear hole.

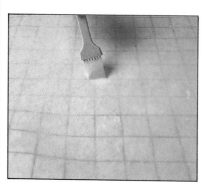

4 Brush immediately with butter to prevent the paste drying out — it becomes brittle alarmingly quickly.

5 Sprinkle the filling on the paste, leaving a clear margin. Use the cloth to help roll it up like a jelly roll, trying to maintain a fairly tight, even roll.

6 Tip the strudel onto a waxed baking sheet and curve it gently into a horse-shoe shape. Brush with butter and bake.

Processor Pastry

1 Put the fat (cut into lumps) into the bowl with the flour and any liquid if used. When processed the mixture will first go crumbly. At this stage, it is suitable for use as a crumble topping.

2 Continue processing until the crumbs are gathered into one lump in the bowl. The mixture is now suitable for pastry. Take care not to overprocess the paste.

Drinks

Banana Shake   347
Bloodshot   347
Buttermilk Liqueur Cooler   347
Citrus Shake   347
Chocolate Egg Nog   347
Hot Chocolate   348
Chocolaccino   348
Choconana Milk Shake   348
Iced Caribbean Chocolate   348
Café Brûlot Diabolique   349
Calypso Coffee   349
Irish Coffee   349
Iced Café au Lait   350
Coffee Noggin   350
Mega Mocha Shake   350
Viennese Coffee   351

Frozen Latin Flip   351
Southern Belle   351
Down Home Shake   352
Singapore Sling   352
Iced Grasshopper   352
Grapefruit Frappé   352
Iced Julep   353
Tomato Cocktail   353
Healthfood Drink   353
Raspberry Yoghurt Drink   354
Pineapple Yoghurt Drink   354
Orange Yoghurt Drink   354
Peach Passion   354

Wine glasses   355

Banana Shake
Serves 2

Ingredients
150ml/¼pt yoghurt
1 banana
honey to taste

Preparation Blend all the ingredients together well.
Serve immediately.

Bloodshot
Serves 4-6

A cross between a Bloody Mary and a Bullshot,
recommended for Sunday Brunch and/or hangovers.

Ingredients
225ml/8fl oz vodka
225ml/8fl oz chilled
*   consommé or beef*
*   bouillon*
350ml/12fl oz chilled
*   tomato juice*
juice of half a lemon
5g/1tsp sugar
10-15ml/2-3tsp garlic juice
*   (optional)*
approx. 5ml/1tsp
*   Worcestershire Sauce*
salt and cayenne pepper or
*   Tabasco to taste*

Preparation Stir the ingredients together in a glass
jug, seasoning to taste, and serve over ice in tall
glasses.

Buttermilk Liqueur Cooler
Serves 4

Use any liqueur you have on hand. Chocolate mint,
orange-flavoured liqueurs, *crème de cassis* — all are
delicious. A miniature, though slightly less than the
stated amount, is a handy measure.

Ingredients
600ml/1pt buttermilk
3 ice cubes
1 egg white
50ml/2fl oz liqueur

Preparation Blend everything together well until
light and fluffy. Serve immediately.

Citrus Shake
Serves 1

This drink contains all the nutrients you need to start
the day.

Ingredients
150ml/¼pt yoghurt
juice of one orange
1 egg
10ml/2tsp clear honey

Preparation Blend everything together well and
drink immediately.

Chocolate Egg Nog
Serves 4-6

Ingredients
2 eggs
30ml/2tbsp sugar
200ml/⅓pt milk
45ml/3tbsp Chocolate
*   Syrup (see recipe for Iced*
*   Caribbean Chocolate)*
30ml/2tbsp Crème de
*   Cacao*
30ml/2tbsp Amaretto
a few drops of vanilla
*   essence*
200ml/⅓pt whipping
*   cream*
grated nutmeg

Preparation Separate the eggs. Put the egg yolks and
15g/1tbsp of sugar into a bowl and whisk until thick
and pale.
    Add milk, chocolate syrup, liqueurs and essence,
and whisk well. Chill.
    Whisk the whipping cream until loosely thick (not
stiff). Whisk the egg whites until stiff and fold in the
remaining sugar.
    Stir the egg yolk mixture into the whipped cream,
fold in the egg white.
    To serve, pour into small glasses and sprinkle with
freshly grated nutmeg.

Hot Chocolate
Serves 3

Ingredients
225g/8oz plain chocolate
300ml/½pt water
450ml/¾pt milk

Preparation Put the chocolate and water into a pan. Heat gently, stirring until dissolved.

Heat the milk just to boiling. Pour the hot milk on to the chocolate and whisk until frothy.

Pour into hot mugs. Add brown sugar if desired. Top with marshmallows or a dollop of whipped cream. Sprinkle with drinking chocolate powder.

Chocolaccino
Serves 1

An excellent variation on *Cappuccino.*

Ingredients
50ml/2fl oz hot milk
50ml/2fl oz hot Italian coffee
30ml/2tbsp double cream, lightly whipped
25g/1oz semi-sweet chocolate, grated

Preparation If you do not have a *cappuccino* maker froth the hot milk in a blender for approximately one minute.

Mix with the hot coffee and pour into a tall cup or glass.

Spoon over the whipped cream and top with grated chocolate. Serve immediately.

Left, Choconana Milk Shake; right, Iced Caribbean Chocolate

Choconana Milk Shake
Serves 2-3

Ingredients
300ml/½pt milk
45ml/3tbsp Chocolate Syrup (see recipe for Iced Caribbean Chocolate)
600ml/1pt chocolate ice cream
1 banana, cut into pieces

Preparation Put milk, chocolate syrup, ice cream and banana into a blender. Cover and blend until smooth.

To serve, pour into glasses and add a chocolate flake to each one.

Iced Caribbean Chocolate
Serves 4

Ingredients
450ml/¾pt milk
150ml/¼pt single cream
2 large pinches of ground nutmeg
2 large pinches of ground cinnamon
a large pinch of ground allspice
75ml/5tbsp Chocolate Syrup (see below)

Preparation Put the milk, cream, spices and syrup into a bowl and whisk well together. Chill well. Before serving, whisk again.

To serve, pour into glasses over ice cubes and top with scoops of coffee ice cream.

Chocolate Syrup Mix 350g/12oz soft brown sugar and 125g/4oz unsweetened cocoa. Add 300ml/½pt boiling water, stirring continuously. Simmer gently for 5 minutes, stirring frequently. Allow to cool and add 10ml/2tsp vanilla essence. Cover and chill.

Café Brulôt Diabolique
Serves 6-8

This punch can be made in a saucepan but it looks far more dramatic when made at the table. Use any deep, heat resistant bowl but a silver bowl is traditional.

Ingredients

8 cloves	45g/3tbsp sugar
1 stick cinnamon	150ml/¼pt brandy
1 vanilla pod	1l/2pt hot coffee
thinly pared rind of 1 orange	75ml/5tbsp Cointreau
thinly pared rind of 1 lemon	

Preparation Put the cloves, cinnamon, vanilla, orange and lemon rind and sugar into a bowl.

Pour the brandy into a warmed ladle a little at a time and heat gently. Ignite it and pour over the ingredients in the bowl. Stir gently.

Slowly add the hot coffee and stir until the flames disappear.

Add the Cointreau and serve in small, warmed cups.

Calypso Coffee
Serves 4

Ingredients

1l/2pt hot coffee	60ml/4tbsp Tia Maria
30ml/2tbsp white rum	150ml/¼pt double cream

Preparation Heat all the ingredients except the cream, but do not boil.

Warm four brandy glasses and divide the liquid between them.

Stir, then add the cream, pouring it slowly over the back of a spoon so that its weight does not pull it straight to the bottom. Serve immediately.

Irish Coffee
Serves 1

It is important to use a strong brew so that the coffee compliments the whiskey rather than being drowned by it.

Ingredients

30ml/1tbsp Irish whiskey
15g/1tsp brown sugar
150ml/¼pt strong coffee
45ml/3tbsp double cream

Preparation Warm an Irish Coffee or long glass, add the sugar and whiskey and pour on the coffee.

To serve, pour the cream over a spoon onto the coffee and drink the warm liquid through the cool layer of cream.

Iced Café au Lait
Serves 4

Ingredients

300ml/½pt hot extra strong   sugar to taste
  coffee, freshly made   60ml/4tbsp double cream,
300ml/½pt hot milk   lightly whipped

Preparation Combine the coffee and milk, and sweeten to taste. Cover and leave to cool, then refrigerate until cold.

Pour into four chilled glasses and serve, topped with the whipped cream.

Coffee Noggin
Serves 6-8

Ingredients

150ml/¼pt milk   4 eggs, separated
150ml/¼pt single cream   20ml/4tsp Crème de Cacao
300ml/½pt hot coffee,   150ml/¼pt double cream
  sweetened   grated nutmeg

Preparation Whisk together in a saucepan over a low heat the milk, single cream and sweetened coffee. Do not boil.

Whisk in the egg yolks and cook until the mixture thickens. Strain and cool.

Stir in the Crème de Cacao. Whisk the double cream until it just holds its peaks and fold into the coffee mixture.

Just before serving, whisk the egg whites until stiff and fold into the Coffee Noggin.

Serve in glass cups, goblets or mugs, sprinkled with nutmeg.

Mega Mocha Shake
Serves 2

Ingredients

3 scoops of coffee ice cream   150ml/¼pt chilled strong
3 scoops of chocolate ice   sweetened coffee
  cream   150ml/¼pt milk

Preparation Combine all the ingredients in a blender until creamy.

To serve, pour out into two chilled tall glasses. Add a wide straw and chocolate flake to each.

Mega Mocha Shake

Viennese Coffee
Serves 4

What makes this Viennese coffee is the 'Schlagobers' — a large spoonful of sweetened whipped cream as topping.

Ingredients
100g/4oz plain chocolate   *150ml/¹/₄pt double cream*
60ml/4tbsp single cream   *5g/1tsp sugar*
600ml/1pt hot strong coffee

Preparation Gently melt the chocolate in a saucepan taking care not to burn it. Stir in single cream.

Pour in the coffee a little at a time, beating well until frothy. Keep warm. Whip the double cream with the sugar. Pour the coffee into four warmed cups and spoon on the whipped cream.

Sprinkle with cinnamon and cocoa to serve.

Frozen Latin Flip
Serves 4

Ingredients
450ml/16fl oz coffee, rum
or chocolate ice cream
125ml/4fl oz Tia Maria,
Kahlua or Crème de
Cacao
225ml/8fl oz milk

Preparation As for iced grasshopper. Garnish wth chocolate strands.

Southern Belle
Serves 2

Ingredients
60ml/4tbsp Southern   *225ml/8fl oz cold black*
Comfort   *coffee*
60ml/4tbsp apricot brandy   *50ml/2fl oz double cream*
   slices of fresh apricot

Preparation Combine all the ingredients except the apricot slices in a blender and pour into chilled glasses.

Serve decorated with apricot slices.

Frozen Latin Flip

Down Home Shake
Serves 4

Ingredients

450ml/16fl oz chocolate,   *15ml/1tbsp honey*
rum or ginger ice cream,   *50ml/2fl oz dark rum*
or lemon sorbet   *225ml/8fl oz milk*

Preparation Combine ingredients in the same way as for iced grasshopper. Omit the mint leaf garnish but serve with either grated chocolate or a sprinkling of cinnamon or ground ginger on top.

Iced Grasshopper
Serves 4

Ingredients

450ml/16fl oz mint or   *50ml/2fl oz Crème de*
pistachio ice cream   *Cacao*
50ml/2fl oz Crème de
Menthe

Preparation Combine all ingredients in a liquidizer, blender or food processor and mix until thick and smooth.
    Pour into tall glasses and garnish with mint leaves dipped into egg white and sugar to give a frosted appearance.

Singapore Sling
Serves 1

This drink was christened the Singapore Sling in 1915 by the head barman at Raffles, whose family are still represented in the long bar even today.

Ingredients

2 measures gin   *few drops Angostura bitters*
1 measure cherry brandy   *few drops Cointreau*
1 measure orange juice   *crushed ice cubes*
1 measure lemon juice   *pineapple and maraschino*
1 measure pineapple juice   *cherry*

Preparation Shake all the ingredients with the ice then strain into a tall glass. Decorate with pineapple and cherry and serve at once.

Grapefruit Frappé
Serves 2-3

This rich and unusual-tasting shake is a meal in itself and, frozen, makes a refreshingly crunchy ice, enough for 4.

Ingredients

75ml/3fl oz frozen   *225ml/8fl oz milk*
concentrated grapefruit   *2 eggs*
juice   *15-30ml/1-2tbsp clear*
225ml/8fl oz vanilla ice   *honey (optional)*
cream

Preparation Liquidize or process all the ingredients together until thick and well blended.
    Serve immediately in tall, chilled glasses.

Iced Julep
Serves 4

Ingredients
450ml/16fl oz mint or
  vanilla ice cream
50ml/2fl oz Crème de
  Menthe

2fl oz Southern Comfort or
  Bourbon

Preparation Combine ingredients in the same way as for Ice Grasshopper. Serve an iced julep over crushed ice and garnish with a sprig of mint.

Tomato Cocktail
Serves 4

Ingredients
3-4 medium/450g/1lb ripe
  tomatoes, skinned
300ml/¹/₂pt yoghurt
fresh basil

salt and pepper
pinch sugar
2 ice cubes

Preparation Halve the tomatoes, squeeze out the seeds (reserve them for use in a soup) and put the flesh in a blender, together with the remaining ingredients.

Blend everything together well and serve immediately in tall glasses, garnished with extra basil.

Healthfood Drink
Serves 1

Ingredients
150ml/¹/₄pt yoghurt
100ml/4fl oz milk
15ml/1tbsp clear honey

20g/2tbsp wheatgerm
50g/2oz strawberries

Preparation Combine everything together in a blender or food processor and blend until smooth. Drink immediately.

Tomato Cocktail

Raspberry Yoghurt Drink
Serves 1-2

Ingredients

600ml/1pt yoghurt	sugar to taste
8 ice cubes	mint sprigs or raspberry
2 egg whites	leaves (optional)
150g/6oz raspberries	

Preparation Blend all the ingredients except the mint sprigs or raspberry leaves until the ice is crushed.

Serve immediately in tall glasses, garnished, if you like, with mint or raspberry leaves.

Variations Instead of raspberries, try 2 large peaches, peeled and sliced; 4 slices pineapple, fresh or canned; 1 large ripe mango; 150g/6oz either strawberries, blackberries, blueberries, blackcurrants or redcurrants.

Pineapple Yoghurt Drink
Serves 1

Ingredients

150ml/¼pt yoghurt
150ml/¼pt pineapple juice
15g/1tbsp crushed
  pineapple, fresh or
  canned
1 ice cube

Preparation Blend everything together well. Serve immediately.

Orange Yoghurt Drink
Serves 2

Ingredients

175ml/6fl oz yoghurt	grated lemon peel
100ml/4fl oz milk	5ml/1tsp honey
grated rind and juice of 1	25g/1oz hazelnuts
orange	(optional)

Preparation Blend all the ingredients together well. Serve immediately or refrigerate until required.

Variation A simpler citrus yoghurt drink can be made by liquidizing either the flesh of an orange or that of a small grapefruit together with ⅝ cup/150ml/¼pt yoghurt and sugar to taste.

Peach Passion
Serves 1

Ingredients

1 small, ripe peach,	1 scoop raspberry water ice
preferably white	champagne to top up

Preparation Peel the peach and slice it into the bottom of a large, chilled wine glass. Add the water ice and top up with champagne.

Variation Instead of the raspberry water ice, try redcurrant or blueberry. Sparkling dry white wine can be used instead of champagne.

Wine Glasses

Any discussion of wines is, of course, outside the scope of this book, but a basic set of wine glasses should contain *(from left to right)*: the all-purpose Paris goblet — available in 100ml/3½fl oz (liqueur), 150ml/5fl oz (sherry), 225ml/8fl oz (white wine) and 350ml/12fl oz (red wine) sizes. The last three tulip-shaped glasses are best for wine — the 175ml/6fl oz for dessert wine or sherry, the 350ml/12fl oz for red wine and the 225ml/8fl oz for white wine.

Confectionery

Coconut Cream Toffee   357
Coconut Ice   357
Coconut Mint Crystals   357
Carrot Halva   358
Colettes   358
Semolina Halva   358
Coffee Mallows   358
Chocolate Caramel Popcorn   359
Coffee Creams   359
Cheese Fudge   360
Coffee Fudge   360
Chocolate Fudge   361

Meringue Mushrooms   361
Rocky Road Fudge   361
Mocha Cups   362
Orange Truffles   362
Coffee Truffles   362
Amaretti Truffles   363
Rich Chocolate Truffles   363
Nougat   364
Praline   364

Testing the Temperature of a Syrup   365

Coconut Cream Toffee
Makes 30-40 pieces

Ingredients
1.5l/3pt single cream
400g/16oz white sugar
flesh of 1 coconut, ground
to a paste

5g/1tsp cardamom seeds,
ground
2.5ml/½tsp rose water

Preparation Mix together the sugar and coconut, gradually add the cream and rose water. Add the cardamom seed and stir thoroughly.

Cook over a gentle heat in a saucepan until the mixture curls off the sides of the pan.

Press the mixture onto a greased baking tray and leave to cool. Score it into squares and finish cutting into squares once it is cold.

Coconut Mint Crystals
Makes 550g/1¼lb

Ingredients
450g/1lb sugar
100g/4oz powdered
glucose
150ml/¼pt water

150g/6oz desiccated
coconut
25g/1oz mint chocolate,
coarsely grated

Preparation In a large heavy-based pan bring the sugar, glucose and water to the boil.

Remove from the heat and stir in the coconut and mint chocolate.

Spoon into small rocky heaps on waxed paper and leave to set.

Serve in small paper cases.

Variation 30ml/2tbsp coffee essence is a good addition.

Coconut Ice

Coconut Ice
Makes 18-24 pieces

Ingredients
450g/1lb granulated sugar
150ml/¼pt milk
150g/5oz desiccated
coconut

30ml/2tbsp coffee essence
OR few drops cochineal

Preparation Put the sugar and milk into a large heavy-based saucepan and gently heat until the sugar has dissolved.

Boil for 10 to 15 minutes. The mixture should form a soft ball when a little is dropped in cold water.

Remove from the heat and stir in the coconut. Pour half the mixture into a greased 15-cm/6-in loose-bottom square cake pan.

Quickly add the coffee essence or cochineal to the remaining mixture and pour into the cake pan.

Smooth the top and mark into squares or bars when half set.

Remove from the pan when cold and set.

Carrot Halva

Ingredients

450g/1lb carrots, peeled
  and grated
900ml/1½pt milk
125g/5oz sugar
3 cardamom pods

60ml/4tbsp Ghee (Clarified
  Butter)
30g/2tbsp raisins
30g/2tbsp pistachio nuts,
  skinned and chopped

Preparation Put the carrots, milk, sugar and cardamom pods in a large saucepan and bring to the boil. Lower heat to a medium low and, stirring occasionally, cook until all the liquid has evaporated.

Heat the clarified butter in a large frying pan over medium heat, add the carrots, raisins and pistachios and, stirring constantly, fry for 15-20 minutes until the mixture is dry and reddish in colour. Serve hot or cold.

Semolina Halva

Ingredients

45ml/3tbsp Ghee (Clarified
  Butter)
25g/1oz almonds,
  blanched and sliced

100g/4oz semolina
15g/1tbsp raisins
400ml/14fl oz milk
60g/2½oz sugar

Preparation Heat the butter in a pan over medium heat. Add the almonds and fry for 1-2 minutes until golden brown. Remove with a slotted spoon and drain on kitchen paper.

Put in the semolina and fry, stirring continuously, until golden. Add the raisins, milk and sugar and continue stirring until the mixture leaves the sides of the pan and a ball forms.

Serve warm or cold, on a flat dish garnished with the almonds.

Colettes

Makes approx. 16

Ingredients

225g/8oz plain chocolate
15ml/1tbsp strong black
  coffee
30ml/2tbsp single cream
450g/2oz butter
2 egg yolks

10-15ml/2-3tsp dark rum
  (or brandy, sherry,
  Cointreau or
  Maraschino)
small pieces of nuts,
  cherries, or crystallized
  flowers

Preparation Melt half the chocolate. Use double layers of paper petit fours cases, or preferably single foil petit fours cases. Spoon a little chocolate into each case. With the handle of a teaspoon, spread evenly around the base and sides of each case.

Turn upside down on to a tray lined with non-stick or waxed paper and leave to set in a cool place.

Melt the remaining chocolate in a bowl over a pan of hot water. Add the coffee and cream and stir.

Remove from the heat. Dice the butter. Beat into the chocolate mixture a little at a time.

Beat in the egg yolks and rum. Leave in a cool place until thick.

Carefully peel the cases away from the chocolate. Using a piping bag fitted with a star nozzle, pipe the filling into each case.

Top with the decorations of your choice and put in clean paper cases, or a decorative box.

Coffee Mallows

Ingredients

450g/1lb sugar
25g/1oz golden syrup (or
  corn syrup)
150ml/¼pt water
30g/2tbsp powdered
  gelatine

150ml/¼pt strong Italian
  coffee
2 egg whites
vanilla essence
icing sugar
cornflour

Preparation Slowly dissolve the sugar, syrup and water in a large, heavy-based pan. Bring to the boil. While the mixture is boiling, dissolve the gelatine in the coffee.

Remove the syrup from the heat and slowly add the gelatine, stirring well.

Whisk the egg whites until just foaming and pour onto the hot syrup in a thin stream, whisking all the time.

Add a few drops of vanilla essence and continue whisking until the mixture is thick and stiff.

Pour into a 25-cm/9-in square loose-bottom cake pan, lined with greased non-stick paper.

Leave uncovered overnight and check that the coffee mallow is completely set before removing from the pan and cutting into squares.

Roll each piece thoroughly in a mixture of one part cornflour and two parts icing sugar.

Variation You can cut the coffee mallow into rounds using biscuit cutters. Dip the cutter into the cornflour and icing sugar mixture between cuts to prevent the cutter from sticking.

Chocolate Caramel Popcorn

Ingredients

50g/2oz brown sugar
25g/1oz butter
20ml/1½tbsp golden syrup
  (or corn syrup)
15ml/1tbsp milk
50g/2oz chocolate chips
pinch bicarbonate of soda
1.2l/2pt popped popcorn

Preparation Put the sugar, butter, syrup and milk into a heavy-based saucepan.

Stir over a gentle heat until the butter and sugar have melted. Boil without stirring for 2 minutes.

Remove from the heat. Add the chocolate and bicarbonate of soda. Stir until the chocolate is melted.

Measure the popped popcorn into a bowl. Pour over the syrup and toss well until evenly coated.

Spread mixture on a large baking tray. Bake in the oven at 150°C/300°F/Gas 2 for about 15 minutes. Test for crispness. Bake for a further 5-10 minutes if necessary.

Cool and break into bite-sized pieces to serve.

Coffee Creams
makes approx. 24

Ingredients

1 egg white
450g/1lb icing sugar
30ml/2tbsp coffee essence,
  or extra strong instant
  coffee

Preparation Beat the egg white until frothy but not stiff. Sift the icing sugar into a bowl and mix with enough of the egg white to make a firm paste.

Add the coffee essence, mix and knead together. Roll out on a board well dusted with icing sugar and cut into small circles.

Transfer onto waxed paper and leave overnight until set and firm to the touch.

Variation Instead of the coffee, add peppermint flavouring to taste.

Cheese Fudge

Ingredients

350g/12oz curd cheese
75g/3oz sugar

15g/1tbsp pistachio nuts,
finely chopped

Preparation Put the curd cheese on a plate and rub with the palm of your hand till smooth and creamy.

Put the cheese in a pan over medium heat, add the sugar and, stirring constantly, cook till it leaves the sides and a ball forms.

Remove from the heat and spread on a plate 1cm/½in thick. Cool slightly, sprinkled with the nuts and cut into small diamonds.

Serve warm or cold.

Coffee Fudge

Ingredients

225g/8oz butter
900g/2lb granulated sugar
450ml/¾pt evaporated
    milk

100ml/4fl oz water
100ml/4fl oz strong coffee
50g/2oz seedless raisins,
    chopped

Preparation Put all the ingredients, except the raisins, into a large heavy-based pan. Stir gently over a low heat until the sugar is dissolved.

Bring to the boil and maintain, stirring occasionally, until a teaspoon of fudge dropped into half a cup of cold water will form a soft ball.

Remove from heat, dip the base of the pan into cold water and leave for 5 minutes. Beat with a wooden spoon until the mixture loses its gloss, looks grainy, thickens a little and will just pour from the pan.

Quickly stir in the raisins and pour into a greased pan 30cm×15cm/12×7in. Leave until cold and set, and cut into squares.

Wrap in waxed paper.

Chocolate Fudge
Makes approx. 700g/1½lb

Ingredients
450g/1lb sugar
150ml/¼pt milk
100g/4oz butter
150g/6oz plain chocolate
50ml/2oz honey

Preparation Put all ingredients into a heavy based saucepan and stir continuously over a gentle heat until the sugar is completely dissolved.

Bring to the boil and cook to the "soft ball" stage, when a teaspoon of the mixture dropped into half a cup of cold water will form a soft ball. If unsure when to stop the cooking, check with a thermometer: the temperature should be around 116°C/240°F.

Remove from the heat and dip the base of the pan in cold water to stop further cooking. Leave for 5 minutes.

Beat the mixture with a wooden spoon until thick and creamy and beginning to "grain". Before it becomes too stiff, pour into a buttered 20cm/8in square pan. Leave to set.

Rocky Road Fudge
Makes approx. 700g/1½lb

Ingredients
450g/1lb milk chocolate
50g/2oz butter
30ml/2tbsp single cream
5ml/1tsp vanilla essence
50g/2oz walnuts, chopped
100g/4oz marshmallows, cut into small pieces with wetted scissors
225g/8oz icing sugar, sieved
75g/3oz plain chocolate

Preparation Melt the chocolate and butter in a bowl over a pan of hot water. Stir in the cream and essence.

Remove from the heat and stir in the walnuts, marshmallows and icing sugar.

Spread in a 20cm/8in square pan, lined with non-stick (waxed) paper, and chill until firm.

Melt the plain chocolate. Using a piping bag fitted with a plain nozzle, drizzle the chocolate over the fudge.

Leave to set, then cut the fudge into diamonds or any other shape that takes your fancy.

Meringue Mushrooms
Makes 6-8

Ingredients
1 egg white
50g/2oz caster sugar
50g/2oz plain chocolate, melted
unsweetened cocoa powder

Preparation Whisk the egg white until stiff, then whisk in the sugar a little at a time until the mixture is stiff and glossy.

Put meringue into a piping bag fitted with a 1cm/½in plain nozzle.

Line a baking sheet with non-stick paper. Pipe 6-8 small mounds of meringue about 2.5cm/1in in diameter to form the mushroom caps.

Next pipe 6-8 smaller mounds, drawing each one up to a point, to represent the stalks.

Bake in the oven at 140°C/275°F/Gas 1 for about 1 hour until dry and crisp. Allow to cool.

Using the point of a sharp knife, make a tiny hole in the base of the mushroom cap.

Spread a little melted chocolate on the underside of each cap and gently push on a stalk. Allow to set.

Before serving, dust the tops of mushrooms with a little cocoa powder.

Mocha Cups
makes 18-20

Ingredients

100g/4oz milk chocolate	50g/2oz butter, softened
125g/5oz plain chocolate	2 egg yolks
60ml/4tbsp strong Italian coffee	rum to taste
	toasted almond slivers

Preparation Melt the milk chocolate in a bowl over hot water until liquid. Pour a teaspoon of chocolate inside each paper sweet case and run it around the inside to line the case completely. Leave to set. Remove the paper cases from the chocolate cups.

Melt the plain chocolate and stir in the coffee. Leave to cool.

Beat in the butter and egg yolks. Add rum to taste.

Pipe or spoon the mocha filling into the chocolate cups and decorate with almond slivers.

Orange Truffles
Makes 12

Ingredients

100g/4oz plain (dark) chocolate in small pieces	finely grated zest of 1 orange
45ml/3tbsp single cream	100g/4oz icing sugar or 50g/2oz chocolate strands
100g/4oz ground almonds	
30ml/2tbsp Cointreau	
225g/8oz biscuit or cake crumbs	

Preparation Melt the chocolate in the top of a double boiler.

Pour the chocolate into a mixing bowl with the cream, ground almonds, Cointreau, crumbs and zest.

Mix well and chill for 1 hour, or until it is firm enough to handle.

Divide the chocolate mixture into 12 pieces. Roll into small balls and toss in sifted sugar or chocolate strands.

Coffee Truffles
Makes 18-24

Ingredients

100g/4oz plain chocolate	1 egg yolk
50g/2oz butter	5ml/1tsp Crème de Cacao
100g/4oz icing sugar	chocolate vermicelli
100g/4oz coffee cake, crumbled	

Preparation Melt the chocolate and butter in a bowl over a saucepan of hot water.

Remove from the heat and stir in remaining ingredients except the chocolate vermicelli.

Chill in the refrigerator until firm enough to handle. Mould into balls the size of a small walnut and roll in the vermicelli.

Leave to set on greaseproof paper before putting in individual paper cases.

Coffee Truffles

Amaretti Truffles
Makes approx. 16

Ingredients

50g/2oz butter, softened	few drops almond essence
150g/6oz icing sugar	approx. 16 small, hard
175g/7oz plain chocolate	macaroons (preferably
5g/1tsp instant coffee	Italian Amaretti)

Preparation Beat together the butter and icing sugar.

Put 75g/3oz of the chocolate into a bowl over a pan of hot water. Dissolve the coffee in a few drops of boiling water and add to the chocolate. Heat until melted.

Remove the chocolate from the heat and add the essence. Stir into the butter mixture. Chill until firm enough to handle.

Roll mixture into balls and press each one on to the flat size of a macaroon.

Melt the rest of the chocolate and dip each "truffle" side of the macaroons. Leave to set, coated sides up.

Rich Chocolate Truffles
Makes approx. 30

Ingredients

225g/8oz plain or milk	2tsp/10ml rum or brandy
chocolate	150g/6oz icing sugar
100g/4oz butter, diced	ground nuts

Preparation Melt the chocolate. Remove from the heat, add the butter and rum or brandy and beat until smooth.

Beat in the icing sugar and chill until firm.

Shape into 2.5-cm/1-in balls and roll in the nuts. Put the truffles in paper cases and keep cool.

Variation The truffles could also be coated in icing sugar, cocoa powder, drinking chocolate powder, Ground Praline, grated chocolate or chocolate vermicelli.

Nougat
Makes 675g/1½lb

Ingredients

100g/4oz whole hazelnuts, toasted
50g/2oz candied orange rind
50g/2oz glacé cherries (of different colours if possible)
450g/1lb sugar
225g/8oz powdered glucose
150ml/¼pt water
2 egg whites
rice paper

Preparation Roughly chop the hazelnuts, candied orange rind and glacé cherries.

In a large heavy-based pan, heat the sugar, glucose and water gently until the sugar dissolves and then boil.

Whisk the egg whites in a bowl until stiff and gradually add the syrup. Keep beating until the mixture thickens. This could take up to 30 minutes but it is important if the nougat is going to set.

Add the nuts, candied orange and cherries, mix well and pour into an 18-cm/7-in square cake pan lined with rice paper. Cover with another sheet of rice paper and press down with a weight.

Leave for 12 hours. Remove from pan and cut into squares.

Variation For Coffee Nougat (illustrated) add 30ml/2tbsp coffee essence with the chopped nuts and fruit.

Praline
Makes 225g/8oz

Ingredients

125g/4oz sugar
125g/4oz blanched almonds
a little oil

Preparation Put the sugar and nuts in the bottom of a heavy based pan. Cook on a very low heat, stirring constantly, until the sugar has melted and turned a golden brown colour. Be sure that all the nuts are well coated.

Brush a flat baking tray with oil. Spread the nuts and syrup onto the tray and leave to set.

Crush the praline with a rolling pin or food processor. It can be coarse or fine, according to personal preference. Alternatively, simply break it into uneven slabs. Use the praline as a garnish, or flavour ice cream with ground praline. Chunks of praline can also be stirred into a softened ice cream or bombe to provide a contrast in texture.

Variation Use peanuts, hazelnuts, walnuts or pecans instead of almonds.

Glazed nuts Melt the sugar as above and dip the nuts in one at a time. Remove and leave to cool on a sheet of greaseproof paper.

Testing the Temperature of a Syrup

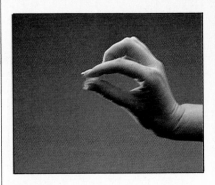

Soft ball 112-116°C/234-240°F
Dip the pan in cold water. Drop a small amount of the syrup into a bowl of very cold water, roll it into a ball in the water, then lift it out.

If the syrup forms a ball whilst in the water but becomes soft and flattens under slight pressure when removed from the water, the correct stage has been reached.

Used for fondants and fudge.

Thread 106-113°C/223-236°F
Dip the pan in cold water. Using a teaspoon, take a small amount of the syrup then gently and slowly pour it over the rim of the spoon.

If a thin thread forms the correct temperature has been reached.

Firm ball 118-121°C/244-250°F
Dip the pan in cold water. Drop a small amount of the syrup into very cold water, roll it into a ball in the water, then lift it out.

If a ball holds its shape when lifted from the water but loses it as it warms up, the correct temperature has been reached.

Used for caramels.

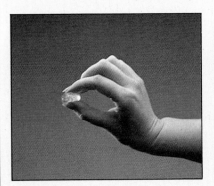

Hard ball 121-130°C/250-266°F
Dip the pan in cold water. Drop a small amount of the syrup into very cold water, form it into a ball in the water, then lift it out.

If the ball holds its shape under slight pressure but is still quite sticky, the correct temperature has been reached.

Used for nougat and marshmallows.

Soft crack 132-143°C/270-290°F
Dip the pan in cold water. Drop a small amount of the syrup into very cold water. Remove it between the fingers then gently separate them.

If the syrup forms threads that are hard but not brittle the correct stage has been reached.

Used for humbugs.

Hard crack 149-154°C/300-310°F
Dip the pan in cold water. Drop a little of the syrup into very cold water, then remove it.

If it is hard and brittle the correct stage has been reached.

Used for hard toffee and rock.

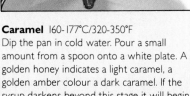

Caramel 160-177°C/320-350°F
Dip the pan in cold water. Pour a small amount from a spoon onto a white plate. A golden honey indicates a light caramel, a golden amber colour a dark caramel. If the syrup darkens beyond this stage it will begin to taste bitter.

Used for pralines.

Sauces, Dressings and Marinades

Bolognese Sauce   367
Curry Sauce   367
Blue Cheese Sauce   367
Cucumber Dill Sauce   368
Dill Sauce   368
Basil Dressing   368
Soured Cream Anchovy Dressing   368
Cheese Herb Dressing   368
Blue Cheese Dressing   368
Chutney dressing   369
Herb Dressing   369
Rich French Dressing   369
Tomato Yoghurt Dressing   369
Mustard Dressing   369
Yoghurt Cream Dressing   369
Aïoli   370
Basic Garlic Dressing   370
Garlic Butter   370
Clarified Garlic Butter   371
Ghee   371
Green Butter   371
Garam Masala   371
Horseradish Sauce, Hot   372
Horseradish Sauce, Cold   372
Béchamel Sauce   372
Chaudfroid Sauce   372
Hollandaise Sauce   372
Mousseline Sauce   372
Mornay Sauce   373
Mustard Sauce   375
Sauce Gribiche   373
Marinara Sauce   373

Mushroom Sauce   374
Putanesca Sauce   374
Ragu Sauce   374
Salsa Verde   374
Spinach and Ricotta Sauce   375
Tuna and Mushroom Sauce   375
Pesto   375
Winter Pesto Sauce   375
Tomato Sauce   376
Concentrated Tomato Sauce   376
Spicy Tomato Sauce   376
Mayonnaise   377
Tartare Sauce   377
Vinaigrette   378
Yoghurt and Tahini Dip   378
Soured Cream Dip   378
Black Cherry Sauce   378
Chocolate Sauce   378
Chocolate Custard   379
Chocolate Syrup   379
Fudge Sauce   379
Mars Bar Sauce   380
Quick Fruit Sauce   380
Summer Sauce   380
Tobler Sauce   380

Crushing Garlic and Making Garlic Paste   381

Bolognese Sauce
Serves 4

Ingredients

1 large onion, peeled and diced	425g/15oz canned tomatoes
1 carrot, scraped and grated	4 tomatoes, skinned and chopped
1 stalk celery, washed and chopped	1 bay leaf
2 cloves garlic, crushed	5g/1tsp origanum
2 slices bacon	½tsp basil
15ml/1tbsp oil	1 bouquet garni
100g/4oz lean minced beef	salt and freshly ground pepper
100g/4oz lean minced veal	15ml/1tbsp tomato purée
300ml/½pt beef stock or water	150ml/¼pt red wine

Preparation Prepare the vegetables making sure that they are diced very finely. Remove strings from the celery with a sharp knife before chopping.

Cut the bacon into small pieces having first removed the rind. Heat the oil in the pan and brown all the meat over a medium heat. Remove with a slotted spoon leaving any fat behind.

Cook the vegetables in the meat fat adding a little extra oil if necessary, over a low heat for 5 minutes.

Put the meat and vegetables into a saucepan with the tomatoes, herbs and seasoning. Lastly add the tomato purée and stir in the wine.

Bring to the boil and simmer gently for 45 minutes. Remove bouquet garni and bay leaf before serving. Serve with spaghetti and other pasta with Parmesan cheese served separately.

Curry Sauce

Ingredients

butter or margarine	300ml/½pt yoghurt
1 medium onion, finely chopped	30ml/2tbsp chutney (optional)
10g/1tbsp curry powder	10g/1tbsp desiccated coconut (optional)
15g/1tbsp cornflour	
30ml/2tbsp water	

Preparation Heat the butter and add the onion. Cook until it has just softened but not browned. Stir in the curry powder and let it cook over a gentle heat for a minute.

Mix the cornflour and water to a smooth paste and add it to the yoghurt. Add this to the pan, stir well and continue cooking for five minutes.

Add the chutney and coconut just before serving.

Curry sauce is so useful for pepping up all sorts of different foods — try it with hard-boiled eggs, or fish, rice, cold meats, chicken, vegetables.

Blue Cheese Sauce
Makes 750ml/1¼pt

Ingredients

600ml/1pt Béchamel Sauce	2.5ml/½tsp French mustard
100g/4oz Roquefort or other blue cheese	pinch of cayenne pepper
salt and freshly ground pepper	

Preparation Make up the Béchamel Sauce. Crumble the cheese and add to the sauce. Stir over a low heat.

Taste for seasoning. Add salt and pepper to taste and then the mustard. Lastly stir in the pinch of cayenne.

This sauce will accompany approximately 450-700g/1-1½lb cooked pasta.

Cucumber Dill Sauce

Ingredients

1 medium sized cucumber, peeled
25g/1oz butter
150ml/¼pt fish or chicken stock
150ml/¼pt dry white wine
15g/2tbsp fresh dill, chopped or 10g/1tbsp dried dill
20g/4tsp cornflour
30ml/2tbsp water
125ml/4fl oz sour cream or yoghurt
salt and pepper

Preparation Coarsely grate the cucumber and put it into a saucepan. Add the butter and cook on a gentle heat just to soften the cucumber. Add the stock, wine and dill and simmer for 5 minutes.

Mix the cornflour with the water. Add it to the pan, cook gently until the sauce begins to thicken, stirring constantly.

Add the sour cream or yoghurt and warm it through. Season to taste.

Serve hot or cold, with salmon or other fish. Also good with poached eggs, potatoes, rice or pasta.

Dill Sauce

Ingredients

50g/2oz butter or margarine
15g/1tbsp flour
250ml/8fl oz water
salt and pepper
10g/1tbsp dried dill
15ml/1tbsp vinegar
5g/1tsp sugar
150ml/¼pt yoghurt or sour cream

Preparation Melt the butter and stir in the flour off the heat. Slowly add the water, stirring constantly to make a smooth paste. Season well and return to the heat.

Add the dill, vinegar and sugar, and cook on a gentle heat for 5 minutes. Stir in the yoghurt or sour cream and warm through gently.

A delicious sauce which can dress up plain chops or steak. It is also excellent with poached fish.

Basil Dressing

Ingredients

250ml/8fl oz yoghurt
10 basil leaves, finely chopped
1 large clove garlic, crushed
salt and pepper

Preparation Blend everything together well. Serve over green or mixed salad or tomato and onion salad.

This also makes a good sauce for pasta, in which case double the quantity.

Soured Cream Anchovy Dressing

Ingredients

150ml/¼pt sour cream
1 clove garlic, crushed
4 anchovy fillets, finely chopped
3 green onions, finely chopped
chopped dill, to taste
juice of 1 lemon
salt and pepper

Preparation Mix everything together well. Refrigerate until required.

Serve as a salad dressing or on hot or cold fish or broiled meats.

Cheese Herb Dressing

Ingredients

225g/8oz curd cheese
200ml/7fl oz sour cream
2 green onions, finely chopped
7g/1tbsp chopped parsley
7g/1tbsp chopped dill
15g/1tbsp sugar
10g/1tbsp chopped onion

Preparation Combine everything together, mixing well to blend the cheese and sour cream.

Serve over plain poached fish or as a salad dressing. Use ricotta instead of curd cheese, if preferred.

Blue Cheese Dressing

Ingredients

150ml/¼pt sour cream
100g/4oz blue cheese
45ml/3tbsp oil
15ml/1tbsp vinegar
salt and pepper

Preparation Blend everything together well, mixing until smooth. If necessary thin the dressing down with a little milk.

Serve over crisp lettuce — chunks of lettuce with blue cheese dressing make a good starter.

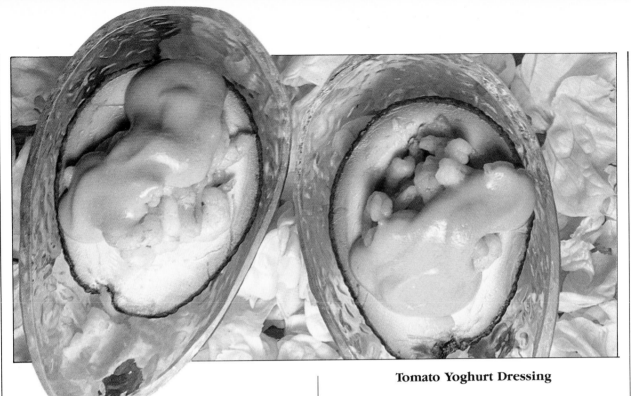

Chutney Dressing

Ingredients

125ml/4fl oz sour cream
125ml/4fl oz buttermilk
30ml/2tbsp mango
  chutney
15ml/1tbsp lemon juice

10ml/2tsp oil
10ml/2tsp mustard
salt and pepper

Preparation Blend everything together well. Refrigerate until required.

Serve on salad or cold vegetables. Use as a dressing for hard-cooked eggs, cold fish or meat.

Herb Dressing

Ingredients

75g/3oz cream cheese
250ml/8fl oz yoghurt or
  buttermilk

salt and pepper
finely chopped fresh herbs

Preparation Blend everything together well. Refrigerate until required. Use on salads or fish.

Rich French Dressing

Ingredients

1 egg
125ml/4fl oz oil
30ml/2tbsp lemon juice
1 clove garlic, crushed

fresh herbs
salt and pepper
250ml/8fl oz yoghurt

Preparation Blend together the egg, oil, lemon juice, garlic, herbs, salt and pepper. Slowly add the yoghurt, with the blender running. Refrigerate until required — it should thicken as it stands.

This makes a delicious salad dressing but if you want to make it thicker, for piping, you can add some gelatine and let it set. Use chives, fennel, parsley, tarragon or any other fresh herbs you have on hand — or a mixture.

For a less rich dressing omit the egg.

Tomato Yoghurt Dressing

Ingredients

150ml/¼pt yoghurt
20ml/4tsp tomato ketchup
dash Worcestershire Sauce

dash tabasco
salt and pepper

Preparation Mix all the ingredients together well. Serve on crisp lettuce or as a seafood dressing.

For a variation add finely chopped green or red pepper, chopped hard-boiled egg, chopped spring onions.

Mustard Dressing

Ingredients

150ml/¼pt yoghurt
15ml/1tbsp mustard

15ml/1tbsp lemon juice
salt and pepper

Preparation Mix all the ingredients together well. Use over green salad or cabbage salad or on steaks, chops or broiled fish.

The flavour of the mustard you use will determine the piquancy of this dressing. *Moutarde de grains* or Dijon mustard works well but it is interesting to try different varieties.

Yoghurt Cream Dressing

Ingredients

600ml/1pt yoghurt
150ml/¼pt whipping
  cream

squeeze of lemon juice
caster sugar to taste

Preparation Drain the yoghurt for 3 hours. Whip the cream and fold into the drained yoghurt. Add the lemon juice and sugar and stir well to dissolve the sugar.

Use as required. It is very good as a dressing over fruit salad, or folded into a fruit salad, or over individual fruits, berries, pineapple, bananas or mangoes.

Add more lemon juice, and some finely grated rind, or orange juice and rind. Substitute 225g/8oz quark, fromage blanc or curd cheese for the yoghurt.

Aïoli
Makes about 500ml/1pt

Aïoli is simply the ultimate garlic sauce. Although originally served with prawns, it is sensational on anything from hamburgers to Bouillabaisse, and a dollop of it will perk up the tiredest vegetable, rev up the blandest soup, and give yesterday's cold cuts a new interest in life. You can, of course, add crushed garlic, or, nicer still, Garlic Purée to home-made or bought mayonnaise. It will taste much better than commercially-produced garlic mayonnaise, but it won't be Aïoli.

Ingredients
*4-6 cloves of garlic (though
    of course you can use
    more)
a pinch of salt
3 egg yolks*
*450ml/16fl oz olive oil
lemon juice to taste
a little water or single
    cream*

Preparation Chop the garlic finely and pound in a mortar with the salt until smooth. Beat in the egg yolks.
   Add the oil, drop by drop at first, then in a thin stream once the mixture is glossy and beginning to thicken.
   Add lemon juice to taste, and if too solid for your liking, add a little water or single cream.
   To stop a skin forming on the Aïoli, cover with a piece of plastic film that touches the surface.

Variations For Almond Skordalia, add 10g/1tbsp of fresh white breadcrumbs, 15g/1tsp of ground almonds, 7g/1tbsp of chopped parsley and a pinch of cayenne for every 300ml/½pt of Aïoli and flavour with lemon or lime juice to taste. This sauce is traditionally served with cold, cooked vegetables.
   For Aïoli Verde, add to each cup of Aïoli a handful of parsley, two or three sprigs of fresh tarragon, two or three sprigs of fresh chervil and half a handful of spinach which have been simmered together in salted water until tender, drained and sieved or blended to a smooth purée.

Basic Garlic Dressing

Ingredients
*1-2 cloves garlic, crushed
5g/1tsp sugar
30ml/2tbsp wine vinegar
    or Garlic Vinegar*
*90ml/6tbsp olive oil
salt and peper*

Preparation Combine all the ingredients in a screw-top jar, cover and shake well. Adjust seasoning before serving.

Variations Include fresh or dried herbs to taste depending on what you are serving the dressing with.
   Substitute different flavoured vinegars.
   Substitute part or all of the oil with walnut oil.
   Replace the oil with sour cream or yoghurt and the vinegar with lemon juice (the cream version is excellent with 10g/1tbsp of freshly grated horse-radish added to it.
   Add 5ml/1tsp of mild French mustard. This dressing is especially good served over warm green beans as a first course.

Garlic Butter

Garlic Butter is a great topping for steaks, hamburgers, grilled fish or chicken and is a handy shortcut to garlic bread. It can also be used to enrich soups, stews and sauces, and, in sandwiches, makes a welcome and tasty change from plain butter.

Ingredients
*100g/4oz butter, softened
3-6 cloves of garlic,
    unpeeled
salt and pepper*

Preparation Cream the butter until light and fluffy. Blanch the garlic in boiling water for 1 minute, drain and peel.
   Crush the garlic to a fine paste with a pinch of salt and gradually mix in the softened butter.
   Season with salt and pepper to taste, wrap in foil and chill until needed.

Green Butter

It is simple to make this savoury butter in a blender or food processor, otherwise all ingredients have to be chopped by hand.

It is usual to make up herb butters in the shape of a round sausage. Wrap the round in foil and cut slices as required after chilling. Cut the rolls into coin-sized pieces when very cold and store in the freezer.

Ingredients

50g/2oz spinach leaves, washed	3 gherkins
1 bunch of watercress, stalks removed	3g/1tsp capers
1 clove of garlic	3 anchovy fillets
fresh tarragon to taste	30ml/2tbsp oil
a few sprigs of parsley	1 egg yolk
fresh chives to taste	1 hard-boiled egg
	100g/4oz butter

Preparation Drop the spinach leaves, watercress, garlic and herbs into the blender to purée. Add the gherkins, capers and anchovy fillets with the oil, egg yolk and hard-boiled egg. Lastly blend in the softened butter.

Chill and serve with grilled fish. This savoury butter is especially good with barbecued food.

Garam Masala

Ingredients

20g/3tbsp cardamom seeds	2.5g/¹⁄₂tsp black peppercorns
3×2.5cm/1in cinnamon sticks	2.5g/¹⁄₂tsp cloves
5g/¹⁄₂tbsp cumin seeds	¹⁄₄ of a nutmeg

Preparation Grind all the spices together until they are finely ground. Store in a spice bottle until required. (The ingredients may be added in different proportions to suit individual tastes).

Variations *Parsley Garlic Butter* add 10g/1¹⁄₂tbsp of chopped fresh parsley.

Herb and Garlic Butter add 10g/1¹⁄₂tbsp of chopped fresh mixed herbs.

Mustard Garlic Butter add 15ml/1tbsp of mild French mustard.

Horseradish Garlic Butter add 10g/1tbsp of grated fresh horseradish.

Chilli Garlic Butter add chilli powder to taste, and 10ml/2tsp of tomato purée.

Tomato Garlic Butter add 15ml/1tbsp tomato purée.

Clarified Garlic Butter

Ingredients

3-6 cloves of garlic, unpeeled
100g/4oz butter
salt and pepper

Preparation Blanch the unpeeled garlic in boiling water for 1 minute, then drain and peel.

Slice the garlic and heat gently in the butter with a little salt and pepper for 5 minutes.

Skim the butter and strain it through a piece of muslin or a very fine sieve. Keep covered in the fridge until needed.

This can be used for frying, especially potatoes, and can be brushed over pastry before baking, and over cooked buns and bagels before heating.

It is also particularly good with vegetables such as asparagus and artichokes, however irreverent this may sound.

Ghee
Clarified Butter

Heat 450g/1lb of unsalted butter in a saucepan over low heat. Let it simmer for 15-20 minutes until all the white residue turns golden and settles at the bottom.

Remove from the heat, strain and cool. Pour into an airtight bottle and store in a cool place.

Horseradish Sauce, Hot

Ingredients

6g/2tsp grated horseradish
150ml/¼pt yoghurt
5ml/1tsp lemon juice
15ml/1tbsp water
5g/1tsp cornflour
salt and pepper

Preparation Combine all the ingredients in a saucepan, with the water and cornflour mixed to a smooth paste.

Cook on a gentle heat, stirring constantly, for 5 minutes.

Horseradish Sauce, Cold

Ingredients

10g/1tbsp freshly grated
horseradish
150ml/¼pt double cream
few drops of olive oil

Preparation Mix horseradish and cream together. Add the olive oil.

Béchamel Sauce
Makes 600ml/1pt

Ingredients

600ml/1pt milk
1 small onion, peeled
1 small carrot, peeled and
sliced
1 bay leaf
6 slightly crushed
peppercorns
1 blade mace
1 stalk parsley
40g/1½oz butter
40g/1½ flour
salt and white pepper

Preparation Pour milk into a saucepan. Add the onion cut into quarters with 2 slices of carrot, bay leaf, peppercorns, mace and parsely stalk.

Cover and allow to heat on low heat without boiling for about 10 minutes. Remove from the heat and allow to infuse for a further 10 minutes, covered.

Make a roux (a blend of butter and flour) by melting the butter in a saucepan. Do not allow the butter to brown. Add the flour and stir well over a medium heat.

Gradually add the strained milk and stir briskly or whisk until a smooth creamy sauce is made, season to taste.

Variation To make a cheese sauce, add 50g/2oz grated cheese, good pinch cayenne pepper and 2.5g/½tsp dried mustard.

Chaudfroid Sauce
Makes 600ml/1pt

Ingredients

450ml/¾pt Béchamel
Sauce
150ml/¼pt aspic jelly
5ml/1 rounded tsp gelatine
30ml/2tbsp boiling water

Preparation Allow the Béchamel Sauce to cool but cover with plastic wrap clingfilm to avoid a skin forming.

Make up the aspic jelly in a jug and sprinkle the gelatine onto the hot water. Make sure the mixture is dissolved by placing the jug in a saucepan of boiling water. Allow to cool before using to coat fish fillets, small fish or fish steaks.

Hollandaise Sauce
Makes 300ml/½pt

Ingredients

30ml/2tbsp water
6 peppercorns, slightly
crushed
15ml/1tbsp white wine
vinegar
175g/6oz butter
2 egg yolks
15ml/1tbsp lemon juice
salt to taste

Preparation Make the sauce in a double boiler or an ovenproof bowl over a saucepan of hot water. If using the latter method make sure that the bottom of the bowl is not touching the hot water or the sauce will set on the bottom of the bowl before it is cooked.

Place the water, crushed peppercorns and white wine vinegar in a small saucepan and reduce to about 15ml/1tbsp liquid. Set aside.

Cut the butter into pieces and soften gently in a small saucepan. Remove from heat.

Whisk the egg yolks, reduced liquid and a little of the butter in the double boiler. When the mixture becomes creamy and slightly thick, pour in the butter in a thin stream, whisking briskly. Add lemon juice and a little salt, and taste for seasoning.

Remove from the heat immediately it is thick. Should the sauce look as if it is curdling, add a few drops of cold water and whisk briskly for a few more minutes.

This sauce can be made in a blender or food processor, but you may find that less butter will be absorbed. The addition of 15ml/1tbsp cold water with the lemon juice will prevent it becoming too thick.

Hollandaise is served hot with grilled fish such as salmon, turbot, halibut and sea bream.

Mousseline Sauce

Preparation Add 60ml/4tbsp whipped cream to the Hollandaise Sauce as it cools and the resulting mousseline sauce can be served cold with fish or vegetables.

Mornay Sauce
Makes approx. 600ml/1pt

Ingredients
600ml/1pt Béchamel Sauce	30ml/2tbsp cream
2 egg yolks	50g/2oz grated cheese

Preparation Place 60ml/4tbsp béchamel sauce in a small bowl and mix with the egg yolks and cream.

Add this mixture to the béchamel sauce and cook over a how heat, stirring well.

Gradually add grated cheese. Parmesan is ideal but individual taste can decide on the type of cheese.

This can be served with poached or steamed fish fillets or cutlets.

Mustard Sauce
Makes 150ml/¼pt

Ingredients
15ml/1tbsp French mustard	150ml/¼pt whipping cream
juice of ½ lemon	
salt and white pepper to taste	

Preparation Mix the mustard, lemon juice and seasoning together.

Whip the cream lightly and stir in the mustard mixture. Chill before using with grilled or fried fish.

Variation Alternatively a hot mustard sauce may be made with 150ml/¼pt Béchamel Sauce. Add 5g/1tsp dried mustard and 5ml/1tsp vinegar to 15ml/1tbsp of the sauce, return to the sauce and stir over the heat for a further minute.

Marinara Sauce

Sauce Gribiche

Ingredients
1 egg	7g/1tbsp freshly chopped parsley
2.5ml/½tsp Dijon mustard	
15g/1tbsp chopped gherkins	5g/1tsp capers, chopped
2g/1tsp fresh tarragon or 2g/½tsp dried	300ml/½pt Mayonnaise

Preparation Add the sieved yolk of the hard-boiled egg, and all the other ingredients to the Mayonnaise. Mix well and serve with cold fish dishes and shellfish.

Marinara Sauce

Ingredients
2 medium onions, thinly sliced	15ml/1tbsp tomato purée
2 cloves garlic, crushed	5g/1tsp sugar
30ml/2tbsp olive oil	5g/1tsp dried oregano
425g/15oz can of tomatoes	5g/1tsp paprika
	salt and pepper

Preparation Fry the onions and garlic in the oil until they begin to brown. Lower the heat and cook for 15 to 20 minutes until soft.

Add the tomatoes, tomato purée, sugar, oregano and paprika. Cook rapidly for about 10 minutes until the tomatoes break down.

Add salt and pepper to taste, and serve. This quantity of sauce is enough for 450g/1lb of pasta. Traditionally this sauce is served without cheese, but if you must, use a strong hard cheese such as Parmesan or pecorino.

Variation Stir 50g/2oz stoned black olives and 30g/2tbsp drained, finely chopped anchovy fillets into the finished sauce and heat through for a few moments before serving.

Mushroom Sauce
Serves 4 to 6

Serve with chops, escalopes of chicken, turkey or veal, or with pasta.

Ingredients
1 small onion, peeled
25g/1oz butter
100g/4oz firm white button mushrooms
15g/½oz flour
150ml/¼pt chicken stock
150ml/¼pt whole milk or light cream

15ml/1tbsp port (optional)
salt and freshly ground pepper
pinch of nutmeg
7g/1tbsp snipped chives
lemon juice to taste

Preparation Finely chop the onion. Heat the butter in a small pan and slowly cook the onion until soft and golden. Slice the mushrooms. Add to the onions and fry over medium heat for 2 minutes. Stir in the stock and milk or cream and bring to the boil, stirring constantly. Add the port, and seasonings. Simmer the sauce for 5 minutes. Chop the chives and stir into the sauce and add a little lemon juice to taste.

Putanesca Sauce
Makes 600ml/1pt

Ingredients
1 onion, peeled and diced
30ml/2tbsp oil
1 carrot, scraped and chopped
425g/15oz canned tomatoes
2 tomatoes, skinned and chopped
60ml/4tbsp white wine
1 bay leaf
3-4 basil leaves or 5g/1tsp dried basil

salt and freshly ground pepper
10g/1tbsp capers, chopped
1 small can anchovies
50g/2oz stoned black olives
3 drops Tabasco sauce
7g/1tbsp freshly chopped parsley

Preparation Put the onion into the oil in a frying saucepan over a low heat. Allow to cook gently for 4 minutes, add the crushed garlic and carrots. Turn in the oil for another minute.

Add the tomatoes, the white wine, bay leaf, basil, some seasoning and 4 anchovy fillets. Bring to the boil and simmer for 30 minutes. Sieve or liquidize into a measuring jug.

Return to the saucepan and add chopped capers, the remainder of the anchovies chopped into small pieces, chopped olives and the spicy Tabasco sauce. Re-heat gently.

Serve with 450g/1lb cooked pasta with Parmesan cheese served separately.

Ragu Sauce
Serves 4

Ingredients
1 onion, peeled
2 cloves garlic, crushed
1 carrot, scraped and grated
1 stalk celery
6 tomatoes, peeled and chopped or 425g/15oz canned tomatoes
60ml/4tbsp oil

225g/8oz lean minced beef
100g/4oz chicken livers
1 bouquet garni
1 bay leaf
300ml/½pt stock and red wine
5g/1tsp origanum
1 stalk parsley

Preparation Cut the onion finely, coarsely grate the carrot. Wash the celery and remove strings with a sharp knife before chopping into very small pieces. Prepare tomatoes.

Heat half the oil in a saucepan and cook the onion and garlic for 3 minutes over a low heat. Add carrot and celery, stir into the oil and allow to cook for a further 3 minutes.

Heat the remaining oil in a frying pan and brown the beef well over a high heat. Turn the heat down to medium and add chopped chicken livers. Mix with the beef and cook until brown.

Add the meat to the vegetables with the herbs and wine, season well, add the stock and simmer for 45 minutes. Taste for seasoning before serving with freshly cooked pasta.

Salsa Verde

Green and piquant, this sauce of fresh herbs is excellent with any fish, hot or cold, and goes well with hard-boiled eggs. Since it is so very good with prawns, try it in a prawn cocktail.

Ingredients
3 cloves of garlic, finely chopped
100g/4oz parsley, finely chopped
10g/1tbsp watercress leaves, finely chopped (optional)

7g/1tbsp mixed fresh herbs, finely chopped (basil, and a little thyme, sage, chervil and dill)
coarse salt
60ml/4tbsp olive oil
juice of 1-2 lemons
5-10g/1-2tsp sugar
black pepper

Preparation Blend or pound together in a mortar, the garlic, parsley, watercress, fresh mixed herbs and a little coarse salt, until they form a smooth paste.

Add the oil, a spoonful at a time, and mix well. Add the lemon juice and season with sugar, salt and pepper to taste.

Spinach and Ricotta Sauce
Makes approx. 600ml/1pt

Ingredients
300ml/¹/₂pt Béchamel
  Sauce
225g/8oz (after cooking),
  fresh or frozen spinach

100g/4oz ricotta cheese
¹/₂tsp nutmeg
salt and freshly ground
  pepper

Preparation Make up the Béchamel Sauce. Cook the spinach for a few minutes and then drain well. Squeeze against the collander to remove the liquid. You will need to cook approx 750g/1¹/₂lb fresh spinach to be left with the amount required by the recipe. Chop or liquidize.

Mix the ricotta with the spinach and season well, add nutmeg. Gradually stir into the Béchamel sauce and re-heat carefully over a low heat.

Serve with approximately 450-700g/1-1¹/₂lb cooked pasta. This sauce is also delicious used in a vegetable or chicken lasagne.

Tuna and Mushroom Sauce
Makes 750ml/1¹/₄pt sauce

Ingredients
25g/1oz butter
15ml/1tbsp oil
100g/4oz mushrooms,
  washed
200g/7oz canned tuna fish

10ml/2tsp tomato purée
30ml/2tbsp white wine
600ml/1pt Béchamel
  Sauce
salt and freshly ground
  pepper

Preparation Heat the butter and oil and cook the mushrooms for 3 minutes, turning from time to time. Flake the tuna fish.

Add the tomato purée, white wine to the Béchamel sauce, mix well. Over a low heat re-heat the sauce and gradually stir in the tuna fish and the drained mushrooms. Cook gently for a few minutes until well mixed and hot. Taste and adjust seasoning.

Mix the sauce with 450g/1lb cooked pasta.

Pesto

Although Pesto is traditionally served as a sauce for pasta, it goes well with cold meats, grilled or broiled fish, in soups or on salads with a little extra oil and a dash of lemon juice. You can buy Pesto but if you can lay your hands on a plentiful supply of fresh basil it really is worth making your own.

Ingredients
75g/3oz fresh basil leaves,
  finely chopped
30g/2tbsp pine kernels
50g/2oz Parmesan cheese,
  finely grated, or half
  Parmesan and half sardo
  cheese

3 cloves of garlic, finely
  chopped
90ml/6tbsp olive oil

Preparation Combine the basil, pine kernels, cheese and garlic in a blender, and reduce to a thick, green, aromatic paste.

Add a little oil, a little at a time, until well incorporated.

Winter Pesto Sauce
Makes approx. 300ml/¹/₂pt

Ingredients
50g/2oz fresh parsley
2 cloves garlic
50g/2oz pine kernels
50g/2oz Parmesan cheese

salt and freshly ground
  pepper
10g/2tsp dried basil
150ml/¹/₄pt olive oil

Preparation Chop the parsley finely in a blender or with a sharp knife if making by hand. Add the garlic crushed to the blender and process for a few seconds. Gradually add the other ingredients through the top of the machine while it is running. When the mixture is puréed add a little olive oil at a time.

Add the dried basil when half the oil has been added. Continue adding oil until a thick creamy mixture is made.

Tomato Sauce
Makes approx. 600ml/1pt

Ingredients

30ml/2tbsp oil
1 large onion, peeled and diced
1-2 cloves garlic, crushed
1 stalk celery, scrubbed
1 carrot, scraped and grated
400g/14oz canned tomatoes
450g/1lb fresh tomatoes, skinned and chopped
1 bouquet garni

2 bay leaves
7g/1tbsp chopped fresh basil, or 5g/1tsp dried basil
parsley sprig
2.5g/¹/₂tsp sugar
salt and freshly ground black pepper
300ml/¹/₂pt fish or chicken stock
30ml/2tbsp red wine

Preparation Heat the oil in a saucepan. Cook the garlic and onions over a low heat for about 4 minutes until transparent.

Remove the strings from the celery stalk and chop into small pieces, then add to the onion and garlic for the last 2 minutes.

Add all the other ingredients, bring to the boil and simmer for 40 minutes on a low heat.

Remove the sprig of parsley, bay leaf and bouquet garni and serve as cooked, or the sauce may be partially blended if a smoother texture is preferred.

Tomato Sauce (shown here with Wholemeal Tagliatelli and Parmesan Cheese)

Concentrated Tomato Sauce

Ingredients

2 medium onions, finely chopped
2-3 cloves garlic, crushed
30ml/2tbsp olive oil
45ml/3tbsp tomato purée

45ml/3tbsp wine or water
5g/1tsp dried oregano
5g/1tsp paprika
5g/1tsp sugar
salt and pepper

Preparation Fry the onions and garlic in the oil until they begin to brown. Turn down the heat and simmer, covered, for 10-15 minutes or until softened.

Add the tomato purée, wine or water, oregano, paprika and sugar, and season with salt and pepper to taste.

Allow the sauce to bubble for 5 minutes, stirring constantly, and serve.

This rich sauce can be served with pasta as it is, or with mince and liquid added. It is delicious poured over chicken pieces or fish steaks before baking, or used to top pizza.

It will also flavour soups and stews and is an excellent relish for cold meats, hamburgers and frankfurters.

Spicy Tomato Sauce
Makes 450ml/³/₄pt

Ingredients

30ml/2tbsp oil
1 large onion, peeled and chopped
1 green pepper, deseeded
1 red pepper, deseeded
1 chilli, deseeded and finely chopped
400-g/14-oz can of tomatoes
2 fresh tomatoes, skinned and chopped

pinch dried mustard
salt and freshly ground pepper
1 bouquet garni
2 bay leaves
¹/₄tsp sugar
150ml/¹/₄pt fish or chicken stock

To garnish
1 green chilli, deseeded and finely chopped

Preparation Heat the oil in a saucepan and sweat the onion on a low heat until transparent.

Dice the peppers finely. Add with the chilli to the onions and cook on a low heat for about 4 minutes.

Add the rest of the ingredients to the onion and pepper mixture. Bring to the boil, reduce the heat and simmer for 30 minutes. Remove bouquet garni and bay leaves.

The sauce may be partially blended if liked. Serve with chopped green chilli on top.

Mayonnaise
Makes approx. 300ml/½pt

Use this recipe as the basis for many interesting and delicious sauces and dressings.

Ingredients

3 egg yolks
2.5g/½tsp mustard powder
salt and pepper
7-15ml/½-1tbsp white wine vinegar

150ml/¼pt sunflower or safflower oil
150ml/¼pt olive oil
15ml/1tbsp hot water

Preparation If using a food processor, process the egg yolks with the mustard powder, a little salt and pepper and ½tbsp of vinegar till well mixed. With the machine running, add the oil, drop by drop, through the feed tube. The mixture should become very thick and emulsified. Taste for seasoning, adding more salt, pepper and vinegar as necessary. Finally, with the machine running, pour the hot water in through the feed tube. If not using a food processor, beat the egg yolks until thick and add the ingredients in the same order, mixing all the time; there is no need to add the hot water.

Store the mayonnaise in a glass or china bowl, cover and chill.

Variations Curry mayonnaise: add 2-3tsp curry paste (or to taste), plus 2tsp mango, apricot, or ginger chutney, and a few chopped fresh coriander leaves to the mayonnaise with the hot water. Serve with hard-boiled eggs, prawns (shrimps), or cold poultry.

Green Mayonnaise: chop 100g/4oz watercress. Add to the mayonnaise with the water. Serve with hard-boiled eggs, cold cooked asparagus or globe artichokes, or cold roast veal or pork.

Watercress Mousseline: chop 100g/4oz watercress. Mix with 150ml/¼pt of the made mayonnaise. Whip 150ml/¼pt of double (whipping) cream and stir in. Taste for seasoning. Serve with cold poached fish — salmon, sole, prawns, shrimps or lobster, or cold roast chicken.

Marie-Rose Mayonnaise: mix 2 to 3 tbsp tomato ketchup and a couple of drops of Tabasco sauce and add to the mayonnaise with the water. Serve with prawns, shrimps, crab, lobster, fish croquettes, fish cakes or egg salads.

Garlic and Herb Mayonnaise: chop ½tbsp each parsley sprigs, tarragon leaves, basil leaves and snipped chives, with 1 to 2 cloves garlic. Add to the mayonnaise with the water. Serve with cold cooked vegetables and salads, or as a dip.

Yoghurt Mayonnaise: mix 150ml/¼pt of plain thick yoghurt with 150ml/¼pt of the mayonnaise, and 1 to 2tbsp snipped chives. Season to taste. Serve with avocados, asparagus, globe artichokes, cold poached fish, green salads and raw vegetables.

Soured Cream Mayonnaise: mix 150ml/¼pt soured cream with an equal quantity of the mayonnaise. Season to taste. Chop ½tbsp mint and 3tbsp cucumber with 2tbsp chopped spring onions. Serve as a dip, or with salads.

Avocado Mayonnaise: process 150ml/¼pt of the mayonnaise with an equal quantity of plain thick yoghurt, 1tsp of lemon juice and a ripe avocado, peeled and diced. Season to taste with salt and cayenne pepper. Serve as a dip, or with green salads and seafood.

Egg and Chive Mayonnaise: add 2 shelled hard-boiled eggs and 2tbsp snipped chives to the mayonnaise with the hot water. Serve with green salads and vegetables or with cold fish and shellfish.

Horseradish Mayonnaise: add 30g/3tbsp freshly grated horseradish to the made mayonnaise. Mix thoroughly and serve with Potato Salad.

Mustard Mayonnaise: use 7.5ml/½tbsp Dijon mustard instead of the mustard powder and add 2.5ml/½tsp Worcestershire sauce and 2-3 drops Tabasco at the same time.

Tartare Sauce
Makes 300ml/½pt

Ingredients

2 hard-boiled eggs
10ml/2tsp French mustard
salt and freshly ground pepper
1 egg yolk
150ml/¼pt vegetable or olive oil

4-6 gherkins
20g/2tbsp capers
15g/2tbsp parsley, finely chopped
5g/1tsp dried chervil or equivalent fresh if available

Preparation Sieve the yolks of the hard-boiled eggs into a bowl and add mustard, salt and pepper. Mix the raw egg yolks into the bowl and cream until the mixture is a smooth paste. Add the oil a few drops at a time until the sauce is thick. If it seems too thick, add a few drops of lemon juice.

Drain and rinse the gherkins and capers in a sieve with cold water as they are usually packed in vinegar or brine, which can overpower the flavour of the sauce. Pat dry with kitchen towels and chop finely. Add to the sauce with the herbs (herbs, gherkins and capers can be chopped in the blender or food processor). Mix well and taste for seasoning. Serve with all types of fried or grilled fish.

Quick Tartare Sauce Add the gherkins, capers, parsley and herbs to 150ml/¼pt mayonnaise.

Tartare Sauce (shown here with Sole en Goujon)

Vinaigrette
Makes approx. 175ml/6fl oz

Ingredients
60ml/4tbsp olive or walnut oil
60ml/4tbsp safflower or sunflower oil
30ml/2tbsp wine or sherry vinegar
2.5g/½tsp freshly ground black pepper
2.5-5g/½-1tsp mustard powder

Preparation Mix all the ingredients together thoroughly, preferably in a blender or food processor.

Variations
Herbed Vinaigrette: chop 15g/2tbsp fresh herbs — parsley, chives, tarragon, mint, basil, etc. Stir into the vinaigrette.

Roquefort Dressing: blend all the ingredients for the vinaigrette, except the salt. Add 50g/2oz crumble Roquefort cheese, 30ml/2tsp lemon juice. Blend until the mixture has emulsified, taste for seasoning.

Chilli Vinaigrette: add 1 to 2 green chilli peppers, seeded, cored and quartered, to the ingredients before blending; or add 1 to 2 crumbled dried red chillis and a few sesame seeds to the ingredients before blending.

Cream Dressing: blend equal quantities of mayonnaise and vinaigrette. Add a few snipped chives, and season to taste, using a couple of drops of Tabasco sauce, if liked.

Yoghurt and Tahini Dip

Tahini paste, which is crushed sesame seeds, is obtainable at Greek stores and healthfood shops and some supermarkets. It is very thick and usually has a layer of oil on top which you should mix in before you use the paste.

Ingredients
2 cloves garlic, crushed
150ml/¼pt tahini paste
150ml/¼pt yoghurt
juice of 2 lemons
salt and pepper
chopped parsley, to taste

Preparation Blend everything together except the parsley until smooth. Taste and add more lemon juice and seasoning if necessary. Turn into a bowl and garnish with the chopped parsley.

Serve as a dip, with pitta or crackers, or as an accompaniment to vegetables, salads or meat or fish dishes.

Soured Cream Dip

Ingredients
150ml/¼pt sour cream
10g/2tsp dried dill
10g/2tsp dried onion flakes
8g/4tsp chopped parsley
2.5ml/½tsp mustard
salt and pepper

Preparation Mix everything together well and leave for the flavours to mingle for 2 hours if possible.

Use as a dip, with carrot sticks, celery, cauliflower etc, or as a salad dressing.

Dried onion is used in this on purpose to give a mild hint of onion. If you use fresh onion, be discreet.

Black Cherry Sauce
Serves 8-10

Ingredients
450g/1b black cherries
50g/2oz sugar
50ml/2fl oz water
5g/1tsp cornflour
15ml/1tbsp water

Preparation Place the fruit, sugar and water in a heavy-bottomed pan on a very low heat. Cook gently until the fruit is soft.

Combine the cornflour and water. Stir into the cooked fruit and bring to the boil, stirring constantly. Heat until the sauce has thickened.

If you are serving black cherry sauce for a special occasion, stir in a few spoonfuls of kirsch.

Chocolate sauce
Serves 3-4

Ingredients
50g/2oz unsweetened cocoa powder
60ml/4tbsp golden syrup
50g/2oz butter
150ml/¼pt milk
2.5ml/½tsp vanilla essence

Preparation Put cocoa, golden syrup and butter into a small pan. Heat gently until well blended. Stir in the milk and essence.

Bring to the boil and simmer gently for about 3 minutes. Serve hot or cold.

Variations *Chocolate/Orange Sauce:* Omit vanilla essence. Add grated rind of ½ orange.

Honey Chocolate Sauce: Use clear honey instead of golden syrup. Add lemon juice instead of vanilla essence.

Choco-Nutty Sauce: Omit vanilla essence. Stir in 15ml/1tbsp peanut butter.

Choco-Ginger Sauce: Add 25g/1oz chopped stem ginger.

Chocolate Custard
Makes 600ml/1pt

Ingredients
600ml/1pt milk
6 egg yolks
50g/2oz sugar

100g/4oz plain chocolate, grated

Preparation Put the milk into a saucepan and bring almost to the boil. Remove from the heat.

Whisk the egg yolks and sugar together until thick and fluffy. Gradually pour the milk on to the eggs and sugar, whisking continuously.

Return mixture to saucepan and stir over a very gentle heat, until it coats the back of a spoon. Remove from the heat and add the chocolate. Stir until dissolved.

Serve the custard hot or cold. To cool the custard, pour into a bowl and place dampened greaseproof paper directly on to the surface to stop a 'skin' from forming. Chill.

Chocolate Syrup

This syrup can be used for milk shakes, to pour over ice cream, pancakes, waffles, etc. To thin it just add a little cream or milk.

Ingredients
350g/12oz soft brown sugar
100g/4oz unsweetened cocoa

300ml/½pt boiling water
10ml/2tsp vanilla essence

Preparation Mix together the sugar and cocoa. Add the water, stirring continuously.

Put the mixture into a small pan and simmer gently for 5 minutes, stirring frequently. Cool, then add the vanilla essence. Cover and chill in the refrigerator.

Fudge Sauce
Serves 4-6

Ingredients
15g/1tbsp unsweetened cocoa powder
175g/6oz evaporated milk
75g/3oz plain chocolate, grated

25g/1oz butter
25g/1oz soft brown sugar

Preparation Put cocoa and evaporated milk into a pan and whisk well together.

Add all the remaining ingredients. Heat gently, stirring until the chocolate, sugar and butter have melted. Do not boil. Serve hot or warm.

Left to right, Chocolate Sauce, Fudge Sauce, Chocolate Syrup

Mars Bar Sauce
Serves 4

This recipe is very quick to make and absolutely delicious.

Ingredients
4 Mars Bars   90ml/6tbsp double cream

Preparation Dice the Mars Bars. Put in a small pan and melt very gently.

Stir in the cream. Mix until smooth and immediately pour over ice cream.

For extra punch, add a little brandy or rum to taste.

Quick Fruit Sauce
Serves 6

Ingredients
450g/1lb fruit   icing sugar

Preparation Stone, liquidize and strain any soft fruit in season, eg peaches, berries, mango etc. Sweeten to taste and spoon over ice cream.

Summer Sauce
Serves 8-10

Ingredients
225g/8oz redcurrants   30ml/2tbsp orange juice
225g/8oz blackcurrants   10g/2tsp cornflour
225g/8oz raspberries   30ml/2tbsp water
100g/4oz sugar

Preparation Place the fruit, sugar and orange juice in a heavy-bottomed pan on a low heat. Cook gently until the fruit is soft.

Combine the cornflour and water. Stir into the cooked fruit and bring to the boil, stirring constantly. Heat until the sauce has thickened.

Tobler Sauce
Serves 4

Ingredients
225g/8oz Toblerone
 Chocolate
150ml/¼pt double cream

Preparation Cut chocolate into very small pieces. Put into a small pan and melt very quickly.

Stir in the cream. Mix until smooth and immediately pour over ice cream or fruit such as bananas or pears, etc.

Crushing Garlic

1 If using many cloves, split a head of garlic with a solid punch of the fist. (Put waxed paper on the board if you want to avoid having to scrub the board later.)

2 To skin a single clove, place it near the edge of a chopping board and lay the flat of a heavy knife over the clove with the handle overlapping the edge of the board. Use a fist to punch down hard on the knife to slightly crush the clove and loosen the skin.

3 The paper skin of the half-crushed garlic clove can now be easily peeled off.

4 To make garlic paste, use the tip of a round-bladed knife and a good quantity of salt to crush the clove, working from tip to 'root' end.

5 Continue the process of crushing and mixing until the paste is smooth.

Pickles and Preserves

Cucumber and Sesame Relish   383
Horseradish and Beetroot Relish   383
Tomato Cucumber and Onion Relish   383
Lime Relish   383
Chilli Vinegar   383
Tomato Chutney   384
Mango Chutney   384
Mint Chutney   384
Tamarind Chutney   384
Pineapple Chutney   385
Coriander Chutney   385
Garlic Purée   386
Worcestershire Sauce   386

Garlic Pepper Essence   386
Garlic Vinegar   386
Fresh Cucumber Pickle   387
Vegetable Pickle   387
Pickled Lemons   387
Pickled Watermelon Rinds   387
Date Jam   387
Strawberry Plum Slatko   388
Java Jam   388
Superior Prunes   388
Vanilla Essence   388

Vinegar Hints   389

Cucumber and Sesame Relish
Serves 4-6

Ingredients
1 large cucumber
600ml/1pt water
juice of ½ lemon
5g/1tsp salt
60ml/4tbsp peanut oil
15ml/1tbsp sesame oil
3 cloves garlic, peeled and
   finely sliced

1 medium onion, peeled,
   finely sliced and dried
   on kitchen paper
10-20g/1-2tbsp roasted
   sesame seeds

Preparation Peel the cucumber, cut it in half and scoop out the seeds. Cut into even-sized chunks.

Put the water into a pan (stainless steel or enamel if possible) and add the lemon and salt. Bring to the boil then lightly cook the cucumber pieces in this, but take care not to overcook. Drain and leave to cool.

Heat the oils and fry the garlic, then lift out the pieces and fry the onion until crisp; lift out and drain. Reserve the oil and when cool pour over the cucumber. Toss well, then mix with the garlic, onion and sesame seeds.

Serve with curries.

Horseradish and Beetroot Relish
Makes 150g/6oz

Ingredients
75g/3oz grated raw
   beetroot
75g/3oz freshly grated
   horseradish
salt and pepper to taste

Preparation Mix the ingredients together, cover and chill.

Serve with grilled fish, boiled fish and meat dishes. Refrigerated, this relish will keep for about a week.

Tomato Cucumber and Onion relish
Serves 4-6

Ingredients
225g/8oz tomatoes,
   chopped into 0.5-cm/¼-
   in chunks
225g/8oz cucumber, cut
   into 0.5-cm/¼-in chunks
1 medium onion, finely
   chopped

2-3 fresh green chillies
2.5g/½tsp salt
2 pinches sugar
45ml/3tbsp lemon juice
15g/2tbsp chopped fresh
   coriander leaves or
   parsley

Preparation Mix all the ingredients together in a small bowl. Cover and chill before serving.

Lime Relish
Makes approx. 1.2l/2pt

Ingredients
12 limes, washed
cold water
350g/12oz sugar

300ml/1½pt vinegar
150ml/¼pt water

Preparation Place the limes in a large pot and add enough cold water to cover. Soak the limes for 24 hours. Drain limes and return to pot. Add enough cold water to cover and cook for 15-20 minutes, or until limes can be easily pierced with a fork. Drain well and set aside to cool.

When the limes are cool, cut into eighths. Remove the seeds. Set the limes aside. Place the sugar, vinegar and water in a saucepan. Cook over a medium-low heat until syrupy, about 15 minutes.

Place the lime pieces into hot sterilized jars. Cover with syrup. Seal, cool, and store.

Chilli Vinegar
Makes approx. 600ml/1pt

Ingredients
25g/1oz dried red hot
   chillies
600ml/1pt vinegar

Preparation Crush the chillies coarsely and steep in the vinegar. Shake daily for 10 days, then strain and bottle.

Mint Chutney

Mint Chutney
Serves 2-4

Ingredients

50g/2oz fresh mint leaves, washed	2 cloves garlic
50ml/2fl oz lemon juice	2cm/³/₄in fresh ginger
1 small onion, finely chopped	2-3 fresh green chillies
	2.5g/¹/₂tsp salt
	2.5g/¹/₂tsp sugar

Preparation Blend or process all the ingredients together until you have a smooth paste.

This chutney can be stored in an airtight jar in the refrigerator for a week.

Tomato Chutney
Makes approx. 450g/1lb

Ingredients

15ml/1tbsp oil	15g/1tbsp sugar
450g/1lb tomatoes, quartered	5g/1tsp cornflour, mixed with a little milk
7.5g/¹/₂tbsp salt	

Preparation Heat the oil in a small saucepan over medium heat.

Add the tomatoes, cover and cook until the tomatoes are soft. Add the salt and sugar and cook a further 10 minutes.

Thicken with the cornflour mixture and remove from the heat.

Chill, before serving.

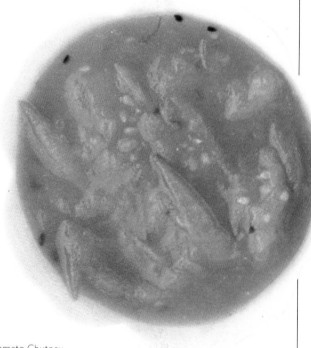

Tomato Chutney

Mango Chutney
Makes approx. 600g/1¹/₄lb

Ingredients

4 green mangoes	2.5g/¹/₂tsp salt
10ml/2tsp oil	60g/4tbsp sugar
2 cardamom pods	5g/1tsp flour mixed to a paste with 30ml/2tbsp milk
2.5-cm/1-in piece stick cinnamon	
450ml/³/₄pt water	

Preparation Wash the mangoes, and pat dry. Cut into 6 pieces, lengthwise.

Heat the oil in a saucepan over a medium high heat. Add the cardamom and cinnamon and let them sizzle for a few seconds. Add the mangoes and stir fry for 2-3 minutes.

Add the water and salt and, when the mixture starts to boil, add the sugar and stir in well. Cover, lower the heat and cook for 15-20 minutes until the mangoes are soft.

Add the flour and milk mixture, stirring constantly to make sure that no lumps can form.

Chill before serving.

Tamarind Chutney
Makes approx. 350ml/12fl oz

Ingredients

100g/4oz dried tamarind	15ml/1tbsp lemon juice
325ml/11fl oz hot water	30g/2tbsp brown sugar
good pinch chilli powder	good pinch salt

Preparation Soak the tamarind in the water for about 30 minutes. Squeeze the liquid from the tamarind and strain.

Combine the tamarind juice with the other ingredients and chill.

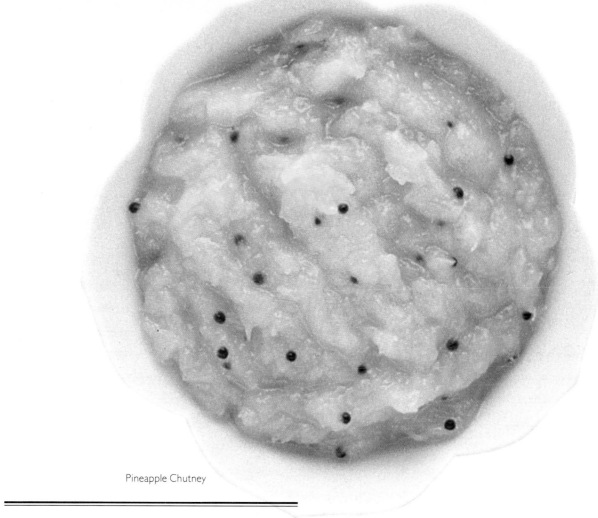

Pineapple Chutney

Pineapple Chutney
Serves 6

Ingredients

7.5ml/¹/₂tbsp oil
2.5g/¹/₂tsp mustard seeds
225g/8oz canned
 pineapple, crushed and
 drained

good pinch salt
5g/1tsp cornflour mixed
 with a little milk

Preparation Heat the oil in a small pan over medium heat. Add the mustard seeds and let them sizzle for a few seconds.

Add the drained pineapple and salt and cook for about 10 minutes, stirring occasionally.

Thicken with the cornflour mixture and remove from the heat. Chill until needed.

Coriander Chutney
Makes approx. 125g/4oz

Ingredients

75g/3oz fresh coriander
 leaves
4 cloves garlic
40g/4tbsp desiccated
 coconut

2 fresh green chillies
30-45ml/2-3tbsp lemon
 juice
2.5g/¹/₂tsp salt
2 pinches sugar

Preparation Chop the sprigs of coriander and throw away the roots and lower stalk.

Blend or process the coriander with all the other ingredients until you have a smooth paste.

This can be stored in an airtight jar in the refrigerator for a week.

Coriander Chutney

Garlic Purée

This is a useful and tasty addition to soups, stews, sauces, salad dressings — especially bought or home-made mayonnaise — and as a relish with cold meat. The cooking takes away any acrid flavours and the purée is far less crude and bitter than the commercially-produced version. It is also delicious spread on toast under poached or scrambled eggs.

Ingredients

*4 heads garlic (about 50   30ml/2tbsp olive oil
    cloves)   salt and pepper*

Preparation Simmer the unpeeled garlic cloves in lightly salted water for about 20-25 minutes, until soft. Drain and cool.

Peel the garlic cloves, cutting off the tough root-end and any discoloured patches, and mash them to a smooth paste with a fork.

Stir in the oil, and season with salt and pepper to taste. Pack into a glass jar and cover securely.

This purée will keep in the fridge for 4-5 days, and can be frozen in cubes, using an ice-cube tray reserved for this purpose.

Worcestershire Sauce
Makes approx. 325ml/11fl oz

Ingredients

*6 cloves garlic, crushed   75ml/3fl oz soy sauce
5g/1tsp black pepper   250ml/8fl oz vinegar
2 pinches chilli powder*

Preparation Liquidize or process the ingredients together until smooth and store in an airtight bottle.
Shake well before use.

Garlic Pepper Essence
Makes approx. 750ml/1¼pt

A few drops of this essence really perks up soups and stews, but because it is very intense, it should be used with caution.

Ingredients
*10 garlic cloves
5 small fresh chilli peppers
cooking sherry*

Preparation Peel and halve the garlic and prick the peppers all over. Mix them together and pack into a wine bottle.

Cover with the sherry and fill the bottle, leaving room for the cork. Cork the bottle securely and leave, undisturbed, for a couple weeks.

The sherry can be topped up from time to time.

Garlic Vinegar
Makes approx. 600ml/1pt

This vinegar is very handy for salad dressing and marinades for fish, shellfish and chicken.

Ingredients
*8-10 cloves garlic   600ml/1pt white wine or
a little coarse salt   tarragon vinegar*

Preparation Crush the garlic finely with the salt and put into a large, heat-proof jar.

Bring the vinegar to the boil and pour over the garlic. Allow to cool and then cover.

Leave to infuse for 2-3 weeks, then strain and bottle for use.

Variation Red wine Garlic Vinegar, for use in strongly flavoured marinades like those for stewing beef, pot roasts and game, is made by saving red wine bottle ends and letting them "turn". Use 10 cloves of garlic to 600ml/1pt of liquid, and warm the vinegar until hand hot before pouring over the crushed garlic.

Fresh Cucumber Pickle
Serves 4-6

Ingredients

1 cucumber	1 fresh red chilli, seeded
salt	and chopped
1 tomato, skinned, seeded	45ml/3tbsp good quality
and diced	vinegar
1 small onion, peeled and	10g/2tsp sugar
finely sliced	pinch salt

Preparation Trim the ends from the cucumber, peel lengthwise but leave some of the skin on to make the pickle look more attractive. Cut into thin slices and lay on a large plate. Sprinkle with salt and leave for 15 minutes. Rinse and dry.

Meanwhile prepare the tomato, onion and chilli. Arrange all the vegetables in a bowl and pour over the vinegar, sugar and salt. Chill before serving.

Vegetable Pickle
Makes approx. 1kg/2lb

Delicious with curries or cold meats.

Ingredients

100g/4oz peanuts	600g/1¼lb mixed
3 small onions, peeled	vegetables and fruits,
2 cloves garlic, peeled	peeled and sliced such
75ml/5tbsp oil	as: carrot, cauliflower,
4 macadamia nuts or	green mango, cabbage,
almonds	cucumber, beans, small
20g/1½tbsp turmeric	onions (leave whole),
300ml/½pt white vinegar	fresh pineapple, green
45g/3tbsp sugar	and red chillies
salt to taste	

Preparation Roast the peanuts in a moderately hot oven until brown, about 10-15 minutes. Rub off the skins and lightly pound; reserve.

Pound the onion and garlic together. Heat the oil and fry the onion and garlic to give off a good smell. Add the macadamia nuts or almonds, fry, then add the turmeric.

Stir in the vinegar, sugar and salt. Add the vegetables and fruit. Cook briefly before adding the peanuts.

Cool and transfer to a screwtop glass jar. Store in the refrigerator.

Pickled Lemons
Makes approx. 1kg/2lb

Ingredients

12 medium lemons, thinly	2 bay leaves
sliced and seeded	350ml/12fl oz corn oil
50g/2oz salt	100ml/4fl oz olive oil
5g/1tsp black peppercorns	

Preparation Arrange the lemon slices in layers in a colander, sprinkling the salt between the layers. Leave them to stand for 24 hours.

Divide the lemon slices among small sterilized glass jars. Divide peppercorns and bay leaves between the jars.

Mix the oils together. Fill each jar with the oil mixture, making sure that no air bubbles are trapped. Seal the jars tightly and store them in the refrigerator for 3 weeks before serving.

Pickled Watermelon Rinds
Makes approx. 1.2l/2pt

Ingredients

1.5kg/3½lb pared	45ml/3tbsp lemon juice
watermelon rinds, white	4 cinnamon sticks, broken
part only, cut into	into 1-in pieces
¼×1in pieces	20g/2tbsp whole cloves
30g/2tbsp salt	20g/2tbsp whole allspice
1kg/2lb sugar	10g/1tbsp whole white
600ml/1pt water	peppercorns
600ml/1pt cider vinegar	10g/1tbsp whole mustard
	seeds

Preparation Toss the watermelon rinds together with salt. Cover with cold water and leave to soak overnight. Drain and rinse well. Put the rinds in a saucepan with enough cold water to cover and bring to the boil over a high heat. Reduce heat and simmer for about 10 minutes. Drain well.

Bring the remaining ingredients to the boil in a large saucepan and simmer, stirring constantly, for about 10 minutes, until the sugar is completely dissolved. Add the watermelon rinds and simmer for about 45 minutes, until rinds are transparent.

Transfer rinds and syrup to sterilized jars and seal. Store pickles for 3-4 weeks before using.

Date Jam
Makes approx. 2.25kg/4½lb

Ingredients

1kg/2lb stoned dates	5g/1tsp ground nutmeg
725ml/1¼pt water	grated peel and juice of 1
1kg/2lb preserving sugar	lemon
5g/1tsp ground cinnamon	30g/2tbsp unsalted butter

Preparation Bring the dates and water to the boil. Simmer gently for 10 minutes.

Add the remaining ingredients and continue to cook, stirring all the time.

When the mixture is thick and smooth, take it off the heat. Pack into sterilized, warmed jars and cover.

Strawberry Plum Slatko
Makes approx. 900g/2lb

Ingredients
450g/1lb preserving sugar
300g/12oz damsons or
 other ripe purple plums,
 pitted and quartered
225g/8oz fresh
 strawberries, quartered
45ml/3tbsp lemon juice

Preparation Combine the sugar, plums and strawberries in a large saucepan. Stir well. Cover and cook over a medium heat for 10 minutes. Stir with a fork to make sure the sugar melts. Cook for a further 20 minutes or until the sugar is completely dissolved.

Add the lemon juice and cook for 10 minutes longer. Remove the saucepan from the heat and leave the slatko to stand, covered, at room temperature for 12 hours.

Store in sterilized glass jars in the refrigerator.

Java Jam
Makes approx. 1kg/2lb

Ingredients
450g/1lb bananas, sliced
600ml/1pt orange juice
600ml/1pt sweetened
 black coffee
300g/10oz soft brown
 sugar
50g/2oz vanilla sugar or
 white sugar

Preparation Put all ingredients into a pan and bring to the boil. Reduce the heat and cook gently, stirring frequently to prevent burning, until the mixture softens and becomes thick.

Spoon into sterilized jars and cover.

Superior Prunes
Makes approx. 1kg/2lb

Ingredients
450g/1lb Demerara sugar
100ml/4fl oz cold coffee
450g/1lb prunes, stoned
450ml/³⁄₄pt Kahlua or
 Crème de Cacao
100ml/4fl oz vodka

Preparation Put the sugar and coffee into a medium heavy-based pan. Bring to the boil, stirring all the time. Reduce the heat and simmer for 5 minutes.

Add the prunes and simmer gently for a further 40 minutes. Remove the prunes with a slotted spoon and put into sterilized jars.

Mix together the Kahlua or Crème de Cacao and vodka and half fill the jars. Cover with the syrup and seal the jars.

Vanilla Essence
Makes approx. 250ml/¹⁄₂pt

Ingredients
2 vanilla pods
300ml/10fl oz brandy

Preparation Partially break vanilla pods and put into the brandy.

Leave in an airtight bottle for 6 weeks before using, shaking every day.

Vinegar Hints

The party is over and you have a few drops of wine left in several bottles. Don't throw it away. Add the wine to your vinegar: red wine to red vinegar and white wine to white vinegar. The wine will naturally sour in the vinegar bottle and create the impression of an endless supply of vinegar. Don't serve a salad with a vinegar dressing on painted plates. The vinegar will soon corrode the paint on the plates.

1 White wine vinegar.

2 Pure red wine vinegar.

3 Rosemary vinegar: vinegars that have been steeped in herbs can transform salad dressings from the commonplace to the extra special.

4 Lemon wine vinegar: the lemon adds a lighter touch.

5 French white wine vinegar: the best wine vinegar comes from Orleans.

6 Raspberry vinegar: adds a light, fresh flavour to dressings.

7 Cider vinegar.

8 French garlic vinegar.

9 Honey and cider vinegar: a favourite with health food devotees.

10 Tarragon vinegar: good with white meat salads.

Appendix

Fibre Facts

It must now be universally acknowledged that the removal of fibre in the commercial processing of our food can lead to ill health: in order to make up the deficit, it is useful to have some idea of the fibre content of natural ingredients and to try to introduce those foods high in fibre into our diet. The tables below show the grams of fibre per 100g/4oz of some of these natural foods. As well as those foods listed, bread (especially wholewheat) and breakfast cereals (especially bran) are of course excellent sources of fibre.

Vegetables	g fibre per 100g/4oz
Aubergine, raw	2.5
Broccoli tops, raw	3.6
Cabbage, white, raw	2.7
Cabbage, red, raw	3.4
Carrots, raw	2.9
Carrots, boiled	3.1
Cauliflower, raw	2.1
Cauliflower, boiled	1.8
Celery, raw	1.8
Celeriac, raw	4.9
Cucumber, raw	0.4
Gourd, bitter, raw, fresh	4.0
Leeks, raw	3.1
Leeks, boiled	3.9
Lettuce, raw	1.5
Mushroom, raw	2.5
Olives in brine	4.4
Parsley, raw	9.1
Parsnip, raw	4.0
Parsnip, boiled	2.5
Pepper, raw and boiled	0.9
Potato, raw	2.1
Potato, baked, flesh only	2.5
Radishes, raw	1.0
Spring onion, flesh of bulb	3.1
Sweetcorn, kernels only, raw	3.7
Sweetcorn, canned, kernels only	5.7
Tomato, raw	1.5
Tomato, canned	0.9
Turnip, raw	2.8
Watercress, raw	3.3

Fruit — fresh and dried	g fibre per 100g/4oz
Apples, eating, with skin and core	1.5
Apples, eating, flesh only	2.0
Apples, cooking, raw, flesh only	2.4
Apricots, dried, raw	24.0
Banana, raw	3.4
Blackberries, raw	7.3
Blackcurrants, raw	8.7
Breadfruit, canned, drained	2.8
Currants, raw	6.5
Dates, dried, raw	8.7
Figs, fresh, raw	2.5
Figs, dried	18.5
Guava, canned, whole	3.6
Loganberries, raw	6.2
Passion fruit, raw	15.9
Peaches, dried, raw	14.3
Pears, eating, with skin and core	1.7
Prunes, raw, with stones	13.4
Prunes, raw, no stones	16.1
Quinces, raw	6.4
Raisins, stoned, raw	6.8
Redcurrants, raw	8.2
Sultanas, raw	7.0
Whitecurrants, raw	6.8

Pulses	g fibre per 100g/4oz
Butter beans, raw	21.6
Butter beans, boiled	5.1
Chickpeas, raw	15.0
Haricot beans, raw	25.4
Haricot beans, boiled	7.4
Kidney beans, raw	25.0
Lentils, red, raw	11.7
Mung beans, raw	22.0
Mung beans, canned	3.0
Peanuts, fresh	8.1
Peas, fresh, raw	12.0
Peas, frozen, boiled	5.3

Nuts	g fibre per 100g/4oz
Almonds	14.3
Barcelona nuts	10.3
Brazil nuts	9.0
Chestnuts	6.8
Cob or hazel nuts	6.1
Coconut, kernel only	13.6
Coconut, desiccated	23.5
Peanuts, fresh	8.1
Peanuts, roasted and salted	8.1
Walnuts	5.2

Pasta and Rice	g fibre per 100g/4oz
Brown rice, raw	4.2
Marcaroni, raw	5.5
Noodles, wheat dried, raw	5.7
Spaghetti, raw	5.6
Wholewheat pasta, uncooked	10.0

Choosing Meat : the Fat Facts

Always choose meat that looks moist and fresh, and which has the least amount of visible fat. This will not only give you more meat for your money, it will make far healthier eating for you and your family.

The tables show the average grams of total fat per 100g/4oz of uncooked meat. Trimming off any visible fat from red meat, and removing the skin from poultry before cooking will considerably reduce the fat content, as the difference in the two sets of figures given here shows.

Beef	Trimmed	Untrimmed
Brisket	3.5	20.5
Forerib	3.3	25.1
Rump Steak	4.0	13.5
Stewing Steak	3.9	10.6
Topside	4.0	11.2

Veal	Trimmed
Fillet	2.7

Lamb	Trimmed	Untrimmed
Leg	7.0	18.7
Loin Chops	5.3	35.4
Rack of Lamb	5.2	36.3
Scrag & Neck	6.2	28.2
Shoulder	6.0	28.0

To trim prepared rack of lamb, the knife must be both sharp and flexible.

Pork	Trimmed	Untrimmed
Loin	4.6	29.5
Leg	5.2	22.5

Ham/Gammon	Trimmed	Untrimmed
Collar	5.2	28.9
Gammon	5.9	18.3

Chicken	Without Skin	With Skin
Roasting	4.3	17.7
Breast (boned)	3.2	
Wing Quarter (including bone)	2.7	
Leg (boned)	5.5	
Leg Quarter (including bone)	3.4	

Turkey	Without Skin	With Skin
Roasting	2.2	6.9
Breast	1.1	
Dark Meat	3.6	

Duck		
	4.8	42.7

Game	Without Skin
Rabbit	4.0
Pheasant	6.2

Offal	Without Skin
Liver — Calves	7.3
— Chicken	6.3
— Lambs	10.3
— Pigs	6.8
Tongue — Calves	14.6
— Ox	17.5

The figures in the tables are taken from *McCance & Widdowson's The Composition of Foods* by A.A. Paul and D.A.T. Southgate (HMSO London, 1978).

Index

A

Acacia Honey Cake, 308
Aïoli, 370
Almond Loaf, 341
Almond Paste, 298
Almond Streussel, 314
Amaretti Truffles, 363
Anise Cookies, 338
Apple Charlotte, 246
Apple Parcels with Coffee Sauce, 278
Apple Sponge Pudding, 280
Apple Strudel, 288
Apple Tart with Cinammon Sticks, 289
Apricot Ice Cream, 242
Artichokes with Tomato Sauce, 9
Asparagus and Egg Napoleon, 53
Asparagus with Hollandaise Sauce, 193
Aubergine Soup, 31
Austrian Bagels, 342
Avocado, Preparing, 273
Avocado, Grapefruit and Prawn or Shrimp, 231
Avocado Dip, 10
Avocado Fish, 11
Avocado Ice Cream, 242
Avocado Mayonnaise, 377
Avocado Soufflé Omelette, 56
Avocado Soup, 31
Avocado with Blue Cheese, 10
Avocado with Honey Sauce, 11

B

Baby Lamb, 123
Bacon, stretching and scoring for crackling, 169
Bacon and Potato Supper, 157
Baked Alaska, 275
Baked Apples with Almonds, 275
Bake Avocado with Crab, 89
Baked Bananas, 276
Baked Eggs with Green Peas and Cream, 53
Baked Grey Mullet, 74
Baked Ham and Broccoli, 161
Baked Perch, 76
Baked Pineapple Rings, 276
Baked Potatoes with Eggs, 203
Baked Red Snapper, 76
Baked Salt Herring, 75
Baked Stuffed Salmon Trout, 77
Baklava, 271
Banana Cake, 322
Banana Choc-Chip Pudding, 280
Banana Custard, 277
Banana Peach and Almond Loaf, 301
Banana Shake, 347
Banana Split, 247
Barbecued Ribs of Beef, 147
Barbecued Spiced Chicken, 97
Basic Buttercream, 296
Basil Dressing, 368
Baumkuchen, 310
Bean, Mushroom and Asparagus Purée, 193
Bean Pancake, 23

Bean Soup, 31
Béchamel Sauce, 372
Beefburgers with Spicy Tomato Sauce, 139
Beef Cobbler, 141
Beef Goulash, 143
Beef Kidney, preparing, 155
Beef Napoleon, 148
Beef Patties, 142
Beef Satay, 144
Beef Stroganoff, 146
Beef Strudel, 147
Beef with Carrots, 140
Beetroot and Cabbage Borscht, 32
Beetroot, Apple, Roquefort and Walnut Salad, 277
Beouf Dijonnaise, 143
Bienenstich, 311
Birnbrot, 339
Bishop's Bread, 340
Black Cherry Sauce, 378
Black Forest Kirschtorte, 310
Bloodshot, 347
Blueberry Buckwheat Pancakes, 278
Blueberry Muffins, 327
Blueberry Tart, 249
Blue Cheese Dressing, 368
Blue Cheese Pâté, 66
Blue Cheese Sauce, 367
Boiled Beef, 148
Bolognese Sauce, 367
Bombe, 235
Boned Highland Chicken, 98
Borscht, 33
Braised Carrots and Onions, 197
Braised Coriander Duck, 117
Braised Veal Chops with Parsley Dressing, 151
Bran and Sultana Muffins, 327
Bread, Wholewheat, 341
Bread Pudding, 280
Broad Bean Pâté, 12
Broccoli and Orange Soup, 32
Broccoli and Tomato Cheesecake, 68
Brownies, 329
Brown Rice Pudding, 281
Brown Stock, 50
Brussel Sprouts with Garlic and Mushrooms, 194
Brussel Sprouts with Hazelnuts, 194
Bulgarian Eggs, 54
Burmese Pork Curry, 162
Butter Bean Salad, 221
Buttercream, Basic, 296
Butterfly Cakes, 330
Buttermilk Liqueur Cooler, 347
Buttermilk Pancakes, 59
Buttermilk Spice Cake, 297
Butterscotch Pudding, 281

C

Cabbage Salad, 215
Caesar Salad, 228
Café Brulôt Diabolique, 349
Calypso Coffee, 349
Canton Barbecued Spare Ribs, 168
Cantonese Chicken, 97

Capered Cutlets, 123
Caramel Ice Cream, 242
Caramel, judging the temperature of, 365
Caraway Cabbage, 195
Carrot and Coriander Soup, 33
Carrot Cake, 313
Carrot Halva, 358
Carrots with Yoghurt, 197
Cauliflower, Blue Cheese and Yoghurt Salad, 228
Celebration Noodles, 172
Celeriac Soup, 33
Celery Mousse, 198
Ceviche, 13
Challah, 342
Chard Soup with Lentils, 33
Charlotte Louise, 265
Charlotte Russe, 267
Chaudfroid Sauce, 372
Cheese and Celery Pancakes, 58
Cheese and Garlic Straws, 23
Cheese and Herb Pâté, 66
Cheese and Onion Soup, 34
Cheese and Spinach Soufflé, 61
Cheese Cutlets, 24
Cheese Fudge, 360
Cheese Herb Dressing, 368
Cheese Pastry, 294
Cheese Sauce, 372
Cheese Shortbreads, 336
Cheese Soufflé, 61
Cheesy Onion Quiche, 64
Cheesy Potato Soup, 44
Cheesy Ratatouille, 205
Chequerboard Cake, 322
Cherries Jubilee, 246
Cherry Chocolate Crunch, 337
Chestnut Mousse, 243
Chestnuts and Vegetables, 206
Chicken, boning, 120
Chicken, jointing, 120
Chicken Avocado Pasta Salad, 98
Chicken Biryani, 99
Chicken Breasts with Sesame Seeds, 101
Chicken Broth, 49
Chicken Buried in Salt, 101
Chicken Casserole with Coconut Milk, 101
Chicken Casserole with Ginger, 100
Chicken Creole, 100
Chicken Curry, 101
Chicken Curry with Noodles, 99
Chicken Escalopes, 103
Chicken Garam Masala, 105
Chicken in Baked Potatoes, 98
Chicken in Coconut Milk, 98
Chicken in Mole Sauce, 111
Chicken in the Pot with Soup, 35
Chicken Livers with Avocado, 12
Chicken Paprika, 102
Chicken Peanut Casserole, 102
Chicken Satay, 103
Chicken Stock, 50
Chicken Stuffed with Fruit and Nuts, 105
Chicken Wings, Fried, 106
Chicken Wings, Glazed, 106
Chicken with Kumquats, 102
Chicken with Mushroom Lasagne, 102
Chicken with Tangerine Peel, 110
Chicory and Walnut Salad, 223
Chicory, Orange and Walnut Salad, 225
Chicory Soufflé, 61
Chilled Borscht, 32
Chilled Orange Soufflé, 244
Chilled Sultana and Orange Cheesecake, 261
Chilli Crab, 88
Chilli Pasta, 174
Chilli Vinaigrette, 378
Chilli Vinegar, 383
Chinese Chicken with Pineapple and Cashew Nuts, 104
Chinese Duck, 116
Choc-Chestnut Mont Blanc, 253
Choc Nut Slice, 254
Chocolaccino, 348
Chocolate and Coffee Bavarois, 252
Chocolate and Orange Sauce, 378
Chocolate and Sour Cream Marble Cake, 320

Chocolate Boxes, 332
Chocolate Caramel Popcorn, 359
Chocolate Caraque, 297
Chocolate Cheesecake Cups, 263
Chocolate Chiffon Pie, 250
Chocolate Chip Cake, 318
Chocolate Custard, 379
Chocolate Egg Nog, 347
Chocolate Fondue, 250
Chocolate Gems, 339
Chocolate Granita, 239
Chocolate Hazelnut Bombe, 252
Chocolate Ice Cream, 238
Chocolate Icing, Soft, 295
Chocolate Icing, Thick, 295
Chocolate Malties, 331
Chocolate Meringue Gâteau, 323
Chocolate Meringues, 330
Chocolate Mousse, 251
Chocolate Orange Pots, 251
Chocolate Pinwheels, 338
Chocolate Ring Doughnuts, 326
Chocolate Roulade, 316
Chocolate Rum Cake, 319
Chocolate Sauce, 378
Chocolate Semolina Pudding, 281
Chocolate Soufflé, 286
Chocolate Spiced Biscuits, 333
Chocolate Syrup, 379
Chocolate Syrup Tart, 289
Chocolate Squares, 332
Chocolate Terrine, 254
Chocolate Upside-Down Pudding, 281
Choconana Milk Shake, 348
Choco-Nutty Sauce, 378
Choco-Ginger Sauce, 378
Cholent, 141
Chop, 24
Chopped Calf's Liver, 11
Chopped Chicken Livers, 12
Chopped Herring Marseilles, 15
Chop Suey, 180
Choux Pastry, 269
"Christmas Pudding" Cakes, 331
Chutney Dressing, 369
Cinnamon Chocolate Pain Perdu, 277
Cinnamon Stars, 333
Citrus Shake, 347
Clam Chowder, 35
Clarified Garlic Butter, 371
Classic Meringue, Basic, 296
Cock-A-Leekie Soup, 37
Coconut Cream Toffee, 357
Coconut Ice, 357
Coconut Mint Crystals, 357
Coconut Rice, 178
Coffee Almond Slice, 318
Coffee and Raspberry Frou Frou, 257
Coffee and Vanilla Jelly, 259
Coffee Apricot Condé, 258
Coffee Bread Pudding, 282
Coffee Brûlée, 268
Coffee Carrot Cake, 319
Coffee Charlotte, 256
Coffee Coconut Soufflé, 256
Coffee Creams, 359
Coffee Fruit Flans, 259
Coffee Fruit Loaf, 321
Coffee Fudge, 360
Coffee Knots, 324
Coffee Macaroons, 334
Coffee Mallows, 358
Coffee Meringue Pyramid, 258
Coffee Noggin, 350
Coffee Nougat, 364
Coffee Orange Soufflés, 287
Coffee Slices, 337
Coffee Spare Ribs, 168
Coffee Sponge with Rum, 304
Coffee Truffles, 362
Cold Apple Soup, 31
Cold Cherry Soup, 34
Cold Chicken Millefoglie, 105
Cold Tomato Soup, 46
Colettes, 358

Coleslaw, 218
Concentrated Tomato Sauce, 376
Consomme, 47
Cooked Egg Yolk and Buttercream, 295
Coriander Chutney, 385
Corn Chowder, 35
Corn Croquettes, 198
Corned Beef Stuffed Potatoes, 143
Cornish Saffron Bread, 340
Cornmeal Pudding, 188
Corn on the Cob with Olive Butter, 13
Cottabulla, 139
Cottage Cheesecake, 262
Coulibiac, 81
Country Vegetable Soup, 48
Courgette and Fennel Soup, 36
Courgettes au Gratin, 198
Courgette Soufflé, 61
Courgettes with Almonds, 198
Court-Bouillon, 50
Couscous, 187
Crab, Dressing, 94
Crab and Asparagus Tart, 62
Crab with Eggs, 89
Cream Dressing, 378
Cream of Corn Soup, 37
Cream of Lentil Soup, 40
Cream of Mushroom Soup, 41
Cream Puffs, 270
Creamed Spinach, 205
Crème Caramel, 266
Crème Pâtissière, 295
Crème Brûlée, 268
Crisp Fried Noodles, 172
Crispy Duck, 115
Crispy Fried Cabbage, 195
Crispy Pork Knuckle, 165
Crispy Potato Cakes, 204
Crispy "Seaweed", 196
Crown Roast of Lamb with Apricot Rice Stuffing, 124
Crudités with Hot Anchovy Dip, 13
Crunchy Apple Crumble, 276
Crunchy Pepper and Tuna Mousse, 63
Crushing Garlic and making Garlic Paste, 381
Cucumber and Sesame Relish, 383
Cucumber Dill Sauce, 368
Cucumber Salad I, 216
Cucumber Salad II, 217
Cucumber Soup, 37
Curd Cheesecake, 261
Curd Cheese Dumplings, 188
Curd Cheese Strudel, 288
Curried Coleslaw, 217
Curried Eggs, 54
Curried Fried Rice, 179
Curried Lentil Soup, 40
Curried Marrow Soup, 41
Curried Vegetables, 207
Curried Vegetable Fritters, 26
Curry-Fried Turkey, 113
Curry Mayonnaise, 377
Curry Noodles, 171
Curry Potatoes, 204
Curry Sauce, 367

D

Danish Pastries, 332
Dark Almond Cake, 304
Date and Cream Cheese Spread, 66
Date Jam, 387
Deep Fried Pastries, 25
Deep-fried Soy Chicken, 106
Deep Fried Wonton and Apricot Sauce, 163
Desdemonas, 312
Devilled Eggs, 24
Devilled Garlic Nuts, 26
Devilled Herring, 75
Devilled Turkey Legs, 113
Devils on Horseback, 25
Dill Sauce, 368
Dobostorta, 307

Double Garlic Chicken, 107
Double Gloucester Salad, 229
Doughnuts, 325
Down Home Shake, 352
Dressed Crab, 88, 94
Dressed Lobster, 90
Dressed Salmon, 78
Drunken Chicken, 107
Duck Breasts with Hazelnuts and Orange Potato Balls, 116
Duck with Pineapple, 117
Dutch Apple Special, 243

E

Easy Ice Cream, 235
Easy Ice Cream Loaf, 240
Eclairs, 270
Egg and Chive Mayonnaise, 377
Egg and Pasta Salad, 225
Egg Salad, 14
Eggs, whisking and preparing a soufflé, 69
Eggs with Curly Kale, 54
Elderflower Water Ice, 236
Eliza Leslie's Ginger Cup Cakes, 324
Engadiner Nusstorte, 298

F

Falafel, 25
Fat-free Sponge, 261
Family Chocolate Cake, 323
Family Fish Pie, 71/72
Family Lentil Soup, 40
Fennel, preparing, 212
Fennel, Stewed, 199
Fennel Mornay, 199
Fennel Salad, 222
Feta Garlic Salad, 228/229
Fettucine alla Romana, 173
Fillets of Sole in White Wine with Mushrooms, 83
Finnish Herring, 15
Fish, selection of, 93
Fish, preparation of, 93
Fish, cleaning and boning, 94
Fish Chowder, 36
Fisherman's Stew, 71
Fish in Bean Paste Sauce, 71
Fish Kebabs, 73
Fish Savouries with Spicy Tomato Sauce, 26
Fish Soup, 38
Fish Stock, 50
Five-Vegetable Gratin, 210
Flan Case, making, 343
Flans aux Fruits, 248
Flapjacks, 335
Flat Fish, cleaning and filleting, 93
Florentines, 336
Fondant Icing, 294
Fragrant Lamb Stew, 123
Frankfurter Kranz, 35
French Bean Salad in Mustard Sauce, 219
French Dressing, Rich, 369
French Onion Soup, 43
Fresh Cucumber Pickle, 387
Fresh Tomato and Vodka Soup, 46
Fried Pork with Mushrooms and Water Chestnuts, 159
Fried Rice, 179
Fritters in Syrup, 285
Frozen Chocolate Sandwiches, 255
Frozen Latin Flip, 351
Fruit Crumble, 277
Fruit Kisel, 246
Fruit Soup, 38
Fruit Surprise, 243
Fudge Sauce, 379

G

Galloping Horses, 27
Garam Masala, 371
Garlic and Herb Mayonnaise, 377
Garlic Butter, 370
Garlic Butter, Clarified, 371
Garlic Buttered Nuts, 26
Garlic Chicken Soup, 38
Garlic, crushing, 381
Garlic Dressing, Basic, 370
Garlic Milk Loaf, 341
Garlic Mushrooms, 14
Garlic Paste, 381
Garlic Pepper Essence, 386
Garlic Purée, 386
Garlic Soup, 38
Garlic Vinegar, 386
Gâteau des Rois, 301
Gâteau Pithiviers, 298
Gazpacho, 38/39
Gefillte Fish Patties, 72
German Carrot Soup, 33
German Herring Salad, 15
Ghee (Clarified Butter), 371
Ginger and Rhubarb Fool, 245
Ginger Ice Cream, 241
Ginger Snaps, 335
Glacé Icing, 294
Glazed Chicken Wings, 106
Globe Artichokes, preparing, 212
Goujons of Sole, 82
Grapefruit Cheese Jelly, 57
Grapefruit Frappé, 352
Greek Salad, 228
Green Banana Balls, 27
Green Bean Salad, 226
Green Beans Paprika, 193
Green Butter, 371
Green Mayonnaise, 377
Green Pea Soup, 42
Green Pea and Lettuce Soup, 43
Green Salad with Coconut Dressing, 225
Green Soup, 39
Grilled Squid with Lime, 84
Ground Beef Curry, 145
Ground Beef with Dill, 145
Gugelhupf, 316

H

Habsburger Torte, 306
Ham and Cheese Mousse, 63
Ham in Sour Cream I, 162
Ham in Sour Cream II, 162
Hard-Boiled Eggs Wrapped in Spiced Meat, 131
Haricot Bean and Cottage Cheese, 221
Haricot Bean Salad, 220
Harvest Soup, 39
Hazelnut and Apricot Crunch, 337
Hazelnut Torte, 308
Healthfood Drink, 353
Hearty Beef Soup, 32
Herb Dressing, 369
Herbed Rice, 179
Herbed Vinaigrette, 378
Herb Roulade, 60
Herring and Apple Salad, 15
Herrings in Oatmeal with Mustard Sauce, 75
Hi-Speed Pizzas, 27
Hobelspänne, 311
Holiday Carrots, 197
Holiday Fried Chicken, 106
Hollandaise Suace, 372
Holyrood Pudding, 281
Honey Chocolate Sauce, 378
Horseradish and Beetroot Relish, 383
Horseradish Mayonnaise, 377
Horseradish Sauce, Cold, 372

Horseradish Sauce, Hot, 372
Hot and Spicy Cucumber Salad, 217
Hot Chocolate, 348
Hot Curd Cheese Cake, 276
Hot Fruit Soufflé, 286
Hot Game Pie with Fried Apples and Onions, 118
Hot Pasta Salad, 229
Hummus, 17
Hunyady Chestnut Torta, 308

I

Iagos, 312
Iced Café au Lait, 350
Iced Caribbean Chocolate, 348
Iced Chocolate Praline Mousse, 257
Iced Grasshopper, 352
Iced Julep, 353
Icing, 294
Indian Cabbage with Peas, 195
Indian Kebab, 140
Indian Potato Salad, 215
Indian Rice Pudding, 282
Irish Coffee, 349
Italian Cheesecake, 260
Italian Meringue, 296

J

Jaffa Cakes, 330
Jambalaya, 178
Java Jam, 388
Jellied Chicken Salad, 108
Jellied Fish, 74
Jellied Lemon Chicken Soup, 34
Julienne Vegetables, preparation, 29

K

Kamla Khir, 244
Kasha, 187
Kashmiri Lamb and Fennel Seeds, 124
Kedgeree, 181
Kedgeree with Cherries, 181
Kidney Bean, Chick Peas and Corn Salad, 221
Kidney Bean Salad, 221
Kipfel, 324
Kipper Mousse Quiche, 65
Kipper Pâté, 16
Kirsch Glaze, 339
Kohlrabi and Chicken Soup, 40
Korean Beef with Vegetable Noodles, 145
Kukuye, 58
Kulfi (Indian Ice Cream), 240

L

La Lechuga, 227
Lamb and Lentil Meatballs, 129
Lamb and Okra Stew, 129
Lamb Biriyani, 125
Lamb Chop Kebabs, 125
Lamb Chops, Marinated, 131
Lamb Chops with Apricot Marsala Sauce, 124
Lamb Curry, Light, 131
Lamb Curry, Simple, 136
Lamb Dhansak, 126
Lamb Extravaganza, 126
Lamb in Dill Sauce with Tagliolini, 127
Lamb Kebabs, 128
Lamb Kidneys, preparing, 137
Lamb Kidneys in red Wine, 128

Lamb Korma, 128
Lamb Stuffed with Artichokes, 130
Lamb Tikka, 130
Lamb with Almonds and Yoghurt, 133
Lamb with Fennel and Lemon Sauce, 127
Lamb with Onions, 130
Lamb with Spinach, 129
Langues de Chat 338
Lardy Cake, 316
Lasagne Al Forno, 173
Leek and Stilton Bake, 62
Leek Quiche, 66
Leg of Lamb Casserole, 135
Lemon and Almond Strudel, 288
Lemon and Clove Cake, 323
Lemon Chicken with Wholewheat Spaghetti, 108
Lemon Meringue Pie, 279
Lemons, Pickled, 387
Lemon Turkey, 113
Lentil and Feta Salad, 223
Lentil and Tomato Soup, 41
Lentil Purée, 199
Lesco, 16
Le Succès, 300
Light Pound Cake, 300
Lime Relish, 383
Linzetorte, 304
Lobster, Dressed, 90
Lobster Newburg, 90
Lion's Head Meatballs, 162
Long Cook Pork Leg Stew, 166
Lox and Onion Omelette, 56
Luxury Mocha Ice Cream, 236

M

Macaroni Cheese with Bacon and Tomato, 173
Madeleines, 327
Magic Chocolate Pudding, 282
Maids of Honour, 328
Malaysian Chicken, 108
Mandarin Pancakes, 58
Mangetout and Carrot Salad, 226
Mango Chutney, 384
Maple Walnut Ice Cream, 241
Marie-Rose Mayonnaise, 377
Marinara Sauce, 373
Marrow or Courgettes, Stuffed, 200
Marrow or Courgettes in Cream Sauce, 200
Mars Bar Sauce, 380
Marshmallow Crunch, 265
Marzipan, 302
Matzo Balls, 189
Matzo Omelette, 279
Mayonnaise, 377
Meatballs, Little, 141
Mediterranean Beef Casserole, 140
Mega Mocha Shake, 350
Melon, Stuffed, 17
Meringue Mushrooms, 361
Meringue Torte, 271
Midwest Corn Chowder, 36
Milanese Risotto, 183
Millefeuilles, 277
Mincemeat Open Tart, 289
Mint Chutney, 384
Mississippi Mud Pie, 237
Mixed Bean Salad, 222
Mixed Herb Platter, 17
Mocha Bombe, 237
Mocha Cups, 362
Mocha Hazelnut Cake, 320
Mohrekopf, 312
Mohr Im Hemd, 253
Morello Cherry Tart, 290
Mornay Sauce, 373
Moules Marinière, 91
Mousseline Sauce, 372
Mozzarella and Avocado Bees, 17
Mozzarella Garlic Salad, 229
Muesli Scones, 326
Mushroom and Herring Salad, 16

Mushroom Cake, 322
Mushroom Omelette Surprise, 57
Mushroom Pancakes, 59
Mushroom Sauce, 374
Mushroom Soup, 42
Mushrooms, Stuffed, 201
Mushroom-Stuffed Artichokes, 193
Mustard Dressing, 369
Mustard Mayonnaise, 377
Mustard Sauce, 375

N

Naan, 341
New Potatoes with Caviar, 18
Noodles with Cottage Cheese, 172
Noodles with Peanut Sauce, 172
Nougat, 364
Nun's Pretzels, 334
Nut Pudding, 245
Nutty Rice Pilau, 184

O

Oatcakes, 336
Oil, hints, 233
Okra with Mustard, 201
Omelette with Cheese and Horseradish, 57
Onions, chopping and slicing, 211
Onion Salad, 224
Onion Tart, 64
Orange Cream, 365
Orange Granita, 239
Orange Lamb Chops, 136
Orange Mousseline Gâteau, 299
Orangen Torte, 305
Orange Pudding, 245
Orange Soufflé, 287
Orange Truffles, 362
Orange Yoghurt Drink, 354
Oriental Chicken and Mushroom Stew, 104
Oriental Chicken Soup, 34
Oriental Cucumber Salad, 216
Oriental Stir-Fry Vegetables with Noodles, 208
Osso Buco, 153
Oysters à l' Américaine, 90
Oysters en Brochette, 91

P

Paella, 180
Paella Marrano, 72
Pamplona Rice, 182
Pancakes, 58
Papaya Crab, 89
Paper-Wrapped Chicken, 110
Paprika Mushrooms, 201
Parsee Beef Curry, 145
Parsley, chopping, 213
Pasta Bows with Buckwheat, 188
Pasta Dough, making by hand, 191
Pasta Salad, 232
Pasta Trio, 175
Pasta Wheels with Salami, 176
Pasta with Aubergine and Apple, 174
Pasta with Mushroom Sauce, 175
Pasta with Spinach Sauce, 175
Pâté à Choux, 269
Pâté Rothschild, 18
Payodhi, 266
Peach Passion, 354
Pears Hélène, 247
Pear Soufflé, 286
Peking Duck, 114
Penang Chicken Curry, 109

Peppers, Stuffed, 18
Peppery Pork, 161
Persian Cucumber Soup, 37
Persian Lamb Stew, 132
Pesto, 375
Petits Pois à la Française, 201
Pheasant Pojarski Cutlets, 118
Pickled Beef Tongue, 148
Pickled Watermelon Rinds, 387
Pike Quenelles, 76
Pilaf, 183
Pilau Rice, 184
Pilchard Pâté, 18
Pineapple, preparing, 273
Pineapple Chutney, 385
Pineapple Coconut Cheesecake, 263
Pineapple Ice Cream, 241
Pineapple Yoghurt Drink, 354
Piperade, 55
Pitta Bread, 342
"Plumb Cake", 303
Poached Salmon, 77
Poached Sole, 82
Polenta, 189
Poori, 340
Poppy Seed or Walnut Roll, 314
Pork and Bean Casserole, 164
Pork and Garlic Satay, 164
Pork Baked Beans, 163
Pork Curry, 164
Pork Dijonnaise, 158
Pork Fillet en Croûte, 160
Pork Fillets in Brandy Cream Sauce, 161
Pork Satay, 160
Pork Soup with Ginger, 42
Pork Spare Ribs in Barbecue Sauce, 168
Pork Spring Roll, 23
Potatoes, Spiced, 202
Potato Gnocchi I, 190
Potato Gnocchi II, 190
Potato Salad with Horseradish I, 216
Potato Salad with Horseradish II, 216
Potato Soup, 43
Poulet au Roquefort, 108
Praline, 364
Prawn and Noodle Balls, 172
Prawn and Pasta Salad, 230
Prawn Bush, 19
Prawn Curry, 91
Processor Pastry, 345
Profiteroles, 272
Provençal Rice Salad, 230
Prune and Noodle Custard, 277
Puff Pastry, 293
Punch Icing, 295
Punschtorte, 305
Purée of Root Vegetables, 210,
Putanesca Sauce, 374

Q

Queen of Puddings, 283
Quick Blue Cheese Pâté, 11
Quick Chilled Summer Soup, 47
Quick Fruit Sauce, 380
Quick Tartare Sauce, 377
Quince Sherbert, 245

R

Rack of Lamb in a Garlic Crust, 132
Ragu Sauce, 374
Rainbow Salad, 225
Raisin Cheesecake, 263
Raisin Chocolate Fudge Cake, 313
Raspberry Chocolate Eclairs, 328
Raspberry Ice Cream, 237

Raspberry Yoghurt Drink, 354
Ravioli, 188
Red Bean Salad, 220
Red Cabbage with Apples, 195
Red-Cooked Chicken, 111
Red Fruit Soufflé, 244
Red Mullet Provençal, 74
Red Snapper à la Creole, 76/77
Red Velvet Cake, 317
Red Wine Garlic Vinegar, 386
Refrigerator Biscuit Cake, 321
Rice à la Provençale, 182
Rice and Raisin Pudding, 269
Rice Cubes, 185
Rice Flour Dessert, 265
Rice with Chicken, 178
Rich Chocolate Meringue Pie, 278
Rich Chocolate Truffles, 363
Rich French Dressing, 369
Rich Salmon Fish Cakes, 79
Risotto, 183
Roast Duck with Spaetzle, 116
Roast Chicken, Traditional, 109
Roast Turkey, 113
Ricotta al Café, 255
Rocky Road Fudge, 361
Roquefort Dressing, 378
Russian Cream Cake, 309
Russian Egg Drop Soup, 44
Russian Potatoes, 202
Russian Salad, 224
Russian Seedcake, 323
Rye Biscuits, 337

S

Sachertorte, 309
Sailor's Delight, 264
Salad of Broad Beans, 220
Salad of Beansprouts and Bean Curd, 223
Salad Niçoise, 231
Salmon, Dressed, 78
Salmon, Poached, 77
Salmon and Chive Cocottes, 63
Salmon and Spinach Pie, 80/81
Salmon Cutlets with Anchovy Butter, 80
Salmon en Croûte, 78/79
Salmon Fish Cakes, 79
Salmon Loaf, 80
Salmon Mousse, 81
Salmon with Lime and Walnut Oil, 79
Salsa Verde, 374
Salt-Grilled Chicken, 110
Salt-Grilled Fish, 72
Saltimbocca, 153
Sandtorte, 302
Sardines Provençal, 82
Sauce Gribiche, 373
Sauerbraten, 149
Sausage and Bacon Kebabs, 157
Sausage and Bacon Rolls with Tomato Rice, 158
Sautéed Sherry Veal, 152
Sauté of Lamb with Cranberries, 132
Savoury Cheesecake, 68
Savoury Cheese Strudel, 58
Savoury Fruit Salad, 231
Savoury Pasties, 26
Savoury Pumpkin Pie, 65
Savoury Spinach Rice, 185
Savoury Sprats, 84
Samosas, 28
Samosas, Wholewheat, 28
Sautéed Chicken Livers, 12
Scallops au Gratin, 92
Scallops with Mushrooms, 92/93
Scarborough Eggs, 55
Scholar's Vegetable Soup, 48
Schraderpuffer, 312
Scotch Barley Soup, 44
Scotch Broth, 44
Scottish Shortbread, 335
Scrambled Eggs with Smoked Salmon, 56

Seafood Salad, 230
Semolina Halva, 358
Semolina Pudding, 264
Sesame Chicken, 112
Sesame Snaps, 336
Shellfish Bisque, 45
Shellfish Paella, 92
Shortcrust Pastry, 293
Shoulder of Veal with Mushrooms and Spinach Fettucini, 152
Shredded Carrot and Cabbage, 196
Shrikhand, 266
Shrimp-Stuffed Courgettes, 92
Shrimp-Stuffed Vine Leaves, 19
Simnel Cake, 302
Simple Cassoulet, 133
Singapore Sling, 352
Skate in Caper Sauce, 82
Smoked Fish Croquettes, 73
Smoked Fish Salad (with Curd Cheese), 73
Smoked Fish Salad (with Pasta Bows), 230
Smoked Haddock Soufflé, 74
Smoked Mackerel Cream, 19
Smoked Mackerel Pâté, 18
Smoked Salmon Pancakes, 59
Smoked Salmon Pâté, 19
Snowball Pie, 238
Soft Chocolate Icing, 295
Sole, Poached, 82
Sole Dugléré, 83
Sole Meunière, 83
Sole Véronique, 83
"Solomon Gundy", 75
Soufflé, whisking eggs and preparing, 69
Soured Cream Anchovy Dressing, 368
Soured Cream Pastry, 294
Soured Cream Dip, 378
Soured Cream Mayonnaise, 377
Sour Potatoes with Pickles, 204
Sour Soup, 45
Southern Belle, 351
Souvlakia, 133
Spaghetti alla Carbonara, 177
Spaghetti con Vongole, 176
Spanish Chicken and Rice, 97
Spanish Rice, 185
Special Pickled Herring, 16
Spice Cake, 298
Spiced Apple Tart, 290
Spiced Brisket I, 150
Spiced Brisket II, 150
Spiced Buttermilk Scones, 326
Spiced Fish, 74
Spiced Lamb and Cheese Meatloaf, 135
Spiced Omelette, 57
Spiced Pork in Coconut Milk, 167
Spiced Potatoes, 202
Spiced Rice Salad, 186
Spiced Bean Salad, 219
Spicy Green Bean and Tomato Pasties, 194
Spicy Lamb Rissoles, 134
Spicy Potato Cakes, 203
Spicy Potato Salad, 215
Spicy Roast Chicken, 111
Spicy Tomato Sauce, 376
Spinach and Carrot Terrine, 20
Spinach and Chickpea Salad, 219
Spinach and Orange Salad, 224
Spinach and Ricotta Sauce, 375
Spinach Pancakes, 59
Spinach Quiche, 65
Spinach Ring, 205
Spinach Roulade, 60
Spinach Soup, 45
Spinach Tagliatelle with Asparagus, 177
Spinach with Ricotta Cannelloni, 177
Sponge, Fat-free, 261
Steak and Sout, 149
Steak au Poivre Verte, 147
Steamed Coffee Pudding, 284
Steamed Fruit Pudding, 283
Steamed Pork Buns, 165
Steamed Puddings, handling, 291
Steamed Trout with Hazelnuts and Courgettes, 86
Stewed Fennel, 199

Stir-Fried Beef with Baby Sweetcorn and Green Peppers, 147
Stir-Fried Cabbage Salad, 215
Stir-Fry Pork, 159
Stock, making, 51
Strawberry and Avocado Salad, 222
Strawberry Granita, 239
Strawberry Peach Sherbet, 268
Strawberry Plum Slatko, 388
Strawberry Shortcake, 248
Streusselkuchen, 314
Strudel Dough, 297
Strudel Paste and making Apple Strudel, 344
Stuffed Aubergines, 9
Stuffed Baked Mackerel, 75
Stuffed Cabbage, 194
Stuffed Cabbage Rolls, 154
Stuffed Date Patties, 12
Stuffed Fish, 73
Stuffed Marrow or Courgettes, 200
Stuffed Melon, 17
Stuffed Mushrooms, 201
Stuffed Pancakes with Cheese and Herbs, 58
Stuffed Pears, 245
Stuffed Pork Chops with Pasta Bows, 158
Stuffed Poussins, 112
Stuffed Tomatoes I, 21
Stuffed Tomatoes II, 21
Stuffed Veal Shoulder, 154
Stuffed Vine Leaves (with Pine Nuts), 14
Stuffed Vine Leaves (with Lamb), 135
Summer Avocado Salad, 10
Summer Lunch Bowl, 20
Summer Posy Mousse, 62
Summer Pudding, 264
Summer Sauce, 380
Summer Vegetable Pasties, 209
Sundae Supreme, 244
Sunshine Cake, 315
Superior Prunes, 388
Sussex Pond Pudding, 284
Sweet and Sour Lamb, 136
Sweet and Sour Pork, 166
Sweet and Sour Salmon, 20
Sweetheart Cookies, 333
Sweet Potato Pie, 279
Sweet Rice Fritters, 278
Sweet Shortcrust Pastry, 293
Switzen Plum Tart, 290
Syrup, testing the temperature of, 365

T

Tabouleh, 226
Tamarind Chutney, 384
Tandoori Chicken, 112
Tapenade, 27
Tarama Salad, 22
Tarragon Lamb, 136
Tartare Sauce, 377
Tea Eggs, 54
Tea Granita, 239
Thai Beef with Spinach, 150
Thai Steamed Rice, 186
Tobler Sauce, 380
Tomato and Sage Derby Quiche, 64
Tomato Chutney, 384
Tomato Cocktail, 353
Tomato, Cucumber and Onion Relish, 383
Tomatoes, preparing, 211
Tomato Salad, 219
Tomato Salad with Olives, 219
Tomato Sauce, 376
Tomato Sauce, Concentrated, 376
Topfen Kuchen, 260
Tortellini Coleslaw, 218
Tortoni, 272
Traditional Roast Chicken, 109
Transylvanian Goulash, 166
Triple Decker Squares, 329
Trout "au Bleu", 84
Trout Chaudfroid, 85

Trout with Almonds, 85
Trout with Avocado and Ham, 85
Truffel Torte, 312
Tsatziki, 227
Tulipes, 338
Turkey, Roast, 113
Turkey Fillets in Wine Sauce, 114
Turkey Mole, 114
Tuna and Mushroom Sauce, 375
Tuna Crêpes, 60
Tuna Mousse, 87
Tuna Pâté, 21
Tuna-Stuffed Potatoes, 87
Tuna Wholewheat Rolls, 87
Twice Cooked Pork, 167
Two Trout Mousse, 86

U

Upside Down Lemon Pudding, 285

V

Vanilla Cream, 267
Vanilla Crescents, 335
Vanilla Essence, 388
Vanilla Sugar, 300
Veal, preparing kidneys and liver, 155
Veal and Aubergine Casserole, 151
Veal Clou de Giroffe, 151
Veal Escalopes with Red Wine, 153
Veal Paprika, 151
Vegetable and Rice Hotch Potch, 209
Vegetable Caviar, 22
Vegetable Cheese Custard, 67
Vegetable Chop Suey, 207
Vegetable Cream Cheese, 22
Vegetable Cream Soup, 47
Vegetable Cutlets, 206
Vegetable Garlic Basil Soup, 47
Vegetable Lasagne, 174
Vegetable Pickle, 387
Vegetable Salad with Hot Peanut Sauce, 222
Vegetables in Aspic, 206

Vegetables in Vinaigrette, 209
Vegetarian "Chopped Liver", 22
Viennese Chocolate Biscuits, 339
Viennese Coffee, 351
Vietnamese Salad, 232
Vinaigrette, 378
Vinegar Hints, 389
Vitello Tonnato, 154

W

Waldorf Salad, 227
Walnut Bread, 341
Walnut Torte, 304
Warm Chicken Liver Salad with Garlic, 232
Warm Potato and Bacon Salad, 231
Waste-Nothing Vegetable Stock, 50
Watercress and Potato Soup, 49
Watercress Mousseline, 377
Watercress Soup, 48
Weight Watcher's Cheesecake, 260
Welsh Rarebit, 67
Wheat Grain Lamb, 134
Whipped Chocolate Cream, 295
Whitebait, 87
Whiting Bercy, 87
Wholefood Pasta Salad, 226
Wine Glasses, 355
Winter Pesto Sauce, 375
Worcestershire Sauce, 386

Y

Yakitori, 112
Yeast Dough and Yeast Sponge Batter, 297
Yeasted Crescents, 324
Yoghurt, Basic, 272
Yoghurt and Tahini Dip, 378
Yoghurt Cream Dressing, 369
Yoghurt Mayonnaise, 377
Yoghurt Pastry, 294
Yoghurt with Cucumbers, 217
Yom Kippur Bread, 342
Yorkshire Curd Tart, 268